Models, Methods, and Applications of Econometrics

A. R. Bergstrom

Models, Methods, and Applications of Econometrics

Essays in Honor of A. R. Bergstrom

edited by

Peter C. B. Phillips

BLACKWELL
Cambridge MA & Oxford UK

First published 1993

Blackwell Publishers
238 Main Street
Cambridge, Massachusetts 02142, USA

108 Cowley Road
Oxford, OX4 1JF, UK

Library of Congress Cataloging-in-Publication Data

Models, methods, and applications of econometrics : essays in honor of
A. R. Bergstrom / edited by Peter C. B. Phillips.
p. cm.
Includes bibliographical references and index.
ISBN 1-55786-110-2 (alk. paper)
1. Econometrics. 2. Bergstrom, A. R. (Albert Rex) I. Bergstrom,
A. R. (Albert Rex) II. Phillips, P. C. E.
HB139.M626 1992
330'.01'5195—dc20 92-27177
CIP

British Library Cataloguing in Publication Data
A CIP catalogue record for this book is available from the British Library.

Typeset in 10pt Times Roman by Keyword Publishing Services

This book is printed on acid-free paper

Contents

List of Contributors

T. D. Agbeyegbe, *Hunter College, USA*
R. J. Bowden, *University of New South Wales, Australia*
M. J. Chambers, *University of Essex, United Kingdom*
G. Ellison, *University of Cambridge, United Kingdom*
G. Gandolfo, *University of Rome, Italy*
D. E. A. Giles, *University of Canterbury, New Zealand*
A. W. Gregory, *Queen's University, Canada*
V. B. Hall, *Victoria University of Wellington, New Zealand*
E. J. Hannan, *Australian National University, Australia*
L. P. Hansen, *University of Chicago, USA*
A. C. Harvey, *London School of Economics, United Kingdom*
D. F. Hendry, *Oxford University, United Kingdom*
G. H. Hillier, *Monash University, Australia*
S. Maheswaran, *University of Minnesota, USA*
V. L. Martin, *University of Melbourne, Australia*
G. Mizon, *University of Southampton, United Kingdom*
P. C. Padoan, *University of Urbino, Italy*
A. R. Pagan, *Australian National University, Australia*
P. C. B. Phillips, *Yale University, USA and University of Auckland, New Zealand*
J. Richmond, *University of Essex, United Kingdom*
P. M. Robinson, *London School of Economics, United Kingdom*
J. D. Sargan, *Theydon Bois, Essex, United Kingdom*
S. E. Satchell, *University of Cambridge, United Kingdom*
C. A. Sims, *Yale University, USA*
C. L. Skeels, *Australian National University, Australia*
G. W. Smith, *Queen's University, Canada*
J. H. Stock, *Harvard University, USA*
R. G. Trevor, *University of New South Wales, Australia*
M. R. Wickens, *London Business School, United Kingdom*
N. S. Wyatt, *New Zealand Ministry of Energy, New Zealand*
C. R. Wymer, *Takapuna, New Zealand*

Preface

This volume of essays has been assembled to honor Rex Bergstrom as a *Festschrift* on the occasion of his sixty-fifth birthday. The scholars who have contributed to the volume form a truly international group. Some have had the good fortune to study under Rex and learn directly from his guidance as a teacher or a thesis adviser. Others have worked with Rex and appreciate his insight and wisdom as a colleague. All of us have been inspired and influenced by his research. As the editor of this volume, it is a privilege for me to bring together and present to Rex this fine collection of essays, which in their breadth of themes and concern for fundamentals together reflect the extent of Rex's own interest in economic modeling and in the theory and application of econometrics.

Some years ago, when he was appointed Professor of Econometrics at the University of Auckland in New Zealand, Rex Bergstrom wrote a short essay entitled "What is Econometrics?" that was published in the *University of Auckland Gazette*. That essay, which is reprinted here with the kind permission of Rex and the University of Auckland, describes the main activities of econometrics in a characteristically lucid and economical way. The title of this present volume and the essays that it includes both reflect these different activities: the formulation of econometric models; statistical estimation and testing; empirical applications and prediction. One of the distinctive features of Rex Bergstrom's own lifetime of research is that he has maintained a strong commitment to the pursuit of excellence in each of these major activities, frequently bringing them together in a powerful way to illustrate the empirical advantages of new econometric methodology.

In teaching as well as in research, Rex Bergstrom has made substantial contributions to the econometrics communities of Britain and New Zealand over the last 40 years. In both countries scholars of many generations have been guided by his example and are proud to carry with them the Bergstrom pedigree in their later careers. In New Zealand some of Rex's former students are now leaders in the business community as well as the university professoriate. Those of us who studied under Rex know well the inspiration and longevity of his teachings and his personal dedication to the best in research.

To honor Rex and to promote the subject of econometrics in his home country of New Zealand, Viv Hall and I have established a Scholarship Fund to support a Prize for research excellence in econometrics among young New Zealanders. Viv Hall helped in the early stages of planning this volume and together we decided to seek funding for an econometrics prize in honor of Rex. The prize is formally announced in this volume as *The A. R. Bergstrom Prize in Econometrics*. It has been established with the financial sponsorship of the Faculty of Commerce and Economics at the University of Auckland, the Economics Department of the University of Canterbury, Lincoln University, the Department of Economics and Marketing at Lincoln University, the Faculty of Commerce and Administration at

Victoria University, and the New Zealand Association of Economists as well as numerous individual sponsorships. Royalties from this *Festschrift* will also contribute to the funding of the Prize. Information about the Prize and its administration are given in the formal announcement in part I of this volume. The sponsors, Viv Hall and I all hope that this Prize will help to promote among young New Zealand scholars the Bergstrom tradition of excellence in econometrics under which many others of an earlier generation were nurtured.

This volume would never have been possible without the willingness of its many contributors to produce this joint mark of respect for Rex Bergstrom. I thank all of the contributing authors for supporting this volume with their research. It is an honor for me to put their essays together in this combined tribute to Rex Bergstrom.

Peter C. B. Phillips
Madison, CT
May 1992

Acknowledgments

The essays in this volume have all been refereed. I thank the contributors and many outside referees for their willingness to aid the preparation of this volume by providing these professional services.

I thank the University of Auckland and Rex Bergstrom for permission to reprint his article "What is Econometrics?", originally published in the *University of Auckland Gazette*, volume 8, no. 1, April 1966, pp. 1–3. Cambridge University Press kindly gave permission to reprint the "*ET* Interview: Professor A. R. Bergstrom," originally published in *Econometric Theory*, volume 4, no. 2, August 1988, pp. 301–27.

It is also a pleasure to thank Elizabeth Dolomont for her excellent secretarial assistance throughout this project, Glena Ames for manuscript typing, and Carmela Quintos for help in proofreading and in preparing the Indexes.

The A. R. Bergstrom Prize in Econometrics

V. B. Hall
Victoria University of Wellington
and
P. C. B. Phillips
Yale University

We are pleased to announce the establishment of *The A. R. Bergstrom Prize in Econometrics.* The Prize is supported by funds that have been generously provided by the following sponsors:

Institutional Sponsors

The New Zealand Association of Economists
The Faculty of Commerce and Economics at the University of Auckland
The Department of Economics at the University of Canterbury
The Faculty of Commerce and Administration at Victoria University of Wellington
Lincoln University
The Department of Economics and Marketing at Lincoln University

Personal Sponsors

A. D. Brownlie
H. A. Fletcher
V. B. Hall
P. C. B. Phillips
R. J. Bowden
R. H. Court
D. M. Emanuel

In addition to these sponsorships, royalties from this *Festschrift* volume will be used to support the Prize. All funds have been set aside in a Trust Account under the name *The A. R. Bergstrom Scholarship Fund.*

The Prize will be awarded once every two years to the most promising young New Zealand econometrician. The award will be made on the basis of a national competition and will be open to all New Zealand citizens or permanent residents of New Zealand who are under the age of 30 years. The criteria for selection will be outstanding research in econometrics evidenced by a research paper in any field of econometrics. The first award of the Prize will be made in 1992.

The purpose of this Prize is to honor Rex Bergstrom, to promote the subject of econometrics in Rex Bergstrom's home country of New Zealand and to encourage research excellence in econometrics among young New Zealanders. Rex Bergstrom was himself educated in New Zealand and a substantial part of his career as an educator and as a researcher was in the New Zealand University system, primarily at Auckland. Over the period 1948–1970 Rex Bergstrom had an enormous influence on the education of New Zealand economics graduates and he has helped to produce some of the country's finest economists. There are few University or Government economics departments in New Zealand now that have not been strongly influenced by his teaching and research or that of his students. We hope that the institution of this Prize will help to advance among young New Zealanders the Bergstrom tradition of research excellence that has set such a fine example to earlier generations of New Zealand economists.

Further particulars and regulations for the administration of this Prize are described in the following rubric.

1. The Prize shall be known as: The A. R. Bergstrom Prize in Econometrics.
2. The objective of the Prize is to reward the achievement of excellence in econometrics. It is intended that the awardee will utilize the proceeds to assist in financing further study or research in econometrics in New Zealand or overseas.
3. The Prize is open to New Zealand citizens or permanent residents of New Zealand who are under the age of 30 years.
4. The Prize shall be awarded on the basis of a national competition by a selection committee consisting of P. C. B. Phillips and V. B. Hall and their nominees. Initial applications will be called for in 1992, and thereafter at two yearly intervals unless determined otherwise by the selection committee. No award shall be made at the time designated if, in the opinion of the selection committee, there is no candidate's work academically worthy of the award. A recipient may be awarded the Prize only once.
5. The value of the Prize shall be as determined from time to time by the committee, having regard to funds available, and in the first instance will be $1,000.
6. Applications/nominations should be sent to Professor V. B. Hall, Economics Department, Faculty of Commerce and Administration, Victoria University of Wellington, by 31 March in the relevant year. The applications/nominations must include:

   - a formal letter of application and, in the case of students, a letter of nomination by their research adviser or chairperson
   - 4 copies of a research paper written by a single author, reporting original research in any area of econometrics
   - a Curriculum Vitae and relevant academic transcripts.

7. Announcements of each award will be made in the *New Zealand Association of Economists Newsletter*, in *New Zealand Economic Papers*, in *Econometric Theory*, and elsewhere, with an accompanying citation describing the research for which the award is made.

Part I

The Contributions of A. R. Bergstrom to Econometrics

1

Rex Bergstrom's Career and Research

Peter C. B. Phillips

Rex Bergstrom* was trained as an economist in New Zealand, earning his B.Com and M.Com degrees in 1946 and 1948 at Canterbury University College, which at that time was a college of the University of New Zealand. He took up his first academic position as an Assistant Lecturer in Economics in 1948 at Massey College in Palmerston North. In 1950 he moved to Auckland University College where he worked until 1962, rising to the rank of Associate Professor of Economics. During the 1950s, Bergstrom became recognized as New Zealand's foremost econometrician, publishing his first applied econometrics article [6] in the *Economic Record* in 1951 and several other papers [5, 7, 8, 11, 12] on empirical aspects of the New Zealand economy over this period. The *Economic Record* paper developed and estimated an export supply function for the New Zealand economy and was the precursor to his famous model of supply and demand for New Zealand exports that was published by *Econometrica* in 1955. The *Econometrica* article [8] was based on Bergstrom's doctoral dissertation at Cambridge, which he had completed while on leave from Auckland during 1952–4, supported by a Travelling Scholarship in Commerce. The article quickly attracted international attention. It reported the largest system of simultaneous equations ever formulated for empirical work up to that time; it was estimated by the new limited-information maximum likelihood (LIML) methodology devised by the Cowles Commission; and its empirical results gave strong support for the new methodology. The skilful mix of economic theory, econometric methodology, and painstaking empirical implementation that was demonstrated in this article became the hallmark of Bergstrom scholarship.

By the end of the 1950s Bergstrom's interests in econometrics had widened considerably beyond empirical research. In search of a more complete understanding of the properties of the LIML procedure that he had used so successfully in his empirical model of New Zealand exports, Bergstrom set about finding the exact finite-sample distributions of the maximum likelihood estimator (MLE) and ordinary least squares (OLS) estimator of the propensity to consume in a simple stochastic income determination model. The Indian econometrician Nagar (1959) had earlier

*References to Bergstrom's articles are in square brackets [ ] and refer to the bibliography of his work in chapter 4.

developed moment approximations for simultaneous equations estimators and his study provided the immediate catalyst for Bergstrom's research. Bergstrom's work turned out to be very different from Nagar's. He derived exact mathematical forms for the density functions of the MLE and OLS estimators, graphed the densities and computed probabilities of concentration about the true value of the parameter for the two estimators. The results were conclusive and provided clear support for the use of simultaneous equations estimators like LIML. Bergstrom's results were published by *Econometrica* in 1962. Remarkable as a first piece of technical research, Bergstrom's paper [13] ushered in a new era of mathematical sophistication in econometrics. Independently, Basmann (1961) had published some related work on the exact density of the two-stage least squares estimator and together their articles are recognized as having opened up a new research field.

In 1962 Bergstrom left Auckland for the London School of Economics (LSE) where he became a Reader in Economics. His arrival coincided with the time when the LSE was rising to prominence in the field of econometrics and overtaking Cambridge as the leading center of econometric research in the UK. Bergstrom joined a burgeoning group of econometricians that included another New Zealand born economist, Bill Phillips, the statistician Jim Durbin and, somewhat later, Denis Sargan, as well as a larger team of economists such as Dick Lipsey, Chris Archibald and Morris Peston all of whom were working vigorously in applied econometrics. The initiatives established during this period at the LSE were to put the School at the forefront of econometric research in the UK for the next two decades.

During his period at the LSE from 1962–4, Bergstrom's own research on econometric modeling moved in decisive new directions. Influenced by the earlier work of Bill Phillips, he embarked on a research agenda concerned with the development of economic models of cyclical growth that synthesized real and monetary phenomena in a growing economy. These models, which were published in *Economica* in 1962 [14] and *Economic Studies Quarterly* in 1966 [17], incorporated a neoclassical production technology, Keynesian-type feedbacks from prices and interest rates to the real sector and adjustment mechanisms to accommodate market disequilibrium. As economic models, they represented an important advance over earlier trade cycle models which set out to explain cyclical behavior in real variables through the multiplier–accelerator mechanism alone. In addition, the new models had particular solutions that corresponded to the steady state paths of the earlier neoclassical growth models of Solow (1956) and Swan (1956). The Bergstrom cyclical growth models therefore provided a synthesis of two earlier strands of research and were the first truly disequilibrium models of neoclassical growth.

The formulation of cyclical growth models as ordinary differential equations with a continuous time parameter leads to econometric specifications as systems of stochastic differential equations. Apart from some isolated early research by Bartlett (1946), Quenouille (1957), Phillips (1959), and Durbin (1961), econometric methodology for estimating systems of stochastic differential equations was completely undeveloped at this time. During his period at the LSE, Bergstrom commenced an ambitious research program that was complementary to his work on economic models of cyclical growth. This research program explicitly addressed the estimation of econometric models in continuous time with discrete data. Bergstrom's research on this topic was motivated by concerns of practical implementation and led to his proposal of nonrecursive discrete approximations to continuous-time systems. The approximations were to be constructed in the form of simultaneous equations models and the proposal had the natural advantage of making available the by-then well-established econometric methodology of simultaneous equations for estimation and inference in continuous-time models formulated as systems of differential equations. The discrete approximation is especially interesting because it shows the precise sense in which a system of simultaneous interdependent equations may be regarded as an approximation to a recursive differential equation system. The approach was systematically explored in an article [16] published in *Econometrica* in 1966 and it laid the foundation for much later empirical econometric work with continuous-time models.

The twin themes of economic models of cyclical growth and econometric estimation in continuous time have remained a major force in Bergstrom's thinking since the 1960s. In 1964 Bergstrom returned to Auckland University as Professor of Econometrics, where he completed his monograph [1] on *The Construction and Use of Economic Models*, published by the English University Press in 1967. This monograph is a masterful synthesis of earlier developments in trade cycle and cyclical growth models and it gives full expression to the disequilibrium modeling methodology that forms the basis of Bergstrom's later research. Indeed, the monograph develops a single-sector disequilibrium growth model that is the prototype for his subsequent empirical work on modeling the UK economy. In its final chapter, this monograph provides a beautifully succinct description of simultaneous equations econometric methodology and its application to the estimation of discrete approximations to stochastic differential equation systems.

In 1970 Bergstrom went back to England as Keynes Visiting Professor at the University of Essex, taking up a permanent Professorship there the following year. Administrative appointments at the senior University level, first as Dean and later as Pro-Vice-Chancellor, as well as a term as Departmental Chairman all reduced Bergstrom's time for research during the ensuing decade. Nevertheless, it was over this period that two of his most significant research accomplishments were completed.

The first of these is a major empirical study of the UK economy based on a continuous time econometric model of disequilibrium growth. This study [23], which was co-authored with Clifford Wymer (a former student from Auckland University who was at that time on the faculty of the LSE), was completed in 1974 and constitutes one of the most innovative empirical econometric exercises ever undertaken up to that time. The Bergstrom–Wymer model (as it soon became known), is a 13-equation continuous-time stochastic system that is based on a formal one-sector model of a macroeconomy. It is heavily constrained by cross-equation restrictions delivered from an underlying neoclassical growth theory. The model is estimated with postwar quarterly data by Gaussian techniques, its long-run properties are examined analytically, a stability analysis is conducted, and impressive out-of-sample forecasting performance is demonstrated. This model is distinguished from other empirical macromodels in many ways but most notably because it has only one exogenous variable, a simple time trend, and performs so well in empirical exercises in spite of this major simplification. The Bergstrom–Wymer model is now a classic study in empirical econometric research. It is a showpiece of careful applied econometrics and is the prototype for many similar models that have since been developed for other countries.

Bergstrom's second major line of research at Essex began in the early 1980s as a theoretical study of Gaussian estimation in continuous-time systems. By the end of the decade it had matured, like his earlier research on discrete approximations, into a complete econometric methodology that involved a theoretical development of inference, computational algorithms, computer programs, and empirical applications. Several doctoral students who worked under Bergstrom's supervision at Essex during the 1980s have helped in the completion of this major research program.

The first step in the new program was the econometric theory. Some earlier work by the author (1972) that was done under Bergstrom's supervision at Auckland University in 1969–70 had indicated that there were definite advantages in terms of bias reduction and efficiency gains from utilizing the exact discrete-time model of a continuous-time system for econometric estimation instead of the discrete approximation. In 1983, Bergstrom published in *Econometrica* an extensive study [25] of exact discrete-time models corresponding to stochastic differential equation systems. This paper broke new ground by allowing for higher order systems of equations and the presence of both stock and flow variables. The form of the exact discrete-time model that accommodated these complexities was found to be a vector autoregressive moving average model (in fact, VARMA(2,2) for a second-order stochastic differential equation system) whose coefficient matrices were highly nonlinear functions of the original system's parameters. Gaussian estimation involved the construction and optimization of the Gaussian likelihood for this discrete-time model. The statistical properties of the resulting estimates then followed from existing asymptotic theory for the estimation of stationary vector time-series models in discrete time, such as that developed by Dunsmuir (1979).

The 1983 paper set the stage for much subsequent research. The next step in Bergstrom's research addressed computational issues. In practical work, the principal difficulty in the implementation of Gaussian maximum likelihood is the construction of the likelihood. The problem is acute when there are data irregularities such as mixed stock and flow variables, missing observations, or initialization on a state vector with unknown elements. Unfortunately, these problems arise regularly in continuous-system estimation. One general approach to the construction of the likelihood is the Kalman filter. The use of this method in continuous-system estimation has been studied recently in a series of articles by Harvey and Stock (1985, 1988a, 1988b). In two papers [29, 30] published in 1985 and 1986, Bergstrom explored another approach that does not rely on the Kalman filter but makes explicit use of the exact discrete model for the observable variables, including the functional dependence of the error covariance matrix (Ω) on the system parameters. The likelihood can then be constructed readily from the conventional Gaussian form, given an initialization of the state vector, by using the Choleski factorization of Ω. The resulting algorithm involves computations that are on the order of Tn^3, where n is the dimension of the system and T is the sample size. Computations of this order within a general algorithm to maximize a likelihood function are well within the capability of modern computing equipment, at least for moderate values of n and T.

With the development of a complete theory of Gaussian estimation of continuous systems and a computational algorithm to implement it, Bergstrom turned to address issues of forecasting, control, and statistical testing. In an article [33] published in *Computers, and Mathematics with Applications* in 1989, Bergstrom showed how to generate optimal forecasts for a continuous system in a simple way from the discrete VARMA model using the Gaussian estimates of the matrix Choleski factorization of the full error covariance matrix. Recursive formulas were provided for the generation of k-period ahead forecasts. A related article [3] dealt with optimal control and provided the solution of a quadratic cost functional optimization problem given stochastic differential equations of motion for the system. This work extended earlier certainty equivalence theory and allowed for weaker conditions on the innovation processes by relaxing the requirement that they be increments of Brownian motion.

Statistical testing and model evaluation of continuous systems form the subject of a very recent article [34] published by Bergstrom (1990) in a volume that brings together his contributions to continuous-time econometric modeling. The subject of [34] is the development of practical statistical tests of the models and explicit parameterizations that arise in discrete versions of continuous systems. Discrete data generated from a continuous system with mixed stock and flow variables satisfy a VARMA model with heavily restricted coefficient matrices. For a second-order system of stochastic differential equations with mixed stock and flow data, the VARMA model is of order (2,2). A further complication is that the MA coefficient matrices are temporarily dependent. [34] gives recursive formulas for the computation of these matrices and shows that the recursion is stable in the sense that the coefficients converge (as $t \rightarrow \infty$) to fixed limit matrices. Several statistical tests are suggested to evaluate the model. These involve three steps:

1. test the hypothesis that a VARMA(2,2) is the data generating mechanism by time-series model selection procedures;
2. test the form of the coefficient matrices in the VARMA(2,2) that are implied by an underlying continuous system using a likelihood ratio test;
3. test the explicit parameterization of the coefficient matrices that are implied by economic theory using a Wald test.

These tests permit an investigator to assess the adequacy of the maintained hypothesis (i.e. a VARMA(2,2) model) within which the continuous system's discrete model is embedded, to test the validity of the restrictions implied by the presence of an underlying continuous time system, and, finally, to test any restrictions delivered by economic theory on the coefficients in the continuous systems.

The article on statistical testing completed Bergstrom's decade-long study of the econometric methodology of higher order continuous-time systems. The empirical implementation of this new methodology is clearly the next phase of research and will carry Bergstrom's commitment to this line of research to its logical conclusion and into the 1990s. The empirical research program has now begun with a joint article [35] with M. J. Chambers (one of Bergstrom's former Ph.D students at Essex) on the demand for durable goods in the UK over the period 1973–84. This article studies dynamic responses of consumer purchases to changes in disposable income and post-sample predictive performance of the model is tested against simpler models. The results are deemed to be a successful empirical implementation of the continuous time econometric methodology.

The most ambitious empirical application of the Bergstrom methodology of Gaussian estimation of higher order continuous systems is to a new continuous-time macroeconometric model of the UK. At the time of writing, this application is nearing completion and is a joint enterprise with Ben Nowman and Clifford Wymer, two of Bergstrom's former students. It promises a major implementation of the latest econometric methodology for continuous-time systems and an important new extension of the earlier Bergstrom–Wymer empirical work on modeling the UK economy. In a very real sense this new empirical application will represent the culmination of a research program that has been ongoing for the last 30 years.

Since the early 1960s Bergstrom has been the world's leading proponent of continuous-time econometric modeling. Few econometricians have ever shown such tremendous dedication to a field of research. These days such dedication is rare even on much shorter time horizons, particularly in North America where funding agencies play a large role in influencing research directions and fads and fashion all too often seem to take the place of serious long-term research agendas. Bergstrom has established a tradition of research wherein a class of exciting economic theory models are formulated and analyzed, econometric methodology is developed, computational algorithms and computer programs are written to permit practical implementation of the methods, and empirical applications are conducted that explore the practical consequences and worldly implications of the new methodology. This must surely be econometrics at its most fully developed. As a paradigm for students and young researchers it is certainly the finest example. As a lifetime achievement in research it is remarkable.

References

Bartlett, M. S. (1946). "On the theoretical specification and sampling properties of autocorrelated time-series," *Journal of the Royal Statistical Society Supplement*, 8, 27–41.

Basmann, R. L. (1961). "A note on the exact finite sample frequency functions of generalized classical linear estimators in two leading overidentified cases," *Journal of the American Statistical Association*, 56, 619–36.

Bergstrom, A. R. (1990). *Continuous Time Econometric Modelling*. Oxford: Oxford University Press.

Dunsmuir, W. (1979). "A central limit theorem for parameter estimation in stationary vector time series and its application to models for a signal observed with noise," *Annals of Statistics*, 7, 490–506.

Durbin, J. (1961). "Efficient fitting of linear models for continuous stationary time series from discrete data," *Bulletin of the International Statistical Institute*, 38, 273–83.

Harvey, A. C., and J. H. Stock (1985). "The estimation of higher-order continuous time autoregressive models," *Econometric Theory*, 1, 97–117.

Harvey, A. C., and J. H. Stock (1988a). "Continuous time autoregressive models with common stochastic trends," *Journal of Economic Dynamics and Control*, 12, 365–84.

Harvey, A. C., and J. H. Stock (1988b). "Estimating integrated higher-order continuous time autoregressions with an application to money-income causality," *Journal of Econometrics*, 42, 319–36.

Nagar, A. L. (1959). "The bias and moment matrix of the general *k*-class estimators of the parameters in structural equations," *Econometrica*, 27, 575–95.

Phillips, A. W. (1959). "The estimation of parameters in systems of stochastic differential equations," *Biometrika*, 46, 67–76.

Phillips, P. C. B. (1972). "The structural estimation of a stochastic differential equation system," *Econometrica*, 40, 1021–41.

Quenouille, M. H. (1957). *The Analysis of Multiple Time Series*. London: Griffin.

Solow, R. M. (1956). "A contribution to the theory of economic growth," *Quarterly Journal of Economics*, 70, 65–94.

Swan, T. (1956). "Economic growth and capital accumulation," *Economic Record*, 32, 334–61.

2

What is Econometrics?*

A. R. Bergstrom

Instead of attempting to give a concise definition of econometrics I shall discuss the activities that it includes. These are: (1) the formulation of econometric models, (2) the statistical testing of these models and the estimation of their parameters, (3) prediction.

The Formulation of Models

Any set of assumptions that approximately describes the behavior of an economy can be called an economic model. Thus all economic theory is concerned with the formulation and analysis of models. But most of these models are too imprecise to be used as a basis for statistical testing and fitting. One of the main tasks of the econometrician is to formulate more precise models which can be tested against statistical observations and whose parameters can be estimated. Such a model is called an econometric model. It usually consists of two parts. The first part is a system of equations relating certain observable economic variables such as incomes, prices, and the quantities of various goods produced and consumed, and unobservable random variables called disturbances. The disturbances represent the influence of a large number of physical and sociological variables which have not been separately introduced into the model and most of which are not directly observable. The second part of the model consists of a set of assumptions about the probability distribution of the disturbances. Some such assumptions are essential if the model is to be statistically testable.

An important consideration influencing the formulation of an econometric model is the amount of data available for the estimation of its parameters. In this respect the task of the econometrician can be contrasted with that of the physical scientist. Whereas the physical scientist can usually generate as much data as is required in order to give reliable estimates of the parameters of his models, the econometrician is faced with the problem of extracting as much information as possible from a given amount of data. The data may, for example, consist of 20 annual observations of each variable. But even an aggregative econometric model (i.e. an econometric model that does not distinguish between different goods, all variables being aggregates or

*First published in *The University of Auckland Gazette*, Vol. 8, No. 1 April 1966.

averages such as the gross national product, the general price level, total consumption, and total capital formation) may involve 20 or more variables each of which is either directly or indirectly influenced by all of the others. Hence, unless same *a priori* information is used to restrict the number of parameters to be estimated it will be impossible to obtain reliable estimates from the limited amount of data available.

The most important source of *a priori* information is the fact that economic behavior is the result of more or less rational decision making. In order to make use of this fact it is necessary to represent it by precise axioms of rational economic behavior from which we can derive behavior relations involving a comparatively small number of parameters. Such axioms are, of course, no more than approximations to reality; and the ultimate test of their usefulness is the predictive power of the equation systems that are derived from them.

A preliminary check on the realism of a model can be obtained by studying its implications. It is important to know whether or not there is any set of values of the parameters for which the paths of the variables generated by the model display certain features of reality. We know, for example, that many of the variables that are to be explained by an econometric model must remain positive. Hence a model that necessarily implies that some of these variables will eventually become negative cannot be a good approximation to reality.

Testing and Estimation

The statistical testing of a model and the estimation of its parameters involve closely related problems. In order to test the model we must find certain properties that have only a small probability of being possessed by a sample (i.e. a series of observations of the variables) that has been generated by the assumed model but a greater probability of being possessed by samples generated by alternative models. If the actual sample possesses one of these properties the model should be rejected in favor of one of the alternatives. The designing of a test involves the derivation of the probability distributions of certain functions of the observations in a sample. The problem of estimation is to find functions of the observations that have suitable properties as estimates of the parameters of the model. Associated with this is the problem of finding confidence intervals which are intervals that have a given probability of containing the true values of the parameters.

Although the general methods relating to the above problems are part of the subject of statistics, the particular methods that are applicable to econometric models have been developed mainly by econometricians and are not yet discussed in treatises on statistical theory. It is mainly because of the importance of *a priori* information in econometric work that the standard statistical methods are inapplicable. Most econometric models can be transformed into one of the standard forms (e.g. a multivariate autogressive system) discussed in the statistical literature. But the parameters of the transformed system would be complicated nonlinear functions of the smaller set of parameters occurring in the economic behavior relations. The standard statistical methods could be applied only by ignoring this restriction or, in other words, making no use of the *a priori* information.

The development of new statistical methods applicable to econometric models continues to be one of the main activities of econometricians, and many important problems remain to be solved. The application of these methods to models of actual economies is, of course, another important activity and one that has been greatly facilitated, in recent years, by the development of electronic computers.

Prediction

The ultimate aim of econometrics is prediction. But here the word "prediction" is used in a broad sense. It includes not only forecasting under the assumption of unchanged structure but also the prediction of the effects of possible changes of structure. It includes, for example, the prediction of the effects of alternative changes of government policy which might be under consideration.

We shall consider first the problem of forecasting under unchanged structure. The problem, in this case, is to predict future observations of the variables assuming that both these and the sample are generated by the assumed model. Even if the assumed model (including the probability distribution of the disturbances) were an exact description of reality and the true values of its parameters were known, it would be impossible to predict the exact values of future observations of the variables. The best that we could do would be to obtain the conditional probability distribution of the values assumed by the variables at any point of time for given values of the variables at previous points of time. Hence, by making use of the values assumed by the variables over the sample period, we could obtain the probability distribution of future observations. In fact the true values of the parameters of the model are unknown. They must be estimated from the sample. All that we can obtain, therefore, are estimates of the parameters of the probability distribution of future observations. An important part of the prediction problem is to obtain confidence intervals for these estimates.

A difficulty that arises in econometric forecasting but not in the forecasting of physical phenomena is that the variables that are being forecast may be influenced by the forecasts. Few econometricians would be so optimistic as to believe that their forecasts have, yet, a sufficient influence on the behavior of businessmen and politicians to make this a serious problem. But, in any case, it can be handled by introducing the model's forecasts as additional variables in the model.

We consider, finally, the problem of predicting the effects of a change of structure. Suppose, for example, that we wish to predict the effect of a new system of automatic control in which certain government policy variables such as taxation rates and the volume of money would be continually adjusted, according to certain formulas, in response to changes in such variables as the level of unemployment, the balance of payments deficit and the rate of increase in prices. The model may contain certain government behavior relations which are assumed to have held over the sample period. These must be retained for the purpose of estimating the parameters of the complete model and then, for the purpose of prediction, replaced by a set of feed-back relations representing the new policy. The econometrician may be required to predict the behavior of the economy for various assumed values of the parameters of the feed-back relations, or alternatively, if the policymakers can provide him with sufficiently precise objectives, to determine the optimum values of these parameters.

3

The *ET* Interview: A. R. Bergstrom*

Interviewed by Peter C. B. Phillips

In the previous interviews in this series, we have learnt from Denis Sargan and Jim Durbin about the role that was played by the London School of Economics (LSE) in shaping the development of econometrics during the 1960s. Two other figures who were central to the initiatives that were taken in this transitional phase at the LSE were the New Zealand born economists Bill Phillips and Rex Bergstrom. Unlike Bill Phillips, who was schooled and apprenticed at the LSE, Rex Bergstrom was trained as an economist in New Zealand and worked there as an academic throughout the 1950s before joining the LSE in 1962. Rex was already an accomplished econometrician when he came to the LSE. His econometric study of supply and demand for New Zealand's exports had attracted international attention in 1955 when it appeared in *Econometrica*. It was the first large-scale macroeconometric model to be estimated by the new Cowles Commission methods and it predated subsequent work on international macroeconometric models by some 15 years.

Since 1966 Rex has been the world's leading proponent of continuous-time econometric modeling. His contributions cover the entire field of research encompassing theoretical work on cyclical growth models, econometric methods of estimation, and a major empirical implementation of the methodology to the UK economy. The latter, which is now popularly known as the Bergstrom–Wymer model, has become the prototype for many subsequent models which have been developed by research teams in the central bands of industralized countries.

Rex Bergstrom's research bears the hallmark of exemplary scholarship. A deep concern for fundamental issues is always evident in his writing; he is a lucid thinker and a fine expositor. There is real follow through in his work, reflecting a desire that is present in all good scholarship to report only what has been properly researched and fully thought out. Above all, Rex is an economist's econometrician with a fervent interest in economics as well as deep respect for mathematics and mathematical statistics.

Only part of Rex's career has been spent in New Zealand but his impact on the professional community of economists in New Zealand has been enormous. Many New Zealand economists themselves carry the Bergstrom pedigree, as do

*First published in *Econometric Theory*, **4**, 1988, 301–27.

many expatriates who live overseas in Australia, England, and North America: some are now in business, some in academe. Many others have been influenced by his work and his style of research through the teachings of his students. All of us who have been fortunate to have had Rex as a teacher know that we have studied under a powerful and intense mind whose lessons and inspirations have the special quality of enduring relevance.

In August 1987, the recently formed Australasian Chapter of the Econometric Society held its annual meeting in New Zealand. These were the first meetings of the Econometric Society to be held in New Zealand and they took place at the University of Canterbury, where Rex had himself studied when it was a College of the University of New Zealand. Before the conference on August 22, Rex and I met in the Economics Department of the University of Canterbury and recorded the following conversation.

Would you like to start by telling us about your schooling in New Zealand? Did you develop academic interests early in life? Were you attracted to the sciences, the humanities, or both?

I attended the Christchurch Boys High for four years, 1938–41. Christchurch Boys High was the leading academic state school then in Christchurch and probably still is. In those days the top form had to do six compulsory subjects for three years. Then we sat the University Entrance examination and later there were opportunities for specialization in the sixth form. The six compulsory subjects were English, Mathematics, Chemistry, Latin, French, and History. Mathematics was my first love, intellectually, and has remained so throughout my life. Mathematics and Chemistry were my best subjects at school and I was at the top all the way through in those subjects. But I dropped chemistry in the fourth year and substituted a course in economics which was being given by one of the teachers on an experimental basis. The reason was that by this stage I had decided to do a commerce degree rather than a science degree, which would have been the obvious thing for me to do on academic grounds. The economics course was fairly general and elementary, but it did stimulate my interest in economics and I looked forward to doing some economics as part of my B.Com degree.

At that time was applied mathematics also a subject in school?

It was. But we didn't take it as a separate subject. It was probably an option for the scholarship examination. Mathematics was all one subject in the mainstream course.

Then you went off to study at Canterbury University College. That must have been during the early war years.

Yes. I left school at the age of 16 and took a full-time job. That was in 1942. At the same time I enrolled as a part-time student for a B.Com at Canterbury University College and commenced studying for the Accountants' Professional Examinations. In those days Canterbury University College was one of the colleges of the University of New Zealand. The University of New Zealand was made up of four main colleges: one in each of the main cities plus two agricultural colleges. The B.Com degree was a very convenient degree to do part time. Normal office hours were from 8:00 a.m.–5:00 p.m., and formal lectures for the B.Com were after 5:00 p.m. It was a fairly hard life. In addition to working in the evenings and weekends, I often used to get up at 5:00 a.m. in the morning and do an hour or two of work before going to the office. That went on for five years. After five years I had completed the B.Com and the Accountants' Professional Examinations. Also in the same period I had a year off in the Air Force.

Was your main objective upon entering university to take up a career in accountancy or did you have other possibilities in mind as well?

I did initially plan to qualify both as an actuary and as an accountant. I thought that actuarial work would give me an opportunity for application in mathematics. In addition, both the actuarial and accountancy professions were quite well paid. I thought it would be useful to have qualifications in both of them. But, in fact, I never started on the actuarial examinations because I soon became very interested in economics and decided to become an economist.

How did your interests in economics develop? Were there teachers that you found particularly stimulating, or was it simply the subject itself?

I think it was the subject itself, although Alan Danks and Wolfgang Rosenberg were my main teachers and they certainly stimulated me to read all the right books. That was probably later on when I took graduate work.

Did you get to read Keynes' General Theory *as an undergraduate?*

This, in fact, was the thing which finally made me make up my mind to become an economist. During the last year of my B.Com I was seriously considering becoming an economist and during the Christmas vacation, following completion of my B.Com, I read the whole of Keynes' *General Theory*. I found it quite exciting to have a complete system of equations determining all the main macroeconomic variables and synthesizing real and monetary phenomena. I decided then definitely to become an economist. I enrolled for the M.Com degree.

How far did you continue with mathematics at university?

When I did the B.Com, mathematics was not on the list of optional subjects, unfortunately. But after completing my B.Com and M.Com degrees and before going to Cambridge, I did do the first two years in pure mathematics for the B.A. in mathematics. That is Stage 1 and Stage 2 mathematics, as they were called in New Zealand. I attended the lectures and sat the examination in Stage 2 mathematics while I was a junior lecturer in economics at Auckland University. That was a year before I went to Cambridge. During that period I also spent a lot of time reading books on mathematics outside of formal course work. I think that the most important book on mathematics I read at that stage was Hardy's *Pure Mathematics*. Although it is only an elementary book, it is beautiful and rigorous and it has had a permanent influence on my approach to mathematics. I also spent a lot of time reading mathematics when I was at Cambridge and I have continued to read many books on mathematics throughout my life. Some of the books which I found most useful were not published until long after I had finished my Ph.D. Examples are Halmos' *Finite Dimensional Vector Spaces* and Kolmogorov and Fomin's *Functional Analysis*, both of which I read completely after I finished my Ph.D.

You mentioned that you served with the Air Force during the War. What was the nature of your work for them?

I went into the Air Force in early 1945 when I was 19. At that stage I had my name down to be a navigator. I had been in the air training corps at school and I knew a bit of navigation, which was just the application of elementary trigonometry. Two months after I went into the Air Force the War ended in Europe and at that stage they decided that it wasn't worthwhile training any more air crew, so I transferred over to the accounts section. The War ended completely when Japan surrendered a few months later and after that there was still a lot of work to do winding down the whole operation. I was in the Air Force for about six months after the War ended. So it occupied about a year all together.

You went on to do your M.Com in economics and got First Class Honors. Did your degree entail course work and a thesis?

It entailed course work and the choice of a thesis or writing an essay, which was on a list of optional topics which one was presented with at the examination. I chose to do the essay. I got quite a good mark for it. But it was during the M.Com work year that I did most of my reading. As I mentioned earlier, my teachers Alan Danks and Wolfgang Rosenberg stimulated me into reading all the right books. The most important book which I read during my M.Com year was Hick's *Value and Capital.* At the time when I read this, it was the most exciting book, intellectually, which I had ever read. More exciting than Keynes' *General Theory*, and I read the complete book, not just the first part, as many people read. For years afterwards I thought that it contained the answer to every economic question that I could think of. I still think that many of the ideas which have subsequently been attributed to other people can be found in *Value and Capital.* Other books which I read during that year were Wicksell's *Lectures in Political Economy*, Marshall's *Principles of Economics*, Pigou's *Economics of Welfare*, Chamberlain's *Monopolistic Competition*, Joan Robinson's *Economics of Imperfect Competition*, Haberler's *Prosperity in Depression*, Ohlin's *Interregional and International Trade*, and there were several others. At that time Samuelson's *Foundations of Economic Analysis* had still not been published. But I did read that several years later, after it was published.

That was a busy year's reading in economics. Did you do any statistics as part of your degree?

I did a statistics course, but it was very elementary. I could do a regression, but I didn't know much about statistical inference at that stage.

After your M.Com degree, you won a scholarship to travel overseas, but before doing so you took up teaching positions at Massey and at Auckland. Can you tell us about this part of your career?

The job at Massey was an assistant lectureship in economics. This was my first academic post. Massey College was an agricultural college and also part of the University of New Zealand. There were only two of us in the department: Brian Low was the head of the department and my job was to give the lectures in pure economics for the students doing the bachelor of agricultural science degree. It was at Massey that I started to be seriously interested in statistics. This was partly because I was surrounded by agricultural scientists who were all working in statistics. It was at Massey, also, that I wrote and published my first paper, which was just a little paper on the application of price discrimination theory to the pricing of dairy products.

After two years at Massey, I moved to Auckland University College. It was only a small department. There were four of us. But it was the best economics department in New Zealand and it was certainly the strongest department in econometrics. The head of the department was Colin Simkin. Although he was not himself an econometrician, Colin was one of the first people in New Zealand to appreciate the importance of econometrics. He had acquired a complete set of back issues of *Econometrica*, as well as the Cowles Commission papers, so there were plenty of things for me to read there. My colleague, Malcolm Fisher, who was a lecturer in the department, was also working in econometrics at that stage. It was at Auckland that I started to work seriously in the field of applied econometrics and it was there that I published my first econometrics paper. This was a paper on New Zealand's export supply function published in the *Economic Record* in 1951. I also had a wide teaching experience at Auckland, as one has to in a small department. I taught courses in money and banking, public finance, and all the third-year economic theory courses. As I have already mentioned, I also spent a lot of time studying mathematics during those years.

In 1952, *you traveled to Cambridge in England to do your Ph.D. What made you select Cambridge University?*

The immediate reason was that Richard Stone was there. I had read his papers on demand analysis and other aspects of econometrics and I hoped that he would agree to be my supervisor, which he did. But there were more general reasons for going to Cambridge. In addition to being a famous center of economics, Cambridge was one of the world's leading centers of science and mathematics. Even when I was at school and still thinking of doing a degree in science, I had aspirations of going to Cambridge. Then, after I had finished my degrees in economics and became intensely absorbed in the study of mathematics, I seriously considered going to Cambridge to do the mathematics tripos. But I decided that in any case I could spend a lot of time reading mathematics while I was at Cambridge doing my Ph.D., and I did. Although I didn't do any formal course work there, a lot of my friends and associates at Cambridge were scientists and mathematicians.

When you went to Cambridge did you already have a topic for doctoral dissertation research in mind?

Yes, I had actually planned and formulated a model which I proposed to estimate. It arose out of my early work on the export supply function. I decided to disaggregate this and have a separate demand and supply equation for various products. I had formulated a complete model before I went to Cambridge and, indeed, had already collected some of the data for the New Zealand side of the model.

In Econometrica *in* 1955 *you published your article on the market for New Zealand exports and this was one of the first, if not the first, empirical implementation of the LIML estimator. Can you tell us about that research?*

It arose out of my doctoral dissertation. The model was quite a large simultaneous equations model involving UK demand equations and New Zealand supply equations. In those days the New Zealand economy was just a subbranch of the UK economy. Almost the entire exports of lamb, mutton, and dairy products went to the UK and these provided most of the export receipts. They were a very important part of the New Zealand economy. The supply side of the model was quite elaborate, with interrelated equations determining output and livestock numbers and based on a dynamic model of the firm. Also, it was necessary to treat all the main New Zealand macroeconomic variables as jointly dependent, endogenous variables because of the important effect that the export market had on the New Zealand economy. The complete model had 27 equations and I estimated 55 parameters by both ordinary least squares and limited-information maximum likelihood. I did most of the calculations on an ordinary electric desk calculator, a MADAS. But I did invert some of the large matrices on the old EDSAC computer, that is, electric delay storage automatic computer, which was one of the first two electronic computers in the UK. But often this machine was broken down just when I wanted to use it and I certainly did invert some 10×10 matrices on the desk calculator. There were no econometric textbooks in those days dealing with LIML. Klein's book had not yet been published, so one had to learn LIML by reading the Anderson and Rubin articles. At the time when my paper was published, I think it was possibly the first paper to give strong empirical support to the new method. I estimated the model from prewar data and then tested the post-sample predictive performance against postwar data. The predictions obtained from the LIML estimator were better not only than those from the least squares estimator, but also than those from the two commonly used naive models in those days. One of these was just that there would be no change between years t and $t + 1$ and the other was that the change between years t and $t + 1$ would be the same as between years $t - 1$ and t. It was considered to be quite an achievement just to get a model which just predicted better than either of these two. In the years following the publication of the article in *Econometrica*, 1955, it got quite a bit of publicity and was referred to by Klein, Koopmans, Wold, and several other leading econometricians.

Your paper must have appeared around the same time as the Klein–Goldberger model?

It was before the Klein–Goldberger model. Klein's first simultaneous equations model was published in 1950 and the Klein–Goldberger model, which was really a sort of Mark II Klein model, was published later. My article was published in between.

Your model also had more endogenous variables and equations than the Klein–Goldberger model.

Yes, it did.

What would you say was the main stimulus to you to work in econometrics?

I think Haavelmo's papers were the main stimulus and then the Anderson and Rubin papers and other Cowles Commission papers. I think another stimulus was Klein's first econometric model, his 1950 econometric model of the USA.

Much of your research in the 1950s was concerned with the New Zealand economy and dealt with various applied macro and international aspects of small open economies. Were there other economists in New Zealand doing empirical research on these issues at that time?

No, I was certainly the first person to apply econometrics to these issues. People were interested in what I was doing.

Did you feel isolated at that time from the growing activity in econometric research overseas, particularly in the UK and in North America?

I suppose I felt a bit isolated. But, as I said, my colleagues in the economics department at Auckland were interested in what I was doing. So also were the mathematicians in New Zealand. I was once invited down to Wellington to talk to the staff seminar of the applied mathematics section of the Department of Scientific and Industrial Research. This was reputed at that stage to be the best mathematics department in New Zealand, better than any of the University departments. One of the participants in the seminar was Peter Whittle, who had recently completed his Ph.D. under Herman Wold in Sweden and had returned to New Zealand for a few years before finally settling in England.

In 1962, Econometrica *published your article on the finite sample distributions of least squares and maximum likelihood estimators of the marginal propensity to consume. Your paper and Basmann's related research marked a watershed in econometric research, opening up a new research program on finite-sample theory. How was it that you came to work on this problem?*

I first started to think about working on this problem when I was at Cambridge, because in those days there was a lot of opposition to the new methods. Whenever I gave seminars, I was in the position of defending the new simultaneous equations methods against least squares. I decided that the most effective way to answer some of the criticisms would be to find the exact distribution of some of these estimators. But I didn't start doing that until several years later when the stimulus was the publication of Nagar's article on approximations to the moment matrix of the k-class estimators. Shortly after that I decided to try to find the exact distribution. I thought that the marginal propensity to consume in the basic stochastic Keynesian model would be a very good point at which to start, because this model had gained a lot of publicity through Haavelmo's famous paper in *JASA* in 1949. I think Theil had also found an approximation to the distribution. So quite a lot of people were interested in the problem.

Did the analytical results come easily?

The maximum likelihood estimator was, of course, quite a straightforward exercise, but finding the distribution of the least squares estimator was much more difficult, because there was no obvious way of proceeding. The key simplifying step was an orthogonal transformation which I made at an early stage of the proof. This is the sort of idea which somehow just comes, if one thinks about a problem for a while. In fact, I think I spent only a few weeks producing the paper and some of this time was spent doing the numerical calculations for the graphs and tables. I first met Haavelmo in 1962 at the LSE, just about the time that the paper was published. When I told him that I had found the exact distribution of the least squares estimator, he said that he didn't think anyone would ever find that in the closed form, in terms of known functions. In fact, it is interesting that it comes out as just a finite number of terms, in terms of just products of rational functions and exponentials of rational functions.

There are few finite-sample distributions which can be expressed so simply and without relying on the special functions of applied mathematics. Have you ever thought of returning to that topic?

I did for many years think of returning to the topic, because to me it is a very attractive topic, mathematically. But I am sure that I will never return to it now because you, in particular, have done so much and pushed it so far forward, that one feels that the field is almost cleaned up.

After working at Auckland University in New Zealand for more than ten years, you moved to the London School of Economics in 1962. *How did this come about?*

I was on leave at the LSE from the University of Auckland in 1962. At that stage, I had either just completed or was working on several topics which were of interest to people at the LSE. I had just published my paper on finite-sample distributions. While I was there, I produced my first paper on cyclical growth models and presented it at the famous Robbins seminar. I was also, in that year, starting to work on my continuous-time estimation problems. They knew that I would be interested in a post if one came up and, in fact, as the result of a resignation, a readership did become vacant. They offered it to me and I accepted. I am sure that, even if the job had not come up at the LSE, I would have stayed in London. London was the center of the world for me and I had never really regarded myself as permanently settled in New Zealand. At that stage, I was seriously considering leaving academic life and taking a job in the city. I did, in fact, have an offer of a job in the city and probably would have accepted it if the job at the LSE had not come up.

What were your impressions of the LSE in the early 1960*s? Was there any sense that this was an important period of transition and development for the LSE in econometrics?*

Yes, there was. I think that, indeed, it was a very important period of transition. It was during this period that the LSE replaced Cambridge as the leading center of econometrics in the UK. After Denis Sargan arrived in 1963, there were four of us working in the field of econometric theory and econometric methodology: Jim Durbin, Bill Phillips, Denis Sargan, and myself. Then, in addition, there was another larger group which was very interested in applied econometrics and there was a regular weekly seminar devoted to applied econometrics. Some of the people who used to come to that seminar were: Dick Lipsey, Max Steuer, Chris Archibald, Morris Peston, and others. In those years, also, we were planning to introduce the first taught Masters course, although that didn't get going until shortly after I left the LSE.

Do you have any special memories of that time; seminars, courses or incidents that seem significant to you now?

I remember Jim Durbin producing his algorithm for obtaining full-information maximum likelihod estimates, which somehow got lost for a number of years, until it was resurrected many years later by other people. He did present it at Copenhagen at the conference and then he got a computer program written to implement it. He asked me to design an econometric model to apply it. We did do this and completed a model but it was never published because after that I returned to New Zealand and I had decided that the best way to do dynamic econometrics was in continuous time.

It was during this period that your research developed two major themes. One was cyclical growth models and the other was continuous-time estimation. Would you like to talk to us about the source of your interest in these fields and the main objectives of your research?

Yes, let me talk first about the cyclical growth model. In 1962, I had been thinking for some time about doing some work on cyclical growth models, with the particular object of introducing more economic theory into the models and introducing a price mechanism. In those days, cyclical growth models were very mechanical. The cycles were produced just by the interaction of the multiplier and accelerator and the growth was produced just by exogenous trends. There was nothing in the models to ensure that over a long period aggregate demand would follow supply. When I had arrived at the LSE in early 1962, I was quite excited to find that Bill Phillips had just published a paper on cyclical growth introducing Keynesian-type feedback mechanisms and synthesizing real and monetary phenomena. This was very much the sort of thing that I had had in mind. Also, I was not surprised to learn that the main stimulus for his work had come from James Meade. James Meade had himself been working on this problem and it was out of his discussions with James Meade that he ended up writing his own paper. There were some aspects of his paper which I found rather unsatisfactory. My first cyclical growth paper, the one published in *Economica* in 1962, was largely an attempt to deal with these, while at the same time keeping as close as possible to Bill Phillips' basic framework. In particular, I retained his rather extreme assumption of a single technology, but I introduced the effect of the price mechanism by developing a pseudo-production function which worked through variations in the age distribution of the stock of capital. At that stage, I was also starting to think about the estimation of continuous-time models. This is really another branch of research which was stimulated by another article by Bill Phillips, his 1959 *Biometrika* paper.

Your monograph on The Construction and Use of Economic Models *brought together many of these developments and is a masterpiece of exposition. Students at Auckland University in my generation used to have competitions among themselves to find even a single typographical error in your book. What inspired you to write it?*

I was invited to write the book by English University Press for their applied mathematics series. The most famous book published in that series was Peter Whittle's *Prediction and Regulation.* The Editor at English University Press who was handling the series told me that Peter Whittle had suggested to him that he invite me to write a book on economic models for the series. I was pleased to do this. My main object in the book was to develop what I called "prototype continuous-time econometric models." Indeed, I think, from this point of view, the book was quite successful because the cyclical growth model developed in the central chapters of the book did, in fact, become the prototype for the first continuous-time econometric model of the UK. The general methodology developed in the central chapters of the book that deal with formulations and stability analysis have since been widely used in continuous-time econometric models.

In 1964, *you returned to the University of Auckland. Did you find it difficult to maintain your ongoing research agenda there, after the lively research activity of the LSE?*

I was very busy during my first year writing my book *The Construction and Use of Economic Models*. I commenced this at the LSE, but I finished it during my first year at Auckland. After that I had a number of other things to do. I had several new books which I wanted to read, including Malinvaud's *Statistical Methods of Econometrics* and a number of new graduate courses to plan. During one long vacation, I also went up to Bangkok and spent nine weeks working as a consultant for the Economic Commission for Asia and the Far East. There was a bit of a lull in my research then as I began to look forward to my next major research project, which would be a new continuous-time model of the UK. I hoped to return to England in a few years and decided that I would start work on that.

During this period at Auckland, you developed a graduate econometrics course based on the most rigorous and general parts of Malinvaud's Statistical Methods of Econometrics. *This course must have been very different in character from typical econometrics courses in other parts of the world. What made you choose to design your graduate econometrics course this way?*

It was really Malinvaud's book itself. I had read enough of the French edition to realize that the book was in a completely different class from any other econometrics book which had been published. I decided then that, as soon as the first English edition came out, I would base a graduate course on it – which I did. The central chapters of that book were very much to my taste. Although general and rigorous, there was a continuous logical development running from the basic linear model in Chapter 5 through to the nonlinear model in Chapter 9, and beyond that into simultaneous equations models. This appealed to me very much as the basis for a course, and I continued to give that course after I moved to the University of Essex. I had a remarkable group of students during that period at Auckland and many of them now have worldwide reputations in econometrics. Apart from yourself, my students at Auckland during that period included Cliff Wymer, who was just finishing off his master's thesis, in 1965. There was also Roger Bowden and Viv Hall. In addition to these students who have made careers in econometrics, I had some brilliant students who did my advanced econometrics course and then moved into completely different fields. Of these the most notable is Hugh Fletcher, who is now the chief executive of the biggest company in New Zealand.

What do you think caused this surge of good students at Auckland during the 1960*s?*

I don't know. Quite a few of them came over from the mathematics department and had done complete degrees in mathematics or the equivalent. You, yourself, virtually did two degrees simultaneously in mathematics and economics. And Roger Bowden had done a degree in mathematics.

Many of these students not only followed your graduate econometrics course but did research for their masters' theses under your supervision.

That's right. I helped Cliff Wymer towards the end of his master's thesis, then I supervised Viv Hall's Ph.D. thesis and your master's thesis.

Looking back on your graduate econometrics course at Auckland now, do you feel that the level of the course was comparable or higher than that of other courses overseas with which you were familiar, like those at the LSE, for example?

I felt that it was at least as high, probably a bit higher. I have subsequently talked to students who have come back from places like Stanford and said that many of the faculty there were surprised at the level of the courses they had already done – people like Hugh Fletcher and George Wheeler, for example, who subsequently went to Stanford.

A second theme to emerge from your research in the 1960s *was econometric modeling in continuous time. This involved both theoretical and empirical research. Can you tell us about this general research program which you initiated in the* 1960s*?*

Yes, the theoretical work was stimulated by reading Bill Phillips' 1959 *Biometrika* paper. I had, several years earlier, read Bartlett's paper in *JRSS* in 1946, but it was not until I read Bill Phillips' paper that I became convinced that continuous-time econometric modeling was really feasible. It was at that stage that I decided to do some work in the field. In fact, I was working on finite-sample distributions at the time, but I decided that as soon as I finished that I would move on to do some work on continuous-time estimation. I had already planned my approach when I arrived at the LSE in 1962. Although Bill Phillips' article was the immediate stimulus to my work, my approach was completely different from his. My approach was to use the exact discrete analog in order to investigate the sampling properties of estimates obtained from an approximate simultaneous equations model. I also aimed to link up this research with the debate on independent versus causal systems, which had been initiated by Herman Wold, a debate which was still quite active at that stage. When I arrived at the LSE and told Bill Phillips what I was planning to do, he was very interested, even though my approach was different from his. He made available computing facilities for me, and I commenced work. Bill Phillips was away himself, on leave at MIT, while the rest of the work was going on, but he arrived back in time to read my paper before I submitted it to *Econometrica* in 1964. Denis Sargan, at that stage, had just arrived at the LSE and he also read the paper. He himself started to work in the field shortly after I left the LSE. I discussed these methodological problems a bit more in my book on *The Construction and Use of Economic Models* and tried there to link it up with my theoretical work on cyclical growth models. I decided that the next major step, having worked on both the econometric methodology and the economic theory, was to combine the two by estimating a continuous-time empirical econometric model. I was thinking about this during my period at Auckland and commenced planning the model shortly before I returned to England in 1970. When I reached Essex in 1970, I had already planned out my model of the United Kingdom, analyzed its mathematical properties, collected the data, and done a transformation to approximately eliminate the autocorrelation resulting from flow data. My former student and colleague, Cliff Wymer was at that stage a lecturer at LSE. When I told him about the project, he was very interested and said that he would like to develop the computer program and do the computing. This was a great help to me. Cliff had already written a computer program for estimating the approximate simultaneous equations model as part of his Ph.D. work and applied it to a model of financial markets. He developed it a lot further in the process of estimating my model. The model was modified a bit during these years, but it's remarkable how close the final estimated model was to the one which I had originally formulated and analyzed. We had to fix a few parameters for which the estimates were too unreliable, but I think that's about all. We estimated the model in two stages. We first estimated it by just estimating the approximate simultaneous equations model but using the transformed data to approximately take account of the flow data and the autocorrelation in the residuals. Then we used these estimates to initiate a second-stage estimation which took account of the restrictions on the matrix of coefficients of the differential equation system through the matrix of coefficients of the discrete model. But we still used only the approximate moving average for the disturbances, we didn't get exact maximum likelihood estimates.

The paper was first presented at the European meeting of the Econometric Society in 1974 and then published in the book that I edited on *Statistical Inferences in Continuous-Time Economic Models* in 1976. I think that the model, in addition to being the first continuous-time macroeconomic model, had a number of other innovative features. In particular, it made much more intensive use of economic theory than previous macroeconomic models. It was the intensive use of economic theory that placed across-equation restrictions on the equations of the model. It also was formulated, following the methodology used in my book *The Construction and Use of Economic Models*, in such a way as to enable us to do a rigorous analysis of the model's asymptotic stability properties. Prior to this, econometricians had tended to use linear approximations about sample means or arbitrary values of the variables in such analyses, for example, in much of the work on the analysis of the Klein–Goldberger model. But nothing can be rigorously deduced from such analyses about the asymptotic stability properties of the underlying nonlinear model. Ours was amenable to rigorous analysis. The model has, of course, become a prototype for many other continuous-time models over the last decade.

Many researchers have pondered the merits of modeling in discrete time and in continuous time. And you have spoken and written about this yourself. Do you have any general thoughts on the subject that you would like to mention now?

I think that it is a fact that the economy does not cease to exist in between observations. This was pointed out by Bartlett in his 1946 article. Nor does the economy move in regular discrete jumps, at quarterly or annual intervals corresponding to the observations. The economy is adjusting in between the observations and it can change at any point of time. This is a fact and I think, therefore, that it must be possible to obtain some gain by taking account of this fact in our empirical work. Another point that I would like to make is that continuous-time modeling is not the same as assuming that the sample paths are continuous functions of time. This is a point which I have stressed in much of my recent work on the mathematical foundations. Many economic variables, particularly financial variables, do make discrete jumps and those jumps can occur at any point of time. I think, therefore, that it is important to formulate our models in continuous time, even though the sample paths may not be continuous functions of time.

Tjalling Koopmans also wrote about this topic in an article in Cowles Commission Volume 10.

I had certainly read the Koopmans article. I remember once discussing it with Bill Phillips. Koopmans, of course, did not get very far, but he did point out that, in principle, it should be possible to derive the exact discrete analog for a continuous-time model but at that stage it would not have been practicable. It looked rather a daunting task and Koopmans said it would be mathematically very difficult. But in the last few years we have, in fact, done this.

Do you find it of interest that leaving aside Koopmans' article on the topic, for many years the entire research program in this field was conducted outside of North America?

It is interesting. It's just hard to know why that is the case. I think it's partly because Bill Phillips was himself at the LSE. I started to do my first work on the topic at the LSE and a nucleus of people working in the field started there. Denis Sargan then came and started to work there. I returned to New Zealand and you and other people like Cliff Wymer, became interested in the field and you both went to the LSE and became Denis Sargan's research students. So there was a nucleus from which the field could develop.

On the other hand, there was a lot of intellectual capital invested in the existing methods. This would tend to perpetuate them unless there was a fairly strong head of steam to push the research in another direction. I think Bill Phillips was never very happy with the simultaneous equations methodology, because he had been trained as an electrical engineer. I think that he was very receptive to the ideas of Herman Wold and the idea of trying to model the economy as a system of causal relations. He had also been influenced by the work of Arnold Tustin, who was also an electrical engineer. I think the first work after Koopmans in the United States was probably Christopher Sims's 1972 paper in *Econometrica.* What stimulated him to think about the problems, I don't know. Telser had also done a little bit of work on the identification problem. After Koopmans, I think that these were the first two on the US scene.

There has recently been a strong resurgence of interest in the field, covering a broad spectrum of research that includes both theoretical and empirical work. This has included a number of researchers in the North American continent, as well as yourself and others in the UK. What factors do you think have led to this revival and what developments do you see on the horizon now?

I think there are three major factors. I think the first one is the enormous development in computing technology which has taken place during the last 10 or 15 years. It would now be feasible to estimate a second-order differential equation, similar to the one which Cliff Wymer and I estimated for the UK, using stock and flow data and taking account of the exact restrictions on the discrete-time analog that are implied by the continuous-time model. Now this would not have been feasible 15 years ago, when we first started working on that model. So I think that the realization that it is now feasible to estimate a model by these exact methods has encouraged a number of others to undertake the rather daunting task of working out the mathematical algorithms. I think the latest phase of this started with my 1983 *Econometrica* article. But this stimulated Harvey and Stock to produce their Kalman filter algorithm and that, in turn, stimulated me to do further work on computational algorithms. There are now a number of other people in the USA working on these problems like Christiano and Zadrozny. Somewhat earlier, Hansen and Sargent had been working on another method which was close to Bill Phillips' procedure and in the context of rational expectations models. There is now quite a lot of trans-Atlantic research. I think that this is the first factor.

The second factor is the effect of the empirical work which has been going on. I think that since we produced our first continuous-time macroeconometric model of the UK, there has been a steady acceleration in the output of papers on the construction and application of continuous-time models. We now have four or five research teams around the world who are very active in continuous-time macro-economic modeling. One of the first was Jonson and his team at the Reserve Bank of Australia. Another is Gandolfo and his team in Italy who have done a lot of work. There is Kirkpatrick and his team in Germany. There is another team at the World Bank. I think this activity has also stimulated people to do more work on the theoretical and methodological issues.

The third factor is the growing interest among economic theorists in continuous-time stochastic models. I am thinking particularly of the work on modeling of asset prices and related issues by Merton and others. There have also been some empirical continuous-time econometric models based on this work.

Many time series from financial and commodity markets are now near continuously observable and one finds, of course, that the variables are not continuous functions of time, as you earlier observed. In fact, they involve jump discontinuities.

That is right. This is one of the factors which has caused me to do more work on the mathematical foundations of continuous-time models and to use assumptions which will allow the innovation processes to include more general processes.

Much of your own work on disequilibrium econometric models has involved tightly specified systems with many prior restrictions delivered from an underlying economic theory. This methodology is very much in line with the original Cowles Commission approach to simultaneous equations. In contrast, alternative methodologies which rely on the use of unrestricted systems of equations have been strongly advocated by Christopher Sims, David Hendry, and others. What is your response to these different methodologies for applied econometric research? Do you see value in both approaches?

I think that given the small samples that we have to work with in econometrics, it is essential to find some way of restricting the number of parameters to be estimated, in addition to the restrictions implied by the assumed order of the system. Christopher Sims, in his important 1972 *Econometrica* article, said that econometric models should be formulated in continuous time. I fully agree with that view. I also think that in order to obtain sufficiently realistic dynamic specifications to make the best use of the data, we need to formulate the continuous-time model as, at least, a second-order differential equation system. The discrete analog of a second-order differential equation system with white-noise disturbance and mixed stock and flow data is an autoregressive moving average system that is of second order in both its autoregressive and moving average parts. So if, for example, one has ten variables, as we had in our model of the UK, then the discrete analog of a second-order differential equation system will have 455 parameters. This is four 10×10 matrices of coefficients plus 55 parameters in the covariance matrix of the innovations. I don't believe it is possible, given the sample sizes that we have in econometric work, to get reliable estimates of so many parameters. I believe that even if the Cowles Commission-type restrictions on the coefficients of a differential equation system are rather approximate, the reduction in variances obtained by taking account of these restrictions, in most cases, far outweighs the bias from imposing those restrictions. I think that we are now reaching a stage where these issues, which have been the subject of methodological debates over the last few years, can be tested empirically. I think that we have reached a stage where you can compare different types of models and their explanatory power by fitting them all to the same data set and computing the value of the likelihood function. Now that we have an algorithm for computing the exact Gaussian likelihood of a second-order differential equation system with mixed stock and flow data, one could fit a model of this sort with, say, ten variables to a set of data and compare the value with the likelihood function of various discrete-time models involving the same number of parameters. This is something which I intend to do.

I would also like to see a competition to find the model which gave the highest value of the likelihood function for a given number of parameters. One could have a competition for various numbers of parameters: for example, the best 100 parameter model, the best 120 parameter model, and so on. The data set might, for example, consist of 60 quarterly observations of the ten leading macroeconomic variables in the UK or the USA. All of the models, both the continuous time and discrete time, would be nested in the very general model which assumes only that the 600 dimensional vector of observations has a multivariate normal distribution. I think it might be necessary to require that the models made some economic sense, but I would interpret this fairly liberally. The criterion would be to find the model with the highest value of the likelihood function.

Apart from this and in a more general context, one criterion which I have emphasized in a number of papers over the last 15 years is the desirability of having a model which generates plausible long-run behavior. I should mention that David Hendry also has, in a number of recent papers, advocated this restriction in dynamic formulations. So, I think we are in agreement on this point. I am also in agreement with Christopher Sims, that there should be much more attention to modeling of complete systems rather than single equation methods.

Christopher Sims has suggested that one achieve parameter economy in vector autoregressive systems by the implementation of Bayesian priors. Do you have any thoughts about the use of Bayesian methodology in this context?

I think the introduction of Bayesian methods is one of the important developments in econometric theory. I hadn't myself thought about it very specifically, although I do to some extent regard just placing the Cowles Commission-type restrictions on models as, to some extent, Bayesian. We know that they are approximate anyway. Ultimately, I suppose, one could do a more exact Bayesian estimation of such a model. I don't know if I will ever get around to doing it. But I think that certainly I would like to see it done.

Another important aspect of econometric modeling is specification testing and in the last decade there has been tremendous interest in this topic. In fact you could go so far as to say that it has become a veritable cottage industry. Do you feel that this is an area to which continuous-time modelers have not yet given enough attention, in contrast to discrete-time modelers?

It certainly has not been given as much attention yet. But I think that this is partly because there has been a lot of other work to do. But I see no reason, in principle, why these tests should not be applied to continuous-time models just as much as they are applied to discrete-time models. In fact, to some extent, by developing algorithms for computing the value of the likelihood we have provided the basic computational procedures for carrying out likelihood ratio tests. Then one can also develop non-nested tests, based on likelihood ratios. I have a preference for likelihood ratio tests as against, for example, Lagrange multiplier tests, because I think one can find cases in nonlinear models where the likelihood ratio tests are more powerful.

One of the main reasons why Lagrange multiplier tests have become so popular is that they are very easy to construct and interpret. One doesn't need to estimate the likelihood function twice. That economy is useful.

That's right. But it is becoming less important as computation technology develops.

Would you like to say more about your idea for a competition among modelers who advocate different methodologies and the criteria to be used in evaluating the competition?

The main criterion would be the value of the likelihood function. I did recently mention this idea to David Hendry. It seemed to appeal to him too. The main thing that one would have to be careful about, though, is to make sure that people didn't cheat by presenting a model which apparently had a small number of parameters but which was really a disguised version of a model with a much larger number of parameters. After preliminary exploration, for example, a simpler model could be formulated by introducing combinations of variables as a single variable. Now in order to avoid that, I think it would have to be necessary to have rules to ensure that the model made economic sense and to prevent people from artificially reducing the number of parameters.

Several other factors seem to be important here. For example, models do have different objectives. Your own models are as much designed to explain medium-term and long-term behavior as to deliver short-term forecasts. Other models are designed more as short-term forecasting instruments and may have poor long-run properties. Do you think it would be important to control these objectives in your competition?

I think we could have several competitions. It would be of interest just to see which sort of model had the greatest explanatory power for a given data set independent of these factors. But then we could also compare their long-term properties.

How would you control for the fact that some models have large numbers of exogenous variables and extract a good deal of leverage from these variables in terms of sample fit?

I think the exogenous variables would have to be specified and this would be part of the competition. We would specify the endogenous variables, say, the ten variables we had in the model of the UK plus three or four exogenous variables to allow for such things as GDP and prices in the rest of the world.

In your teaching and in your research you have always been very much of an economist as well as an econometrician. I think that this has come over clearly in the conversation that we have already had. But one of the things that I have known about you for many years is that you have a very healthy respect for mathematics and for mathematical statistics. How do you feel about the possibility of training new generations of econometricians as the subject has become so much broader in scope and its mathematical requirements have continued to deepen?

I think it is really a very daunting task now for a new graduate student in econometrics. I don't think one could expect a graduate student to master the contents of the three volumes of the *Handbook of Econometrics*. I think that it is very important, therefore, for a student to concentrate on the fundamentals. I think it is particularly important for a graduate who wants to be an expert econometrician, rather than just a user of econometrics, to have a very good background in mathematics. Ideally, I think that he/she should do a degree in mathematics followed by a master's degree, including courses in economic theory, econometric theory, and applied econometrics. I think that the econometric theory course would be based mainly on the fundamentals and very much along the lines of the Malinvaud course I used to give and then perhaps with a choice of optional topics. After all, the student is going to learn a lot about some particular field or fields when he/she gets on to his/her Ph.D. work.

So you don't believe that the gap between current econometric courses at the graduate level and research activity in econometrics is so wide that it's impossible for students to bridge the gap?

No, I don't think so. I think that once a student starts working on his/her Ph.D. then he/she can be directed to reading the particular papers in that field.

I wonder if we can change our subject of conversation. For many years at Essex you have been involved with high-level administration for the University as well as the Department of Economics. Can you tell us about these administrative responsibilities? Have they placed a major burden on your time for reading and research?

I spent about ten years altogether in major administrative roles at Essex. I was successively Dean of the School of Social Sciences, Chairman of the Department of Economics, and a Pro-Vice-Chancellor, with gaps of just a year or two in between these posts. They certainly took a lot of time away from my research. For example, when I was Pro-Vice-Chancellor I was on 15 different committees and chairman of five of them. I think that I was a very efficient administrator but, even so, it took a lot of time away from my research. I tried to keep up with my reading so that whenever I did have a few weeks to spare, I could get back to some research.

Have there been any positive externalities to you from those administrative responsibilities?

I think so. One of the positive externalities was meeting and working with men from outside academia on the council, and various committees of the council. Often they were men who had got first class degrees about 40 years ago and then got into management and were now chief executives of their companies. I think another externality was being involved in the central financial planning of the university during a very difficult period. I was on all the key committees and, in particular, the important finance committees which were involved with the planning of the university and university finances. And I am pleased to say that during the three years that I was the Pro-Vice-Chancellor chairing the main subcommittees of the Finance Committee, the university accounts show a healthy financial surplus. This was during a period when many other universities in the country were close to insolvency.

During the course of your career you must have seen many phases in the development of econometrics as a discipline. Looking back, do any milestones seem particularly important to you now?

I think 1943 was certainly a milestone year. This was the year of Haavelmo's first paper on simultaneous equations models and also the Mann and Wald paper which was the beginning of rigorous asymptotic theory. The next milestone was in 1949 with the Anderson and Rubin papers, which was the beginning of single equations methods and which made simultaneous equations models feasible in applied econometric work. After that I think the subject began to develop very rapidly and it's easier to pick out important developments, rather than particular milestones. I have always tried, myself, to work in the fields which seemed to me to be the most important. So obviously I must regard both the finite-sample theory and continuous-time modeling as two of the important developments. In finite-sample theory, work on Edgeworth approximation theory is another development and here the important early papers are by Sargan and Mikhail and Anderson and Sawa in the early 1970s. Another important development during my period as an econometrician was the development of Fourier methods of time-series analysis, which began with the important papers of Peter Whittle in the 1950s. But then it was extensively developed by Ted Hannan. Although the methods have not been much used in econometrics, I think they have been important in developing the asymptotic sampling properties of estimators. There has, of course, been a move back towards time-domain methods. I think another important development is the rigorous analysis of the asymptotic properties of estimation of nonlinear models in which the early papers by Malinvaud and Jennrich in the late 1960s and early 1970s were important. Although I have not myself done any work on Bayesian economics, I think that this has been another important development which I particularly associate with Dreze and Zellner.

Within each of these fields, one could pick out milestones. Certainly in the field of finite-sample theory there are several of your own papers that I am sure will come to be regarded as milestones. Particularly important, I think, are your 1980 and 1985 *Econometrica* articles dealing with instrumental variables estimation in the most general case, and then later the complete SUR regression model. These involved the introduction of your application of zonal polynomials and then the fractional matrix calculus.

Another major area of development has been microeconometrics.

I should have mentioned microeconometrics and I think I should have mentioned some more applied work. All of the things I mentioned earlier were theoretical developments. In applied econometrics, the Klein models were certainly milestones: the first Klein model of the USA in 1950 and later, in 1955, the Klein–Goldberger model. In applied microeconometric work, I think one of the important early milestones was another English contribution: Stone's original work on the linear expenditure system, which was one of the earliest papers on demand systems. Most recently, there has been rational expectations.

In your own research you have achieved a balance between empirical research and theoretical work in econometrics. Have you been happy with this balance?

I think I've personally been fairly happy with it. Although I sometimes wonder if I tried to spread the field too widely. But I think this reflects my general approach to econometrics and to some extent I think I was influenced in this way back in Cambridge by Stone. This was very much his approach: to formulate a 12-year project, develop a model, devise methods of estimating it, then set about estimating it and so on. I think that this is very much what I have done in terms of my continuous-time modeling work right from the theoretical model to the development of the estimation techniques and through to the application.

I have always found you to be a tremendously optimistic person about econometrics generally and econometric research in particular. Is there any particular reason for this? How useful do you now see econometrics to be in terms of understanding economic phenomena?

Given the limitations of the phenomena we are trying to model, I think econometrics certainly must be the basis for a scientific approach to economics. But I sometimes get a bit depressed about economics and think how nice it would be to be a physicist or a chemist where things remained unchanged. One feels that the structure of the economy is continually changing and as soon as one can get to the stage of explaining one period or another, the economy changes. You make some mention of this in one of your own finite-sample papers: that one of the important reasons for finite-sample theory is that the longer the period we estimate, the more parameters one must introduce and the more variables we have in order to allow for structural changes. I think there are some relations and some parameters which will remain fairly constant over a long period, but mixed up with these are other things which are changing all the time, this makes modeling the economy very difficult over a long period.

It is interesting that we are doing this interview now in New Zealand where there has recently been a most dramatic instance of institutional economic change through comprehensive financial deregulation. As someone who has seen both the European and American systems from the comparative isolation of New Zealand, do you perceive major differences in thinking about economics and econometrics between the two continents?

I think I am not really very qualified to answer that question because I have spent most of my active academic working life in England and I have never worked at all in an American university. Also, probably because I've been so heavily involved with university administration and never even visited an American university for more than a few days. I do think that Europe and England, in particular, have fallen behind America in economic theory during the last 40 years. Forty years ago when I was a student, most of the most important recent developments in economic theory had been made in England by Keynes, Hicks, and others. But I think that most of the important theoretical developments in the last 20 years have been made in America. On the other hand, I do think that in England we are still quite strong in econometrics as compared to America, especially if one takes account of the differences between the populations of the two countries. So I think that there has been a shift in the relative balance between economic theory and econometrics between England and America. Now I know that that doesn't really answer your question, but I think that is about all I can say.

Do you feel that you had any particular advantages coming from a small country like New Zealand or do you feel that it was a disadvantage?

I think it may have had the advantage that I've been less likely to be indoctrinated with a particular point of view. I read rather widely and I think that throughout my life books have probably had a more important influence on me than personal contacts with people. Of the important books I've read, and I've already mentioned Keynes' *General Theory*, Hick's *Value and Capital*, and Hardy's *Pure Mathematics*, there is one which I haven't mentioned and this is Cramer's *Mathematical Methods of Statistics*. This was one of the most important books that I read when I was at Cambridge and this became the bible of statistics for me. Of all the books on my shelf, it is the book that I have used most.

What thoughts do you have about the future of econometrics in the course of the next ten years, let us say?

I think that among the most important developments will be those which take advantage of the enormous changes in computing technology that have taken place over the last few years. I have already said a lot about continuous-time modeling, and obviously this is one of the important developments which is going to continue but there are also others. The development of more exact methods of hypothesis testing and confidence intervals based, for example, on Edgeworth approximations, will be important and I think the development of nonparametric models will also be important. I think, generally, we are going to have also more emphasis on complete systems rather than single equation methods.

This question is a bit out of the blue. Did you ever think of writing a textbook of econometrics at any stage?

I once thought of writing an elementary, but at its level fairly rigorous, textbook on statistics for econometrics, very much based on the sort of undergraduate statistics course that I had given for many years. I have also thought of writing a book on continuous-time econometrics. I haven't ever thought of writing a 600 or 700 page treatise on econometrics.

A final question. What advice or encouragement would you offer young scholars who are thinking of doing research in econometrics?

I think that I have already mentioned some of them. I certainly think that they should get a very good basis in mathematics and also do some good graduate courses in economic theory. I think they should concentrate on the fundamentals and then branch off into specific areas of research. One other thing I should mention is that I think they should not be afraid of writing their own computer programs. I think that the proliferation of packaged programs that are available these days has a tendency to encourage students to just look around for packaged programs. But I think that if someone is ever going to become an econometric theorist, it's useful to write some computer programs at some stage. I think it is also useful to do some empirical work. A few random thoughts.

4

The Publications of A. R. Bergstrom

Books

[1] *The Construction and Use of Economic Models.* 1967. London: English Universities Press; also published as *Selected Economic Models and their Analysis.* 1967. New York: American Elsevier; also translated into Japanese.

[2] *Statistical Inference in Continuous Time Economic Models* (edited). 1976: Amsterdam: North-Holland Publishing Company.

[3] *Stability and Inflation: Essays in Memory of A. W. Phillips* (edited with A. J. L. Catt, M. H. Peston and B. D. J. Silverstone). 1978. New York: John Wiley & Sons.

[4] *Continuous Time Econometric Modelling.* 1990. Oxford: Oxford University Press.

Articles

1949

[5] "The guaranteed price for dairy products," *Economic Record*, 25, 91–7.

1951

[6] "New Zealand's export supply function," *Economic Record*, 27, 21–9.

1952

[7] "Report of the taxation committee, New Zealand 1951," *Economic Record*, 28, 88–90.

1955

[8] "An econometric study of supply and demand for New Zealand's exports," *Econometrica*, 23, 258–76.

1956

[9] "The use of index numbers in demand analysis," *Review of Economic Studies*, 23, 17–26.

1957

[10] "A reply to Mr. Kemp," *Review of Economic Studies*, 24, 215.

1958

[11] "The New Zealand economy, 1957–8," *Economic Record*, 34, 306–16.

1960

[12] "Linear programming, import controls and the exchange rate where the supply of exports is inelastic," *Economic Record*, 36, 385–93.

1962

[13] "The exact sampling distributions of least squares and maximum likelihood estimators of the marginal propensity to consume," *Econometrica*, 30, 480–90.

[14] "A model of technical progress, the production function and cyclical growth," *Economica*, 29, 357–70.

1965

[15] "An econometric model of the New Zealand economy" (with A. D. Brownlie), *Economic Record*, 41, 125–6.

1966

[16] "Nonrecursive models as discrete approximations to systems of stochastic differential equations," *Econometrica*, 34, 173–82.

[17] "Monetary phenomena and economic growth: A synthesis of neoclassical and Keynesian theories," *Economic Studies Quarterly*, 17, 1–8.

[18] "What is econometrics?", *The University of Auckland Gazette*, 8, 1–3.

1967

[19] "Mathematical restatement of the profit guidance problem" (with A. Zauberman) in *Aspects of Planometrics*, by A. Zauberman. London: Athlone Press.

[20] "Monetary and fiscal policy in a growing economy," *New Zealand Economic Papers*, 31–9.

[21] "Forecasting the New Zealand Economy" (with A. D. Brownlie), *Economic Record*, 43, 303–5.

1972

[22] "The covariance matrix of the limited information maximum likelihood estimator," *Econometrica*, 40, 899–900.

1976

[23] "A model of disequilibrium neoclassical growth and its application to the United Kingdom" (with C. R. Wymer), *Statistical Inference in Continuous Time Econometric Models* (edited by A. R. Bergstrom). Amsterdam: North-Holland Publishing Company.

1978

[24] "Monetary policy in a model of the United Kingdom," in *Stability and Inflation* (edited by A. R. Bergstrom et al.). New York: Wiley.

1983

[25] "Gaussian estimation of structural parameters in higher order continuous time dynamic models," *Econometrica*, 51, 117–52.

1984

[26] "Continuous time stochastic models and issues of aggregation over time," in *Handbook of Econometrics*, Vol. 2 (edited by Z. Griliches and M. D. Intriligator). Amsterdam: North-Holland Publishing Company.

[27] "Monetary fiscal and exchange rate policy in a continuous time econometric model of the United Kingdom," in *Contemporary Macroeconomic Modelling* (edited by P. Malgrange and P. Muet). London: Blackwell.

1985

[28] "The estimation of nonparametric functions in a Hilbert space," *Econometric Theory*, 1, 7–26.

[29] "The estimation of parameters in nonstationary higher order continuous time dynamic models," *Econometric Theory*, 1, 369–86.

1986

[30] "The estimation of open higher order continuous time dynamic models with mixed stock and flow data," *Econometric Theory*, 2, 350–73.

1987

[31] "Optimal control of wide-sense stationary continuous time stochastic models," *Journal of Economic Dynamics and Control*, 11, 425–43.

1988

[32] "The history of continuous-time econometric models," *Econometric Theory*, 4, 365–83.

1989

[33] "Optimal forecasting of discrete stock and flow data generated by a higher order continuous time system," *Computers and Mathematics with Applications*, 17, 1203–14.

1990

[34] "Hypothesis testing in continuous time econometric models," in *Continuous Time Econometric Modelling* (by A. R. Bergstrom). Oxford: Oxford University Press.

[35] "Gaussian estimation of a continuous time model of demand for consumer durable goods with applications to demand in the United Kingdom, 1973–84" (with M. J. Chambers) in *Continuous Time Econometric Modelling* (by A. R. Bergstrom). Oxford: Oxford University Press.

Part II

Continuous-Time Models

5

Forecasting with Continuous-Time and Discrete-Time Series Models: An Empirical Comparison

Marcus J. Chambers

Introduction

A great deal of attention has been paid by economists and econometricians to the problem of forecasting economic time series beyond the sample period. Indeed, most of the industrialized nations devote considerable resources (both private and public) to producing forecasts of the key economic variables over varying horizons. Yet, despite such intensive effort, there appears to be no consensus view as to the appropriate methods to be used for obtaining the "best" forecasts of any particular variable, or group of variables.

The problem of prediction is one which has been considered by Rex Bergstrom in a number of his publications on continuous-time models, both at the theoretical level (for example, Bergstrom (1966, 1983, 1985)) and in applied studies (Bergstrom and Wymer (1976), Bergstrom and Chambers (1990)). In this contribution we consider the post-sample forecasts obtained from a continuous-time model and compare them with those obtained from a discrete-time series model. Such a comparison is of interest because although both models use precisely the same data set, the continuous-time model imposes complicated restrictions on its discrete representation, which can be important in reducing not only the variance of the estimates, but also the variance of the forecasts.

The particular continuous-time model under consideration is a model of consumers' demand developed and estimated by Chambers (1992). It was applied to three broad categories of consumers' expenditure in the UK and is obtained from a two-stage optimization procedure by consumers. The novel features of this model are the inclusion of parameters in the utility function which reflect the durability and stock effects of the commodities, and the use of user cost instead of pure prices. Thus the inclusion of interest rates is motivated theoretically, rather than just including them as additonal explanatory variables in a fairly *ad hoc* fashion. A description of the model is given in the next section, but further details are to be found in Chambers (1992).

As the discrete analog of an open continuous-time system takes the form of a vector autoregressive moving average model with exogenous variables, i.e. a VARMAX model, the natural model to use in a comparative study like this is a

VARMAX model of the same order, but without the parameter restrictions associated with the continuous-time model. Although this type of exercise can act as a further specification test of the underlying structure of the continuous-time system, the estimation of VARMAX models can pose further problems due to the greater number of parameters to be estimated. A discussion of the estimation of VARMAX models appears in the third section.

The estimates of both models, obtained using UK seasonally adjusted quarterly data for nondurables, semidurables, and durables, are given in the fourth section, where we also consider various measures proposed to compare forecasts generated by different models. The empirical results, whilst not being entirely conclusive, do lend support to the use of continuous-time models to describe and predict economic time series relationships. Some concluding comments are given.

The Continuous-time Model

Specification

The continuous-time model of demand involves consumers engaging in a two-stage optimization process. In the first stage, consumers choose their desired (long-run, steady state) levels of demand by maximizing the following modified Stone–Geary utility function

$$u(q_1, \ldots, q_n) = \sum_{i=1}^{n} (q_i - d_i a_i)^{d_i b_i} \tag{1}$$

subject to the long-run budget constraint

$$\sum_{i=1}^{n} v_i q_i = y, \tag{2}$$

where q_i denotes the purchases of good i, y denotes personal disposable income, and v_i denotes the user cost of the ith commodity. In equation (1), the term $d_i a_i$ is often interpreted as a committed quantity of purchases, and $d_i b_i$ represents the marginal budget share. The novel feature here is the introduction of the d_i parameters, which depend both on the durability of the good, and the effect of stocks on purchases. More precisely, denoting the depreciation rate by δ, and the stock effect by β, we have

$$d_i = \frac{\delta_i}{\delta_i - \beta_i}, \qquad i = 1, \ldots, n. \tag{3}$$

Thus, if a good has a relatively high depreciation rate or is subject to a positive stock effect (habit formation), then the consumer gives this good greater weight in his consumption plans, not only because it needs to be purchased more frequently, but also because of its habit-forming effect.

The user cost terms in the budget constraint (2) reflect elements of price, interest charge and durability, and are specified as follows

$$v_i = p_i(1 + r/\delta_i), \qquad i = 1, \ldots, n, \tag{4}$$

where p_i denotes the price of good i, and r denotes the rate of interest. This definition is motivated by using the stock adjustment relationship

$$ds_i(t) = [q_i(t) - \delta_i s_i(t)]\,dt, \qquad i = 1, \ldots, n, \tag{5}$$

where s_i denotes the stock of good i held by the consumer.

The solution to the optimization problem given by (1) and (2) yields the following long-run demand functions

$$q_i^* = d_i a_i + d_i b_i\left(y - \sum_j d_j a_j v_j\right)\bigg/ v_i, \qquad i = 1, \ldots, n \tag{6}$$

which may be written in vector form as

$$\mathbf{q}^* = \delta^0 S \mathbf{z} \tag{7}$$

where $\mathbf{q}^*$ is the $n \times 1$ vector $(q_1^*, \ldots, q_n^*)'$, δ^0 is an $n \times n$ matrix with the vector $\boldsymbol{\delta} = (\delta_1, \ldots, \delta_n)$ on the principal diagonal, S is a matrix of known functions of the parameters of the utility function (1), and $\mathbf{z}$ is the $m \times 1$ vector of explanatory variables, containing income and user cost ratio terms. Note that imposing additivity of long-run demands, so that $\Sigma_i v_i q_i^* = y$, necessitates the restriction $\Sigma_i d_i b_i = 1$. But this is unrealistic, since it does not allow for the possibility of savings in the long run. The constraint $\Sigma_i d_i b_i = 1 - \tau$ is therefore imposed, where τ denotes the proportion of supernumerary income $(= y - \Sigma_i d_i a_i v_i)$ that is saved.

Since consumers are unable to obtain the desired levels of demand in the short run, due to adjustment costs, for example, it is assumed that they continually minimize the following cost function

$$C = \int_t^\infty \{[\mathbf{s}(r) - \mathbf{s}^*]'C_1[\mathbf{s}(r) - \mathbf{s}^*] + [\mathbf{q}(r) - \mathbf{q}^*]'C_2[\mathbf{q}(r) - \mathbf{q}^*]$$
$$+ [d\mathbf{q}(r)/dr]'C_3[d\mathbf{q}(r)/dr]\}\,dr \tag{8}$$

subject to the stock depreciation relationship (5), where C_1, C_2, and C_3 are $n \times n$ matrices. Using well-known results from optimal control theory (see for example Bergstrom (1987)), it can be shown that the optimal feedback is given by the following differential equation in purchases

$$d\mathbf{q}(t) = \pi^0[\Gamma(\alpha)\mathbf{z}(t) + \beta^0\mathbf{s}(t) - \mathbf{q}(t)]\,dt, \tag{9}$$

where $\Gamma(\alpha) = (\delta^0 - \beta^0)S$, and it is assumed that π^0 and β^0 are diagonal matrices in order to reduce the number of parameters to be estimated (see Chambers (1992) for full details of this model). By appending a vector of white-noise disturbances, $\boldsymbol{\mu}(dt)$, to equation (9), where $E[\boldsymbol{\mu}(dt)] = 0$ and $E[\boldsymbol{\mu}(dt)\boldsymbol{\mu}(dt)'] = (dt)\Sigma$, we may write a representative equation as

$$\mathrm{d}\mathbf{q}_i(t) = \pi_i\left\{\mathbf{a}_i + \mathbf{b}_i\left[y(t) - \sum_j d_j a_j v_j(t)\right]\Big/ v_i(t) + \beta_i \mathbf{s}_i(t) - \mathbf{q}_i(t)\right\}\mathrm{d}t + \boldsymbol{\mu}_i(\mathrm{d}t), \quad (10)$$

where $\boldsymbol{\mu}_i(\mathrm{d}t)$ is the random disturbance term. Note that there are a number of parameter restrictions to be taken into account, both within and across equations.

Note, also, that unlike many demand systems, the system of equations (10) is not characterized by a singular disturbance covariance matrix. This arises mainly because of the influence of stocks on the right-hand side of (10), which are not governed by additivity constraints, even though the long-run demands are additive. Another reason is that we are using personal disposable income rather than total expenditure as our income variable, allowing for the possibility (indeed, the necessity) of consumers borrowing and saving in the short run when adjusting their demands.

Estimation

As we do not have a continuous record of the variables over time, it is necessary, for the purposes of estimation, to obtain a discrete representation of the continuous-time model. This is achieved using the general methodology of Bergstrom (1983, 1985, 1986), rather than the precise formulas in those articles. The additional problem here is that the stock variables, $s(t)$, are unobservable, even at discrete intervals of time. The estimates therefore have to be based on the discrete observations on purchases and the exogenous variables, given by $\mathbf{q}_t = \int_{t-1}^{t} \mathbf{q}(r)\,\mathrm{d}r$ and $\mathbf{z}_t = \int_{t-1}^{t} \mathbf{z}(r)\,\mathrm{d}r$ respectively (these variables are flows measured as integrals over the unit time period). The procedure is, therefore, to first obtain from equations (5) and (10) a system of first-order stochastic difference equations in purchases and stocks, and then eliminate the unobservable stock component to obtain a second-order stochastic difference equation in purchases (see also Bergstrom and Chambers (1990)).

Application of the above method results in the following equation

$$\mathbf{q}_t = K_1\mathbf{q}_{t-1} + K_2\mathbf{q}_{t-2} + J_0\mathbf{z}_t + J_1\mathbf{z}_{t-1} + J_2\mathbf{z}_{t-2} + \boldsymbol{\varepsilon}_t, \qquad t = 3, \ldots, T, \quad (11)$$

$$\boldsymbol{\varepsilon}_t = \int_{t-1}^{t} \phi_1(t-r)\boldsymbol{\mu}(\mathrm{d}r) + \int_{t-2}^{t-1} \phi_2(t-1-r)\boldsymbol{\mu}(\mathrm{d}r) + \int_{t-3}^{t-2} \phi_3(t-2-r)\boldsymbol{\mu}(\mathrm{d}r)$$

and the matrices K_1, K_2, J_0, J_1, J_2, and functions $\phi_1(r)$, $\phi_2(r)$, and $\phi_3(r)$ depend in a complicated manner on the underlying structural parameters of the continuous-time model. It should be pointed out that the diagonality of the continuous-time system feeds through into the matrices K_1 and K_2, and that the J_i matrices contain a large number of zero elements, as only the relevant elements of the $\mathbf{z}_t$, namely those with the deflator $v_i(t)$ and the constant term, enter into equation i.

For estimation purposes, the initial observations, $\mathbf{q}_1$ and $\mathbf{q}_2$, are also incorporated, for the reasons discussed in Bergstrom (1985). The actual estimates obtained are reproduced from Chambers (1992) and are given in the fourth section. These estimates are obtained by maximizing the likelihood function based on the discrete observations, under the assumption that the discrete disturbances have a multivariate Gaussian distribution. Under suitable regularity conditions, it can be shown that the

Gaussian estimator is asymptotically normally distributed, and the asymptotic covariance matrix is derived in Chambers (1992).

Forecasting

The problem of producing forecasts from the estimated model (11) has been dealt with neatly by Bergstrom (1989), who considers a model with both stock and flow data. The model here only contains flow data, but the procedure remains the same. Assuming that the model holds over the interval $[0, T+K]$, where K represents the number of forecast periods, we may write the $n(T+K) \times n(T+K)$ covariance matrix of the $n(T+K)$ vector $\boldsymbol{\varepsilon}^* = [\varepsilon_1', \varepsilon_2', \ldots, \varepsilon_T', \ldots, \varepsilon_{T+K}']'$ as

$$\Omega^* = \underset{\begin{matrix} nT & \quad nK \end{matrix}}{\begin{bmatrix} \Omega & \vdots & \Omega_{12} \\ \cdots & \cdots & \cdots \\ \Omega_{21} & \vdots & \Omega_{22} \end{bmatrix}} \begin{matrix} nT \\ nK \end{matrix}, \tag{12}$$

$$\Omega_{12} = \Omega_{21}' = \begin{bmatrix} 0 & 0 & 0 & \cdot & \cdot & 0 \\ \cdot & \cdot & \cdot & \cdot & \cdot & \cdot \\ \cdot & \cdot & \cdot & \cdot & \cdot & \cdot \\ 0 & \cdot & \cdot & \cdot & \cdot & 0 \\ \Omega_2' & 0 & 0 & \cdot & \cdot & 0 \\ \Omega_1' & \Omega_2' & 0 & \cdot & \cdot & 0 \end{bmatrix},$$

$$\Omega_{22} = \begin{bmatrix} \Omega_0 & \Omega_1' & \Omega_2' & 0 & \cdot & \cdot & \cdot & \cdot & \cdot & 0 \\ \Omega_1 & \Omega_0 & \Omega_1' & \Omega_2' & \cdot & \cdot & \cdot & \cdot & \cdot & \cdot \\ \Omega_2 & \Omega_1 & \Omega_0 & \Omega_1' & \cdot & \cdot & \cdot & \cdot & \cdot & \cdot \\ 0 & \Omega_2 & \Omega_1 & \Omega_0 & \cdot & \cdot & \cdot & \cdot & \cdot & \cdot \\ \cdot & \cdot & \cdot & \cdot & \cdot & \cdot & \cdot & \cdot & \cdot & \cdot \\ \cdot & \cdot & \cdot & \cdot & \cdot & \cdot & \cdot & \cdot & \cdot & \cdot \\ \cdot & \cdot & \cdot & \cdot & \cdot & \cdot & \cdot & \cdot & \cdot & \cdot \\ \cdot & \cdot & \cdot & \cdot & \cdot & \cdot & \Omega_2 & \Omega_1 & \Omega_0 & \Omega_1' \\ 0 & \cdot & \cdot & \cdot & \cdot & \cdot & 0 & \Omega_2 & \Omega_1 & \Omega_0 \end{bmatrix},$$

$$\Omega_0 = E(\boldsymbol{\varepsilon}_t\boldsymbol{\varepsilon}_t'), \qquad t = 3, \ldots, T+K,$$

$$\Omega_1 = E(\boldsymbol{\varepsilon}_t\boldsymbol{\varepsilon}_{t-1}'), \qquad t = 4, \ldots, T+K,$$

$$\Omega_2 = E(\boldsymbol{\varepsilon}_t\boldsymbol{\varepsilon}_{t-2}'), \qquad t = 3, \ldots, T+K.$$

Now, using the Cholesky factorization of Ω^*, such that

$$\Omega^* = M^*M^{*\prime}, \tag{13}$$

$$M^* = \begin{bmatrix} M & \vdots & 0 \\ \cdots & \vdots & \cdots \\ M_{21} & \vdots & M_{22} \end{bmatrix} \begin{matrix} nT \\ \\ nK \end{matrix},$$
$$\qquad nT \qquad nK$$

we may write the $nT \times 1$ vector $\mathbf{p}$ as

$$\mathbf{p} = M^{-1}\boldsymbol{\varepsilon} \tag{14}$$

(where $\boldsymbol{\varepsilon}$ is the $nT \times 1$ vector of residuals), from which we may obtain the $nK \times 1$ vector of forecast disturbances

$$\begin{aligned} \boldsymbol{\xi} &= M_{21}\mathbf{p} \\ &= [\xi'_{T+1}, \xi'_{T+2}, 0, \ldots, 0]'. \end{aligned} \tag{15}$$

The dynamic forecasts, conditional on the observed values of the exogenous variables, are obtained as follows

$$\mathbf{q}^*_{T+1} = K_1\mathbf{q}_T + K_2\mathbf{q}_{T-1} + J_0\mathbf{z}_{T+1} + J_1\mathbf{z}_T + J_2\mathbf{z}_{T-1} + \boldsymbol{\xi}_{T+1}, \tag{16}$$

$$\mathbf{q}^*_{T+2} = K_1\mathbf{q}^*_{T+1} + K_2\mathbf{q}_T + J_0\mathbf{z}_{T+2} + J_1\mathbf{z}_{T+1} + J_2\mathbf{z}_T + \boldsymbol{\xi}_{T+2}, \tag{17}$$

$$\mathbf{q}^*_{T+i} = K_1\mathbf{q}^*_{T+i-1} + K_2\mathbf{q}^*_{T+i-2} + J_0\mathbf{z}_{T+i} + J_1\mathbf{z}_{T+i-1} + J_2\mathbf{z}_{T+i-2} \tag{18}$$

with equation (18) holding for $i = 3$ through K, the forecast horizon. Such forecasts have been shown by Bergstrom (1989) to be optimal in the sense that the forecasts are exact maximum likelihood estimates of the conditional expectation of the post-sample observations, conditional on all the information in the sample, when the innovations are Gaussian. Indeed, for the system of equations estimated here, the assumption of normality was not rejected by the estimated residuals (see the fourth section).

The form of discrete model (11) contains additional parsimony over an unrestricted vector autoregressive moving average model, while at the same time retaining a rich dynamic structure. It is therefore natural to compare the forecast performance of the model (11), containing the complex restrictions implied by the continuous-time model, with an unrestricted time-series model. The estimation of such models is discussed in the next section.

Estimating VARMAX Models

This section concentrates primarily on models analogous to equation (11), the discrete analog of the continuous-time system, but which do not contain parameter restrictions. In particular, in order to maintain as much coherence with (11) as possible, the following model is considered

$$\mathbf{q}_t = \boldsymbol{\Phi}_0 + \sum_{i=1}^{2} q^0_{t-i}\boldsymbol{\Phi}_i + \sum_{i=0}^{2} B_i\mathbf{z}_{t-i} + \sum_{i=0}^{2} \theta_i\boldsymbol{\varepsilon}_{t-i}, \tag{19}$$

where $\mathbf{q}_t$ is the $n \times 1$ vector of purchases, q^0_{t-i} is an $n \times n$ matrix of zeros with $\mathbf{q}_{t-i}$ on the principal diagonal, $\mathbf{z}_t$ is the $m \times 1$ vector of exogenous variables, and $\boldsymbol{\varepsilon}_t$ is an $n \times 1$ vector of disturbances. The parameters to be estimated are the (unrestricted) elements of the $n \times 1$ vectors $\boldsymbol{\Phi}_i$, the $n \times m$ matrices B_i, and the $n \times n$ matrices θ_i. In fact, most of the elements of the B_i matrices will be zero to conform to the J_i matrices in equation (11) (this results from the diagonality of the continuous-time system and the form of the variables which constitute $\mathbf{z}_t$). Without loss of generality, θ_0 is set equal to an identity matrix, and it is further assumed that $E(\boldsymbol{\varepsilon}_t) = 0$, $E(\boldsymbol{\varepsilon}_t\boldsymbol{\varepsilon}_t') = V$, and $E(\boldsymbol{\varepsilon}_t\boldsymbol{\varepsilon}_s') = 0$, $s \neq t$. Given the above assumptions and definitions, we are therefore dealing with a VARMAX model of second order in each of its AR, MA, and X components.

The estimation of vector time-series models has received a great deal of attention in the literature, and a number of useful asymptotic results have been derived for a large class of quite general linear models; see for example Hannan *et al.* (1980), and Kohn (1979). One of the problems to be confronted is how to treat the initial observations. Taking account of the distribution of $\mathbf{q}_1$ and $\mathbf{q}_2$ in order to obtain exact maximum likelihood estimates would be difficult for the model (19). Instead, it will be assumed that $\boldsymbol{\varepsilon}_1 = \boldsymbol{\varepsilon}_2 = 0$, which implies that $\mathbf{q}_1$ and $\mathbf{q}_2$ are fixed (nonrandom). This greatly facilitates the computation of, and maximization of, the conditional likelihood function, which may be written

$$\log L = -\frac{nT}{2}\log 2\pi - \frac{T}{2}\log|V| - \frac{1}{2}\sum_{t=3}^{T} \boldsymbol{\varepsilon}_t' V^{-1}\boldsymbol{\varepsilon}_t. \tag{20}$$

Concentrating V out of (20) yields the estimator

$$V^* = T^{-1}\Sigma\boldsymbol{\xi}_t\boldsymbol{\xi}_t', \tag{21}$$

where the $\boldsymbol{\xi}_t$ are the sample estimates of the residuals $\boldsymbol{\varepsilon}_t$. Maximizing (20) is therefore equivalent to minimizing the following expression, making use of (21):

$$S(\boldsymbol{\alpha}) = \left|\sum_{t=3}^{T} \boldsymbol{\varepsilon}_t(\boldsymbol{\alpha})\boldsymbol{\varepsilon}_t'(\boldsymbol{\alpha})\right|, \tag{22}$$

where $\boldsymbol{\alpha}$ is the vector of unrestricted parameters to be estimated.

An obvious candidate for the minimization of (22) is the Gauss–Newton algorithm. Conditional on V, the estimate of $\boldsymbol{\alpha}$ at iteration i is updated by the formula

$$\boldsymbol{\alpha}^i = \boldsymbol{\alpha}^{i-1} + \tau[\Sigma Z_t V^{-1} Z_t']^{-1}\Sigma Z_t V^{-1}\boldsymbol{\varepsilon}_t \tag{23}$$

where $Z_t = -\partial\boldsymbol{\varepsilon}_t'/\partial\boldsymbol{\alpha}$, and τ is a variable step length. In order to compute the matrix Z_t of derivatives, the disturbance term, $\boldsymbol{\varepsilon}_t$, from the model (19) can be written

$$\boldsymbol{\varepsilon}_t = \mathbf{q}_t - \boldsymbol{\Phi}_0 - \Sigma q^0_{t-i}\boldsymbol{\Phi}_i + \Sigma[I \otimes \mathbf{z}_{t-i}'] \operatorname{vec}(B_i') - \Sigma[I \otimes \boldsymbol{\varepsilon}_{t-i}'] \operatorname{vec}(\theta_i') \tag{24}$$

where $\operatorname{vec}(\cdot)$ is the operator which stacks the columns of an $h \times j$ matrix vertically to form an $hj \times 1$ vector. The relevant derivatives are given by equations (25) through

(28) below.

$$-\partial\varepsilon_t'/\partial\Phi_0 = I + \Sigma[\partial\varepsilon_{t-i}'/\partial\Phi_0]\theta_i, \tag{25}$$

$$-\partial\varepsilon_t'/\partial\Phi_j = q_{t-j}^0 + \Sigma[\partial\varepsilon_{t-i}'/\partial\Phi_i]\theta_i, \qquad j = 1, 2 \tag{26}$$

$$-\partial\varepsilon_t'/\partial\text{vec}\,(\theta_j') = [I \otimes \varepsilon_{t-j}'] + \Sigma[\partial\varepsilon_{t-i}'/\partial\text{vec}\,(\theta_i')]\theta_i, \quad j = 1, 2 \tag{27}$$

$$-\partial\varepsilon_t'/\partial\text{vec}\,(B_j') = [I \otimes \mathbf{z}_{t-j}'] + \Sigma[\partial\varepsilon_{t-i}'/\partial\text{vec}\,(B_i')]\theta_i, \quad j = 0, 1, 2 \tag{28}$$

with the summations running from $i = 1$ to 2. Hence $\boldsymbol{\alpha}$ is the vector $\boldsymbol{\alpha} = [\Phi_0', \Phi_1', \Phi_2', \text{vec}\,(\theta_1')', \text{vec}\,(\theta_2')', \text{vec}\,(B_0'), \text{vec}\,(B_1')', \text{vec}\,(B_2')']'$ where only the nonzero elements of the B_i matrices are included. In this system of equations, there are a total of 54 parameters to be estimated, which is a much greater number of parameters than in the continuous-time model.

Under suitable regularity conditions relating to the differentiation of log L under the integral sign, and given certain conditions relating to the asymptotic behavior of the exogenous variables, it can be expected that

$$\sqrt{T}(\boldsymbol{\alpha}^* - \boldsymbol{\alpha}^0) \rightarrow N(0, W) \tag{29}$$

where $W = [\text{plim}\, T^{-1}\Sigma Z_t V^{-1} Z_t']^{-1}$ evaluated at the true value $\boldsymbol{\alpha}^0$, and $\boldsymbol{\alpha}^*$ is the estimated value. In practice, the asymptotic covariance matrix of $\boldsymbol{\alpha}^*$ may be approximated by the sample analog $[\Sigma Z_t V^{-1} Z_t']^{-1}$, which is used to calculate the standard errors of the estimates in the empirical application.

The optimal forecasts from the estimated time-series model are obtained in a similar manner to those from the continuous-time model, making use of the lagged fitted residuals from periods T and $T - 1$. As with the continuous-time forecasts, these forecasts are conditional on the observed values of the exogenous variables. The estimates of the continuous time and VARMAX models, and the forecasts obtained from these models, are presented in the next section.

Empirical Results

The continuous-time and VARMAX models were estimated using UK seasonally adjusted quarterly data on three broad commodity groupings, namely nondurables, semidurables, and durables. The estimation period covered 1973(1) to 1982(4), with eight further observations, from 1983(1) to 1984(4), retained for forecasting purposes. More details regarding the data are to be found in the appendix.

Estimates of the Continuous-time Model

The estimates of the parameters of the continuous time system are presented in table 5.1, along with some summary statistics for each equation. Note that Σ represents the covariance matrix of the continuous-time innovation vector $\boldsymbol{\mu}(dt)$.

On the whole, the estimates in table 5.1 are well determined and are all plausible. The high depreciation rate for the semi-durables category is rather surprising, but is consistent with the model, since δ also reflects consumers' preferences for new goods in addition to purely physical depreciation. For a fuller discussion of the estimated model, see Chambers (1992).

Table 5.1 Estimates of the continuous-time model

Coefficient	Equation: Non-durables	Semi-durables	Durables
π_i	0.0203	0.0528	0.3466
	(0.0129)	(0.0046)	(0.1546)
β_i	0.6942	−0.2134	−0.2984
	(0.4142)	(0.2855)	(0.1108)
δ_i	1.1154	5.8697	0.3826
	(0.8206)	(0.1688)	(0.0962)
a_i	52.0477	235.2171	90.5175
	(19.9290)	(101.4168)	(12.5847)
b_i	0.0656	0.4332	0.0399
	(0.0073)	(0.0850)	(0.0051)
Σ	32.7953	—	—
	(2.3695)		
	5.9803	41.7698	—
	(0.6370)	(3.2567)	
	24.8621	60.3298	165.1442
	(5.4364)	(5.9007)	(33.0683)
DW	2.8888	1.4855	2.4476
BP(8)	10.5952	13.9368	2.7323
LB(8)	11.6021	16.4286	3.1753
W	0.9624	0.9496	0.9841
BJ	1.9144	4.5027	2.5955

Note: Figures in parentheses are standard errors; DW is the Durbin–Watson statistic; BP and LB are the Box–Pierce and Ljung–Box statistics, each having approximate asymptotic chi-squared distributions with four degrees of freedom; W is the Shapiro–Wilk statistic for normality of the residuals; and BJ is the Bera–Jarque skewness-kurtosis test for normality of the residuals, having an asymptotic chi-squared distribution with two degrees of freedom. Reproduced from Chambers (1992).

With regard to the diagnostic statistics, these are based on a vector of transformed residuals, for the following reason. We know that the discrete innovation, $\boldsymbol{\varepsilon}_t$, is serially correlated over time by definition (see equation (6)). Denoting the covariance matrix of the $nT \times 1$ vector $\boldsymbol{\varepsilon} = (\varepsilon_1', \ldots, \varepsilon_T')$ by Ω, and the Choleski decomposition of Ω by M (where $\Omega = MM'$), then the vector $\mathbf{p} = M^{-1}\boldsymbol{\varepsilon}$ has the properties $E(\mathbf{p}) = 0$ and $E(\mathbf{pp}') = I$, under the assumption that the model is correctly specified. In other words, $\mathbf{p}$ should be serially uncorrelated, and, if the innovations are indeed Gaussian, should also be normally distributed. The diagnostic tests, checking for the presence of serial correlation and evidence of non-normality, are therefore applied to the vector $\mathbf{p}$, rather than $\boldsymbol{\varepsilon}$.

By examining these statistics, it would appear that the model is adequately specified, with the exception that there may be a degree of serial correlation in the nondurables and semidurables categories. However, Davies and Newbold (1979) and Hall and McAleer (1987) have presented Monte-Carlo evidence which puts into question the reliability of the Box–Pierce and Ljung–Box statistics. Since the role of stocks is less clear for these two categories of expenditure, this evidence may suggest that a different approach, possibly reflecting habit persistence in a different manner, is called for.

A further test of the model was carried out using the method of Chambers (1990), whereby the property of symmetric compensated price responses, exhibited by the long-run demands (6), may be tested against a more general alternative. The likelihood ratio statistic of 5.3246 fails to reject the symmetry hypothesis for a test with three degrees of freedom. This further specfication test, combined with the comments made above, suggests that this model may be a reasonable representation of the data.

Estimates of the VARMAX model

The estimated parameters of the VARMAX model are given in table 5.2. These estimates tend to have large sampling variances, mainly because so many parameters (54) are being estimated from a fairly small sample of 40 observations. In addition, there is also evidence of serial correlation in the residuals, and non-normality in equation (3), as indicated by the diagnostic statistics reported.

Clearly, the unconstrained VARMAX model being considered here is overparameterized, and if the exercise was model building rather than forecasting, the results in table 5.2 would be rather unsatisfactory. A more parsimonious model might be obtained by using data based methods of model selection along the lines discussed in Hannan and Deistler (1988), with the key reference for vector systems being Hannan and Kavalieris (1984). Although we are using a second-order VARMAX system for this forecasting exercise, this is dictated solely by the fact that the continuous-time model produces such a discrete analog. The use of data-based order estimation methods may possibly suggest a system of different order to that being assumed here. Indeed, this type of approach has been suggested as the first stage of a modeling strategy by Bergstom (1990).

A number of procedures have been suggested to estimate the order of a system. The criteria reviewed by Hannan and Deistler (1988) are of the form

$$C(n) = \log \det \Sigma_n + d(n)C_T/T, \tag{30}$$

where $d(n)$ is the dimension of the vector of system parameters, dependent on the order n, Σ_n is the estimated covariance matrix, and C_T is a constant that needs to be determined which satisfies

$$C_T > 0 \qquad \text{and} \qquad T^{-1}C_T \to 0 \quad \text{as } T \to \infty.$$

The order of the system is then chosen as the value of n that minimizes (30). Note that although increasing the order of the system, which involves the estimation of additional parameters, will lead to a lower value of log det Σ_n in (30), such action is penalized by the second term, which increases with $d(n)$ (and hence n). Special cases of (3) which are often employed are Akaike's information criterion

$$\text{AIC}(n) = \log \det \Sigma_n + 2d(n)/T \tag{31}$$

(Akaike 1973), and the Schwarz information criterion

$$\text{BIC}(n) = \log \det \Sigma_n + [d(n) \log T]/T \tag{32}$$

(see Schwarz 1978). Further criteria, such as those proposed by Parzen (1974), and Mallows (1973), can be shown to be closely related to AIC(n).

Table 5.2 Estimates of the VARMAX model

Explanatory variables	*Dependent variable* $\mathbf{q}_{it}$		
	Non-durables	*Semi-durables*	*Durables*
Constant	324.9422	274.6227	−624.6534
	(108.7970)	(1603.8467)	(332.6367)
$\mathbf{q}_{i,t-1}$	−0.5988	1.8418	0.5004
	(0.4535)	(0.4808)	(0.3833)
$\mathbf{q}_{i,t-2}$	−0.4301	−0.8411	−0.0280
	(0.3176)	(0.5244)	(0.3163)
$\varepsilon_{1,t-1}$	0.1859	0.0070	0.0653
	(0.5608)	(0.2237)	(0.1892)
$\varepsilon_{2,t-1}$	0.1141	−1.0332	−0.1621
	(0.4337)	(0.5803)	(0.2097)
$\varepsilon_{3,t-1}$	−0.4243	−0.4722	−0.1904
	(0.7963)	(0.5693)	(0.5102)
$\varepsilon_{1,t-2}$	−0.0056	−0.0261	0.0425
	(0.4136)	(0.1422)	(0.1550)
$\varepsilon_{2,t-2}$	0.6908	0.0395	−0.0496
	(0.4904)	(0.3233)	(0.2218)
$\varepsilon_{3,t-2}$	0.6127	−0.2271	0.0464
	(0.8075)	(0.5109)	(0.4238)
$(y/v_i)_t$	−0.0035	0.1168	−0.0338
	(0.0257)	(0.0265)	(0.0170)
$(y/v_i)_{t-1}$	0.1685	−0.0642	−0.0306
	(0.0365)	(0.0544)	(0.0186)
$(y/v_i)_{t-2}$	0.0060	0.0009	0.0009
	(0.0682)	(0.0280)	(0.0173)
$(v_j/v_i)_t$	−299.9363	−266.8816	−28.0946
	(301.3802)	(300.7365)	(43.5177)
$(v_k/v_i)_t$	13.6392	136.2835	143.3395
	(14.4419)	(59.6868)	(86.5190)
$(v_j/v_i)_{t-1}$	524.3957	488.2516	−67.0100
	(390.1073)	(383.1133)	(49.7917)
$(v_k/v_i)_{t-1}$	−5.7952	81.6515	181.1239
	(12.0528)	(88.2470)	(100.7992)
$(v_j/v_i)_{t-2}$	−377.4707	−339.9125	59.4646
	(413.7458)	(407.7054)	(51.1723)
$(v_k/v_i)_{t-2}$	−10.3572	80.2389	66.7497
	(17.2622)	(80.3858)	(110.6570)
V	[6.7259	—	—
	2.1070	6.3456	—
	14.3114	7.6575	44.4528]
DW	0.7074	2.4526	0.3803
BP(8)	13.3705	10.4186	14.8795
LB(8)	14.9521	12.4959	16.6813
W	0.9660	0.9772	0.8956
BJ	8.7532	1.5482	4.2122

Note: The same notes as to table 5.1 apply.

Although in principle the minimization of the above criteria is a useful way of proceeding with a modeling strategy, the method is not without its disadvantages. The main problem is the number of parameters that need to be estimated when dealing with an unconstrained system. The VARMAX(2,2,2) model used here involves 54 unrestricted parameters. Increasing the order of each component would, in general, add a further nine parameters, so that the corresponding VARMAX(3,3,3) would contain 75 parameters (recall that here the autoregressive matrices are diagonal, and the matrices on the exogenous variables contain a number of zeros). The estimation of VARMAX models of this type of order is cumbersome, to say the least, and the reliability of such estimates is questionable, particularly when most of the useful results are asymptotic. However, such data-based order estimation techniques provide great scope in univariate or bivariate models, or where the sample size is large. The model here belongs to neither category.

The unrestricted VARMAX model also offers potential in terms of testing the restrictions implicit in the discrete form of the continuous-time model, suggesting the possibility of conducting likelihod ratio tests of these restrictions. But the continuous-time model is not exactly nested within the VARMAX model, for the moving average coefficient matrices in the former are time-dependent, whereas those in the latter are assumed constant over time. However, it is shown in Bergstrom (1990) that the MA coefficient matrices for the continuous-time model converge fairly rapidly to constant matrices, so Bergstrom bases his test of the continuous-time restrictions on the subsample ($t = t_1, \ldots, T$) in which these matrices have converged. One could then conduct a likelihood ratio test using the maximized likelihood ratio values for this restricted sample. This approach has not been implemented here, for the restricted sample is likely to be too small to base valid inferences upon.

The Comparison of Forecasts

As detailed by Fair (1986), the three most commonly used measures of the accuracy of forecasts are root mean squared error (RMSE), mean absolute error (MAE), and Theil's inequality measure (U). In addition to these three measures, the mean error (ME) of the forecasts will also be given. Denoting the forecast value of $\mathbf{q}_{it}$ by $\mathbf{q}_{it}^*$, the four measures are defined by

$$\text{RMSE} = \sqrt{[T^{-1}\Sigma(\mathbf{q}_{it} - \mathbf{q}_{it}^*)^2]} \tag{33}$$

$$\text{MAE} = T^{-1}\Sigma|\mathbf{q}_{it} - \mathbf{q}_{it}^*| \tag{34}$$

$$\text{ME} = T^{-1}\Sigma(\mathbf{q}_{it} - \mathbf{q}_{it}^*) \tag{35}$$

$$U = \sqrt{[T^{-1}\Sigma(D\mathbf{q}_{it} - D\mathbf{q}_{it}^*)^2]}/\sqrt{[T^{-1}\Sigma(D\mathbf{q}_{it})^2]} \tag{36}$$

where $D\mathbf{q}_{it} = \mathbf{q}_{it} - \mathbf{q}_{i,t-1}$ and the summations run from $t = T + 1$ to $T + K$. If the forecasts are perfect (made without error), then each of the above measures is zero, while the MAE penalizes large errors less severely than the RMSE measure. Note that the value of U is equal to one for a no-change forecast ($D\,\mathbf{q}_{it}^* = 0$). Thus a value of U greater than one indicates that the forecasts are less accurate than those obtained assuming $\mathbf{q}_{it}^*$ is constant over the forecast period. It should also be mentioned that a naive (random walk) model produces one-step-ahead forecasts based on knowledge of the actual value of $\mathbf{q}_{it}$ in the previous period. The forecasts from the continuous-time and VARMAX models, on the other hand, are not based on this information, for they are dynamic K-step-ahead forecasts, conditional on the exogenous variables. This must be borne in mind when assessing the results of the forecasting exercise presented below.

The Forecasts

The forecasts generated by the continuous-time and VARMAX models are presented in table 5.3 for each of the three commodity groupings under consideration.

The VARMAX model tends to over-predict for the nondurables and durables categories, but seems to perform better for the semidurables category. The continuous-time forecasts, on the other hand, appear to be more evenly dispersed, but a proper comparison must rely on the relevant statistics. These are given in table 5.4.

The forecasts from the continuous-time model have an unambiguous advantage over those from the VARMAX model for the nondurables and durables categories, while the VARMAX model performs better than the continuous-time model for the semidurables category. Although the naive model seems to dominate the other two models for all categories, this is not evidence in itself to suggest that consumption necessarily follows a random walk.

It is worth re-emphasizing the point made in the previous subsection that the forecasts from the continuous-time and VARMAX models are K-step-ahead forecasts, conditional on the exogenous variables, whereas those from the naive random walk model are one-step-ahead forecasts. It is possible that if the forecasts were put

Table 5.3 Forecasts from the continuous time and VARMAX models

Commodity	*Quarter*	*Actual*	*Continuous-time*	*VARMAX*
Nondurables	1983(1)	210.9204	211.0280	207.8425
	(2)	213.4544	210.7175	209.4386
	(3)	214.3934	214.1523	211.0967
	(4)	214.7985	214.5418	211.6032
	1984(1)	214.8678	214.7863	206.5492
	(2)	213.3055	214.7903	206.4777
	(3)	211.0153	212.6952	209.4345
	(4)	213.1246	210.1587	214.5623
Semidurables	1983(1)	345.7668	345.2490	349.9327
	(2)	349.7020	346.5491	348.1235
	(3)	355.1705	353.5092	353.8588
	(4)	355.9235	360.5918	361.9744
	1984(1)	356.3000	357.4218	357.3556
	(2)	364.4751	347.1312	360.5894
	(3)	365.9098	372.5569	371.9407
	(4)	368.3382	367.1547	369.7564
Durables	1983(1)	72.2943	66.5873	75.2741
	(2)	71.8493	70.2281	81.4824
	(3)	75.1946	69.4660	77.2885
	(4)	74.2231	73.9935	84.5487
	1984(1)	73.2762	71.3702	72.1103
	(2)	75.2749	70.6226	82.7838
	(3)	71.3236	73.5337	80.8042
	(4)	76.0591	67.3247	85.5736

Table 5.4 Summary statistics for the forecasts

	Nondurables	*Semidurables*	*Durables*
RMSE			
Continuous-time	1.6377	4.1161	4.6706
VARMAX	4.5698	3.7546	7.5069
Naive	1.5685	3.7373	2.7578
MAE			
Continuous-time	1.1943	3.2871	3.8486
VARMAX	4.0793	3.1872	6.5878
Naive	1.2729	2.7071	2.3446
ME			
Continuous-time	0.3762	0.1778	3.2961
VARMAX	3.6094	−1.4932	−6.2963
Naive	0.3098	2.7071	0.7660
U			
Continuous-time	1.3999	1.8767	1.9634
VARMAX	1.8420	1.5108	2.6151
Naive	1.2492	1.1290	1.7038

on the same basis, for example by making the continuous-time and VARMAX forecasts one-step-ahead (using actual values in preceding periods rather than predicted values), then the random walk model may lose its apparent advantage. If this turned out to be the case, then this could be constituted as evidence against the naive model. But we are not in a position to do this on the strength of the results in table 5.4. Another possibility for the naive model's success is that there is actually a unit root in the consumption series, or, alternatively, a unit root in the exogenous series, for example, income. If this is the case, then by imposing a unit root prior, it is possible that the continuous-time and VARMAX models might perform better. But the dynamic lead time involved with these models may still enable the random walk model to dominate. These possibilities have not been explored empirically.

One of the assumptions made, with respect to both the continuous-time and time-series models, is that the covariance matrix of the disturbance terms is constant over the sample period. Indeed, this is a common assumption in many econometric models. However, this assumption may be rather unrealistic when using real consumers' expenditure as the endogenous variable. Although the covariance structure of real expenditure may be more stable than for current expenditure, it may be preferable to model consumption in terms of budget shares, which may have an impact on the estimated behavior of the models. However, it is not entirely clear how a budget-share interpretation of the continuous-time model may be developed, in view of the form of the stock adjustment relationship being used. Such a problem would not occur, however, if we ignored the role of stocks in a demand system for nondurable consumption, based for example on the almost-ideal-demand system of Deaton and Muellbauer (1980).

It is also worth commenting on recent work regarding consumption behavior in a more general context. One implication of the results of Hall (1978) is that the best predictor of consumption in period t is its value in period $t-1$ – additional explanatory variables yield no improvement in forecasting accuracy. This result seems to have been supported to some extent here in view of the superior performance of the naive model, but the earlier comments regarding the basis of the forecasts (K-step as opposed to one-step) must be reasserted, and thus no firm conclusion can be drawn. An explicit test of the life cycle/permanent income/ rational expectations hypothesis would be worth investigating in the context of a continuous-time model, particularly regarding the ability to forecast (see also Christiano *et al.* (1991)).

Putting aside the comments contained in the last paragraphs, and returning to the original comparison of the continuous-time and VARMAX models, it does seem clear from the results obtained that the restrictions imposed by a continuous-time model, on the discrete data, can be important in not only reducing the variances of the estimated parameters, but also in producing more accurate forecasts. It is also worth pointing out that the methodology proposed by Bergstrom for estimating continuous-time models provides a good basis for general diagnostic and specification testing, whether by Wald, Lagrange multiplier or likelihood ratio methods. In addition to testing the continuous-time restrictions against the VARMAX model, as mentioned earlier, other hypotheses of interest relate to the comparison of competing specifications of the continuous-time model, such as the test of symmetry restrictions in the demand model reported here. It therefore seems that a continuous-time modeling strategy offers a great deal of potential in analyzing time series relationships, which will no doubt be exploited in due course.

Conclusions

The objective of this paper was to examine the relevant forecasting performance of a particular continuous-time model against the performance of a discrete time-series (VARMAX) model. Quasi-maximum likelihood estimates of both models were obtained using quarterly data and highlighted the fact that the restricted number of parameters in the continuous-time model can be estimated with much greater precision than in the VARMAX model. The overall forecasting performance was also better for the continuous-time model, but a naive random walk dominated both models. This is not regarded here as being a serious problem, for the random walk is based on knowledge that the other models do not possess, namely the value of the endogenous variable in the preceding period.

Although both models could be refined further and respecified in the light of the diagnostic statistics reported, and could possibly perform even better over the post-sample period as a consequence, the exercise conducted here nevertheless shows the potential importance of taking into account the restrictions on the discrete data imposed by an underlying continuous-time model. It is intuitively clear that agents do not change their behavior once every period coinciding with the unit of observation. Indeed, it is only with continuous-time models, formulated as systems of stochastic differential equations, that we will be able to take account of the dynamic features of economic behavior, and test more precisely the hypotheses suggested by economic theory. There is thus much scope for further work testing appropriate specifications of continuous-time models, particularly with a view to producing more accurate forecasts. Much of this potential research activity is only possible due to the work of Rex Bergstrom.

Appendix

The data used in the study spans the period 1973(1) to 1984(4). Esimates were obtained using 40 observations, from 1973(1) to 1982(4), with eight further observations, from 1983(1) to 1984(4), retained for forecasting purposes. Definitions of the data are given below; all data are taken from *Economic Trends*.

Variable	Definition
q	Real per capita consumers' expenditure.
p	Real price of the category of expenditure, defined as the implicit price deflator divided by the price deflator for total consumers' expenditure.
y	Real per capita personal disposable income.
r	Real interest rate, defined as the average percentage yield on Treasury Bills, minus the annual percentage change in the consumers' price deflator.

All the data are seasonally adjusted, and have 1980 as their base. Quarterly population figures were obtained by the method of quadratic Lagrange interpolation from the annual series.

As the data are quarterly, it is necessary to calculate the quarterly rate of interest from the annual data. Denoting the annual rate by r_a, the following formula is used to obtain the quarterly equivalent:

$$r = \tfrac{1}{4}\log(1 + r_a).$$

The commodity groupings used to define the three broad categories of expenditure are as follows.

Nondurables	Food, alcoholic drink and tobacco.
	Energy products.
Semidurables	Clothing and footwear.
	Other goods.
	Other services.
Durables	Furniture and floor coverings.
	Cars and motorcycles.
	Other durable goods.

Such a classification is difficult in the absence of prior knowledge regarding depreciation rates, but is not crucial in this study, as the depreciation rate constitutes one of the parameters to be estimated. The above categorization was chosen so that the groupings were roughly equal in terms of expenditure. In fact, the main difficulty arises in specifying the nondurable and semidurable groupings.

Note

I would like to thank two anonymous referees for their helpful comments. Particular thanks go to the editor, Peter Phillips, for his advice and suggestions in helping me revise this paper, which is based on a chapter in my Ph.D. thesis supervised by Rex Bergstrom (see Chambers (1989)).

References

Akaike, H. (1973). "Information theory and an extension of the maximum likelihood principle," in B. N. Petrov and F. Csaki (eds) *Second International Symposium on Information Theory*. Budapest: Akademiai Kiadó.

Bergstrom, A. R. (1966). "Non-recursive models as discrete approximations to systems of stochastic differential equations," *Econometrica*, 34, 173–82.

Bergstrom, A. R. (1983). "Gaussian estimation of structural parameters in higher-order continuous time dynamic models," *Econometrica*, 51, 117–52.

Bergstrom, A. R. (1985). "The estimation of parameters in non-stationary higher-order continuous time dynamic models," *Econometric Theory*, 1, 369–85.

Bergstrom, A. R. (1986). "The estimation of open higher-order continuous time dynamic models with mixed stock and flow data," *Econometric Theory*, 2, 350–73.

Bergstrom, A. R. (1987). "Optimal control in wide sense stationary continuous time stochastic models," *Journal of Economic Dynamics and Control*, 11, 425–43.

Bergstrom, A. R. (1989). "Optimal forecasting of discrete stock and flow data generated by a higher order continuous time system," *Computers and Mathematics with Applications*, 17, 1203–14.

Bergstrom, A. R. (1990). "Hypothesis testing in continuous time models," chapter 7 in A. R. Bergstrom *Continuous Time Econometric Modelling*, Oxford: Oxford University Press.

Bergstrom, A. R., and M. J. Chambers (1990). "Gaussian estimation of a continuous time model of demand for consumer durable goods with applications to demand in the United Kingdom, 1973–1984," in A. R. Bergstrom *Continuous Time Econometric Modelling*. Oxford: Oxford University Press.

Bergstrom, A. R., and C. R. Wymer (1976). "A model of disequilibrium neoclassical growth and its application to the United Kingdom," in A. R. Bergstrom (ed.) *Statistical Inference in Continuous Time Economic Models*. Amsterdam: North-Holland.

Chambers, M. J. (1989). *Durability and Consumers' Demand: Gaussian Estimation of some Continuous Time Models*. Unpublished Ph.D. thesis, University of Essex.

Chambers, M. J. (1990). "Forecasting with demand systems: a comparative study," *Journal of Econometrics*, 44, 363–76.

Chambers, M. J. (1992). "Estimation of a continuous time dynamic demand system," *Journal of Applied Econometrics*, 7, 53–64.

Christiano, L., M. Eichenbaum, and D. Marshall (1991). "The permanent income hypothesis revisited," *Econometrica*, 59, 397–423.

Davies, N., and P. Newbold (1979). "Some power studies of a portmanteau test of time series model specification," *Biometrika*, 66, 153–5.

Deaton, A. S., and J. Muellbauer (1980). "An almost ideal demand system," *American Economic Review*, 70, 312–36.

Fair, R. C. (1986). "Evaluating the predictive accuracy of models", in Z. Griliches and M. D. Intriligator (eds) *Handbook of Econometrics*, volume 3, Amsterdam: North-Holland.

Hall, A. D., and M. McAleer (1987). "A Monte Carlo study of some tests of model adequacy in time series analysis," Australian National University Working Paper No. 148.

Hall, R. E. (1978). "Stochastic implications of the life cycle–permanent income hypothesis: theory and evidence", *Journal of Political Economy*, 86, 971–87.

Hannan, E. J., and M. Deistler (1988). *The Statistical Theory of Linear Systems*. New York: John Wiley.

Hannan, E. J., and L. Kavalieris (1984). "Multivariate linear time series models," *Advances in Applied Probability*, 16, 492–561.

Hannan, E. J., W. Dunsmuir, and M. Deistler (1980). "Estimation of vector ARMAX models," *Journal of Multivariate Analysis*, 10, 275–95.

Kohn, R. (1979). "Asymptotic estimation and hypothesis testing results for vector linear time series models," *Econometrica*, 47, 1005–30.

Mallows, C. L. (1973). "Some comments on C_P," *Technometrics*, 15, 661–75.
Parzen, E. (1974). "Some recent advances in time series modelling," *IEEE Transactions on Automatic Control*, 19, 723–30.
Schwarz, G. (1978). "Estimating the dimension of a model," *Annals of Statistics*, 6, 461–4.

6

Estimation, Smoothing, Interpolation, and Distribution for Structural Time-Series Models in Continuous Time

A. C. Harvey and James H. Stock

Introduction

Rex Bergstrom's work has stressed not just the technical aspects but also the philosophical basis for applying continuous time models to time-series data; see Bergstrom (1966, 1976, 1984). Because many economic variables are essentially continuous and decisions are made continuously, it is often more appealing to set up models in continuous time even though observations are made at discrete intervals. The dynamic structure of a model is then not dependent on the observation interval, something which may bear no relation to the underlying data generation process.

An application of continuous-time models emphasized in this paper is their use to estimate intermediate values of a discretely sampled time series. Adopting Litterman's (1983) terminology, estimation at points between observations will be termed interpolation for a stock variable (sampled at a point in time) and distribution for a flow (sampled as an integral over a time interval). Using a continuous-time model in this context is appealing for several reasons. First, as emphasized by the contributors to Bergstrom (1976), the continuous-time framework provides a logically consistent basis for the handling of stocks and flows. Second, it provides a natural conceptual framework, with considerable technical simplifications, for handling irregularly spaced observations. Third, it provides a well-defined framework for interpolation and distribution to arbitrary subintervals.

Historically, a key technical hurdle in applying continuous-time models to economic data has been the difficulty of evaluating the exact Gaussian likelihood for flow data and for mixed stock-flow systems. These problems have largely been solved for large classes of models by Bergstrom (1983, 1984, 1985, 1986) and by his students and collaborators. Here, we consider interpolation for stocks and distribution for flows. To simplify the discussion, we restrict attention to univariate series.

This article studies continuous-time formulations within the context of structural time-series models in the sense of Harvey (1989). Structural models are formulated directly in terms of components of interest, such as trends, seasonals, and cycles. These components are functions of time and it is natural to regard them as being continuous. The essence of a structural time-series model is that its components are stochastic rather than deterministic. A continuous-time model can be set up to parameterize these stochastic movements. It can then be shown that, for the principal structural time-series models, the implied discrete-time model is, apart from some minor differences, of the same form as a discrete-time model which one would set up without reference to the continuous-time formulation. This is true for both stocks and flows. Thus there is a logical consistency in the structural class.

Since the components of structural time-series models have a direct interpretation, these models can often be specified without a detailed initial analysis of the data. The appropriateness of a particular specification is then checked by various diagnostics, and the whole model selection exercise is much more akin to what it is in econometrics; see for example Harvey (1985). Thus although data are not available on a continuous basis, the greater emphasis on prior considerations in model specification means that it is just as easy to adopt a continuous-time model formulation as a discrete one.

The next two sections examine the exact discrete-time models implied by the underlying continuous-time structural models sampled at the observation timing interval. This is straightforward for stock variables, less so for flows. In each case we consider the following statistical problems: time domain estimation of the model parameters by maximum likelihood; prediction of future observations; estimation of the unobserved components at the observation points and at intermediate points; and estimation of what the observations themselves would have been at intermediate points.

Structural Time-series Models in Discrete Time

A structural time-series model is one which is set up in terms of components which have a direct interpretation. For an economic time series, these components will typically consist of a trend, a seasonal, an irregular, and perhaps even a cycle. Examples of the application of such models can be found in Engle (1978), Harvey (1985), and Kitagawa (1981). Other components can be brought into the model. For example, daily or weekly components can be included if appropriate data are available. A general review can be found in Harvey (1989). In the present article, attention is restricted primarily to trend, cycle, seasonal, and irregular components, defined as follows.

Trend The level, μ_t, and slope, β_t, are generated by the multivariate random walk process,

$$\mu_t = \mu_{t-1} + \beta_{t-1} + \eta_t, \tag{1a}$$

$$\beta_t = \beta_{t-1} + \zeta_t, \tag{1b}$$

where η_t and ζ_t are mutually uncorrelated white-noise processes with zero means and variances σ_η^2 and σ_ζ^2 respectively.

Cycle The cycle, ψ_t, is stationary and is centered on a frequency λ_c, which lies in the range $[0, \pi]$. Its statistical formulation is

$$\begin{bmatrix} \psi_t \\ \psi_t^* \end{bmatrix} = \rho \begin{bmatrix} \cos\lambda_c & \sin\lambda_c \\ -\sin\lambda_c & \cos\lambda_c \end{bmatrix} \begin{bmatrix} \psi_{t-1} \\ \psi_{t-1}^* \end{bmatrix} + \begin{bmatrix} \kappa_t \\ \kappa_t^* \end{bmatrix}, \tag{2}$$

where κ_t and κ_t^* are uncorrelated white-noise disturbances with a common variance σ_κ^2, and ρ is a damping factor which lies in the range $0 \leqslant \rho \leqslant 1$.

Seasonal The seasonal component, γ_t, is defined as the sum of an appropriate number of trigonometric terms, γ_{jt}, each having a specification of the form (2) with ρ equal to unity and λ_c equal to a given seasonal frequency, $\lambda_j = 2\pi j/s$. Thus $\gamma_t = \sum_{j=1}^{s/2} \gamma_{jt}$, where s is the number of "seasons" (assumed to be even) and where

$$\begin{bmatrix} \gamma_{jt} \\ \gamma_{jt}^* \end{bmatrix} = \begin{bmatrix} \cos \lambda_j & \sin \lambda_j \\ -\sin \lambda_j & \cos \lambda_j \end{bmatrix} \begin{bmatrix} \gamma_{j,t-1} \\ \gamma_{j,t-1}^* \end{bmatrix} + \begin{bmatrix} \omega_{jt} \\ \omega_{jt}^* \end{bmatrix} \tag{3}$$

with $\text{Var}\,(\omega_{jt}) = \text{Var}\,(\omega_{jt}^*) = \sigma_\omega^2$ for all j.

Irregular The irregular term, ε_t, is generally taken to be a white-noise process, with variance σ_ε^2, unless there are strong *a priori* grounds to assume otherwise, as in Hausman and Watson (1985).

These components – trend, cycle, seasonal, and irregular – combine in various ways to give the principal structural time-series models for an observed series, Y_t, $t = 1, \ldots, T$. These models are:

1. *Local Linear Trend* The discrete-time process obeys

$$Y_t = \mu_t + \varepsilon_t, \tag{4}$$

where μ_t is a stochastic trend of the form (1) and ε_t is a white-noise irregular term.

2. *Local Level* This is a special case of the local linear trend in which μ_t is just a random walk:

$$\mu_t = \mu_{t-1} + \eta_t. \tag{5}$$

3. *Basic Structural Model with Cycles* Both seasonal and cyclical components may be brought into the model by expanding (4) to give

$$Y_t = \mu_t + \gamma_t + \psi_t + \varepsilon_t. \tag{6}$$

Each of these models can be handled statistically by putting them in state space form:

$$\boldsymbol{\alpha}_t = T_t \boldsymbol{\alpha}_{t-1} + R_t \boldsymbol{\eta}_t, \ \text{Var}\,(\boldsymbol{\eta}_t) \equiv Q_t \tag{7a}$$

$$Y_t = z_t' \boldsymbol{\alpha}_t + \varepsilon_t, \ \text{Var}\,(\varepsilon_t) \equiv h_t \tag{7b}$$

where $\boldsymbol{\alpha}_t$ is an $m \times 1$ state vector and ε_t and $\boldsymbol{\eta}_t$ are respectively scalar and $g \times 1$ zero mean white-noise disturbances which are mutually uncorrelated. The matrices z_t, T_t, R_t, and Q_t are $m \times 1$, $m \times m$, $m \times g$ and $g \times g$ respectively. These matrices may depend on a number of parameters, known as hyperparameters. Thus, for example, in the local linear trend model, (4), the hyperparameters are the variances σ_η^2, σ_ζ^2 and σ_ε^2. In some circumstances z_t and R_t will depend on time, say if there are some missing observations. More often, z_t and R_t will be time-invariant and henceforth will be denoted by z and R.

The state vector may be estimated by the Kalman filter. Furthermore, if the disturbances are normally distributed, the unknown hyperparameters may be estimated by maximum likelihood via the prediction error decomposition; see Ansley and Kohn (1985), De Jong (1991) and Harvey (1989, chapter 4).

General State Form of Continuous Time Models with Stocks and Flows

This section summarizes some results for the general continuous-time model when the data are observed at T irregular observation times $\{t_\tau\}$, $\tau = 1, \ldots, T$. These observation times are separated by calendar time units δ_τ, so that $t_\tau \equiv t_{\tau-1} + \delta_\tau$. The continuous-time state vector is denoted by $\boldsymbol{\alpha}(t)$; at the observation times, it is denoted by $\boldsymbol{\alpha}_\tau \equiv \boldsymbol{\alpha}(t_\tau)$. Thus, in the notational convention adopted here, $\boldsymbol{\alpha}(t)$, $y(t)$, etc. denote continuous-time processes, and $\boldsymbol{\alpha}_\tau$, y_τ, etc. denote these processes at the appropriate discrete-time sampling dates. The observable (discrete time) process is Y_τ, and the data are T observations on the (discrete time) time series $(Y_1, \ldots, Y_T)$.

The continuous-time analog of the time-invariant discrete-time transition equation in (7a) is

$$\mathrm{d}\boldsymbol{\alpha}(t) = A\boldsymbol{\alpha}(t)\,\mathrm{d}t + R\,\mathrm{d}\boldsymbol{\eta}(t) \tag{8}$$

where the matrices A and R are $m \times m$ and $m \times g$ respectively and may be functions of hyperparameters and $\boldsymbol{\eta}(t)$ is a $g \times 1$ continuous-time multivariate Wiener process. For a discussion of the formal interpretation of linear stochastic differential equations, see Bergstrom (1983). The Wiener process has independent increments that are Gaussian with mean zero and covariance matrix

$$E\left[\int_r^s \mathrm{d}\boldsymbol{\eta}(t) \int_r^s \mathrm{d}\boldsymbol{\eta}(t)'\right] = (s-r)Q.$$

Suppose we have a univariate series of observations at time $\{t_\tau\}$ for $\tau = 1, \ldots, T$. For a stock variable the observations are defined by

$$\mathrm{Y}_\tau = z'\boldsymbol{\alpha}(t_\tau) + \boldsymbol{\varepsilon}_\tau,\ \tau = 1, \ldots, T, \tag{9}$$

where $\boldsymbol{\varepsilon}_\tau$ is white-noise disturbance term with mean zero and variance σ_ε^2 which is uncorrelated with differences of $\boldsymbol{\eta}(t)$ in all time periods. For a flow

$$\mathrm{Y}_\tau = \int_{t_{\tau-1}}^{t_\tau} z'\boldsymbol{\alpha}(r)\,\mathrm{d}r + \int_{t_{\tau-1}}^{t_\tau} \mathrm{d}\boldsymbol{\varepsilon}(r),\ \tau = 1, \ldots, T, \tag{10}$$

where $\boldsymbol{\varepsilon}(t)$ is a continuous-time Gaussian process with uncorrelated increments, mean zero and variance σ_ε^2, which is uncorrelated with $\boldsymbol{\eta}(t)$ in all time periods in that

$$E\left[\int_r^s \mathrm{d}\boldsymbol{\eta}(t) \int_p^q \mathrm{d}\varepsilon(r)\right] = 0$$

for all $r < s$ and $p < q$.

The state space formulation of continuous-time models derives from the stochastic integral equations that properly define the stochastic differential equations (8). The relationship between the state vector at time t_τ and time $t_{\tau-1}$ is given by

$$\boldsymbol{\alpha}(t_\tau) = \mathrm{e}^{A\delta_\tau}\boldsymbol{\alpha}(t_{\tau-1}) + \int_{t_{\tau-1}}^{t_\tau} \mathrm{e}^{A(t_\tau - s)} R \,\mathrm{d}\boldsymbol{\eta}(s). \tag{11}$$

This yields the discrete-time transition equation,

$$\boldsymbol{\alpha}_\tau = T_\tau \boldsymbol{\alpha}_{\tau-1} + \boldsymbol{\eta}_\tau, \; \tau = 1, \ldots, T, \tag{12}$$

where $T_\tau = \mathrm{e}^{A\delta_\tau}$, $\boldsymbol{\alpha}_\tau \equiv \boldsymbol{\alpha}(t_\tau)$, and $\boldsymbol{\eta}_\tau$ is a multivariate white-noise disturbance term with mean zero and covariance matrix

$$Q_\tau = \int_0^{\delta_\tau} \mathrm{e}^{A(\delta_\tau - s)} RQR' \, \mathrm{e}^{A'(\delta_\tau - s)} \,\mathrm{d}s. \tag{13}$$

The condition for $\boldsymbol{\alpha}(t)$ in (8) to be stationary is that the real parts of the characteristic roots of A are negative. Then

$$\boldsymbol{\alpha}(t) = \int_{-\infty}^{t} \mathrm{e}^{A(t-s)} R \,\mathrm{d}\boldsymbol{\eta}(s)$$

so that $E\boldsymbol{\alpha}(t) = 0$ and

$$\mathrm{Var}\,\{\boldsymbol{\alpha}(t)\} = \int_0^{\infty} \mathrm{e}^{As} RQR' \, \mathrm{e}^{As'} \,\mathrm{d}s \tag{14}$$

which provides initial conditions for $\boldsymbol{\alpha}(t)$ in the Kalman filter.

Structural Components in Continuous Time

The main structural components have the following natural formulations in continuous time.

Trend The linear trend component is

$$\mathrm{d}\begin{bmatrix} \mu(t) \\ \beta(t) \end{bmatrix} = \begin{bmatrix} 0 & 1 \\ 0 & 0 \end{bmatrix} \begin{bmatrix} \mu(t) \\ \beta(t) \end{bmatrix} \mathrm{d}t + \begin{bmatrix} \mathrm{d}\boldsymbol{\eta}(t) \\ \mathrm{d}\zeta(t) \end{bmatrix}, \tag{15}$$

where the continuous time processes $\boldsymbol{\eta}(t)$ and $\zeta(t)$ have mutually and serially uncorrelated increments and variances σ_η^2 and σ_ζ^2, respectively. The local level model obtains as a special case of (15) with $\beta(0) = 0$ and $\sigma_\zeta^2 = 0$.

Cycle The continuous-time cycle component is

$$\mathrm{d}\begin{bmatrix} \Psi(t) \\ \Psi^*(t) \end{bmatrix} = \begin{bmatrix} \log\rho & \lambda_c \\ -\lambda_c & \log\rho \end{bmatrix} \begin{bmatrix} \Psi(t) \\ \Psi^*(t) \end{bmatrix} \mathrm{d}t + \begin{bmatrix} \mathrm{d}\kappa(t) \\ \mathrm{d}\kappa^*(t) \end{bmatrix}, \tag{16}$$

where $\kappa(t)$ and $\kappa^*(t)$ have mutually and serially uncorrelated increments and the same variance, σ_κ^2, and ρ, and λ_c are parameters, the latter being the frequency of the cycle. The characteristic roots of the matrix containing these parameters are $(\log\rho) \pm i\lambda_c$. Since the general condition for stationarity of a model of the form (8) is that the characteristic roots must have negative real parts, the condition for $\Psi(t)$ to be a stationary process is $\log\rho < 0$, which corresponds to $\rho < 1$.

Seasonal The continuous-time seasonal component is the sum of a suitable number of trigonometric components, $\gamma_j(t)$, generated by processes of the form (16) with ρ equal to unity and λ_c set equal to the appropriate seasonal frequency λ_j. That is, for $j = 1, \ldots, s/2$,

$$\mathrm{d}\begin{bmatrix} \gamma_j(t) \\ \gamma_j^*(t) \end{bmatrix} = \begin{bmatrix} 0 & \lambda_j \\ -\lambda_j & 0 \end{bmatrix} \begin{bmatrix} \gamma_j(t) \\ \gamma_j^*(t) \end{bmatrix} \mathrm{d}t + \begin{bmatrix} \mathrm{d}\omega_j(t) \\ \mathrm{d}\omega_j^*(t) \end{bmatrix}, \tag{17}$$

where $\omega_j(t)$ and $\omega_j^*(t)$ are processes with serially and mutually uncorrelated increments and with equal variance σ_ω^2.

Continuous-time structural models constructed from these components constitute special cases of the general process (8) and of more general continuous-time processes such as those studied by Phillips (1988). The aim of these structural models is to provide a practical framework for forecasting and – in the continuous-time setting – interpolation and distribution.

Stock Variables

The discrete state space form for a stock variable generated by a continuous-time process consists of the transition equation (12) together with the measurement equation (9). The Kalman filter can therefore be applied in a standard way. When the observations are equally spaced the implied discrete time model is time-invariant and typically it is convenient to set $\delta_\tau = 1$. One of the main practical advantages, however, of the continuous-time framework is the easy handling of irregularly spaced observations, so the case of general δ_τ is considered here. For related applications, see Jones (1984) and Kitagawa (1984).

Structural Models
The continuous-time components defined above can be combined to produce a continuous-time structural model. As in the discrete case, the components are usually assumed to be mutually uncorrelated. Hence the A and Q matrices in (13) are block diagonal and so the discrete-time components can be evaluated separately.

Trend For the local linear trend model (15), $T_\tau = e^{A\delta_\tau}$ is

$$T_\tau = \exp\left\{\begin{bmatrix} 0 & 1 \\ 0 & 0 \end{bmatrix}\delta_\tau\right\} = I + \begin{bmatrix} 0 & \delta_\tau \\ 0 & 0 \end{bmatrix} = \begin{bmatrix} 1 & \delta_\tau \\ 0 & 1 \end{bmatrix}.$$

Thus the exact discrete-time representation of (15) is

$$\begin{bmatrix} \mu_\tau \\ \beta_\tau \end{bmatrix} = \begin{bmatrix} 1 & \delta_\tau \\ 0 & 1 \end{bmatrix}\begin{bmatrix} \mu_{\tau-1} \\ \beta_{\tau-1} \end{bmatrix} + \begin{bmatrix} \eta_\tau \\ \zeta_\tau \end{bmatrix}. \tag{18a}$$

In view of the simple structure of this matrix exponential, the evaluation of the covariance matrix of the discrete-time disturbances can be carried out explicitly, yielding

$$\operatorname{Var}\begin{bmatrix} \eta_\tau \\ \zeta_\tau \end{bmatrix} = \delta_\tau \begin{bmatrix} \sigma_\eta^2 + \delta_\tau^2\sigma_\zeta^2/3 & \frac{1}{2}\delta_\tau\sigma_\zeta^2 \\ \frac{1}{2}\delta_\tau\sigma_\zeta^2 & \sigma_\zeta^2 \end{bmatrix}. \tag{18b}$$

When δ_τ is equal to unity, (18) reduces to the discrete-time local linear trend (1). However, while in (1) the disturbances are uncorrelated, (18b) shows that uncorrelatedness of the continuous-time disturbances implies that the corresponding discrete-time disturbances are correlated.

The discrete-time model for the local level trend obtains by setting $\beta_0 = 0$ and $\sigma_\zeta^2 = 0$ in (18), in which case μ_t evolves in discrete time as a random walk. Thus with only a local level trend and the irregular term ε_t, $Y_\tau = \mu_\tau + \varepsilon_\tau$, $\tau = 1, \ldots, T$, so that Y_τ evolves according to the familiar random-walk-plus-noise model.

Cycle For the cycle model (16), use of the matrix exponential definition together with the power series expansions for the cosine and sine functions gives the discrete-time model

$$\begin{bmatrix} \Psi_\tau \\ \Psi_\tau^* \end{bmatrix} = \rho^{\delta_\tau}\begin{bmatrix} \cos\lambda_c\delta_\tau & \sin\lambda_c\delta_\tau \\ -\sin\lambda_c\delta_\tau & \cos\lambda_c\delta_\tau \end{bmatrix}\begin{bmatrix} \Psi_{\tau-1} \\ \Psi_{\tau-1}^* \end{bmatrix} + \begin{bmatrix} \kappa_\tau \\ \kappa_\tau^* \end{bmatrix}. \tag{19}$$

When δ_τ is one, the transition matrix corresponds exactly to the transition matrix of the discrete-time cyclical component (2). As regards the properties of the disturbances, specifying that $\kappa(t)$ and $\kappa^*(t)$ be mutually uncorrelated with equal variances means that in the corresponding discrete time model κ_τ and κ_τ^* will also be uncorrelated with the same variance for any δ_τ. In fact, the covariance matrix of $(\kappa_\tau, \kappa_\tau^*)'$ is $(-\sigma_\kappa^2/2\log\rho)(1-\rho^{2\delta_\tau})I$.

There are three noteworthy parallels between (19) and the cyclical process as originally defined in discrete time. First, as in the discrete analog, letting $\kappa(t)$ and $\kappa^*(t)$ be uncorrelated with equal variances imposes one more restriction than is necessary for identifiability. However, it ensures that the specification of the discrete-time model is consistent with the continuous-time model. Second, setting λ_c equal to zero in (19) means that Ψ_t collapses to a continuous-time AR(1) process exhibiting positive autocorrelation. Third, a pseudocyclical process is also obtained from a continuous time AR(2) or ARMA(2,1) model since, as shown in Phadke and Wu (1974), the roots of the corresponding discrete time AR(2) polynomial are typically complex. One attraction of working with the cycle model is that it is easier to handle as well as being set up in terms of the parameters of interest.

Seasonal For a trigonometric seasonal component, (17), the discrete time specification is similar to (19) with $\rho = 1$. The covariance matrix of the disturbance is $\sigma_\omega^2 \delta_\tau I$. When $\delta_\tau = 1$, this specification corresponds exactly to that given in (3).

As regards starting values for the Kalman filter for irregularly spaced observations, the considerations which arise are almost exactly as for a conventional discrete-time model. Thus, if the state vector contains d nonstationary components, d observations are needed before the elements of the state vector can be estimated with finite MSE. A diffuse prior can be used to initiate the nonstationary elements of the state vector. The starting values for the stationary components are provided by their respective unconditional distributions. Thus for the stationary cyclical component (16), the unconditional mean of $[\Psi(t), \Psi^*(t)]'$ is zero while the covariance matrix is obtained by evaluating (14). Thus, because $RQR' = \sigma_\kappa^2 I$, $\text{Var}(\boldsymbol{\alpha}_0) = \sigma_\kappa^2 \int_0^\infty e^{(A+A')s}\,ds$. However $A + A' = (2 \log \rho)I$, so $\text{Var}(\boldsymbol{\alpha}_0) = (-\sigma_\kappa^2/2 \log \rho)I$.

In summary, putting the various continuous-time components together yields discrete-time models which, for regularly spaced observations, are almost identical to the discrete-time models set up in equations (1) to (7). In fact, the only case where the implied discrete time model is different from the model originally formulated is the local linear trend and there the difference is minor. Thus, for a stock variable, the principal discrete-time structural models are consistent with the corresponding continuous-time models. The continuous-time models are more general, however, in that they can handle irregularly spaced observations and interpolate at any point.

Smoothing and Interpolation

Interpolation is the estimation of the series and/or its components at some point between observations. This may be carried out by defining the required points, constructing the appropriate transition equations, and treating the corresponding observations as missing. Thus, suppose interpolation is to be carried out at J points $t_\tau + r_1$, $t_\tau + r_2$, and so on where $0 < r_1 < r_2 < \cdots < r_J \leqslant \delta_{\tau+1}$. All that is required is the definition of the discrete-time transition equation (12) at $t_\tau + r_1, t_\tau + r_2, \ldots, t_{\tau+1}$ and the subsequent applications of the Kalman filter. The optimal estimators of $y(t)$ at these intermediate points are then obtained by applying a suitable smoothing algorithm; see for example Anderson and Moore (1979) or Harvey (1989, chapter 3). The estimators at time $t_\tau + r_j$ may be written as $y(t_\tau + r_j | T)$. This yields the minimum MSE linear estimator of an observation at time $t_\tau + r_j$, $y(t_\tau + r_j | T) = z'a(t_\tau + r_j | T)$, where $a(t|\tau)$ denote the optimal predictor of $\boldsymbol{\alpha}(t)$ using data through the τth observation (i.e. the observable time series through calendar date t_τ). The corresponding MSE is $\text{MSE}[y(t_\tau + r_j | T)] = z'P(t_\tau + r_j | T)z + \sigma_\varepsilon^2$, $j = 1, 2, \ldots, J$, where $P(t_\tau + r_j | T)$ is the MSE matrix of $\boldsymbol{\alpha}(t_\tau + r_j | T)$, the smoothed estimator of the state vector at time $t_\tau + r_j$.

Prediction

Let $a_\tau \equiv a(t_\tau | \tau)$. In the general model (8), the optimal predictor of the state vector for any positive lead time, l (i.e. at time $t_T + l$, given data through calendar time t_T), is given by the forecast function $a(t_T + l|T) = e^{Al}a_T$. The state vector at lead time l satisfies:

$$\boldsymbol{\alpha}(t_T + l) = e^{Al}\boldsymbol{\alpha}_T + \int_{t_T}^{t_T+l} e^{A(t_T+l-s)}R\, d\boldsymbol{\eta}(s) \tag{20}$$

and so the MSE matrix associated with $a(t_T + l|T)$ is $P(t_T + l|T) = T_l P_T T_l' + Q_l$, where $T_l = e^{Al}$ and Q_l is given by (13) evaluated with $\delta_\tau = l$.

The forecast function for the systematic part of the series, $\bar{y}(t) \equiv z'\boldsymbol{\alpha}(t)$, can also be expressed as a continuous function of l, namely $\bar{y}(t_T + l|T) = z'\, e^{Al}a_T$. Note that, if this is considered to be the forecast of an observation to be made at time $t_T + l$, then we can simply set $\delta_{T+1} \equiv l$, so that $Y_{T+1|T} = \bar{y}(t_T + l|T)$. Thus $Y_{T+1|T} = z'\, e^{Al}a_T$. Here, the observation to be forecast has arbitrarily been classified as the one indexed by $\tau = T + 1$. The MSE of this forecast obtains directly as $\text{MSE}\,(Y_{T+1|T}) = E(Y_{T+1} - Y_{T+1|T})^2 = z'P(t_T + l|T)z + \sigma_\varepsilon^2$.

The evaluation of forecast functions for the various structural models is relatively straightforward. For example, consider the local level model with measurement equation $Y_\tau = \mu(t_\tau) + \varepsilon_\tau$, $\tau = 1, \ldots, T$, where $\text{Var}\,(\varepsilon_\tau) = \sigma_\varepsilon^2$. This model has the forecast function, $y(t_T + l|T) = \mu(t_T + l|T) = \mu_{T|T}$, which is simply a horizontal straight line passing through the final estimate of the trend. The MSE of the forecast of the $(T + 1)$th observation (to be made at calendar time $t_T + l$) is $\text{MSE}\,(Y_{T+1|T}) = P_T + l\sigma_\eta^2 + \sigma_\varepsilon^2$.

The forecast functions for more complicated components models obtain directly. For example, introducing a slope component into the trend – the local linear trend model – yields the straight line forecast function, $y(t_T + l|T) = \mu(t_T + l|T) = \mu_{T|T} + \beta_{T|T}l$. Also, the forecast function for a cyclical component takes the form of a damped cosine wave, $\Psi(t_T + l|T) = \rho^l[(\cos \lambda_c l)\Psi_{T|T} + (\sin \lambda_c l)\Psi^*_{T|T}]$. The forecast function for the seasonal component has the form of the cyclical component with $\rho = 1$ (no damping factor).

Estimation

The estimation of Gaussian continuous-time structural models poses no new problems when the observations are regularly spaced: algorithms already developed can be applied directly with only a minor modification needed to handle the covariance matrix of the disturbances of the local linear trend model in (18b). On the other hand, when the observations are irregularly spaced, the time domain estimation procedure must be adapted to account for the fact that the state space model is no longer time invariant. Once this has been done, the construction of the likelihood function can proceed via the prediction error decomposition as implemented by the Kalman filter; see for example Jones (1981) or Harvey and Stock (1985).

Flow Variables

Observed flow variables were defined in (10). To develop a state-space model of flow variables in continuous time, it is useful to introduce a continuous time cumulator (or integrator) variable, $\mathbf{y}^{f}(t)$. This cumulator is defined as

$$\mathbf{y}^{f}(t_\tau + l) = \int_{t_\tau}^{t_\tau + l} \mathbf{y}(r)\,\mathrm{d}r, \qquad 0 < l \leqslant \delta_\tau. \tag{21}$$

Thus $\mathbf{Y}_\tau = \mathbf{y}^{f}(t_\tau)$ for $\tau = 1, \ldots, T$. This definition, (10) and (11) imply that the cumulator at time t_τ can be written as

$$\begin{aligned}
\mathbf{y}^{f}(t_\tau) &= \int_0^{\delta_\tau} y(t_{\tau-1} + r)\,\mathrm{d}r = z' \int_0^{\delta_\tau} \boldsymbol{\alpha}(t_{\tau-1} + r)\,\mathrm{d}r + \int_{t_{\tau-1}}^{t_\tau} \mathrm{d}\boldsymbol{\varepsilon}(r) \\
&= z' \int_0^{\delta_\tau} \left[\mathrm{e}^{Ar}\boldsymbol{\alpha}(t_{\tau-1}) + \int_{t_{\tau-1}}^{t_{\tau-1}+r} \mathrm{e}^{A(t_{\tau-1}+r-s)} R\,\mathrm{d}\boldsymbol{\eta}(s) \right] \mathrm{d}r + \int_{t_{\tau-1}}^{t_\tau} \mathrm{d}\boldsymbol{\varepsilon}(r) \\
&= z' \left[\int_0^{\delta_\tau} \mathrm{e}^{Ar}\,\mathrm{d}r \right] \boldsymbol{\alpha}(t_{\tau-1}) + z' \int_0^{\delta_\tau} \int_{t_{\tau-1}}^{t_{\tau-1}+r} \mathrm{e}^{A(t_{\tau-1}+r-s)} R\,\mathrm{d}\boldsymbol{\eta}(s)\,\mathrm{d}r + \int_{t_{\tau-1}}^{t_\tau} \mathrm{d}\boldsymbol{\varepsilon}(r) \\
&= z' W(\delta_\tau)\boldsymbol{\alpha}(t_{\tau-1}) + z'\boldsymbol{\eta}^{f}(t_\tau) + \boldsymbol{\varepsilon}^{f}(t_\tau),
\end{aligned} \tag{22}$$

where $\boldsymbol{\eta}^{f}(t_\tau) = \int_{t_{\tau-1}}^{t_\tau} W(t_\tau - s)R\,\mathrm{d}\boldsymbol{\eta}(s)$, $\boldsymbol{\varepsilon}^{f}(t_\tau) = \int_{t_{\tau-1}}^{t_\tau} \mathrm{d}\boldsymbol{\varepsilon}(s)$, and $W(r) = \int_0^r \mathrm{e}^{As}\,\mathrm{d}s$. Now letting $\boldsymbol{\eta}_\tau^{f} \equiv \boldsymbol{\eta}^{f}(t_\tau)$, $\boldsymbol{\varepsilon}_\tau^{f} \equiv \boldsymbol{\varepsilon}^{f}(t_\tau)$, and $\mathbf{y}_\tau^{f} \equiv \mathbf{y}^{f}(t_\tau)$, and remembering that $\mathbf{y}^{f}(t_\tau) = \mathbf{Y}_\tau$, we have, on combining (12) with (22), the augmented state space form

$$\begin{bmatrix} \boldsymbol{\alpha}_\tau \\ \mathbf{y}_\tau^{f} \end{bmatrix} = \begin{bmatrix} \mathrm{e}^{A\delta_\tau} & 0 \\ z'W(\delta_\tau) & 0 \end{bmatrix} \begin{bmatrix} \boldsymbol{\alpha}_{\tau-1} \\ \mathbf{y}_{\tau-1}^{f} \end{bmatrix} + \begin{bmatrix} I & 0 \\ 0 & z' \end{bmatrix} \begin{bmatrix} \boldsymbol{\eta}_\tau \\ \boldsymbol{\eta}_\tau^{f} \end{bmatrix} + \begin{bmatrix} 0 \\ \boldsymbol{\varepsilon}_\tau^{f} \end{bmatrix}, \tag{23a}$$

$$\mathbf{Y}_\tau = (0 \quad 1) \begin{bmatrix} \boldsymbol{\alpha}_\tau \\ \mathbf{y}_\tau^{f} \end{bmatrix} \tag{23b}$$

with $\mathrm{Var}\,(\boldsymbol{\varepsilon}_\tau^{f}) = \delta_\tau \sigma_\varepsilon^2$ and

$$\mathrm{Var}\begin{bmatrix} \boldsymbol{\eta}_\tau \\ \boldsymbol{\eta}_\tau^{f} \end{bmatrix} = \int_0^{\delta_\tau} \begin{bmatrix} \mathrm{e}^{Ar}RQR'\,\mathrm{e}^{A'r} & \mathrm{e}^{Ar}RQR'W(r)' \\ W(r)RQR'\,\mathrm{e}^{A'r} & W(r)RQR'W(r)' \end{bmatrix} \mathrm{d}r \equiv Q_\tau^{\dagger}. \tag{24}$$

Maximum likelihood estimators of the hyperparameters can be computed via the prediction error decomposition by running the Kalman filter on (23). No additional starting value problems are caused by bringing the cumulator variable into the state vector as $\mathbf{y}^{f}(t_0)$ is zero by construction.

An alternative, numerically equivalent approach is to treat the second equation in (23a) as a measurement equation rather than a state equation. Define $\boldsymbol{\alpha}_\tau^{*} \equiv \boldsymbol{\alpha}_{\tau-1}$. Then (23) can be rewritten as

$$\boldsymbol{\alpha}_{\tau+1}^{*} = T_{\tau+1}^{*}\boldsymbol{\alpha}_\tau^{*} + \boldsymbol{\eta}_\tau, \tag{25a}$$

$$Y_\tau = z_\tau^{*\prime}\boldsymbol{\alpha}_\tau^{*} + \boldsymbol{\varepsilon}_\tau^{*}, \tag{25b}$$

where $z_\tau^{*\prime} \equiv z'W(\delta_\tau)$, $\boldsymbol{\varepsilon}_\tau^{*} \equiv z'\boldsymbol{\eta}_\tau^{f} + \boldsymbol{\varepsilon}_\tau^{f}$, and $T_{\tau+1}^{*} \equiv \mathrm{e}^{A\delta_\tau}$. Taken together equations (25) are a state model in which the measurement equation disturbance, $\boldsymbol{\varepsilon}_\tau$, and the transition equation disturbance, η_τ, are correlated, in contrast to the standard formulation with uncorrelated disturbances. The covariance matrix of $(\boldsymbol{\eta}_\tau', \boldsymbol{\varepsilon}_\tau^*)'$ is given by

$$\text{Var}\begin{bmatrix}\boldsymbol{\eta}_\tau \\ \boldsymbol{\varepsilon}_\tau^*\end{bmatrix} = \begin{bmatrix} Q_\tau & G_\tau \\ G_\tau' & H_\tau \end{bmatrix} = \begin{bmatrix} I & 0 \\ 0 & z' \end{bmatrix} Q_\tau^\dagger \begin{bmatrix} I & 0 \\ 0 & z \end{bmatrix} + \begin{bmatrix} 0 & 0 \\ 0 & \delta_\tau \sigma_\varepsilon^2 \end{bmatrix}. \tag{26}$$

The modified version of the Kalman filter needed to handle such systems is described in Jazwinski (1970, chapter 7) and Harvey (1989, chapter 3).

Structural Models

The various matrix exponential expressions which need to be computed for the flow variable are relatively easy to evaluate for trend and seasonal components. The formulas for a stationary cyclical component are rather more tedious to derive and so will not be given here explicitly. Because the components in a basic structural model are typically assumed to be independent of each other, the various blocks in (24) can be treated separately, as though there were only a single component in the model. This simplifies the development for general structural models. Because the top left-hand block in (24) is the same as the corresponding Q_τ matrix evaluated for a stock variable in the second section of this article, only the remaining two terms are derived here.

Trend For the local linear trend component (15),

$$W(r) = \int_0^r \begin{bmatrix} 1 & s \\ 0 & 1 \end{bmatrix} ds = \begin{bmatrix} r & \frac{1}{2}r^2 \\ 0 & r \end{bmatrix}. \tag{27}$$

Thus, in (24), the lower right-hand matrix is

$$\text{Var}\,(\boldsymbol{\eta}_\tau^{\text{f}}) = \int_0^{\delta_\tau} W(r)RQR'W(r)'\,dr = \begin{bmatrix} \delta_\tau^3\sigma_\eta^2/3 + \delta_\tau^5\sigma_\zeta^2/20 & \delta_\tau^4\sigma_\zeta^2/8 \\ \delta_\tau^4\sigma_\zeta^2/8 & \delta_\tau^3\sigma_\zeta^2/3 \end{bmatrix}, \tag{28}$$

where in this case $\boldsymbol{\eta}_\tau^{\text{f}}$ is the 2×1 vector $(\eta_\tau^{\text{f}} \quad \zeta_\tau^{\text{f}})'$.

The off-diagonal blocks are derived in a similar way. Thus

$$\text{Cov}\,(\eta_\tau^{\text{f}}, \eta_\tau') = \int_0^{\delta_\tau} W(r)RQR'\,e^{A'r}\,dr = \begin{bmatrix} \frac{1}{2}\delta_\tau^2\sigma_\eta^2 + \delta_\tau^4\sigma_\zeta^2/8 & \delta_\tau^2\sigma_\zeta^2/6 \\ \delta_\tau^3\sigma_\zeta^2/3 & \frac{1}{2}\delta_\tau^2\sigma_\zeta^2 \end{bmatrix}. \tag{29}$$

The local level model is just a special case in which Var (η_τ^{f}) and Cov $(\eta_\tau^{\text{f}}, \eta_\tau)$ are scalars consisting of the top left-hand elements of (27) and (28), respectively, with $\sigma_\zeta^2 = 0$.

Seasonal For a trigonometric component in the seasonal model (17),

$$W(r) = \int_0^r \begin{bmatrix} \cos\lambda s & \sin\lambda s \\ -\sin\lambda s & \cos\lambda s \end{bmatrix} ds = \lambda^{-1}\begin{bmatrix} \sin\lambda r & 1-(\cos\lambda r) \\ (\cos\lambda r)-1 & \sin\lambda r \end{bmatrix}. \tag{30}$$

Thus, if η_τ^f in (23) relates to the disturbances in a trigonometric term,

$$\text{Var}\,(\eta_\tau^f) = 2\delta_\tau\sigma_\omega^2/\lambda^2\begin{bmatrix}1-(1/\lambda\delta_\tau)(\sin\lambda\delta_\tau) & 0\\ 0 & 1-(1/\lambda\delta_\tau)(\sin\lambda\delta_\tau)\end{bmatrix}, \tag{31}$$

$$\text{Cov}\,(\eta_\tau^f, \eta_\tau') = \sigma_\omega^2/\lambda^2\begin{bmatrix}1-(\cos\lambda\delta_\tau) & (\sin\lambda\delta_\tau)-\lambda\delta_\tau\\ \lambda\delta_\tau-(\sin\lambda\delta_\tau) & 1-(\cos\lambda\delta_\tau)\end{bmatrix}. \tag{32}$$

The state space form with correlated disturbances in the measurement and transition equations, (25), shows that the structure of the discrete-time model corresponding to a particular continuous-time model is essentially the same for a flow as for a stock. For example, consider the continuous-time local level model $\mathbf{y}(t) = \boldsymbol{\mu}(t) + \boldsymbol{\varepsilon}(t)$, with $\boldsymbol{\mu}(t)$ given by the local level specialization of (15). In terms of (25), the state equation is $\boldsymbol{\mu}_{\tau+1}^* = \boldsymbol{\mu}_\tau^* + \boldsymbol{\eta}_\tau$ and the measurement equation is $\mathbf{Y}_\tau = \delta_\tau\boldsymbol{\mu}_\tau^* + \boldsymbol{\varepsilon}_\tau^*$, with

$$\text{Var}\begin{bmatrix}\boldsymbol{\eta}_\tau\\ \boldsymbol{\varepsilon}_\tau^*\end{bmatrix} = \begin{bmatrix}\delta_\tau\sigma_\eta^2 & \frac{1}{2}\delta_\tau^2\sigma_\eta^2\\ \frac{1}{2}\delta_\tau^2\sigma_\eta^2 & \delta_\tau^3\sigma_\eta^2/3+\delta_\tau\sigma_\varepsilon^2\end{bmatrix}. \tag{33}$$

When the observations are evenly spaced, δ_τ can be set equal to unity. The forecasts formed by the steady-state Kalman filter for the local level model with flows are then equivalent to the exponentially weighted moving average,

$$Y_{\tau+1|\tau} = (1-\lambda)Y_{r|\tau-1} + \lambda Y_\tau, \tag{34}$$

where $0 < \lambda \leqslant 1.27$. Note that the smoothing constant has a maximum value of 1.27 (to two decimal places) rather than unity. The reason is that this model has a wider range of dynamic properties than the discrete-time model formulated in (4) and (5). Taking first differences of (34) with $\delta_\tau = 1$, and evaluating the autocorrelations, one obtains $\rho(1) = (q-6)/(4q+12)$, where $q = \sigma_\eta^2/\sigma_\varepsilon^2$ and, for $\tau \geqslant 2$, $\rho(\tau) = 0$. Whereas in (4) and (5), $\rho(1)$ is always negative, lying in the range $[-0.5, 0]$, in this case $\rho(1) \in [-0.5, 0.25]$.

One interesting consequence is that a series with a first-order autocorrelation of 0.25 in first differences can be modeled simply by a time-aggregated Brownian motion; compare Working (1960). A second point is that ΔY_τ follows a discrete-time random walk when $q = 6$. This means that a discrete-time random walk can be smoothed to a limited extent since the corresponding continuous-time model contains an additive disturbance term. Of course the same can be done when a discrete-time random-walk-plus-noise model is formulated at a finer timing interval than the observation interval; see Harvey (1989, chapter 6).

Smoothing and Distribution

Suppose that the observations are evenly spaced at intervals of δ and that one wishes to estimate certain integrals of linear combinations of the state vector at evenly spaced intervals Δ time periods apart where δ/Δ is a positive integer. For example, it might be desirable to distribute quarterly observations to a monthly level. The quantities to be estimated may be written in an $m^* \times 1$ vector as

$$\boldsymbol{\alpha}^{\Delta}(t_i) \equiv \boldsymbol{\alpha}_i^{\Delta} = \int_0^{\Delta} Z'\boldsymbol{\alpha}(t_{i-1} + s)\,\mathrm{d}s, \qquad t_i, i = 1, \ldots, (\delta/\Delta)T, \tag{35}$$

where Z is an $m^* \times m$ selection matrix. In the continuous-time basic structural model, the components of interest might be (for example) the level of the trend, the slope and the seasonal, in which case $Z'\boldsymbol{\alpha}(t) = \{\mu(t), \beta(t), \gamma(t)\}'$. In addition it may be desirable to estimate the values of the series itself,

$$\mathbf{y}_i^{\Delta} \equiv \mathbf{y}(t_i) = \int_0^{\Delta} z'\boldsymbol{\alpha}(t_{i-1} + s)\,\mathrm{d}s + \int_{t_{i-1}}^{t_i} \mathrm{d}\boldsymbol{\varepsilon}(s). \tag{36}$$

Smoothed estimates of the quantities of interest may be obtained from an augmented discrete-time state space model. The transition equation is

$$\boldsymbol{\alpha}_i^{\dagger} = \begin{bmatrix} \boldsymbol{\alpha}_i \\ \mathbf{y}_i^{\mathrm{f}} \\ \boldsymbol{\alpha}_i^{\Delta} \\ \mathbf{y}_i^{\Delta} \end{bmatrix} = \begin{bmatrix} \mathrm{e}^{A\Delta} & 0 & 0 & 0 \\ z'W(\Delta) & \phi_i & 0 & 0 \\ Z'W(\Delta) & 0 & 0 & 0 \\ z'W(\Delta) & 0 & 0 & 0 \end{bmatrix} \begin{bmatrix} \boldsymbol{\alpha}_{i-1} \\ \mathbf{y}_{i-1}^{\mathrm{f}} \\ \boldsymbol{\alpha}_{i-1}^{\Delta} \\ \mathbf{y}_{i-1}^{\Delta} \end{bmatrix} + \begin{bmatrix} I & 0 \\ 0 & z' \\ 0 & Z' \\ 0 & z' \end{bmatrix} \begin{bmatrix} \boldsymbol{\eta}_i \\ \boldsymbol{\eta}_i^{\mathrm{f}} \end{bmatrix} + \begin{bmatrix} 0 \\ 1 \\ 0 \\ 1 \end{bmatrix} \boldsymbol{\varepsilon}_i^{\mathrm{f}}, \tag{37}$$

with $\phi_i = 0$, $i = (\delta/\Delta)(\tau - 1) + 1$, $\tau = 1, \ldots, T$, and $\phi_i = 1$ otherwise. The covariance matrix of $(\eta_i', \eta_i^{\mathrm{f}\prime})'$ is defined as in (24) with δ_τ replaced by Δ, while $\mathrm{Var}(\varepsilon_i^{\mathrm{f}}) = \Delta\sigma_\varepsilon^2$. The corresponding measurement equation is only defined at observation times and can be written as $\mathbf{Y}_\tau = [0' \quad 1 \quad 0' \quad 0]\boldsymbol{\alpha}_i^{\dagger}$ for $i = (\delta/\Delta)\tau$, $\tau = 1, \ldots, T$.

The distributed values of the series (the $\mathbf{y}_i^{\Delta}$ terms) could alternatively be estimated by differencing the estimators of the $\mathbf{y}_i^{\mathrm{f}}$ terms. The appearance of $\mathbf{y}_i^{\Delta}$ in the state is really only necessary if the MSE of its estimator is required. Of course if $\Delta = \delta$, it becomes totally superfluous.

Predictions

In making predictions for a flow it is necessary to distinguish between the total accumulation from time t_τ to time $t_\tau + l$, which might include several unit time intervals, and the amount of the flow in a single time period ending at time $t_\tau + l$. The latter concept corresponds to the usual idea of prediction in a discrete model. Cumulative predictions are perhaps more natural in a continuous-time model, particularly when the observations are made at irregular intervals. Here, three types of predictions are discussed: cumulative predictions, predictions over the unit interval, and predictions over a variable lead time.

Cumulative Predictions Predictions for the cumulative effect of $\mathbf{y}(t)$ are obtained by noting that the quantity required is $\mathbf{y}^{\mathrm{f}}(t_\tau + l)$ which in terms of the state space model (23) is $\mathbf{y}_{T+1}$ with $\delta_{T+1} = l$, where it is assumed that $l \geqslant 0$. The optimal predictor can therefore be obtained directly from the Kalman filter as can its MSE. Written out explicitly, $\mathbf{y}^{\mathrm{f}}(t_T + l \,|\, T) = \mathbf{Y}_{T+1\,|\,T} = z'W(l)\mathbf{a}_T$. Because the quantity to be estimated is

$\mathbf{y}^f(t_T + l) = \int_0^l y(t_T + r)\,dr = z'W(l)\boldsymbol{\alpha}_T + z'\boldsymbol{\eta}_{T+1}^f + \boldsymbol{\varepsilon}_{T+1}^f$, the prediction MSE is

$$\text{MSE}\,[\mathbf{y}^f(t_T + l|T)] = z'W(l)P_T W(l)'z + z'\,\text{Var}\,(\boldsymbol{\eta}_\tau^f)z + \text{Var}\,(\boldsymbol{\varepsilon}_{T+1}^f). \tag{38}$$

Note that if the modified Kalman filter based on (25) is run, $\mathbf{a}_T = \mathbf{a}_{T+1|T}^*$ (because $\boldsymbol{\alpha}_{T+1}^* = \boldsymbol{\alpha}_T$) and so $\mathbf{a}_{T+1|T}^*$ is the optimal estimator of $\boldsymbol{\alpha}_T$ based on all the observations.

As a simple example, consider the local level model. For $l > 0$,

$$\mathbf{y}^f(t_T + l|T) = l\boldsymbol{\mu}_{T|T}, \qquad \text{MSE}\,[\mathbf{y}^f(t_T + l|T)] = l^2 P_T + l^3\sigma_\eta^2/3 + l\sigma_\varepsilon^2. \tag{39}$$

Corresponding expressions for the discrete-time models can be obtained; see for example Johnson and Harrison (1986). However, the derivation of (39) is both simpler and more elegant. For the local linear trend, (27) gives

$$\mathbf{y}^f(t_T + l|T) = l\boldsymbol{\mu}_{T|T} + \tfrac{1}{2}l^2\beta_{T|T}, \tag{40}$$

$$\text{MSE}\,[\mathbf{y}^f(t_T + l|T)] = l^2 P_{11T} + l^3 P_{12T} + l^4 P_{22T}/4 + l^3\sigma_\eta^2/3 + l^5\sigma_\zeta^2/20 + l\sigma_\varepsilon^2, \tag{41}$$

where P_{ijT} is the (i, j) element of P_T.

Predictions over the Unit Interval Predictions over the unit interval emerge quite naturally from the state space form (23) as the predictions of $\mathbf{Y}_{T+l}$, $l = 1, 2, \ldots$ with δ_{T+l} set equal to unity for all l. The forecast function for the state vector, $\mathbf{a}_{T+l} = e^{Al}\mathbf{a}_T$, has the same form as in the corresponding stock variable model. The presence of the term $W(1)$ in (23a) leads to a slight modification when these forecasts are translated into a prediction for the series itself. Specifically,

$$\mathbf{Y}_{T+l|T} = z'W(1)\mathbf{a}_{T+l-1|T} = z'W(1)\,e^{A(l-1)}\mathbf{a}_T, \qquad l = 1, 2, \ldots. \tag{42}$$

As a special case, in the local linear trend model $\mathbf{a}_{T+l-1|T} = [\boldsymbol{\mu}_{T|T} + (l-1)\boldsymbol{\beta}_{T|T}, \boldsymbol{\beta}_{T|T}]'$, so $\mathbf{Y}_{T+l|T} = \boldsymbol{\mu}_{T|T} + (l - \tfrac{1}{2})\boldsymbol{\beta}_{T|T}$ for $l = 1, 2, \ldots$. The one-half arises here because each observation is cumulated over the unit interval.

Predictions over a Variable Lead Time In some applications the lead time itself can be regarded as a random variable. This happens, for example, in inventory control problems where an order is put in to meet demand, but the delivery time is uncertain. In such situations it may be useful to determine the unconditional distribution of the cumulation of $\mathbf{y}(t)$ from the current point in time, T. Assume the random lead time is independent of $\{\mathbf{y}(s)\}$. The unconditional PDF of this cumulation from t_T to $t_T + l$ is

$$p(\mathbf{y}^f(t_T + l)|M_T) = \int p(\mathbf{y}^f(t_T + l)|M_T, l)\,dF(l), \tag{43}$$

where $F(l)$ is the distribution of lead times and $p(\mathbf{y}^f(t_T + l)|M_T, l)$ is the predictive distribution of $\mathbf{y}^f(t)$ at time $t_T + l$, that is the distribution of $\mathbf{y}^f(t_T + l)$ conditional on l and on $M_T = \{Y_1, Y_2, \ldots, Y_T\}$, i.e. the information available at time t_T. In a

Gaussian model, the mean of $\mathbf{y}^{\mathrm{f}}(t_T + l)$ (conditional on l and M_T) is given by $\mathbf{y}^{\mathrm{f}}(r_T + l) = z' W(l)\mathbf{a}_T$ and its conditional variance is the MSE given in (39). Although it can be difficult to derive the full PDF $p(\mathbf{y}^{\mathrm{f}}(t_T + l)|M_T)$, expressions for the mean and variance of this distribution may be obtained for the principal structural time series models; see Harvey and Snyder (1990). If the lead time distribution is taken to be discrete, the derivation of such expressions is much more tedious. Of course, in concrete applications the integral (43) can be evaluated numerically.

Conclusion

The formulas provided here for univariate stocks or flows are readily extended to multivariate mixed stock-flow systems; compare Harvey and Stock (1985) and Zadrozny (1988). Harvey and Stock (1988) develop this extension for a model in which the variables are cointegrated (so that the stochastic trend term is common among several multivariate time series); they also provide an empirical application to the estimation of the common stochastic trend among consumption and income using a mutivariate continuous-time components model.

An advantage of the continuous-time framework is that, in multivariate applications, the observational frequency need not be the same for all the series. As a concrete example, weekly observations on interest rates (a "stock" variable), observations on some of the components of investment that are available monthly (a "flow"), and quarterly observations on total investment could be used to distribute total quarterly investment to a monthly level. Some of the components – say, trend and cycle – could be modeled as common among these series, and some could be modeled as independent (or perhaps correlated) across series. It should be emphasized, however, that the distributed values (or, for stocks, the interpolated values) resulting from the procedures outlined in this article have unavoidable measurement error. Moreover, this article has not addressed issues of aliasing, which could pose additional difficulties for interpolation and distribution. Thus care must be taken in using these values in subsequent statistical analysis.

Structural time-series models are based on fitting stochastic functions of time to the observations. A continuous-time formulation of structural models both is intuitively appealing and provides a logical consistency for both stock and flow data. The form of the model does not depend on the observation timing interval and hence can be applied to irregular observations. From the technical point of view, estimation, prediction, interpolation, and distribution can all be based on state space algorithms.

Note

Stock thanks the Sloan Foundation and the National Science Foundation for financial support through grants SES-86-18984 and SES-89-10601.

References

Anderson, B. D. O., and J. B. Moore (1979). *Optimal Filtering.* Englewood Cliffs: Prentice-Hall.
Ansley, C. F., and R. Kohn (1985). "Estimation, filtering and smoothing in state space models with incompletely specified initial conditions". *Annals of Statistics*, 13, 1286–316.

Bergstrom, A. R. (1966). "Non-recursive models as discrete approximations to systems of stochastic differential equations," *Econometrica*, 34, 173–82.

Bergstrom, A. R. (1976) (ed.). *Statistical Inference in Continuous Time Economic Models*. Amsterdam: North-Holland.

Bergstrom, A. R. (1983). "Gaussian estimation of structural parameters in higher-order continuous time dynamic models," *Econometrica*, 51, 117–52.

Bergstrom, A. R. (1984). "Continuous time stochastic models and issues of aggregation over time," in Z. Griliches and M. D. Intrilligator (eds) *Handbook of Econometrics*, volume 2, pp. 1145–212. Amsterdam: North-Holland.

Bergstrom, A. R. (1985). "The estimation of parameters in non-stationary higher-order continuous time dynamic models," *Econometric Theory*, 1, 369–85.

Bergstrom, A. R. (1986). "The estimation of open higher-order continuous time dynamic models with mixed stock and flow data," *Econometric Theory*, 2, 350–73.

De Jong, P. (1991). "The Diffuse Kalman Filter," *Annals of Statistics*, 19, 1073–83.

Engle, R. F. (1978). "Estimating structural models of seasonality," in A. Zellner (ed.) *Seasonal Analysis of Economic Time Series*, pp. 281–308. Washington: Bureau of the Census.

Harvey, A. C. (1985). "Trends and cycles in macroeconomic time series," *Journal of Business and Economic Statistics*, 3, 216–27.

Harvey, A. C. (1989). *Forecasting, Structural Time Series Models, and the Kalman Filter*. Cambridge: Cambridge University Press.

Harvey, A. C., and R. D. Snyder (1990). "Structural time series models in inventory control," *International Journal of Forecasting*, 6, 187–98.

Harvey, A. C., and J. H. Stock (1985). "The estimation of higher order continuous time autoregressive processes," *Econometric Theory*, 1, 97–117.

Harvey, A. C., and J. H. Stock (1988). "Continuous time autoregressive models with common stochastic trends", *Journal of Economic Dynamics and Control*, 12, 365–84.

Hausman, J. A., and M. W. Watson (1985). "Errors in variable and seasonal adjustment procedures," *Journal of the American Statistical Association*, 80, 541–52.

Jazwinski, A. H. (1970). *Stochastic Processes and Filtering Theory*. New York: Academic Press.

Johnston, F. R., and P. J. Harrison (1986). "The variance of lead time demand," *Journal of the Operational Research Society*, 37, 303–8.

Jones, R. H. (1981). "Fitting a continuous time autoregression to discrete data," in D. F. Findley (ed.) *Applied Time Series Analysis II*. New York: Academic Press.

Jones, R. H. (1984). "Fitting multivariate models to unequally spaced data," in E. Parzen (ed.) *Time Series Analysis of Irregularly Observed Data*, pp. 158–88. New York: Springer-Verlag.

Kitagawa, G. (1981). "A nonstationary time series model and its fitting by a recursive filter," *Journal of Time Series Analysis*, 2, 103–16.

Kitagawa, G. (1984). "State space modelling of nonstationary time series and smoothing of unequally spaced data," in E. Parzen (ed.) *Time Series Analysis of Irregularly Observed Data*, pp. 189–210. New York: Springer-Verlag.

Litterman, R. B. (1983). "A random walk Markov model for the distribution of time series," *Journal of Business and Economic Statistics*, 1, 169–73.

Phadke, M. S., and S. M. Wu (1974). "Modelling of continuous stochastic processes from discrete observations with application to sunspots data," *Journal of the American Statistical Association*, 69, 325–9.

Phillips, P. C. B. (1988). "Error correction and long run equilibrium in continuous time," Cowles Foundation Discussion Paper 882, Yale University.

Working, H. (1960). "Note on the correlations of first differences of a random chain," *Econometrica*, 28, 916–18.

Zadrozny, P. (1988). "Gaussian likelihood of continuous-time ARMAX models when data are stocks and flows at different frequencies," *Econometric Theory*, 4, 108–24.

7

Continuous-Time Models in Econometrics: Closed and Open Systems, Stocks and Flows

Peter M. Robinson

Introduction

This paper describes frequency domain approaches to the estimation of continuous-time parametric and semiparametric econometric models on the basis of observations recorded at discrete, equally spaced intervals of time. We focus on differential equation systems, though some of our methods can be applied to other models. Both closed and open systems are treated. Some of the economic variables can be stocks, the underlying continuous process being "skip-sampled"; others can be flows, the underlying continuous process being "temporally aggregated". It is assumed that all processes are covariance stationary; because only a large-sample discussion is possible, this might be relaxed to some kind of "asymptotic covariance stationarity" condition, entailing the sample autocovariances converging stochastically to the autocovariances of a stationary sequence. Both assumptions require that the differential equations satisfy "stability" conditions. In some alternative "time domain", approaches to the same problem, stationarity assumptions have been less explicit, but existing theory is again only large-sample, and, for the standard theory usually claimed to hold, these approaches also require similar asymptotic stationarity, and thus stability, assumptions.

In the frequency domain, models can be described by restrictions on the spectral density matrix of the economic variables, that is the Fourier transform of the autocovariance sequence of the variables. Estimates are expressed in terms of the discrete Fourier transforms of the data. Some difficulties inherent in continuous-time model estimation will be resolved in a manner that seems natural in the frequency domain.

In closed systems, the spectral density is a known function of frequency and of a finite-dimensional vector of unknown parameters. In the time domain, this can correspond to modeling the economic variables as a linear filter of a vector unobservable "continuous white noise" process, the coefficients being parametric functions. Because a differential equations system is assumed, the spectral density is a rational function of frequency. It is possible to relax the specification by assuming that the parametric model for the spectral density holds only over a proper subset of the frequencies, so that a form of semiparametric modeling of the economic variables is involved.

In open systems, the economic variables are categorized under two headings, termed "endogenous" and "exogenous" for convenience. There is a set of homogeneous linear restrictions linking the cross-spectral density between endogenous and exogenous variables and the spectral density of the exogenous variables. The coefficients of the restrictions depend on frequency, and are known up to finitely many unknown parameters. In a complete system there are as many restrictions as endogenous variables; in an incomplete system there are fewer. This model corresponds in the time domain to a vector of "disturbances" (which are linear filters of the observables) being incoherent with the exogenous variables. There may be additional moment restrictions; the spectral density matrix of the disturbances may or may not be parametric. As in all methods of estimation of continuous-time systems, some specification of how the continuous-time paths interpolate the discrete paths of the exogenous variables must be introduced. We allow for a wide class of such specifications, but also specialize to one which allows limited information estimation of incomplete systems, and relatively easily programmable closed-form estimation of linear-in-parameters systems. Moreover, if we impose the parametric specification over only a proper subset of the frequencies, a less complete specification of the continuous-time paths of the exogenous variables is entailed. Other senses in which the modeling may be only semiparametric are the allowances for an incomplete system and for a nonparametric disturbance spectral density.

Such frequency domain approaches to the estimation of open and closed differential equation systems were set down earlier by the author. We elaborate on and extend this work here. In Robinson (1977), frequency domain estimates of closed systems were discussed. They require a formula for the spectral density of the discretely observed economic variables. Formulas in limited, scalar settings were given by Robinson (1980a, 1980b). Here, we present generally applicable, compact formulas for multivariate models of mixed stock and flow data. In Robinson (1972, 1976a, 1976b, 1977) frequency domain estimates of open systems from skip-sampled data were considered, and some asymptotic statistical theory based on an identified model with fixed sampling interval given. Here, we express the model in a slightly more general and modern way, in terms of orthogonality restrictions; describe inference rules which are somewhat more robust; note that earlier assumptions that the smoothing in the estimation of the nonparametric frequency response functions and disturbance spectral density does not depend on the data can now be relaxed; and allow some or all of the observables to be temporally aggregated. The paper emphasizes models, methods, and useful results; asymptotic statistical theory is dealt with in a formal way, without detailed regularity conditions, indeed rigorous theory seems not to be currently available to justify all the methods in the generality in which they are presented.

Serious econometric research on the estimation of linear differential equation systems was begun by Bergstrom (1966, 1967), who among others proposed rival, "time domain" methods for estimation of closed and open systems involving skip-sampled and temporally aggregated data (see for example Bergstrom (1983, 1985, 1986)). Bergstrom (1966) approximated the exact discrete model for a first-order closed system in the presence of skip-sampled data by a form that is much easier to estimate. Sargan (1974) extended this approach to open systems, and Phillips (1978) proposed an alternative type of approximation for a first-order model with temporally aggregated data. The latter two authors provided asymptotic theory in which the sampling interval converges to zero after sample size has tended to infinity. Bartlett (1946) had obtained the exact discrete model for a simple continuous-time system, and Phillips (1959), Phillips (1972) and subsequent authors discussed estimation of the exact discrete model for other closed systems. Jones (1981) and subsequent authors employed the Kalman filter in estimation; this can be especially useful in case of missing observations. Bergstrom (1983, 1985) rigorously discussed solution and estimation of first- and second-order closed systems in the presence of both skip-sampled and temporally aggregated data. The identification problem for closed systems had been discussed by Telser (1967), Phillips (1973) and others. Time domain estimates of the exact discrete model of a first-order open model in the presence of skip-sampled and temporally aggregated data, employing an interpolation of the continuous-time paths of the exogenous variables that is not in the class we consider, were proposed by Phillips (1974, 1976a, 1976b), and extended to second-order systems by Bergstrom (1986) and others. Another important component to the literature has been the work of Sims (1971) and subsequent authors on nonparametric continuous-time distributed lags.

Closed Systems

The Model

Let $\mathbf{z}(t)$, $-\infty < t < \infty$, be a D-dimensional vector of real-valued covariance stationary processes, such that

$$\operatorname{Cov}\{\mathbf{z}(0), \mathbf{z}(t)\} = \int_{-\infty}^{\infty} f_z(\lambda)\, \mathrm{e}^{\mathrm{i}t\lambda}\, \mathrm{d}\lambda, \quad -\infty < t < \infty. \tag{1}$$

Here $f_z(\lambda)$, the spectral density matrix of $\mathbf{z}(t)$, is assumed to have the form

$$f_z(\lambda) = (2\pi)^{-1} A(\lambda)^{-1} B(\lambda) B^*(\lambda) A^*(\lambda)^{-1}, \quad -\infty < \lambda < \infty \tag{2}$$

where the asterisk denotes transposition combined with complex conjugation,

$$A(\lambda) = \sum_{j=0}^{p} A_j(-\mathrm{i}\lambda)^j, \qquad B(\lambda) = \sum_{j=0}^{q} B_j(-\mathrm{i}\lambda)^j, \tag{3}$$

in which $p > q$ and the A_j, B_j are $D \times D$ matrices such that $A_p \neq 0$. We can express this model in time domain form,

$$\sum_{j=0}^{p} A_j \frac{\mathrm{d}^j}{\mathrm{d}t^j}[\mathbf{z}(t) - E\mathbf{z}(t)] = \sum_{j=0}^{q} B_j \frac{\mathrm{d}^j}{\mathrm{d}t^j} \boldsymbol{\eta}(t), \quad -\infty < t < \infty, \tag{4}$$

where $\boldsymbol{\eta}(t)$ is a D-dimensional zero-mean process with spectral density $I_G/(2\pi)$ at all frequencies, I_G being the G-rowed identity matrix, and $\det\{A(\mathrm{i}s)\} \neq 0$ for all complex s with non-negative real part; a more rigorous description is omitted because we focus on the spectral form (2). Note that no extra generality would be gained by allowing the spectral density of $\boldsymbol{\eta}(t)$ to be a general, constant positive definite matrix. It is assumed that at least the coefficients A_j, B_j are identifiable from (2); conditions for this are equivalent to ones for discrete-time rational systems, see for example Hannan (1969).

We partition $\mathbf{z}(t)$ as

$$\mathbf{z}(t) = \begin{bmatrix} \mathbf{z}^{S}(t) \\ \mathbf{z}^{F}(t) \end{bmatrix}, \tag{5}$$

where $\mathbf{z}^{S}(t)$ is a vector of stock variables, whereas $\mathbf{z}^{F}(t)$ is a vector of flow variables. We partition $f_z(\lambda)$ corresponding to the partitioning of $\mathbf{z}(t)$ as

$$f_z(\lambda) = \begin{bmatrix} f_z^{SS}(\lambda) & f_z^{SF}(\lambda) \\ f_z^{FS}(\lambda) & f_z^{FF}(\lambda) \end{bmatrix}. \tag{6}$$

Consider the process

$$\mathbf{Z}(t) = \begin{bmatrix} \mathbf{Z}^{S}(t) \\ \mathbf{Z}^{F}(t) \end{bmatrix} = \begin{bmatrix} \mathbf{z}^{S}(t) \\ \dfrac{1}{\delta}\displaystyle\int_{t-\delta}^{t} \mathbf{z}^{F}(u)\,\mathrm{d}u \end{bmatrix} \tag{7}$$

for some $\delta > 0$. The spectral density of $\mathbf{Z}(t)$, $-\infty < t < \infty$, is

$$f_Z(\lambda) = \begin{bmatrix} f_z^{SS}(\lambda) & \dfrac{1 - \mathrm{e}^{-\mathrm{i}\delta\lambda}}{\mathrm{i}\delta\lambda} f_z^{SF}(\lambda) \\ \dfrac{\mathrm{e}^{\mathrm{i}\delta\lambda} - 1}{\mathrm{i}\delta\lambda} f_z^{FS}(\lambda) & \dfrac{4\sin^2 \frac{1}{2}\delta\lambda}{\delta^2\lambda^2} f_z^{FF}(\lambda) \end{bmatrix}. \tag{8}$$

Now suppose only $\mathbf{Z}_t = \mathbf{Z}(\delta t)$, $t = 0, \pm 1, \ldots,$ is observable. A representation for the spectral density of the sequence $\mathbf{Z}_t$ is

$$\bar{f}_Z(\lambda) = \frac{1}{\delta} \sum_{j=-\infty}^{\infty} f_Z\left(\frac{\lambda + 2\pi j}{\delta}\right), \qquad -\infty < \lambda < \infty. \tag{9}$$

Parameter Estimation

We allow for identifying or over-identifying restrictions on the A_j, B_j by introducing the r-dimensional unknown vector $\boldsymbol{\theta}_0$, where $r \leqslant D^2(p + q) + \frac{1}{2}D(D + 1)$. We introduce a function $f_z(\lambda; \boldsymbol{\theta})$ such that $f_z(\lambda) = f_z(\lambda; \boldsymbol{\theta}_0)$, and correspondingly $\bar{f}_Z(\lambda; \boldsymbol{\theta})$ such that $\bar{f}_Z(\lambda) = \bar{f}_Z(\lambda; \boldsymbol{\theta}_0)$. The objective is to estimate $\boldsymbol{\theta}_0$ on the basis of observations $\mathbf{Z}_t$, $t = 1, \ldots, N$.

The discrete Fourier transform of the $\mathbf{Z}_t$ is given by

$$w_Z(\lambda) = (2\pi N)^{-1/2} \sum_{t=1}^{N} h_{tT}(\mathbf{Z}_t - \bar{\mathbf{Z}})\,\mathrm{e}^{\mathrm{i}t\lambda}, \tag{10}$$

where h_{tT} is a data-taper (Brillinger 1975), introduced to reduce bias due to leakage from neighboring frequencies at which spectral peaks occur, and $\bar{\mathbf{Z}}$ is the sample mean of $\mathbf{Z}_t$.

The estimate of $\boldsymbol{\theta}_0$ considered by Robinson (1977) is

$$\hat{\boldsymbol{\theta}} = \arg\min_{\boldsymbol{\theta}\in\boldsymbol{\Theta}} L(\theta), \tag{11}$$

where

$$L(\boldsymbol{\theta}) = \frac{1}{N}\sum_{\lambda_j\in B}\{\log\det \bar{f}_Z(\lambda_j;\boldsymbol{\theta}) + \mathrm{Tr}[\bar{f}_Z(\lambda_j;\boldsymbol{\theta})^{-1}I_Z(\lambda_j)]\}, \tag{12}$$

$\lambda_j = 2\pi_j/N$, B is a symmetric subset of $(-\pi, \pi)$ that omits $\lambda_0 = 0$ for purposes of mean-correction, $I_Z(\lambda_j) = w_Z(\lambda_j)w_Z^*(\lambda_j)$, and $\boldsymbol{\theta}$ is a set of admissible values of $\boldsymbol{\theta}_0$. We take B to be a proper subset of $(-\pi, \pi)$ if it is desired to filter out frequencies at which seasonal or other measurement error is likely to be substantial. When $B = (-\pi, \pi)$ the objective function (12) is one of several which under similar regularity conditions produce estimates with the same first-order asymptotic properties, and the same ones as maximum likelihood estimates when $\mathbf{Z}_t$ is Gaussian. Whittle (1951) found that $-\frac{1}{2}$ times the Gaussian likelihood can be approximated up to a constant by

$$L_1(\boldsymbol{\theta}) = \log\det\Sigma(\boldsymbol{\theta}) + \frac{1}{2\pi}\int_{-\pi}^{\pi}\mathrm{Tr}\,[\bar{f}_Z(\lambda;\boldsymbol{\theta})^{-1}I_Z(\lambda)]\,\mathrm{d}\lambda, \tag{13}$$

where

$$\log\det\Sigma(\boldsymbol{\theta}) = \frac{1}{2\pi}\int_{-\pi}^{\pi}\log\det\,[2\pi\bar{f}_Z(\lambda;\boldsymbol{\theta})]\,\mathrm{d}\lambda \tag{14}$$

and $\Sigma = \Sigma(\boldsymbol{\theta}_0)$ is the innovations covariance matrix in the Wold representation for $\mathbf{Z}_t$. The modification

$$L_2(\boldsymbol{\theta}) = \log\det\Sigma(\boldsymbol{\theta}) + \frac{1}{N}\sum_{j=1}^{N-1}\mathrm{Tr}\,[\bar{f}_Z(\lambda_j;\boldsymbol{\theta})^{-1}I_Z(\lambda_j)], \tag{15}$$

can make more direct use of the fast Fourier transform algorithm. In standard parameterizations of time-series models, such as standard autoregressive moving average (ARMA) parameterizations, $\boldsymbol{\theta}$ can be split into two variation-free subvectors, $\boldsymbol{\theta}_1$ and $\boldsymbol{\theta}_2$, where $\boldsymbol{\theta}_1$ parameterizes the coefficients of the Wold representation and $\boldsymbol{\theta}_2$ parameterizes Σ, and moreover $\Sigma(\boldsymbol{\theta})$ is a known, closed-form function of $\boldsymbol{\theta}_2$. Thus the term (14) in $L_1(\boldsymbol{\theta})$ or $L_2(\boldsymbol{\theta})$ causes no difficulty, and indeed contributes nothing to the $\boldsymbol{\theta}_1$ normal equations. However, when the integral in (14) instead extends only over a proper subset, B, of frequencies, the integral will be a function also of the parameters of interest, and when $\bar{f}_Z$ is generated by models such as (2) this will be the case even when $B = (-\pi, \pi)$, and no convenient closed-form expression in terms of the underlying parameters is available. Some other parametric time-series models in which L_1 and L_2 are inconvenient to use were described by Robinson (1978). In such models, and in (2), $L(\boldsymbol{\theta})$ seems preferable, entailing summation rather than integration.

Asymptotic theory for versions of estimates minimizing $L_1(\boldsymbol{\theta})$ or $L_2(\boldsymbol{\theta})$ has been given by Whittle (1951, 1962), Davies (1973), Hannan (1973), Dunsmuir and Hannan (1976), and Dunsmuir (1979), for example. Asymptotic theory for some cases of $\hat{\boldsymbol{\theta}}$ was given by Davies (1973), Robinson (1978), and Thomson (1986). Under regularity conditions, $\hat{\boldsymbol{\theta}}$ is consistent for $\boldsymbol{\theta}_0$ and moreover $N^{1/2}(\hat{\boldsymbol{\theta}} - \boldsymbol{\theta}_0) \to_d N(0, \Xi)$. When $\mathbf{z}(t)$ is Gaussian, $\hat{\boldsymbol{\theta}}$, like the estimates minimizing L_1 or L_2, achieves the asymptotic Cramer–Rao bound, and $\Xi = 2\Omega^{-1}$, where Ω has (k, l)th element

$$\frac{1}{2\pi}\int_B \operatorname{Tr}\,[\beta_k(\lambda; \boldsymbol{\theta}_0)\beta_l(\lambda; \boldsymbol{\theta}_0)]\,\mathrm{d}\lambda, \tag{16}$$

and is consistently estimated by $\hat{\Omega}$, which has (k, l)th element

$$\frac{1}{2N}\sum_B \operatorname{Tr}\,[\beta_k(\lambda_j; \hat{\boldsymbol{\theta}})\beta_l(\lambda_j; \hat{\boldsymbol{\theta}})], \tag{17}$$

where $\beta_k(\lambda; \boldsymbol{\theta}) = \bar{f}_Z^{-1}(\lambda; \boldsymbol{\theta})(\partial/\partial\theta_k)\bar{f}_Z(\lambda; \boldsymbol{\theta})$, where θ_k is the k-th element of $\boldsymbol{\theta}$. However, Ξ in general differs from $2\Omega^{-1}$ when $\mathbf{z}(t)$ is non-Gaussian. In the standard parameterizations of discrete-time models referred to above, it turns out that under Gaussianity Ω is block diagonal so that $N^{1/2}(\hat{\boldsymbol{\theta}}_1 - \boldsymbol{\theta}_{01})$ and $N^{1/2}(\hat{\boldsymbol{\theta}}_2 - \boldsymbol{\theta}_{02})$ are asymptotically independent and indeed the limiting covariance matrix $2\Omega_1^{-1}$, say, of the former is invariant to departures from the Gaussianity assumption. Because $\boldsymbol{\theta}_1$ is usually the main component of interest, and because Gaussianity is a restriction that one might wish to avoid, this is practically a valuable property. Unfortunately, no natural parameterization of the underlying continuous-time system (2) in general affords a decomposition of this form in the discrete model, which is a "nonstandard" ARMA, and in the absence of Gaussianity any element of Ξ might depend on third or fourth cumulants of $\mathbf{z}(t)$, and thus differ from the corresponding element of $2\Omega^{-1}$. Thus, use of $2\hat{\Omega}^{-1}$ in inference rules can produce invalid hypothesis tests and inconsistent interval estimates. Tests for Gaussianity are available, though application of standard tests, many of which are designed for scalar, serially independent observations, may not be very efficient when applied to a multivariate, dynamic system. In any event, one needs a consistent estimate of Ξ should a test for Gaussianity reject.

A similar problem arises in a number of models, not only for time series but for cross-sectional and panel data also. Some of these were listed by Robinson (1988), who provided a number of proposals for robust estimation of the limiting covariance matrix of Gaussian estimates when Gaussianity is not assumed, following an earlier proposal of White (1982) in a still more general context. All those proposals were, however, formulated in the time domain. One frequency domain estimate of Ξ that would be consistent under regularity conditions is $\hat{\Omega}^{-1}\hat{\Sigma}\hat{\Omega}^{-1}$, where $\hat{\Sigma}$ has (k, l)th element

$$\frac{1}{N}\sum_{B} \text{Tr}\,[\beta_k(\lambda_j;\hat{\boldsymbol{\theta}})\gamma(\lambda_j;\hat{\boldsymbol{\theta}})]\,\text{Tr}\,[\beta_l(\lambda_j;\hat{\boldsymbol{\theta}})\gamma(\lambda_j;\hat{\boldsymbol{\theta}})], \tag{18}$$

in which $\gamma(\lambda;\boldsymbol{\theta}) = I_D - \bar{f}_Z^{-1}(\lambda;\boldsymbol{\theta})I_Z(\lambda)$.

A necessary condition for the usual asymptotic theory under our stationarity assumptions (see Phillips (1988, 1989) for alternative theories) is that $\boldsymbol{\theta}_0$ be identifiable, that is $\boldsymbol{\theta}_0$ is the only $\boldsymbol{\theta}$ in Θ satisfying

$$\bar{f}_Z(\lambda;\boldsymbol{\theta}) = \bar{f}_Z(\lambda;\boldsymbol{\theta}_0), \qquad \lambda \in B. \tag{19}$$

Of course this requires that (4) be identifiable from a continuous record and that a value of δ be prescribed. Even then, Telser (1967) indicated that as a consequence of the familiar aliasing problem countably many $\boldsymbol{\theta}$ satisfy (19), in which case $\boldsymbol{\Theta}$ would need to be chosen suitably small to afford a global identification. In a first-order model, Phillips (1973) showed how this might be achieved by means of suitable linear restrictions on the coefficients of (4), and Hansen and Sargent (1983) showed that the global identifiability problem may be less serious than previously expected. Pandit and Wu (1975) suggested that, in a second-order scalar model, identifiability is possible without restrictions, but in this model Robinson (1980a) found that the objective function (12) can be multimodal as $N \to \infty$ with modes of similar height, so that sampling variability with a finite N might lead to a $\hat{\boldsymbol{\theta}}$ far from $\boldsymbol{\theta}_0$. We know of no complete account of the identifiability problem in the generality of our current setting.

Formulas for f_Z

A remaining problem is to obtain a manageable expression for the $\bar{f}_Z(\lambda_j;\boldsymbol{\theta})$ in $L(\boldsymbol{\theta})$, which will need to be evaluated at several $\boldsymbol{\theta}$ in order to compute $\hat{\boldsymbol{\theta}}$. We suppress reference to $\boldsymbol{\theta}$, and take $\delta = 1$ for simplicity of notation. To evaluate the infinite series in (9) we adopt an approach and notation similar to that employed in a somewhat different setting by Robinson (1976a). Alternative approaches are possible, see for example Phillips (1959).

Denote by ζ_j, $j = 1, \ldots, n$, the distinct zeros of det $\{A(s)\}$ on the complex plane; these are the poles of $f_z(s)$. Because the A_j are real, the ζ_j are either imaginary or the $\mathrm{i}\zeta_j$ occur in conjugate pairs, but we reserve no special notation for these possibilities. Denote by m_j the multiplicity of ζ_j, so $\sum_{j=1}^{n} m_j \leqslant pG^2$. The poles of $f_z(\lambda + 2\pi j)$ are $(\zeta_j - \lambda)/2\pi$.

We apply theorem 9.3.1 of Hille (1959) to obtain

$$\bar{f}_Z^{\text{SS}}(\lambda) = -\sum_{j=1}^{n} \rho_j^{\text{SS}}\left(\frac{\zeta_j - \lambda}{2\pi}\right), \tag{20}$$

where

$$\rho_j^{\text{SS}}(v) = \frac{1}{(m_j - 1)!}\frac{\partial^{m_j - 1}}{\partial v^{m_j - 1}}\left[(\pi \cot \pi v)\left(v - \frac{\zeta_j - \lambda}{2\pi}\right)^{m_j} f_Z^{\text{SS}}(\lambda + 2\pi v)\right]. \tag{21}$$

Note that the elements of the summand in (20) are the residues of the corresponding elements of $(\pi \cot \pi v) f_z^{SS}(\lambda + 2\pi v)$ at $v = (\zeta_j - \lambda)/2\pi$. It is possible that a residue can be zero for all values of $\boldsymbol{\theta}$. Proceeding similarly,

$$\bar{f}_Z^{SF}(\lambda) = e^{-i\lambda/2}(\cos \tfrac{1}{2}\lambda) f_z^{SF}(0) - (1 - e^{-i\lambda}) \sum_{j=1}^{n} \rho_j^{SF}\left(\frac{\zeta_j - \lambda}{2\pi}\right), \tag{22}$$

where

$$\rho_j^{SF}(v) = \frac{1}{(m_j - 1)!} \frac{\partial^{m_j - 1}}{\partial v^{m_j - 1}} \left[(\pi \cot \pi v) \left(v - \frac{\zeta_j - \lambda}{2\pi} \right)^{m_j} \frac{f_z^{SF}(\lambda + 2\pi v)}{\lambda + 2\pi v} \right]. \tag{23}$$

Note that $\bar{f}_z^{FS}(\lambda) = \bar{f}_z^{SF}(\lambda)^*$. Finally

$$\bar{f}_Z^{FF}(\lambda) = f_z^{FF}(0) - (\sin \lambda) \frac{\partial f_Z^{FF}(0)}{\partial v} - 4(\sin^2 \tfrac{1}{2}\lambda) \sum_{j=1}^{n} \rho_j^{FF}\left(\frac{\zeta_j - \lambda}{2\pi}\right), \tag{24}$$

where

$$\rho_j^{FF}(v) = \frac{1}{(m_j - 1)!} \frac{\partial^{m_j - 1}}{\partial v^{m_j - 1}} \left[(\pi \cot \pi v) \left(v - \frac{\zeta_j - \lambda}{2\pi} \right)^{m_j} \frac{f_z^{FF}(\lambda + 2\pi v)}{(\lambda + 2\pi v)^2} \right]. \tag{25}$$

The derivatives of the cotangent function are easily calculated, and using the above formulas we can, in principle, compute $L(\boldsymbol{\theta})$ for any admissible (stable) $\boldsymbol{\theta}$-value irrespective of the pole multiplicities it implies. It may, however, be desired to compute $L(\boldsymbol{\theta})$ only at simple poles, in which case the formulas simplify substantially. We take $m_j = 1$, and write $f_{zj}^{SS}(v) = (v - \zeta_j) f_z^{SS}(v)$, $f_{zj}^{SF}(v) = (v - \zeta_j) f_z^{SF}(v)$, $f_{zj}^{FF}(v) = (v - \zeta_j) f_z^{FF}(v)$. Then

$$\bar{f}_Z^{SS}(\lambda) = -\frac{1}{2} \sum_{j=1}^{n} \cot\left(\frac{\zeta_j - \lambda}{2}\right) f_{zj}^{SS}(\zeta_j), \tag{26}$$

$$\bar{f}_Z^{SF}(\lambda) = e^{-i\lambda/2}(\cos \tfrac{1}{2}\lambda) f_z^{SF}(0) - \frac{1}{2}(1 - e^{-i\lambda}) \sum_{j=1}^{n} \cot\left(\frac{\zeta_j - \lambda}{2}\right) \frac{f_{zj}^{SF}(\zeta_j)}{\zeta_j}, \tag{27}$$

$$\bar{f}_Z^{FF}(\lambda) = f_z^{FF}(0) - (\sin \lambda) \frac{\partial f_z^{FF}(0)}{\partial v} - 2(\sin^2 \tfrac{1}{2}\lambda) \sum_{j=1}^{n} \cot\left(\frac{\zeta_j - \lambda}{2}\right) \frac{f_{zj}^{FF}(\zeta_j)}{\zeta_j^2}. \tag{28}$$

For computational purposes, note that for real a, b, $\cot[\tfrac{1}{2}(a + ib)] = 2Q(e^{-b}, a) - 2iP(e^{-b}, a)$, where

$$P(e^{-b}, a) = \frac{1 - e^{-2b}}{2|1 - e^{-b+ia}|^2} = \frac{\sinh b}{2(\cosh b - \cos a)}, \tag{29}$$

$$Q(e^{-b}, a) = \frac{e^{-b} \sin a}{|1 - e^{-b+ia}|^2} = \frac{\sin a}{2(\cosh b - \cos a)}, \tag{30}$$

the middle expressions most clearly illustrating the well-known ARMA structure of $\mathbf{Z}_t$.

To form (17), we have to compare $(\partial/\partial\boldsymbol{\theta}_k)\bar{f}_Z(\lambda_j; \hat{\boldsymbol{\theta}})$, and similar derivatives also must be calculated in iterative methods of locating $\hat{\boldsymbol{\theta}}$, such as the scoring one in Robinson (1977). Note that $(\partial/\partial\boldsymbol{\theta}_k)f_Z(\lambda + 2\pi v; \boldsymbol{\theta})$ is also a rational function of v, with the same poles as $f_Z(\lambda + 2\pi v; \boldsymbol{\theta})$ (but possibly different multiplicities). With obvious substitutions, we can then apply formulas (20), (22), and (24). An alternative approach employed in Robinson (1980a, 1980b) is to parameterize in terms of the ζ_j and then differentiate after summation, that is differentiate (20), (22), and (24) directly.

Open Systems

The Model

In an open system, f_z is not a parametric function, but it satisfies parametric, frequency-dependent linear restrictions of a certain type. The basic restrictions distinguish between components of a partition of $\mathbf{z}(t)$,

$$\mathbf{z}(t) = \begin{bmatrix} \mathbf{y}(t) \\ \mathbf{x}(t) \end{bmatrix}, \tag{31}$$

where $\mathbf{x}(t)$ is $H \times 1$ and $\mathbf{y}(t)$ is $J \times 1$, and $H \geqslant 1$, $J \geqslant 1$. Correspondingly, partition $f_z(\lambda)$ as

$$f_z(\lambda) = [\, f_{zy}(\lambda), f_{zx}(\lambda)]. \tag{32}$$

We assume that

$$A(\lambda)f_{zx}(\lambda) = 0, \qquad -\infty < \lambda < \infty, \tag{33}$$

where A is as given by (3) but it has $K \leqslant J$ rows. The time domain motivation for (33) is that the unobservable process

$$\mathbf{u}(t) = \sum_{j=0}^{p} A_j \frac{\mathrm{d}^j}{\mathrm{d}t^j}[\mathbf{z}(t) - E\mathbf{z}(t)] \tag{34}$$

is incoherent with the process $\mathbf{x}(t)$. Thus we term $\mathbf{y}(t)$, $\mathbf{x}(t)$ endogenous, exogenous. When $K = J$ the system is said to be "complete"; when $K < J$ it is "incomplete". The principal difference between an "open" system and a "closed" one is that in the former case $\mathbf{x}(t)$ is not assumed to be generated by a parametric model, that is its spectral density is not assumed rational.

Again we allow for both stock and flow variables, writing

$$\mathbf{y}(t) = \begin{bmatrix} \mathbf{x}^{\mathrm{S}}(t) \\ \mathbf{x}^{\mathrm{F}}(t) \end{bmatrix}, \qquad \mathbf{x}(t) = \begin{bmatrix} \mathbf{y}^{\mathrm{S}}(t) \\ \mathbf{y}^{\mathrm{F}}(t) \end{bmatrix}, \tag{35}$$

where $\mathbf{x}^S$ is $H_S \times 1$, $\mathbf{x}^F$ is $H_F \times 1$, $\mathbf{y}^S$ is $J_S \times 1$, $\mathbf{y}^F$ is $J_F \times 1$. Consider the processes

$$\mathbf{Y}(t) = \begin{bmatrix} \mathbf{Y}^S(t) \\ \mathbf{Y}^F(t) \end{bmatrix} = \begin{bmatrix} \mathbf{y}^S(t) \\ \int_{t-1}^{t} \mathbf{y}^F(u)\,du \end{bmatrix},$$
$$\mathbf{x}(t) = \begin{bmatrix} \mathbf{x}^S(t) \\ \mathbf{x}^F(t) \end{bmatrix} = \begin{bmatrix} \mathbf{x}^S(t) \\ \int_{t-1}^{t} \mathbf{x}^F(u)\,du \end{bmatrix}. \tag{36}$$

This definition corresponds to (7), but with a different partition and taking $\delta = 1$ at the outset. In view of (8), $\mathbf{X}(t)$ has spectral density

$$f_X(\lambda) = L_x(\lambda) f_x(\lambda) L_x^*(\lambda), \tag{37}$$

and $\mathbf{Y}(t)$ and $\mathbf{X}(t)$ have cross-spectral density matrix

$$f_{YX}(\lambda) = L_y(\lambda) f_{yx}(\lambda) L_x^*(\lambda), \tag{38}$$

where we have partitioned f'_{zx} as $(f'_{xy}, f'_x)'$, and where

$$L_x(\lambda) = \begin{bmatrix} I_{H_S} & 0 \\ 0 & \dfrac{e^{i\lambda} - 1}{i\lambda} I_{H_F} \end{bmatrix}, \qquad L_y(\lambda) = \begin{bmatrix} I_{J_S} & 0 \\ 0 & \dfrac{e^{i\lambda} - 1}{i\lambda} I_{J_F} \end{bmatrix}. \tag{39}$$

For $\lambda \neq 2\pi j$, $j = \pm 1, \pm 2, \ldots$, (where some elements of f_X and f_{YX} vanish) we can write

$$\tilde{A}(\lambda) f_{ZX}(\lambda) = 0 \tag{40}$$

where $\tilde{A}(\lambda) = A(\lambda) L^{-1}(\lambda)$, in which

$$L(\lambda) = \begin{bmatrix} L_y(\lambda) & 0 \\ 0 & L_x(\lambda) \end{bmatrix}. \tag{41}$$

Suppose only

$$\mathbf{X}_t = \mathbf{X}(t), \qquad \mathbf{Y}_t = \mathbf{Y}(t), \qquad t = 0, \pm 1, \ldots, \tag{42}$$

are observable. The spectral density of $\mathbf{X}_t$ and cross-spectral density between $\mathbf{Y}_t$ and $\mathbf{X}_t$ are

$$\bar{f}_X(\lambda) = F\{f_X; \lambda\}, \qquad \bar{f}_{YX}(\lambda) = F\{f_{YX}; \lambda\}, \tag{43}$$

where we introduce the folding operator

$$F\{f; \lambda\} = \sum_{j=-\infty}^{\infty} f(\lambda + 2\pi j). \tag{44}$$

For λ such that $\det\{f_X(\lambda)\} \neq 0$ put $m(\lambda) = f_{YX}(\lambda) f_X^{-1}(\lambda)$, then we can write

$$\begin{aligned} M(\lambda) &\triangleq \bar{f}_{YX}(\lambda)\bar{f}_X^{-1}(\lambda) \\ &= F\{m\phi; \lambda\}, \end{aligned} \tag{45}$$

where

$$\phi(\lambda) = f_X(\lambda)\bar{f}_X^{-1}(\lambda). \tag{46}$$

The function $\phi(\lambda)$, which we term the distributor, distributes mass in $\bar{f}_X(\lambda)$ across λ, where $\lambda \in (-\pi, \pi)$, and its aliases $\lambda + 2\pi j, j \neq 0$: $F\{\phi; \lambda\} = I_H$. ϕ is the same as ρ in Robinson (1977), and corresponds to the Fourier transform of the function r_x of Sims (1971). When m is a parametric function, a different choice of distributor leads via (45) in general to a different identification of the parameters. For each λ there are uncountably many possible distributors, and thus uncountably many different identifications. The basic identifiability problem caused by the discrete sampling is thus one of local identification for (semiparametric) open systems with prescribed sampling interval, whereas for (parametric, rational) systems with prescribed sampling interval it is the less acute one of global identification. For given, say rational, f_x, expressions for ϕ can be calculated, but may be complicated.

When (33) is a complete system, make the partition $A(\lambda) = (C(\lambda), D(\lambda))$ in ratio $H:J$, and assume $\det\{C(\lambda)\} \neq 0$, where $C(\lambda)$ is a polynomial of degree at least one. Thus

$$m(\lambda) = -\tilde{C}^{-1}(\lambda)\tilde{D}(\lambda), \tag{47}$$

with $\tilde{A}(\lambda) = (\tilde{C}(\lambda), \tilde{D}(\lambda))$. We study the identification problem for parameters in $A(\lambda)$ via (45). A simple distributor is

$$\phi(\lambda + 2\pi j) \begin{cases} = I_H, & j = 0, \\ = 0, & j \neq 0, \end{cases} \tag{48}$$

for some $\lambda \in (-\pi, \pi]$. For this λ, (48) is equivalent to

$$f_X(\lambda + 2\pi j) = 0, \qquad j \neq 0. \tag{49}$$

Under (48), it follows from (45) and (47) that

$$M(\lambda) = -\tilde{C}^{-1}(\lambda)\tilde{D}(\lambda) \tag{50}$$

for complete systems. Then the identification problem of determining C and D from M is equivalent to that for systems with rational transfer function (see for example

Hannan (1971)). In both complete and incomplete systems we can derive a linear restriction on $\bar{f}_X, \bar{f}_{YX}$ under (48). Using also (45),

$$\bar{f}_{YX}(\lambda) = m(\lambda)\bar{f}_X(\lambda) = m(\lambda) f_X(\lambda) = f_{YX}(\lambda). \tag{51}$$

Applying (33),

$$\tilde{A}(\lambda)\bar{f}_{ZX}(\lambda) = 0. \tag{52}$$

A parametric model is sometimes also prescribed for the spectral density of $u(t)$ in (34),

$$f_u(\lambda) = A(\lambda) f_z(\lambda) A^*(\lambda) \tag{53}$$

This has further implications for the identification problem. Denoting by $f_y(\lambda)$ the spectral density of $\mathbf{y}(t)$, that of $\mathbf{Y}(t)$ is $f_Y(\lambda) = L_y(\lambda) f_y(\lambda) L_y^*(\lambda)$. We can rewrite (53) as

$$f_Y(\lambda) = m(\lambda) f_X(\lambda) m^*(\lambda) + f_V(\lambda) \tag{54}$$

where $f_V(\lambda) = \tilde{C}^{-1}(\lambda) f_u(\lambda) \tilde{C}^{-1}(\lambda)^*$. The spectral density of the sequence $\mathbf{Y}_t$ is thus

$$\bar{f}_Y(\lambda) = F\{f_Y; \lambda\} = F\{m f_X m^*; \lambda\} + \bar{f}_V(\lambda), \tag{55}$$

where $\bar{f}_V(\lambda) = F\{f_V; \lambda\}$. Incorporating (45),

$$\begin{aligned} \bar{f}_W(\lambda) &\triangleq \bar{f}_Y(\lambda) - \bar{f}_{YX}(\lambda)\bar{f}_X^{-1}(\lambda)\bar{f}_{XY}(\lambda) \\ &= F\{(m - M) f_X (m - M)^*; \lambda\} + \bar{f}_V(\lambda). \end{aligned} \tag{56}$$

Given $\bar{f}_W(\lambda)$, which like $M(\lambda)$ is a function of spectra of observables, and given also a choice of distributor ϕ and prior identification of $m(\lambda)$, the problem becomes one of identifying the remaining parameters from $\bar{f}_V(\lambda)$, which is of the type mentioned in the previous section when $f_u(\lambda)$ is rational. Note that the simplest situation again arises under (48), when $\bar{f}_V(\lambda) = \bar{f}_W(\lambda)$. More generally, the identification problem posed by (45) and (56) might be considered simultaneously.

Pseudomaximum Likelihood Estimation of Complete Systems

In a complete system, let $A(\lambda; \theta)$ and $f_u(\lambda; \theta)$ be given functions of λ and the r-dimensional vector $\boldsymbol{\theta}$, such that for some $\boldsymbol{\theta}_0$ $A(\lambda) = A(\lambda; \boldsymbol{\theta}_0)$, $f_u(\lambda) = f_u(\lambda; \boldsymbol{\theta}_0)$. Correspondingly introduce $m(\lambda; \boldsymbol{\theta})$, $\tilde{C}(\lambda; \boldsymbol{\theta})$, $f_V(\lambda; \boldsymbol{\theta})$. Denote by $M(\lambda; \boldsymbol{\theta})$ (45) with $m(\lambda)$ replaced by $m(\lambda; \boldsymbol{\theta})$, following a given choice of distributor ϕ, and by $\bar{f}_W(\lambda; \boldsymbol{\theta})$ (56) with $f_u(\lambda)$, $\tilde{C}(\lambda)$, $m(\lambda)$, $M(\lambda)$, and $f_X(\lambda)$ replaced by $f_u(\lambda; \boldsymbol{\theta})$, $\tilde{C}(\lambda; \boldsymbol{\theta})$, $m(\lambda; \boldsymbol{\theta})$, $M(\lambda; \boldsymbol{\theta})$, and $\{\phi(\lambda)\hat{f}_X^2(\lambda)\phi(\lambda)^*\}^{1/2}$ respectively. The latter of these expressions employs a smoothed nonparametric estimate $\hat{f}_X(\lambda)$ of $\bar{f}_X(\lambda)$ (see for example Brillinger (1975), chapter 5); note that the more obvious use of $\phi(\lambda)\hat{f}_X(\lambda)$ would not guarantee a positive semidefinite $\bar{f}_W(\lambda; \theta)$. When ϕ is chosen to be (48) we have simply $\bar{f}_W(\lambda; \boldsymbol{\theta}) = \bar{f}_V(\lambda; \boldsymbol{\theta})$.

For a given $\boldsymbol{\theta}$ and a rational choice of $f_u(\lambda)$ (often f_u has been chosen constant over $(-\infty, \infty)$), we can calculate $\bar{f}_W(\lambda; \boldsymbol{\theta})$ via the techniques described in formulas (20)–(30).

We can construct a Gaussian estimate after a factorization of the Gaussian pseudolikelihood (12),

$$\boldsymbol{\theta} = \arg\min_{\boldsymbol{\Theta}} \tilde{L}(\boldsymbol{\theta}), \tag{57}$$

where

$$\tilde{L}(\boldsymbol{\theta}) = \frac{1}{N} \sum_{\lambda_j \in B} \{\log \det \bar{f}_W(\lambda_j; \boldsymbol{\theta}) + \mathrm{Tr}\,[\bar{f}_W^{-1}(\lambda_j; \boldsymbol{\theta}) I_W(\lambda_j; \boldsymbol{\theta})]\}, \tag{58}$$

in which

$$I_W(\lambda; \boldsymbol{\theta}) = [w_Y(\lambda) - M(\lambda; \boldsymbol{\theta}) w_X(\lambda)][w_Y(\lambda) - M(\lambda; \boldsymbol{\theta}) w_X(\lambda)]^*, \tag{59}$$

$$w_X(\lambda) = (2\pi N)^{-1/2} \sum_{t=1}^{N} h_{tT}(X_t - \bar{\mathbf{X}})\, \mathrm{e}^{\mathrm{i}t\lambda}, \tag{60}$$

$$w_Y(\lambda) = (2\pi N)^{-1/2} \sum_{t=1}^{N} h_{tT}(Y_t - \bar{\mathbf{Y}})\, \mathrm{e}^{\mathrm{i}t\lambda}. \tag{61}$$

Note that even under Gaussian assumptions (58) does not give the actual log likelihood.

In the generality of the set-up considered here, the asymptotic properties of $\boldsymbol{\theta}$ are not covered by existing theory of which we are aware. The case of ϕ given by (48), and f_u nonparametric, was covered by Robinson (1972) (see below). Results of Dunsmuir (1979), for example, in effect treat parametric f_u but do not allow for the presence of $\hat{f}_X$ and ϕ, or for B being a proper subset of $(-\pi, \pi)$, and also treat objective functions in which $N^{-1}\Sigma \log\det \bar{f}_W(\lambda_j; \boldsymbol{\theta})$ is replaced by $(2\pi)^{-1}\int \log\det \bar{f}_W(\lambda; \boldsymbol{\theta})\, \mathrm{d}\lambda$ (cf. (14)). Under suitable conditions it seems that $N^{1/2}(\hat{\boldsymbol{\theta}} - \boldsymbol{\theta}_0) \to_{\mathrm{d}} N(0, \Xi)$, for some Ξ. When $\mathbf{z}(t)$ is Gaussian, $\Xi = 2\Omega^{-1}$, where Ω has (k, l)th element

$$\frac{1}{2\pi} \int_B \mathrm{Tr}\,[\beta_k(\lambda; \boldsymbol{\theta}_0)\beta_l(\lambda; \boldsymbol{\theta}_0) + 2M_k(\lambda; \boldsymbol{\theta}_0)\bar{f}_X(\lambda) M_k^*(\lambda; \boldsymbol{\theta}_0)\bar{f}_W^{-1}(\lambda; \boldsymbol{\theta}_0)]\, \mathrm{d}\lambda, \tag{62}$$

where now $\beta_k(\lambda; \boldsymbol{\theta}) = \bar{f}_W^{-1}(\lambda; \boldsymbol{\theta})(\partial/\partial\boldsymbol{\theta}_k)\bar{f}_W(\lambda; \boldsymbol{\theta})$, and $M_k(\lambda; \boldsymbol{\theta}) = (\partial/\partial\boldsymbol{\theta}_k)M(\lambda; \boldsymbol{\theta})$. When ϕ is chosen as (48), we still obtain $\Xi = 2\Omega^{-1}$ if only the disturbance process $\mathbf{u}(t)$ is Gaussian. We can estimate $2\Omega^{-1}$ by $2\hat{\Omega}^{-1}$, where $\hat{\Omega}$ has (k, l)th element

$$\frac{1}{N} \sum_{B} \mathrm{Tr}\,[\beta_k(\lambda_j; \hat{\boldsymbol{\theta}})\beta_l(\lambda_j; \hat{\boldsymbol{\theta}}) + 2M_k(\lambda_j; \hat{\boldsymbol{\theta}}) I_X(\lambda_j) M_l^*(\lambda_j; \hat{\boldsymbol{\theta}})\bar{f}_W^{-1}(\lambda_j; \hat{\boldsymbol{\theta}})], \tag{63}$$

where $I_X(\lambda) = w_X(\lambda)w_X^*(\lambda)$. However, this will not be consistent for Ξ if the aforementioned Gaussianity conditions are violated. A robust estimate of Ξ is given by $\hat{\Omega}^{-1}\hat{\Sigma}\hat{\Omega}^{-1}$, where $\hat{\Sigma}$ has (k, l)th element

$$\frac{1}{N}\sum_{B} \mathrm{Tr}\,[\beta_k(\lambda_j; \hat{\boldsymbol{\theta}})\gamma(\lambda_j; \hat{\boldsymbol{\theta}}) - \delta_k(\lambda_j; \hat{\boldsymbol{\theta}})]\,\mathrm{Tr}\,[\beta_l(\lambda_j; \hat{\boldsymbol{\theta}})\gamma(\lambda_j; \hat{\boldsymbol{\theta}}) - \delta_l(-\lambda_j; \hat{\boldsymbol{\theta}})] \tag{64}$$

where now $\gamma(\lambda; \boldsymbol{\theta}) = I_J - \hat{f}_{\bar{W}}^{-1}(\lambda; \boldsymbol{\theta})I_W(\lambda)$, and

$$\delta_K(\lambda; \boldsymbol{\theta}) = M_k(\lambda; \boldsymbol{\theta})[I_{XY}(\lambda) - I_X(\lambda)M^*(\lambda; \boldsymbol{\theta})] + [I_{YX}(\lambda) - M(\lambda; \boldsymbol{\theta})I_X(\lambda)]M_k^*(\lambda; \boldsymbol{\theta}). \tag{65}$$

Parametric assumptions on the disturbance spectral density play a less crucial role in open systems than in closed systems. Though use of such parametric assumptions, in the way just described, is desirable for efficiency purposes, there are also substantial advantages in avoiding them. Note that if $f_u(\lambda)$ is nonparametric then so are $\hat{f}_V(\lambda)$ and $\bar{f}_W(\lambda)$. If $\bar{f}_W(\lambda; \boldsymbol{\theta})$ is replaced in $\tilde{L}(\boldsymbol{\theta})$ by $\bar{f}_W(\lambda)$, then $\hat{\boldsymbol{\theta}}$ is also given by

$$\hat{\boldsymbol{\theta}} = \arg\min_{\Theta} \frac{1}{N}\sum_{B} \mathrm{Tr}\,[I_W(\lambda_j; \boldsymbol{\theta})\bar{f}_{W}^{-1}(\lambda_j)]. \tag{66}$$

Because $\bar{f}_W$ is unknown, $\hat{\boldsymbol{\theta}}$ is now infeasible. With no loss of first-order asymptotic performance, we can replace $\bar{f}_W(\lambda)$ by a consistent estimate $\hat{f}_W(\lambda)$:

$$\hat{\boldsymbol{\theta}} = \arg\min_{\Theta} \frac{1}{N}\sum_{B} \mathrm{Tr}\,[I_W(\lambda_j; \boldsymbol{\theta})\hat{f}_{\bar{W}}^{-1}(\lambda_j)]. \tag{67}$$

Under regularity conditions (Robinson 1972) $\hat{\boldsymbol{\theta}}$ is consistent and $N^{1/2}(\hat{\boldsymbol{\theta}} - \boldsymbol{\theta}_0) \to_d N(0, \Omega^{-1})$, where Ω has (k, l)th element

$$\frac{1}{2\pi}\int_{B} \mathrm{Tr}\,[M_k(\lambda; \boldsymbol{\theta}_0)\bar{f}_X(\lambda)M_l^*(\lambda; \boldsymbol{\theta}_0)\bar{f}_{\bar{W}}^{-1}(\lambda)]\,\mathrm{d}\lambda, \tag{68}$$

which can be estimated by

$$\frac{1}{N}\sum_{B} \mathrm{Tr}\,[M_k(\lambda_j; \hat{\boldsymbol{\theta}})I_X(\lambda_j)M_l^*(\lambda_j; \hat{\boldsymbol{\theta}})\hat{f}_{\bar{W}}^{-1}(\lambda_j)]. \tag{69}$$

Note that the form Ω^{-1} does not rely on any Gaussianity assumptions on $\mathbf{z}(t)$ or $\mathbf{u}(t)$. An estimate $\hat{f}_W(\lambda)$ is

$$\hat{f}_W(\lambda) = \hat{f}_Y(\lambda) - \hat{f}_{YX}(\lambda)\hat{f}_{\bar{X}}^{-1}(\lambda)\hat{f}_{XY}(\lambda), \tag{70}$$

where $\hat{f}_Y$ and $\hat{f}_{YX}$, $\hat{f}_{XY}$ are smoothed nonparametric spectral and cross-spectral estimates. Note that alternative weightings of $\hat{f}_{\bar{W}}^{-1}$ are possible in (67), but $\hat{f}_{\bar{W}}^{-1}$

provides the most efficient one. However, "adapting" to $\bar{f}_W$ by employing the slowly converging nonparametric estimate (70) is only likely to be successful if N is large; otherwise the asymptotic performance may be poorly approximated, and the estimates might be worse than ones based on a misspecified parametric f_u. Whatever the weighting employed, a minimum distance estimate like $\hat{\boldsymbol{\theta}}$ is generally less efficient asymptotically than $\hat{\boldsymbol{\theta}}$ if it uses a correct parametric f_u and $\mathbf{u}(t)$ is Gaussian, but not necessarily otherwise. Confident specification of f_u is particularly difficult because it is the spectral density of a continuous-time process that is not even directly observable in discrete time, and a misspecified f_u can be a source of inconsistency.

Instrumental Variables Estimates of Complete, Incomplete and Linear-in-parameter Systems

It cannot be stressed too strongly that the desirable asymptotic properties just claimed depend crucially on a correct choice of distributor ϕ. Because ϕ is bound in practice to be picked incorrectly, specification error and asymptotic bias is bound to occur. Moreover the motivation for the approach assumes stationarity of $\mathbf{z}(t)$, as does existing theoretical justification, and stationarity entails a restriction on the observed discrete data, and thus one that is capable of being rejected by a statistical test. Of course, alternative approaches also rely on a precise, accurate interpolation of $\mathbf{z}(t)$ for consistent estimation based on a fixed sampling interval, and also appear to entail some restriction on the discrete data, or to have been justified only under restrictive conditions on the discrete data. The approach used by Bergstrom (1986), who assumes $p = 2$ and $J = K$ in (34), yields an exact discrete model for given integer t when $\mathbf{z}(t)$ is quadratic in t on $[t - 3, t]$, that is, through four consecutive data points (unlike the three points used by Phillips (1974)), which if true for each $t = 1, \dots, N$ implies not merely a certain interpolation entailing first and second derivatives of $\mathbf{z}(t)$ in the model to be linear in t and constant respectively and all derivatives of order three or more to be zero, but also that all discrete time $\mathbf{Z}_1, \dots, \mathbf{Z}_n$ lie on a quadratic; the latter restriction may be approximately satisfied by various time series but it is capable of being rejected by a statistical test based on the observed data, it logically entails multicollinearity if H is large enough, and it provides parameter estimates requiring a different fixed sampling interval asymptotic justification from that in the existing literature which assumes the $\mathbf{Z}_t$ are asymptotically stationary. When $\mathbf{u}(t)$ is white noise the exact discrete model of Bergstrom (1986) for his $z(t)$ is of ARMAX form, and an ARMAX results also if $\mathbf{z}(t)$ has instead a rational spectral density, though the parameterization differs. Simple estimates based on (48) can be approximately corrected to allow for an actual rational f_x, as in Robinson (1976a). Notice that we have allowed again for summation over only a proper subset B of $(-\pi, \pi)$, and in open systems this is perhaps of particular value in that the smaller B the smaller the range of λ within $(-\pi, \pi)$ for which ϕ must be prescribed, and thus the smaller the scope for misspecification. Notice also that because the function $(e^{i\lambda} - 1)/i\lambda$ is zero at $\lambda = 2\pi j, j = \pm 1, \pm 2, \dots$, and close to zero near these points, (48) will tend to be closer to the truth for the temporally aggregated version of a process than the skip-sampled one. However, although we might expect spectral mass to often be greater over the sampling frequencies than over any other interval of length 2π, (48) is an extreme choice. In the estimates just discussed, (48) was found to be the choice of ϕ affording the most simplicity. If we do select this ϕ, and if we are willing to take f_u to be nonparametric, we can obtained computationally still simpler estimates than $\hat{\boldsymbol{\theta}}$, with no further loss of asymptotic efficiency. More important, we can perform limited information estimation of incomplete systems, again with good asymptotic efficiency. Moreover, when $A(\lambda; \boldsymbol{\theta})$ is linear in $\boldsymbol{\theta}$, we can obtain estimates that are defined in closed form.

We commence with (52), deducing that

$$\frac{1}{2\pi}\int_B F^*(\lambda)\{\bar{f}'_{ZX}(\lambda) \otimes I_K\} \operatorname{vec}\{\tilde{A}(\lambda; \boldsymbol{\theta}_0)\}\, \mathrm{d}\lambda = 0, \tag{71}$$

for any $HK \times r$ function $F(\lambda)$ with even real parts and odd imaginary parts. Let

$$s(\boldsymbol{\theta}; F) = \frac{1}{N}\sum_B F^*(\lambda_j)\{I'_{ZX}(\lambda_j) \otimes I_K\} \operatorname{vec}\{\tilde{A}(\lambda_j; \boldsymbol{\theta}),\tag{72}$$

$$\hat{\boldsymbol{\theta}}(F) = \arg\min_{\boldsymbol{\Theta}} s'(\boldsymbol{\theta}, F) s(\boldsymbol{\theta}, F).\tag{73}$$

Under regularity conditions (that do not require any Gaussianity) $N^{1/2}\{\hat{\boldsymbol{\theta}}(F) - \boldsymbol{\theta}_0\} \to_{\mathrm{d}} N(0, \Xi)$, where Ξ can be minimized by

$$F_0(\lambda) = \{(m(\lambda), I_H)' \otimes [\tilde{C}(\lambda)\bar{f}_V(\lambda)\tilde{C}^*(\lambda)]^{-1}\}\tilde{\alpha}(\lambda; \boldsymbol{\theta}_0),\tag{74}$$

where $\tilde{\alpha}(\lambda; \boldsymbol{\theta}) = (\partial/\partial\boldsymbol{\theta}) \operatorname{vec}\{\tilde{A}(\lambda; \boldsymbol{\theta})\}$. The minimized Ξ is

$$\Xi_0 = \left\{\frac{1}{2\pi}\int_B \tilde{\alpha}^*(\lambda; \boldsymbol{\theta}_0)\left\{\begin{pmatrix} m(-\lambda) \\ I_H\end{pmatrix}\bar{f}'_X(\lambda)\begin{pmatrix} m(\lambda) \\ I_H\end{pmatrix}' \otimes [\tilde{C}(\lambda)\bar{f}_V(\lambda)C^*(\lambda)]^{-1}\right\}\tilde{\alpha}(\lambda; \boldsymbol{\theta}_0)\, \mathrm{d}\lambda\right\}^{-1}.\tag{75}$$

To obtain a feasible version of F_0, first consider an arbitrary F that produces an $N^{1/2}$-consistent $\hat{\boldsymbol{\theta}}(F)$. Let

$$\hat{F}(\lambda) = \{(\hat{m}(\lambda), I_H)' \otimes [\tilde{C}(\lambda; \hat{\boldsymbol{\theta}}(F))\hat{f}_V(\lambda)\tilde{C}^*(\lambda; \hat{\boldsymbol{\theta}}(F))]^{-1}\}\tilde{\alpha}(\lambda; \hat{\boldsymbol{\theta}}(F)),\tag{76}$$

where $\hat{m}(\lambda) = \hat{f}_{YX}(\lambda)\hat{f}_X^{-1}(\lambda)$, using smoothed nonparametric spectral estimates, and $\hat{f}_V(\lambda) = \hat{f}_{\hat{W}}(\lambda)$ is given by (70). Then under regularity conditions (Robinson 1972) $N^{1/2}\{\hat{\boldsymbol{\theta}}(\hat{F}) - \boldsymbol{\theta}_0\} \to_{\mathrm{d}} N(0, \Xi_0)$, with Ξ_0 given by (73). We can estimate Ξ_0 by

$$\hat{\Xi} = \left\{\frac{1}{N}\sum_B \tilde{\alpha}(\lambda_j; \hat{\boldsymbol{\theta}})\left[\begin{pmatrix} \hat{m}(-\lambda_j) \\ I_H\end{pmatrix} I'_X(\lambda_j)\begin{pmatrix} \hat{m}(\lambda_j) \\ I_H\end{pmatrix}' \otimes [\tilde{C}(\lambda_j; \hat{\boldsymbol{\theta}}(F))\hat{f}_V(\lambda_j)\tilde{C}^*(\lambda_j; \hat{\boldsymbol{\theta}}(F))]^{-1}\right]\tilde{\alpha}^*(\lambda_j; \hat{\boldsymbol{\theta}}(F))\right\}^{-1}.\tag{77}$$

In complete systems $\tilde{m}(\lambda)$ might be replaced by $-\tilde{C}^{-1}(\lambda; \hat{\boldsymbol{\theta}}(F))^{-1}\tilde{D}(\lambda_j; (F))$ in $\hat{F}(\lambda)$, and by $-\tilde{C}^{-1}(\lambda; \hat{\boldsymbol{\theta}}(\hat{F}))^{-1}\tilde{D}(\lambda; \hat{\boldsymbol{\theta}}(\hat{F}))$ in $\hat{\Xi}$. It may be checked that when the system is complete, Ξ_0 is identical to the matrix given by (68) under (48), so the optimal instrumental variables estimate $\hat{\boldsymbol{\theta}}(\hat{F})$ does as well as the minimum distance estimate $\hat{\boldsymbol{\theta}}$. However, unlike $\hat{\boldsymbol{\theta}}$, $\hat{\boldsymbol{\theta}}(\hat{F})$ is available also for incomplete systems. Moreover, the nonlinear optimization problem (73) seems more attractive than (67). When $A(\lambda; \boldsymbol{\theta})$ is bilinear in $\boldsymbol{\theta}$ (as in a model of Houthakker and Taylor (1970), p. 11, for example), we can optimize (73) by a simple back-and-forth procedure. When $A(\lambda; \boldsymbol{\theta})$ is linear in $\boldsymbol{\theta}$, $\hat{\boldsymbol{\theta}}(\hat{F})$ is given in closed form. The instrumental variables procedure we have described for differential equation systems entails only a mild extension to the mixed stock and flow case of that of Robinson (1976b) for the stock case. However, a more modern asymptotic theory for estimates of more general systems was given by Robinson (1991). A feature of this is the allowance for a data-dependent bandwidth in the smoothed nonparametric spectral estimation used in $\hat{\boldsymbol{\theta}}(\hat{F})$. Data-dependent methods of bandwidth choice can be less subjective than data-free ones and help to avoid some of the problems of ambiguity in nonparametric estimation. A specific, automatic, method of bandwidth choice was discussed by Robinson (1991).

Final Comments

The estimation of continuous-time systems from equally spaced discrete time series data may be an unusually ambitious venture by the standards of econometric research. In closed systems, the exact discrete model, whether expressed in time- or frequency-domain form, is liable to be a highly complicated function of the parameters of the underlying model, and there is evidence that it may only locally identify these parameters, or at least that it may identify them insufficiently strongly to rule out the possibility of sampling variability contributing to misleading estimates. In open systems, the cost of lack of knowledge of how the continuous exogenous processes interpolate the discrete ones is an apparently hopeless identification problem, and the interpolation employed for the sake of obtaining estimates corresponding to a particular identification, whether formulated in the time or frequency domain, is bound to be more or less arbitrary and to produce specification errors, which possibly could dominate sampling error. However, as Professor Bergstrom has argued in his important writings, econometric models may be naturally formulated in continuous time, and in view of the limited length of many macroeconomic time series the effort to estimate parameters of the underlying model, rather than a less parsimonious, *ad hoc* discrete approximation, may pay off in enabling us to answer questions of economic interest formulated in terms of the parameters, answer them reliably, and obtain reliable forecasts. In this paper we have described frequency-domain approaches to large-sample inference on both closed and open, stable, continuous-time systems, from data that can be a mixture of both stocks and aggregate flow variables. We briefly summarize the main features of our work.

1 All the methods involve discrete Fourier transforms of the data, which can be computed once and for all at the start of the analysis by the fast Fourier transform algorithm. This algorithm can be computationally more efficient and may

introduce less round-off error than more naive methods of computing discrete Fourier transforms.

2 The objective function $L(\boldsymbol{\theta})$ in (12) could be approximated in the time domain, as well as by L_1 or L_2, the corresponding estimates possibly differing significantly in finite samples, despite having similar asymptotic properties. Time-domain representations involve the inverse and determinant of a $DN \times DN$ block Toeplitz matrix, which the frequency-domain from $L(\boldsymbol{\theta})$ conveniently replaced by inverses and determinants of the $D \times D$ $\bar{f}_Z(\lambda_j; \boldsymbol{\theta})$. Similar remarks apply to the objective functions in (58), (67), and (73).

3 We have provided compact formulas for $\bar{f}_Z(\lambda; \boldsymbol{\theta})$, and thus for the exact discrete model of a continuous closed system, that can be used in systems of general order, involving both stock and flow data and allowing for the possibility of multiple roots.

4 All our estimates are of a Gaussian nature. The form of the limiting covariance matrix of some but not all of the estimates can be more or less affected by departures from Gaussianity. Covariance matrix estimates that are consistent both under Gaussianity and non-Gaussianity have been given.

5 The approach to estimating open differential equations applies simultaneously to models with derivatives of any finite order in both the endogenous and exogenous variables; it is not necessary to carry out side calculations peculiar to a continuous model of given order in order to obtain a working model for the discrete data. The approach can be extended to other forms of linear-in-variable continuous-time model, such as delay-differential equations, possibly with unknown, non-integral lags.

6 We have exploited the property that the Fourier transform of a convolution is simply the product of the Fourier transforms, to obtain a working model for open systems in which parametric functions are separable from discrete Fourier transforms. Temporal aggregation merely results in multiplication by a simple function of frequency, an insignificant further complication of the formulas.

7 The initial approach to estimating open systems in the second subsection of the third section stresses the severity of the identification problem posed by the discrete sampling of the continuous exogenous processes. It allows for a variety of solutions ϕ to the problem, and thus for sensitivity of the estimates of $\boldsymbol{\theta}_0$ to different ϕ to be assessed.

8 With a particular choice of ϕ, which seems likely to be a better approximation in flow than stock data, we obtain a working model which does not mix across equations the coefficients in the underlying system, and thus allows limited-information estimation of incomplete systems, via instrumental variables techniques.

9 For that ϕ, the remaining identification problem is equivalent to the well-known and extensively treated one for discrete-time systems with rational transfer function.

10 For that ϕ, when the underlying structural form is linear in parameters, we obtain closed-form parameter estimates.

11 In open systems, we can allow the spectral density of continuous-time disturbances to be nonparametric, thereby failing to reach the efficiency bound for Gaussian, correctly parameterized disturbances but avoiding a source of asymptotic bias due to an incorrect parametric model for the disturbances. We obtain

estimates with optimal asymptotic properties in the presence of a nonparametric disturbance spectral density, though their finite-sample properties might possibly be inferior to estimates based on an incorrect parametric density.

12 Smoothed nonparametric spectral estimation plays a significant role in the estimates of at the end of the third section, where recent developments in the methodology and theory of automatic bandwidth determination may be useful.

Note

This article is based on research funded by the Economic and Social Research Council (ESRC) reference number: R000231441. I thank Peter Phillips and a referee for suggestions leading to an improved presentation.

References

Bartlett, M. S. (1946). "On the theoretical specification of sampling properties of autocorrelated time series," *Journal of the Royal Statistical Society*, 8 (Supplement), 27–41.

Bergstrom, A. R. (1966). "Nonrecursive models as discrete approximations to systems of stochastic differential equations," *Econometrica*, 34, 173–82.

Bergstrom, A. R. (1967). *The Construction and Use of Economic Models*. London: English Universities Press.

Bergstrom, A. R. (1983). "Gaussian estimation of structural parameters in higher-order continuous-time dynamic models," *Econometrica*, 51, 117–52.

Bergstrom, A. R. (1985). "The estimation of parameters in nonstationary higher order continuous-time dynamic models," *Econometric Theory*, 1, 369–85.

Bergstrom, A. R. (1986), "The estimation of open higher-order continuous-time dynamic models with mixed stock and flow data," *Econometric Theory*, 2, 350–73.

Brillinger, D. R. (1975). *Time Series, Data Analysis and Theory*. San Francisco: Holden-Day.

Davies, R. B. (1973). "Asymptotic inference in stationary Gaussian time-series," *Advances in Applied Probability*, 5, 469–97.

Dunsmuir, W. (1979). "A central limit theorem for parameter estimation in stationary vector time series and its application to models for a signal observed with noise," *Annals of Statistics*, 7, 490–506.

Dunsmuir, W., and E. J. Hannan (1976). "Vector linear time series models," *Advances in Applied Probability*, 8, 339–64.

Hannan, E. J. (1969). "The identification of vector mixed autoregressive-moving average systems," *Biometrika*, 56, 223–5.

Hannan, E. J. (1971). "The identification problem for multiple equation systems with moving average errors," *Econometrica*, 39, 751–65.

Hannan, E. J. (1973). "The asymptotic theory of linear time series models," *Journal of Applied Probability*, 10, 130–45.

Hansen, L. P., and T. J. Sargent (1983). "The dimensionality of the aliasing problem," *Econometrica*, 51, 377–88.

Hille, E. (1959). *Analytic Function Theory*, volume I. Waltham, Massachusetts: Blaisdell.

Houthakker, H. S., and L. D. Taylor (1970). *Consumer Demand in the United States: Analyses and Projections*. Cambridge, Massachusetts: Harvard University Press.

Jones, R. H. (1981). "Fitting a continuous-time autoregression to discrete data," in D. F. Findlay (ed.) *Applied Time Series Analysis*, pp. 651–74. New York: Academic Press.

Pandit, S. M., and S. M. Wu (1975). "Unique estimates of the parameters of a continuous stationary process," *Biometrika*, 62, 497–501.

Phillips, A. W. (1959). "The estimation of parameters in systems of stochastic differential equations," *Biometrika*, 46, 67–76.

Phillips, P. C. B. (1972). "The structural estimation of a stochastic differential-equation system," *Econometrica*, 40, 1021–41.

Phillips, P. C. B. (1973). "The problem of identificaton in finite parameter continuous-time models," *Journal of Econometrics*, 1, 351–62.
Phillips, P. C. B. (1974). "The estimation of some continuous-time models," *Econometrica*, 42, 803–24.
Phillips, P. C. B. (1976a). "The estimation of linear stochastic differential equation models with exogenous variables," in A. R. Bergstrom (ed.), *Statistical Inference in Continuous-Time Economic Models*, pp. 135–73. Amsterdam: North-Holland.
Phillips, P. C. B. (1976b). "Some computations based on observed data series of the exogenous variable component of continuous systems," in *Statistical Inference in Continuous-Time Economic Models* (A. R. Bergstrom, ed.), pp. 174–214. Amsterdam: North-Holland.
Phillips, P. C. B. (1978). "The treatment of flow data in the estimation of continuous-time systems," in A. R. Bergstrom et al. (eds), *Stability and Inflation*, pp. 257–74. New York: Wiley.
Phillips, P. C. B. (1988). "Error correction and long run equilibria in continuous time," Cowles Foundation discussion paper 882.
Phillips, P. C. B. (1989). "Partially identified econometric models," *Econometric Theory*, 5, 181–240.
Robinson, P. M. (1972). *The Estimation of Continuous Time Systems Using Discrete-Time Data*, Ph.D. thesis, Australian National University.
Robinson, P. M. (1976a). "The aliasing problem in differential equation estimation," *Journal of the Royal Statistical Society B*, 38, 180–8.
Robinson, P. M. (1976b). "Instrumental variables estimation of differential equations," *Econometrica*, 44, 765–76.
Robinson, P. M. (1977). "The construction and estimation of continuous time models and discrete approximations in econometrics," *Journal of Econometrics*, 6, 173–97.
Robinson, P. M. (1978). "Alternative models for stationary stochastic processes," *Stochastic Processes and Applicatons*, 8, 141–52.
Robinson, P. M. (1980a). "Continuous model fitting from discrete data," in D. R. Brillinger and G. C. Tiao (eds) *Directions in Time Series*, pp. 263–77. Hayward, CA: Institute of Mathematical Statistics.
Robinson, P. M. (1980b). "The efficient estimation of a rational spectral density," in M. Kunt and F. de Coulon (eds) *Signal Processes: Theories of Applications*, pp. 701–4. Amsterdam: North-Holland.
Robinson, P. M. (1988). "Using Gaussian estimators robustly," *Oxford Bulletin of Economics and Statisics*, 50, 97–106.
Robinson, P. M. (1991). "Automatic frequency-domain inference on semiparametric and nonparametric models," *Econometrica*, 59, 1329–63.
Sargan, J. D. (1974). "Some discrete approximations to continuous-time stochastic models," *Journal of the Royal Statistical Society B*, 36, 74–90.
Sims, C. A. (1971). "Discrete approximations to continuous-time distributed lags in econometrics," *Econometrica*, 39, 545–63.
Telser, L. G. (1967). "Discrete samples and moving sums in stationary stochastic processes," *Journal of the American Statistics Association*, 62, 484–99.
Thomson, P. J. (1986). "Band-limited spectral estimation of autoregressive-moving-average processes," *Journal of Applied Probability*, 23A, 143–255.
White, H. (1982). "Maximum likelihood estimation of misspecified models," *Econometrica*, 50, 1–25.
Whittle, P. (1951). *Hypothesis Testing in Time-Series Analysis.* Stockholm: Almqvist and Wicksell.
Whittle, P. (1962). "Gaussian estimation in stationary time series," *Bulletin of the International Statistical Institute*, 39, 105–129.

8

Estimation of Nonlinear Continuous-Time Models from Discrete Data

Clifford R. Wymer

Introduction

Differential equation models have been used in economics for a large number of years but the estimation of the parameters of these models has been developed during only the past 25 years, although based on earlier work. The reasons for using such models in econometrics have been discussed by a number of authors, for example, Koopmans (1950), Bergstrom (1967), and Wymer (1976), and Bergstrom (1988) provides a review of the development of the estimators of these models. A detailed introduction to continuous-time estimators and references to their use is given in Gandolfo (1981) and Bergstrom (1984).

The difficulty of using differential equation systems in economics compared with other disciplines is due to the nonexperimental nature of almost all econometric work so that the parameters of the system cannot be measured directly but must be inferred from a sample of observations of the variables of the model measured at discrete points in time. While discrete observations of variables such as stocks, prices, interest rates, and exchange rates can be obtained at a point in time, other variables are flows which are observed only as an integral over some observation period. It is assumed, at present, that all observations in the sample are equispaced but it is possible to relax this restriction and the estimator discussed in this paper may facilitate this for both linear and nonlinear models.

In the development of estimators of continuous-time models from discrete data it has generally been assumed that the model being estimated is linear in the variables and of the form, written imprecisely but conveniently,

$$\mathrm{D}\mathbf{y}(t) = A(\boldsymbol{\theta})\mathbf{y}(t) + B(\boldsymbol{\theta})\mathbf{z}(t) + \boldsymbol{\xi}(t), \tag{1}$$

where $\mathbf{y}(t)$ is a vector of m continuous endogenous variables, $\mathbf{z}(t)$ is a vector of n continuous exogenous variables, $\boldsymbol{\theta}$ is a vector of p parameters, and $\boldsymbol{\xi}(t)$ is a vector of white-noise errors. $A(\boldsymbol{\theta})$ and $B(\boldsymbol{\theta})$ are matrices whose elements are specified functions of the set of parameters $\boldsymbol{\theta}$. Since the spectral density matrix of $\boldsymbol{\xi}(t)$ is constant, $\boldsymbol{\xi}(t)$ cannot be rigorously defined and the derivative $\mathrm{D}\boldsymbol{\xi}(t)$ does not exist, but for specification purposes the model may be viewed as though it does exist; a more precise definition of the system is given below. In this paper, apart from the introduction, D is the differential operator d/dt defined in the mean square sense. The assumption of a linear model allows estimators to be derived with well-defined properties.

Economic models, however, are often nonlinear. Economic theory often leads to nonlinear functions and some economic systems may be better represented by a nonlinear model. The use of a nonlinear model may be necessary to represent certain features of an economy or market as it allows dynamic behavior, including the possibility of limit cycles, which is precluded by a linear system as discussed, for example, in Bergstrom (1967), Wymer (1976, 1979a), Bergstrom and Wymer (1976), Gandolfo (1981), and Bailey et al. (1987). Nonlinearities may be due to the basic theoretical structure which is assumed to be underlying the economic system, such as the form of a utility or production function, or due to the institutional or market structure in which the utility or production functions are imbedded. Behavioral functions, perhaps derived from utility or profit maximization, are often highly nonlinear, and perhaps of a logarithmic or transcendental form, while other equations may be linear or simple multiplicative functions of the variables. The institutional or market structure may also be non-linear. These non-linearities may have significant implications both in the long run and in the adjustment from one state to another. In a dynamic adjustment model, for example, the rate of adjustment may vary according to the state of the economy or of the market; thus the model could allow for an acceleration in prices and wages or a rise in interest rates as the economy approaches full capacity or full employment and thus incorporate the conditions for a contraction better than a linear model.

Although a general model of such an economic system may be written

$$\mathbf{\Phi}\{\mathrm{D}\mathbf{y}(t), \mathbf{y}(t), \mathbf{z}(t), \boldsymbol{\theta}\} = \mathbf{v}(t), \tag{2}$$

if the system is recursive this becomes

$$\mathrm{D}\mathbf{y}(t) = \boldsymbol{\phi}\{\mathbf{y}(t), \mathbf{z}(t), \boldsymbol{\theta}\} + \boldsymbol{\xi}(t), \tag{3}$$

where $\mathbf{y}(t)$, $\mathbf{z}(t)$, $\boldsymbol{\xi}(t)$ and $\boldsymbol{\theta}$ are defined as in (1), and $\boldsymbol{\phi}$ is a vector of continuous functions of all variables and the set of parameters. The reasons for using recursive systems have been discussed elsewhere, for instance in Bergstrom (1966, 1984), Wymer (1976) and Gandolfo (1981), which also contain extensive references.

The aim of much of the applied econometric work on continuous systems, such as that discussed, for example, in Wymer (1976, 1979a) but also in many other papers, has been to develop models of the economic system and then to use those models as directly as possible to estimate the parameters of that system. The estimates of these parameters may then be used for hypothesis testing, analysis, and prediction. Owing to the difficulty of estimating the parameters $\boldsymbol{\theta}$ of the nonlinear system (3), this model may be approximated by a Taylor series expansion about some appropriate point or path to give a linearized model of the same form as (1) and then, given (1), the parameters may be estimated subject to all the over-identifying restrictions implied by the structure of (3) and its linearization. Since the parameters $\boldsymbol{\theta}$ of the linearized model (1) are those of the nonlinear model (3), once (1) is estimated the nonlinear model (3) can be used for analysis or prediction.

The problem with this approach is that the errors implicit in the linearization of (3) are generally not known. The linearization may bias the estimates of the parameters and prevent nonlinear effects showing in any analysis of the nonlinear system. Moreover, the linearization of (3) may mean that some parameters become poorly identified or even unidentified in the linear model. For example, in the linearized version of the Bergstrom and Wymer (1976) and the Knight and Wymer (1978) models of the UK, the estimates of the parameter $\boldsymbol{\beta}_4$ which determines the elasticity of substitution had large asymptotic standard errors and it was necessary to restrict this parameter. Although the parameter was formally identifiable in both the nonlinear and linearized versions of the models, it is considered that because the variance of capital was relatively small over the sample period and because the form of the linearized expressions were such that the full nonlinear effects of variations in capital were obscured, it became poorly identified in the linearized model. Preliminary estimates of the nonlinear version of the model suggest that estimating the nonlinear model directly, without linearization, may eliminate some identification problems which arise in linearized models and hence remove, or at least reduce, the problem of aliasing.

Another problem which arises with linearization is that the error process of the linearized model may be non-Gaussian even though the errors of the nonlinear model are Gaussian. In particular, this problem arises if the underlying system generating the data is highly nonlinear but it may be eliminated by estimating the nonlinear model directly by a nonlinear estimator. Some specifications of the monetary sector of the Knight and Wymer (1978) model of the UK economy exhibited this problem. Another example is the monetary model of the German hyperinflation of 1920–3 in Sommariva and Tullio (1987). In the last six months of the hyperinflation even the rate of acceleration of prices was so great that it could not be well-represented by a linear second-order system and it seems that a nonlinear model, perhaps with a third-order process, may be necessary to obtain a satisfactory representation of this phenomenon.

The properties of the estimators of linear models are now well known. As the broad approach to the estimation of nonlinear systems is similar to that of linear models, and as some properties of the nonlinear estimators must, at present, be inferred from those of the linear estimators, the linear estimators will be reviewed briefly. The nonlinear model and the exact estimator of the "pure" case where instantaneous observations exist for all variables will then be examined, "exact" estimators of mixed stock/flow and higher order models are considered next, and then the use of mixed frequency data. Finally, empirical applications of the estimators are discussed.

Linear Estimators

It is assumed that the stochastic linear differential equation system, defined more precisely than in (1), is

$$\mathrm{d}\mathbf{y}(t) = A(\boldsymbol{\theta})\mathbf{y}(t)\,\mathrm{d}t + B(\boldsymbol{\theta})\mathbf{z}(t)\,\mathrm{d}t + \zeta(\mathrm{d}t) \tag{4}$$

where $\mathbf{y}(t)$ is a vector of m continuous endogenous variables, $\mathbf{z}(t)$ is a vector of n continuous exogenous variables, $\boldsymbol{\theta}$ is a vector of p parameters, and $\zeta(\mathrm{d}t)$ is a vector of white-noise innovations such that $E[\zeta(\mathrm{d}t)] = 0$, $E[\zeta(\mathrm{d}t)\zeta'(\mathrm{d}t)] = |\mathrm{d}t|\Omega$ where Ω is a positive definite matrix, and $E[\zeta(\Delta t_1)\zeta'(\Delta t_2)] = 0$ for disjoint Δt_1 and Δt_2. $A(\boldsymbol{\theta})$ is a matrix of order m and $B(\boldsymbol{\theta})$ is a matrix of dimension $m \times n$ with the elements of both matrices being functions of the set of parameters $\boldsymbol{\theta}$. The assumptions can be easily modified to allow some equations to be identities. The matrix $A(\boldsymbol{\theta})$ must be restricted in order to identify the model, as shown by Phillips (1973). The models are often heavily over-identified, however, and the relatively small size of samples available for many econometric studies has required all the restrictions to be imposed in order to obtain efficient estimates.

The solution of (4) has the integral form

$$\mathbf{y}(t) = \mathrm{e}^{\delta A(\boldsymbol{\theta})}\mathbf{y}(t-\delta) + \int_{t-\delta}^{t} \mathrm{e}^{(t-s)A(\boldsymbol{\theta})}B(\boldsymbol{\theta})\mathbf{z}(s)\,\mathrm{d}s + \int_{t-\delta}^{t} \mathrm{e}^{(t-s)A(\boldsymbol{\theta})}\zeta(\mathrm{d}s). \tag{5}$$

Assume that the continuous variables are observed every δ time units (so that δ is the length of the observation interval in terms of the basic time unit of the system) and let x_τ be the discrete observation of a continuous variable $x(t)$ at time t, so that $x_\tau = x(\tau\delta)$ for integral τ. The exact discrete model is then

$$\mathbf{y}_\tau = \mathrm{e}^{\delta A}\mathbf{y}_{\tau-1} + \boldsymbol{\psi}_\tau + \boldsymbol{\omega}_\tau, \tag{6}$$

where

$$\mathbf{y}_\tau = \mathbf{y}(\tau\delta), \qquad \mathbf{z}_\tau = \mathbf{z}(\tau\delta), \qquad \boldsymbol{\psi}_\tau = \int_{\tau\delta-\delta}^{\tau\delta} \mathrm{e}^{(\tau\delta-s)A}B\mathbf{z}(s)\,\mathrm{d}s,$$

and $\boldsymbol{\omega}_\tau = \int_{\tau\delta-\delta}^{\tau\delta} \mathrm{e}^{(\tau\delta-s)A}\zeta(ds)$. For the purposes of the discussion here, it will also be assumed that the integral $\boldsymbol{\psi}_\tau$ can be evaluated exactly; this will be true if the $\mathbf{z}(t)$ are analytic functions of time. From the properties of the disturbances

$$E[\boldsymbol{\omega}_\delta] = E\left[\int_{t-\delta}^{t} \mathrm{e}^{(t-s)A}\zeta(\mathrm{d}s)\right] = 0, \tag{6a}$$

$$\begin{aligned} E[\boldsymbol{\omega}_t\boldsymbol{\omega}_t'] &= E\left\{\left[\int_{t-\delta}^{t} \mathrm{e}^{(t-s)A}\zeta(\mathrm{d}s)\right]\left[\int_{t-\delta}^{t} \mathrm{e}^{(t-s)A}\zeta(\mathrm{d}s)\right]'\right\}, \\ &= \int_0^{\delta} \mathrm{e}^{sA}\Omega\,\mathrm{e}^{sA'}\,\mathrm{d}s, \end{aligned} \tag{6b}$$

$$\begin{aligned} E[\boldsymbol{\omega}_r\boldsymbol{\omega}_t'] &= E\left\{\left[\int_{r-\delta}^{r} \mathrm{e}^{(r-s)A}\zeta(\mathrm{d}s)\right]\left[\int_{t-\delta}^{t} \mathrm{e}^{(t-s)A}\zeta(\mathrm{d}s)\right]'\right\}, \\ &= 0 \quad \text{for } r \neq t. \end{aligned} \tag{6c}$$

Thus, even if the variance matrix Ω is diagonal, this will not be true of the variance matrix of the errors of the exact discrete model, so that the errors $\boldsymbol{\omega}_t$ are not independent; they will, however, be serially uncorrelated under the assumptions above. Following Bergstrom (1983), the estimates considered in this paper would be maximum likelihood estimates if the integral of the white-noise disturbances $\zeta(dt)$ were a Gaussian process, but it is not assumed that the disturbances themselves have this property.

If the system contains identities, the estimator is still well defined, and unchanged, providing that the error variance matrix of the exact discrete model given by the integral in (6b) is positive definite. If the system has m_1 stochastic equations and m_2 identities, the model may be written

$$\mathrm{d}\begin{bmatrix} \mathbf{y}_1(t) \\ \mathbf{y}_2(t) \end{bmatrix} = \begin{bmatrix} A_{11} & A_{12} \\ A_{21} & A_{22} \end{bmatrix}\begin{bmatrix} \mathbf{y}_1(t) \\ \mathbf{y}_2(t) \end{bmatrix} \mathrm{d}t + B\mathbf{z}(t)\,\mathrm{d}t + \begin{bmatrix} \zeta_1(\mathrm{d}t) \\ 0 \end{bmatrix}, \tag{7}$$

where $\mathbf{y}_1(t)$ and $\zeta_1(\mathrm{d}t)$ have m_1 elements, $\mathbf{y}_2(t)$ has m_2 elements and A is partitioned accordingly. Phillips (1974) has shown, in particular, that if the number of stochastic equations is at least as great as the number of identities, a sufficient condition for the error variance matrix to be positive definite is that the submatrix A_{21} has rank m_2, that is, it is of full rank. First-order models are likely to have relatively few identities and it is likely, but not certain, that this condition will hold. Phillips also considered another special, but common, case which arises when an underlying mixed-order differential equation system is reduced to first order by defining additional variables and identities $\mathrm{D}y_j(t) = y_i(t)$ for some $i, j, i > j$; in this case the error variance matrix is always nonsingular. The general first-order model includes both structural identities and identities which arise from redefining a higher order system. The error covariance matrix of such models will usually, but not necessarily, be nonsingular.

A simpler, but approximate, discrete model can be obtained directly by integrating (4) over the observation interval to give

$$\int_{t-\delta}^{t} \mathrm{d}\mathbf{y}(s) = A\int_{t-\delta}^{t} \mathbf{y}(s)\,\mathrm{d}s + B\int_{t-\delta}^{t} \mathbf{z}(s)\,\mathrm{d}s + \int_{t-\delta}^{t} \zeta(\mathrm{d}s), \tag{8}$$

and thus, approximating $\int_{t-\delta}^{t} \mathbf{y}(s)\,\mathrm{d}s$ by $\frac{1}{2}(\mathbf{y}_t + \mathbf{y}_{t-\delta})$,

$$\Delta\mathbf{y}_t = A\tfrac{1}{2}(\mathbf{y}_t + \mathbf{y}_{t-\delta}) + B\int_{t-\delta}^{t} \mathbf{z}(s)\,\mathrm{d}s + \int_{t-\delta}^{t} \zeta(\mathrm{d}s), \quad \text{or} \tag{9}$$

$$\mathbf{y}_t = (I - \tfrac{1}{2}A)^{-1}(I + \tfrac{1}{2}A)\mathbf{y}_{t-\delta} + (I + \tfrac{1}{2}A)^{-1}B\int_{t-\delta}^{t} \mathbf{z}(s)\,\mathrm{d}s + (I - \tfrac{1}{2}A)^{-1}\int_{t-\delta}^{t} \zeta(\mathrm{d}s), \tag{10}$$

which can be compared with the exact discrete model (6). Again, the errors are not independent. It may be noted that, unlike the exact discrete model (6), the approximate discrete model (9) has the same form as the differential equation system (4).

An important feature of continuous-time models is that the observations generated by the differential equation system (4) will satisfy the exact discrete model (6) irrespective of the observation interval, so that the properties of the estimates of the parameters of the differential system may be derived from the sampling properties of the exact discrete model. A full-information maximum likelihood estimator is used to estimate both the exact and approximate discrete models because of the interdependence of the error terms and the need to impose all the constraints inherent not only in the restrictions on A and B but also in the form of the discrete model. The exact discrete estimator gives consistent estimates of the parameters $\boldsymbol{\theta}$ irrespective of the observation period, and as Phillips (1991) has shown the asymptotic convergence properties of this estimator mean that it will be more efficient. The approximate discrete estimator is asymptotically biased, with the bias depending on the length of the observation period, but this bias rapidly tends to zero as the observation length decreases. In practice, the point estimates of approximate linear models are often not significantly different from those of the exact estimator but the exact estimator is much more precise in the sense that the asymptotic standard errors are much smaller as shown, for example, in Phillips (1972) and Bergstrom and Wymer (1976).

A difficulty arises with flow variables, and with variables which are derivatives of other variables, since only the integrals of these variables can be observed. Although exact estimators were developed by Phillips (1978) for flow models and by Bergstrom (1983, 1985, 1986) and Agbeyegbe (1984) for higher order and mixed stock/flow systems[1] which take account of the measurement of these variables, the complexity of these estimators led to a class of "exact" estimators which are derived from the solution of the differential system as though point observations existed for all variables. As this is not the case with flow variables, the system must be integrated to provide variables which can be observed, or approximated by observable variables where necessary, but the errors in this model are no longer Gaussian. A model with Gaussian errors, at least to an approximation, may be derived by prewhitening the data, and this model is used to provide the "exact" estimates. Such estimators are derived and discussed in Wymer (1970, 1976) and Bergstrom and Wymer (1976). An "exact" estimator may also be defined for models where the exogenous variables do not satisfy the strict conditions necessary for it to be exact, as discussed in Wymer (1970, 1976) and Phillips (1974, 1976a). In this case, the approximation is such that the estimator would be exact if the exogenous variables were polynomials in time.

Nonlinear Estimators

The general nonlinear model to be considered in this paper is a recursive system of first-order stochastic differential equations of the form

$$\mathrm{d}\mathbf{y}(t) = \boldsymbol{\phi}\{\mathbf{y}(t), \mathbf{z}(t), \boldsymbol{\theta}\}\, \mathrm{d}t + \boldsymbol{\zeta}(\mathrm{d}t) \tag{11}$$

where $\mathbf{y}(t)$, $\mathbf{z}(t)$, $\boldsymbol{\zeta}(\mathrm{d}t)$ and $\boldsymbol{\theta}$ are defined as in (4). $\boldsymbol{\phi}\{\mathbf{y}(t), \mathbf{z}(t), \boldsymbol{\theta}\}$ is a vector of continuous and differentiable functions of all variables and the set of parameters $\boldsymbol{\theta}$. Some equations may be identities with the corresponding elements of $\boldsymbol{\zeta}(\mathrm{d}t)$ zero, in which case the equations of the model may be written

$$\mathrm{d}y_i(t) = \phi_i\{\mathbf{y}(t), \mathbf{z}(t), \boldsymbol{\theta}\}\, \mathrm{d}t + \zeta_i(\mathrm{d}t), \qquad i = 1, \ldots, m_1, \tag{11a}$$

$$\mathrm{d}y_i(t) = \phi_i\{\mathbf{y}(t), \mathbf{z}(t)\}\, \mathrm{d}t, \qquad i = m_1 + 1, \ldots, m, \tag{11b}$$

where the first m_1 equations (11a) are stochastic with $\zeta(dt)$ a vector of white-noise innovations such that $E[\zeta(dt)] = 0$, $E[\zeta(dt)\zeta'(dt)] = |dt|\Omega$ where Ω is a positive definite matrix, and $E[\zeta(\Delta t_1)\zeta'(\Delta t_2)] = 0$ for disjoint Δt_1 and Δt_2. A precise interpretation of the disturbances $\zeta(dt)$ and their relationship to $\xi(t)$ in (3) is given in Wymer (1972) and Bergstrom (1983, 1984).[2]

Although the system is defined to be of first order, higher order systems may formally be reduced to first order by introducing additional variables and corresponding definitional equations of the form $Dy_j(t) = y_i(t)$ where $y_j(t)$ is mean square differentiable. Usually only the integrals of these additional variables will be observable, as the variables themselves cannot be observed directly, and hence such systems must be considered specifically; such models are discussed later. Initially, it will be assumed that all variables can be observed instantaneously; the estimation of flow and higher order systems will be considered in the next section.

Let $\boldsymbol{\omega}(t)$ be the vector of errors in the trajectories of the system such that $\boldsymbol{\omega}(t) = \mathbf{y}(t) - \hat{\mathbf{y}}(t)$ where $\mathbf{y}(t)$ is the solution to (11) given initial conditions $\mathbf{y}(t-\delta)$ and $\hat{\mathbf{y}}(t)$ satisfies $d\hat{\mathbf{y}}(t) = \boldsymbol{\phi}\{\hat{\mathbf{y}}(t), \mathbf{z}(t), \boldsymbol{\theta}\}$ given the same initial conditions. This is analogous to the corresponding errors in the trajectories of the linear model (5). $E[\boldsymbol{\omega}(t)\boldsymbol{\omega}'(t)]$ is then the integral of an (unknown) function of the $\zeta(dt)$ over the interval $(t-\delta, t)$ and it follows from the properties of the error process $\zeta(dt)$ that the errors $\boldsymbol{\omega}(t)$ are interdependent but serially uncorrelated. $E[\boldsymbol{\omega}(t)\boldsymbol{\omega}'(t)]$ will generally be positive definite.

The model may include both structural identities and identities which allow an underlying higher order system to be reduced to first order. Unlike a linearized model, however, where some "structural" identities may be approximations and hence not true identities, properly specified identities in the nonlinear model will be exact. Like the linear estimator, the nonlinear estimator will be well defined only if the error covariance matrix is nonsingular, and although explicit conditions for this do not exist, it is considered most unlikely that the matrix would be singular.

It is assumed that the model is to be estimated using a sample of $T + 1$ equispaced observations of the variables $\mathbf{y}(t)$ and $\mathbf{z}(t)$ with an observation length of δ; for estimation purposes the basic time unit is chosen such that $\delta = 1$. Although many parameters will be independent of the basic time unit, some parameters, such as rates of adjustment or their reciprocal, may vary in accordance with the basic time unit and must be defined in terms of this unit. For discussion of some of the properties of the estimator, the basic time unit will be fixed so that the limit as δ tends to zero can be considered. For simulation and prediction, δ may take on any value irrespective of the observation length used in estimation.

One approach to the estimation of the nonlinear model was that of Bailey et al. (1987), who used a nonlinear discrete approximation to (11).[3] Instead of linearizing (11) and then using the linear model to estimate the parameters, the nonlinear system is integrated over the observation interval and then approximated to give a system of nonlinear functions of discrete variables which could be estimated by a quasi-full-information maximum likelihood estimator. This estimator is analogous to the approximate discrete estimator for linear models (8); if (11) were linear the two estimators would be almost the same. Sargan (1976) showed that the asymptotic bias in the approximate linear estimator is of $O(\delta^2)$ as δ tends to zero. Although the Bailey et al. estimator removes the questions raised by linearization, the estimates will be asymptotically biased and the analogy with the approximate discrete estimator for linear systems suggests that they will not be as efficient as those of an exact nonlinear discrete estimator.

The exact nonlinear discrete estimator described here is an obvious next step and was proposed in Wymer (1979a). Although the exact discrete estimator for linear models is derived using the analytical solution to the differential equation system, for nonlinear models the system must be solved by numerical integration, but the principle is the same in both cases. In the "pure" case, where all variables are observed at a point in time, the estimator will be consistent and efficient and is analogous to the exact discrete estimator for linear models which provides estimates which are superefficient. If this estimator were applied to a linear model, the estimates would be the same as the exact linear discrete estimator.

In the "pure" case, the endogenous variables $\mathbf{y}(t)$ are assumed to be observable at a point in time, such as stocks, prices, interest and exchange rates, and it will also be assumed that the exogenous variables are given analytic functions of time. For a given set of initial values of the parameters $\boldsymbol{\theta}$ and a set of initial values for the variables at the point $t-1$, the solution trajectories of (11) can be found by a numerical integration procedure. Let the vector of solution trajectories at t given the observed $\mathbf{y}(t-1)$ as initial values and the given set of $\boldsymbol{\theta}$ be $\hat{\mathbf{y}}(t;\boldsymbol{\theta})$. The residual between the observations of the endogenous variables at t, $\mathbf{y}(t)$, and the solution trajectory at this point is then

$$\mathbf{u}(t) = \mathbf{y}(t) - \hat{\mathbf{y}}(t;\boldsymbol{\theta}). \tag{12}$$

This procedure may then be repeated for all observations, with the integration procedure being reinitialized using the observed $\mathbf{y}(t-1)$ for each observation period[4], to form a set of residuals $\mathbf{u}(t)$, $t = 1, \ldots, T$. It follows from the properties of the error process $\zeta(\mathrm{d}t)$ that the residuals are serially uncorrelated. The logarithm of the determinant of the residual covariance matrix

$$L(\boldsymbol{\theta}) = \ln \det \left[\frac{1}{T} \sum_{t=1}^{T} \{\mathbf{y}(t) - \hat{\mathbf{y}}(t;\boldsymbol{\theta})\}\{\mathbf{y}(t) - \hat{\mathbf{y}}(t;\boldsymbol{\theta})\}' \right] \tag{13}$$

can then be formed and minimized with respect to the parameters $\boldsymbol{\theta}$ to give full-information maximum likelihood estimates of the parameters.

The "pure" exact nonlinear discrete estimator described above requires that the exogenous variables (or forcing functions) be analytic functions of time so that the integration procedure is exact. Under those conditions the exact linear and nonlinear discrete estimators are the same for linear models but this will not be true for more general exogenous variables. In most econometric models (Bergstrom and Wymer (1976), for example, is an exception) the exogenous variables are defined only by a series of discrete observations. As in the linear estimators, the continuous path of exogenous variables may be approximated using a polynomial fitted to nearby observations. In the linear case, the asymptotic bias of the approximate discrete estimator is of $O(\delta^2)$ as δ tends to zero where δ is the length of the observation interval, while for the exact linear discrete estimator using a quadratic, Phillips (1974, 1976a) has shown that, providing the exogenous variables are sufficiently smooth nonrandom variables, or that they are stationary stochastic processes differentiable in the mean square, the asymptotic bias in the parameter estimates is of $O(\delta^3)$ as δ tends to zero. Moreover, for a fixed observation interval, the asymptotic bias of the exact estimator decreases more rapidly in more heavily damped systems than the approximate estimator. If the smoothness conditions do not hold, however, the asymptotic bias of the exact model may be greater than that of the approximate estimator.

In the nonlinear estimator, the numerical integration procedure uses intermediate values within the observation interval $(t-1, t)$ interpolated from a third-order polynomial fitted to the discrete observations $\mathbf{z}(t-2)$, $\mathbf{z}(t-1)$, $\mathbf{z}(t)$ and $\mathbf{z}(t+1)$. Assume

$$\mathbf{z}(t+s) = \mathbf{a}_3 s^3 + \mathbf{a}_2 s^2 + \mathbf{a}_1 s + \mathbf{a}_0, \tag{14}$$

and, for each integer t, let $\mathbf{z}_{t+s}$ be the discrete observation at the point $t+s$ for $s = -2, -1, 0, 1$. Solving for $\mathbf{a}_3$, $\mathbf{a}_2$, $\mathbf{a}_1$, $\mathbf{a}_0$ gives

$$\mathbf{a}_3 = \tfrac{1}{6}(\mathbf{z}_{t+1} - \mathbf{z}_{t-2}) - \tfrac{1}{2}(\mathbf{z}_t - \mathbf{z}_{t-1}), \tag{15}$$

$$\mathbf{a}_2 = \tfrac{1}{2}(\mathbf{z}_{t+1} + \mathbf{z}_{t-1}) - \mathbf{z}_t, \tag{16}$$

$$\mathbf{a}_1 = \tfrac{1}{3}\mathbf{z}_{t+1} + \tfrac{1}{2}\mathbf{z}_t - \mathbf{z}_{t-1} + \tfrac{1}{6}\mathbf{z}_{t-2}, \tag{17}$$

$$\mathbf{a}_0 = \mathbf{z}_t. \tag{18}$$

As the difference between the exact linear and nonlinear estimators for linear models is only the form of polynomial approximation to the exogenous variables, and as the approximation used here will be as accurate as that used in the exact linear discrete estimator, the asymptotic bias in the exact nonlinear estimator will be no greater than $O(\delta^3)$ and the difference in the bias between the estimators will be negligible. It is suggested that the asymptotic bias in the exact nonlinear estimator of the parameters of a nonlinear model with general exogenous variables will be of the same order. It is also suggested that the asymptotic bias of the "exact" nonlinear estimator will usually be smaller than that of the approximate estimator. This "exact" estimator will provide Gaussian estimates if the exogenous variables are analytical functions of time.

"Exact" Nonlinear Estimation of Mixed Stock/Flow and Higher Order Models

Many economic models include flow variables such as production, consumption, demand, and supply. These variables cannot be observed at a point in time but are measured only as an integral over some interval so that the "pure" case needs to be extended. Other variables such as implicit price deflators, which are usually defined as the ratio of two flows, are also measured as an integral over some interval. Moreover, the basic model underlying (11) may be a second-order system so that the functions $\boldsymbol{\phi}$ in (11) would include rates of change of other variables in the model. The approximate nonlinear discrete estimator of Bailey et al. (1987) incorporated stocks and flows using approximations similar to those of the linear approximate estimator. The exact nonlinear estimator can also be extended to include stock/flow and higher order models but, as with the "exact" estimator of linear stock/flow models, the estimator is no longer exact; it can, however, be expected to be a good approximation to an exact estimator. The analogy with the estimators of linear models suggests that the asymptotic bias of the "exact" estimator of such models will be less than that of the approximate estimator.

Variables which are averages, such as price deflators, and which therefore are integrals, are treated in the same way as flows, except that the integral must be divided by the length of the observation δ measured in terms of the basic time unit in the model. Thus there is no need to discuss such variables specifically. Usually the basic time unit is defined such that $\delta = 1$, so that even the averaging becomes trivial.

In the numerical integration of the nonlinear model, it is necessary to have initial values for the endogenous variables for the solution over each observation period. In the "pure" exact estimator, observations of the variables at the beginning of each observation period, $\mathbf{y}(t - \delta)$, can be used where δ is the length of the observation interval. Flow variables, however, are observed as integrals over time so that each observation, say $\mathbf{y}^0(t)$, is

$$\mathbf{y}^0(t) = \int_{t-\delta}^{t} \mathbf{y}(s)\,\mathrm{d}s \qquad \text{for all } t; \tag{19}$$

initial values of the flow variables at the point $t - \delta$ must be approximated from these observations.

Two approaches to this problem are considered followed by a brief discussion of an "exact" discrete estimator of higher order systems and the use of higher frequency observations to provide a better approximation to the initial values of flow variables and to the path of exogenous variables.

Approximation of Initial Values of Flow Variables

Initial values of the flow variables at the point $t - \delta$, $\mathbf{y}(t - \delta)$, may be interpolated from a quadratic fitted to the discrete observations for successive periods $\mathbf{y}^0(t - 2\delta)$, $\mathbf{y}^0(t - \delta)$, $\mathbf{y}^0(t)$.

Let

$$\mathbf{y}_{t+s} = \int_{s-1}^{s} \mathbf{y}(t + \tau)\,\mathrm{d}\tau, \tag{20}$$

and assume

$$\mathbf{y}(t + s) = \mathbf{a}_2 s^2 + \mathbf{a}_1 s + \mathbf{a}_0. \tag{21}$$

Integrating $\mathbf{y}(t + s)$ over the intervals $(-2, -1)$, $(-1, 0)$ and $(0, 1)$, equating to $\mathbf{y}^0_{t-1}$, $\mathbf{y}^0_t$, $\mathbf{y}^0_{t+1}$, and solving for $\mathbf{a}_2$, $\mathbf{a}_1$, $\mathbf{a}_0$ gives

$$\mathbf{a}_2 = \tfrac{1}{2}(\mathbf{y}^0_{t+1} + \mathbf{y}^0_{t-1}) - \mathbf{y}^0_t, \tag{22}$$

$$\mathbf{a}_1 = \mathbf{y}^0_{t+1} - \mathbf{y}^0_t, \tag{23}$$

$$\mathbf{a}_0 = \tfrac{1}{3}\mathbf{y}^0_{t+1} + \tfrac{1}{6}(5\mathbf{y}^0_t - \mathbf{y}^0_{t-1}) \tag{24}$$

so that if $s = 0$ the estimate of the flow at the point t is $\tilde{\mathbf{y}}(t) = \mathbf{a}_0$. Hence

$$\tilde{\mathbf{y}}(t-1) = -\tfrac{1}{6}\mathbf{y}^0_{t-2} + \tfrac{5}{6}\mathbf{y}^0_{t-1} + \tfrac{1}{3}\mathbf{y}^0_t. \tag{25}$$

If a flow or averaged variable $\mathbf{y}(t)$ in the model is defined as a logarithm, the approximation $\tilde{\mathbf{y}}(t-1)$ should be made in terms of $e^{y^0_t}$, that is, using the observed values of the variables as natural numbers, and then

$$\tilde{\mathbf{y}}(t-1) = \ln\left(-\tfrac{1}{6}\, e^{y^0_{t-2}} + \tfrac{5}{6}\, e^{y^0_{t-1}} + \tfrac{1}{3}\, e^{y^0_t}\right). \tag{26}$$

The error of approximation $\mathbf{y}(t-\delta) - \tilde{\mathbf{y}}(t-\delta)$ is of $O(\delta^3)$ as δ tends to zero.

The solution trajectories of the system are calculated numerically over the interval $(t-1, t)$, for $\delta = 1$, and the flow and averaged variables are simultaneously integrated. The residuals for such variables are then

$$\mathbf{u}(t) = \mathbf{y}^0(t) - \int_{t-1}^{t} \hat{\mathbf{y}}(s; \boldsymbol{\theta})\, ds \qquad \text{for } t = 1, \ldots, T, \tag{27}$$

where $\hat{\mathbf{y}}(s; \boldsymbol{\theta})$ is the value of the variable at each point of the solution of the system. The integration of the flow variable means that the errors in the trajectory $\boldsymbol{\omega}(t)$ are also an integral over the observation period $(t-1, t)$. If the initial values of the variables at $t-1$ were given, the properties of the errors would mean that the residuals would be serially uncorrelated and this would provide an exact estimator. However, as the initial values $\mathbf{y}(t-1)$ are approximated as a function of observed variables $\mathbf{y}^0(t-1)$, which are integrals over $(t-2, t-1)$, $E[\boldsymbol{\omega}(r)\, \boldsymbol{\omega}'(t)]$ will contain the product of terms involving the disturbances $\zeta(ds)$ where the $\zeta(ds)$ are not disjoint. Thus the errors $\boldsymbol{\omega}(t)$ and the residuals $\mathbf{u}(t)$ will be serially correlated and hence no longer white noise.

For linear flow models, Phillips (1978) has shown that the asymptotic bias of the "exact" discrete estimator is of $O(\delta)$ as δ tends to zero but the approximate discrete estimator is asymptotically biased even in the limit as the observation interval tends to zero. This suggests that the asymptotic bias in the estimator being considered here would also be of $O(\delta)$ but, since it is the approximation of the initial values which introduces serial correlation into the residuals, it may be possible to reduce this bias. In particular, the asymptotic bias will be affected by the use of a linear or quadratic interpolation procedure to approximate the $\mathbf{y}^0(t-1)$. The implications of this, even for a linear model, are not clear; quadratic interpolation provides a more accurate approximation but may introduce greater serial correlation and a larger bias. It may be noted that in the linear estimators the serial correlation may be eliminated, at least to an approximation, by transforming the data; such a transformation is precluded by a nonlinear system.

An Alternative Approximation to the Initial Values of Flow Variables

Another approach, suggested by Bergstrom, to obtaining the initial values of flow variables required to solve the system over each observation interval $(t-1, t)$ is to linearize the model in the neighborhood of each initial point $t-1$ for each

$t = 1, \ldots, T$ and to use the resulting system to interpolate $\mathbf{y}(t-1)$. A Taylor series expansion of the nonlinear system (11) about a point $\mathbf{y}^0(t)$ is

$$\mathrm{d}\mathbf{y}(t) = A\{\boldsymbol{\theta}, \mathbf{y}^0(t)\}\mathbf{y}(t)\,\mathrm{d}t + B\{\boldsymbol{\theta}, \mathbf{y}^0(t)\}\mathbf{z}(t)\,\mathrm{d}t + \boldsymbol{\eta}(\mathrm{d}t), \tag{28}$$

where A and B are the matrices given by the linearization about $\mathbf{y}^0(t)$ and $\boldsymbol{\eta}(\mathrm{d}t)$ is assumed to be a vector of white-noise innovations with properties similar to the disturbances in (4). Integrating (28) over the interval $(t-1, t)$ gives

$$\mathbf{y}(t) - \mathbf{y}(t-1) = A\int_{t-1}^{t} \mathbf{y}(s)\,\mathrm{d}s + B\int_{t-1}^{t} \mathbf{z}(s)\,\mathrm{d}s + \int_{t-1}^{t} \boldsymbol{\eta}(\mathrm{d}s). \tag{29}$$

The solution of (28) is

$$\mathbf{y}(t) = \mathrm{e}^{A}\mathbf{y}(t-1) + \int_{t-1}^{t} \mathrm{e}^{(t-s)A}B\mathbf{z}(s)\,\mathrm{d}s + \int_{t-1}^{t} \mathrm{e}^{(t-s)A}\boldsymbol{\eta}(\mathrm{d}s) \tag{30}$$

so that from (29) and (30) and the properties of $\boldsymbol{\eta}(\mathrm{d}s)$, the best linear unbiased estimator of $\mathbf{y}(t)$ is

$$\tilde{\mathbf{y}}(t) = [\mathrm{e}^{A} - I]^{-1}\,\mathrm{e}^{A}A\int_{t-1}^{t} \mathbf{y}(s)\,\mathrm{d}s + [\mathrm{e}^{A} - I]^{-1}\,\mathrm{e}^{A}\int_{t-1}^{t} [I - \mathrm{e}^{(t-s-1)A}]B\mathbf{z}(s)\,\mathrm{d}s. \tag{31}$$

For flow variables, $\int_{t-1}^{t} \mathbf{y}(s)\,\mathrm{d}s = \mathbf{y}^0(t)$, the observed values of the flow variables over the observation interval $(t-1, t)$, so that the values of the flow variables at the point $t-1$, which are required to initialize the system for the solution over interval $(t-1, t)$, are given by

$$\tilde{\mathbf{y}}(t-1) = [\mathrm{e}^{A} - I]^{-1}\,\mathrm{e}^{A}A\mathbf{y}^0(t-1) + [\mathrm{e}^{A} - I]^{-1}\,\mathrm{e}^{A}\int_{t-2}^{t-1} [I - \mathrm{e}^{(t-s-2)A}]B\mathbf{z}(s)\,\mathrm{d}s, \tag{32}$$

where A and B are calculated for each $t-1$ by linearizing the nonlinear system about the point $\mathbf{y}^0(t-1)$, $\mathbf{z}^0(t-1)$.

In a mixed stock/flow system, some of the integrals in the vector $\int_{t-1}^{t} \mathbf{y}(s)\,\mathrm{d}s$ in (31) would need to be approximated. If $\mathbf{y}_f(s)$ in the integral is a flow or averaged variable, the integral is equal to the observed value of the variable; if $\mathbf{y}_f(s)$ is an instantaneously observable variable such as a stock or price, the integral would need to be replaced by an approximation, for instance,

$$\int_{t-1}^{t} \mathbf{y}_s(s)\,\mathrm{d}s = \tfrac{1}{2}[\mathbf{y}_s(t) + \mathbf{y}_s(t-1)], \tag{33}$$

and this approximation should also be used in each successive linearization to form

A and B in (32). The integral of the exogenous variables could be calculated as in the linear exact discrete estimator (Wymer 1976). The values of the variables required to initialize the system at the point $t - 1$ would be the observation $\mathbf{y}_s(t-1)$ for stock and price variables and the interpolated value $\tilde{\mathbf{y}}_f(t-1)$ for flow variables.

This procedure is attractive in that it uses all the information available in the model to estimate the initial values of the flow variables for each solution interval and it is particularly so if all the variables in the model are flows. The errors introduced by the linearization of the system and by any approximation of other variables, however, raise the question of whether this procedure would be more accurate than the direct interpolation of initial values from the discrete series in a general model.

Higher Order Systems

Economic models are often higher order systems of differential equations so that the set of functions $\boldsymbol{\phi}$ will contain variables which are derivatives of other variables in the system. For example, the model may contain investment, I, defined as the rate of change of the capital stock or the rate of change of an exchange rate, π, where only the level of capital stock, K, or exchange rate, e, is observed at a point in time. The model will therefore include equations such as $\mathrm{D}K(t) = I(t)$ or $\mathrm{D}e(t) = \pi(t)$ and the functions $\boldsymbol{\phi}$ will contain $I(t)$, $K(t)$, $\pi(t)$ and $e(t)$ as arguments. A mixed second-order model, for example, may be written

$$\mathrm{d}[\mathrm{D}\mathbf{y}_1(t)] = \boldsymbol{\phi}_1[\mathrm{D}\mathbf{y}_1(t), \mathbf{y}_2(t), \mathbf{y}_1(t), \mathbf{z}(t), \boldsymbol{\theta}] + \boldsymbol{\zeta}_1(\mathrm{d}t), \tag{34}$$

$$\mathrm{d}\mathbf{y}_2(t) = \boldsymbol{\phi}_2[\mathrm{D}\mathbf{y}_1(t), \mathbf{y}_2(t), \mathbf{y}_1(t), \mathbf{z}(t), \boldsymbol{\theta}] + \boldsymbol{\zeta}_2(\mathrm{d}t), \tag{35}$$

where $\mathbf{y}_1(t)$ is assumed to be mean square differentiable and D is the mean square differential operator. Although such higher order systems may formally be reduced to first order by introducing additional variables and identities of the form

$$\mathrm{D}\mathbf{y}_1(t) = \mathbf{y}_3(t), \tag{36}$$

generally only the level of the variable $\mathbf{y}_1(t)$ is observed at a point in time. Thus the estimation of such systems is not a simple extension of the first-order case but must be considered specifically. As suggested by Bergstrom (1984), the assumption that the disturbances of the differential equation system are white-noise innovations may more easily be justified in higher order systems than in first-order ones.

In the second-order model (34) and (35), and similarly in higher order models, the initial conditions $\tilde{\mathbf{y}}_3(t-1)$ necessary to calculate the trajectories of the system for each observation period may be derived from the derivative of a cubic fitted through the points $\mathbf{y}_1(t-3)$, $\mathbf{y}_1(t-2)$, $\mathbf{y}_1(t-1)$ and $\mathbf{y}_1(t)$, the derivative being evaluated at the point $t-1$, or they may be derived in a way similar to the flow variables in (32). The reason for using a cubic to interpolate stock or price variables which are observed at a point in time, and a quadratic to interpolate flow or averaged variables which are observed as integrals over time, is to allow the interpolation to be made over the same period and to allow one observation on either side of the period for which the solution trajectory is being found. For the trajectory in the interval $(t-1, t)$, a quadratic is used directly to approximate the initial condition for endogenous flow variables at each discrete point $t-1$, and the derivative of a cubic is used to estimate the initial value of endogenous rates of change at the same point. For the same trajectory, exogenous stocks and flows are interpolated from a cubic and a quadratic respectively. Derivatives of these variables can be calculated if required.

The residual for this variable over the observation period is

$$\mathbf{u}_3(t) = \int_{t-1}^{t} \mathbf{y}_3(s)\,\mathrm{d}s - \int_{t-1}^{t} \hat{\mathbf{y}}_3(s;\boldsymbol{\theta})\,\mathrm{d}s \tag{37}$$

or, from (36), for stock variables,

$$\mathbf{u}_3(t) = \mathbf{y}_1(t) - \mathbf{y}_1(t-1) - \int_{t-1}^{t} \hat{\mathbf{y}}_3(s;\boldsymbol{\theta})\,\mathrm{d}s. \tag{38}$$

Again, as in the flow model, the use of information prior to the point $t-1$ in the interpolation of the initial values of $\mathbf{y}_3(t-1)$ means that the integral forms residuals which are serially correlated. This "exact" estimator will again be asymptotically biased and that bias will depend on the interpolation procedure.

Higher Frequency Observations

The discussion so far assumes that the observations being used are equispaced. Although the national income statistics of most developed countries are now available quarterly, some price, employment and financial data such as the volume of money are monthly and other data such as interest rates, exchange rates, and commodity and financial prices are observed at high frequency. It is usually necessary to estimate macro-models using quarterly data, but commodity and financial markets, for example, may be estimated with higher frequency data. Maximum likelihod estimators of linear mixed stock and flow models using the Kalman filter have been developed by Harvey and Stock (1985) and Zadrozny (1988) to allow the parameters to be estimated from data observed at different frequencies.

In special cases, higher frequency data for some variables may be utilized in the exact nonlinear discrete estimator. High-frequency observations of exogenous variables, for example, could be used directly to give much more accurate interpolation of points on the continuous path of these variables; these data need not be equispaced. Phillips (1976a) has discussed the use of intermediate observations of exogenous variables in the context of the exact and approximate estimators of linear models. The error of approximation in the "exact" discrete estimator of a linear model with sufficiently smooth exogenous variables is of $O(\delta^{k+4})$ where k is the number of additional equispaced observations of the exogenous variables in each basic observation period δ and the variables are approximated using a polynomial of order $k+2$. If ε is the length of each intermediate observation period, then $\delta = (k+1)\varepsilon$. Thus if the basic time unit in the model is three months (say) and $\varepsilon = \frac{1}{3}\delta$ (that is, the intermediate observations are monthly) then $k = 2$ and the error of approximation as δ tends to zero is of order $O(\delta^6)$. For less stringent conditions on the form of the exogenous variables, the error of approximation and the corresponding asymptotic bias of the linear estimator will be greater. The extent to which these assumptions are realistic and their importance for empirical work is discussed in Phillips (1976b).

In the exact nonlinear discrete estimator, where higher frequency observations are available on exogenous variables, it is suggested that values on the continuous paths of the exogenous variables $\mathbf{z}(t)$ may be interpolated from a quadratic or higher order polynomial fitted to successive observations in the neighborhood of t. The observations need not be equispaced. If the higher frequency observations are equispaced with an observation interval ε, the error of approximation $\mathbf{z}(t) - \tilde{\mathbf{z}}(t)$ using a cubic interpolation at each point t will be of $O(\varepsilon^4)$ as ε tends to zero. This error would be negligible if ε were small relative to δ and the results for the linear model suggest that the corresponding asymptotic bias in the quasi-full-information maximum likelihood nonlinear estimator will also be small providing the exogenous variables are sufficiently smooth.

Similar data for some endogenous flow or rate of change variables could improve the estimation of initial values for the solution trajectory; the high-frequency data now available for interest rates, exchange rates and commodity prices, for instance, could be used for determining initial values for rates of change of these variables in second-order models of financial or commodity markets to a high accuracy. In these cases, levels of these variables can be observed directly as $\mathbf{y}(t)$, while rates of change can be observed almost directly as $(1/2\varepsilon)[\mathbf{y}(t + \varepsilon) - \mathbf{y}(t - \varepsilon)]$, with the high-frequency observation interval ε small relative to the observation period δ, instead of having to approximate the rates of change from $\mathbf{y}(t - 1)$, $\mathbf{y}(t)$, and $\mathbf{y}(t + 1)$. A higher order polynomial fitted to several observations in the neighborhood of t, $\mathbf{y}(t)$, $\mathbf{y}(t)$, $\mathbf{y}(t \pm \varepsilon)$, $\mathbf{y}(t \pm 2\varepsilon), \ldots$ would give an even better approximation. Thus, if ε is sufficiently small, using this approximation allows rates of change in the model to be treated as (almost) instantaneously observable variables with serially uncorrelated residuals as in (12), rather than as in (38).

An Exact Nonlinear Estimator Using Mixed Frequency Data

A more general Gaussian maximum likelihood estimator of nonlinear models using mixed frequency data can be derived. The model is assumed to be that given in (11) with all variables being observed instantaneously at points in time but with differing observation intervals; the observations on each variable are assumed to be equispaced. It will also be assumed that the basic time unit of the model is chosen to equal the longest observation interval; this interval will be defined as unity. The sample is assumed to consist of $T + 1$ observations of the least frequently observed variable with all variables $\mathbf{y}(t)$ being observed at the beginning and end points of the sample $t = 0$ and $t = T$.

Let the variables be ranked into l groups in order of frequency such that $\mathbf{y}(t)$ is a vector of variables with observation interval δ_i such that $\delta_i = 1/k_i$ for some integer k_i, $\mathbf{y}'(t) = \{\mathbf{y}'_1(t), \mathbf{y}'_2(t), \ldots, \mathbf{y}'_l(t)\}$. Thus for each δ_i and k_i the corresponding set of variables $\mathbf{y}_i(t)$ have $k_i T$ observations $\mathbf{y}_i(t - 1 + s\delta_i)$ for $t = 1, \ldots, T$, $s = 1, \ldots, k_i$, and observation $\mathbf{y}(0)$ is available for all variables. The discrete observations will be denoted $\mathbf{y}_i(t, s) = \mathbf{y}_i(t - 1 + s\delta_i)$, so that $\mathbf{y}_i(t, s)$ is observation s of variables of frequency group i in the interval $(t - 1, t)$. Let ε be the longest interval which is an integer fraction of all the observation intervals; that is, for each $i = 1, \ldots, l$ there is an integer k such that $k\varepsilon = \delta_i$. Let λ be such that $\lambda\varepsilon = \delta_l = 1$. Often $\varepsilon = \delta_1$. For instance, in the case of a sample with weekly, monthly, quarterly, and annual observations on different variables (assuming a 52 week year and neglecting the variation in the length of a month) $\delta_1 = 1/52$, $\delta_2 = 1/12$, $\delta_3 = 1/4$, $\delta_4 = 1$, and $\varepsilon = 1/156$. Thus $\mathbf{y}_2(t, 4)$ refers to the fourth monthly observation in year t.

Let $\hat{\mathbf{y}}(t)$ be the solution trajectory satisfying the model $d\hat{\mathbf{y}}(t) = \boldsymbol{\phi}\{\hat{\mathbf{y}}(t), \mathbf{z}(t), \boldsymbol{\theta}\}\,dt$ for given initial conditions and let $\boldsymbol{\omega}(t)$ be the error in these trajectories under the same conditions; the initial conditions, the solution, and the corresponding errors are defined as follows. For each integral t, the initial values are given for all variables at the point $t - 1$ and the model is integrated over each successive interval of length ε, that is, $(t - 1 + (s - 1)\varepsilon,\ t - 1 + s\varepsilon)$, for successive $s = 1, 2, \ldots, \lambda$ to give the solution $\hat{\mathbf{y}}(t - 1 + s\varepsilon)$. For each point $t - 1 + s\varepsilon$ which corresponds to an observation point $t - 1 + s_i\delta_i$ for some $s_i = 1, \ldots k_i$, the corresponding error in the solution trajectory is $\boldsymbol{\omega}_i(t, s) = \mathbf{y}_i(t, s_i) - \hat{\mathbf{y}}_i(t, s_i)$ where the discrete observations, solutions and errors at this point are denoted by $\mathbf{y}_i(t, s_i)$, $\hat{\mathbf{y}}_i(t, s_i) = \hat{\mathbf{y}}_i(t - 1 + s_i\delta_i)$ and $\boldsymbol{\omega}_i(t, s_i) = \boldsymbol{\omega}_i(t - 1 + s_i\delta_i)$. At this point, the initial conditions for the next interval of length ε are revised by setting the solution vector $\hat{\mathbf{y}}_i(t - 1 + s_i\delta_i)$ in $\hat{\mathbf{y}}(t)$ equal to the observation $\mathbf{y}_i(t, s_i)$. If $t - 1 + s\varepsilon$ does not correspond to an observation point, the initial conditions are unchanged; if $\varepsilon = \delta_1$ each point $t - 1 + s\varepsilon$ will be an observation point of variables $\mathbf{y}_1(t - 1 + s\delta_1)$ but may or may not be an observation point for other variables. The model is then integrated to find the solution at the next point $t - 1 + (s + 1)\varepsilon$. Thus for all $i = 1, \ldots, l$ such that $s\varepsilon = s_i\delta_i$, $s_i = 1, \ldots, k_i$, $s = 1, \ldots, l$, the solution $\hat{\mathbf{y}}_i(t, s_i)$ is conditional on the initial values $\mathbf{y}_i(t, s_i - 1)$, $s_i = \max(s_i\delta_i < s\varepsilon)$.

The corresponding errors are $\boldsymbol{\omega}_i(t, s_i) = \mathbf{y}_i(t, s_i) - \hat{\mathbf{y}}_i(t, s_i)$. Although each vector of errors $\boldsymbol{\omega}_i(t, s)$, $i = 1, \ldots, l$, $s = 1, \ldots, k_i$, is obtained from the integration of the model over an interval of length δ_i, where $\delta_l = 1$, the solution of the model depends on initial conditions for at least some variables as far back as $t - 1$ so that, in general, these errors are functions of all disturbances $\boldsymbol{\zeta}(ds)$ in the interval $(t - 1, t - 1 + s_i\delta_i)$. It follows from the properties of the disturbances that the vectors $\boldsymbol{\omega}_i(t, s_i)$, $\boldsymbol{\omega}_j(t, s_j)$ are correlated for all s_i, s_j within each interval $(t - 1, t)$. Thus the covariance matrices $E[\boldsymbol{\omega}(t, s_i)\boldsymbol{\omega}'(t, s_j)]$ will be nonzero for all $s_i = 1, \ldots, k_i$, $s_j = 1, \ldots, k_j$, $i, j = 1, \ldots, l$. The convolution integral which defines these covariances is such that for $i < j$ the covariances of $\boldsymbol{\omega}_i(t, s_i)$ and $\boldsymbol{\omega}_j(t, s_j)$ decline as s_i becomes smaller, that is, for given j and s_j $E[\boldsymbol{\omega}_i(t, s_i - 1)\boldsymbol{\omega}_j'(t, s_j)] < E[\boldsymbol{\omega}_i(t, s_i)\boldsymbol{\omega}_j'(t, s_j)]$ for all s_i. There is no correlation between errors in the intervals $(t - 1, t)$ and $(r - 1, r)$ for $t, r = 1, \ldots, T$, $t \neq r$, so that $E[\boldsymbol{\omega}_i(t - s, s_i)\boldsymbol{\omega}_j'(t, s_j)] = 0$ for all $s > 0$ and integral t.

In principle, the model may be estimated by a quasi-full-information maximum likelihood procedure. For a given set of initial values of the parameters $\boldsymbol{\theta}$ the solution trajectory can be found by a numerical integration procedure using successive observations as initial conditions. Within each interval $(t - 1, t)$, $t = 1, \ldots, T$, the observation $\mathbf{y}(t - 1)$ is used to initialize the integration procedure, which then provides the solution $\hat{\mathbf{y}}(t - 1 + \varepsilon)$ where ε is defined as above.[5] The derivation of the residuals $\mathbf{u}(s)$ is similar to that of the errors $\boldsymbol{\omega}(s)$ above.

The log likelihood function is

$$L^*(\boldsymbol{\theta}, \boldsymbol{\Omega}) = c^* - \tfrac{1}{2}\ln\det\Gamma^*(\boldsymbol{\theta}, \boldsymbol{\Omega}) - \tfrac{1}{2}\{u^{*\prime}(1)u^{*\prime}(2)\ldots u^{*\prime}(T)\}\Gamma^*(\boldsymbol{\theta}, \boldsymbol{\Omega})^{-1}\begin{bmatrix} u^*(1) \\ \vdots \\ u^*(T) \end{bmatrix}, \tag{39}$$

where

$$u^{*\prime}(t) = \{u_1(t, 1)\ u_1(t, 2) \ldots u_1(t, k_1)\ u_2(t, 1) \ldots u_l(t, 1)\} \tag{40}$$

and $\Gamma^*(\boldsymbol{\theta}, \Omega) = \{W_t^*(\boldsymbol{\theta}, \Omega)\}$ is a block diagonal matrix where each of the T blocks takes the form

$$W_t^*(\boldsymbol{\theta}, \Omega) = \begin{bmatrix} W_{11}(1,1) \cdots W_{11}(1,k_1) & W_{12}(1,1) \cdots W_{12}(1,k_2) & \cdots W_{1l}(1,1) \\ \vdots \quad \cdots \quad \vdots & \vdots \quad \cdots \quad \vdots & \cdots \quad \vdots \\ W_{11}(k_1,1) \cdots W_{11}(k_1,k_1) & W_{12}(k_1,1) \cdots W_{12}(k_1,k_2) & \cdots W_{1l}(k_1,1) \\ \vdots \quad \cdots \quad \vdots & \vdots \quad \cdots \quad \vdots & \cdots \quad \vdots \\ W_{l1}(1,1) \cdots W_{l1}(1,k_1) & W_{l2}(1,1) \cdots W_{l2}(1,k_2) & \cdots W_{ll}(1,1) \end{bmatrix}. \tag{41}$$

Each submatrix $W_{ij}(s_i, s_j) = E[\boldsymbol{\omega}_i(t, s_i)\boldsymbol{\omega}_j'(t, s_j)]$ for $i, j = 1, \ldots, l$, $s_i = 1, \ldots, k_i$, $s_j = 1, \ldots, k_j$. The matrix $W_t^*(\boldsymbol{\theta}, \Omega)$ is of order $\sum_{i=1}^{l} k_i m_i$ where k_i is the number of intervals of length δ_i in each interval $(t-1, t)$ and m_i is the number of variables in frequency group i. As the matrices $W_t^*(\boldsymbol{\theta}, \Omega)$ are independent of t, the subscript t will be dropped and the likelihood function written

$$L^*(\boldsymbol{\theta}, \Omega) = c^* - \tfrac{1}{2}T \ln \det \{W^*(\boldsymbol{\theta}, \Omega)\} - \tfrac{1}{2} \sum_{t=1}^{T} u^{*\prime}(t) W^*(\boldsymbol{\theta}, \Omega)^{-1} u^*(t). \tag{42}$$

The implicit restrictions on the covariance matrix $W^*(\boldsymbol{\theta}, \Omega)$ which would be inherent in the derivation from the integral of the error process would make the maximization of this function extremely difficult, if not virtually impossible. If T is sufficiently large, however, the matrix could be estimated without constraint and although this would be less efficient than the fully restricted model if it could be defined, it would be more efficient than neglecting the higher frequency data.

An alternative estimator can be defined which uses the extra observations on the higher frequency variables to give a better estimate of the variance and covariance of the errors $\boldsymbol{\omega}_i(t, s_i)$ than the single-frequency estimator, but under the assumptions that, to a reasonable approximation, for each $i, j = 1, \ldots, l$ the errors $\boldsymbol{\omega}_i(t, s_i)$ are serially uncorrelated, the variances of $\boldsymbol{\omega}_i(t, s_i)$ are the same for all s_i, and the covariances between $\boldsymbol{\omega}_i(t, s_i)$ and $\boldsymbol{\omega}_j(t, s_j)$ are the same for all s_i, s_j. In order for the residual covariance matrix to be well defined, it is necessary to restrict the frequencies of observation such that each δ_i is an integer multiple of δ_{i-1}, $i = 2, \ldots, l$. Hence, $\varepsilon = \delta_1$, and each higher frequency observation interval is fully enclosed within all lower frequency ones. For instance, this would exclude the use of a sample containing weekly and monthly observations.

Using the set of residuals $\mathbf{u}_i(t, s_i)$ for $t = 1, \ldots, T$, $s_i = 1, \ldots, k_i$ and $i = 1, \ldots, l$, the residual covariance matrix $V^* = (V_{ij})$ is defined as

$$V_{ii} = \frac{1}{T} \sum_{t=1}^{T} \sum_{s=1}^{k_i} \mathbf{u}_i(t, s)\mathbf{u}_i'(t, s) \qquad \text{for } i = 1, \ldots, l, \tag{43}$$

and

$$V_{ij} = \frac{1}{T} \sum_{t=1}^{T} \sum_{r=1}^{k_j} \left[\mathbf{u}_j(t, r) \sum_{s=1}^{k} \mathbf{u}_i'(t, (r-1)k + s) \right] \tag{44}$$

or

$$V_{ij} = \frac{1}{T} \sum_{t=1}^{T} \sum_{r=1}^{k_j} \sum_{s=1}^{k} \mathbf{u}_j(t, r)\mathbf{u}_i'(t, (r-1)k + s), \tag{45}$$

where $k = k_i/k_j$, $i = 1, \ldots, l$, $j = i + 1, \ldots, l$, and $V_{ij} = V_{ji}$.

Although it might seem that the double summation

$$V_{11} = \frac{1}{T} \sum_{t=1}^{T} \sum_{s=1}^{k_1} \mathbf{u}_1(t, s)\mathbf{u}_1'(t, s)$$

should be multiplied by $1/k_1T$ rather than $1/T$, the summation must be multiplied by $1/\delta_1 k_1 T$, that is $1/T$, in order to take account of the observation interval δ_1. This follows from the derivation of $E[\boldsymbol{\omega}_1(t)\boldsymbol{\omega}_1'(t)]$. Similarly, all the summations must be multiplied by $1/T$ only. Under the assumptions above, quasi-maximum likelihood estimates could be found by minimizing $L(\boldsymbol{\theta}) = \ln \det V^*$ with respect to the parameters $\boldsymbol{\theta}$. This estimator would be consistent under those assumptions, and, because of the additional observations being used, more efficient than the single-frequency estimator. In general, however, the assumptions will not hold, so that the estimator will be asymptotically biased but this deficiency may be offset by the greater efficiency of the estimator.

As an example, it may be useful to review the estimator for a model with some variables observed at monthly intervals, others quarterly, and the remainder annually. The basic time unit in the model is one year. The variation in the exact length of these intervals is ignored. Thus the sets of variables are $\mathbf{y}_1(t)$ with $\delta_1 = 1/12$ and $k_1 = 12$, $\mathbf{y}_2(t)$ with $\delta_2 = 1/4$ and $k_2 = 4$ and $\mathbf{y}_3(t)$ with $\delta_3 = k_3 = 1$, $\varepsilon = \delta_1 = 1/12$. For each interval $(t-1, t)$, $t = 1, \ldots, T$, the observation $\mathbf{y}(t-1)$ is used to initialize an integration procedure which provides the solution $\hat{\mathbf{y}}(t - 1 + 1/12)$. The residual of $\hat{\mathbf{y}}_1(t - 1 + 1/12)$ in the solution trajectory $\mathbf{u}_1(t, 1) = \mathbf{y}_1(t, 1) - \hat{\mathbf{y}}(t, 1)$ is calculated and the solution vector is then reinitialized by replacing $\hat{\mathbf{y}}_1(t - 1 + 1/12)$ by the observed value $\mathbf{y}_1(t, 1)$. The model is integrated to the point $t - 1 + 2/12$, the residual $\mathbf{u}_1(t, 2)$ calculated and $\hat{\mathbf{y}}_1(t - 1 + 2/12)$ replaced by $\mathbf{y}_1(t, 2)$ in the solution vector. Integrating to the point $t - 1 + 3/12$ gives the solution $\hat{\mathbf{y}}_1(t, 3)$ and the corresponding residual $\mathbf{u}_1(t, 3)$. Since $\delta_2 = 3\delta_1$, the residual $\mathbf{u}_2(t, 1)$ may be calculated from the observation $\mathbf{y}_2(t, 1)$ and the trajectory solution $\hat{\mathbf{y}}_2(t, 1)$ at that point. $\hat{\mathbf{y}}_2(t - 1 + 1/4)$ is then replaced by $\mathbf{y}_2(t, 1)$ and the procedure is then repeated for each successive observation interval $\{t - 1 + (s-1)/12,\ t - 1 + s/12\}$, $s = 1, \ldots, 12$. When $s = 12$ the solution of the full vector $\mathbf{y}(t)$ is used to form the residuals $\mathbf{u}(t)$ and the integration procedure is fully reinitialized. The covariance matrix of the residuals $V^* = (V_{ij})$ is given by

$$V_{11} = \frac{1}{T}\sum_{t=1}^{T}\sum_{s=1}^{12} \mathbf{u}_1(t, s)\mathbf{u}_1'(t, s), \quad V_{22} = \frac{1}{T}\sum_{t=1}^{T}\sum_{r=1}^{4} \mathbf{u}_2(t, r)\mathbf{u}_2'(t, r),$$
$$V_{33} = \frac{1}{T}\sum_{t=1}^{T} \mathbf{u}_3(t)\mathbf{u}_3'(t), \quad V_{12} = \frac{1}{T}\sum_{t=1}^{T}\sum_{r=1}^{4} \mathbf{u}_2(t, r)\sum_{s=1}^{3} \mathbf{u}_1'\{t, 3(r-1)+s\}, \tag{46}$$
$$V_{13} = \frac{1}{T}\sum_{t=1}^{T} \mathbf{u}_3(t)\sum_{s=1}^{12} \mathbf{u}_1'(t, s), \quad V_{23} = \frac{1}{T}\sum_{t=1}^{T} \mathbf{u}_3(t)\sum_{r=1}^{4} \mathbf{u}_2'(t, r).$$

Although the estimator has been defined for nonlinear models, it could, of course, be used to estimate linear models as a special case. The estimator may be extended to take account of occasional missing observations by continuing the integration procedure over two observation intervals without reinitializing; the corresponding residuals would be neglected. It may also be extended to mixed-frequency mixed-stock/flow models by combining the procedures suggested in the previous two sections. The errors of this "exact" nonlinear estimator would be serially correlated.

Empirical Applications

A computer program (Wymer 1990) has been developed to support applied work using the exact nonlinear discrete estimator.[6] The program calculates quasi-full-information maximum likelihood estimates of the nonlinear model as described above and these become true full-information maximum likelihood estimates for the "pure" exact model. The program is designed to estimate the more general model

$$\mathbf{\Phi}_1[\mathrm{d}\mathbf{y}(t), \mathbf{y}(t), \mathbf{z}(t)] = \mathbf{v}_1(\mathrm{d}t), \tag{47}$$

$$\mathbf{\Phi}_2[\mathrm{d}\mathbf{y}(t), \mathbf{y}(t), \mathbf{z}(t)] = 0, \tag{48}$$

providing that it can be written, at least implicitly, as (11). The set of variables $\mathbf{y}(t)$ and $\mathbf{z}(t)$ may include first- or second-order derivatives of other variables, and the model may also include zero-order identities. Thus the underlying general model, written in recursive form, is

$$\mathrm{d}D^2\mathbf{y}_1(t) = \boldsymbol{\phi}_1[D^2\mathbf{y}_1(t), D\mathbf{y}_2(t), \mathbf{y}_3(t), \mathbf{y}_4(t), D\mathbf{y}_1(t), \mathbf{y}_2(t), \mathbf{y}_1(t), \mathbf{z}(t), \boldsymbol{\theta}] + \boldsymbol{\zeta}_1(\mathrm{d}t), \tag{49}$$

$$\mathrm{d}D\mathbf{y}_2(t) = \boldsymbol{\phi}_2[D^2\mathbf{y}_1(t), D\mathbf{y}_2(t), \mathbf{y}_3(t), \mathbf{y}_4(t), D\mathbf{y}_1(t), \mathbf{y}_2(t), \mathbf{y}_1(t), \mathbf{z}(t), \boldsymbol{\theta}] + \boldsymbol{\zeta}_2(\mathrm{d}t), \tag{50}$$

$$\mathrm{d}\mathbf{y}_3(t) = \boldsymbol{\phi}_3[D^2\mathbf{y}_1(t), D\mathbf{y}_2(t), \mathbf{y}_3(t), \mathbf{y}_4(t), D\mathbf{y}_1(t), \mathbf{y}_2(t), \mathbf{y}_1(t), z(t), \boldsymbol{\theta}] + \boldsymbol{\zeta}_3(\mathrm{d}t), \tag{51}$$

$$\mathbf{y}_4(t) = \boldsymbol{\phi}_4[D^2\mathbf{y}_1(t), D\mathbf{y}_2(t), \mathbf{y}_3(t), \mathbf{y}_4(t), D\mathbf{y}_1(t), \mathbf{y}_2(t), \mathbf{y}_1(t), \mathbf{z}(t)], \tag{52}$$

where some of the $\boldsymbol{\zeta}_i(\mathrm{d}t)$ may be identically zero; in that case, the corresponding functions $\boldsymbol{\phi}_i$ will be nonparametric. Additional variables must be defined to reduce the system to first order as in (47) and (48).

The variables $\mathbf{y}(t)$ in (47) and (48) are defined as stocks (or other instantaneously observable variables), flows, averages, logarithms of flows or averages or first or second derivatives of these variables in the input, and the program then handles these variables and their residuals appropriately during estimation. The exogenous variables $\mathbf{z}(t)$ are defined in a similar way so that an (almost) continuous path can be interpolated at each step of the integration process. As the model is nonlinear, analytical functions of time may be specified. The program also allows exogenous variables which are constant through the observation interval to be specified, so that jump discontinuities may be defined. Endogenous switching functions, whereby certain parameters or functions become effective in the model depending on functions of endogenous variables, may also be defined by the appropriate use of transcendental functions. Such functions, and other discontinuities, must, however, be treated with caution.

The choice of defining endogenous variables $y(t)$ as natural numbers or as logarithms (or as some other function) will usually affect the properties of the model and the estimates of the parameters. The choice depends on the nature of the variables and the process being modeled. Unlike the linear estimators, the exact nonlinear estimator can treat these variables properly. Let $Y(t)$ be an endogenous variable defined as a natural number and $y(t)$ be the corresponding logarithm. With stock variables the relationship is simply $Y(t) = e^{y(t)}$ and $\mathrm{d}Y(t) = e^{y(t)}\,\mathrm{d}y(t)$. With flow variables, the observed value is defined as a natural number such that $Y^0(t) = \int_{t-1}^{t} Y(s)\,\mathrm{d}s$ and the logarithm of the observation is $y^0(t) = \ln Y^0(t)$. If the variable defined in the model is the logarithm of a flow $y(t)$, the estimator treats the variable similarly to a flow, except that it is the exponential of the variable which is integrated and the residual is defined as

$$u(t) = y^0(t) - \ln \int_{t-1}^{t} e^{y(s)}\,\mathrm{d}s. \qquad (53)$$

Average variables are treated in a similar way.

A variable-order variable-step Adams numerical integration procedure[7] is used to solve the system over each interval $(t-1, t)$, given the observed or interpolated values of the endogenous variables at the point $t-1$, and to integrate variables which are flows or rates of change as required. Let the system of first-order equations be

$$\mathrm{D}\mathbf{y}(t) = f[\mathbf{y}(t), t] \qquad (54)$$

the solution of which may be written

$$\mathbf{y}(t_{n+1}) = \mathbf{y}(t_n) + \int_{t_n}^{t_n+i} f[\mathbf{y}(s), s]\,\mathrm{d}s. \qquad (55)$$

Adams methods approximate this solution by replacing the integral by a polynomial, interpolating the computed derivative values of $f^{(i)}$, and then integrating the polynomial. The procedure used here allows both the step length $h = t_{n+1} - t_n$ and the order of the polynomial to vary to attain rapid solution to some specified accuracy. At the $(n+1)$th step, for a constant step size and constant order of the interpolating polynomial, the (PECE) algorithm on which the procedure is based predicts the value of $\mathbf{y}_{n+1}$ from the polynomial, evaluates the function f using that value, corrects the value of $\mathbf{y}_{n+1}$, and then evaluates the function using the corrected value of $\mathbf{y}_{n+1}$. The second evaluation is not made unless the estimated error at that point satisfies a local accuracy criterion; if not, the maximum step length that can be used, subject to the error test being satisfied, is calculated. The estimated errors for higher and lower order polynomials can be approximated at this point, without recalculating the function, and a decision made whether to increase or reduce the order of the interpolating polynomial.

Although the algorithm incorporates procedures to modify the order and/or step size at each step, it is designed to ensure that most steps are taken in groups with constant step size and constant order, since this increases the efficiency of the program. The program generally requires two function evaluations in each step, but if required the error in approximation of the integral can be obtained by evaluating the error at the midpoint of each step, in which case the number of evaluations per step is increased to three. The program incorporates measures to deal with discontinuities in the system which may be important in economic models. It should be noted that if the general form (47) and (48) is used, the cost of evaluating the implicit functions $\boldsymbol{\phi}$ is high since the system must be solved iteratively for every function evaluation.

Unlike earlier full-information maximum likelihood estimation programs developed by the author which use second-order Newton–Raphson iterative methods with analytical derivatives being evaluated explicitly, the complexity of the derivatives of the likelihood function of the exact nonlinear estimator makes it necessary to use a numerical minimization procedure. Whereas the earlier programs impose strict criteria for convergence, and hence find the maximum of the likelihood function with a high degree of certainty, the criteria for convergence used in this program are inherently weaker.

The program has been used in some preliminary work. Estimation of the 13 equation nonlinear model of the UK economy of Bergstrom and Wymer (1976) takes about 14 hours on an IBM PS/2 Model 80 to complete 29 iterations using the exact discrete estimates of the linearized model as initial values of the parameters. This model has 34 parameters and a sample of 48 observations. The time taken for estimation is much more heavily affected by the sample size in the exact nonlinear discrete estimator than in corresponding linear estimators, owing to the integration procedure used to solve the differential equation system, particularly if the model is written in the implicit form (47) and (48), rather than as an explicit recursive system. Other major determinants are the number of parameters in the model, the number of equations and, to a lesser extent, the proportion of endogenous flow or rate of change variables.

The program is also being used by Giancarlo Gandolfo and Pier Carlo Padoan to estimate their model of the Italian economy (Gandolfo and Padoan 1987) and by Kieran Donaghy and Denis Richard in estimating a model of exchange and interest rates, prices and money demand in the G5 countries (Donaghy and Richard 1992). The Italian model has 24 equations and 77 parameters and is being estimated with a sample of 100 observations on an IBM computer in the University of Rome. The exchange rate model has 13 equations and 88 parameters and is being estimated using a sample of 135 observations on an IBM supercomputer at Cornell University and a Cray X-MP/48 at the University of Illinois at Urbana-Champaign.

Notes

I am most grateful to Peter Phillips, Vivian Hall, Giancarlo Gandolfo and Denis Richard for their encouragement to write this paper and for their comments and to Rex Bergstrom for his interest and suggestions. I should also like to thank Peter Robinson, Pier Carlo Padoan and two anonymous referees for their comments on the paper. I wish to acknowledge the financial assistance of the Consiglio Nazionale delle Richerche in enabling me to visit the University of Rome at the invitation of Giancarlo Gandolfo to discuss this research with him and his colleagues. This paper was presented at The International Symposium on Economic Modelling, University of Urbino, Italy, 23–25 July, 1990.

1. Other estimators of general linear continuous-time systems such as those developed by Robinson (1976a, 1976b, 1976c) and others are discussed in Bergstrom (1988).
2. The stochastic properties of the equation

$$\mathrm{d}x(t) = m\{t, x(t)\}\,\mathrm{d}t + \sigma\{t, x(t)\}\zeta(\mathrm{d}t)$$

   where m and σ are non-linear functions of $x(t)$ and t are considered by Doob (1953).
3. This paper by Bailey et al. (1987) is essentially the same as an earlier version entitled *A Model of Output, Employment and Inflation in an Open Economy* which was presented at the 49th ANZAAS Congress in Auckland, New Zealand, in January, 1979.
4. As Bailey et al. (1987) have suggested, it is important to reinitialize the system for each observaton period in order to obtain consistent estimates of the parameters.
5. For the purposes of explanation it is assumed that the range of integration is always ε. In practice, the observation points on all variables are ordered in time and the model integrated from one observation point to the next irrespective of which variable is observed at that point. The solution and corresponding residual at each point would be better denoted by $\hat{\mathbf{y}}_i(t - 1 + s_i\delta^i; \hat{\boldsymbol{\theta}}, I)$ and $\mathbf{u}_i(t - 1 + s_i\delta_i; \hat{\boldsymbol{\theta}}, I)$ where $\hat{\boldsymbol{\theta}}$ refers to the current estimate of $\boldsymbol{\theta}$ and I is the set of initial conditions on which the solution is based. For simplicity of notation, the current estimate of $\boldsymbol{\theta}$ and the conditions I are omitted.
6. The program, called Escona, is written in Fortran 77 and versions are available for IBM mainframes and compatible machines and for personal computers. The PC version requires the Microway NDP Fortran compiler and Phar Lap assembler.
7. This procedure is based on algorithms of Krogh (1973, 1974) and implemented by Wymer (1979b). Discussions of these methods, and comparisons with other numerical integration procedures such as Runge Kutta, are contained in Hall and Watt (1976). It is considered that the method used here is numerically stable and requires significantly fewer derivative evaluations than other methods such as Runge Kutta, but has greater overhead. The procedure appears to be particularly robust, a necessary requirement given that the model must be integrated over each observation interval for each evaluation of the likelihood function, including those required for the approximations to the Hessian and gradient of the likelihood function.

References

Agbeyegbe, T. D. (1984). "The exact discrete analog to a closed linear mixed-order system," *Journal of Economic Dynamics and Control* 7, 363–75.

Bailey, P. W., V. B. Hall, and P. C. B. Phillips (1987). "A model of output, employment, capital formation and inflation," in G. Gandolfo, and F. Marzano (eds), *Keynesian Theory, Planning Models and Quantitative Economics: Essays in Memory of Vittorio Marrama*, Vol. 2, pp. 703–68. Milan: Giuffrè.

Bergstrom, A. R. (1966). "Non-recursive models as discrete approximations to systems of stochastic differential equations," *Econometrica* 34, 173–82.

Bergstrom, A. R. (1967). *The Construction and Use of Economic Models*, London: English Universities Press.

Bergstrom, A. R. (1978). "Monetary policy in a model of the United Kingdom," in A. R. Bergstrom, A. J. L. Catt, M. H. Preston, and B. D. J. Silverstone (eds), *Stability and Inflation*, chapter 6, pp. 89–102. New York: Wiley.

Bergstrom, A. R. (1983). "Gaussian estimation of structural parameters in higher order continuous-time dynamic models," *Econometrica* 51, 117–52.

Bergstrom, A. R. (1984). Continuous-time stochastic models and issues of aggregation over time," in A. Griliches and M. D. Intriligator (eds), *Handbook of Econometrics*, chapter 20, pp. 1146–212. Amsterdam: North-Holland.

Bergstrom, A. R. (1985). "The estimation of parameters in non-stationary higher-order continuous time dynamic models," *Econometric Theory* 1, 369–85.

Bergstrom, A. R. (1986). "The estimation of open higher-order continuous time dynamic models with mixed stock and flow data," *Econometric Theory* 2, 350–73.

Bergstrom, A. R. (1988). "The history of continuous-time econometric models," *Econometric Theory* 4, 365–83. Reprinted in G. Gandolfo (ed.) (1993). *Continuous Time Econometrics: Theory and Applications*, chapter 2, pp. 13–33. London: Chapman and Hall. (To appear.)

Bergstrom, A. R., and C. R. Wymer (1976). "A model of disequilibrium neoclassical growth and its application to the United Kingdom," in Bergstrom, A. R. (ed.) (1976). *Statistical Inference in Continuous-time Economic Models*, chapter 10, pp. 267–328. Amsterdam: North-Holland.

Donaghy, K., and D. M. Richard (1992). "Flexible functional forms and generalized dynamic adjustment in the specification of the demand for money," in G. Gandolfo (ed.) (1993). *Continuous Time Econometrics: Theory and Applications*, chapter 10, pp. 229–59. London: Chapman and Hall. (To appear.)

Doob, J. L. (1953). *Stochastic Processes*. chapter 6, pp. 273–91. New York: Wiley.

Gandolfo, G. (1981). *Quantitative Analysis and Econometric Estimation of Continuous-Time Dynamic Models*, Amsterdam: North-Holland.

Gandolfo, G., and P. C. Padoan (1987). *The Mark V Version of the Italian Continuous-Time Model*, Istituto di Economia della Facolta di Scienze Economiche e Bancarie, Sienna.

Hall, G., and J. M. Watt (eds) (1976). *Modern Numerical Methods for Ordinary Differential Equations*, Oxford: Clarendon Press.

Harvey, A. C., and J. H. Stock (1985). "The estimation of higher order continuous-time autoregressive models," *Econometric Theory* 1, 97–117.

Knight, M. D., and C. R. Wymer (1978). "A macroeconomic model of the United Kingdom," *IMF Staff Papers*, 25, 742–78.

Koopmans, T. C. (1950). "Models involving a continuous-time variable," in T. C. Koopmans (ed), *Statistical Inference in Dynamic Economic Models*, chapter 16, pp. 384–92. New York: Wiley.

Krogh, F. T. (1973). "Algorithms for changing the step size," *SIAM Journal of Numerical Analysis* 10, 949–65.

Krogh, F. T. (1974). "Changing stepsize in the integration of differential equations using modified divided differences," in *Lecture Notes in Mathematics No. 362*; *Proceedings of the Conference on the Numerical Solution of Ordinary Differential Equations*, pp. 22–71, New York: Springer-Verlag.

Phillips, P. C. B. (1972). "The structural estimation of a stochastic differential equation system," *Econometrica* 40, 1021–41. Reprinted in A. R. Bergstrom (ed.) (1976). *Statistical Inference in Continuous-time Economic Models*, chapter 5, pp. 97–122. Amsterdam: North-Holland.

Phillips, P. C. B. (1973). "The problem of identification in finite parameter continuous-time models," *Journal of Econometrics* 1, 351–62. Reprinted in A. R. Bergstrom (ed.) (1976). *Statistical Inference in Continuous-Time Economic Models*, chapter 6, pp. 123–34. Amsterdam: North-Holland.

Phillips, P. C. B. (1974). "The estimation of some continuous-time models," *Econometrica* 42, 803–24.

Phillips, P. C. B. (1976a). "The estimation of linear stochastic differential equations with exogenous variables," in A. R. Bergstrom (ed.) (1976). *Statistical Inference in Continuous-Time Economic Models*, chapter 7, pp. 135–74. Amsterdam: North-Holland.

Phillips, P. C. B. (1976b). "Some computations based on observed data series of the exogenous variable component in continuous systems," in A. R. Bergstrom (ed.) (1976). *Statistical Inferrence in Continuous-time Economic Models*, chapter 8, pp. 175–214. Amsterdam: North-Holland.

Phillips, P. C. B. (1978). "The treatment of flow data in the estimation of continuous-time systems," in A. R. Bergstrom, A. J. L. Catt, M. H. Preston, and B. D. J. Silverstone (eds) *Stability and Inflation*, chapter 15, pp. 257–74, New York: Wiley.

Phillips, P. C. B. (1987). "Asymptotic expansions in non-stationary vector autoregressions," *Econometric Theory* 3, 45–68.

Phillips, P. C. B. (1991). "Error correction and long-run equilibrium in continuous-time," *Econometrica*, 59, 967–80.

Robinson, P. M. (1976a). "Fourier estimation of continuous-time models," in A. R. Bergstrom (ed.) (1976). *Statistical Inference in Continuous-time Economic Models*, chapter 9, pp. 215–26. Amsterdam: North-Holland.

Robinson, P. M. (1976b). "The estimation of linear differential equations with constant coefficients," *Econometrica* 44, 751–64.

Robinson, P. M. (1976c). "Instrumental variable estimation of differential equations," *Econometrica* 44, 765–76.

Sargan, J. D. (1976). "Some discrete approximations to continuous-time stochastic models," in A. R. Bergstrom (ed.) (1976). *Statistical Inference in Continuous-time Economic Models*, chapter 3, pp. 27–80. Amsterdam: North-Holland. Previously published (1974) in abridged form in *Journal of the Royal Statistical Society*, Series B, 36, 74–90.

Sommariva, A., and G. Tullio (1987). *German Macro-economic History: 1880–1979; A Study of the Effects of Economic Policy on Inflation, Currency Depreciation and Growth*, chapter 3, pp. 121–59. London: Macmillan.

Wymer, C. R. (1970). *Computer Program: Discon*, London School of Economics and Political Science, mimeo.

Wymer, C. R. (1972). "Econometric estimation of stochastic differential equation systems," *Econometrica*, 40, 565–77. Reprinted in A. R. Bergstrom (ed.) (1976), *Statistical Inference in Continuous Economic Models*, chapter 4, pp. 81–95. Amsterdam: North-Holland.

Wymer, C. R. (1976). "Continuous time models in macro-economics: specification and estimation," mimeo. Paper prepared for the SSRC-Ford Foundation Conference on *Macroeconomic Policy and Adjustment in Open Economies* at Fanhams Hall, Ware, England, 28 April–1 May, 1976. Published in extended form in G. Gandolfo (ed.) (1993). *Continuous Time Econometrics: Theory and Applications*, chapter 3, pp. 35–79. London: Chapman and Hall. (To appear.)

Wymer, C. R. (1979a). "The use of continuous time models in economics," International Monetary Fund, unpublished manuscript.

Wymer, C. R. (1979b). *Program Manual: Apredic* (and supplement), International Monetary Fund, mimeo.

Wymer, C. R. (1990). *Program Manual: Escona*, mimeo.

Zadrozny, P. A. (1988). "Gaussian likelihood of continuous-time ARMX models when data are stocks and flows at different frequencies," *Econometric Theory* 4, 108–24.

Part III

Finite-Sample Theory

9

Some Further Exact Results for Structural Equation Estimators

Grant H. Hillier and Christopher L. Skeels

Introduction

The study of exact distribution theory for the statistics used in structural econometric models was pioneered by Basmann (1961) and Bergstrom (1962) 30 years ago. The subject is notoriously difficult and, notwithstanding a surge of progress in the 1980s, it is probably fair to say that our understanding of the properties of the various estimators and tests that are used remains far from satisfactory. Vastly improved computing technology may soon improve matters – in particular, by bringing higher order asymptotic results within reach – but the challenge to provide a coherent structure for inference in this model remains. Moreover, the lessons to be learned from these efforts are not confined to the structural model, for this model has much in common with the multivariate time-series models that are currently of such interest to econometricians generally – see Phillips (1988, 1989).

This paper extends the results available for the single structural equation model in two ways. First, we derive both a conditional and an unconditional version of the density of the limited-information maximum likelihood (LIML) estimator for the coefficients of the endogenous variables. Primitive versions of these results were initially given in Hillier (1987). The unconditional result provides an alternative to the expression given in Phillips (1985) for the density of the LIML estimator for these coefficients, and permits an immediate extension of the results in Phillips (1984a) for the ordinary least squares (OLS) and two-stage least squares (TSLS) estimators of the coefficients of the exogenous variables to the LIML case. Second, we provide exact expressions for the mean square error of the OLS and TSLS estimators of the coefficients of the exogenous variables. These results supplement the results in Phillips (1984a), Skeels (1989a, 1989b), and Hillier (1985b).

The conditional result for LIML hinges on a decomposition for positive definite symmetric matrices – theorem 1 in the fourth section – that is apparently new. This is a key result for this model, for the following reason. The single structural equation model is an example of a curved exponential model – that is, a model in which the dimension of the minimal sufficient statistic exceeds that of the parameter space, see Efron (1975), Barndorff-Nielson (1980), Hillier (1987), and Hosoya et al. (1989). In such models, marginal distributions of the type traditionally studied for this model are not the "relevant" bases for judging the merits of the procedures of interest, but should be replaced by particular conditional distributions. Theorem 1 in the fourth section provides a means of obtaining both a variety of joint distributions, and the conditional distributions relevant in this context. In our final section we briefly indicate how these results follow from theorem 1, but a detailed study of the curved exponential character of this model is not attempted here.

Model and Canonical Forms of Estimators

We consider a single (normalized) structural equation

$$y = Y\beta^* + Z_1\gamma^* + u, \tag{1}$$

with corresponding reduced form

$$(y, Y) = (Z_1, Z_2)\begin{bmatrix} \pi_1 & \Pi_1 \\ \pi_2 & \Pi_2 \end{bmatrix} + (v, V). \tag{2}$$

Here y is $N \times 1$, Y is $N \times n$, Z_1 is $N \times K_1$ and Z_2 is $N \times K_2$. We assume that $K_2 \geqslant n$, so that (1) is apparently identified, that $Z = (Z_1, Z_2)$ is fixed and of full column rank $K = K_1 + K_2$, and that the rows of (v, V) are independent normal vectors with mean zero and common covariance matrix

$$\Omega = \begin{bmatrix} \omega_{11} & \omega_{21}' \\ \omega_{21} & \Omega_{22} \end{bmatrix} \begin{matrix} 1 \\ n \end{matrix}. \tag{3}$$

We shall also refer to an un-normalized version of (1):

$$(y, Y)\beta_\Delta = Z_1\gamma^* + u. \tag{4}$$

The compatibility of (1) with (2) entails the relations

$$\pi_1 - \Pi_1\beta^* = \gamma^*, \qquad ((\pi_1, \Pi_1)\beta_\Delta = \gamma^*), \tag{5}$$

$$\pi_2 - \Pi_2\beta^* = 0, \qquad ((\pi_2, \Pi_2)\beta_\Delta = 0), \tag{6}$$

and $u = v - V\beta^*$ $(u = (v, V)\beta_\Delta)$, where the relations in brackets refer to the un-normalized equation (4). We shall assume that (1) (and (4)) are compatible with (2), but defer for the moment any assumption on the identification of (1) and (4).

The OLS and TSLS estimators for γ^* in (1) are of the form

$$g = (Z_1'Z_1)^{-1}Z_1'(y - Yb), \tag{7}$$

where b denotes the OLS or TSLS estimator for β^* in (1). The LIML estimator for

γ^* is given by

$$g_1 = (Z_1'Z_1)^{-1}Z_1'(y, Y)\tilde{\beta}_\Delta, \tag{8}$$

where $\tilde{\beta}_\Delta$ is any $(n + 1) \times 1$ vector that maximizes

$$\beta_\Delta'(y, Y)'P(y, Y)\beta_\Delta/\beta_\Delta'(y, Y)'(P_1 - P)(y, Y)\beta_\Delta, \tag{9}$$

where $P = I - Z(Z'Z)^{-1}Z'$ and $P_1 = I - Z_1(Z_1'Z_1)^{-1}Z_1'$. Now, $\tilde{\beta}_\Delta$ is determined by (9) only up to a scalar multiple, or, to put this another way, only the direction of $\tilde{\beta}_\Delta$ is determined, not its length. Thus, g_1 in (8) is well-defined only when $\tilde{\beta}_\Delta$ is normalized in some way, and $\tilde{\beta}_\Delta$ can, but need not, be normalized to correspond with (1). Partitioning $\tilde{\beta}_\Delta$ as $\tilde{\beta}_\Delta = (\tilde{\beta}_{\Delta 1}, \tilde{\beta}_{\Delta 2}')'$, with $\tilde{\beta}_{\Delta 2}$ $n \times 1$, we set $b = -\tilde{\beta}_{\Delta 1}^{-1}\tilde{\beta}_{\Delta 2}$ (note that b is uniquely defined even though $\tilde{\beta}_\Delta$ is not), and define the LIML estimator for γ^* in the normalized equation, (1), as in (7). Since this normalization for the LIML estimator is probably the most common, (7) covers all of the estimators for γ^* that are in common use, and is the version of the LIML estimator that we shall discuss. However, it would be of considerable interest to study the impact (if any) of the normalization rule adopted for $\tilde{\beta}_\Delta$ on the estimator g_1 in (8), but that is a subject for another paper. The effect of the normalization rule on the properties of the estimators for β^* and β_Δ is studied in Hillier (1990).

Joint sufficient statistics for (π_1, Π_1), (π_2, Π_2), and Ω are $(\tilde{\pi}_1, \tilde{\Pi}_1) = (Z_1'Z_1)^{-1}Z_1'(y, Y)$, $(\hat{\pi}_2, \hat{\Pi}_2) = (Z_2'P_1Z_2)^{-1}Z_2'P_1(y, Y)$, and $S^* = (y, Y)'P(y, Y)$. Let

$$T = \begin{bmatrix} 1/\omega & , & 0 \\ -\alpha/\omega & , & \Omega_{22}^{-1/2} \end{bmatrix}, \tag{10}$$

where $\omega^2 = \omega_{11} - \omega_{21}'\Omega_{22}^{-1}\omega_{21}$ and $\alpha = \Omega_{22}^{-1}\omega_{21}$, so that $T'\Omega T = I_{n+1}$, and define

$$(x_1, X_1) = (Z_1'Z_1)^{1/2}(\tilde{\pi}_1, \tilde{\Pi}_1)T, \tag{11}$$

$$(x, X) = (Z_2'P_1Z_2)^{1/2}(\hat{\pi}_2, \hat{\Pi}_2)T, \tag{12}$$

$$S = T'S^*T. \tag{13}$$

It is straightforward to check that (x_1, X_1), (x, X), and S are mutually independent, that $S \sim W_{n+1}(m, I_{n+1})$, where $m = N - K$, and that the rows of both (x_1, X_1) and (x, X) are independent normal vectors with covariance matrix I_{n+1}, with

$$E(x_1, X_1) = (Z_1'Z_1)^{-1/2}Z_1'Z(\pi, \Pi)T = (m_1, M_1), \tag{14}$$

say, and

$$E(x, X) = (Z_2'P_1Z_2)^{1/2}(\pi_2, \Pi_2)T = (\mu, M), \tag{15}$$

say, where $\pi = (\pi_1', \pi_2')'$ and $\Pi = (\Pi_1', \Pi_2')'$.

The canonical forms of the OLS, LIML, and TSLS estimators for β^* are

$$r_0 = (X'X + S_{22})^{-1}(X'x + s_{21}), \tag{16}$$

$$r_1 = -h_1^{-1}h_2, \tag{17}$$

$$r_2 = (X'X)^{-1}X'x \tag{18}$$

respectively, where S has been partitioned to conform with the partition of Ω above, and $h = (h_1, h_2')'$ is any characteristic vector satisfying $[S - f_1(x, X)'(x, X)]h = 0$, with f_1 the largest root of $|S - f(x, X)'(x, X)| = 0$. It is easy to check that, in each case, r and b are related by

$$r = \Omega_{22}^{1/2}(b - \alpha)/\omega. \tag{19}$$

Defining $s = (Z_1'Z_1)^{1/2}g/\omega$, the canonical statistics to be studied below for the normalized case are of the form

$$s_i = x_1 - X_1 r_i, \qquad i = 0, 1, 2. \tag{20}$$

The statistics r_i $(i = 0, 1, 2)$, and hence the s_i in (20), are well-defined as long as $N - K \geqslant n + 1$ and $K_2 \geqslant n + 1$, whether or not equation (1) (or (4)) is identified. In what follows, special cases of some results are given under various simplifying assumptions, some of which imply lack of identification. The implications of these assumptions will be discussed below, but for the moment we note that if rank $(\Pi_2) = n$ and rank $(\pi_2, \Pi_2) = n$, both β^* and β_Δ in (5) are uniquely defined except that β_Δ is determined only up to scale. Equation (5) is then a *definition* of γ^* as a function of (π_1, Π_1) and β^* (or β_Δ), and hence as a function of (π_1, Π_1) and (π_2, Π_2). Defining

$$\beta = \Omega_{22}^{1/2}(\beta^* - \alpha)/\omega, \qquad \eta = T^{-1}\beta_\Delta, \tag{21}$$

and $\gamma = (Z_1'Z_1)^{1/2}\gamma^*/\omega$, these too are uniquely defined and, in (14) and (15), we have

$$m_1 = E(x_1) = \gamma + M_1\beta, \qquad \gamma = (m_1, M_1)\eta, \tag{22}$$

and $\mu = E(x) = M\beta$, $(\mu, M)\eta = 0$. Note that $\beta = 0$ if and only if Y is independent of u in (1).

Some Conditional Results

Since (x_1, X_1) is independent of (x, X) and S, it is independent of all functions of (x, X) and S, including the three statistics r_0, r_1, and r_2, and the largest root, f_1, associated with the LIML procedure. Using r to denote any one of r_0, r_1, r_2, and setting $s = x_1 - X_1 r$, it follows at once that, given r,

$$s|r \sim N(m_1 - M_1 r, (1 + r'r)I). \tag{23}$$

The densities of r_0, r_1, and r_2 are known – see the next two sections – so that the joint density PDF(s, r) is easily obtained, and the marginal density of s can, in principle, be obtained from the relation

$$\text{PDF}(s) = \int_{R^n} \text{PDF}(s|r)\,\text{PDF}(r)\,\mathrm{d}r. \tag{24}$$

This is the procedure followed in Phillips (1984a), who gives results for the OLS and TSLS estimators. Skeels (1989a, 1989b) also obtains results for the OLS/TSLS estimators using a somewhat different approach. In the next section, we derive an expression for the density of the LIML estimator r_1 that makes it possible to evaluate the integral in (24) for the LIML case by exactly the method that Phillips (1984a) uses to evaluate (24) for the OLS/TSLS estimators. In the remainder of this section we derive some simple consequences of (23) and (24).

First, it is known that the densities of the OLS and TSLS estimators r_0 and r_2 are identical except in respect of a single "degrees of freedom" parameter, v, which is $N - K_1$ for OLS, K_2 for TSLS (see equation (62) below). Hence, (24) implies that PDF(s) also differs between these two cases only in respect of v, and we shall henceforth make no distinction between these two estimators.

Next, consider an arbitrary fixed linear combination of r and s:

$$w = a_1'r + a_2's = a_2'x_1 + (a_1 - X_1'a_2)'r \tag{25}$$

with $a_2 \neq 0$, and a_2 normalized, if necessary, so that $a_2'a_2 = 1$. It follows from (23) that, given r,

$$w|r \sim N(a_2'm_1 - (M_1'a_2 - a_1)'r, (1 + r'r)). \tag{26}$$

The unconditional density of w can be obtained from (26) by the analog of (24), and it follows from this that the density of an arbitrary linear combination of r and s has precisely the same form as the density of s itself upon making the substitutions $m_1 \to a_2'm_1$; $M_1 \to (M_1'a_2 - a_1)'$; $K_1 \to 1$ for terms that originate from PDF$(s|r)$. The results in Phillips (1984a) and Skeels (1989a, 1989b) therefore cover not just the density of s for the OLS/TSLS estimators, but also the densities of arbitrary linear combinations of r and s. The results below for the LIML estimator extend in the same way, but we leave the details to the reader.

It is clear from (23) and (26) that the LIML estimator s_1 has no moments, because r_1 has none, and that for the OLS and TSLS estimators the moments of s exist up to the same order as those of the r from which it was constructed (i.e. $v - n$). Note also that, for OLS and TSLS,

$$E(w) = a_2'm_1 - (M_1'a_2 - a_1)'E(r). \tag{27}$$

In the case of an identified equation it follows from (22) that w is an unbiased estimator for $w_0 = a_1'\beta + a_2'\gamma$ only if either $E(r) = \beta$, which is true only if $\beta = 0$, or $a_1 = M_1'a_2$, a very special case. The moments of w are discussed in detail in Skeels (1989a) and will not be considered further here.

For an identified, normalized, equation we have $m_1 = \gamma + M_1\beta$, and (23) can be written as

$$s|r \sim N(\gamma + M_1(\beta - r), (1 + r'r)I). \tag{28}$$

Hence, in this case, given r,

$$[(s - \gamma)'(s - \gamma)/(1 + r'r)]|r \sim \chi'^2(K_1, (r - \beta)'M'_1M_1(r - \beta)/(1 + r'r)). \tag{29}$$

Defining, for the identified case, $q = (s - \gamma)'(s - \gamma)$, the conditional density of q given r can be found easily from (29), and the unconditional density from a formula analogous to (24). The unconditional distribution function of q gives the probability content of spherical regions centered at γ. Some properties of q for the OLS/TSLS estimators are given later.

The mean of q (i.e. MSE (s) in the identified case) does not exist for the LIML estimator, but for the OLS/TSLS estimators is given by (if $v - n > 2$)

$$\text{MSE}(s) = E_r[K_1(1 + r'r) + (r - \beta)'M'_1M_1(r - \beta)]. \tag{30}$$

Several properties of the OLS/TSLS estimators can be deduced fairly easily from (30). First, it is clear that MSE (s) $\geqslant K_1$, its value in the simple regression ($\beta^* = 0$) case. However, a greater lower bound can be obtained by completing the square in r in (30) and noting that the expectation of the resulting quadratic term in r cannot be negative. This gives the lower bound

$$\text{MSE}(s) \geqslant K_1 + \beta'M'_1[I_{K_1} - M_1A_1^{-1}M'_1]M_1\beta, \tag{31}$$

where $A_1 = K_1I_n + M'_1M_1$. Second, it follows from (18) and the properties of the matrix (x, X) that, given X, $r_2|X \sim N((X'X)^{-1}X'M\beta, (X'X)^{-1})$. Evaluating the expectation in (30) conditionally, given X, we see that

$$\begin{aligned} \text{MSE}(s) = E_X\{&K_1 + \text{Tr}[A_1(X'X)^{-1}] \\ &+ \beta'[K_1M'X(X'X)^{-2}X'M \\ &+ (X - M)'X(X'X)^{-1}M'_1M_1(X'X)^{-1}X'(X - M)]\beta\}. \end{aligned} \tag{32}$$

Since the matrix [...] in the third term here is positive semidefinite for all X, and the density of X does not depend on β, it follows that, for the TSLS estimator, MSE (s) is necessarily larger when $\beta \neq 0$ (i.e. when Y is correlated with u in (1)) than it is when $\beta = 0$. The same result is easily obtained for the OLS estimator.

In some of the cases to be considered below, the structural equation is not identified, and in such cases q should be defined as either $q = (s - m_1)'(s - m_1)$, with a suitable definition of m_1, or, if $m_1 = 0$, simply as $q = s's$.

Density of the LIML Estimator for Endogenous Coefficients

Phillips (1985) has obtained an expression for the density of r_1 in an operator form. In this section we derive an expression for PDF (r_1) that is analogous to results obtained earlier for the OLS/TSLS estimators (see the next section). The approach used is quite different from that used in Phillips (1984b, 1985), and is based on a decomposition for positive definite symmetric matrices that is of independent interest (theorem 1 below). Symmetrically normalized analogs of the OLS/TSLS estimators for β_Δ in the unnormalized equation (4) may be defined and have densities identical to that of the LIML estimator except for certain numerical coefficients – see Hillier (1990). The results below for LIML can be extended to cover these estimators as well.

Since r_1 is a function of the independent matrices S and (x, X) we shall first find the conditional density of r_1 given the matrix (x, X). This can then be converted into the unconditional density by averaging with respect to the density of (x, X). Let

$$Q = \begin{bmatrix} t_2 & 0 \\ (X'X)^{1/2} r_2 & (X'X)^{1/2} \end{bmatrix}, \tag{33}$$

with r_2 as in (18) and $t_2^2 = x'[I - X(X'X)^{-1}X']x$, so that $Q'Q = (x, X)'(x, X) = W$, say, and define $R = (QS^{-1}Q')^{-1}$. Since S is independent of (x, X), it follows from Muirhead (1982, theorem 3.2.11) that, conditional on (x, X), $R|(x, X) \sim W_{n+1}(m, V)$, with $V = (QQ')^{-1}$. That is,

$$\text{PDF}\,(R|(x, X)) = C_1 \operatorname{etr}\{-\tfrac{1}{2}V^{-1}R\}|R|^{(m-n-2)/2}|V|^{-m/2}, \tag{34}$$

where $C_1 = [2^{m(n+1)/2}\Gamma_{n+1}(m/2)]^{-1}$.

If $\tilde{\mathbf{h}} = (\tilde{h}_1, \tilde{h}_2')'$ (with $\tilde{h}_2$ $n \times 1$) is a characteristic vector satisfying $[S - f_1 W]\tilde{\mathbf{h}} = 0$, with f_1 the largest root of $|S - fW| = 0$, then $r_1 = -\tilde{h}_1^{-1}\tilde{h}_2$. On the other hand, if $\mathbf{h} = (h_1, h_2')'$ is a characteristic vector satisfying $[R - f_1 I]\mathbf{h} = 0$, then $Q^{-1}\mathbf{h} \propto \tilde{\mathbf{h}}$ and, defining $r = -h_1^{-1}h_2$, we have $r = t_2^{-1}(X'X)^{1/2}(r_1 - r_2)$, or

$$r_1 = r_2 + t_2(X'X)^{-1/2}r. \tag{35}$$

That is, for fixed (x, X), r_1 is a simple function of r. Thus, we shall first find the conditional joint density of r, f_1, and another matrix B (defined in theorem 1 below), given (x, X), and then transform to PDF $(r_1, f_1, B|(x, X))$ using (35). The following theorem and its corollaries (proved in the appendix) give the details of the transformation $R \to (f_1, r, B)$, the corresponding transformation of the measure $dR = \bigwedge_{i \leq j} dR_{ij}$, and various joint and marginal densities when $R \sim W_{n+1}(k, V)$. Here, and throughout, we use the notational shorthand for various volume elements explained in Muirhead (1982, chapter 2).

Theorem 1 (a) *Let $R((n+1) \times (n+1))$ be a positive definite symmetric matrix, let $F = \operatorname{diag}\{f_1, f_2, \ldots, f_{n+1}\}$, with $f_1 > f_2 > \cdots > f_{n+1} > 0$, be a diagonal matrix containing the ordered characteristic roots of R, and let $H \in O(n+1)$ be an orthogonal matrix with columns the orthonormal characteristic vectors of R corresponding to the roots $f_1, f_2, \ldots, f_{n+1}$ respectively, with the elements in the first row of H positive. F and H as*

$$F = \begin{pmatrix} f_1 & 0 \\ 0 & F_2 \end{pmatrix}, \qquad H = \left(\begin{array}{c|c} h_1 & H_2 \\ h_2 & \end{array}\right), \tag{36}$$

with F_2 $n \times n$ and h_2 $n \times 1$, and define $r = -h_1^{-1}h_2$ and

$$B = f_1^{-1}(I + rr')^{-1/2}(r, I)H_2F_2H_2'(r, I)'(I + rr')^{-1/2},$$

so that $r \in R^n$ and $0 < B < I$. Then, the transformation $R \to (f_1, r, B)$ is one-to-one, and the volume element transforms as

$$\mathrm{d}R = f_1^{n(n+3)/2}(1 + r'r)^{-(n+1)/2}|I - B|\,\mathrm{d}f_1\left(\prod_{i=1}^{n}\mathrm{d}r_i\right)\mathrm{d}B \tag{37}$$

(b) *$R \sim W_{n+1}(m, V)$, then the joint density of (f_1, r, B) is given by*

$$\begin{aligned}\mathrm{PDF}\,(f_1, r, B) = {} & C_1 f_1^{m(n+1)/2-1}|B|^{(m-n-2)/2}|I - B|(1 + r'r)^{-(n+1)/2}|V|^{-m/2} \\ & \times \mathrm{etr}\left\{-\tfrac{1}{2}f_1 V^{-1}\left[(1 + r'r)^{-1}\begin{pmatrix}1\\ -r\end{pmatrix}\begin{pmatrix}1\\ -r\end{pmatrix}'\right.\right. \\ & \left.\left. + (r, I)'(I + rr')^{-1/2}B(I + rr')^{-1/2}(r, I)\right]\right\}.\end{aligned} \tag{38}$$

Note that, if $V = I$, r is independent of f_1 and B because the last term in (38) *does not depend on r.*

Corollary 1.1 *Assuming $R \sim W_{n+1}(m, V)$, the marginal density of (r, f_1) is given by*

$$\begin{aligned}\mathrm{PDF}\,(r, f_1) = {} & C_1^* f_1^{m(n+1)/2-1}(1 + r'r)^{-(n+1)/2}\,\mathrm{etr}\,\{-\tfrac{1}{2}f_1 V^{-1}\}|V|^{-m/2} \\ & \times {}_1F_1((n + 3)/2, (m + n + 2)/2; \\ & \qquad \tfrac{1}{2}f_1(I + rr')^{-1/2}(r, I)V^{-1}(r, I)'(I + rr')^{-1/2}),\end{aligned} \tag{39}$$

where $C_1^* = [C_1\Gamma_n((m - 1)/2)\Gamma_n((n + 3)/2)/\Gamma_n((m + n + 2)/2)]$.

Corollary 1.2 *Assuming $R \sim W_{n+1}(m, V)$, the marginal density of f_1 is*

$$\begin{aligned}\mathrm{PDF}\,(f_1) = {} & C_1^{**} f_1^{m(n+1)/2-1}\,\mathrm{etr}\,\{-\tfrac{1}{2}f_1 V^{-1}\}|V|^{-m/2} \\ & \times {}_2F_2(n/2, (n + 3)/2; (m + n + 2)/2, (n + 1)/2; \tfrac{1}{2}f_1 V^{-1}),\end{aligned} \tag{40}$$

where $C_1^{**} = 2\pi^{(n+1)/2}C_1^*/\Gamma((n + 1)/2)$.

By applying corollary 1.2 to PDF $(f_1 | W)$, this result can be used to obtain the unconditional density of f_1. Rhodes (1981) has obtained a result of this type for f_1, but his expression for PDF (f_1) involves unknown coefficients; we leave it to the reader to confirm that the expression obtained by using corollary 1.2 does not (set $V^{-1} = W$ in (40), multiply by PDF (W) in (44) below, and then integrate over $W > 0$).

Applying corollary 1.1 to the matrix $R = (QS^{-1}Q')^{-1}$, with $V = (QQ')^{-1}$, we obtain the conditional joint density PDF $(r, f_1 | (x, X))$. Transforming $r \to r_1$ using

(35) (Jacobian $t_2^{-n}|X'X|^{1/2}$) and simplifying, we obtain

$$\begin{aligned}\text{PDF}\,(r_1, f_1|(x, X)) = C_1^* \operatorname{etr}\{-\tfrac{1}{2}f_1 W\} f_1^{m(n+1)/2-1}|W|^{(m+1)/2} \\ \times (1 + r_1'r_1)^{-(n+1)/2}[h'Wh]^{-(n+1)/2} \\ \times {}_1F_1((n+3)/2, (m+n+2)/2; \tfrac{1}{2}f_1(G'W^{-1}G)^{-1}),\end{aligned} \quad (41)$$

where we have put

$$h = \begin{pmatrix} 1 \\ -r_1 \end{pmatrix}(1 + r_1'r_1)^{-1/2}, \qquad G = \begin{pmatrix} r_1' \\ I_n \end{pmatrix}(I + r_1r_1')^{-1/2}, \quad (42)$$

and $W = (x, X)'(x, X)$. Note that PDF $(r_1, f_1|(x, X))$ depends upon (x, X) only through W, and that

$$\begin{aligned}(G'W^{-1}G)^{-1} &= (I + r_1r_1')^{1/2}[(X'X)^{-1} + t_2^{-2}(r_1 - r_2)(r_1 - r_2)']^{-1}(I + r_1r_1')^{1/2} \\ &= (I + r_1r_1')^{1/2}X'[I - (x - Xr_1)[(x - Xr_1)'(x - Xr_1)]^{-1} \\ &\quad \times (x - Xr_1)']X(I + r_1r_1')^{1/2}.\end{aligned} \quad (43)$$

The conditional result in equation (41) can be used to obtain a number of interesting results that are useful for inference in this model. For example, on multiplying (41) by PDF (W), and then transforming $W \to (r_2, t_2^2, X'X)$, we obtain PDF $(r_1, r_2, f_1, t_2^2, X'X)$, and from this we can obtain, for instance, the joint density of the TSLS and LIML estimators, PDF (r_1, r_2). Some further results that follow from (41) are mentioned in the final section.

The matrix $W = (x, X)'(x, X)$ has the noncentral Wishart distribution with K_2 degrees of freedom and noncentrality matrix $(\beta, I)'M'M(\beta, I)$. That is,

$$\text{PDF}\,(W) = C_2 \operatorname{etr}(-\tfrac{1}{2}W)|W|^{(K_2-n-2)/2}{}_0F_1(K_2/2, (\beta, I)'M'M(\beta, I)W/4), \quad (44)$$

where $C_2 = [\operatorname{etr}\{-M'M(I + \beta\beta')/2\}/[2^{(n+1)K_2/2}\Gamma_{n+1}(K_2/2)]]$. Now,

$$\text{PDF}\,(r_1, f_1) = \int_{W>0} \text{PDF}\,(r_1, f_1|W)\,\text{PDF}\,(W)(\mathrm{d}W), \quad (45)$$

with PDF $(r_1, f_1|W)$ given by (41), and PDF (W) by (44). To evaluate the integral, we first transform to $\bar{W} = (h, G)'W(h, G)$ (the Jacobian is unity because $(h, G) \in O(n+1)$). Partitioning $\bar{W}$ as

$$\bar{W} = \begin{bmatrix} \bar{w}_{11} & \bar{w}_{21}' \\ \bar{w}_{21} & \bar{W}_{22} \end{bmatrix} \begin{matrix} 1 \\ n \end{matrix}, \quad (46)$$

we then put $U = \bar{W}_{22} - \bar{w}_{11}^{-1}\bar{w}_{21}\bar{w}_{21}'$, $z = \bar{w}_{21}$, and $w = \bar{w}_{11}$, the Jacobian again being unity. Note that, in (41), $h'Wh = w$ and, because $[(h, G)'W^{-1}(h, G)] = [(h, G)'W(h, G)]^{-1}$, $(G'W^{-1}G)^{-1} = U$. The argument of the ${}_0F_1$ function in (44) becomes

$$\bar{M}(\beta, I)'(h, G)\begin{bmatrix} w & z' \\ z & U + w^{-1}zz' \end{bmatrix}(h, G)'(\beta, I)\bar{M}'/4, \tag{47}$$

where $\bar{M}$ is any $n \times n$ matrix such that $\bar{M}'\bar{M} = M'M$. We can write this function as an inverse Laplace transform:

$$a_n\Gamma_n(K_2/2)\int_{\mathrm{Re}(Z)>0} \mathrm{etr}\,(Z)|Z|^{-K_2/2}\,\mathrm{etr}\,\{A_{22}U/2\}$$
$$\times \exp\,[wa_{11} + 2z'a_{21} + w^{-1}z'A_{22}z)/2](\mathrm{d}Z), \tag{48}$$

where $a_n = [2^{n(n-1)/2}/(2\pi \mathrm{i})^{n(n+1)/2}]$ and we have put

$$A = \begin{bmatrix} a_{11} & a'_{21} \\ a_{21} & A_{22} \end{bmatrix} = (h, G)'(\beta, I)'\bar{M}'Z^{-1}\bar{M}(\beta, I)(h, G)/2 \tag{49}$$

(cf. Herz (1955), Constantine (1963), and James (1964)). Since $|W| = |\bar{W}| = w|U|$, and $\mathrm{Tr}\,(W) = \mathrm{Tr}\,(\bar{W}) = w + w^{-1}z'z + \mathrm{Tr}\,(U)$, it is reasonably straightforward to integrate over $U > 0$ (using Constantine (1963, theorem 1)), and over $z \in R^n$ (by completing the square). This leaves

$$\mathrm{PDF}\,(r_1, f_1, w) = [(2\pi)^{n/2}2^{n(m+K_2)/2}\Gamma_n((m + K_2)/2)C_1^*C_2]$$
$$\times f_1^{m(n+1)/2-1}(1 + f_1)^{-n(m+K_2+1)/2}(1 + r_1'r_1)^{-(n+1)/2}w^{(m+K_2-n)/2-1}$$
$$\times a_n\Gamma_n(K_2/2)\int_{\mathrm{Re}(Z)>0} \mathrm{etr}\,(Z)|Z|^{-K_2/2}|I_n - A_{22}/(1 + f_1)|^{-(m+K_2+1)/2}$$
$$\times {}_2F_1((m + K_2)/2, (n + 3)/2; (m + n + 2)/2; f_1[(1 + f_1)I_n - A_{22}]^{-1})$$
$$\times \exp\,\{-\tfrac{1}{2}w(1 + f_1 - a_{11} - a'_{21}[(1 + f_1)I_n - A_{22}]^{-1}a_{21})\}(\mathrm{d}Z). \tag{50}$$

The term in the exponent of the last term in the integrand in (50) may be written as

$$-\tfrac{1}{2}w(1 + f_1)|I_n - \bar{M}(I + \beta\beta')\bar{M}'Z^{-1}/2(1 + f_1)|/|I_n - A_{22}/(1 + f_1)|. \tag{51}$$

Hence, integrating over $w > 0$, we obtain an expression which can be written in the form

$$\mathrm{PDF}\,(r_1, f_1) = C_3 f_1^{m(n+1)/2-1}(1 + f_1)^{-(m+K_2)(n+1)/2}(1 + r_1'r_1)^{-(n+1)/2}$$
$$\times [a_n\Gamma_n(K_2/2)/\Gamma_n((n + 1)/2)]\int_{\mathrm{Re}(Z)>0}\int_{R>0} \mathrm{etr}\,(Z)|Z|^{-K_2/2}$$
$$\times \mathrm{etr}\,\{-[I - G'(\beta, I)'\bar{M}'Z^{-1}\bar{M}(\beta, I)G/2(1 + f_1)]R\}$$

$$\times |I - \bar{M}(I + \beta\beta')\bar{M}'Z^{-1}/2(1 + f_1)|^{-(m+K_2-n)/2}$$
$$\times {}_2F_2((m + K_2)/2, (n + 3)/2; (m + n + 2)/2, (n + 1)/2;$$
$$f_1 R/(1 + f_1))(\mathrm{d}R)(\mathrm{d}Z), \quad (52)$$

where $C_3 = [2^{(m+K_2)(n+1)/2}\Gamma_{n+1}((m + K_2)/2)C_1^* C_2]$.

In the totally unidentified case with $M = 0$, we obtain at once from (52) PDF (r_1, f_1) = PDF (r_1) PDF (f_1) with

$$\text{PDF}\ (r_1) = \Gamma((n + 1)/2)[\pi(1 + r_1'r_1)]^{-(n+1)/2} \quad (53)$$

(cf. Phillips (1984b, 1985)), and

$$\text{PDF}\ (f_1) = C_4 f_1^{m(n+1)/2-1}(1 + f_1)^{-(m+K_2)(n+1)/2}$$
$$\times {}_2F_1((m + K_2)/2, (n + 3)/2; (m + n + 2)/2; f_1 I_n/(1 + f_1)) \quad (54)$$

with

$$C_4 = \frac{\pi^{(n+1)/2}\Gamma_n((m - 1)/2)\Gamma_n((n + 3)/2)\Gamma_{n+1}((m + K_2)/2)}{\Gamma((n + 1)/2)\Gamma_n((m + n + 2)/2)\Gamma_{n+1}(m/2)\Gamma_{n+1}(K_2/2)}. \quad (55)$$

Thus, in this leading case, r_1 and f_1 are independent. We shall see shortly that this it not true in general.

In the general case, first notice that (52) is invariant under $G \to GH$, $H \in O(n)$, because on making this substitution we can then transform $R \to HRH'$ and leave the integral unchanged. Hence, replacing G by GH and averaging over $O(n)$, the term etr $\{G'(\beta, I)'\bar{M}'Z^{-1}\bar{M}(\beta, I)GR/2(1 + f_1)\}$ in (52) is replaced by the generalized hypergeometric series ${}_0F_0^{(n)}(\bar{M}(\beta, I)GG'(\beta, I)'\bar{M}'Z^{-1}/2(1 + f_1), R)$. We may then use results from Davis (1979) to evaluate the inverse Laplace transform and obtain

$$\text{PDF}\ (r_1, f_1) = C_4\Gamma((n + 1)/2)[\pi(1 + r_1'r_1)]^{-(n+1)/2}\ \text{etr}\ \{-M'M(I + \beta\beta')/2\}$$
$$\times f_1^{m(n+1)/2-1}(1 + f_1)^{-(m+K_2)(n+1)/2}$$
$$\times \sum_{\alpha, \kappa; \phi} \frac{((m + K_2 - n)/2)_\kappa}{j!k!(K_2/2)_\phi}\, \theta_\phi^{\alpha,\kappa} C_\phi^{\alpha,\kappa}(\bar{M}(\beta, I)GG'(\beta, I)'\bar{M}'/2,$$
$$\bar{M}(I + \beta\beta')\bar{M}'/2) \times (1 + f_1)^{-(j+k)}\mathcal{G}_\alpha(f_1), \quad (56)$$

where

$$\mathcal{G}_\alpha(f_1) = [\Gamma_n((n + 1)/2)]^{-1}\int_{R>0} \text{etr}\,(-R)[C_\alpha(R)/C_\alpha(I)]$$
$$\times {}_2F_2((m + K_2)/2, (n + 3)/2; (m + n + 2)/2, (n + 1)/2; f_1 R/(1 + f_1))(\mathrm{d}R)$$
$$= \sum_{l=0}^{\infty}\sum_{\lambda} \frac{((m + K_2)/2)_\lambda((n + 3)/2)_\lambda}{l!((m + n + 2)/2)_\lambda((n + 1)/2)_\lambda}[f_1/(1 + f_1)]^l g(\alpha, \lambda), \quad (57)$$

with

$$g(\alpha, \lambda) = \sum_{\rho \in \alpha \cdot \lambda} \left\{ \sum_{\rho^* \equiv \rho} (\theta_{\rho^*}^{\alpha, \lambda})^2 \right\} ((n+1)/2)_\rho C_\rho(I)/C_\alpha(I). \tag{58}$$

The notation used here is explained in detail in Davis (1979) and Chikuse and Davis (1986).

The marginal density of r_1 itself may be obtained at once from equation (56) by simply integrating over $f_1 > 0$. This gives the density in the form

$$\text{PDF}(r_1) = C_5 \Gamma((n+1)/2)[\pi(1 + r_1' r_1)]^{-(n+1)/2} \operatorname{etr}\{-M'M(I + \beta\beta')/2\}$$
$$\times \sum_{\alpha, \kappa; \phi} \frac{a(\alpha, \kappa; \phi)}{j!k!} C_\phi^{\alpha, \kappa}(\bar{M}(\beta, I)GG'(\beta, I)'\bar{M}'/2, \bar{M}(I + \beta\beta')\bar{M}'/2), \tag{59}$$

with $C_5 = [\Gamma(m(n+1)/2)\Gamma(K_2(n+1)/2)C_4/\Gamma((m+K_2)(n+1)/2)]$, and

$$a(\alpha, \kappa; \phi) = \frac{((m + K_2 - n)/2)_\kappa (K_2(n+1)/2)_{j+k}}{(K_2/2)_\phi ((m + K_2)(n+1)/2)_{j+k}} \theta_\phi^{\alpha, \kappa}$$
$$\times \sum_{l=0}^{\infty} \sum_{\lambda} \frac{((m + K_2)/2)_\lambda ((n+3)/2)_\lambda (m(n+1)/2)_l \, g(\alpha, \lambda)}{l!((m + n + 2)/2)_\lambda ((n+1)/2)_\lambda (j + k + (m + K_2)(n+1)/2)_l}. \tag{60}$$

Equation (58) is exactly analogous to equation (63) below for the OLS/TSLS estimators.

When $n = 1$ (58) simplifies to

$$\text{PDF}(r_1) = C_5[\pi(1 + r_1^2)]^{-1} \exp(-d^2/2)$$
$$\times \sum_{j,k=0}^{\infty} \frac{a(j, k)}{j!k!} (d^2/2)^{j+k} [(1 + r_1\beta)^2/(1 + r_1^2)(1 + \beta^2)]^j, \tag{61}$$

where, from (60),

$$a(j, k) = [((m + K_2 - 1)/2)_k (K_2)_{j+k} (1)_j / (K_2/2)_{j+k} (m + K_2)_{j+k}$$
$${}_4F_3((m + K_2)/2, 2, m, j + 1; (m + 3)/2, 1, j + k + m + K_2; 1), \tag{62}$$

and we have put $d^2 = M'M(1 + \beta^2)$, a scalar in this case.

Densities of OLS/TSLS Estimators and Special Cases

The density functions of the OLS/TSLS estimators have the form (see Phillips (1980), Phillips (1983), and Hillier (1985a)),

$$\text{PDF}(r) = C_6(1 + r'r)^{-(\nu+1)/2} \operatorname{etr}\{-M'M(I + \beta\beta')/2\}$$
$$\times \sum_{\alpha,[k];\phi} \frac{c_\nu(\alpha, [k]; \phi)}{j!k!} C_\phi^{\alpha,[k]}(M'M(I + \beta r')(I + rr')^{-1}(I + r\beta')/2, M'M\beta\beta'/2) \tag{63}$$

where $\nu = N - K_1$ for OLS, $\nu = K_2$ for TSLS, the constant C_6 is given by

$$C_6 = [\Gamma((\nu + 1)/2)/\pi^{n/2}\Gamma((\nu - n + 1)/2)], \tag{64}$$

and the numerical coefficients $c_\nu(\alpha, [k]; \phi)$ are given by

$$c_\nu(\alpha, [k]; \phi) = ((\nu + 1)/2)_\alpha((\nu - n)/2)_k \theta_\phi^{\alpha,[k]}/(\nu/2)_\phi. \tag{65}$$

The remaining notation is explained in the references above.

Equation (63) for the OLS/TSLS estimators is evidently analogous to equation (59) for the LIML estimator, except that the numerical coefficients $a(\alpha, k; \phi)$ are much more complicated than the $c_\nu(\alpha, [k]; \phi)$ in (63), and the powers of $(1 + r'r)$ in the leading terms differ.

The special cases to be considered below are as follows.

Case A $(m_1, M_1) = 0$, $(\mu, M) = 0$. Here $E(y, Y) = 0$, equations (1) and (3) are totally unidentified, (23) becomes simply $s|r \sim N(0, (1 + r'r)I)$, (53) applies and (63) simplifies to

$$\text{PDF}(r) = C_6(1 + r'r)^{-(\nu+1)/2}. \tag{66}$$

In this case we take $q = s's$.

Case B $(\mu, M) = 0$, $(m_1, M_1) \neq 0$. Here Z_2 is not involved in the reduced form, and again the model is totally unidentified. This case yields the leading terms in the series expansions of PDF (s) and PDF (q) for the general case, and hence embodies some of the important properties of s and q. Here (23) and (66) apply, and $q = (s - m_1)'(s - m_1)$, with $m_1 = (Z_1'Z_1)^{1/2}(\pi_1 - \Pi_1\alpha)/\omega$ (not $\gamma + M_1\beta$, because β and γ are undefined).

Case C $\beta = 0$ (rank $(\mu, M) =$ rank $(M) = n$). Here the model is identified but Y is independent of u in (1). The density of the OLS/TSLS estimators in (63) simplifies to

$$\text{PDF}(r) = C_6(1 + r'r)^{-(\nu+1)/2} \operatorname{etr}\{-M'M/2\}\,{}_1F_1((\nu + 1)/2, \nu/2; M'M(I + rr')^{-1}/2). \tag{67}$$

The density of the LIML estimator in (59) does not simplify greatly. Here we may take $q = (s - \gamma)'(s - \gamma)$ and $\gamma \equiv m_1$.

We also give a number of results for the special case $n = 1$, because the general expressions are exceedingly complicated and difficult to evaluate numerically except when $n = 1$, or perhaps $n = 2$.

Mean and Density of q: OLS/TSLS Estimators

Case A $(m_1, M_1) = 0$, $(\mu, M) = 0$. Since, in this case, $s|r \sim N(0, (1 + r'r)I)$,

$$\text{PDF}\,(q|r) = [2^{K_1/2}\Gamma(K_1/2)]^{-1}(1 + r'r)^{-K_1/2}\exp[-q/2(1+r'r)]q^{K_1/2-1}, \quad (68)$$

and PDF (r) is given by (66). Multiplying (68) by (66), setting $r = vt$ $(v = r(r'r)^{-1/2}$, $t^2 = r'r$, $(dr) = 2^{-1}(t^2)^{n/2-1}(dt^2)(v'\,dv))$, and integrating over $v'v = 1$ and $t^2 > 0$, we obtain

$$\text{PDF}\,(q) = [2^{K_1/2}\Gamma(K_1/2)]^{-1}\exp(-q/2)q^{K_1/2-1}C(\nu, n)\,{}_1F_1(n/2, (\nu + K_1 + 1)/2; q/2), \quad (69)$$

where

$$C(\nu, n) = \Gamma((\nu + 1)/2)\Gamma((\nu + K_1 - n + 1)/2)/\Gamma((\nu + K_1 + 1)/2)\Gamma((\nu - n + 1)/2). \quad (70)$$

Also, it is straightforward to show that

$$E(q) = (\nu - 1)K_1/(\nu - n - 1). \quad (71)$$

Case B $(\mu, M) = 0$, $(m_1, M_1) \neq 0$. Using (23), we find that

$$\begin{aligned}\text{PDF}\,(q|r) = {} & [2^{K_1/2}\Gamma(K_1/2)]^{-1}(1 + r'r)^{-K_1/2}\exp[-q/2(1 + r'r)]\,q^{K_1/2-1} \\ & \times \exp[-r'M_1'M_1r/2(1 + r'r)]\,{}_0F_1(K_1/2; qr'M_1'M_1r/4(1 + r'r)^2). \quad (72)\end{aligned}$$

Multiplying (72) by (66), the integration over $r \in R^n$ can be accomplished as in case A above and we find

$$\begin{aligned}\text{PDF}\,(q) = {} & [2^{K_1/2}\Gamma(K_1/2)]^{-1}\exp(-q/2)\,q^{K_1/2-1} \\ & \times C(\nu, n)\sum_{j,k=0}^{\infty}\frac{(-1)^k}{j!k!}a_\nu^*(j, k)(q/2)^j C_{j+k}(M_1'M_1/2) \\ & \times {}_1F_1(j + k + n/2, 2j + k + (\nu + K_1 + 1)/2; q/2), \quad (73)\end{aligned}$$

with

$$a_\nu^*(j, k) = (\tfrac{1}{2})_{j+k}((\nu + K_1 - n + 1)/2)_j/(K_1/2)_j((\nu + K_1 + 1)/2)_{2j+k}. \quad (74)$$

The mean of q in this case is most easily obtained from

$$E(q) = E_r[K_1(1 + r'r) + r'M'_1M_1r]. \tag{75}$$

Multiplying (75) by (76), and integrating over r as before, gives

$$E(q) = [(v - 1)K_1 + \mathrm{Tr}\,(M'_1M_1)]/(v - n - 1). \tag{76}$$

Case C $\beta = 0$. Consider first the mean of q (=MSE (s)). Rewrite (75) in the form

$$E(q) = K_1 + E_r\{(1 + r'r)\,\mathrm{Tr}\,[A_1rr'(I + rr')^{-1}]\}. \tag{77}$$

Multiplying (77) by PDF (r) in (67), the resulting integral over r is evidently invariant under the simultaneous transformations $A_1 \to H'A_1H$, $M'M \to H'M'MH$, $H \in O(n)$, because, after making these transformations, we can then transform $r \to Hr$, leaving the integral unchanged. Hence, averaging the integral over $O(n)$, we find that the expectation of the second term in (77) is given by

$$C_6\,\mathrm{etr}\,\{-M'M/2\} \int_{r\in R^n} (1 + r'r)^{-(v-1)/2}$$

$$\times \sum_{\alpha,[1];\phi} \frac{((v + 1)/2)_\alpha C_\phi^{\alpha,[1]}(M'M/2), A_1)C_\phi^{\alpha,[1]}((I + rr')^{-1}, rr'(I + rr')^{-1})}{j!(v/2)_\alpha C_\phi(I_n)}\,(dr). \tag{78}$$

To evaluate the coefficients in (78) we use:

Lemma 1 *For* Re (t) > −1,

$$\int_{x\in R^n} (1 + x'x)^{-(t+n+1)/2} C_\phi^{\alpha,[k]}((I + xx')^{-1}, xx'(I + xx')^{-1})\,dx$$

$$= \frac{\pi^{n/2}\Gamma((t + 1)/2)((t + n)/2)_\alpha(\tfrac{1}{2})_k}{\Gamma((t + n + 1)/2)((t + n + 1)/2)_\phi}\,\theta_\phi^{\alpha,[k]}C_\phi(I_n). \tag{79}$$

Proof The integral on the left-hand side in (79) may be written as the Laplace transform (with $p = (n + 1)/2$):

$$\int_{R^n}\int_{S>0} \frac{\mathrm{etr}\,\{-S(I + xx')\}|S|^{(t+n+1)/2-p}C_\phi^{\alpha,[k]}(S, xx'S)}{\Gamma_n((t + n + 1)/2)((t + n + 1)/2)_\phi}\,dS\,dx.$$

Transform to $z = S^{1/2}x$ and evaluate the Laplace transform using Davis (1979), equations (2.12) and (2.2), to obtain

$$\frac{\Gamma_n((t+n)/2)((t+n)/2)_\alpha(\tfrac{1}{2})_k}{\Gamma_n((t+n+1)/2)((t+n+1)/2)_\phi(n/2)_k}\,\theta_\phi^{\alpha,[k]}C_\phi(I_n)\int_{R^n}\exp(-z'z\}(z'z)^k\,dz,$$

and this yields the right-hand side of (79).

Using (79) in (78) with $t = v - n - 2$, $k = 1$, gives (for $v > n + 1$)

$$E(q) = K_1 + \frac{(v-1)}{(v-n-1)}\operatorname{etr}\{-M'M/2\}P(M'M, A_1),$$

$$P(M'M, A_1) = \sum_{\alpha,[1];\phi}\frac{((v-2)/2)_\alpha((v+1)/2)_\alpha}{j!(v/2)_\alpha((v-1)/2)_\phi}\,\theta_\phi^{\alpha,[1]}C_\phi^{\alpha,[1]}(M'M/2, A_1/2) \qquad (80)$$

is a polynomial in the matrices $M'M$ and A_1, invariant under $M'M \to H'M'MH$, $A_1 \to H'A_1H$, $H \in O(n)$. When $n = 1$, (80) simplifies to

$$E(q) = K_1 + \left(\frac{\lambda_1 + K_1}{v-2}\right)\exp(-\lambda/2)\,{}_1F_1((v-2)/2, v/2; \lambda/2), \qquad (81)$$

where $\lambda_1 = M_1'M_1$ and $\lambda = M'M$. The second term in (81) is an increasing function of λ_1, a decreasing function of λ, and a decreasing function of v ($=K_2$ for the TSLS estimator).

The density of $q = (s-\gamma)'(s-\gamma)$ can be obtained by much the same argument and we find that

$$\text{PDF}(q) = [q^{K_1/2-1}/2^{K_1/2}\Gamma(K_1/2)]\operatorname{etr}\{-M'M/2\}\,C(v, n)$$
$$\times\sum_{i,j,k,l=0}^{\infty}\frac{(-1)^{i+k}(q/2)^{i+l}}{i!j!k!l!}\sum_{\alpha,\phi\in\alpha\cdot[k+l]}e_\phi^{i,\alpha,k,l}C_\phi^{\alpha,[k+l]}(M'M/2, M_1'M_1/2), \qquad (82)$$

with coefficients $e_\phi^{i,\alpha,k,l}$ equal to

$$\frac{((v+1)/2)_\alpha(i+l+(v+K_1)/2)_\alpha((v+K_1-n+1)/2)_{i+l}(\tfrac{1}{2})_{k+l}}{(v/2)_\alpha(K_1/2)_l(i+l+(v+K_1+1)/2)_\phi((v+K_1+1)/2)_{i+l}}\,\theta_\phi^{\alpha,[k+l]}. \qquad (83)$$

When $n = 1$ this reduces to

$$\text{PDF}(q) = \exp(-q/2)\,q^{K_1/2-1}/[2^{K_1/2}\Gamma(K_1/2)]C(v, 1)$$
$$\times\sum_{k,l=0}^{\infty}\frac{(\tfrac{1}{2})_l((v+K_1)/2)_{k+l}}{k!l!(K_1/2)_l((v+K_1+1)/2)_{k+2l}}(\lambda_1 q/4)^l p_k(\lambda, \lambda_1)$$
$$\times\,{}_1F_1(l+1/2, k+2l+(v+K_1+1)/2; q/2), \qquad (84)$$

where

$$p_k(\lambda, \lambda_1) = \exp[-(\lambda + \lambda_1)/2] \sum_{j=0}^{k} \binom{k}{j} [((v+1)/2)_j/(v/2)_j](\lambda/2)^j(\lambda_1/2)^{k-j}. \quad (85)$$

The General Case

To evaluate $E(q) = \text{MSE}(s)$ in the general case, first write (29) in the form

$$E(q) = K_1 + \beta' M'_1 M_1 \beta + \text{Tr}[A_1 E(rr')] - 2\beta' M'_1 M_1 E(r). \quad (86)$$

Now, using equations (46) and (48) from Hillier (1985a), the terms $E(rr')$ and $E(r)$ in (86) can be expressed as inverse Laplace transforms, and these can be evaluated using results from Davis (1979). Thus,

$$\begin{aligned} 2\beta' M'_1 M_1 E(r) = {} & \Gamma_n(v/2)\,\text{etr}\{-M'M/2\} a_n \int_{\text{Re}(W)>0} \text{etr}(W)|W|^{-v/2} \\ & \times {}_1F_0(v/2; M'MW^{-1}/2) \\ & \times \text{Tr}[\bar{M}(\beta\beta' M'_1 M_1 + M'_1 M_1 \beta\beta')\bar{M}' W^{-1}/2](\mathrm{d}W) \\ = {} & \text{etr}\{-M'M/2\} \sum_{\alpha,[1];\phi} \frac{(v/2)_\alpha}{j!(v/2)_\phi} \theta_\phi^{\alpha,[1]} \\ & \times C_\phi^{\alpha,[1]}(M'M/2, M'M(\beta\beta' M'_1 M_1 + M'_1 M_1 \beta\beta')/2), \end{aligned} \quad (87)$$

where $a_n = [2^{n(n-1)/2}/(2\pi \mathrm{i})^{n(n+1)/2}]$ and, as before, $\bar{M}$ is any $n \times n$ matrix such that $\bar{M}'\bar{M} = M'M$. Also,

$$\begin{aligned} \text{Tr}[A_1 E(rr')] = {} & \Gamma_n(v/2)\,\text{etr}\{-M'M/2\} a_n \int_{\text{Re}(W)>0} \text{etr}(W)|W|^{-v/2} \\ & \times {}_1F_0(v/2; M'MW^{-1}/2)\{\text{Tr}[\bar{M}A_1\bar{M}'W^{-1}\bar{M}\beta\beta'\bar{M}'W^{-1}]/4 \\ & + (1 + \beta'\bar{M}'W^{-1}\bar{M}\beta/2) \\ & \times \text{Tr}[A_1(I - \bar{M}'W^{-1}\bar{M}/2)]/(v-n-1)\} \\ & \times (\mathrm{d}W). \end{aligned} \quad (88)$$

This integral can be resolved into the following three terms:

$$\frac{\text{Tr}(A_1)}{(v-n-1)} \left\{1 + \text{etr}\{M'M/2\} \sum_{\alpha,[1];\phi} \frac{(v/2)_\alpha}{j!(v/2)_\phi} \theta_\phi^{\alpha,[1]} C_\phi^{\alpha,[1]}(M'M/2, M'M\beta\beta'/2)\right\},$$

(89a)

$$\frac{(v-n-2)}{(v-n-1)} \operatorname{etr}\{-M'M/2\}\left\{ \sum_{\alpha,[1];\phi} \frac{(v/2)_\alpha}{j!(v/2)_\phi} \theta_\phi^{\alpha,[1]} C_\phi^{\alpha,[1]}(M'M/2, M'MA_1/2) \right.$$

$$+ \sum_{\alpha,[1],[1];\rho} \frac{(v/2)_\alpha}{j!(v/2)_\rho}$$

$$\left. \times\, \theta_\rho^{\alpha,[1],[1]} C_\rho^{\alpha,[1],[1]}(M'M/2, M'MA_1/2, M'M\beta\beta'/2) \right\}, \tag{89b}$$

$$-\operatorname{etr}\{-M'M(I+\beta\beta')/2\}\left\{ \sum_{\alpha,[1];[l];\rho} \frac{(v/2)_\alpha (1)_l}{j!l!(v/2)_\rho} \theta_\rho^{\alpha,[1],[l]} \right.$$

$$\left. \times\, C_\rho^{\alpha,[1],[l]}(M'M(I+\beta\beta')/2, M'MA_1/2, M'M\beta\beta'/2) \right\}. \tag{89c}$$

Inserting equations (88) and (89a–c) into equation (86) yields an expression for $E(q)$ in the general case. These equations simplify greatly, of course, when $n = 1$, and we find

$$E(q) = K_1(1+\beta^2) + \beta^2(v-3)(\lambda_1 + K_1)/2$$

$$+ [2\lambda_1\beta^2 + (\lambda_1 + K_1)[1 - \beta^2 - \beta^2(v+\lambda)(v-3)/2]/(v-2)]$$

$$\times\, e^{-\lambda/2} {}_1F_1((v-2)/2, v/2; \lambda/2). \tag{90}$$

This reduces to equation (81) when $\beta = 0$.

The density of q may be obtained by similar but much more tedious calculations and we omit this result.

The LIML Estimator for the Exogenous Coefficients

The joint density PDF (r_1, s_1) is simply the product of equation (58) with the conditional normal density PDF $(s_1 | r_1)$ in equation (23), and this might well be the most useful result for these estimators from the point of view of hypothesis testing. However, to integrate out r_1 it is a simple matter to adapt the argument in Phillips (1984a) to this case, and hence to obtain an expression for PDF (s_1) in an operator form. We omit the details of this calculation, and give here instead the results for cases A and B that provide the leading terms in the more general expression for the density.

Case A $(m_1, M_1) = 0$, $(\mu, M) = 0$. Since (omitting the subscripts on s and r for simplicity) $s|r \sim N(0, (1 + r'r)I)$, and PDF (r) is as in (52), it is reasonably straightforward to obtain:

$$\text{PDF}(s) = (2\pi)^{-K_1/2} \exp(-s's/2)\, C(n,n)\, {}_1F_1(n/2, (n+K_1+1)/2; s's/2), \tag{91}$$

where $C(v, n)$ is defined in (69). Transforming to $q = s's$ then yields PDF (q) in exactly the form (68), but with v replaced by n. Hence, in this case the densities of the OLS, TSLS, and LIML estimators have exactly the same form apart from a degrees of freedom parameter v, which takes the values $N - K_1$, K_2, and n respectively.

Case B $(\mu, M) = 0, (m, M) \neq 0$. Here (23) and (52) hold for PDF $(s|r)$ and PDF (r) respectively. Using the same approach as in the previous section to integrate out r, we find that

$$\begin{aligned}\text{PDF}(s) = {} & (2\pi)^{-K_1/2} \exp[-(s - m_1)'(s - m_1)/2]\, C(n, n) \\ & \times \sum_{j,k=0}^{\infty} \frac{(-1)^k(\frac{1}{2})_{j+k}((K_1 + 1)/2)_j}{j!k!(\frac{1}{2})_j((n + K_1 + 1)/2)_{2j+k}} C_{j+k}^{j,k}(M'_1(s - m_1)(s - m_1)'M_1/4, \\ & M'_1M_1/2)\,{}_1F_1(j + k + n/2, 2j + k + (n + K_1 + 1)/2; \\ & (s - m_1)'(s - m_1)/2). \end{aligned} \tag{92}$$

Transforming to $q = (s - m_1)'(s - m_1)$ yields PDF (q) exactly as in (72) except that v is replaced by n throughout, so again the densities of the three estimators differ only in respect of the degrees of freedom parameter, v.

Unfortunately, case C $(\beta = 0)$ is no simpler in the case of the LIML estimator than is the general case (see equation (51) above for evidence of this), so this special case must be treated by the methods described above for the general case. It does not seem possible to obtain expressions analogous to (91) and (92) for the general case.

Extensions

As indicated in the fourth section, the result in equation (40) can be used to obtain, for instance, the joint density of the LIML and TSLS estimators, PDF (r_1, r_2). By an obvious extension of the argument leading to equation (23), we also have the conditional result

$$(s_1, s_2)|(r_1, r_2) \sim N\left((m_1, M_1)\begin{pmatrix} 1 & 1 \\ -r_1 & -r_2 \end{pmatrix}, I_{K_1} \otimes \begin{pmatrix} 1 + r'_1r_1 & 1 + r'_1r_2 \\ 1 + r'_2r_1 & 1 + r'_2r_2 \end{pmatrix}\right), \tag{93}$$

so that the joint density PDF (r_1, s_1, r_2, s_2) is easily obtained. Such results may be useful in comparing the properties of the two estimators.

More generally, theorem 1 provides (after transforming $r \to r_1$ in equation (37)) the joint density PDF $(r_1, f_1, B, (x, X))$. Multiplying by PDF (x_1, X_1) then gives PDF $(r_1, f_1, B, (x, X), (x_1, X_1))$, which is equivalent to the joint distribution of the (canonical) minimal sufficient statistic $t = (S, (x, X), (x_1, X_1))$. A variety of useful joint distribution results can then be obtained by transformation in this distribution. In particular, motivated by the curved exponential character of this model, one can consider the family of (one-to-one) transformations $t \to (\hat{\theta}(t), a(t))$ in which $\hat{\theta}(t)$ is the LIML estimate for all of the parameters in (2) (subject to (5) and (6)), and the

$a(t)$ are statistics defined on the manifold (in t-space) defined by $\hat{\theta}(t) = \text{constant}$ that essentially capture the information lost in the reduction $t \to \hat{\theta}(t)$ (Barndorff-Neilson 1980). Of particular interest is the question of whether or not there exists an exactly ancillary statistic $a(t)$. These matters will be pursued in future work.

Appendix

Proof of theorem 1 The transformation $R \to (F, H)$ described in the theorem is one-to-one, and the volume element transforms as

$$(\mathrm{d}R) = \prod_{i<j} (f_i - f_j) \prod_{i=1}^{n+1} \mathrm{d}f_i (H' \, \mathrm{d}H) \tag{A1}$$

Partitioning $H = (\mathbf{h}, H_2)$, H_2 is an element of the Stiefel manifold orthogonal to $\mathbf{h}$. That is, $H'_2 H_2 = I_n$ and $H'_2 \mathbf{h} = 0$. This manifold may be generated by choosing, for each fixed $\mathbf{h}$, a fixed matrix G, say, on the manifold (i.e. $G'G = I_n$, and $G'\mathbf{h} = 0$, and so $GG' = I - \mathbf{hh}'$), and then setting $H_2 = GH_1$, where H_1 ranges over the orthogonal group $O(n)$. To ensure that the transformation $R \to (F, \mathbf{h}, H_1)$ is one-to-one, we can replace the condition that the elements in the first row of H_2 are positive by the condition that the elements in the first row of H_1 are positive. The volume element on $O(n+1)$ transforms as

$$(H' \, \mathrm{d}H) = (\mathbf{h}' \, \mathrm{d}\mathbf{h})(H'_1 \, \mathrm{d}H_1), \tag{A2}$$

where $(\mathbf{h}' \, \mathrm{d}\mathbf{h})$ denotes the invariant measure on the surface of the unit $(n+1)$-sphere, and $(H'_1 \, \mathrm{d}H_1)$ that on $O(n)$ (see Muirhead (1982, lemma 9.5.3, p. 397)).

Next, partition $\mathbf{h} = (h_1, h'_2)'$, with $h_2 \; n \times 1$, and define $r = -h_1^{-1} h_2$. The transformation $\mathbf{h} \to r$ is one-to-one because h_1 is taken to be positive, and the transformation of the volume element is given in Phillips (1984b) as

$$(\mathbf{h}' \, \mathrm{d}\mathbf{h}) = (1 + r'r)^{-(n+1)/2} \bigwedge_{i=1}^{n} \mathrm{d}r_i. \tag{A3}$$

The matrix G that defines the transformation $H \to (\mathbf{h}, H_1)$ may be defined in terms of r by

$$G = \begin{pmatrix} r' \\ I_n \end{pmatrix} (I + rr')^{-1/2}, \tag{A4}$$

since, under the transformation $r = -h_1^{-1} h_2$,

$$\mathbf{h} = \begin{pmatrix} 1 \\ -r \end{pmatrix} (1 + r'r)^{-1/2}. \tag{A5}$$

Now define $\bar{F}_2$ by $F_2 = f_1\bar{F}_2$, so that $1 > \bar{f}_2 > \bar{f}_3 > \cdots > \bar{f}_{n+1} > 0$, and

$$\prod_{i<j}^{n+1} (f_i - f_j) \bigwedge_{j=1}^{n+1} \mathrm{d}f_i = (f_1^{n(n+3)/2}\,\mathrm{d}f_1)\left(\prod_{j=2}^{n+1} (1 - \bar{f}_j) \prod_{\substack{i,j=2\\ i<j}}^{n+1} (\bar{f}_i - \bar{f}_j) \bigwedge_{j=2}^{n+1} \mathrm{d}\bar{f}_j\right). \quad \text{(A6)}$$

Finally, set $B = H_1\bar{F}_2H'_1$, $0 < B < I$. Since the elements in the first row of H_1 are positive, and the elements on the diagonal of $\bar{F}_2$ are ordered, the transformation $(\bar{F}_2, H_1) \rightarrow B$ is one-to-one and we have

$$\prod_{\substack{i,j=2\\ i<j}}^{n+1} (\bar{f}_i - \bar{f}_j) \bigwedge_{j=2}^{n+1} \mathrm{d}\bar{f}_j(H'_1\,\mathrm{d}H_1) = (\mathrm{d}B). \quad \text{(A7)}$$

Combining (A1)–(A7), and noting that, in (A7), $\prod_{j=2}^{n+1} (1 - \bar{f}_j) = |I - B|$, we have

$$R = f_1\left[(1 + r'r)^{-1}\begin{pmatrix}1\\ -r\end{pmatrix}\begin{pmatrix}1\\ -r\end{pmatrix}' + (r, I)'(I + rr')^{-1/2}B(I + rr')^{-1/2}(r, I)\right] \quad \text{(A8)}$$

$$(\mathrm{d}R) = f_1^{n(n+3)/2}(1 + r'r)^{-(n+1)/2}|I - B|\,\mathrm{d}f_1 \bigwedge_{i=1}^{n} \mathrm{d}r_i\,(\mathrm{d}B). \quad \text{(A9)}$$

Since $H_2 = GH_1$, $H_1 = G'H_2$ and we can express B in terms of r, $\bar{F}_2$, and H_2 as

$$B = (I + rr')^{-1/2}(r, I)H_2\bar{F}_2H'_2(r, I)'(I + rr')^{-1/2}, \quad \text{(A10)}$$

thus completing the proof of part (a).

Part (b) follows from equations (34), (A8), and (A9) on noting that $|R|^{(m-n-2)/2} = f_1^{(n+1)(m-n-2)/2}|B|^{(m-n-2)/2}$.

Proof of corollary 1.1 The matrix B may be integrated out of PDF (r, f_1, B) in equation (37) by using Muirhead (1982, theorem 7.4.2). This gives

$$\begin{aligned}\mathrm{PDF}\,(r, f_1) = {} & C_1^* f_1^{m(n+1)/2-1}(1 + r'r)^{-(n+1)/2}|V|^{-m/2}\\ & \times \exp\left[-\tfrac{1}{2}f_1(1, -r')V^{-1}(1, -r')'/(1 + r'r)\right]\\ & \times {}_1F_1((m-1)/2, (m+n+2)/2, -\tfrac{1}{2}f_1G'V^{-1}G)\end{aligned} \quad \text{(A11)}$$

with G as in (A3) above. Equation (38) then follows on using the Kummer formula for the confluent hypergeometric function (James 1964, equation (51)): ${}_1F_1(a, c; S) = \mathrm{etr}\,\{S\}\,{}_1F_1(c - a, c; -S)$.

Proof of corollary 1.2 To integrate out r in equation (38), we can invert the transformation $\mathbf{h} \rightarrow r$ used above to define

$$\mathbf{h} = \begin{pmatrix}1\\ -r\end{pmatrix}(1 + r'r)^{-1/2}. \quad \text{(A12)}$$

Then, only the confluent hypergeometric function in (38) involves **h** and its argument is, apart from the factor $(f_1/2)$, the rank-n matrix $(I - \mathbf{hh}')V^{-1}$. Integrating term by term we have

$$\int_{\mathbf{h}'\mathbf{h}=1} C_\lambda((I - \mathbf{hh}')V^{-1})(\mathbf{h}'\,d\mathbf{h}) = \frac{2\pi^{(n+1)/2}}{\Gamma((n+1)/2)} \int_{O(n+1)} C_\lambda\left(H\begin{pmatrix} I_n & 0 \\ 0 & 0 \end{pmatrix} H'V^{-1}\right)(dH)$$
$$= \frac{2\pi^{(n+1)/2}}{\Gamma((n+1)/2)} C_\lambda\begin{pmatrix} I_n & 0 \\ 0 & 0 \end{pmatrix} C_\lambda(V^{-1})/C_\lambda(I_{n+1}), \quad \text{(A13)}$$

which vanishes unless l_{n+1}, the $(n+1)$th part of the partition λ, is zero, and is equal to

$$\frac{2\pi^{(n+1)/2}}{\Gamma((n+1)/2)} \frac{(n/2)_\lambda}{((n+1)/2)_\lambda} C_\lambda(V^{-1}) \quad \text{(A14)}$$

when $l_{n+1} = 0$. Since $(n/2)_\lambda = 0$ unless $l_{n+1} = 0$, this yields equation (39).

References

Barndorff-Nielson, O. E. (1980). "Conditionality resolutions," *Biometrika*, 67, 293–310.

Basmann, R. L. (1961). "Note on the exact finite sample frequency functions of generalized classical linear estimators in two leading overidentified cases," *Journal of the American Statistical Association*, 56, 619–36.

Bergstrom, A. R. (1962). "The exact sampling distributions of least squares and maximum likelihood estimators of the marginal propensity to consume," *Econometrica*, 30, 480–90.

Chikuse, Y., and A. W. Davis (1986). "A survey on the invariant polynomials with matrix arguments in relation to econometric distribution theory", *Econometric Theory*, 2, 232–48.

Constantine, A. G. (1963). "Some noncentral distribution problems in multivariate analysis," *Annals of Mathematical Statistics*, 34, 1270–85.

Davis, A. W. (1979). "Invariant polynomials with two matrix arguments, extending the zonal polynomials: Applications to multivariate distribution theory," *Annals of the Institute of Statistical Mathematics* A, 31, 465–85.

Efron, B. (1975). "Defining the curvature of a statistical problem (with application to second order efficiency)," *Annals of Statistics*, 3, 1189–242.

Herz, C. S. (1955). "Bessel functions of matrix argument," *Annals of Mathematics*, 61, 474–523.

Hillier, G. H. (1985a). "On the joint and marginal densities of instrumental variable estimators in a general structural equation", *Econometric Theory*, 1, 53–72.

Hillier, G. H. (1985b). "Marginal densities of instrumental variables estimators: further exact results," mimeo, Monash University.

Hillier, G. H. (1987). "Joint distribution theory for some statistics based on LIML and TSLS," Cowles Foundation Discussion Paper 840.

Hillier, G. H. (1990). "On the normalization of structural equations: properties of direction estimators," *Econometrica*, 58, 1181–94.

Hosoya, Y., Y. Tsukuda, and N. Terui (1989). "Ancillarity and the limited information maximum likelihood estimation of a structural equation in a simultaneous equation system," *Econometric Theory*, 5, 385–404.

James, A. T. (1964). "Distribution of matrix variates and latent roots derived from normal samples," *Annals of Mathematical Statistics*, 35, 475–501.

Muirhead, R. J. (1982). *Aspects of Multivariate Statistical Theory*. New York: Wiley.

Phillips, P. C. B. (1980). "The exact finite sample density of instrumental variable estimators in an equation with $n + 1$ endogenous variables," *Econometrica*, 48, 861–78.

Phillips, P. C. B. (1983). "Exact small sample theory in the simultaneous equations model," in M. D. Intriligator and Z. Griliches (eds) *Handbook of Econometrics*. Amsterdam: North-Holland.

Phillips, P. C. B. (1984a). "The exact distribution of exogenous variable coefficient estimators," *Journal of Econometrics*, 26, 387–98.

Phillips, P. C. B. (1984b). "The exact distribution of LIML: I," *International Economic Review*, 25, 249–61.

Phillips, P. C. B. (1985). "The exact distribution of LIML: II," *International Economic Review*, 26, 21–36.

Phillips, P. C. B. (1988). "Reflections on econometric methodology," *The Economic Record*, Dec.

Phillips, P. C. B. (1989). "Partially identified econometric models," *Econometric Theory*, 5, 181–240.

Rhodes, G. F. (1981). "Exact density functions and approximate critical regions for likelihood ratio identifiability test statistics," *Econometrica*, 49, 1035–226.

Skeels, C. L. (1989a). "Estimation in misspecified systems of equations: some exact results," unpublished Ph.D. Thesis, Monash University.

Skeels, C. L. (1989b). "The exact distribution of exogenous variable coefficient estimators," Australian National University, Working Papers in Economics and Econometrics, Working Paper 178.

10

Operational Algebra and Regression t-Tests

Peter C. B. Phillips

Introduction

In an article published by *Econometrica*, Rex Bergstrom (1962) derived the exact sampling distributions of least squares and maximum likelihood estimators of the marginal propensity to consume in a two-equation Keynesian model of income determination. This article emphasized the importance of a mathematical study of the small-sample behavior of econometric estimators. Bergstrom's objective was to evaluate the performance characteristics of the new simultaneous equations estimators in relation to least squares and his conclusion, at least for the model studied, was unambiguous: "... for samples of ten or more observations ... the maximum likelihood estimator of the marginal propensity to consume is the 'better' general purpose estimator of this parameter."

The Bergstrom article, together with a related paper by Basmann (1961), created a field of research that became known as finite-sample theory in econometrics. Progress in the field was intermittent through the 1960s and 1970s, with few spectacular advances. This is in part explained by the mathematical difficulty of the research, but another factor was the rapid development in computer technology during this period. This opened the way to large-scale simulation exercises that provided quick and easy numerical information about the sampling characteristics of estimators and tests in stochastic environments similar to those in which they were to be used. The 1980s witnessed even greater enhancements in computer technology. With the advent of cheap personal computers and workstations capable of 32-bit arithmetic and with simulation-based statistical methods like the bootstrap, it seems likely that attention will continue to move away from mathematical studies of the Bergstrom type.

Nevertheless, mathematical studies remain fascinating and have continued to attract a few dedicated researchers. Perhaps the biggest obstacle to research in the field is the specificity of individual studies. Each new estimator or test seems to bring with it a new set of mathematical difficulties that sustained effort, ingenuity, and technical skill are not always sufficient to resolve. As a result, graduate students and young researchers are naturally more easily drawn into asymptotic analyses where there is the rich reservoir of theorems and methods from probability theory to draw upon when there is a need to demonstrate hard quantitative conclusions, and into simulation exercises when there is a need to illustrate sampling performance. The latter exercises have themselves been facilitated by the widespread availability of matrix programming languages such as GAUSS (1989), which is one of the more popular packages among econometricians. Software packages like GAUSS allow formulas to be programmed much as they are written down in matrix format, so that the transition from econometric formula to computer program is enormously simplified. Moreover, the graphics facilities that GAUSS supports are sophisticated and easy to use. With such software, it is nowadays usual practice to have simulations up and running with accompanying graphics within a few days of developing the theory or, indeed, as work on the theory is itself under way. What might have taken six months developmental work in the 1960s is now done in a week. And the programming skills that support the use of software like GAUSS are now as much a part of the econometrician's tool kit as linear algebra.

The model that I have just described of theoretical quantitative research underpinned by asymptotics and simulation has become widespread in recent years. It might easily be taken as the standard research paradigm of today's young econometric theorist. It seems likely that it will become almost universal during the 1990s.

This combination of asymptotics and simulation is usually highly productive and informative, but it is not without drawbacks, perhaps the most important of which is that it diverts attention from some vital issues. Econometrics, like statistics, is concerned with data reduction. Estimators and test statistics are summary measures and the formulas that give rise to them carry with them certain characteristics. The characteristics of the mapping from data to statistics are often of primary importance in understanding the statistical properties of a given procedure. Indeed, the physical form of the statistic as a function of the data itself induces an operation on the probability law of the sample from which the statistic is derived. The situation is exhibited in the following scheme:

data reductions	:	data y	$\rightarrow$	sample moments $m(y)$	$\rightarrow$	estimators and tests $r(m)$
induced reductions of probability measures	:	μ_y	$\rightarrow$	μ_m	$\rightarrow$	μ_r

In many cases, the probability measure μ_y of the data will be absolutely continuous with respect to Lebesgue measure and the transition at the second level can be formulated in terms of probability densities as PDF $(y) \rightarrow$ PDF $(m) \rightarrow$ PDF (r). The fundamental question addressed in a mathematical study that seeks to derive PDF (r) is this: can the operations on PDF (y) that are induced by the data maps $y \rightarrow m \rightarrow r$ be formalized algebraically and reduced to give a solution in a closed form or a series representation?

Of course, understanding the transition $y \rightarrow m \rightarrow r$ and what this reduction loses in the way of information in the sample is critical to virtually all statistical theory. But solutions are available only in specific instances and no one seems yet to have attempted a general theory. The present paper is designed to offer some thoughts on how to tackle this general problem and to illustrate an algebraic approach that seems promising. Let it be clear at the outset that I am not proposing an operational procedure for practical applications. So what I have to say will in no way be competitive with the ongoing research paradigm of "asymptotic theory plus illustrative simulations" that I described above. However, the idea that I am going to put forward has the merit of providing a general mathematical framework for solving distributional problems. In this sense, it follows the spirit of the original Bergstrom (1962) study and eschews the research direction that has been followed by much of the profession since then.

On matters of notation I shall use the symbol "$\equiv$" to signify equivalence in distribution, and "$\sim$" to signify asymptotic equivalence. Lt $(\cdot)$ and PDF $(\cdot)$ represent the Laplace transform and probability density of a distribution, $\Gamma(\cdot)$ is the gamma function and $B(\cdot,\cdot)$ the beta function. $\chi_n^2(\cdot)$ is the density of the chi-squared distribution with n degrees of freedom and $N(0, 1)$ is the standard normal density, usually with argument r, viz. $(2\pi)^{-1/2}\,e^{-r^2/2}$.

Functions of Differential Operators, Pseudodifferential and Fourier Integral Operators

At the outset it is useful to start with a space of functions that have nice properties, not all of which are really needed. Accordingly, we let C_∞ be the space of infinitely differentiable functions $f(x)$ on the real line $(-\infty, \infty)$. If $D = d/dx$ represents the usual operation of differentiation then D may be interpreted as the mapping $D: C_\infty \to C_\infty$ defined by $Df(x) = f'(x) \in C_\infty$, $\forall f \in C_\infty$. In a similar way we may attach a meaning to polynomial functions of D such as $p_n(D): C_\infty \to C_\infty$, $p_n(D) = \sum_{i=0}^n a_i D^i$ which are defined according to the relation $p_n(D)f(x) = \sum_{i=0}^n a_i f^{(i)}(x)$ setting $f^{(0)} = f$ and using $f^{(i)}$ to signify the ith derivative of f. Such a class of operators is useful in solving ordinary differential equations with constant coefficients.

It is also useful to attach a meaning to nonintegral powers of D. This leads to the concept of fractional differentiation (and integration). The simplest approach is to rely on the gamma integral for a complex power which yields the formula

$$D^{-\alpha}f(x) = \Gamma(\alpha)^{-1}\int_0^\infty [e^{-Dt}f(x)]t^{\alpha-1}\,dt = \Gamma(\alpha)^{-1}\int_0^\infty f(x-t)t^{\alpha-1}\,dt, \qquad (1)$$

which is valid for complex α with Re $(\alpha) > 0$ provided the integral converges. Note that the final integral representation in (1) is induced via the Taylor formula $\exp(-Dt)f(x) = f(x-t)$, which holds for $f(\cdot)$ analytic; but this final representation takes on an independent life as a definition of $D^{-\alpha}f(x)$ provided the integral converges. Moreover, quite general complex powers such as D^μ may now be defined by setting $D^\mu f(x) = D^{-\alpha}\{D^m f(x)\}$ with $\mu = m - \alpha$, Re $(\alpha) > 0$ and m a non-negative integer. Fractional operators defined this way form a Weyl calculus (see for example Miller (1974)) and can be easily extended to matrices using the multivariate gamma integral in place of (1). Such extensions were introduced independently by the author (1985) and by Richards (1984) in quite different contexts. The use of such operators in resolving problems of distribution theory is illustrated in the author's papers (1984, 1985, 1986, 1987).

More general functions than powers of D can be accommodated through use of Fourier transforms. Suppose $g(z)$ has Fourier transform $\tilde{g}(p) = \int_{\mathbb{R}} e^{ipz}g(z)\,dz$. Then we define the operator $g(D)$ by its action on f through the inverse transform as follows:

$$g(\mathrm{D})f(x) = (2\pi)^{-1} \int_{-\infty}^{\infty} [\mathrm{e}^{-\mathrm{i}p\mathrm{D}} f(x)]\tilde{g}(p)\,\mathrm{d}p = (2\pi)^{-1} \int_{-\infty}^{\infty} f(x - \mathrm{i}p)\tilde{g}(p)\,\mathrm{d}p, \quad (2)$$

provided the integral converges.

It is easy to see that with this definition $g(\mathrm{D})\,\mathrm{e}^{ax} = \mathrm{e}^{ax}g(a)$, as in elementary calculus. Moreover

$$g(\mathrm{D})\,\mathrm{e}^{ax}f(x) = \mathrm{e}^{ax}g(\mathrm{D} + a)f(x), \quad (3)$$

just as when $g(\mathrm{D})$ is a polynomial. These rules for operating on exponentials can then be employed to deal with other elementary functions. For instance, if $\mathrm{Re}\,(\beta) > 0$ we have

$$f(\mathrm{D})(1 - x)^{-\beta} = (1/\Gamma(\beta)) \int_{0}^{\infty} \exp\left[-(1 - x)t\right] t^{\beta - 1} f(t)\,\mathrm{d}t, \quad (4)$$

which for $f(\mathrm{D}) = \mathrm{D}^{\mu}$ leads to

$$\mathrm{D}^{\mu}(1 - x)^{-\beta} = [\Gamma(\beta + \mu)/\Gamma(\beta)](1 - x)^{-\beta - \mu} = (\beta)_{\mu}(1 - x)^{-\beta - \mu}, \quad (5)$$

where $(\beta)_{\mu} = \beta(\beta + 1)\ldots(\beta + \mu - 1)$ is the forward factorial, with the convention that $(0)_0 = 1$. Note that the final formula then holds by analytic continuation irrespective of the values of β and μ.

Formula (2) has a natural multivariate extension. Suppose $x \in R^n$ and let $\partial x = \partial/\partial x$. We define

$$g(\partial x)f(x) = (2\pi)^{-n} \int_{\mathbb{R}^n} [\mathrm{e}^{-\mathrm{i}p'\partial x} f(x)]\tilde{g}(p)\,\mathrm{d}p = (2\pi)^{-n} \int_{\mathbb{R}^n} f(x - \mathrm{i}p)\tilde{g}(p)\,\mathrm{d}p, \quad (6)$$

where g and $\tilde{g}$ are again a Fourier transform pair. Since the Fourier transform of a generalized function always exists, it is often useful to work with generalized functions or ordinary functions that are used as generalized functions in this representation. For example, suppose in (6) that $g(z) = \exp(b'z)$ and z is an n-vector. Then $\tilde{g}(p) = (2\pi)^n \delta(p - \mathrm{i}b)$ where $\delta(\cdot)$ is the dirac generalized function (cf. Gelfand and Shilov (1964), pp. 169–90). We deduce from (6) that

$$g(\partial x)f(x) = \int_{\mathbb{R}^n} f(x - \mathrm{i}p)\delta(p - \mathrm{i}b)\,\mathrm{d}p. \quad (7)$$

Upon deforming the contour of integration from $\mathbb{R}^n$ to $\mathrm{i}b + \mathbb{R}^n$ in $\mathbb{C}^n$, we obtain

$$g(\partial x)f(x) = \int_{\mathrm{i}b + \mathbb{R}^n} f(x - \mathrm{i}p)\delta(p - \mathrm{i}b)\,\mathrm{d}p = f(x - \mathrm{i}^2 b) = f(x + b), \quad (8)$$

which corresponds with the usual Taylor formula, viz. $\mathrm{e}^{b'\partial x}f(x) = f(x + b)$. The same result can be obtained by using the Fourier transform $\tilde{f}(p)$ of $f(\cdot)$ rather than $g(\cdot)$ in the definition (6). We would then have

$$g(\partial x)f(x) = (2\pi)^{-n} \int_{\mathbb{R}^n} g(\partial x)\, \mathrm{e}^{-\mathrm{i}p'x}\tilde{f}(p)\,\mathrm{d}p = (2\pi)^{-n} \int_{\mathbb{R}^n} \mathrm{e}^{-\mathrm{i}p'x} g(-\mathrm{i}p)\tilde{f}(p)\,\mathrm{d}p. \quad (9)$$

When $g(z) = \exp(b'z)$ the right-hand side of (9) is trivially $f(x + b)$. Note finally that we can invert the Fourier transform in (9), giving us the representation

$$g(\partial x)f(x) = (2\pi)^{-n} \int_{\mathbb{R}^{2n}} \mathrm{e}^{-\mathrm{i}p'(x-\xi)} g(-\mathrm{i}p) f(\xi)\,\mathrm{d}\xi\,\mathrm{d}p. \quad (10)$$

As given above, (2), (6), and especially (9) are all closely related to the concept of a pseudodifferential operator. Suppose f has Fourier transform $\tilde{f}$ in R^n. Then a pseudodifferential operator $k(x, \mathrm{i}\,\partial x)$ is usually defined as

$$k(x, \mathrm{i}\,\partial x)f(x) = (2\pi)^{-n} \int_{\mathbb{R}^n} k(x, p)\tilde{f}(p)\,\mathrm{e}^{-\mathrm{i}x'p}\,\mathrm{d}p. \quad (11)$$

Again the representation retains its meaning for generalized functions and their transforms. The operator $k(x, \mathrm{i}\,\partial x)$ is generally noncommutative in its arguments and the action of the operators x and ∂x is taken in the given order, i.e. $k(x, \mathrm{i}\,\partial x)$, with the elements of ∂x acting before those of x. Note that in contrast to (6) we are now employing the Fourier transform of the operand f in (11) as distinct from that of the operator as in (6). Thus, (11) may be interpreted as a natural extension of (9).

There is now a vast literature on the properties of such operators and they are extensively used in the theory of partial differential equations. Treves (1982, volume 1) and Dieudonné (1988) provide a detailed study. An example of the use of a special case of (11) is the Laplace equation

$$\nabla^2 y(x) = f(x), \quad \nabla^2 = \partial x'\,\partial x, \quad (12)$$

which is solved by

$$y(x) = \nabla^{-2} f(x) = -(2\pi)^{-n} \int_{\mathbb{R}^n} \mathrm{e}^{-\mathrm{i}x'p}(p'p)^{-1}\tilde{f}(p)\,\mathrm{d}p. \quad (13)$$

Partial differential equations with variable coefficients then lead to solutions that involve noncommutative operators of the form given in (9).

Further extensions of operators based on (9) are available in which $x'p$ in the exponent is replaced by a real-valued C_∞ function $\varphi(x, p)$. Such extended operators are known as Fourier integral operators and they are discussed in Treves (1982, volume 2). We shall have no need for them in the present work.

We end this section with the following lemma that reports two useful results on nonlinear functions of operators induced by the standard normal density. We employ the notation

$$N(0, 1/\partial y) = (2\pi)^{-1/2}(\partial y)^{1/2} \exp[-\tfrac{1}{2}r^2\, \partial y]. \tag{14}$$

Lemma

$$N(0, 1/\partial y)\, e^y y^m = N(0, 1)\, e^y \sum_{j=0}^{m} \binom{m}{j} (-1)^j(-\tfrac{1}{2})_j (y - r^2/2)^{m-j}; \tag{15}$$

$$[N(0, n/\partial \mathbf{x}'\, \partial \mathbf{x})\, e^{\mathbf{x}'\mathbf{x}/2}]_{\mathbf{x}=0} = [N(0, n/\partial y)(1 - 2y)^{-n/2}]_{y=0}; \tag{16}$$

where y is a scalar in (15) and $\mathbf{x}$ is an n-vector in (16).

Proof. To prove (15) we introduce the auxiliary variable α and write

$$\begin{aligned}
N(0, 1/\partial y)\, e^y y^m &= [N(0, 1/\partial y)\, \partial\alpha^m\, e^{\alpha y}]_{\alpha=1} \\
&= [(\partial\alpha)^m N(0, 1/\partial y)\, e^{\alpha y}]_{\alpha=1} = [\partial\alpha^m\, e^{\alpha y} N(0, 1/\alpha)]_{\alpha=1} \\
&= [(\partial\alpha)^m \{e^{\alpha y}(2\pi)^{-1/2}\alpha^{1/2}\, e^{-\alpha r^2/2}\}]_{\alpha=1} \\
&= (2\pi)^{-1/2}[\partial\alpha^m(\alpha^{1/2}\, e^{\alpha(y-r^2/2)})]_{\alpha=1} \\
&= (2\pi)^{-1/2}\left[\sum_{j=0}^{m}\binom{m}{j}(\partial\alpha^j\alpha^{1/2})(\partial\alpha^{m-j}\, e^{\alpha(y-r^2/2)})\right]_{\alpha=1} \\
&= (2\pi)^{-1/2}\left[\sum_{j=0}^{m}\binom{m}{j}(-1)^j(-\tfrac{1}{2})_j\alpha^{1/2-j}(y - r^2/2)^{m-j}\, e^{\alpha(y-r^2/2)}\right]_{\alpha=1} \\
&= (2\pi)^{-1/2}\, e^{-r^2/2}\, e^y \sum_{j=0}^{m}\binom{m}{j}(-1)^j(-\tfrac{1}{2})_j(y - r^2/2)^{m-j}
\end{aligned} \tag{17}$$

as stated. To prove (16) we let $\xi \equiv N(0, I)$ so that $E(e^{\mathbf{x}'\xi}) = e^{\mathbf{x}'\mathbf{x}/2}$ is the Laplace transform. Then

$$\begin{aligned}
N(0, n/\partial \mathbf{x}'\, \partial \mathbf{x})\, e^{\mathbf{x}'\mathbf{x}/2} &= N(0, n/\partial \mathbf{x}'\, \partial \mathbf{x}) E(e^{\mathbf{x}'\xi}) \\
&= E[N(0, n/\partial \mathbf{x}'\, \partial \mathbf{x})\, e^{\mathbf{x}'\xi}] \\
&= E[N(0, n/\xi'\xi)\, e^{\mathbf{x}'\xi}].
\end{aligned} \tag{18}$$

Next write ξ in polar coordinates as $\xi = r^{1/2}\mathbf{h}$ where $r = \xi'\xi \equiv \chi_n^2$ and $\mathbf{h}$ is uniformly distributed on the unit sphere in $\mathbb{R}^n$. Then, upon evaluation at $x = 0$, (18) becomes

$$\begin{aligned}
E[N(0, n/r)\, e^{\mathbf{x}'r^{1/2}\mathbf{h}}]_{x=0} &= E[N(0, n/\partial y)\, e^{yr + \mathbf{x}'r^{1/2}\mathbf{h}}]_{y=0, x=0} \\
&= [N(0, n/\partial y) E(e^{yr})]_{y=0} \\
&= [N(0, n/\partial y)(1 - 2y)^{-n/2}]_{y=0}
\end{aligned} \tag{19}$$

as required.

The Regression t-Statistic: I

The operational algebra can be illustrated in the case of conventional regression test statistics such as the t-ratio. We shall proceed under the usual Gaussian assumptions and show how to use the methods to extract the exact distribution theory, the asymptotic distributions and the full asymptotic series expansions. It will be assumed that the reductions from the original data to appropriate sample moments have already been performed.

The sample moments that appear in the usual regression t statistic are assumed to have been centered and scaled and we write them as $X \equiv N(0, 1)$, $s \equiv \chi_n^2$. Then, by independence and in an obvious notation, we have

$$r = \frac{X}{(s/n)^{1/2}} \equiv \frac{N(0,1)}{(\chi_n^2/n)^{1/2}} \equiv t_n. \tag{20}$$

We write the conditional density of r given s and the marginal density of s as PDF $(r \mid s) \equiv N(0, n/s)$, PDF $(s) = \chi_n^2(s)$.

The density of r is

$$\begin{aligned} \text{PDF }(r) &= \int_{s>0} N(0, n/s)\chi_n^2(s)\,\mathrm{d}s \\ &= \int_{s>0} [N(0, n/\partial z)\,\mathrm{e}^{zs}]_{z=0}\chi_n^2(s)\,\mathrm{d}s \\ &= \left[N(0, n/\partial z)\int_{s>0} \mathrm{e}^{zs}\chi_n^2(s)\,\mathrm{d}s\right]_{z=0} \\ &= [N(0, n/\partial z)\,\mathrm{Lt}\,(z)]_{z=0} \\ &= [N(0, n/\partial z)(1-2z)^{-n/2}]_{z=0} \\ &= [N(0, n/2\,\partial u)(1-u)^{-n/2}]_{u=0}, \end{aligned} \tag{21}$$

setting $u = 2z$ so that $\partial z = 2\,\partial u$, and

$$\begin{aligned} \text{PDF }(r) &= (2\pi)^{-1/2}[\mathrm{e}^{-(r^2/n)\,\partial u}(2/n)^{1/2}\,\partial u^{1/2}(1-u)^{-n/2}]_{u=0} \\ &= (\pi n)^{-1/2}[\mathrm{e}^{-(r^2/n)\,\partial u}\{\Gamma((n+1)/2)/\Gamma(n/2)\}(1-u)^{-(n+1)/2}]_{u=0} \\ &= \{n^{1/2}B(n/2, 1/2)\}^{-1}(1 + r^2/n)^{-(n+1)/2}, \end{aligned} \tag{22}$$

using (5) above.

The asymptotic distribution as $n \to \infty$ can be derived from (21) by noting that $(1-u)^{-n/2} \sim \mathrm{e}^{-nu/2}$ and then

$$\text{PDF }(r) \sim [N(0, n/2\,\partial u)\,\mathrm{e}^{-nu/2}]_{u=0} = N(0, 1) \tag{23}$$

directly from (3).

To develop a complete asymptotic series expansion about the limit (23), we start by writing (21) in the form

$$\mathrm{PDF}(r) = [N(0, 1/\partial v)(1 - 2v/n)^{-n/2}]_{v=0} \tag{24}$$

using the transformation $u \to v = nu/2$. Next, we expand the operand in (24) in the conventional way for large n, viz.

$$\begin{aligned}(1 - 2v/n)^{-n/2} &= \exp[-(n/2)\ln(1 - 2v/n)] \\ &= \exp\left[+(n/2)\sum_{k=1}^{\infty}(1/k)(2v/n)^k\right] \\ &= e^v \exp\left[\sum_{j=1}^{\infty} 2^j v^{j+1}/n^j(j+1)\right] \\ &= e^v\left[1 + \sum_{k=1}^{\infty}\left(\frac{2}{n}\right)^k \sum_{l=1}^{k}\frac{v^{k+l}}{l!}\sum{}^{*}\{(j_1+1)\cdots(j_l+1)\}^{-1}\right]\end{aligned} \tag{25}$$

where $\sum^*$ signifies summation over all $j_1, \ldots, j_l$ ($\geqslant 1$) for which $\sum_1^l j_i = k$. Direct application of the operator in (24) now yields

$$\mathrm{PDF}(r) \sim N(0, 1) + \sum_{k=1}^{\infty}\left(\frac{2}{n}\right)^k \sum_{l=1}^{k}[N(0, 1/\partial v)\, e^v v^{k+l}]_{v=0}\frac{1}{l!}\sum{}^{*}\{(j_1+1)\cdots(j_l+1)\}^{-1} \tag{26}$$

which by result (15) of the lemma reduces to

$$\mathrm{PDF}(r) \sim N(0, 1)\left[1 + \sum_{k=1}^{\infty}\left(\frac{2}{n}\right)^k \sum_{l=1}^{k} p_{k+l}(r)\right], \tag{27}$$

where

$$p_{k+l}(r) = \left[\frac{1}{l!}\sum{}^{*}\{(j_1+1)\cdots(j_l+1)\}^{-1}\right]\sum_{j=0}^{k+1}\binom{k+l}{j}(-1)^j(-\tfrac{1}{2})_j\left(-\frac{r^2}{2}\right)^{k+l-j}. \tag{28}$$

Expression (27) gives a full asymptotic series representation of PDF (r) about its limit density, the standard normal $N(0, 1)$. Note that we use the asymptotic equivalence symbol "$\sim$" in place of "$=$", since the series is asymptotic and not convergent. Including terms up to order n^{-2} in (27), we have

$$\begin{aligned}\mathrm{PDF}(r) \sim N(0, 1)[&1 + (4n)^{-1}(r^4 - 2r^2 - 1) \\ &+ (96n^2)^{-1}(3r^8 - 28r^6 + 30r^4 + 12r^2 + 3) + o(n^{-2})],\end{aligned} \tag{29}$$

which is the same as the expression to this order that was originally found by Fisher (1925).

In a similar way, we can extract an alternate asymptotic series based on Appell polynomials that was suggested by Dickey (1967). In place of (21) we now use (22) for the calculation of the expansion. Specifically, we have

$$[e^{-(r^2/n)\,\partial u}(1-u)^{-(n+1)/2}]_{u=0}$$
$$= [e^{-(r^2/n)\,\partial u} \exp[-((n+1)/2)\ln(1-u)]]_{u=0}$$
$$= \left[e^{-(r^2/n)\,\partial u} \exp\left[((n+1)/2)\sum_{k=1}^{\infty} u^k/k\right]\right]_{u=0}$$
$$= \left[e^{-(r^2h/2)\,\partial v} \exp\left[((n+1)/2)\sum_{k=1}^{\infty} (v^k/k)(2/(n+1))^k\right]\right]_{v=0},$$
$$v = (n+1)u/2, \quad h = (n+1)/n$$
$$= \left[e^{-(r^2h/2)\,\partial v} e^{v}\left[1+\sum_{k=1}^{\infty}\left(\frac{2}{n+1}\right)^k \sum_{l=1}^{k}\frac{v^{k+l}}{l!}\Sigma^*\{(j_1+1)\ldots(j_l+1)\}^{-1}\right]\right]_{v=0}$$
$$= e^{-r^2h/2}\sum_{k=0}^{\infty}\left(\frac{2}{n+1}\right)^k A_k(-hr^2/2), \tag{30}$$

where

$$A_k(x) = \sum_{l=1}^{k}(1/l!)x^{k+l}\Sigma^*\{(j_1+1)\cdots(j_l+1)\}^{-1} = x^k\sum_{l=1}^{k} B_{k,l}x^l, \tag{31}$$

say.

In this case the series (30) is convergent for $r^2 < n$. The polynomials $A_k(x)$ are called Appell's polynomials and the coefficients $B_{k,l}$ may be computed by simple recursion formulas (see Erdélyi (1953) p. 256). Expression (30) leads to a corresponding expansion for the density in terms of Appell polynomials. Dickey (1967) concludes that the accuracy of this expansion is about the same as that of the Edgeworth series (27). The present development helps to show how closely related the two expansions are.

Similar operational methods may be used in the case of the regression F statistic. Some of the calculations leading to the exact density and distribution function, the χ^2 asymptotics and full asymptotic series are given in a paper by the author (1987) on fractional operators.

The Regression *t*-Statistic: II

The results of the previous section can be derived by conventional methods. The main role of the operational algebra is therefore to simplify the derivations and the final formulas, to bring them all within the same analytical framework and to codify the operations on the probability densities that are induced by the data reductions from sample moments to test statistic.

As a nontrivial application of the techniques, we shall now consider the linear model

$$y = X\boldsymbol{\beta} + u, \quad u \equiv N(0, \Omega) \tag{32}$$

whose error covariance matrix $\Omega = \Omega(\boldsymbol{\theta})$ is generally nonscalar and depends on a p-vector $\boldsymbol{\theta} \in \boldsymbol{\Theta} \subset \mathbb{R}^p$, which is variation-independent of the parameter vector $\boldsymbol{\beta}$ and whose true value is denoted $\boldsymbol{\theta}_0$. It will be assumed that X is nonrandom and of full column rank $k \leqslant n$ and $\Omega(\boldsymbol{\theta})$ is nonsingular $\forall \boldsymbol{\theta} \in \boldsymbol{\Theta}$ and analytic. We shall use $V(\boldsymbol{\theta}) = \Omega(\boldsymbol{\theta})^{-1}$ to represent the precision matrix. The model is the same as that studied by Rothenberg (1984a, 1984b).

The minimum variance unbiased estimator of $\boldsymbol{\beta}$ in (32) is given by generalized least squares (GLS) when $\boldsymbol{\theta}_0$ is known, i.e.

$$\bar{\boldsymbol{\beta}} = [X'VX]^{-1}[X'Vy], \quad V = V(\boldsymbol{\theta}_0). \tag{33}$$

When $\boldsymbol{\theta}_0$ is unknown, it is usual to employ a feasible GLS procedure based on a preliminary estimator $\hat{\boldsymbol{\theta}}$ of $\boldsymbol{\theta}_0$, i.e. $\hat{\boldsymbol{\beta}} = [X'V(\hat{\boldsymbol{\theta}})X]^{-1}[X'V(\hat{\boldsymbol{\theta}})y]$.

Let $\mathbf{c}'\boldsymbol{\beta}$ be some linear combination of $\boldsymbol{\beta}$ for some known vector $\mathbf{c} \neq 0$. Then the corresponding GLS estimate is $\mathbf{c}'\hat{\boldsymbol{\beta}}$ and its asymptotic t-ratio is

$$t_c = \mathbf{c}'(\hat{\boldsymbol{\beta}} - \boldsymbol{\beta})/\{\mathbf{c}'[X'V(\hat{\boldsymbol{\theta}})X]^{-1}\mathbf{c}\}^{1/2}. \tag{34}$$

Our object is to derive a distribution theory for $\mathbf{c}'\hat{\boldsymbol{\beta}}$ and t_c. To make headway we need to be more explicit about $\hat{\boldsymbol{\theta}}$. Since $\boldsymbol{\theta}$ is usually estimated from the residuals of a first-stage regression on (32), we could let $\hat{\boldsymbol{\theta}}$ be some function of the residuals from this regression. In fact, it will be more general if we allow $\hat{\boldsymbol{\theta}}$ to be a function, say

$$\hat{\boldsymbol{\theta}} = \boldsymbol{\theta}(Qu), \quad Qu = (I - X(X'VX)^{-1}X'V)u \tag{35}$$

of the residuals, Qu, from the GLS regression leading to (33). Here $Q = Q(\boldsymbol{\theta}_0)$ depends on the true vector $\boldsymbol{\theta}_0$. Note that the representation (35) includes all estimators of $\boldsymbol{\theta}$ that rely on the least squares residuals since $\hat{u} = (I - P_X)u = (I - P_X)Qu$.

The formulation (35) also includes the maximum likelihood estimator of $\boldsymbol{\theta}$. In this case the log likelihood, after concentrating out $\boldsymbol{\beta}$, is

$$\begin{aligned} L(\boldsymbol{\theta}) &= \tfrac{1}{2}\ln|V(\boldsymbol{\theta})| - \tfrac{1}{2}y'Q(\boldsymbol{\theta})'V(\boldsymbol{\theta})Q(\boldsymbol{\theta})y \\ &= \tfrac{1}{2}\ln|V(\boldsymbol{\theta})| - \tfrac{1}{2}y'Q'Q(\boldsymbol{\theta})'V(\boldsymbol{\theta})Q(\boldsymbol{\theta})Qy. \end{aligned} \tag{36}$$

Since $L(\boldsymbol{\theta})$ depends on y only through Qy, so too does its optimum and hence (35) applies in this case also.

We now write the estimator $\hat{\boldsymbol{\beta}}$ in terms of $\bar{\boldsymbol{\beta}}$ and Qu as $\hat{\boldsymbol{\beta}} = \bar{\boldsymbol{\beta}} + (\hat{\boldsymbol{\beta}} - \bar{\boldsymbol{\beta}}) = \bar{\boldsymbol{\beta}} + \mathbf{d}$, where $\mathbf{d} = [X'V(\hat{\boldsymbol{\theta}})X]^{-1}X'V(\hat{\boldsymbol{\theta}})Qu = \mathbf{d}(Qu)$, say, is statistically independent of $\bar{\boldsymbol{\beta}}$. Let $r = \mathbf{c}'\hat{\boldsymbol{\beta}} = \mathbf{c}'\bar{\boldsymbol{\beta}} + \mathbf{c}'\mathbf{d}$ and we have the conditional density

$$\text{PDF}(r \mid Qu) = N(\mathbf{c}'\boldsymbol{\beta} + \mathbf{c}'\mathbf{d}, \mathbf{c}'(X'VX)^{-1}\mathbf{c}). \tag{37}$$

Next Qu is singular $N(0, QV^{-1}Q)$ and using $P(\cdot)$ to represent the probability measure of this distribution, we deduce that

$$\begin{aligned}
\text{PDF}(r) &= \int N(\mathbf{c}'\boldsymbol{\beta} + \mathbf{c}'\mathbf{d}, \mathbf{c}'(X'VX)^{-1}\mathbf{c})\, \mathrm{d}P(Qu) \\
&= \int [N(\mathbf{c}'\boldsymbol{\beta} + \mathbf{c}'\mathbf{d}(\partial w), \mathbf{c}'(X'VX)^{-1}\mathbf{c})\, \mathrm{e}^{w'Qu}]_{w=0}\, \mathrm{d}P(Qu) \\
&= \left[N(\mathbf{c}'\boldsymbol{\beta} + \mathbf{c}'\mathbf{d}(\partial w), \mathbf{c}'(X'VX)^{-1}\mathbf{c}) \int \mathrm{e}^{w'Qu}\, \mathrm{d}P(Qu) \right]_{w=0} \\
&= [N(\mathbf{c}'\boldsymbol{\beta} + \mathbf{c}'\mathbf{d}(\partial w), \mathbf{c}'(X'VX)^{-1}\mathbf{c})\, \mathrm{e}^{w'QV^{-1}Qw/2}]_{w=0}. \qquad (38)
\end{aligned}$$

Note that in this formula $\mathbf{d}(\partial w)$ and hence $N(\mathbf{c}'\boldsymbol{\beta} + \mathbf{c}'\mathbf{d}(\partial w), \mathbf{c}'(X'VX)^{-1}\mathbf{c})$ are analytic functions of the differential operator ∂w and can be interpreted according to the definition (6).

Expression (38) shows the distribution of $\hat{\boldsymbol{\beta}}$ to be a form of normal mixture. There is no linear term in the exponent of the operand $\exp(w'QV^{-1}Qw/2)$ since this is the Laplace transform of the distribution of Qu, whose mean is zero. Upon replacement of this operand with the approximation $\exp(0'w) = 1$ we see that (38) reduces to

$$N(\mathbf{c}'\boldsymbol{\beta}, \mathbf{c}'(X'VX)^{-1}\mathbf{c}), \qquad (39)$$

which is the usual first-order asymptotic approximation to the distribution of $\mathbf{c}'\hat{\boldsymbol{\beta}}$. Higher order approximations may also be obtained. Note that when $\hat{\boldsymbol{\theta}} = \boldsymbol{\theta}(Qu)$ is taken to be an even function of Qu, as it is in most practical situations, it is easy to show from (38) that the next term in the expansion leads only to an adjustment in the asymptotic variance term in (39). The normal approximation itself is retained. This corresponds with the main conclusion of Rothenberg (1984a).

The distribution of the t-ratio t_c in (34) may be handled in the same way as $\hat{\boldsymbol{\beta}}$. With t_c we have the additional dependence of the denominator on $\hat{\boldsymbol{\theta}}$. However, this presents no further complication in the operational algebra. Following the same steps as those employed in deriving (38), we find

$$\text{PDF}(t) = [N(\mathbf{c}'\mathbf{d}(\partial w), \mathbf{c}'(X'VX)^{-1}c/c'(X'V(\partial w)X)^{-1}\mathbf{c})\, \mathrm{e}^{w'QV^{-1}Qw/2}]_{w=0}. \qquad (40)$$

This formula can be interpreted as an extension to the general regression case of formula (21) given earlier for the distribution of the usual t-ratio. In that case the error covariance matrix $\boldsymbol{\Omega} = \sigma^2 I$ was scalar. Writing $V(\hat{\boldsymbol{\theta}}) = (1/\hat{\sigma}^2)I$ with $\hat{\sigma}^2 = \hat{u}'\hat{u}/n$ and $n = T - k$, we see that $\mathbf{d}(\partial w) = 0$, $V(\partial w) = (1/\partial w'\, \partial w)I$ and formula (40) above reduces to

$$[N(0, n\sigma^2/\partial w'\, \partial w)\, \mathrm{e}^{\sigma^2 w' Q_X w/2}]_{w=0}, \qquad (41)$$

where $Q_X = I - P_X$. Let C be an orthogonal matrix for which $C'Q_X C = \operatorname{diag}(I_n, 0)$. Transform $w \to z = \sigma C'w$ and note that the operators transform according to the relation $\partial w = \sigma C\, \partial z$.

Under this transformation (41) becomes

$$[N(0, n/\partial z' \partial z)\, e^{z_1' z_1/2}]_{z=0} = [N(0, n/\partial z_1' \partial z_1)\, e^{z_1' z_1/2}]_{z_1=0}, \tag{42}$$

where z is partitioned as $(z_1', z_2')'$, conformably with the block diagonal decomposition of $C'Q_XC$. The expression on the right-hand side of (42) now simplifies by a change of dummy variables to $[N(0, n/\partial u)(1 - 2u)^{-n/2}]_{u=0}$ as in result (16) of the lemma in the second section. The density given in (42) therefore reduces to that of the usual t-ratio in this case.

In general, of course, the symbolic representations (38) and (40) rely on the form of the dependence of $V(\boldsymbol{\theta})$ on $\boldsymbol{\theta}$. In models with heterogeneity, the dependence is straightforward. In finite-order autoregressive error models, $V(\boldsymbol{\theta})$ has the usual finite-band matrix format associated with the inverse of the covariance matrix. For more general ARMA models the dependence is more complex but formulas are known (Zinde-Walsh 1988).

Conclusion

The methods introduced in this paper belong to a class of operational techniques that have been used for some time by mathematicians in studying solutions to systems of partial differential equations. The literature in this field is vast; but it is also rather abstract, as is evident in the works of Hormander (1971), Treves (1982) and Dieudonné (1988). Little attention seems yet to be have been given to the development of practical rules for working with nonlinear functions of operators in specific cases of interest. Nevertheless, it would appear from the regression examples studied here that the methods offer some prospect for dealing with rather complex distributional problems in an economical and efficient way. Indeed, as is apparent from the previous section, the regression estimator and t-statistic in the general linear model with a nonscalar covariance matrix are as easy to handle with the operational algebra as are the OLS estimator and t-ratio in the classical regression model.

Notes

My thanks go to a referee for helpful comments, to Glena Ames for her talents in word-processing this essay and to the NSF for research support.

References

Basmann, R. L. (1961). "Note on the exact finite sample frequency functions of generalized classical linear estimators in two leading overidentified cases," *Journal of the American Statistical Association*, 55, 619–36.

Bergstrom, A. R. (1962). "The exact sampling distributions of least squares and maximum likelihood estimators of the marginal propensity to consume," *Econometrica*, 30, 480–90.

Dieudonné, J. (1988). *Treatise on Analysis*, volume 8. New York: Academic Press.

Dickey, J. M. (1967). "Expansions of t densities and related complete integrals," *Annals of Mathematical Statistics*, 503–10.

Erdélyi, A. (1953). *Higher Transcendental Functions*, volume 3. New York: McGraw-Hill.

Fisher, R. A. (1925). "Expansion of Student's integral in powers in n^{-1}," *Metron*, 5, 109–12.

GAUSS (1989). *Gauss Version 2.0*. Kent: Aptech Systems Inc.

Gelfand, I. M. and G. E. Shilov (1964). *Generalized Functions*, volume 1. New York: Academic Press.

Hormander, L. (1971). "Fourier integral operators," *Acta Mathematica*, 127, 79–183.

Miller, K. S. (1974). "The Weyl fractional calculus," in B. Ross (ed.) *Fractional Calculus and its Applications*. Berlin: Springer-Verlag.

Phillips, P. C. B. (1984). "The exact distribution of the Stein-rule estimator," *Journal of Econometrics*, 25, 123–31.

Phillips, P. C. B. (1985). "The exact distribution of the SUR estimator," *Econometrica*, 53, 745–56.

Phillips, P. C. B. (1986). "The exact distribution of the Wald statistics," *Econometrica*, 54.

Phillips, P. C. B. (1987). "Fractional matrix calculus and the distribution of multivariate tests," in I. B. MacNeil and G. J. Umphrey (eds) *Time Series and Econometric Modeling*. Dordrecht: Reidel Publishing Company.

Richards, D. (1984). "Hyperspherical models, fractional derivatives and exponential distributions on matrix spaces," *Sankhya* A, 45, 155–65.

Rothenberg, T. J. (1984a). "Approximate normality of generalized least squares estimates," *Econometrica*, 52, 811–26.

Rothenberg, T. J. (1984b). "Hypothesis testing in linear models when the error covariance matrix is nonscalar," *Econometrica*, 52, 827–42.

Treves, F. (1982). *Pseudodifferential and Fourier Integral Operators*, volumes 1 & 2. New York: Plenum Press.

Zinde-Walsh, V. (1988). "Some exact formulae for autoregressive moving average processes," *Econometric Theory*, 4, 384–402.

11

Multiple Comparisons Emphasizing Incremental Effects

J. Richmond

Introduction

A wide class of multiple comparisons problems can be viewed in the following way. An observation is available on a K-variate random variable $\mathbf{x} = (x_1, \ldots, x_K)'$ which has the $N(\boldsymbol{\mu}, \sigma^2\Omega)$ distribution, where $\boldsymbol{\mu} = (\mu_1, \ldots, \mu_K)'$ and Ω is a known positive definite matrix. In addition an estimator s^2 of σ^2 is available that is independent of $\mathbf{x}$ and is distributed as $\sigma^2\chi_\nu^2/\nu$. In a linear subspace $L \subset R^K$, a certain spanning set $P = \{\mathbf{l}_1, \ldots, \mathbf{l}_q\}$ is regarded as *primary* in the sense that the researcher is particularly interested in obtaining confidence intervals for the linear combinations $\mathbf{l}_1'\boldsymbol{\mu}, \ldots, \mathbf{l}_q'\boldsymbol{\mu}$ of elements of the vector $\boldsymbol{\mu}$. At the same time, those linear combinations $\mathbf{l}'\boldsymbol{\mu}$ where $\mathbf{l} \in L - P$ may also be of *secondary* interest, and confidence intervals for some or all of these may be required. For example, the generalized Tukey procedure (Miller 1966) may be intepreted as one in which L is the space of all contrasts among means and the $K(K-1)/2$ differences $(\mu_i - \mu_j)$ $(i, j = 1, \ldots, K$ and $i \neq j)$ are regarded as primary. A further example in which L is also the space of all contrasts is the extension of Dunnett's procedure given by Shaffer (1977). In this case the $(K-1)$ differences $(\mu_1 - \mu_i)$ $(i = 2, \ldots, K)$ between a control mean μ_1 and the remaining means are regarded as primary.

In Richmond (1982), a general procedure for dealing with problems of this type was described. Let

$$A(\mathbf{l}) = \left\{(a_1, \ldots, a_q) : \sum_{i=1}^{q} \mathbf{l}_i a_i = \mathbf{l}\right\} \tag{1}$$

and define

$$\phi(\mathbf{l}) = \min_{(a_1, \ldots, a_q) \in A(\mathbf{l})} \sum_{i=1}^{q} (\mathbf{l}_i'\Omega\mathbf{l}_i)^{1/2}|a_i|. \tag{2}$$

It was shown in Richmond (1982) that, given C, the set of confidence intervals

$$\{\mathbf{l}'\mathbf{x} \pm Cs\phi(\mathbf{l}) : \mathbf{l} \in Q\} \tag{3}$$

has an overall confidence level that is the same for all choices of Q such that $P \subset Q \subset L$. This confidence level can in some cases be controlled exactly by a suitable choice of the critical value C, but in any case, if we let $C = m(\alpha : q, v)$, the upper 100α percent critical value of the Studentized maximum modulus (SMM) distribution, the overall confidence level will be at least $100(1 - \alpha)$ percent. (If $(z_1, \ldots, z_q)'$ are independent $N(0, \sigma^2)$ random variables and vs_z^2/σ_z^2 is χ_v^2, the Studentized maximum modulus is $m_{q,v} = \max_i |z_i|/s_z$. See Hahn and Hendrickson (1971) for details.) For future reference we note the following facts.

1. The value $\phi(\mathbf{l})$ can always be computed by solving a linear programming problem.
2. When $\mathbf{l}_1, \ldots, \mathbf{l}_q$ are linearly independent, computation of $\phi(\mathbf{l})$ is often trivial because the set $A(\mathbf{l})$ contains only one element.
3. For $i = 1, \ldots, q$, $\phi(\mathbf{l}_i) = (\mathbf{l}_i'\Omega\mathbf{l}_i)^{1/2}$.

In this article, we consider the one-way analysis of variance model in which $\Omega = \text{diag}\,(1/n_1, \ldots, 1/n_K)$ where the n_i are the numbers of observations per treatment. In many models of this type, primary interest lies in the total effects $\mu_1, \ldots, \mu_K$ and the incremental effects $(\mu_{i+1} - \mu_i)$ $(i = 1, \ldots, K - 1)$. Other linear combinations of the means may be of only secondary interest. In the next section, we describe a method that can be used to construct confidence intervals for any linear combinations of the means, while treating μ_i $(i = 1, \ldots, K)$ and $(\mu_{i+1} - \mu_i)$ $(i = 1, \ldots, K - 1)$ as primary. A table of critical values for use with the new method is given. The third section compares this method with three other multiple comparisons procedures.

An Incremental Effects Method

The theory developed in this section is a straightforward application of the general method in Richmond (1982). Our aim is to design a multiple comparisons procedure that gives special emphasis to the individual means $\mu_1, \ldots, \mu_K$ and to the incremental effects $(\mu_{i+1} - \mu_i)$ $(i = 1, \ldots, K - 1)$, a total of $q = 2K - 1$ objects of primary interest. Let $P = \{\mathbf{l}_1, \ldots, \mathbf{l}_{2K-1}\}$ where the $\mathbf{l}_i \in R^K$ are the vectors indicated in the following array.

$$
\begin{array}{cccccccc}
\mathbf{l}_1 & \mathbf{l}_2 & & \mathbf{l}_K & \mathbf{l}_{K+1} & \mathbf{l}_{K+2} & & \mathbf{l}_{2K-1} \\
1 & 0 & & 0 & -1 & 0 & & 0 \\
0 & 1 & & \cdot & 1 & -1 & & \cdot \\
\cdot & 0 & \cdots & \cdot & 0 & 1 & \cdots & \cdot \\
\cdot & \cdot & & \cdot & \cdot & 0 & & 0 \\
\cdot & \cdot & & 0 & \cdot & \cdot & & -1 \\
0 & 0 & & 1 & 0 & 0 & & 1
\end{array}
$$

The space L spanned by the vectors in P is the whole of R^K. For $\mathbf{l}_i \in P$, confidence interval width is determined by the value $\phi(\mathbf{l}_i) = (\mathbf{l}_i'\Omega\mathbf{l}_i)^{1/2}$, giving

$$
\phi(\mathbf{l}_i) = \begin{cases} (1/n_i)^{1/2}, & 1 \leqslant i \leqslant K, \\ (1/n_{i-K} + 1/n_{i-K+1})^{1/2}, & K + 1 \leqslant i \leqslant 2K - 1. \end{cases} \tag{4}
$$

More generally, for arbitrary $\mathbf{l} = (\lambda_1, \ldots, \lambda_K)' \in R^K$, $\phi(\mathbf{l})$ can be calculated as the value of a linear program that is dual to, and therefore has the same value as, the program

$$\begin{aligned} &\max \sum_{i=1}^{K} \lambda_i y_i, \\ &|y_i| \leqslant (1/n_i)^{1/2}, \quad 1 \leqslant i \leqslant K, \\ &|y_{i+1} - y_i| \leqslant (1/n_i + 1/n_{i+1})^{1/2}, \quad i = 1, \ldots, K-1. \end{aligned} \tag{5}$$

Equation (5) can easily be solved by a computational algorithm, but for several of the cases of interest a simple analytic solution can be obtained.

We consider first the case in which $\lambda_i \geqslant 0$ for each $i = 1, \ldots, K$. Then clearly the value of the program (5) cannot exceed $\sum_{i=1}^{K} \lambda_i (1/n_i)^{1/2}$. Furthermore, the choice $y_i = (1/n_i)^{1/2}$ $(i = 1, \ldots, K)$ is feasible for the program since $|(1/n_{i+1})^{1/2} - (1/n_i)^{1/2}| \leqslant (1/n_{i+1} + 1/n_i)^{1/2}$. It follows that this choice of $y_1, \ldots, y_K$ solves (5); thus $\lambda_i \geqslant 0$ $(i = 1, \ldots, K)$ implies

$$\phi(\mathbf{l}) = \sum_{i=1}^{K} (1/n_i)^{1/2} \lambda_i. \tag{6}$$

Now consider the case in which only λ_r and λ_s are nonzero with $\lambda_i = 0$ $(i \neq r, s)$; we allow for the possibility that λ_r or λ_s may be negative (this case includes all the differences $(\mu_r - \mu_s)$). It is obvious that in this situation many of the constraints in problem (5) are redundant. If $|r - s| > 1$, (5) can be solved by setting $y_i = 0$ for $i \neq r, s$ and choosing y_r and y_s to solve

$$\begin{aligned} &\max (\lambda_r y_r + \lambda_s y_s), \\ &|y_r| \leqslant (1/n_r)^{1/2}, \\ &|y_s| \leqslant (1/n_s)^{1/2}. \end{aligned} \tag{7}$$

Equation (7) is solved by letting $y_r = (1/n_r)^{1/2}$ if $\lambda_r \geqslant 0$ and $y_r = -(1/n_r)^{1/2}$ if $\lambda_r < 0$; similarly for y_s. Hence, in this case $|r - s| > 1$ implies

$$\phi(\mathbf{l}) = (1/n_r)^{1/2} |\lambda_r| + (1/n_s)^{1/2} |\lambda_s|. \tag{8}$$

When $|r - s| = 1$, problem (5) may similarly be reduced to that of choosing y_r and y_s to solve

$$\begin{aligned} &\max (\lambda_r y_r + \lambda_s y_s), \\ &|y_r| \leqslant (1/n_r)^{1/2}, \\ &|y_s| \leqslant (1/n_s)^{1/2}, \\ &|y_s - y_r| \leqslant (1/n_r + 1/n_s)^{1/2}. \end{aligned} \tag{9}$$

The solution of (9) is fairly simple to obtain by using graphical methods in (y_r, y_s) space to construct the feasible region and the level sets of the objective function.

These level sets are straight lines sloping upward if λ_r and λ_s are of opposite sign, downward sloping otherwise. In the latter case the solution is simple: sign $(\lambda_r) =$ sign (λ_s) implies

$$\phi(\mathbf{l}) = (1/n_r)^{1/2}|\lambda_r| + (1/n_s)^{1/2}|\lambda_s|. \tag{10}$$

When λ_r and λ_s are of opposite sign, a graphical analysis shows that the solution depends on whether $|\lambda_r/\lambda_s|$ is less than one or greater than or equal to one. The result of the analysis shows that sign $(\lambda_r) \neq$ sign (λ_s) and $|\lambda_r/\lambda_s| \geqslant 1$ implies

$$\phi(\mathbf{l}) = |\lambda_r|(1/n_r)^{1/2} + |\lambda_s|((1/n_r + 1/n_s)^{1/2} - (1/n_r)^{1/2}) \tag{11}$$

and that sign $(\lambda_r) \neq$ sign (λ_s) and $|\lambda_r/\lambda_s| < 1$ implies

$$\phi(\mathbf{l}) = |\lambda_r|((1/n_r + 1/n_s)^{1/2} - (1/n_s)^{1/2}) + |\lambda_s|(1/n_s)^{1/2}. \tag{12}$$

The results in (4), (6), (8), (10), (11) and (12) cover most of the cases likely to be of interest in practice, and in those cases they simplify considerably. Since there are (2K − 1) vectors in the primary set, we use the critical value $m(\alpha:2K-1, \nu)$. In particular we obtain the following confidence intervals ($\hat{\mu}_i$ denotes the estimator of μ_i).

Total effects:

$$\hat{\mu}_i \pm m(\alpha:2K-1, \nu)s(1/n_i)^{1/2}, \quad i = 1, \ldots, K. \tag{13}$$

Incremental effects:

$$(\hat{\mu}_{i+1} - \hat{\mu}_i) \pm m(\alpha:2K-1, \nu)s(1/n_{i+1} + 1/n_i)^{1/2}, \quad i = 1, \ldots, K-1. \tag{14}$$

Other differences in means:

$$(\hat{\mu}_j - \hat{\mu}_i) \pm m(\alpha:2K-1, \nu)s((1/n_i)^{1/2} + (1/n_j)^{1/2}), \quad i, j = 1, \ldots, K, |i-j| > 1. \tag{15}$$

This set of confidence intervals has an overall confidence level of at least $100(1-\alpha)$ percent, and may be appropriately augmented by intervals for *any* other linear combination of the means without affecting the overall confidence level. In the remainder of this paper, we shall refer to the technique described in this section as the incremental effects method (IEM).

Published tables such as those in Hahn and Hendrickson (1971), Stoline and Ury (1979), or Hochberg and Tamhane (1987) are not really adequate for using the IEM. We therefore conclude this section with Tables 11.1–11.3 which give for $K = 2(1)20$ and for $\alpha = 0.01, 0.05, 0.10$ the upper α critical values of the Studentized maximum modulus distribution required for use with the IEM. The table was computed using the Fortran program in Stoline et al. (1979). Values in the table are believed to be accurate to within ± 0.001.

Table 11.1 Upper 1 percent points of SMM distribution: $m(0.01 : K^*, v)$. Parameters $K^* = (2K - 1)$; v

K	K^*	v = 5	7	10	12	16	20
2	3	5.105	4.297	3.801	3.631	3.434	3.323
3	5	5.625	4.678	4.099	3.899	3.669	3.540
4	7	5.969	4.930	4.295	4.076	3.823	3.682
5	9	6.227	5.119	4.441	4.208	3.938	3.787
6	11	6.430	5.270	4.559	4.313	4.029	3.871
7	13	6.600	5.395	4.655	4.400	4.105	3.939
8	15	6.742	5.502	4.738	4.476	4.170	3.999
9	17	6.869	5.596	4.811	4.541	4.227	4.051
10	19	6.980	5.678	4.875	4.599	4.276	4.097
11	21	7.078	5.752	4.934	4.650	4.321	4.138
12	23	7.168	5.818	4.986	4.697	4.362	4.175
13	25	7.250	5.881	5.033	4.740	4.400	4.209
14	27	7.326	5.938	5.078	4.780	4.435	4.240
15	29	7.395	5.988	5.119	4.817	4.467	4.270
16	31	7.461	6.037	5.157	4.852	4.496	4.296
17	33	7.521	6.082	5.193	4.884	4.524	4.321
18	35	7.578	6.125	5.227	4.914	4.550	4.346
19	37	7.633	6.166	5.258	4.942	4.575	4.368
20	39	7.684	6.203	5.288	4.970	4.599	4.390

K	K^*	v = 24	30	40	60	120	∞
2	3	3.253	3.185	3.119	3.055	2.994	2.934
3	5	3.458	3.379	3.303	3.229	3.158	3.089
4	7	3.592	3.505	3.421	3.340	3.263	3.188
5	9	3.690	3.598	3.509	3.422	3.339	3.260
6	11	3.770	3.672	3.578	3.487	3.400	3.316
7	13	3.834	3.732	3.635	3.540	3.450	3.362
8	15	3.890	3.785	3.684	3.586	3.492	3.402
9	17	3.938	3.830	3.726	3.625	3.528	3.436
10	19	3.981	3.870	3.763	3.660	3.561	3.466
11	21	4.020	3.906	3.796	3.691	3.590	3.493
12	23	4.055	3.938	3.827	3.719	3.616	3.517
13	25	4.086	3.968	3.854	3.745	3.640	3.539
14	27	4.116	3.996	3.880	3.769	3.662	3.559
15	29	4.143	4.021	3.904	3.791	3.682	3.578
16	31	4.168	4.045	3.926	3.811	3.701	3.595
17	33	4.192	4.067	3.946	3.830	3.718	3.611
18	35	4.215	4.088	3.966	3.848	3.735	3.626
19	37	4.235	4.107	3.984	3.865	3.750	3.641
20	39	4.255	4.126	4.001	3.881	3.765	3.654

Table 11.2 Upper 5 percent points of SMM distribution: $m(0.05: K^*, \nu)$. Parameters $K^* = (2K - 1)$; ν

		ν					
K	K^*	5	7	10	12	16	20
2	3	3.399	3.055	2.829	2.747	2.650	2.594
3	5	3.789	3.376	3.103	3.004	2.866	2.819
4	7	4.044	3.585	3.281	3.171	3.039	2.963
5	9	4.233	3.740	3.413	3.294	3.152	3.070
6	11	4.382	3.863	3.517	3.391	3.241	3.154
7	13	4.506	3.965	3.603	3.472	3.314	3.223
8	15	4.610	4.051	3.677	3.541	3.377	3.282
9	17	4.701	4.126	3.741	3.600	3.431	3.333
10	19	4.782	4.192	3.797	3.653	3.479	3.378
11	21	4.854	4.252	3.848	3.700	3.522	3.419
12	23	4.918	4.306	3.894	3.743	3.561	3.456
13	25	4.977	4.354	3.935	3.782	3.597	3.489
14	27	5.032	4.399	3.974	3.818	3.629	3.520
15	29	5.082	4.441	4.009	3.851	3.660	3.548
16	31	5.128	4.480	4.042	3.882	3.688	3.575
17	33	5.171	4.516	4.073	3.911	3.714	3.600
18	35	5.212	4.550	4.102	3.938	3.739	3.623
19	37	5.250	4.582	4.129	3.963	3.762	3.645
20	39	5.287	4.612	4.155	3.987	3.784	3.665

		ν					
K	K^*	24	30	40	60	120	∞
2	3	2.558	2.522	2.488	2.454	2.420	2.388
3	5	2.775	2.732	2.690	2.649	2.608	2.569
4	7	2.914	2.866	2.819	2.772	2.727	2.683
5	9	3.016	2.964	2.913	2.863	2.814	2.766
6	11	3.097	3.042	2.987	2.934	2.881	2.830
7	13	3.164	3.105	3.048	2.992	2.937	2.883
8	15	3.220	3.160	3.100	3.041	2.984	2.928
9	17	3.269	3.207	3.145	3.084	3.025	2.966
10	19	3.313	3.248	3.184	3.122	3.061	3.000
11	21	3.352	3.285	3.220	3.156	3.093	3.031
12	23	3.387	3.319	3.252	3.186	3.121	3.058
13	25	3.419	3.349	3.281	3.214	3.148	3.083
14	27	3.448	3.377	3.308	3.239	3.172	3.106
15	29	3.475	3.404	3.333	3.263	3.194	3.127
16	31	3.501	3.428	3.356	3.285	3.215	3.146
17	33	3.525	3.450	3.377	3.305	3.234	3.165
18	35	3.547	3.472	3.397	3.324	3.252	3.182
19	37	3.568	3.492	3.417	3.343	3.269	3.198
20	39	3.587	3.510	3.435	3.359	3.286	3.213

Table 11.3 Upper 10 percent points of SMM distribution: $m(0.10 : K^*, v)$. Parameters $K^* = (2K - 1)$; v

		v					
K	K^*	5	7	10	12	16	20
2	3	2.769	2.556	2.410	2.357	2.293	2.255
3	5	3.116	2.856	2.678	2.612	2.532	2.486
4	7	3.341	3.050	2.850	2.776	2.686	2.634
5	9	3.507	3.193	2.977	2.896	2.799	2.742
6	11	3.638	3.306	3.077	2.991	2.887	2.826
7	13	3.746	3.399	3.159	3.070	2.960	2.896
8	15	3.837	3.478	3.229	3.136	3.022	2.956
9	17	3.916	3.547	3.290	3.194	3.076	3.007
10	19	3.986	3.607	3.343	3.244	3.123	3.052
11	21	4.048	3.661	3.391	3.290	3.166	3.093
12	23	4.104	3.710	3.434	3.331	3.204	3.129
13	25	4.155	3.754	3.474	3.368	3.239	3.163
14	27	4.202	3.795	3.510	3.403	3.271	3.193
15	29	4.245	3.833	3.543	3.434	3.301	3.221
16	31	4.286	3.868	3.574	3.464	3.328	3.248
17	33	4.323	3.900	3.603	3.492	3.354	3.272
18	35	4.358	3.931	3.631	3.517	3.378	3.295
19	37	4.393	3.960	3.656	3.542	3.401	3.317
20	39	4.422	3.987	3.680	3.565	3.422	3.337

		v					
K	K^*	24	30	40	60	120	∞
2	3	2.231	2.207	2.183	2.160	2.137	2.114
3	5	2.456	2.426	2.396	2.367	2.339	2.311
4	7	2.599	2.565	2.532	2.499	2.466	2.434
5	9	2.704	2.667	2.630	2.594	2.558	2.523
6	11	2.786	2.747	2.708	2.669	2.630	2.592
7	13	2.854	2.812	2.771	2.730	2.689	2.649
8	15	2.911	2.868	2.825	2.782	2.739	2.697
9	17	2.961	2.916	2.871	2.826	2.782	2.738
10	19	3.005	2.958	2.912	2.866	2.820	2.774
11	21	3.044	2.996	2.948	2.901	2.854	2.807
12	23	3.080	3.030	2.981	2.933	2.884	2.836
13	25	3.112	3.062	3.011	2.962	2.912	2.862
14	27	3.142	3.090	3.039	2.988	2.937	2.887
15	29	3.169	3.117	3.065	3.013	2.961	2.909
16	31	3.194	3.141	3.088	3.035	2.982	2.930
17	33	3.218	3.164	3.110	3.056	3.003	2.949
18	35	3.240	3.186	3.131	3.076	3.022	2.967
19	37	3.261	3.206	3.150	3.095	3.040	2.984
20	39	3.281	3.225	3.169	3.113	3.056	3.000

Alternatives to the IEM

In this section we describe some variants of the Dunnett and Tukey methods for the purposes of comparison with the IEM. Note that the IEM gives confidence intervals for arbitrary linear combinations of the means, that is the space L is the whole of R^K. The Dunnett method as extended by Shaffer (1977) requires that the sample sizes per treatment be the same (except possibly for one treatment regarded as the control). Furthermore, Shaffer's extension is to the space L_C of all contrasts among means, not to the complete set of arbitrary linear combinations of means. The Tukey method was originally designed for the case of equal sample sizes and the for the space L_C; however a modified version, the T' method of Spjøtvoll and Stoline (1973), can be used in the case of unequal sample sizes over the whole of R^K. Hochberg's (1974) GT2 method for multiple comparisons in the space of all contrasts can also be used when sample sizes are unequal, and coverage can be extended to the whole of R^K in a variety of ways.

In order to make comparisons with the method of the previous section, we first show how to augment the Dunnett method and the GT2 method to include confidence intervals for any linear combination of the means. In each case the extension from L_C to $L = R^K$ is easily achieved by including μ_1 in the primary set. In many applications, μ_1 can be interpreted as a control mean and the special emphasis it receives by being included in the primary set is amply justified. In what follows we refer to these modified multiple comparisons procedures as the augmented Dunnett method (ADM) and the augmented Tukey method (ATM).

Consider first the ADM. The primary set $P_{\text{ADM}} = \{\mathbf{l}_1, \dots, \mathbf{l}_K\}$ where $\mathbf{l}_1' = (1, 0, \dots, 0)$ and for $j = 2, \dots, K$ the vector $\mathbf{l}_j$ has first element -1, jth element $+1$, all other elements zero. These vectors are linearly independent and span R^K. For any $\mathbf{l} = (\lambda_1, \dots, \lambda_K)' \in R^K$ the solution to $\sum_{i=1}^K \mathbf{l}_i a_i = \mathbf{l}$ is

$$a_1 = \sum_{i=1}^{K} \lambda_i, \qquad a_j = \lambda_j, j = 2, \dots, K. \tag{16}$$

The length of the confidence interval for $\mathbf{l}'\boldsymbol{\mu}$ where $\mathbf{l} \in R^K$ is then determined by the value

$$\phi(\mathbf{l}) = (1/n_1)^{1/2} \left| \sum_{i=1}^{K} \lambda_i \right| + \sum_{i=2}^{K} (1/n_1 + 1/n_i)^{1/2} |\lambda_i|. \tag{17}$$

Choosing as critical value $m(\alpha : K, \nu)$ gives us the following ADM confidence intervals, which have an overall confidence level of at least $100(1 - \alpha)$ percent.

Total effects:

$$\hat{\mu}_1 \pm m(\alpha : K, \nu) s (1/n_1)^{1/2},$$
$$\hat{\mu}_j \pm m(\alpha : K, \nu) s ((1/n_1)^{1/2} + (1/n_1 + 1/n_j)^{1/2}), \qquad j = 2, \dots, K. \tag{18}$$

Incremental effects:

$$(\hat{\mu}_2 - \hat{\mu}_1) \pm m(\alpha : K, v)s(1/n_1 + 1/n_2)^{1/2},$$
$$(\hat{\mu}_{i+1} - \hat{\mu}_i) \pm m(\alpha : K, v)s((1/n_1 + 1/n_i)^{1/2} + (1/n_1 + 1/n_{i+1})^{1/2}), \quad (19)$$
$$i = 2, \ldots, K-1.$$

Other differences in means:

$$(\hat{\mu}_j - \hat{\mu}_1) \pm m(\alpha : K, v)s(1/n_1 + 1/n_j)^{1/2}, \qquad j = 2, \ldots, K,$$
$$(\hat{\mu}_j - \hat{\mu}_i) \pm m(\alpha : K, v)s((1/n_1 + 1/n_j)^{1/2} + (1/n_1 + 1/n_i)^{1/2}), \quad (20)$$
$$2 \leqslant i < j \leqslant K;\ i < j-1.$$

Moving now to the ATM method, we take as primary set $P_{\text{ATM}} = \{\mathbf{l}_1, \ldots, \mathbf{l}_q\}$ where $q = K(K-1)/2 + 1$, $\mathbf{l}_1 = (1,0,\ldots,0)'$ and the remaining $(q-1)$ vectors have the form $(0,\ldots,0,-1,0,\ldots,0,+1,0,\ldots,0)$ with -1 appearing in the ith place and $+1$ in the jth place for $1 \leqslant i < j \leqslant K$. The value $\phi(\mathbf{l})$ which determines the length of the confidence intervals can in this case be computed as the solution to the problem

$$\max \sum_{i=1}^{K} \lambda_i y_i,$$
$$|y_1| \leqslant (1/n_1)^{1/2}, \quad (21)$$
$$|y_i - y_j| \leqslant (1/n_i + 1/n_j)^{1/2}, \qquad 1 \leqslant i < j \leqslant K.$$

It is not easy to give a general analytic solution to (21) except in special cases. For the purposes of this paper, recall that $\phi(\mathbf{l}_i) = (\mathbf{l}_i'\Omega\mathbf{l}_i)^{1/2}$ for $i = 1, \ldots, q$. This covers all the pairwise differences in means and also the control mean. Now consider the jth mean where $j \neq 1$. It is easy to show that in this case problem (21) reduces to

$$\max y_j,$$
$$|y_j| \leqslant (1/n_j + 1/n_k)^{1/2}, \qquad k = 1, \ldots, K\ (k \neq j). \quad (22)$$

The solution to (22) gives

$$\phi(\mathbf{l}) = \min_{k \neq j} (1/n_j + 1/n_k)^{1/2}. \quad (23)$$

For an overall confidence level of at least $100(1-\alpha)$ per cent, use the critical value $m(\alpha : q, v)$ with $q = K(K-1)/2 + 1$. This gives the following set of intervals.

Total effects:

$$\hat{\mu}_1 \pm m(\alpha : q, v)s(1/n_1)^{1/2},$$
$$\hat{\mu}_j \pm m(\alpha : q, v)s \min_{k \neq j} (1/n_j + 1/n_k)^{1/2}, \qquad j = 2, \ldots, K. \quad (24)$$

Incremental effects:

$$(\hat{\mu}_{i+1} - \hat{\mu}_i) \pm m(\alpha : q, v)s(1/n_{i+1} + 1/n_i)^{1/2}, \qquad i = 1, \ldots, K-1. \tag{25}$$

Other differences in means:

$$(\hat{\mu}_i - \hat{\mu}_j) \pm m(\alpha : q, v)s(1/n_i + 1/n_j)^{1/2}, \qquad 1 \leqslant i < j \leqslant K, i < j-1. \tag{26}$$

For ease of reference, the corresponding T' confidence intervals of Spjøtvoll and Stoline (1973) are given in (27)–(29).

Total effects:

$$\hat{\mu}_i \pm q'(\alpha : K, v)s(1/n_i)^{1/2}, \qquad i = 1, \ldots, K. \tag{27}$$

Incremental effects:

$$(\hat{\mu}_{i+1} - \hat{\mu}_i) \pm q'(\alpha : K, v)s \max((1/n_{i+1})^{1/2}, (1/n_i)^{1/2}), \qquad i = 1, \ldots, K-1. \tag{28}$$

Other differences in means:

$$(\hat{\mu}_j - \hat{\mu}_i) \pm q'(\alpha : K, v)s \max((1/n_j)^{1/2}, (1/n_i)^{1/2}), \qquad 1 \leqslant i < j \leqslant K, i < j-1. \tag{29}$$

In (27)–(29), $q'(\alpha : K, v)$ denotes the $100(1-\alpha)$ percent critical value of the Studentized augmented range distribution with K and v degrees of freedom (Stoline 1978).

Some numerical comparisons

In order to assess how the methods described in the last section are likely to differ in practical applications, we report in this section the results of some numerical comparisons between the IEM and the alternative methods. Some indication of the differences among the confidence intervals in (13)–(15) compared with those of (18)–(20), (24)–(26), and (27)–(29) is displayed in tables 11.4 and 11.5. In constructing the tables, critical values of the Studentized maximum modulus distribution were computed using the Fortran program in Stoline et al. (1979); values for the Studentized augmented range distribution were taken from Stoline (1978) and the table in Scheffé (1959). Table 11.4 gives the ratios of the width of the IEM intervals in (13)–(15) to those of the ADM, ATM, and T' intervals, for three values of K, $\alpha = 0.05$ and $v = 60$ in the case of the balanced model for which $n_1 = n_2 \cdots = n_K$. Qualitatively, the results reported conform closely to the expectation that the narrower confidence intervals will be obtained for each type of interval by a method which treats that type of interval as primary. In addition, if two methods both treat a particular type of interval as primary, then usually the method with the smaller number of elements in the primary set will generate the narrower interval (these comments do not apply to the T' method). Quantitatively, the different methods can yield very substantial differences in the width of confidence intervals, as is apparent in the values appearing in the table. Similar tables for $v = 20$ and $v = 120$ show results both qualitatively and quantitatively very similar to those shown in table 11.4.

Table 11.5 gives the ratios of the confidence interval widths for a small unbalanced

Table 11.4 Ratios of confidence interval widths: balanced model ($\nu = 60$, $\alpha = 0.05$)

Type of interval	K	Methods compared: IEM/ADM	IEM/ATM	IEM/T'
Total effects				
μ_1	5	1.081	0.976	0.719
	10	1.077	0.915	0.671
	20	1.070	0.872	0.641
$\mu_j (2 \leqslant j \leqslant K)$	5	0.448	0.690	0.719
	10	0.446	0.647	0.671
	20	0.443	0.617	0.641
Incremental effects				
$\mu_2 - \mu_1$	5	1.081	0.976	1.017
	10	1.077	0.915	0.949
	20	1.070	0.872	0.907
$\mu_{i+1} - \mu_i (2 \leqslant i \leqslant K - 1)$	5	0.541	0.976	1.017
	10	0.538	0.915	0.949
	20	0.535	0.872	0.907
Other				
$\mu_j - \mu_1 (3 \leqslant j \leqslant K)$	5	1.529	1.380	1.438
	10	1.523	1.294	1.342
	20	1.513	1.233	1.282
$\mu_j - \mu_i (2 \leqslant i < j \leqslant K; i < j - 1)$	5	0.764	1.380	1.438
	10	0.761	1.294	1.342
	20	0.757	1.233	1.282

Table 11.5 Ratios of confidence interval widths: unbalanced model ($K = 4$, $n_1 = 6$, $n_2 = 14$, $n_3 = 15$, $n_4 = 10$; $\nu = 41$, $\alpha = 0.05$)

Type of interval	Methods compared: IEM/ADM	IEM/ATM	IEM/T'
Total effects			
μ_1	1.083	1.000	0.744
μ_2	0.323	0.719	0.744
μ_3	0.312	0.695	0.744
μ_4	0.371	0.775	0.744
Incremental effects			
$\mu_2 - \mu_1$	1.083	1.000	0.889
$\mu_3 - \mu_2$	0.415	1.000	1.034
$\mu_4 - \mu_3$	0.443	1.000	0.960
Other			
$\mu_3 - \mu_1$	1.495	1.380	1.214
$\mu_4 - \mu_1$	1.520	1.403	1.320
$\mu_4 - \mu_2$	0.629	1.409	1.624

model, again for $\alpha = 0.05$. The parameters used to construct the table were $K = 4$, $n_1 = 6$, $n_2 = 14$, $n_3 = 15$, and $n_4 = 10$; the value used for v was $(n_1 + n_2 + n_3 + n_4) - K = 41$. Qualitatively, the results are comparable to those in table 11.4; as might be expected the quantitative differences in the widths of the intervals are even more widespread than in table 11.4. For the intervals in table 11.5, we find the IEM intervals are on average 0.76 times the width of the ADM intervals, 1.04 times the width of the ATM intervals and 1.00 times the width of the T' intervals. However, when we confine ourselves to the intervals for total and incremental effects only (which are treated as primary by the IEM) these averages are 0.58, 0.88, and 0.84 respectively.

Conclusions

In many practical experiments, treatment levels can be ordered in a natural way and the investigator may be particularly interested not only in responses to different treatment levels but also in the effect of moving from one treatment level to the next (examples: effect of increased exposure to radiation hazard, effect of movement from one social class to another, etc.). The IEM method described above treats the means and the $(K - 1)$ differences in adjacent means as primary while at the same time allowing the investigator to construct confidence intervals for any other linear combination of the means with no effect on the overall confidence level. Comparisons with three other methods that can be used to construct intervals for arbitrary linear combinations of the means suggest that the IEM could be a useful tool in applied research.

References

Hahn, G. J., and R. W. Hendrickson (1971). "A table of percentage points of the distribution of the largest absolute value of k student t variates and its applications," *Biometrika*, 58, 323–32.

Hochberg, Y. (1974). "Some generalizations of the T-method in simultaneous inference," *Journal of Multivariate Analysis*, 4, 224–34.

Hochberg, Y., and C. A. Tamhane (1987). *Multiple Comparison Procedures*. New York: John Wiley.

Miller, R. G. (1966). *Simultaneous Statistical Inference*. New York: McGraw-Hill.

Richmond, J. (1982). "A general method for constructing simultaneous confidence intervals," *Journal of the American Statistical Association*, 77, 455–60.

Scheffé, H. J. (1959). *The Analysis of Variance*. New York: John Wiley.

Shaffer, J. P. (1977). "Multiple comparisons emphasizing selected contrasts: an extension and generalization of Dunnett's procedure," *Biometrics*, 33, 293–303.

Spjøtvoll, E., and M. R. Stoline (1973). "An extension of the T-methods of multiple comparison to include cases with unequal sample sizes," *Journal of the American Statistical Association*, 68, 975–8.

Stoline, M. R. (1978). "Tables of the Studentized augmented range and applications to problems of multiple comparison," *Journal of the American Statistical Association*, 73, 656–60.

Stoline, M. R., B. T. Mitchell, and H. K. Ury (1979). "Fortran program: double precision generation of the upper α-points for the Studentized maximum modulus distribution," *Western Michigan University Mathematics Report*. 57.

Stoline, M. R., and H. K. Ury (1979). "Tables of the Studentized maximum modulus distribution and an application to multiple comparison among means," *Technometrics*, 21, 87–93.

12

Some Alternatives to the Edgeworth Approximation for Econometric Statistics

J. D. Sargan

Introduction

Twenty years ago when I first considered the use of Edgeworth approximations to approximate the distributions of econometric estimators and test statistics, it seemed likely that here was a comparatively easy way of improving the performance of many test statistics which might be used in applied contexts. This paper consists of two sections, a technical section on the Edgeworth approximations, and a final section discussing the general problem of improving the tests used in applied studies.

In linear models these statistics could be expressed as functions of the data second moments, and the data second moments had asymptotically normal distributions from which the asymptotic distributions of the more general statistics could be derived. Denoting the data second moments arranged as a vector by $\mathbf{p}$ and a scalar function of these, representing some statistic whose distribution it is desired to approximate, by $\phi(\mathbf{p})$, the asymptotic distribution of ϕ depends only on the first derivatives of ϕ at the expected values of $\mathbf{p}$ and on the asymptotic distribution of $\mathbf{p}$, which can be regarded as only depending on the asymptotic variance matrix of $\mathbf{p}$. Edgeworth approximations require only the specification of the higher order derivatives of the ϕ and the higher order moments of $\mathbf{p}$. They can be applied easily to a very wide range of such functions.

It would be ideal if, for the types of model and sizes of sample which are used in applied econometrics, the Edgeworth approximation gives a value for the probability attributed to the confidence intervals of various test statistics which have relatively trivial errors. The accuracy of the approximation is very model-dependent, so that the size of the sample T which is required for a given accuracy, measured in terms of the maximal error for some interval of the distribution, depends very much on the statistic and the parameters of the model from which the statistic is generated. The size of the error is made very dependent on these factors because the approximation to the distribution function, $F(x)$, need not have the property that it increases as a function of x for all values of x, and tends to $+1$ as x tends to $+\infty$ and tends to 0 as x tends to $-\infty$. This is particularly serious when it is required to develop approximations to the probabilities of being outside a 95 percent or 99 percent confidence interval, since the approximations are particuarly poor on the tails of the distributions. (In the rest of this paper, an approximation to a cumulative distribution function which has the property of being always increasing between its lower limit 0 and its upper limit 1 will be referred to as behaving satisfactorily.) The failure of the Edgeworth approximation to behave satisfactorily can be corrected by using modified Edgeworth approximations which are rather arbitrarily modified to ensure that they do satisfy the requirement that they are always increasing, as in Arellano and Sargan (1990). The approximation then takes the form $I(\psi(x))$, where $I(\cdot)$ is the standard normal cumulative distribution function, and $\psi(x)$ is a function always increasing in x, and chosen so that its third-order Taylor series expansion at the origin equals the third-order polymomial used for the second-order Edgeworth approximation. Appendix A has the details of this approximation. Later references to the modified Edgeworth approximation refer to this approximation.

Both the original and the modified Edgeworth approximations have the defect that their tails tend to zero or one exponentially, i.e. the $F(x)$ is of order $\exp(-g(x))$ where $g(x)$ is some positive polynomial in x as $x \to -\infty$ and $1 - F(x)$ is of similar order as $x \to +\infty$. Since the tails of the exact distributions of these estimators and test statistics are usually of order some negative power of x, for sufficiently large values of x the approximation error may be relatively large on the tails. This paper suggests alternative forms of Edgeworth approximation designed to correct these defects.

Modified Forms which do not Require Further Information

There are some simple forms of modification which do not attempt to have tail distributions of the correct order in x as $x \to \infty$. The first is obtained by introducing a change of variable into the distribution function, transforming the variable using a function $w(x)$ increasing from $-\infty$ to $+\infty$, such that $w(0) = 0$, and with derivatives up to the third order at $x = 0$. Then

$$\Pr(T^{1/2}\phi(\mathbf{p}) > r) = \Pr(T^{1/2}w(\phi(\mathbf{p}) > T^{1/2}w(T^{-1/2}r)). \tag{1}$$

This probability can then be approximated by using the Edgeworth expansion for $w(\phi(\mathbf{p}))$. This gives a wide range of alternative expansions, all with errors of the same order of magnitude. It is also true that the behavior of the approximation on the tail can be made of the correct inverse power of x type if $w(x)$ is of the form $(\log(x + a) + b)^{1/6}) - (\log a + b)^{1/6}$. However, the approximation is only good on one tail of the distribution, and a simpler approach is that of the next section, which fits both tails of the distribution equally well.

A second type of modification, originally discussed by Arellano and Sargan (1990), was motivated by the idea that most poor Edgeworth approximations are poor because of one of two causes: either the function $\phi(\mathbf{p})$ is poorly approximated by its Taylor expansion, and/or the distribution of $\mathbf{p}$ is poorly approximated by a multivariate Edgeworth expansion. In the latter case it may be better to consider approximations of the following general type. Suppose that $H(x)$ is a cumulative distribution function, and consider the approximation equal to $H(h(r))$ where

$$h(r) = r/\sigma + (h_0 + h_2 r^2/\sigma^2)/T^{1/2} + (h_1 r/\sigma + h_3 r^3/\sigma^3)/T. \tag{2}$$

This is a possible form of approximation for a general distribution function $H(x)$, but its particular simplicity of use arises when $H(x)$ has a valid Edgeworth expansion, so that

$$H(x) = I(x/\sigma^* + (h_0^* + h_2^* x^2/\sigma^2)/T^{1/2} + (h_1^* x/\sigma + h_3^* x^3/\sigma^3)/T) + O(T^{-3/2}), \quad (3)$$

where $I(z)$ is the standard normal distribution function.

Using this formula to approximate $H(h(r))$, it follows that

$$H(h(r)) = I(h^\dagger(r)) + O(T^{-3/2}), \quad (4)$$

where

$$h^\dagger(r) = r/\sigma^\dagger + (h_0^\dagger + h_2 r^2/\sigma^{\dagger 3})/T^{1/2} + (h_1^\dagger r/\sigma^\dagger + h_3^\dagger r^3/\sigma^{\dagger 3})/T \quad (5)$$

and $\sigma^\dagger = \sigma\sigma^*$, and

$$h_0^\dagger = h_0^* + h_0/\sigma^*, \quad (6)$$

$$h_2^\dagger = h_2^* + h_2\sigma^*, \quad (7)$$

$$h_1^\dagger = h_1^* + h_1 + 2h_2^* h_0/\sigma^*, \quad (8)$$

$$h_3^\dagger = h_3^* + h_3\sigma^{*2} + 2h_2^* h_2\sigma^*. \quad (9)$$

If now the $h_i^\dagger$, i = 0, 1, 2, 3 are the coefficients of the Edgeworth approximation to the distribution under consideration, then we get an equally valid approximation with the same property that the error in the approximation is of order $T^{-3/2}$ if the h_i, $i = 0, 1, 2, 3$, are chosen to satisfy the latter equations. This leads to the equations

$$h_0 = \sigma^*(h_0^\dagger - h_0^*), \quad (10)$$

$$h_2 = (h_2^\dagger - h_2^*)/\sigma^*, \quad (11)$$

$$h_1 = h_1^\dagger - h_1^* - 2h_2^*(h_0^\dagger - h_0^*), \quad (12)$$

$$h_3 = (h_3^\dagger - h_3^*)/\sigma^{*2} - 2h_2^*(h_2^\dagger - h_2^*), \quad (13)$$

This is a quite general result for any suitable function $H(x)$. Arellano and Sargan (1990) considered the case where $\phi(\mathbf{p})$ can be approximated closely by a linear function of **p**, and $H(x)$ is then taken as the cumulative distribution of this linear function. Then, since the second moments of **p** are quadratic functions of the data variables, the linear function of **p** is a quadratic function of the data. If the data are normally distributed, then $H(x)$ can be computed numerically using the Imhof method. The approximation might be expected to improve on the Edgeworth approximation, particularly when the data is generated by an autoregressive model with roots near the unit circle, since in this case the distribution of **p** is particularly non-normal. However, the requirement that $\phi(\mathbf{p})$ is nearly linear is rather restrictive. Note, however, that both approximations have errors of the same order of magnitude, and there is no reason why one should generally be better than the other. It might then be reasonable to use the Imhof approximation generally, since it is certainly better in the special cases specified above. It is also possible to modify the general approximation of this section so that it behaves satisfactorily by using the technique of the last section; in fact using the form $H(\psi(x))$, where $\psi(x)$ is defined as in Appendix A, so that its Taylor series expansion is equal to $h(r)$.

Finally, it is possible to choose the $H(x)$ distribution function so as to obtain inverse power tails, but the methods suggested in the next section are easier to specify and apply.

Improving the Tail Distribution Approximation

The first method of this section is simply to express the approximation as a mixture of the Edgeworth approximation and a suitable cumulative t-ratio distribution. Define $g(x)$ as

$$g(x) = c_k \int_{-\infty}^{x} (1 + [(z - \alpha)/\beta)]^2)^{-(k+1)/2}\, dz, \tag{14}$$

where c_k is a factor to scale $g(x)$ to be 1 for $x = \infty$, and define $J(x)$ as the modified Edgeworth approximation. Then the mixture approximation can be written

$$(1 - \lambda)J(r) + \lambda g(T^{-1/2}r). \tag{15}$$

This always behaves satisfactorily if $0 < \lambda < 1$, and depends on the three extra parameters α, β, and λ. It is found that λ is always of order $O[\exp(-KT)]$ in T for some positive K, and so for finite r the first term of (15) dominates the second term for large T. To discuss the tails of this distribution, it is useful to write $R = T^{-1/2}r$ and then consider the two terms for large R. For large modulus, $RJ(r)$ is of order $\exp[-T(K^*(R)^2)]$, where $K^*(R)$ is, of order of magnitude, a cubic in $|R|$ (for details see appendix A). Thus, for large negative R, the second term dominates the first term and (15) can be approximated by

$$\lambda c_k[\beta^k|R - \alpha|^{-k}/k - \tfrac{1}{2}(k + 1)\beta^{k+2}|R - \alpha|^{-k-2}/k + 2]. \tag{16}$$

This formula is also the approximation to one minus (15) for large positive R.[1]

An alternative approximation with similar properties is obtained by using a change of variables, as in the previous section, but defining

$$w(x) = x/(1 + \mu^k|x|^k)^{1/k}, \tag{17}$$

where μ takes two different values, μ_+ or μ_-, depending on whether x is positive or negative. Note that $w(x)$ tends to $1/\mu_+$ as $x \to +\infty$ and to $-1/\mu_-$ as $x \to -\infty$, so that $w(x)$ increases between $J(-T^{1/2}/\mu_-)$ and $J(T^{1/2}/\mu_+)$. This is easily corrected by defining $\delta_- = J(-T^{1/2}/\mu_-)$ and $\delta_+ = 1 - J(T^{1/2}/\mu_+)$, and then using

$$E(w(r)) - \delta_-/(1 - \delta_+ - \delta_-). \tag{18}$$

Equation (16) then behaves suitably, and since both δs are of order $\exp(-K^*T)$,

(16) has errors of order $T^{-3/2}$ for all finite values of r. It is then possible to choose μ_- and μ_+ so that the tail distribution of (16) is of the form

$$\lambda|R|^{-k} \tag{19}$$

by suitably choosing μ_- and μ_+. The upper and lower approximations do not have all their derivatives continuous at $r = 0$, but if $k > 3$ it can be shown that both sets of Edgeworth coefficients corresponding to the upper and lower approximations are equal, and that the derivatives of the two approximants at $r = 0$ are equal if the order is less than k. Even for $k = 1$ or 2, the derivatives of order $\leqslant 3$ can be equalized by making negligible changes in the Edgeworth coefficients. The detail of this is given in an unpublished working paper and will be supplied by the author to any inquirer.

However, comparing (16) and (19), it is clear that (16) can be expected to give a better approximation on the tails of the distribution since it gives two more terms in the expansion in terms of inverse powers of r, and, in fact, allows the three parameters α, β, and λ to be independently determined whereas in (19) only λ can be determined. These approximations are similar to the Pade approximations discussed by Phillips (1982) in that they have parameters which primarily determine the shape of the approximation near the origin, and a second set that determine the shape of the tails of the distribution. They have the advantages that they behave satisfactorily without arbitrary adjustments, and that the coefficients of the Edgeworth coefficients are relatively easily computed from a knowledge of the model and the definition of the sample function even for large and complicated models. But the difficulty of using the tail-adjusted Edgeworth approximations is to find some method of computing the parameters α, β, and λ for any except the simplest of models and sample functions. It is usually possible to determine k for a wide range of cases, but the other parameters are known only for some static models and some very simple autoregressive models and for some simple estimators. If it is necessary to use some crude approximation to α and β, based for example on some very specialized version of the general class of models which is being considered, then perhaps the mixture approximation is no better than the truncated model approximation.

Discussion and General Conclusions

On first considering this type of approximation, the hope was that the Edgeworth approximation provided a method of improving on the asymptotic approximation for the significance tests used in applied work for models of any size or complexity. It is difficult to assess the accuracy of these approximations for large models, since for large models little is known about the exact distributions of even the simplest sample statistics, and even for small models exact distributions are not known for any except a few statistics. On *a priori* grounds it is clear that the Edgeworth coefficients increase with the size of the model more than linearly, and the error on the approximation is likely to do the same. Thus, for large models, the size of T required to ensure that the Edgeworth approximation is better than the asymptotic approximation may be as large as 1,000 compared with the sample size in the region of 100 which we are used to having, and which may be about the maximum period of time for which our models may be unchanged.

To assess the accuracy of the approximations for any except the simplest cases, it is necessary to use Monte Carlo simulation. If simple sample-proportion estimates are used of the probability attached to a given limit for some sampling statistic to obtain a standard error of 0.005, corresponding to an approximate probability of 0.05 of being more than 0.01 in error from the true probability, the application of the binomial theorem shows that, for the worst case, a total simulation sample of 160,000 is needed. This level of standard error seems to be appropriate to give a smooth curve to the estimated probability distribution to be compared with the various theoretical approximation functions. Recent developments in parallel or distributed array computing make it much less expensive, so that one might contemplate regularly using such a number of simulations for relatively small models with an explicit reduced form. One proposal which would make this sort of simulation available for econometricians on a personal computer is that for some set of standard models the statistics **p** should be simulated and stored, so that they could be transferred to the hard disk of any researcher wishing to work in this field. The vectors **p** would be stored in random order with each element of **p** in the form of a fixed point number as a 16-bit byte, this form giving an adequate accuracy for the purpose. Suppose that **p** has 100 elements; then the sample of 160,000 simulations can be accommodated on a disk on 20 megabytes with some room to spare. Then, all that is required to simulate, is to write a simple subroutine to compute the various estimators and test statistics as functions of **p**, and a fairly simple master program to compute the estimates of simulation probabilities and incidental statistics such as the moments of the simulated statistics. Even a quite large model could be simulated and stored, and then **p** split into subvectors suitable for particular problems, e.g. to be used in studying single equations estimators and small subsector estimators and test statistics for some submodel. Note also that for models with a large number of parameters, a much larger set of models will have to be simulated to obtain any idea how the errors in the approximations depend on the parameters.

Now, returning to the use of the Edgeworth approximations, however modified, to applied significance testing, especially those derived from realistic models which include a rather larger number of variables, the whole process of validating these approximations will be very time consuming, and if it turns out that the approximations are poor then the Edgeworth approximations cannot be used. The use of "empirical Edgeworth" methods in models of any size may require the estimation of very large numbers of cumulants up to fourth order. In this context, the size which is relevant is the total number of variables required to form the basis of some complete model sufficient to determine the endogenous variables. For example, if a model containing 20 variables is required to explain a statistic which only depends on some of these variables, the total number of cumulants to be estimated is some 10,000, and increases with the fourth power of the model size. It seems likely that if each cumulant is estimated from a relatively small sample (e.g. a sample size T of 20 or 50) the difference between the empirical Edgeworth and the simple Edgeworth approximations will be large, not only because of large sampling errors, but because, except in the important second-order case, where the approximation to the size of a symmetric confidence interval for a t-ratio is being considered, the form of the Edgeworth approximations may be changed by the use of estimated cumulants.[2]

It may then be better to consider the alternative of using a bootstrap procedure to simulate the model and its test statistics immediately after it has been estimated, using the estimated parameters. This is particularly so, since a theoretical comparison of the bootstrap and the empirical Edgeworth procedures shows that there is no advantage in a wide class of time-series models in terms of the order of magnitude of the errors in the approximation in using the empirical Edgeworth approximation. (See Bhattacharaya (1987).) For the purpose of computing the bootstrap estimates, it seems that we might be satisfied to estimate the probablities of our various confidence intervals to within 0.01, and this could be achieved by using a simulation sample of only 1,600, reducing the amount of computing required to 1 percent of that suggested above.[3]

Bootstrap simulations for large models may be very time consuming. If they are to be used for routine applied testing, some of the earlier ideas in this section might be valuable. In so far as attempts are being made to improve some small sector of a large model which is regarded as giving a reasonable explanation of the data in the sample period, it might be worthwhile to compute all the **p** for the model in the given sample period and store them suitably. (Of course, for a really large model, a laser storage disk might be required to give a single store for all the relevant **p**. However the cost of the use of this medium would be relatively trivial compared with the cost of the computing time required to generate the simulated **p**.) Because of the high cost of simulation on a large model, the number of simulations stored might be set at somewhere near the lower limit suggested above, say 5,000 simulations. Then, if the required test statistics for the modified version of the model could be expressed as functions of some subvector of **p**, the stored sample of **p** could be used to give Monte Carlo estimates of confidence intervals for each statistic. Note that this method has the limitation that it does not allow the introduction of completely new variables into the model, and if it is required to consider transformed variables which are nonlinear transforms of other variables, then these must be included in the set of variables for which the **p** statistics are computed.

Appendix A. An Increasing Function of r

The standard Edgeworth approximation function can be written $I(h(r))$ where

$$h(r) = r/\sigma + (h_0 + h_2 r^2/\sigma^2)T^{-1/2} + (h_1 r/\sigma + h_3 r^3/\sigma^3)/T. \tag{A1}$$

It is convenient to rewrite this as a function of $y = T^{-1/2} r/\sigma$, so that

$$T^{-1/2} h(r) = h_0/T + h^* y + h_2 y^2 + h_3 y^3, \tag{A2}$$

where $h^* = 1 + h_1/T$, and is assumed to be always positive. It is required to replace this by a function of y, with the same first three derivatives at the origin, which is an increasing function for all values of y. If $3h_3 h^* \geqslant h_2^2$, then no change is required since the first derivative of this function of y is a quadratic in y which is always positive.

Supposing now that $3h_3 h^* < h_2^2$, then it is suggested that a modified function using the inverse tangent is used. This has the property that it contains an appropriate negative cubic term in its Taylor series expansion and yet tends to a constant asymptote at both $\pm\infty$. If this is added to a general increasing cubic, there are superfluous parameters to be arbitrarily chosen and it is necessary to satisfy the criterion that the cubic is increasing. A specialization which avoids these problems is to add the third power of a linear factor as below:

$$a[1 + 3(1 + c)h_3 y/h_2]^3 + 3ch_3/b^3 \tan^{-1}(by) - a + h_0/T. \tag{A3}$$

This has the correct coefficients of both y^2 and y^3 if

$$a = h_2^3/27(1 + c)^2 h_3^2, \tag{A4}$$

and both terms are increasing if $a(1 + c)h_3/h_2 > 0$ and $ch_3 > 0$.

The coefficient of y is correct if

$$\begin{aligned} h^* &= 9a(1 + c)h_3/h_2 + 3ch_3/b^2 \\ &= h_2^2/3(1 + c)h_3 + 3ch_3/b^2. \end{aligned} \tag{A5}$$

The previous inequalities and the last equation show that c must be chosen so that $ch_3 > 0$, $(1 + c)h_3 > 0$, and $h^* > h_2^2/3(1 + c)h_3$.

It is then arbitrary what choice of c is made, but a convenient choice is to take $b^2 = c(1 + c)$, which is always possible since c and $1 + c$ have the same sign. Then

$$1 + c = (h_2^2 + 9h_3^2)/3h_3 h^*. \tag{A6}$$

Note that c has the same sign as $h^* h_3$, but that

$$b^2 = c(1 + c) = (h_2^2 + 9h_3^2)(h_2^2 - 3h^* h_3 + 9h_3^2)/9h^{*2} h_3^2. \tag{A7}$$

Expression (A7) is always positive, since $h_2^2 > 3h^* h_3$, so that b can be determined from this equation. Its sign is arbitrary, but might be standardized as positive. The corresponding $\psi(r)$ is then

$$\begin{aligned} \psi(r) = h_0/T^{1/2} &+ T^{1/2}(1 + c)h_3[r/\sigma T^{1/2} + h_2/3(1 + c)h_3]^3 \\ &+ 3ch_3 T^{1/2}/b^3 \tan^{-1}(br/\sigma T^{1/2}) - T^{1/2} h_2^3/27h_3^2(1 + c)^2. \end{aligned} \tag{A8}$$

The modified Edgeworth approximation is then $E(r) = I(\psi(r))$, where $I(\cdot)$ is the standard normal CDF. This method can also be used for the Imhof approximation or, in general, by using $H(\psi(r))$ for any appropriate distribution function H.

If $r = T^{1/2}R$, then

$$\begin{aligned} \psi(r) = T^{-1/2}h_0 + T^{1/2}(1 + c)h_3\{R/\sigma + h_2/[3(1 + c)h_3]^3 + 3(ch_3/b_3) \\ \times [\tan^{-1}(bR/\sigma) - h_2^3/27h_3^2(1 + c)^2]\}, \end{aligned} \tag{A9}$$

which is dominated by its second term when R is large. Then using the inequality $I(z) < (2\pi)^{-1/2} \exp(-\frac{1}{2}z^2)/|z|$, $I(\psi(r))$ is of order $\exp[-\frac{1}{2}T(K^*(R))^2]$ for large negative

R, where

$$K^*(R) = (1 + c)h_3\{R/\sigma + h_2/[3(1 + c)h_3]^3\}. \quad \text{(A10)}$$

The same formula can be proved also for the top tail probability. A very similar formula can be proved by the same methods for the case where $3h_3h^* > h_2^2$.

Appendix B. Transforming the Variable in the Edgeworth Approximation

Suppose that, as in appendix A the distribution of $\phi(\mathbf{p})$ has a valid Edgeworth approximation $I(h(r))$, and that $w(\phi(\mathbf{p}))$ has a valid Edgeworth approximation $I(h^*(r)$, where $h^*(r)$ is defined similarly to equation (A1), except that σ^*, and h_i^* are substituted for σ and h_i, $i = 1, 2, 3, 4$. Writing

$$r^* = T^{1/2}w(T^{-1/2}r), \quad \text{(B1)}$$

since $\Pr(T^{1/2}\phi > r) = \Pr(T^{1/2}w(\phi) > r^*)$,

$$h^*(r^*) = h(r) + O(T^{-3/2}). \quad \text{(B2)}$$

In this equation we can use (B1) to approximate

$$r^* = w_1r + T^{-1/2}w_2r^2 + w_3/Tr^3 + O(T^{-3/2}), \quad \text{(B3)}$$

where w_i is the ith-order Taylor series coefficient of $w(r)$ at the origin (i.e. the ith-order derivative divided by factorial i). Substituting (B3) into (B2), and equating the coefficients of powers of r up to the third power, gives

$$\sigma^* = \sigma w_1, \quad \text{(B4)}$$

$$h_1/\sigma = h_1^*w_1/\sigma^*, \quad \text{(B5)}$$

$$h_2/\sigma^2 = h_1^*w_2/\sigma^* + h_2^*w_1^2/\sigma^{*2}, \quad \text{(B6)}$$

$$h_3/\sigma^3 = h_1^*w_3/\sigma^* + 2h_2^*w_1w_2/\sigma^{*2} + h_3^*w_1^3/\sigma^{*3}. \quad \text{(B7)}$$

These equations can then be solved recursively to give

$$h_0^* = h_0, \quad \text{(B8)}$$

$$h_1^* = h_1, \quad \text{(B9)}$$

$$\mathrm{h}_2^* = h_2 - h_1w_2\sigma/w_1, \quad \text{(B10)}$$

$$\mathrm{h}_3^* = h_3 - 2h_2w_2\sigma/w_1 + h_1(2w_2^2 - w_1w_3)\sigma^2/w_1^2. \quad \text{(B11)}$$

Then the alternative approximation to $\Pr(T^{1/2}\phi(\mathbf{p}) < r)$ is

$$I\{w(r)/\sigma^* + T^{-1/2}[h_0^* + h_2^*(w(r))^2/\sigma^{*2}] + [h_1^*w(r)/\sigma^* + h_3^*(w(r))^3/\sigma^{*3}]/T\}. \quad \text{(B12)}$$

If this is not increasing in r, it should be modified by using $I[\psi^*(w(r))]$, where $\psi^*(\cdot)$ is determined from $h^*(\cdot)$ as in appendix A.

As an example, if $w(r) = r/(1 + \mu^k r^k)^{1/k}$, then if $k > 2$, $\sigma^* = \sigma$, $w_1 = 1$, and $w_i = 0$ for $i = 1, 2, 3$. Thus $\sigma^* = \sigma$ and $h_i^* = h_i$ for $i = 0, 1, 2, 3$, whatever the value of μ. In the case considered in the body of the article, where two separate approximations are used for r positive and r negative, the positive and negative approximants only differ because of the difference between $w_+(r)$ and $w_-(r)$, and all the derivatives at the origin of these functions are the same up to kth order. It follows that the corresponding derivatives of the two approximant functions are continuous at the origin up to kth order.

Notes

1. Note that, as a very special case, the approximation is exact for a classical t-ratio with $\lambda = 1$.
2. For an early example of the discussion of empirical Edgeworth approximations see my (1975) paper.
3. The author has discussed in (1981) a modified bootstrap procedure, where the errors are generated from normal distributions, since it was considered that, if the sample size is 20 or 100, the use of the empirical distribution of the errors gives a poor approximation to an underlying continuous distribution function. It might be worthwhile to use the empirical or the normal distribution, depending on some criterion for the normality of the observed errors. At the same time, with this size of sample, there is some doubt whether the asymptotic theory gives a good guide to the accuracy of the bootstrap procedure. This was considered for the case where the distributions were of the t-ratios of the 3SLS estimates of the coefficients of a simple dynamic two-equation model by simulating the whole process of generating bootstrap estimates. Each bootstrap estimator for the size of a given confidence interval was based on 1,000 simulations, and the estimate of the true size of the interval was based on a similar number of replications generated from the true model. The estimation of the model followed by a bootstrap estimate of the sizes was then resimulated 50 times. Various sets of parameters, and sample sizes $T = 20$ and 50, were used. From this overall simulation, it was possible to estimate the bias and the standard error of the bootstrap estimate of the size of the various confidence intervals. It was found that in the worst cases the standard error was relatively large, (up to five times the s.e. which would be expected if the simulation was done using the true model). The bootstrap procedure gave some very poor estimates of the true sizes.

References

Arellano, M., and J. D. Sargan (1990). "Imhof approximations to econometric estimators," *The Review of Economic Studies*, 57, 627–46.

Bhattacharya, R. N. (1987) "Some aspects of Edgeworth expansions in statistics and probability," in M. L. Puri, J. P. Vilaplana, and W. Wertz (eds) *New Perspectives in Theoretical and Applied Statistics*. New York: Wiley.

Phillips, P. C. B. (1982). "Best uniform and modified Pade approximations of probability densities in econometrics," in W. Hildenbrand (ed.) *Advances in Econometrics*. Cambridge: Cambridge University Press.

Sargan, J. D. (1975) "Gram–Charlier approximations applied to *t*-ratios of *k*-class estimators," *Econometrica*, 43, 76–97.

Sargan, J. D. (1981) "Some experiments with post estimation simulation," Working Paper, LSE Econometrics Research Programme.

13

The Finite-Sample Properties of Cointegration Estimators with Applications to Testing

Glenn Ellison and Stephen E. Satchell

Introduction

In the last few years, cointegration has become a popular methodology for exploring relationships between economic variables. Cointegration is a general linking relationship allowing ties between different variables to be tested outside the framework of causation. The prototypical example of cointegration is the relationship between consumption and income. Each of the two variables seems to wander randomly over time, and they are nonstationary in that they have an upward trend. However, while each wanders a great deal, in some sense, they are wandering together, and measured appropriately, the gap between them remains small.

Engle and Granger (1987) have made a valuable contribution in investigating the properties of cointegrated models and developing tests for the presence of cointegration. In their paper they consider seven tests and assess their power properties, they use their results to reduce the number of competing procedures to three, and on the basis of their Monte Carlo experiments, recommend one of these as their choice for applied work. Economists have followed their recommendations and used their tests, for a sample of applied work in this area, see Giovannetti (1988), Hall (1986), and Jenkinson (1986). Our aim is to investigate the properties of these three tests in a situation where there exists a cointegrating relationship. To do this we study a very simple bivariate model and derive the finite-sample distribution of the parameter estimator underlying all the test procedures. We do this to study the bias of the least squares estimator in the cointegrating relationship. Phillips has analyzed the bias of such estimators in more general models, but using asymptotic results (Philips 1989). Our model can be seen to be a special case of his. We show that the bias of this estimator increases as a fundamental parameter, essentially the ratio of variances of the two underlying *variables*, changes; further the finite-sample distribution of the estimator (suitably normalized) depends only on the aforementioned parameter. We are able to use this parameter as the key input in our Monte Carlo experiments in more realistic models, the purpose of these experiments being power comparisons for the three tests. Our results differ from those of Engle and Granger: their preferred test, the Augmented Dickey–Fuller test, does very badly for certain parameter values and rarely seems to do particularly well. Finally, we construct a new test which is invariant to changes in the underlying parameter and which is easy for the applied economist to implement. Methodologically, our approach has been to use finite-sample theory to direct the design of our Monte Carlo work, this being a synthesis of two methods which have often been seen as substitutes. Our new test is based on a new estimation procedure, we minimize the first-order autocorrelation of the cointegration residuals rather than the sum of squares of the cointegration residuals which has been the traditional procedure. This method is of interest in its own right. We show that the resulting estimator is consistent (theorem 6), and derive the asymptotic distributions of the least squares and least autocorrelation estimators (theorem 7). In the second section, we present our model and finite-sample and numerical results for our biases. In the third section, we calculate the powers of the tests and present our new test and conclusions. An appendix contains some of the longer proofs.

The Cointegration Model

In this paper, we shall adopt a simple model of cointegration to allow us to compute the finite-sample properties theoretically. We have

$$x_t = \alpha y_t + v_t, \quad v_t = \rho v_{t-1} + \omega_t, \quad \omega_t \sim IN(0, \sigma_\omega^2), \tag{1}$$

$$y_t = \beta x_t + u_t, \quad u_t = u_{t-1} + \varepsilon_t, \quad \varepsilon_t \sim IN(0, \sigma_\varepsilon^2). \tag{2}$$

There are T observations, $t = 1, 2, \ldots, T$. Alternatively we may also write

$$x_t = \alpha y_t + v_t, \tag{3}$$

$$x_t = \frac{y_t}{\beta} + W_t, \quad W_t = -u_t/\beta. \tag{4}$$

Assuming that $\alpha\beta \neq 1$, we find the reduced form

$$x_t = \frac{\alpha}{1 - \alpha\beta} u_t + \frac{1}{1 - \alpha\beta} v_t, \tag{5}$$

$$y_t = \frac{1}{1 - \alpha\beta} u_t + \frac{\beta}{1 - \alpha\beta} v_t, \tag{6}$$

We shall specialize our model in this section by letting $\rho = 0$, so that $v_t \sim IN(0, \sigma_v^2)$.

We can replace u by ε in the equations to give

$$y_t = \frac{1}{1 - \alpha\beta}\left(\beta v_t + \sum_{j=1}^{t} \varepsilon_j\right). \tag{7}$$

Now,

$$\hat{\alpha} = \frac{\sum_t x_t y_t}{\sum_t y_t^2} \tag{8}$$

is the standard OLS estimate which we are interested in, and upon which Engle and Granger base their tests. Making the usual substitution from (3), we see that

$$\hat{\alpha} - \alpha = \frac{\sum_t y_t v_t}{\sum_t y_t^2}, \tag{9}$$

$$\frac{\hat{\alpha} - \alpha}{1/\beta - \alpha} = \beta \frac{\sum_t \left(\beta v_t + \sum_{j=1}^{t} \varepsilon_j\right) v_t}{\sum_t \left(\beta v_t + \sum_{j=1}^{t} \varepsilon_j\right)^2}. \tag{10}$$

Equations (1) and (2) are the model in Engle and Granger (1987, equations (4.7) and (4.8)), where we have taken the true value of the covariance of v_t and ε_t to be zero and we have assumed the covariance matrix of v_t and ε_t to be

$$\begin{bmatrix} \sigma_v^2 & 0 \\ 0 & \sigma_\varepsilon^2 \end{bmatrix}$$

rather than I_2. We also assume normality, as is usual in finite-sample work; we should note that Engle and Granger assume the covariance matrix to be I_2 because they show that any residual-based test will be similar for any choice of positive definite covariance matrix, while we are testing that $\rho = 1$. However, similarity, will not hold when $|\rho| < 1$, as we have in our case, thus assumptions about the relative magnitudes of σ_v^2 *and* σ_ε^2 are going to be important when we consider power evaluations. A more complete discussion would consider nonzero covariance between v_t and ε_t, but this would complicate the finite-sample theory, we hope that readers will look sympathetically on our choices as being a reasonable tradeoff between tractability and generality. We now simplify $\hat{\alpha} - \alpha$ into a ratio of quadratic forms in normal variables. Let

$$s = \begin{pmatrix} \varepsilon^* \\ v^* \end{pmatrix} \sim N(0, I_{2T}), \tag{12}$$

$$\varepsilon_t = \sigma_\varepsilon \varepsilon_t^*, \tag{13}$$

$$v_t = \sigma_v v_t^*, \tag{14}$$

$$\sum_t \left(\beta v_t + \sum_{j=1}^{t} \varepsilon_j\right)\beta v_t = \sum_t \left(\beta^2\sigma_v^2 v_t^{*2} + \sum_{j=1}^{t} \varepsilon_j^* v_t^* \beta\sigma_\varepsilon\sigma_v\right)$$
$$= \sum a_{ij}s_i s_j, \tag{15}$$

where

$$A = \begin{pmatrix} 0 & \dfrac{\beta\sigma_\varepsilon\sigma_v}{2}P \\ \dfrac{\beta\sigma_\varepsilon\sigma_v}{2}P' & \beta^2\sigma_v^2 I_T \end{pmatrix} \tag{16}$$

$$P = \begin{pmatrix} 1 & 1 & 1 & \cdots & 1 \\ 0 & 1 & 1 & \cdots & 1 \\ 0 & 0 & 1 & \cdots & 1 \\ \vdots & \vdots & \vdots & \vdots & \vdots \\ 0 & 0 & 0 & \cdots & 1 \end{pmatrix}. \tag{17}$$

The denominator is

$$\sum_t \left(\beta\sigma_v v_t^* + \sum_{j=1}^{t} \varepsilon_j^*\sigma_\varepsilon\right)^2 = \sum b_{ij}s_i s_j, \tag{18}$$

$$B = \begin{pmatrix} \sigma_\varepsilon^2 J & \beta\sigma_\varepsilon\sigma_v P \\ \beta\sigma_\varepsilon\sigma_v P' & \beta^2\sigma_v^2 I_T \end{pmatrix}, \tag{19}$$

$$J = \begin{pmatrix} T & T-1 & T-2 & \cdots & 1 \\ T-1 & T-1 & T-1 & \cdots & 1 \\ T-2 & T-2 & T-2 & \cdots & 1 \\ \vdots & \vdots & \vdots & \vdots & \vdots \\ 1 & 1 & 1 & 1 & 1 \end{pmatrix}. \tag{20}$$

As a sum of squares, B is positive semidefinite. We will need this fact later on. It is interesting to note that $PP' = J$, so J is positive semidefinite as well.

In the remainder of this paper, we will examine the distribution of

$$\frac{\hat{\alpha} - \alpha}{1/\beta - \alpha} = \frac{s'As}{s'Bs}. \tag{21}$$

We shall be particularly concerned with the impact on the distribution of changes in the relative variances of v_t and w_t. To this end, we set

$$k = \frac{\sigma_v}{\sigma_\varepsilon/\beta}, \tag{22}$$

and rewrite (16) and (19) as

$$A = \begin{pmatrix} 0 & \frac{1}{2}kP \\ \frac{1}{2}kP' & k^2 I_T \end{pmatrix}, \tag{23}$$

$$B = \begin{pmatrix} J & kP \\ kP' & k^2 I_T \end{pmatrix}. \tag{24}$$

The parameter k will be central to our study of finite-sample biases. In order to do this, we first calculate the joint moment generating function, MGF (t_1, t_2), of $s'As$ and $s'Bs$. We shall present two theorems.

Theorem 1 *The joint moment generating function of $s'As$ and $s'Bs$ is given by*

$$\text{MGF}\,(t_1, t_2) = \sum_{j=1}^{T} [1 - 2k^2(t_1 + t_2) - \lambda_{j,T}(k^2 t_1^2 - 2t_2)]^{-1/2}, \tag{25}$$

where

$$\lambda_{j,T} = \frac{1}{4} \frac{1}{\sin^2\left(\dfrac{(j - 1/2)}{2T + 1}\pi\right)}. \tag{26}$$

Proof See the appendix.

An alternative representation for MGF (t_1, t_2) is given by theorem 2.

Theorem 2 *The moment generating function of $s'As$ and $s'Bs$ can be represented as*

$$\text{MGF}\,(t_1, t_2) = (-k^2 t_1^2 - 2t_2)^{-T/2} CP_T^{-1/2}(\phi) \tag{27}$$

where

$$\phi = \frac{1 - 2k^2(t_1 + t_2)}{k^2 t_1^2 + 2t_2}, \tag{28}$$

and $CP_T(x)$ is the characteristic polynomial of the matrix J defined in (20), *$CP_T(x)$ is calculated in the appendix.*

Proof See the appendix.

The advantage of the first expression will be in analytic work. For computational work, however, the second expression is better, since it does not use summations or products, nor does it need calculation or use of $\lambda_{j'T}$.

Phillips (1986, chapter 8) gives several expressions which allow us to deduce the moments of the ratio of the quadratic forms $s'As$ and $s'Bs$ from their joint moment generating function. For X, Y random variables he expresses Y^{-r} as a gamma integral, and multiplies by X^r to show that

$$E\left[\left[\frac{X}{Y}\right]^r\right] = \frac{1}{\Gamma(r)} \int_{-\infty}^{0} (-t_2)^{r-1} \left[\frac{\partial^r \mathrm{MGF}\,(t_1, t_2)}{\partial t_1^r}\right]_{t_1=0} dt_2 \tag{29}$$

with MGF (t_1, t_2) the joint moment generating function of X, and Y. We shall only attempt to find the first two moments of $\hat{\alpha}$. For $r = 1$, and $r = 2$, (29) reduces to

$$E\left[\frac{X}{Y}\right] = \int_{-\infty}^{0} \left[\frac{\partial \mathrm{MGF}\,(t_1, t_2)}{\partial t_1}\right]_{t_1=0} dt_2, \tag{30}$$

and

$$E\left[\left[\frac{X}{Y}\right]^2\right] = \int_{-\infty}^{0} (-t_2) \left[\frac{\partial^2 \mathrm{MGF}\,(t_1, t_2)}{\partial t_1^2}\right]_{t_1=0} dt_2. \tag{31}$$

We now prepare to evaluate these by computing the derivatives of the moment generating function as given by equations (A6) and (A7) and (A21)–(A23) in the appendix. First we do this in the product expression (A6) and (A7).

$$\begin{aligned}
\frac{\partial \mathrm{MGF}\,(t_1, t_2)}{\partial t_1} &= \frac{\partial}{\partial t_1} u^{-1/2}, \qquad u = 1 - 2k^2(t_1 + t_2) - \lambda(k^2 t_1^2 - 2t_2) \\
&= -\tfrac{1}{2} u^{-1/2} \frac{\partial u/\partial t_1}{u} = -\tfrac{1}{2} u^{1/2} \frac{\partial}{\partial t_1} \log(u) \\
&= -\tfrac{1}{2} u^{-1/2} \sum_{j=1}^{T} \frac{-2k^2 - 2k^2 \lambda_j t_1}{1 - 2k^2(t_1 + t_2) - \lambda_j(k^2 t_1^2 - 2t_2)},
\end{aligned} \tag{32}$$

$$\left.\frac{\partial \mathrm{MGF}\,(t_1, t_2)}{\partial t_1}\right|_{t_1=0} = \prod_{j=1}^{T} [1 - 2(k^2 - \lambda_j)t_2]^{-1/2} \sum_{j=1}^{T} \frac{1}{1 - 2(k^2 - \lambda_j)t_2}. \tag{33}$$

Calculating the second derivative is a similar but exceedingly tedious calculation. Omitting pages of equations, we eventually find

$$\begin{aligned}
\left.\frac{\partial^2 \mathrm{MGF}\,(t_1, t_2)}{\partial t_1^2}\right|_{t_1=0} &= k^2 \prod_{j=1}^{T} [1 - 2(k^2 - \lambda_j)t_2]^{-1/2} \left[k^2 \left[\sum \frac{1}{d_j}\right]^2 + \sum \frac{1}{d_j^2}\right], \\
d_j &= [1 - 2(k^2 - \lambda_j)t_2].
\end{aligned} \tag{34}$$

In the next section, we will use these formulas to examine the finite sample biases of $\hat{\alpha}$. Before we do that though, we will also compute the derivative of our other expression for the moment generating function in line (A22). We had

$$\mathrm{MGF}\,(t_1, t_2) = (-k^2t_1^2 - 2t_2)^{-T/2}CP_T^{-1/2}(\phi), \tag{35}$$

$$\left.\frac{\partial \mathrm{MGF}\,(t_1, t_2)}{\partial t_1}\right|_{t_1=0} = (-k^2t_1^2 - 2t_2)^{-T/2}|_{t_1=0}CP_T^{-3/2}(\phi)\left.\frac{\mathrm{d}CP_T(\phi)}{\mathrm{d}\phi}\right|_{\phi(0,t_2)}\left.\frac{\partial\phi}{\partial t_1}\right|_{t_1=0}$$

$$+ CP_T^{-1/2}(\phi)\frac{T}{2}(2k^2t_1)(-k^2t_1 - 2t_2)^{-T/2}|_{t_1=0}. \tag{36}$$

The second term contains a factor of t_1, and thus equals zero. As for the first term,

$$\left.\frac{\partial\phi}{\partial t_1}\right|_{t_1=0} = \frac{-k^2}{t_2}, \tag{37}$$

$$\phi(0, t_2) = \frac{1}{2t_2} - k^2, \tag{38}$$

with a, b, u, v, as before (A15)–(A20),

$$CP_T(x) = au^T + bv^T, \tag{39}$$

Note that $\mathrm{d}u/\mathrm{d}x = -2a$, and $\mathrm{d}v/\mathrm{d}x = -2b$, so

$$\frac{\mathrm{d}}{\mathrm{d}x}CP_T(x) = a\frac{\mathrm{d}}{\mathrm{d}x}u^T + u^T\frac{\mathrm{d}a}{\mathrm{d}x} + b\frac{\mathrm{d}}{\mathrm{d}x}v^T + v^T\frac{\mathrm{d}b}{\mathrm{d}x}$$

$$= aTu^Tu^{T-1}(-2a) + u^T(-1/2)(1/2)(-4)\left(\frac{1}{(1-4x)^{3/2}}\right) + bTv^{T-1}(-2b)$$

$$+ v^T(-1/2)(1/2)(-4)\left(\frac{1}{(1-4x)^{3/2}}\right)$$

$$= -2a^2Tu^{2T-1} + \frac{1}{(1-4x)^{3/2}}u^T - 2b^2Tv^{T-1} + \frac{1}{(1-4x)^{3/2}}v^T. \tag{40}$$

Finally, we obtain the desired equation:

$$\left.\frac{\partial \mathrm{MGF}\,(t_1, t_2)}{\partial t_1}\right|_{t_1=0} = (-2t_2)^{-T/2-1}k^2\frac{(\mathrm{d}/\mathrm{d}x)CP_T(1/2t_2 - k^2)}{CP_T(1/2t_2 - k - k^2)^{3/2}}, \tag{41}$$

with $(\mathrm{d}/\mathrm{d}x)CP_T(x)$ and $CP_T(x)$ as given above and (A20), (A21). We now move on to study the finite-sample properties of $\hat{\alpha}$.

With the derivatives computed above, we can now apply our earlier results on moments of ratios to get exact expressions for the finite-sample biases. From (29) and (40), we have

$$E(\hat{\alpha} - \alpha) = (1/\beta - \alpha) \int_{-\infty}^{0} \left[\frac{\partial \text{MGF}(t_1, t_2)}{\partial t_1}\right]_{t_1=0} dt_2$$
$$= (1/\beta - \alpha)k^2 \int_{-\infty}^{0} \sum_{j=1}^{T} [1 - 2(k^2 + \lambda_j)t_2]^{-1/2} \sum_{j=1}^{T} \frac{1}{1 - 2(k^2 + \lambda_j)t_2} dt_2. \tag{42}$$

The form of this equation is particularly interesting. Note that α does not appear except in the term $(1/\beta - \alpha)$. We have an expression of the form:

$$E(\hat{\alpha}) = \alpha + (1/\beta - \alpha)g(k^2, T). \tag{43}$$

Thus, to the extent that we can evaluate the integral, we know with one calculation the expected bias for all α. For any given k, the expected error is proportional to $(1/\beta - \alpha)$. We now ask how $g(k^2, T)$ behaves as k varies.

If we look at our original formulation of the model in (3) and (4), we can get some notion of the limiting behavior. As $k \to 0$, the variance of v_t becomes negligible relative to the variance of w_t. Intuitively, the limiting behavior of the system is approaching that of $x_t = \alpha t_t$, $x_t = (y_t/\beta) + w_t$. In this system, the first equation is exact, so the OLS estimate of α should be exact as well. Thus, in our system we would expect α to be approaching consistently. A similar analysis applies as $k \to 0$, thus we can show the following.

Theorem 3 *For the model given by* (1) *and* (2) *with* $\rho = 0$, $\hat{\alpha}$ *the OLS estimator, and* $k = \sigma_v/(\sigma_t/\beta)$

$$\lim_{k \to 0} E(\hat{\alpha} - \alpha) = 0,$$

$$\lim_{k \to 0} E[(\hat{\alpha} - \alpha^2)] = 0,$$

$$\lim_{k \to \infty} E(\hat{\alpha} - \alpha) = \frac{1}{\beta} - \alpha$$

$$\lim_{k \to \infty} E[(\hat{\alpha} - \alpha)^2] = \left(\frac{1}{\beta} - \alpha\right)^2.$$

Proof This is available from the authors upon request.

This theorem has the obvious implications that $\mathbf{plim}_{k \to 0}\, \hat{\alpha} = \alpha$ and $\mathbf{plim}_{k \to \infty}\, \hat{\alpha} = 1/\beta$. This can be proved by convergence in mean square, in both cases the variance of $\hat{\alpha}$ is tending to zero. Thus, the variance of $\hat{\alpha}$ will tend to zero at each extreme of k, and will be greatest at some intermediate value.

To get a sharper idea about the behavior of $\hat{\alpha}$, we will evaluate the integrals in (42) and (43) numerically. Before we begin with this though, it is useful to go back to our alternative expression in theorem 2 for the derivative of the moment generating function. From it, we get another formula for the finite sample bias:

$$E\left[\frac{\hat{\alpha}-\alpha}{(1/\beta-\alpha)}\right]=\int_{-\infty}^{0}(-2t_2)^{-T/2-1}k^2\,\frac{(d/dx)CP_T(1/2t_2-k^2)}{CP_T T(1/2t_2-k^2)^{3/2}}\,dt_2, \qquad (44)$$

with $(d/dx)CP_T(x)$, and $CP_T(x)$ as given in (34) and (A21).

The reader who actually looks back at those lines will realize that this is rather a messy equation. As it involves only elementary operations and square roots, however, it may be more useful for some theoretical calculations. In particular, it is probably much easier to use this formula to investigate behavior as T changes. Equation (42) involves a product with both the number of terms and the eigenvalues changing as T changes; (44) is easier to handle in this respect, and also can be simplified asymptotically for T large as v^T becomes insignificant relative to u^T.

More importantly though, this expression, while having many terms, is in closed form with no need to evaluate a product of T terms as in (42). Thus, for numerical computation, it will be far more efficient.

The intuition behind our calculations now becomes transparent and is worthy of a brief comment. If we go back to equations (3) and (4), we see that x_t can be related to y_t in two different ways, one with a coefficient of α, the other with a coefficient of $1/\beta$, the variances of the two equations are, for $\rho = 0$, σ_v^2 and $T\sigma_\varepsilon^2/\beta^2$ respectively. If we fix T, then increasing k is to increase σ_v relative to σ_ε or to decrease σ_ε relative to σ_v. Taking the latter interpretation, this makes (4) tend to an exact relationship, so that $\hat{\alpha}$ converges in probability to $1/\beta$. Likewise, sending $k \to 0$ makes $\hat{\alpha}$ converge in probability to α, this is the essence of theorem 3.

We calculate numerically the biases. To do this, the integrals in (43) and (44) were approximated numerically on a MicroVax computer. The negative real axis was partitioned into intervals concentrated around the origin, and Simpson's rule was used to approximate the integral on each interval. In practice, the integrands were sharply peaked at the origin, and it was only necessary to evaluate the integral over an interval like $(-0.2, 0)$ rather than $(-\infty, 0)$. The programs were designed to guarantee at least three significant figures in the final result.

To begin, we look at how the bias, $E(\hat{\alpha}) - \alpha$, varies as we change k. We found that, for all parameter values chosen, the bias is an increasing function of k, although we could not derive a proof. Theorem 3 does tell us, however, that by fixing T and letting k increase, we can get the bias up to $1/\beta - \alpha$ for any sample size. We repeated the calculations for fixed k, again we found a monotonic *decrease* in bias as T increases to infinity, reflecting the consistency property. However, for $k = 4$, for example, the bias $T = 250$ was the same as the bias at $T = 20$ and $k = 1$, thus, for large k, we may need very large samples before we can conclude that our estimator is nearly unbiased.

A k-invariant Test

From the previous sections, we have a fairly good knowledge of the finite-sample properties of the OLS estimator $\hat{\alpha}$, of the cointegrating parameter α. We know that

$\hat{\alpha} - \alpha$ is a fraction, $g(k^2, T)$ of $(1/\beta - \alpha)$. In the previous section, we have tried to explain how this fraction varies with the sample size and the ratio of the variances of the noise terms. One thing we have seen is that the finite-sample biases can be large even for large samples.

At this point, we will briefly discuss possible implications for cointegration testing. After all, when an economist is investigating whether consumption and income are cointegrated, he may have little interest in the particular constant α which acts as a scaling factor between them. Rather, he may be interested simply in whether they are or are not cointegrated. To this end, we would like to know how errors in $\hat{\alpha}$ affect the standard test for cointegration.

We have remarked that Engle and Granger consider several tests for cointegration, and that the tests have the following form:

1 Use OLS to find the estimate $\hat{\alpha}$ in $x_t = \alpha y_t + e_t$.
2 Apply some test to the residuals $x_t - \hat{\alpha} y_t$ to see whether they are integrated of order zero.

We shall follow them in this procedure, first estimating $\hat{\alpha}$, calculating the residuals, and applying the Durbin–Watson (DW), Dickey–Fuller (DF), and augmented Dickey–Fuller (ADF) tests, the three tests that seem to be contenders among the seven originally chosen. Our purpose is to calculate the power of these three tests when $\rho = 0$, $T = 100$, and α, β are chosen to be the same as the values chosen by Engle and Granger; we only vary k. If these tests are to be of any practical use we would expect them to be very powerful as $\rho = 0$ is an extreme case, the series is ergodic, and not typical of economic time series.

We checked our computer programs by recalculating the critical values of the test statistics; these agreed to a fair degree of accuracy. For each test we took only 1,000 replications, this was not intended to achieve precise results but rather to unveil any patterns that might emerge. Table 13.1 gives the powers of the three tests as the 1, 5, and 10 percent level for a range of different k values. The results are very interesting: apart from exhibiting the usual properties of power functions with respect to changes in type 1 error, all three tests show a monotonic decrease in power as k increases at all critical values chosen. For the DW and DF tests, this decline in power seems quite smooth and the tests seem to be relatively powerful against different values of k.

In contrast, for the ADF test, the collapse in power is dramatic and occurs very quickly. On the evidence of this experiment, the ADF test is not to be used. Of course Engle and Granger chose the ADF test more on the basis of its behavior when the alternative hypotheses were very close to unit root situations; all we have shown so far is that, if we are a long way from a unit root model, the ADF test is inappropriate. This may have no practical significance, since in models of this sort one may expect substantial positive correlation in the errors.

We therefore chose a second experiment where the alternative hypothesis involved values of ρ equal to 0.8 or 0.9 and we let k vary as before. Although the finite-sample distribution may not depend on k in the simple way that it did for the $\rho = 0$ case discussed in the previous section, the results of table 13.1 suggest that it may be a sensible parameter to vary. The results are presented in table 13.2, again power is always a decreasing function of k for both $\rho = 0.8$ and $\rho = 0.9$, the DW is better than the DF test, which is better than the ADF test, and for large k and ρ all three are very bad. Finally, we allow our models to incorporate fourth-order lags, this

Table 13.1 Power of test statistics. Behavior of various models with the following parameters: $(\alpha = -2, \beta = -1)y_t + 2x_t = v_t$, $u_t = u_{t-1} + \varepsilon_t$, $\rho = 0$, $x_t + y_t = u_t$, $v_t = N(0, \sigma_v^2)$, $T = 100$, 1,000 replications

		DW	DF	ADF
1% Critical vajues				
k	0.000001	100	100	88.2
	0.1	100	100	88.3
	0.5	100	100	73.7
	1.0	100	100	49.0
	2.0	100	100	9.6
	4.0	95.2	91.6	0.4
	8.0	35.3	30.2	0.2
	12.0	8.9	5.7	0.2
	20.0	1.3	0.7	0.3
5% Critical values				
k	0.000001	100	100	99
	0.1	100	100	99
	0.5	100	100	96.8
	1.0	100	100	94
	2.0	100	100	34.4
	4.0	99.5	98.9	4.4
	8.0	60.5	56.5	1.3
	12.0	23.8	22.2	1.4
	20.0	4.8	5.8	2.2
10% Critical values				
k	0.000001	100	100	99.8
	0.1	100	100	99.8
	0.5	100	100	99.4
	1.0	100	100	94.0
	2.0	100	100	55.1
	4.0	100	99.9	11.2
	8.0	76.6	73.5	4.9
	12.0	40.3	38.3	3.8
	20.0	10.7	7.4	4.8

corresponds to table III in Engle and Granger and should allow the more general structure of the ADF test to come into its own. Again we vary k, keeping the other parameters as they were before, and letting our error dynamics be

$$\Delta v_t = (\rho - 1)v_{t-1} + 0.8\,\Delta v_{t-4} + u_t, \tag{45}$$

$$\Delta v_t = 0.8\,\Delta v_{t-1} + \varepsilon_t. \tag{46}$$

In this case, if $\rho = 1$, v_t has a unit root and there exists no cointegrating relationship. We find the power of our three tests for $\rho = 0.8$ and 0.9, our results are presented in table 13.3.

While our experiments have been carried out only to discern broad trends, several results emerge very clearly. Firstly, as k increases so that the bias of $\hat{\alpha}$ increases, the

Table 13.2 Power of test statistics. Behavior of various models with the following parameters: $(\alpha = -2, \beta = -1)y_t + 2x_t = v_t$, $u_t = u_{t-1} + \varepsilon_t$, $y_t + x_t = u_t$, $v_t = \rho v_{t-1} + \sigma_t$, $T = 100$, 1,000 replications

	DW	DF	ADF
$\rho = 0.8$			
1% Critical value			
0.5	41.6	26.5	12.6
1.0	28.8	17.9	7.6
2.0	15.6	9.3	4.1
4.0	2.6	1.6	0.6
5% Critical values			
0.5	79.8	69.4	39.5
1.0	62.1	52.3	28.5
2.0	37.4	32.5	14.3
4.0	12.2	11.2	4.0
10% Critical value			
0.5	93.1	87.5	61.7
1.0	81.3	72.2	47.7
2.0	54.5	48.0	27.7
4.0	21.0	20.3	12.1
$\rho = 0.9$			
1% Critical value			
0.5	7.7	3.9	4.7
1.0	5.7	3.1	3.0
2.0	2.4	1.4	1.9
4.0	1.1	1.4	1.6
5% Critical value			
0.5	26.9	20.6	16.8
1.0	19.1	16.2	12.8
2.0	10.6	10.1	7.4
4.0	5.1	6.5	5.7
10% Critical value			
0.5	45.2	38.9	31.2
1.0	31.4	27.6	24.8
2.0	21.0	20.1	17.6
4.0	11.0	13.5	11.4

power of all tests decreases, this is true for all models investigated. Secondly, on the basis of power comparisons, the DW test outperforms the DF test, which outperforms the ADF test. The only exception to this case is for model III of Engle and Granger, where the structure of the model under H_1 is sufficiently complex to benefit the ADF test. However, the ADF test only outperforms for $\rho = 0.9$ *not* $\rho = 0.8$, where the three tests revert to their usual ordering, and, even in the $\rho = 0.9$ case, the relative advantage of the ADF decreases very quickly for k large, in fact all three tests become very poor indeed. Thus, our initial conjecture seems confirmed, namely that these

Table 13.3 Power of test statistics. Behavior of various models in the following parameters: $y_t + 2x_t = v_t$, $\Delta v_t = (\rho - 1)v_{t-1} + 0.8\,\Delta v_{t-4} + u_t$, $y_t + x_t = u_t$, $\Delta u_t = 0.8\,\Delta u_{t-4} + \varepsilon_t$, $\rho = 0.9$ or 0.8, $T = 100$, 1,000 replications

	Statistic	DW	DF	ADF
$\rho = 0.8$				
1% Critical value				
k	1.0	82.9	59.1	68.8
	2.0	59.1	44.9	54.6
	4.0	38.5	28.5	27.1
	8.0	17.4	12.1	5.3
5% Critical value				
k	1.0	94.5	86.4	89.3
	2.0	85.4	74.9	77.4
	4.0	68.7	54.7	49.4
	8.0	38.2	28.3	18.1
10% Critical value				
k	1.0	97.9	93.3	93.8
	2.0	95.4	83.8	85.9
	4.0	80.3	67.4	60.9
	8.0	52.2	38.4	28.5
$\rho = 0.9$				
1% Critical value				
k	1.0	12.2	7.5	37.8
	2.0	9.5	5.5	22.9
	4.0	5.1	3.5	9.7
	8.0	2.1	1.1	2.1
5% Critical value				
k	1.0	36.6	22.8	64.1
	2.0	26.6	16.4	46.2
	4.0	15.6	10.5	26.3
	8.0	7.0	5.1	6.7
10% Critical value				
k	1.0	56.9	34.8	78.6
	2.0	43.9	26.5	56.7
	4.0	27.7	17.1	36.6
	8.0	13.1	7.8	12.2

tests are not terribly good as $\hat{\alpha}$ becomes biased and driving k up leads to the power tending to zero. This is most unsatisfactory for both the applied economist and the theoretical econometrician and we shall try to develop in this section a testing procedure whose power is independent of k. For this purpose, we shall rewrite our bivariate model as a reduced form

$$\Delta x_t = \varepsilon_{1t}, \quad \Delta y_t = \varepsilon_{2t}, \tag{47}$$

where Δ is the usual difference operator, and it is assumed that H_0 holds, i.e. both original error terms are random. Engle and Granger go on to show that, for this particular model, the composite null hypothesis $\{\rho = 1, \Omega\}$, where Ω is the contemporaneous covariance matrix of the two errors, has the same distribution if the test statistic is based on OLS residuals, for all Ω positive definite. The proof assumes that ε_{1t} and ε_{2t} are independent and identically distributed.

Notice that this will be true under H_0 but not under H_1. Under H_1, ε_{1t}, and ε_{2t} are serially correlated and nonstationary, so that Ω, under H_1, is a function of t. Tests based on residuals, as are our three test statistics in the previous section, will have distributions which are not invariant under H_1 to changes in Ω, which in our simple case is summarized by k. Since our results show that the power of our tests can be made very small for large k, it is worthwhile to ask the question as to whether we can construct a test which has a k-invariant power function and whose invariant power compares not too unfavorably with that of the previous test statistics. An intuitive approach would be to look at other properties of the error in the nonintegrating regression besides the variance, which is the Engle and Granger approach. If we consider the measure $r = \sum v_t v_{t-1}/\sum v_t^2$, which loosely can be thought of as the first-order autocorrelation, this should take a value of one under H_0 but ρ under H_1. So, instead of choosing α to minimize the residual variance, it may be just as sensible to choose α to minimize r. However, we would expect that changes in the underlying variance of v_t should leave the value of r unchanged, thus this test statistic should have constant power against changes in k.

Another feature that makes r a sensible basis for testing is that both the Durbin–Watson and the Dickey–Fuller tests are transformations of r if we approximate $\sum v_t^2$ by $\sum v_{t-1}^2$, which under H_1 should be reasonably accurate. Thus, not only will these tests be invariant for different k, they should have approximately the same power functions, the augmented Dickey–Fuller test will become k invariant, but its power function should differ from that of the other test statistics.

We wish to show that $r_{\min} = \min_\alpha(\sum v_t v_{t-1}/\sum v_t^2)$ is independent of k. First, we show how our new estimator of α, $\hat{\alpha}$ is calculated. Let

$$r(\alpha) = \frac{\sum v_t v_{t-1}}{\sum v_t^2}$$

$$= \frac{\sum (x_t - \alpha y_t)(x_{t-1} - \alpha y_{t-1})}{\sum (x_t - \alpha y_t)^2}. \tag{48}$$

We differentiate $r(\alpha)$ with respect to α and equate to zero. After simplification, we see that

$$a_T\tilde{\alpha}^2 + b_T\tilde{\alpha} + c_T = 0, \tag{49}$$

where

$$a_T = -2\sum_{t=1}^{T} x_t y_t \sum_{t=1}^{T} x_t x_{t-1} + \sum_{t=1}^{T} x_t^2 \sum_{t=1}^{T} x_t y_{t-1} + \sum_{t=1}^{T} x_t^2 \sum_{t=1}^{T} y_t x_{t-1}, \tag{50}$$

$$b_T = 2\sum_{t=1}^{T} y_t^2 \sum_{t=1}^{T} x_t x_{t-1} - 2\sum_{t=1}^{T} x_t^2 \sum_{t=1}^{T} y_t v_{t-1}, \tag{51}$$

Table 13.4 Behavior of various models with the following parameters: $T=100$, $\Delta x_t = \varepsilon_t$, $\varepsilon_t \sim N(0, 1)$, $\Delta y_t = v_t$, $v_t \sim N(0, 1)$, 10,000 replications

	DW	DF	ADF
Critical value			
1%	0.463	3.53	3.55
5%	0.341	2.95	2.89
10%	0.256	2.65	2.58
Power of tests for $\alpha = 2, \beta = -1$, 1,000 replications			
1%	100	100	90.5
5%	100	100	99.3
10%	100	100	100
$\rho = 0$			
1%	100	100	90.5
5%	100	100	99.3
10%	100	100	100
$\rho = 0.8$			
1%	45.5	48.7	15.6
5%	86.2	86.5	49.6
10%	95.5	95.3	68.8
$\rho = 0.9$ ($k = 1$)			
1%	8.2	8.3	4.7
5%	30.6	29.7	22.0
10%	47.8	48.4	37.1

$$c_T = 2\sum_{t=1}^{T} x_t y_t \sum_{t=1}^{T} y_t y_{t-1} - \sum_{t=1}^{T} y_t^2 \sum_{t=1}^{T} x_t y_{t-1} - \sum_{t=1}^{T} y_T^2 \sum_{t=1}^{T} y_1 x_{t-1}. \tag{52}$$

Equation (49) has two solutions, in $\hat{\alpha}$, one corresponding to a maximum, the other to a minimum. Computationally this is very simple to carry out.

Our testing procedure is to use $\tilde{\alpha}$ instead of $\hat{\alpha}$ to construct minimum autocorrelation residuals. These are then used in the DW, DF, and ADF tests. The powers of these tests are given in table 13.4 for the same values as before, except that we no longer need to change k. We did change k to check our program (and our theorem!) and found, for the same random numbers, the same power, as one would expect. We see that the results of table 13.4 give a reasonably powerful test, which is better than OLS-based tests for even moderate k. Also, DW and DF tests have virtually identical power, as we predicted, since they are monotonic transformations of each other, except for end effects. Both dominate the ADF test. However, we have lost the property of similarity referred to after equation (47), so that different parametrizations of the covariance matrix might lead to different tests.

We now show that

$$\hat{\rho} = \min_{\alpha}\left(\frac{\sum (x_t - \alpha y_t)(x_{t-1} - \alpha y_{t-1})}{\sum (x_t - \alpha y_t)^2}\right) \tag{53}$$

is invariant to changes in k. Now

$$x_t = \frac{\alpha}{1 - \alpha\beta} u_t + \frac{1}{1 - \alpha\beta} v_t, \tag{54}$$

$$y_t = \frac{u_t}{1 - \alpha\beta} + \frac{\beta}{1 - \alpha\beta} v_t. \tag{55}$$

Suppose, without loss of generality, that we consider the new model

$$v_t' = p v_{t-1}' + \delta_t', \qquad p \leqslant 1, \tag{56}$$

$$u_t' = u_{t-1}' + \varepsilon_t', \tag{57}$$

$$\varepsilon_t' \sim IN(0, k^2\sigma_\varepsilon^2), \tag{58}$$

so that $u_t' = k u_t$, $v_t' = v_t$, and

$$x_t = \frac{\alpha}{1 - \alpha\beta} u_t' + \frac{1}{1 - \alpha\beta} v_t' = \frac{\alpha k}{1 - \alpha\beta} u_t + \frac{1}{1 - \alpha\beta} v_t \tag{59}$$

$$y_t = \frac{u_t'}{1 - \alpha\beta} + \frac{\beta}{1 - \alpha\beta} v_t' = \frac{k u_t}{1 - \alpha\beta} + \frac{\beta}{1 - \alpha\beta} v_t. \tag{60}$$

Reparameterize the model by letting $\alpha_1 = \alpha k$, $\beta_1 = \beta/k$, $\alpha_1\beta_1 = \alpha\beta$,

$$x_t(\alpha) = \frac{\alpha_1 u_t}{1 - \alpha_1\beta_1} + \frac{1}{1 - \alpha_1\beta_1} v_t, \tag{61}$$

$$y_t(\alpha) = k\left(\frac{y_t}{1 - \alpha_1\beta_1} + \frac{\beta_1 v_1}{1 - \alpha_1\beta_1}\right), \quad x_t - \alpha y_t = x_t - \alpha k y_t$$
$$= x_t - \alpha_1 y_t. \tag{62}$$

This implies that the minimum over α_1 and α will be the same, thus $\hat{\rho}$ is invariant, of course, the minimizing value $\hat{\alpha} = \hat{\alpha}_1/k$.

In what follows we shall refer to H_1 as being when $\rho < 1$, the coefficients of equations (49)–(51), a_T, b_T, and c_T can be written, using vector notation so that $\mathbf{u}'\mathbf{u}_1 = \sum u_t u_{t-1}$, as

$$\frac{(1 - \alpha\beta)^3 a_T}{2} = -\mathbf{u}'\mathbf{v}\mathbf{u}'\mathbf{u}_1 + \mathbf{u}'\mathbf{u}\tilde{\mathbf{u}}\mathbf{v} - \beta\mathbf{v}'\mathbf{v}\mathbf{u}'\mathbf{u}_1 + \beta\mathbf{u}'\mathbf{u}\mathbf{v}'\mathbf{v}_1 - \beta^2\mathbf{v}'\mathbf{v}\mathbf{u}\tilde{\mathbf{v}} + \beta^2\mathbf{u}'\mathbf{v}\mathbf{u}'\mathbf{v}_1, \tag{63}$$

$$\frac{(1 - \alpha\beta)^3 b_T}{2} = -2\alpha\mathbf{u}'\mathbf{v}\mathbf{u}'\mathbf{u}_1 + 2\alpha\mathbf{u}'\mathbf{u}\tilde{\mathbf{u}}\mathbf{v} + (1 + \alpha\beta)\mathbf{v}'\mathbf{v}\mathbf{u}'\mathbf{u}_1$$
$$- (1 + \alpha\beta)\mathbf{u}'\mathbf{u}\mathbf{v}'\mathbf{v}_1 + 2\beta\mathbf{v}'\mathbf{v}\tilde{\mathbf{u}}\mathbf{v} - 2\beta\mathbf{u}'\mathbf{v}\mathbf{v}'\mathbf{v}_1, \tag{64}$$

$$\frac{(1-\alpha\beta)^3 c_T}{2} = -\alpha^2\mathbf{u'vu'u_1} + \alpha^2\mathbf{u'u\tilde{u}v} + -\alpha\mathbf{v'vu'u_1} + \alpha\mathbf{u'uv'v_1} - \mathbf{v'v\tilde{u}v} + \mathbf{u'vv'v_1} \quad (65)$$

where $\mathbf{\tilde{u}v} = \frac{1}{2}(\sum u_t v_{t-1} + \sum v_t u_{t-1})$; and equations (63) to (65) result from direct substitution into (49)–(51) using (3)–(5).

We can use the above relationships to investigate the asymptotic properties of $\tilde{\alpha}$. These are presented below:

Lemma 1 *Under H_1 and under the assumption that* $\mathrm{cov}(u_t, v_s) = 0$ *for all t and s, and u_t, v_s normal, and $u_0 = 0$, $v_0 \sim N(0, \sigma\omega^2/1 - \rho^2)$,*

$$\lim_{T\to\infty} E\left(\frac{a_T}{T^3}\right) = \frac{-\beta\sigma_\omega^2\sigma\varepsilon^2}{(1-\alpha\beta)^3(1+\rho)},$$

$$\lim_{T\to\infty} E\left(\frac{b_T}{T^3}\right) = \frac{(1+\alpha\beta)\sigma_\omega^2\sigma_\varepsilon^2}{(1-\alpha\beta)^3(1+\rho)},$$

$$\lim_{T\to\infty} E\left(\frac{c_T}{T^3}\right) = \frac{-\alpha\sigma_\omega^2\sigma_\varepsilon^2}{(1-\alpha\beta)^3(1+\rho)}.$$

Proof This is a simple exercise in taking expectations in (63)–(65) and deleting lower order terms.

Lemma 2 *Under the same assumptions as lemma* 1, *the limiting variance of a_T, b_T, and c_T are given by*

$$\lim_{T\to-\infty} V\left(\frac{a_T}{T^3}\right) = 0,$$

$$\lim_{T\to-\infty} V\left(\frac{b_T}{T^3}\right) = 0,$$

$$\lim_{T\to-\infty} V\left(\frac{c_T}{T^3}\right) = 0.$$

Proof We shall only solve for the variance of b_T. From (63) and noting that $\mathbf{u'u}$, $\mathbf{u'u_1}$ are $O_P(T^2)$, $\mathbf{u'v}$, $\mathbf{\tilde{u}v}$, etc. are $O_P(T)$, we need only consider

$$\mathrm{Var}(b_T) = \mathrm{Var}[(1+\alpha\beta)(\mathbf{v'vu'u_1} - \mathbf{u'uv'v_1}) + 2\alpha(\mathbf{u'vu'u_1} - \mathbf{u'u\tilde{u}v})] + \text{lower order terms}$$

and we need only consider terms of $O_P(T^6)$ or greater. Now

$$\mathrm{Var}(\mathbf{v'vu'u_1} - \mathbf{u'uv'v_1}) = E[(\mathbf{v'vu'u_1})^2] + E[(\mathbf{u'u})^2(\mathbf{v'v_1})^2] - 2E[(\mathbf{v'vu'u_1u'uv'v_1})]$$

and these expressions can be calculated using formulas given in theorem 5.1 in

Magnus (1987), the details are rather tedious and have been omitted, but one can show by direct evaluation that the highest order term in each expectation is $O_p(T^6)$, and these terms cancel out leaving an overall expression of lower order.

Theorem 6 *Under the assumptions that u_t, v_s are normal and* cov $(u_t, v_s) = 0$ *for all t and s and that H_1 holds, then the correlation minimizing estimator, $\tilde{\alpha}$, is consistent.*

Corollary *The value of*

$$r(\tilde{\alpha}) = \frac{\sum (x_t - \tilde{\alpha} y_t)(x_{t-1} - \tilde{\alpha} y_{t+1})}{\sum (x_t - \tilde{\alpha} y_t)^2}$$

converges in probability to ρ as $\tilde{\alpha}$, the minimizing value, converges in probability to α and to 1 as the maximizing value tends to $1/\beta$.

It is also worth noting that it is the larger of the two solutions in (49) that tends to α and the smaller to $1/\beta$. Also, this result should be expected to hold under much weaker assumptions than the ones made in theorem 6. A full treatment of the properties of $\tilde{\alpha}$ under the sort of assumptions used by Phillips and Durlauf (1986) would be of interest.

We shall end this section by deriving the asymptotic distributions of $\hat{\alpha}$ and $\tilde{\alpha}$. Phillips and Durlauf (1986, theorem 4.1) have found the asymptotic distribution of $\hat{\alpha}$ under very general conditions. We shall stay within the framework of multivariate normality and independence between u_t and v_t, whilst recognizing the limitations of our approach. The arrows $\xrightarrow{d}$ and $\xrightarrow{p}$ will be used for convergence in distribution and probability, $W(r)$ will be two-dimensional Brownian motion with covariance matrix I_2. Readers should refer to Phillips (1987) for a detailed discussion of the mathematics and meaning of large-sample theory involving Brownian motion.

Theorem 7 *Under the assumption of theorem* 6

$$\frac{T(\hat{\alpha} - \alpha)}{(1/\beta) - \alpha} \xrightarrow{d} \frac{\dfrac{k}{\sqrt{1 - \rho^2}} \displaystyle\int_0^1 W_1(r)\, \mathrm{d}W_2(r) + \dfrac{k^2}{1 - \rho^2}}{\displaystyle\int_0^1 W_1^2(r)\, \mathrm{d}r},$$

$$\frac{T(\tilde{\alpha} - \alpha)}{(1/\beta) - \alpha} \xrightarrow{d} \frac{\dfrac{k}{\sqrt{- \rho^2}} \displaystyle\int_0^1 W_1(r)\, \mathrm{d}W_2(r)}{\displaystyle\int_0^1 W_1^2(r)\, \mathrm{d}r}.$$

Corollary 7 *If $\rho = 0$, the asymptotic distribution of*

$$\frac{T(\hat{\alpha} - a)}{1/\beta - \alpha} \xrightarrow{d} \frac{k\int_0^1 W_1(r)\,\mathrm{d}W_2(r) + k^2}{\int_0^1 W_1^2(r)\,\mathrm{d}r}.$$

This confirms our findings in theorems 2 and 3, that is, the distribution of $T(\hat{\alpha} - \alpha)/(1/\beta - \alpha)$ depends only on k and T, notice that $\tilde{\alpha}$ has a limiting distribution which is a homogeneous function of k. The interesting point that comes out of theorem 7 is that $\tilde{\alpha}$ has the same asymptotic distribution as the maximum likelihood estimates given in theorem 1 of Phillips (1989). Thus, analogous to the least squares interpretation of the maximum likelihood estimates in the linear regression model with normal errors, we have a minimum correlation interpretation of the maximum likelihood estimates sense of equality of asymptotic distribution. Finally, one can use the "t-statistic" analog for our estimates $\tilde{\alpha}$. It is a straightforward extension of theorem 7 to show that it will be asymptotically distributed as a standard normal, and one might hope that it might have good power properties in finite samples. The properties of the t-statistic await further investigation.

Appendix

Proof of theorem 1 Looking at the integral which defines it, it is easy to see that

$$\begin{aligned}
\text{MGP}\,(t_1, t_2) &= \text{Det}\,(I - 2t_1 A - 2t_2 B)^{-1/2} \\
&= \text{Det}^{-1/2}\left(\begin{pmatrix} I_T & 0 \\ 0 & I_T \end{pmatrix} - 2t_1\begin{pmatrix} 0 & \tfrac{1}{2}kP \\ \tfrac{1}{2}kP' & k^2 I_T \end{pmatrix} - 2t_2\begin{pmatrix} J & kP \\ kP' & k^2 I_T \end{pmatrix}\right) \\
&= \text{Det}^{-1/2}\begin{pmatrix} I_T - 2t_2 I & -k(t_1 + 2t_2)P \\ -k(t_1 + 2t_2)P' & (1 - 2k^2(t_1 + t_2))I_T \end{pmatrix} \\
&= \text{Det}^{-1/2}\begin{pmatrix} A_{11} & A_{12} \\ A_{21} & A_{22} \end{pmatrix} \\
&= \text{Det}^{-1/2}\,(A_{22})\,\text{Det}^{-1/2}\,(A_{11} - A_{12}A_{22}^{-1}A_{21}). \qquad \text{(A1)}
\end{aligned}$$

The left-hand term of the above product is simply

$$[1 - 2k^2(t_1 + t_2)]^{-T/2}. \qquad \text{(A2)}$$

The right-hand term is

$$\text{Det}^{-1/2}\left(I_T - 2t_2J - [-k(t_1+2t_2)P]\frac{I_T}{1-2k^2(t_1+T_2)}[-k(t_1+2t_2)P']\right)$$

$$= \text{Det}^{-1/2}\left(I_T - 2t_2J - \frac{k^2(t_1+2t_2)^2}{1-2k^2(t_1+t_2)}J\right), \quad PP' = J$$

$$= \text{Det}^{-1/2}(I_T + \theta J),$$

$$= \frac{k^2(t_1^2+4t_1t_2+4t_2^2) - 2t_2 + 4k^2(t_1t_2+t_2^2)}{1-2k^2(t_1+t_2)}, \tag{A3}$$

$$\theta = \frac{-k^2t_1^2 - 2t_2}{1-2k^2(t_1+t_2)} \tag{A4}$$

$$\text{Det}^{-1/2}(I_T+\theta J) = \prod_{j=1}^{T}(1+\theta\lambda_j)^{-1/2} \tag{A5}$$

where the λ_j are the eigenvalues of J. (We are assuming that J is a $T \times T$ matrix. When T is unclear, we will write $\lambda_{j,T}$).

Now, going back to (A5), we have

$$\text{MGF}(t_1,t_2) = [1-2k^2(t_1+t_2)]^{-T/2}\prod_{j=1}^{T}\left(1+\lambda_j\frac{k^2t_1^2-2t_2}{1-2k^2(t_1+t_2)}\right)^{-1/2}$$

$$= \prod_{j=1}^{T}[1-2k^2(t_1+t_2) - \lambda_j(k^2t_1^2+2t_2)]^{-1/2}. \tag{A6}$$

The eigenvalues of J are well known, they are given by

$$\lambda_{j,T} = \frac{1}{4}\frac{1}{\sin^2\left(\dfrac{t-\frac{1}{2}}{2T+1}\pi\right)}. \tag{A7}$$

Thus we have a complete expression for the moment generating function.

Proof of theorem 2.

$$\text{MGF}(t_1,t_2) = [1-2k^2(t_1+t_2)]^{-T/2}\prod_{j=1}^{T}(1+\theta\lambda_j)^{-1/2}. \tag{A8}$$

Note that

$$\sum_{j=1}^{T}(1+\theta\lambda_j) = \theta^T\sum_{j=1}^{T}(\lambda_j+1/\theta). \tag{A9}$$

The characteristic polynomial of the $T \times T$ matrix J, $CP_T(x)$ is given by

$$CP_T(x) = \prod_{j=1}^{T} (\lambda_j - x). \tag{A10}$$

Hence,

$$\text{MGF}\,(t_1, t_2) = (-k^2 t_1^2 - 2t_2)^{-T/2} CP_T^{-1/2}(-1/\theta). \tag{A11}$$

We now derive an expression for $CP_T(-1/\theta)$.

$$CP_T(x) = \text{Det}\begin{pmatrix} T-x & T-1 & T-2 & \cdots & 1 \\ T-1 & T-1-x & T-2 & \cdots & 1 \\ T-2 & T-2 & T-2-x & \cdots & 1 \\ \vdots & \vdots & \vdots & \cdots & \vdots \\ 1 & 1 & 1 & 1 & 1-x \end{pmatrix} \tag{A12}$$

By standard manipulations on the columns, we get the difference equation.

$$CP_T(x) = (1 - 2x)CP_{T-1}(x) - x^2 CP_{T-2}(x). \tag{A13}$$

This recursive equation has a solution of the form

$$CP_T(x) = au^T + bv^T, \tag{A14}$$

where u, v are the roots of $u^2 - (1 - 2x)u + x^2 = 0$. We solve for

$$u = \frac{1 - 2x + \sqrt{1 - 4x}}{2}, \tag{A15}$$

$$v = \frac{1 - 2x - \sqrt{1 - 4x}}{2}. \tag{A16}$$

The first two values of $CP_T(x)$ are $CP_1(x) = 1 - x$ and $CP_2(x) = 1 - 3x + x^2$. Iterating backwards in equation (A13), we find $CP_0(x) = 1$. Now, $au^0 + bv^0 = a + b = 1$.

$$a\left(\frac{1 - 2x + \sqrt{1 - 4x}}{2}\right) + (1 - a)\left(\frac{1 - 2x - \sqrt{1 - 4x}}{2}\right) = 1 - x, \tag{A17}$$

therefore

$$\frac{1 - 2x}{2} - \frac{\sqrt{1 - 4x}}{2} + a(\sqrt{1 - 4x}) - 1 + x = 0 \tag{A18}$$

and

$$a = \frac{1}{\sqrt{1-4x}} \frac{1+\sqrt{1-4x}}{2} = \frac{1}{2}\left(1 + \frac{1}{\sqrt{1-4x}}\right), \tag{A19}$$

$$b = \frac{1}{2}\left(1 + \frac{1}{\sqrt{1-4x}}\right). \tag{A20}$$

Hence, we get the expressions

$$CP_T(x) = \frac{1}{2}\left(1 + \frac{1}{\sqrt{1-4x}}\right)\left(\frac{1-2x+\sqrt{1-4x}}{2}\right)^T$$

$$+ \frac{1}{2}\left(1 - \frac{1}{\sqrt{1-4x}}\right)\left(\frac{1-2x-\sqrt{1-4x}}{2}\right)^T \tag{A21}$$

$$\text{MGF}\,(t_1, t_2) = (-k^2t_1^2 - 2t_2)^{-T/2} CP_T^{-1/2}(\phi), \tag{A22}$$

$$\phi = \frac{1 - 2k^2(t_1 + t_2)}{k^2t_1^2 + 2t_2}. \tag{A23}$$

Notes

We would like to thank P. C. B. Phillips and two anonymous referees for several important improvements to this paper.

References

Amemiya, T. (1985). *Advanced Econometrics.* London: Basil Blackwell.

Engle, R. F., and C. W. J. Granger. (1987). "Co-integration and error correction: representation, estimation and testing," *Econometrica*, 55, 251–76.

Griliches, Z., and M. D. Intrilligator. *Handbook of Econometrics*, volume 1, pp. 444–516. Amsterdam: North Holland.

Giovannetti, G. (1988). "The purchasing power in the long run: an application of cointegration," unpublished manuscript.

Hall, S. G. (1986). "An application of the Granger and Engle two-step estimation procedure to United Kingdom aggregate wage data," *Oxford Bulletin of Economics and Statistics*, 48, 229–39.

Jenkinson, T. J. (1986). "Testing neo-classical theories of labour demand: an application of co-integration techniques," *Oxford Bulletin of Economics and Statistics*, 48, 241–51.

Magnus, J. R. (1987). "The moments of products of quadratic forms in normal variables," Overdrukken, 24, Instituut Voor Actuariaat en Econometrie, University of Amsterdam.

Phillips, P. C. B. (1986). "Exact small sample theory in the simultaneous equation model," in Z. Griliches and M. D. Intrilligator. *Handbook of Econometrics*, volume 1. Amsterdam: North Holland.

Phillips, P. C. B. (1987). "Time series regression with a unit root," *Econometrica*, 55, 277–301.

Phillips, P. C. B. (1989). "Optimal inference in cointegrated systems," Cowles Foundation Discussion Paper 866R.

Phillips, P. C. B., and S. N. Durlauf. (1986). "Multiple time series regression with integrated processes," *Review of Economic Studies*, LIII, 473–95.

Part IV

Dynamic Econometric Modeling

14

Reference Cycles in the Time and Frequency Domains: Duality Aspects of the Business Cycle

Roger J. Bowden and Vance L. Martin

Introduction and Review

The identification and measurement of business cycles has had a long if on the whole informal history in the literature of statistical economics. It has nevertheless been a history marked by methodological controversy, starting with the famous "measurement without theory" charge leveled by Koopmans (1947) at the work of the National Bureau of Economic Research (NBER). On the other hand, it surely could not be claimed that the empirical representation of more explicit economic theorizing in the form of econometric modeling has contributed much more to our understanding of business cycles with respect, in particular, to the measurement of their incidence and timing. So the NBER methodology survives. In recent years, it has become a little more sophisticated both conceptually and methodologically, with the selection of indicators being based upon, at least, an implied economic model. An important aspect of indicator analysis is in the classification of series into leading, coincident, and lagging indicators. The coincident indicators are intended to encapsulate the actual course of macroeconomic events (GNP, sales, employment, etc.) while the leading indicators (such as new orders, increases in overdraft limits, etc.) are measurements of commitments with respect to future activity. The remaining group, the lagging indicators, are viewed as consequential entailments of general economic activity. For a general review, we refer the reader to Moore (1983) and for different approaches to the construction of composite indexes, see Auerbach (1982), Hymans (1973), Martin (1987), and Sargent and Sims (1977).

However the basic methodology of the NBER approach remains one of identifying the turning points and lead–lag relationships of the constituent series and composite indexes by means of an eyeballing process, or a computer recreation thereof. The subjectivity of such procedures led to attempts to enlist techniques of time-series analysis. Empirical spectral analyses of the business cycle showed early on that cycles of regular periodicity did not, on the whole, appear to exist. In some measure this highlighted the deficiencies in the subjective approach which up to that point (the mid to late sixties) had indeed claimed regular periodicity, although few if any practitioners could now make such a claim in the light of intervening economic experience. However, a focus on the spectral behavior of individual series missed some points of substance. In the first place, it has come to be recognized that there is no real requirement for regular periodicity. Over an extended time interval, business cycles can be of any length. Instead, cycles are to be identified by their coherence aspect: the collection of series must move together (or exhibit some such tendencies) as if driven by a common underlying machine, in spite of their differing lead-lag relationships (Koopmans 1947, Sargent 1979). The identification of regularities between principal economic time series in terms of coherence as well as phase for a number of countries led Lucas (1977, p. 9) to conclude that all business cycles are alike.[1]

An early approach to the general coherence problem is contained in Bowden (1972). The spectral density matrix embodies all the mutual information of a set of covariance-stationary time series.[2] A one-dimensional manifold of the required kind therefore exists in the frequency domain if the first principal component of the spectral density matrix dominates the others, in the sense of representing most of the variance of the system. The corresponding loadings can be used to establish what we refer to as a spectral reference cycle, in terms of which phase relationships are easily identified with regard to the individual constituents series. Recently Martin (1987) resurrected the general idea, but applied it to a pre-existing classification of coincident and leading indicators, by utilizing techniques of canonical correlation in the frequency domain to establish optimum weights for each constituent series in the weighted sums comprising the coincident and leading indexes. Sargent and Sims (1977) took yet a different tack, but again based on a multivariate analysis in the frequency domain. They proposed that, as a generalization of the one-dimensional manifold idea, the individual series could be driven by more than one factor. For example, a two-index model could arise if two basic factors, "real" and "monetary," provided the motive force. They proposed a testing procedure for the number of such factors, or indexes, based on an extension to the frequency domain of testing procedure for classical factor analysis. In the Sargent and Sims model, one might not be surprised to find that the second principal component of the spectral density matrix exhibits substantial power, for it may well be that this corresponds to a second basic factor at work, and that independent contributions accrue from each.

Turning to the time domain, dual representations to the above spectral representations or conceptualizations do exist, at least in principle. Dual to the spectral reference cycle is a time domain index of the following form:

$$y_{jt} = a_j * \zeta_t + u_{jt}, \tag{1}$$

where $a_j * \zeta_j = \sum_{\tau=-\infty}^{\infty} a_\tau^j \zeta_{t-\tau}$, or $= \sum_{\tau=0}^{\infty} a_\tau^j \zeta_{t-\tau}$, is either a two-sided or one-sided convolution in terms of a simple index ζ_t respectively, while u_{jt} is a disturbance. The latter is uncorrelated with the index ζ_t but may itself be serially correlated and might also be correlated with some but not all other u_{kt} for $k \neq j$. Now if a business cycle can be said to exist, then we should expect that over a range of "business cycle" frequencies (collectively called w_B) or periods (T_B), then the power of the disturbances u_{jt} should be small over those frequencies. On the other hand, at very high frequencies the general business cycle might be overlain with individualized short-period "noise" or extraneous fluctuations; something similar might also be true of very low frequencies. Such behavior would give rise to what is commonly observed (see for instance the third section), namely that overall spectral coherence is high over certain frequencies (the 2–5-year band) and lower elsewhere. The above decomposition would also imply a type of quasi-prediction property. Suppose that we attempted to predict y_{jt+T_B}, i.e. T_B periods ahead. The $a_j * \zeta_{t+T_B}$ should constitute a good prediction. On the other hand $a_j * \zeta_{t+T}$ might well constitute a poor prediction for $T \ll T_B$ or even $T \gg T_B$. Of course, the "predictions" involved here are all ex-post, in the sense that we are assuming that future values of ζ_t are available.

The Sargent and Sims multi-index model can be represented in the same general form as (1) except that $\boldsymbol{\zeta}_t$ is now a k-dimensional vector and a^j an $n \times k$ matrix series. From the outset, they choose the convolution to be one-sided, and also specify that the u_{jt} are uncorrelated across j (the factor analysis model) and should have low power, uniformly over all frequencies. Whether one chooses a single-index representation or multi-index model depends on the ultimate purpose of the exercise. Sargent and Sims are more concerned with the implied underlying structures. If (to take one of their examples) one can show that two indexes are involved, they might perhaps be identified with "real" and "monetary" influences, leading, one hopes, to a settlement of some outstanding issues in macroeconomic theory. The Sargent–Sims methodology does not, however, lead directly to a time domain representation of the relevant indexes.

In the present paper we are concerned, as are the National Bureau and many statistical agencies, with questions of a more empirical and in some respects, more basic, nature. We ask whether an overall cycle does exist, defining this in terms of the dominance of the first principle component of the spectral density matrix over at least a certain range, the business cycle range, of frequencies. Once we are satisfied that such a spectral reference cycle does exist, we then turn to the temporal characterization of this cycle, as a single index.

The notion of a spectral reference cycle is a useful device for examination of frequency-specific effects, but it does suffer from the defect that it is in many ways more natural to think of a reference cycle in the time rather than the frequency domain. Thus, from the point of view of economic history, one would like to know the timing of the peaks and troughs of the reference cycle. Or, in terms of current or real time, one would like to be able to assess aggregate developments in terms of the current position of the reference cycle indicator. And in terms of the study of the leads and lags, frequency-specific phase differences cannot be integrated over all frequency bands to derive a time domain estimate of the extent to which a constituent index leads, lags, or is coincident with the aggregate cycle. Such questions can be properly answered only in the time domain, and it is our purpose to provide such a resolution. Our methodology basically proceeds by finding the temporal inversion of the first principal component of the empirical spectral density matrix. Our discussion assumes that the spectral density matrix does indeed exist, either in theory or else as an acceptable empirical regularity predicated on an agreed meaning for the processes of detrending that may be necessary for such a regularity to exist. In this respect, we are well aware of the unsettled state of opinion in the profession regarding the problem of stationarity or of achieving stationarity, in economic time series. Pending a resolution of the solution structure of macroeconomic models (where the work of Bergstrom (1962) may well constitute a good starting point), we simply assume that an empirical spectral matrix does exist for a suitably transformed set of the economic time series under discussion.

The central idea of the present paper is that systematic information about the individual time series and their interrelationships is contained in the spectral density matrix. It can be extracted, particularly in its mutual coherence aspect, by means of principal component analysis. Fourier inversion of the resulting spectral single index results in a temporal index whose dynamic behavior is a temporal recreation of the collective information revealed in the spectral density matrix. This leads (the second section of the paper) to a temporal reference cycle, in one of two forms. A classical Fourier inversion results in a two-sided reference cycle, in which constituent series appear with positive and negative lags. This two-sided cycle (we call it RCYCLE2) can be utilized for validation purposes and for historical studies. For purposes of current observation – "in real time" as it were – future values of the constituent series are not available, and the need is for a one-sided composite index that receives contributions from only the past of the constituent series. Such a one-sided cycle – we call it RCYCLE1 – is outlined in the third section.

A calculus of lead/lag measurement in the time domain is also suggested. Whether a series leads or lags the general cycle can in principle be established by examining the implied loading or weights obtained from the Fourier inversion of the spectral reference cycle, and we propose one methodology for doing this, which is in fact derived directly from the frequency domain. In practice, however, such leads or lags can also be effectively presented in the form of a contribution to the stepwise R^2 in a Granger–Sims type regression of a certain kind, and the existence of leads tested in terms of the F-test for the existence of causality. It turns out that the statistical paradigm resulting from the Fourier inversion has a fairly close correspondence with that required for such causality testing.

The fourth section is an empirical application to the USA business cycle. We run through the methodology established in preceding sections utilizing the Centre for International Business Cycle Research (CIBCR) leading and coincident indicators and consider whether and to what extent the post-war USA economy supports the idea of a spectral or temporal reference cycle, or whether existing decompositions using NBER methodology into leading and coincident indicators have any more formal support.

The limited information nature of our methodology should be stressed at the outset. Like the NBER methodology, it takes as given the choice as to which constituent series are to enter into the putative reference cycle, and findings as to the existence or otherwise of spectral or temporal reference cycles are not invariant to the composition of the subject set of time series. As with the NBER methods, the choice of constituent series must be informed by at least a residue of economic principles, so that this is never entirely a measurement without theory. To a greater extent than the NBER techniques, our methodology does appear to offer a more systematic basis for the inclusion or exclusion of constituent series into or from the index pool, but again this is based upon statistical technology rather than economic theory. Thus, while the charge of measurement without economic theory can also be leveled at the methodology proposed in the present paper, at least a somewhat less subjective kind of statistical decision theory is involved.

The Reference Index: Frequency and Time Domains

In order to motivate the basic theoretical development of this and the following section, consider a set of n regular jointly covariance stationary processes $y_{1t}, y_{2t}, \ldots, y_{nt}$.[3]

These are assumed to be of zero mean and in order to avoid arbitrary reassignments of influence resulting from simple rescaling, we shall suppose that each series has been normalized by dividing by its standard deviation σ_j. The symmetric positive definite (or semidefinite perhaps) spectral density matrix $G(w)$ may be factorized as

$$G(w) = U(w)\Lambda(w)U^*(w), \tag{2}$$

where the asterisk denotes conjugate transpose, $\Lambda(w) = \mathrm{diag}(\lambda_k(\mathrm{w}))$ contains the eigenvalues of $G(w)$ in descending order of magnitude and the columns of $U(w)$ are the corresponding eigenvectors, all at the indicated frequency w. The matrix $U(w)$ is normalized to be unitary. Note, however, that this is insufficient to uniquely determine $U(w)$, for postmultiplication by any diagonal matrix $\mathrm{e}^{-\mathrm{i}D(w)} = [\mathrm{e}^{-\mathrm{i}d_1(w)}, \mathrm{e}^{-\mathrm{i}d_2(w)}, \ldots, \mathrm{e}^{-\mathrm{i}d_n(w)}]$, where the $d_k(w)$ are possibly arbitrary functions of w, will yield a set of eigenvectors $\tilde{\mathrm{U}}(w) = U(w)\,\mathrm{e}^{-\mathrm{i}D(w)}$ that are also unitary and satisfy (2). We shall return to this point below, and in the meantime proceed in terms of any arbitrary normalizaton.

The Cramer representation of y_{jt} is $y_{jt} = \int_{-\pi}^{\pi} \mathrm{e}^{\mathrm{i}wt}\, \mathrm{d}y_j(w)$, so that $y_j(w)$ is a process in the frequency domain with orthogonal increments $\mathrm{d}y_j(w)$. In terms of the principal component analysis of $G(w)$, let us define at each frequency a vector of increments

$$\mathrm{d}\boldsymbol{\zeta}(w) = U^*(w)\,\mathrm{d}\mathbf{y}(w). \tag{3}$$

Evidently $E\,\mathrm{d}\boldsymbol{\zeta}(w)\,\mathrm{d}\boldsymbol{\zeta}^*(w) = \Lambda(w)\,\mathrm{d}w$, where the decomposition (2) has been utlized, together with $E\,\mathrm{d}\mathbf{y}(w)\,\mathrm{d}\mathbf{y}^*(w) = G(w)\,\mathrm{d}w$. In other words, the linear combination of the right-hand side of (3) behaves as the increments of a vector process $\boldsymbol{\zeta}(w)$ in the frequency domain such that $E|\mathrm{d}\zeta_j(w)|^2 = \lambda_j(w)\,\mathrm{d}w$ and $E\,\mathrm{d}\zeta_j(w)\,\mathrm{d}\bar{\zeta}_k(w) = 0, j \neq k$.

Suppose in particular that the first principle component is associated with a dominant eigenvalue $\lambda_1(w)$, and moreover exhibits a high degree of coherence with all constituent series. One could then say that a spectral reference cycle existed at that particular frequency. Writing $u_{1j}^*(w) = a_j(w)$, one would then have

$$\mathrm{d}\zeta_1(w) = \sum_j a_j(w)\,\mathrm{d}y_j(w). \tag{4}$$

The phase difference between the spectral reference cycle and the constituent series j is given at frequency w by

$$\theta_{1j}(w) = -\tan^{-1}[\mathrm{Im}\,(a_j(w))/\mathrm{Re}\,(a_j(w))]. \tag{5}$$

For a derivation of these and related coherence formulas, we refer the reader to Bowden (1972) and Brillinger (1975). Empirically, however, Bowden worked with the coherence matrix, which is real, and did not notice the lack of uniqueness in the matrix $U(w)$, and therefore $\mathbf{a}(w)$, referred to above. However a suitable normalization can be derived as follows. Define $\tilde{\mathbf{a}}(w)$ as corresponding to $\tilde{U}^*(w)$, so that $\tilde{a}_j(w) = \mathrm{e}^{\mathrm{i}d_1(w)}a_j(w)$. In terms of this alternative normalization, the phase difference at frequency w between series j and the alternative $\mathrm{d}\tilde{\zeta}_1(w) = \mathrm{e}^{\mathrm{i}d_1(w)}\,\mathrm{d}\zeta_1(w)$, is given by $\tilde{\theta}_{1j}(w) = \theta_{1j}(w) - d_1(w)$.

Our rule is to normalize so that $\sum_j \tilde{\theta}_{1j}(w) = 0$. In other words, we normalize so that the average phase difference at each frequency between the proposed spectral reference cycle and the constituent series is zero. To accomplish this, we start with any arbitrary normalization (unitary solution $U^*(w)$ to the diagonalization (2)), and normalize the resulting weights $a_j(w)$ in (4) by multiplying each by $e^{id_1(w)}$, where $d_1(w) = \sum_j \theta_{1j}(w)/n$. Although alternative normalization procedures are available, the above appears to be the most natural.

Suppose now that the first principal component $d\zeta_1(w)$ exhibits some characterisic of special interest. For example, it may be that this component dominates the variance of the system uniformly across all frequency bands. Or it may be that $d\zeta_1(w)$ dominates in a more local sense at some particular frequency band of prime interest, as described in the first section. In either case, we can invert the component to provide a time index ζ_{1t} that will encapsulate in the time domain the feature of special interest. Reconsidering equation (4), we note that $U(w)$ has period 2π, so that the following Fourier transform (FT) pair is supported:

$$a_j(w) = \frac{1}{2\pi} \sum_{\tau=-\infty}^{\infty} a_\tau \, e^{-iw\tau}, \tag{6a}$$

$$a_\tau^j = \int_{-\pi}^{\pi} e^{iw\tau} a_j(w) \, dw. \tag{6b}$$

Given the process $\zeta_1(w)$ with orthogonal increments $d\zeta_1(w)$, define a time function ζ_{1t} by the stochastic integral

$$\begin{aligned}\int_{-\pi}^{\pi} e^{iwt} \, d\zeta_1(w) &= \frac{1}{2\pi} \sum_j \int_{-\pi}^{\pi} e^{iwt} \left[\sum_\tau a_\tau^j \, e^{-iw\tau} \right] dy_j(w) \\ &= \frac{1}{2\pi} \sum_j \sum_\tau a_\tau^j \int_{-\pi}^{\pi} e^{iw(t-\tau)} \, dy_j(w) \\ &= \frac{1}{2\pi} \sum_j \sum_\tau a_\tau^j y_{jt-\tau}. \end{aligned} \tag{7}$$

Thus

$$\zeta_{1t} = \sum_j \zeta_{1t}^j, \tag{8}$$

where

$$\zeta_{1t}^j = \frac{1}{2\pi} \sum_{\tau=-\infty}^{\infty} a_\tau^j y_{jt-\tau}, \tag{9}$$

is that part of the index originating in series j. Equation (8) provides the required temporal inversion of the spectral reference cycle. The index ζ_{1t} has spectrum $\lambda(w)$ and the relationship of the y_{jt} with ζ_{1j} display the features described in connection with the decomposition (1). The index is two-sided since both positive and negative lags of the various constituent series y_{jt} contribute to its formation; for this reason we shall refer to it in empirical work as RCYCLE2.

Some very convenient symmetry relationships connect the series ζ_{1t} with the constituent y_{jt}. Premultiplying equation (3) by $U(w)$, we have $\mathbf{dy}(w) = U(w)\,\mathrm{d}\boldsymbol{\zeta}(w)$, whence in particular for series j,

$$\mathrm{d}y_j(w) = \sum_{k=1}^{n} u_{jk}(w)\,\mathrm{d}\zeta_k(w). \tag{10}$$

Hence

$$\mathrm{d}y_j(w) = u_{j1}(w)\,\mathrm{d}\zeta_1(w) + \mathrm{d}\varepsilon_j(w), \tag{11}$$

where $\mathrm{d}\varepsilon_j(w) = \sum_{k=2}^{n} u_{jk}(w)\,\mathrm{d}\zeta_k(w)$ is uncorrelated with $\mathrm{d}\zeta_1(w)$. Now $u_{j1}(w) = \bar{u}^*_{1j}(w) = \bar{a}_j(w)$, where $a_j(w)$ is defined in terms of equation (4). Applying the Cramer representation to equation (11) we therefore get

$$y_{jt} = \int_{-\pi}^{\pi} \mathrm{e}^{\mathrm{i}wt}\bar{a}_j(w)\,\mathrm{d}\zeta_1(w) + \int_{-\pi}^{\pi} \mathrm{e}^{\mathrm{i}wt}\,\mathrm{d}\varepsilon_j(w). \tag{12}$$

Using the FT (6a), we obtain

$$\int_{-\pi}^{\pi} \mathrm{e}^{\mathrm{i}wt}\bar{a}_j(w)\,\mathrm{d}\zeta_1(w) = \frac{1}{2\pi}\int_{-\pi}^{\pi} \mathrm{e}^{\mathrm{i}wt}\left[\sum_{\tau'=-\infty}^{\infty} a^j_{-\tau'}\,\mathrm{e}^{-\mathrm{i}w\tau'}\right]\mathrm{d}\zeta_1(w)$$

$$= \frac{1}{2\pi}\sum_{\tau=-\infty}^{\infty} a^j_{-\tau}\zeta_{1t-\tau}. \tag{13}$$

In summary, we have

$$y_{jt} = \frac{1}{2\pi}\sum_{\tau=-\infty}^{\infty} a^j_{-\tau}\zeta_{1t-\tau} + \varepsilon_{jt}, \tag{14}$$

where the residual ε_{jt} is uncorrelated with the $\zeta_{1t-\tau}$.

Equations (8) and (14) give the reciprocal relationship between the two-sided principal spectral reference cycle and its constituent indexes. The relationship may be summarized thus

$$\zeta_{1t} = \sum_j \zeta^j_{1t}, \tag{15}$$

$$2\pi\zeta^j_{1t} = \cdots a^j_2 y_{jt-2} + a^j_1 y_{jt-1} + a^j_0 y_{jt} + a^j_{-1} y_{jt+1} + a^j_{-2} y_{jt+2} + \cdots; \tag{15a}$$

$$2\pi y_{jt} = \cdots a^j_{-2}\zeta_{1t-2} + a^j_{-1}\zeta_{1t-1} + a^j_0\zeta_{1t} + a^j_1\zeta_{1t+1} + a^j_2\zeta_{1t+2} + \cdots + \varepsilon_{jt}, \tag{15b}$$

where the a^j_τ are defined in terms of equations (4) and (6) as the Fourier transforms of the principal eigenvector of $G(w)$. The antisymmetry should be noted – the weights run one way in (15a), the reverse way in (15b). These equations will play an important role in the lead–lag discussions of the next section.

Leads, Lags, and the One-Sided Reference Cycle

Leads, Lags, and Causality

One of the disadvantages of the phase difference (5) is that it is frequency specific; no natural integration procedure exists that will convert it to a time domain measure of the extent to which an individual series leads or lags the reference cycle. Formulas (15a) and (15b) allow us to derive such a measure in terms of the arithmetic mean lag (i.e. y_{jt} lags ζ_{jt}) defined for a two-sided relationship by

$$L_j = -\sum_{\tau=-\infty}^{\infty} \tau a_\tau^j \Big/ \sum_{\tau=-\infty}^{\infty} a_\tau^j, \tag{16a}$$

provided that the denominator exists. By differentiating both sides of equation (6a) and setting $w = 0$, we obtain $L_j = -ia_j'(0)/a_j(0)$.

Let $v_j(w)$ be the imaginary part of $a_j(w)$ and – at a slight risk of a notational clash with the elements of U^* – let $u_j(w)$ denote the corresponding real part. Then if we write $a_j(w) = u_j(w) + iv_j(w)$, it follows from (6a) that $u_j(w) = u_j(-w)$ and $v_j(w) = -v_j(-w)$: the real part is symmetric about zero and the imaginary part is antisymmetric. In particular, $v_j(0) = 0$ so that $a_j(0) = u_j(0)$ and since the constituent time series are by assumption regular $u_j'(0) = 0$, so that $a_j'(0) = iv_j'(0)$.

Computationally, therefore, we have

$$L_j = v_j'(0)/u_j(0). \tag{16b}$$

The mean lag L_j bears an interesting relationship with the phase difference $\theta_{1j}(w)$ defined by equation (5). We have $\tan \theta_{1j}(w) = -v_j(w)/u_j(w)$.

Differentiating both sides and setting $w = 0$ we obtain

$$\frac{d}{dw} \tan \theta_{1j}(w)_{w=0} = -v_j'(0)/u_j(0) = -L_j.$$

The mean lag can therefore also be calculated in terms of the derivative of the tangent of the phase difference, evaluated at $w = 0$,[4]

$$L_j = -\frac{d}{dw} \tan \theta_{1j}(0). \tag{16c}$$

In practice, the differentiation will have to be executed numerically, but of course there are many standard routines available for this.

It must be remarked, however, that the choice of the arithmetic mean is perhaps a little arbitrary. Moreover it is handy to have a formal testing procedure available for whether series y_{jt} leads or lags as a whole the reference cycle ζ_{1t}; the rationale behind such a test also gives rise to some further useful descriptive measures for lead–lag behavior. Recall the Granger–Sims tests for causality (see Granger (1969) and Sims (1972), also Pierce and Haugh (1977)). In our context, series y_{jt} might be said to "cause" ζ_{1t} if, in the regression (15b), the future coefficients $(a_1^j, a_2^j, \ldots)$ were statistically significant in the regression of y_{jt} on ζ_{1t+r}: $r \lessgtr 0$. Leaving aside the causality connotation, which may be unacceptable here, we should certainly be able to say that series y_{jt} lagged ζ_{1t} if the relevant F test showed that the future coefficients were statistically insignificant. We observe that equation (15b) fulfils a necessary condition for a test of this type, namely that the disturbance ε_{jt} is independent of the regressors. On the other hand, the disturbance is not necessarily serially uncorrelated, so that some bias may exist in the classical testing procedure. It should also be noted that lead–lag testing cannot be based on (15a), since the regressors $(y_{jt+\tau})$ are in this case not independent of the implied disturbance.

A less formal procedure, but one that is more independent of distributional assumptions, is to conduct a series of stepwise regressions based on equation (15b) and graph the progressive R^2 as more terms on the right-hand side are introduced. The progressive R^2 may be plotted against τ in a graph where the horizontal axis is reversed so that τ-values to the right-hand side of the origin are negative, indicating leads. The next section contains some examples of such plots In general terms, if the R^2 graph climbs steeply after $\tau = 0$, this would be taken to indicate that series j leads the principal reference cycle, whereas if R^2 remains relatively stationary after the origin, then series j lags – or is simply unrelated to – the general reference cycle. Reconsidering (16b), the theoretical maximum for the regression sum of squares (equal to R^2, since the variances are normalized at unity) may be derived from equation (11) to be

$$R^2_{\max} = \int_{-\pi}^{\pi} |a_j(w)|^2 \lambda_1(w)\, dw. \tag{17}$$

Thus one can have a flat R^2 graph either if $\lambda_1(w)$ is uniformly low, which means that no reference cycle can be said to exist, or if $|a_j(w)|$ is uniformly low, so that series y_j does not enter into the principal reference cycle. In this respect it may be noted that these techniques can also be applied where several principal components obviously exist, so that the system is effectively split into several blocks.

A final remark concerns sampling variability. We have hitherto been implicitly assuming that the spectral density matrix $G(w)$ is measured with a high degree of accuracy, so that the effects of sampling fluctuation are negligible. Assuming that the σ_j are known, the asymptotic sampling theory of $G(w)$ is that of a complex Wishart distributed matrix. The distribution of $\sqrt{n}(\hat{\lambda}_1(w) - \lambda_1(w))$ is asymptotically $N(0, \lambda_1^2(w))$; $w \neq 0$ or $N(0, 2\lambda_1^2(w))$; $w = 0$ with the subdominant roots distributed in similar fashion (Bowden 1970, chapter 4). Unfortunately, the sampling distribution of the eigenvectors is more complicated. Thus far the sampling distribution of the derived measures such as L_j, $R^2_{\max}$ and confidence bounds for the spectral reference cycle have still to be worked out. It would seem unwise to place too much reliance on the results unless the underlying spectral estimation is supported by a fairly lengthy run of data.

The One-Sided Reference Cycle

As equations (15a) and (15b) make clear, the two-sided reference cycle ζ_{1t} depends upon future constituent values as well as present and past values. For purposes of current monitoring of the cycle (as distinct from historical examinations or validational procedures) it would be useful to have available an index that relies only upon currently available information .... $y_{jt-2}, y_{jt-1}, y_{jt}$. Thus we should like to form an index

$$\zeta_{1t}^{(1)} = \sum_j \zeta_{1t}^{(1)j}; \tag{18}$$

$$\begin{aligned} 2\pi\zeta_{1t}^{(1)j} &= \cdots \alpha_2 y_{jt-2} + \alpha_1 y_{jt-1} + \alpha_0 y_{jt} \\ &= \alpha(z) y_{jt}, \end{aligned} \tag{19}$$

where $\alpha(z)$ is a one-sided filter in the lag operator z. Unfortunately, there is no way that this can be accomplished exactly; the problem has some parallels with the problem of achieving a one-sided factorization of the spectrum (Whittle 1963, chapter 2) and the method that we propose has some analogies with the empirical resolution of the latter problem.

Thus let us in the first instance form the two-sided cycle ζ_{1t}(RCYCLE2). Then we find weights $\alpha_0, \alpha_1, \alpha_2, \ldots$ such that $\zeta_{1t}^{(1)j}$ as defined by equation (18) most closely approximates, in the least squares sense, the given series ζ_{1t}^j. In other words,

$$\zeta_{1t}^{(1)j} = E[\zeta_{1t}^j \mid I_t], \tag{20}$$

where I_t is the available information set, in this case the set of current and historical data on all the constituent series y_{jt-r}: $r \geqslant 0$.

While a theoretical expression can be given for the conditional expectation (20) in terms of the MA representation of the vector process $(\mathbf{y}_t)$, it is in practice probably easier to limit the information set for ζ_{1t}^j to $I_t^j = (\cdots y_{t-2}^j, y_{t-1}^j, y_t^j)$; in other words, its current and own past. We should then obtain $\zeta_{1t}^{(1)j}$ by regressing RCYCLE2 or its jth component on y_t^j and its past few lags – various autoregressive transformations may help to identify this process. The estimated $\hat{\zeta}_{1t}^{(1)j}$ are then added to form RCYCLE1, the estimated one-sided reference cycle. Finally it should be remarked that the causality-type decomposition (15b) does not exist for the one-sided reference cycle, so that detection of leads and lags must of necessity be an informal process.

Application to the USA Business Cycle

In this section, the methodology developed in the previous two sections is applied to the construction of spectral reference cycles for the USA economy. The constituent series consist of the 12 leading and 6 coincident indicators used by the CIBCR in the construction of leading and coincident composite indexes respectively. Sources and descriptions are given in Table 14.1. The data are monthly, with the exception of corporate profits, business inventories, ratio of price to unit labor costs, and GNP, which are quarterly. These quarterly series, however, are converted to monthly series by using a linear interpolation. Where appropriate, data are seasonally adjusted by the X-11 method.[5] The sample period starts in 1948(2) and ends in 1988(11), a total of 481 observations. All series are expressed in logarithms, with the exception of consumer credit, business inventories and industrial material prices. Stationarity in the mean is achieved by regressing each series on a constant and the series lagged one month and using the residuals as the "stationarized" series.[6] The data are then standardized to have unit variance by dividing each resulting series by its empirical standard deviation.

Table 14.1 CIBCR Indicators for the USA

Leading indicators
Net business formation
Change in consumer installment credit
Stock price index
Corporate profits after taxes
Change in business inventories
New building permits, housing
Change in industrial materials prices
Average workweek, manufacturing
Average weekly initial claims, unemployment insurance
New orders, consumer goods and materials
Contracts and orders, plant and equipment
Ratio, price to unit labor cost, manufacturing
Coincident indicators
Personal income
Gross national product
Industrial production
Unemployment rate, inverted
Manufacturing and trade sales
Employees on nonfarm payrolls

Source: *International Economic Indicators*, various issues.

Spectra and cross-spectra are computed using the fast Fourier transform with the ordinates evaluated at $w_j = 2\pi j/N, j = 0, 1, 2, \ldots, N$, where N is chosen to be 600.[7] The number of moving average parameters is chosen to be 25, which means that the spectral density matrix $G(w)$, is evaluated at frequencies starting at zero and incremented by $2\pi/25$. Consistent estimates of the spectral density matrices are obtained using a Daniell window of length 23. This choice ensures that $G(w)$ both has full rank and is independent over the frequencies $w_k = 2\pi k/25$, $k = 0, 1, 2, \ldots, 24$. The spectrum is "recolored" by using the transfer function of the equation used to render the data stationary in the mean. Each spectral density matrix is factorized by using the IMSL subroutine EVLHF to compute the eigenvalues $a_j(w_k)$, in (6a). The eigenvalues corresponding to each constituent series are then grouped together over the 25 frequencies and transformed using a discrete inverse fast Fourier transform to generate the moving average parameters in (6b).

The Reference Cycle

Table 14.2 gives the dominant eigenvalue expressed as a proportion of the total, of the spectral density matrix for various business cycle frequencies. The results show that a spectral reference cycle does exist for a wide band of business cycle frequencies. The dominant frequency occurs at $w = 0.52\pi/12$ which corresponds to a cycle of length 46.14 months, with the proportion of variation of the system that is explained by the first principal component being 78.7 percent. This contrasts with the nonbusiness cycle frequencies $w > 0.96\pi/12$, as the dominant eigenvalue declines quickly.

The coherence structure given in Table 14.3 shows that all six coincident indicators cohere with the first principal component ζ_1. Of the leading indicators, only corporate profits, average workweek, unemployment insurance, new orders, and contracts and orders, cohere with the spectral reference cycle.[8]

Table 14.2 Dominant eigenvalue (proportion of 18)

Frequency (w)	*Period* (*months*)	λ_1
0	—	0.8898
$0.40\pi/12$	60.00	0.7577
$0.44\pi/12$	54.54	0.7681
$0.48\pi/12$	50.00	0.7735
$0.52\pi/12$	46.15	0.7887
$0.56\pi/12$	42.86	0.7788
$0.60\pi/12$	40.00	0.7814
$0.64\pi/12$	37.50	0.7778
$0.68\pi/12$	35.29	0.7773
$0.72\pi/12$	33.33	0.7805
$0.76\pi/12$	31.58	0.7741
$0.80\pi/12$	30.00	0.7782
$0.84\pi/12$	28.57	0.7657
$0.88\pi/12$	27.27	0.7691
$0.92\pi/12$	26.09	0.7588
$0.96\pi/12$	25.00	0.7553
$1.92\pi/12$	12.50	0.3818
$2.88\pi/12$	8.33	0.3716
$3.84\pi/12$	6.25	0.2829
$4.80\pi/12$	5.00	0.2686
$5.76\pi/12$	4.17	0.2343
$6.72\pi/12$	3.57	0.2734

The spectral reference cycle, RCYCLE2, is constructed by using equation (8), where the order of the moving average is chosen as 25 months. The one-sided reference cycle, RCYCLE1, is constructed by using for each constituent series a 12th-order univariate autoregression to generate forecasts for the next 12 periods. A 25th-order moving average is then used to combine the observed (lagged) and unobserved (forecast) sample values. A comparison of the two series in figure 14.1 shows that both series are nearly coincident, with RCYCLE2 tending to lead RCYCLE1.[9]

For comparison, both the two-sided spectral reference cycle and the CIBCR composite coincident index and composite leading index are displayed in figure 14.2 Both CIBCR composite indexes are transformed by a logarithmic filter, detrended by using the residuals from an AR(1) regression equation as the "stationarized" series, and are standardized to have unit variance. A more detailed comparison of the growth cycle turning points of the principal composites is given in table 14.4, together with the CIBCR's growth cycle chronology.[10] The results show that the timing of the reference cycle RCYCLE2 and the coincident index turning points are very close, with the reference cycle turning points tending to lead the coincident index turning points. This last result reflects the influence of the leading indicators on the reference cycle and shows that the lead–lag patterns between the leading and coincident indicators, used in the construction of the composite indexes for the USA, are by and large preserved when all the indicators are combined into a spectral reference index.

Table 14.3 (Squared) coherence structure between the constituent series and principal components

Series	ζ_1	ζ_2	ζ_3
Business formation	0.6357	0.1130	0.0283
Consumer credit	0.3215	0.0941	0.0550
Stock price	0.4722	0.0099	0.2989
Corporate profits	0.8625	0.0328	0.0009
Business inventories	0.6176	0.0573	0.1691
Business permits	0.6704	0.0799	0.0056
Materials prices	0.5287	0.3618	0.0186
Average workwork	0.9147	0.0045	0.0012
Unemployment insurance	0.9291	0.0107	0.0104
New orders	0.8826	0.0248	0.0304
Contracts and orders	0.8020	0.0422	0.0395
Unit labor cost	0.5820	0.2825	0.0642
Personal income	0.7541	0.0723	0.0234
Gross national product	0.8899	0.0424	0.0078
Industrial production	0.9553	0.0033	0.0083
Unemployment rate	0.9181	0.0090	0.0094
Sales	0.8611	0.0238	0.0174
Employees	0.9459	0.0028	0.0279

Note: Squared coherences evaluated at frequency $w = 0.60\pi/12$, the 40 month cycle. The dominant principal component is given by ζ_1, while ζ_2 and ζ_3 represent the second and third largest principal components respectively.

Examination of the CIBCR Classification of Indicators

The mean lags in table 14.5, between the spectral reference cycle and the constituent series, provide strong support for the CIBCR classification of series into leading and coincident indicators. All six coincident indicators lag the reference cycle on average by between five and 16 months, while seven of the 12 leading indicators lead the reference cycle by between three and 26 months. Of the five leading indicators which

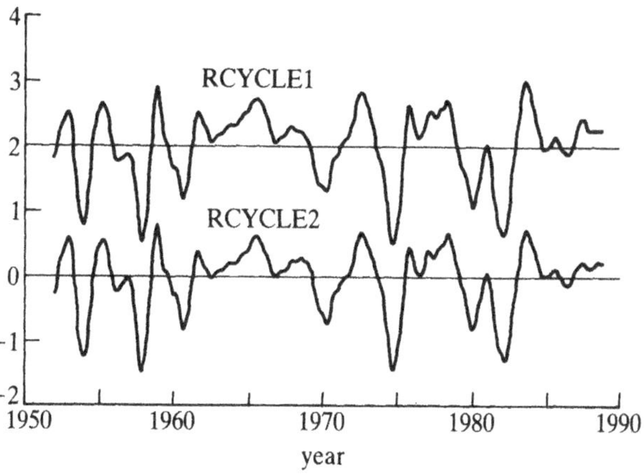

Figure 14.1 The two-sided and one-sided spectral reference cycles RCYCLE2 and RECYCLE 1

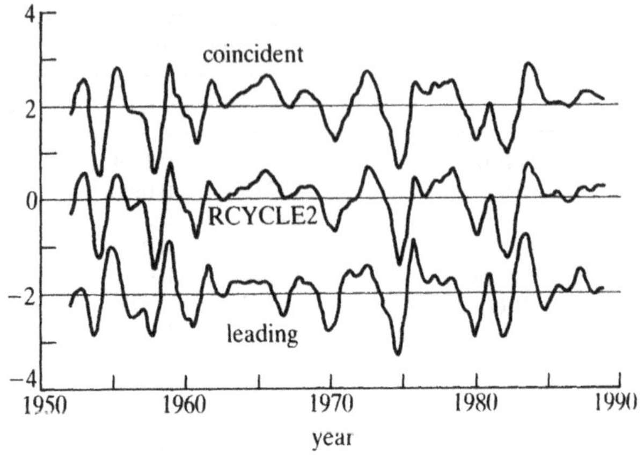

Figure 14.2 The two-sided spectral reference cycle and CIBCR composite indexes

lag the reference cycle, only two indicators: consumer credit (11.71 months) and average workweek (7.16 months), have lag times comparable with the coincident indicators. However, in the case of consumer credit, the results of table 14.3 show that this indicator is not strongly associated with the reference cycle, and suggest that this indicator be excluded from the CIBCR complement of indicators. This contrasts with the series average workweek, which from table 14.3 has high coherence with the reference cycle. Given the coherence and mean lag properties of this series, it would seem that the average workweek is more of a coincident indicator than a leading indicator.

The lead–lag relationship between the constituent series and the reference cycle is also highlighted by graphing the progressive R^2 statistics from a stepwise regression using equation (15b).[11] A selection of the plots are given in figure 14.3.[12] The results show that the two coincident indicators, gross national product and industrial production, lag the reference cycle, as there is a sharp climb in the graphs at zero followed by a flat region for negative lags. Similar results occur for the leading indicators, business inventories and unemployment insurance. For the leading

Table 14.4 Growth cycle turning points: 1952(1) to 1988(11)

CIBCR		*RCYCLE2*		*Coincident*		*Leading*	
Peak	*Trough*	*Peak*	*Trough*	*Peak*	*Trough*	*Peak*	*Trough*
—	52/7	—	—	—	—	—	—
53/3	54/8	—	53/11	—	53/12	52/9	53/9
57/2	58/4	55/1	58/2	54/11	58/2	55/1	58/2
60/2	61/2	58/11	60/11	58/11	60/11	58/11	—
62/5	64/10	61/11	62/5	61/11	62/6	—	62/5
66/6	67/10	64/1	67/3	65/9	67/2	62/11	66/5
69/3	70/11	68/6	70/1	67/11	70/10	67/8	69/11
73/3	75/3	72/9	75/1	72/11	74/12	70/12	75/1
78/12	82/12	78/4	81/12	78/4	82/1	75/1	81/10

Note: CIBCR classification from *International Economic Indicactors*, 1988.

Table 14.5 Mean lags between the constituent series and RCYCLE2 (months)[(a)]

Series	*Mean lag*[(b)]
Business formation	+3.3207
Consumer credit	−11.7131
Stock price	+17.7890
Corporate profits	+5.0458
Business inventories	−3.8582
Building permits	+16.5548
Materials prices	+21.1394
Average workweek	−7.1646
Unemployment insurance	−4.5988
New orders	+3.3236
Contracts and orders	−3.6919
Unit labor cost	+25.0416
Personal income	−8.6009
Gross national product	−5.0880
Industrial production	−6.2377
Unemployment rate	−14.6893
Sales	−5.8939
Employees	−15.1310

(a) A + (−) shows that the constituent leads (lags) RCYCLE2.

(b) Based on a finite difference approximation of equation (16c) with a step length of $2\pi/150$.

indicators, business formation and stock price, the graphs continually rise, suggesting that these indicators lead the reference cycle.

Conclusion and Suggestions for Future Research

This paper has provided a framework for a dual reference cycle methodology based upon a principal component decomposition of the spectral density matrix. By working with the spectral density matrix, systematic information in terms of coherency aspects for various cycles is extracted by means of the first principal component to construct a spectral index. This index is inverted to generate a temporal reference index which can then be used to identify the peaks and troughs in the business cycle. An alternative one-sided reference cycle, which incorporates only current and past indicator values, can be devised as a predictive approximation to identify the current state of the economy. Ancillary to and emerging from the two-sided index, is a range of measuring and testing procedures to determine whether individual series lead, lag or are coincident with the general cycle.

The methodology developed in the paper was applied to the CIBCR postwar business cycle data for the USA. The main result of the paper is that a reference cycle does exist for the USA. Important cycles were identified over a wide band of business cycle frequencies, and for each cycle the coherence between the reference cycle and the constituent series, with the exception of only two leading indicators – consumer credit and business inventories, was high. A number of tests in both the time and the frequency domain were then employed to examine the CIBCR classification of series

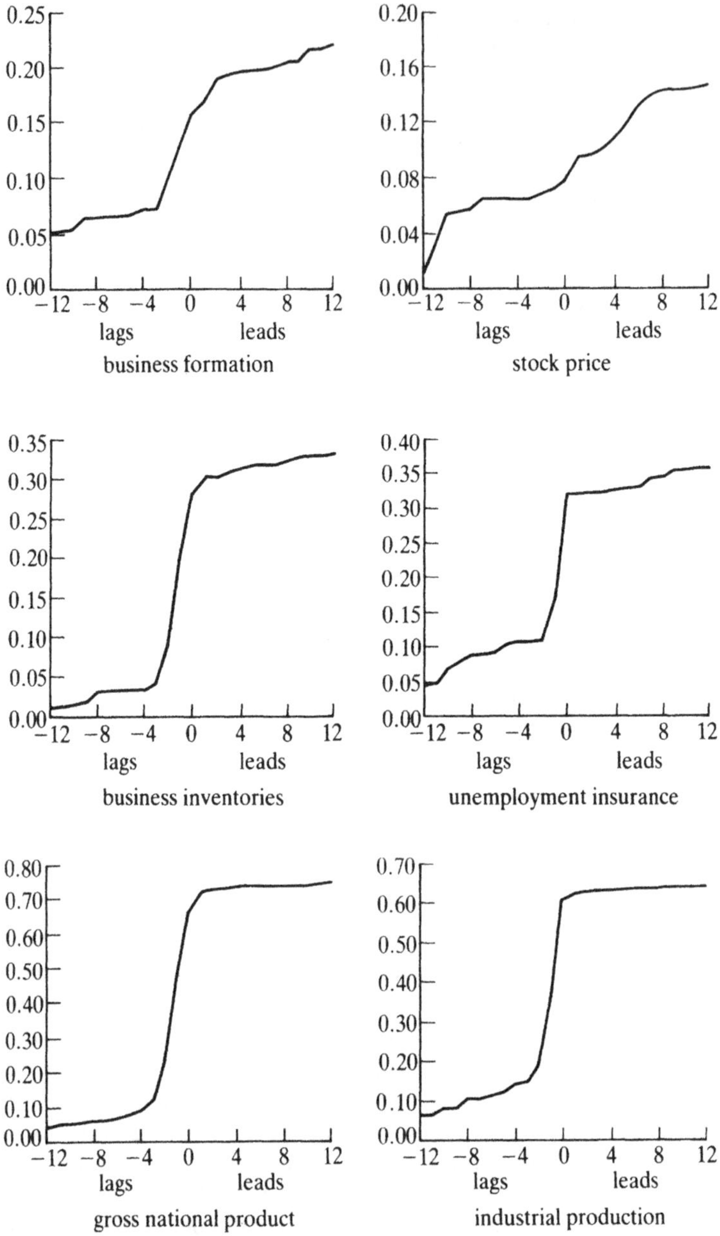

Figure 14.3 Lead–lag relationship between constituent series and RCYCLE2 with R^2 from stepwise regressions

into leading and coincident indicators. Overall, the results of the tests supported the CIBCR classification with the exception of average workweek, which was found to be more of a coincident indicator than a leading indicator.

The potential applications of the methodology are by means limited to the kind of empirical questions described in the previous section. A more or less immediate extension is to apply the methodology of the paper to an international comparison of business cycles in terms of their national coherence and lead–lag patterns to determine if business cycles are indeed all alike. Some preliminary work we have done suggests that not all countries, even among apparently rather similar members of the OECD, share the strong coherence aspect of the USA business cycle. Indeed, it could legitimately be argued that at least one stylized fact that forms the maintained hypothesis of much causal model building, namely that a business cycle does exist as a widely observed fact of western economic experience, may be more stylized than fact. The precision with which judgements can now be made on such issues may enable us to throw some light on the success or otherwise of causal model building. Turning to a somewhat different line of enquiry, an international comparison of turning points between countries can be used to identify if one country acts as the "engine of growth" by having turning points which lead the turning points of other countries. One thinks in particular of the changing views as to which, if any, of the USA, Japanese or EEC economies have assumed dominance, or at least have acquired additional weight, as a motive force for international economic activity.

Notes

An earlier draft of this paper was presented at the 1988 Australasian Meeting of the Econometric Society in Canberra, and also at seminars of the University of Monash, NSW and British Columbia. The authors would like to thank participants and readers, especially P. C. B. Phillips, E. J. Hannan, and an anonymous referee, for their comments.

1. Defining business cycles in terms of the coherence between economic time series also forms the basis of models of real business cycles (Prescott 1986, p. 13).
2. In the case where the set of time series is nonstationary but forms a cointegrated system, stationarity is achieved as the cointegrating vector reduces the spectral power at the origin to zero (Engle and Granger 1987, Phillips 1986, Phillips and Ouliaris 1988).
3. Since the constituent series are assumed to be covariance stationary, the business cycle studied in this paper may also be referred to as a growth cycle (Boehm and Moore 1984). This approach of decomposing series into a nonstationary trend and a stationary cycle component underlines the statistical procedures established by the NBER.
4. A referee has noted the potential applicability of the group delay concept (see for example Zadeh and Desoer (1963, 9.11)) as a way of representing or measuring lags. In the engineering literature, the differential $\theta'(w)$ of the phase of a transfer function can be taken as a measure of the time taken by an input sinusoid e^{iwt} to impact maximally on the output of a system with the given transfer function. One could adapt this idea so that $\theta'_{ij}(w_B)$ would measure the lead or lag (in temporal terms) that the business cycle components of y_{jt} would have with respect to ζ_{1t}, or vice-versa. Perhaps one could relate this also to the predictive interpretation mentioned in the first section (which itself needs to be developed further). So far as leads and lags are concerned, we have elected to stay with the arithmetical mean lag, more familiar to economists.
5. The X-11 seasonal adjustment procedure is used by the CIBCR in the construction of composite indexes, and has been chosen here to make our results more compatible with the CIBCR results. However, as observed by both Sims (1974) and Wallis (1974), the X-11 seasonal adjustment procedure can introduce distortions into the lag distribution.
6. Stationarity tests based on both the autocorrelation function, the Dickey–Fuller unit root test (Fuller 1976), and the Schmidt–Phillips unit root test (Schmidt and Phillips 1989), all supported the hypothesis that the filtered series are stationary.
7. The fast Fourier transform and all subsequent calculations, with the exception of the eigenvalues and eigenvectors of the spectral density matrix, are carried out using the regression package RATS (Doan and Litterman 1981).

8. Similar eigenvalue spectrum and coherence structure are obtained when an AR(2) is used to render the data stationary.
9. A number of tests were carried out to analyze the lead–lag behavior of RCYCLE2 and RCYCLE1, such as the identification of turning points and Granger causality tests, which showed that RCYCLE2 tended to lead RCYCLE1.
10. The identification of turning points is based on the rules established by the NBER.
11. An information test of the lead–lag patterns between the constituent series and the two-sided reference cycle was also performed by utilizing the Granger test of causality. The results of this procedure tended to support the CIBCR classification.
12. For each constituent series, the series is initially regressed on a constant and the two-sided reference cycle lagged 12 months. Lower order lags are continually included in the regression with the final regression containing the two-sided reference cycle 12 months ahead.

References

Auerbach, A. J. (1982). "The index of leading indicators: 'Measurement without theory' thirty-five years later," *Review of Economics and Statistics*, 64, 589–95.

Bergstrom, A. R. (1962). "A model of technical progress, the production function and cyclical growth," *Economica*, 29, 357–70.

Boehm, E. A., and G. H. Moore (1984). "New economic indicators for Australia, 1949–84," *Australian Economic Review*, 4th Quarter, 34–56.

Bowden, R. J. (1970). *Towards a Stochastic Dynamics*, unpublished Ph.D. thesis, University of Manchester.

Bowden, R. J. (1972). "More stochastic properties of the Klein–Goldberger model," *Econometrica*, 40, 87–98.

Brillinger, D. R. (1975). *Time Series: Data Analysis and Theory*. New York: Holt, Rinehart and Winston Inc.

Doan, T. A., and R. B. Litterman (1981). *RATS User's Manual*, VAR Econometrics, Minneapolis, MN 55419.

Engle, R. F., and C. W. J. Granger (1987). "Co-integration and error correction: representation, estimation and testing," *Econometrica*, 55, 251–76.

Fuller, W. A. (1976). *Introduction to Statistical Time Series*. New York: John Wiley and Sons.

Granger, C. W. J. (1969). "Investigating causal relations by econometric models and cross-spectral methods," *Econometrica*, 37, 424–38.

Hymans, S. H. (1973). "On the use of leading indicators to predict cyclical turning points," *Brookings Papers on Economic Activity*, 2, 339–75.

International Economic Indicators, various issues.

Koopmans, T. C. (1947). "Measurement without theory," *Review of Economics and Statistics*, 29, 161–72.

Lucas, R. E. (1977). "Understanding business cycles," in K. Brunner and A. H. Meltzer (eds) *Stabilization of the Domestic and International Economy*, volume 5 of Carnegie-Rochester Series on Public Policy, pp. 7–29. Amsterdam: North-Holland.

Martin, V. L. (1987). "Leads and lags in the Australian business cycle: a canonical approach in the frequency domain," *Australian Economic Papers*, Dec. 188–96.

Moore, G. H. (1983). *Business Cycles, Inflation and Forecasting*, second revised edition. Cambridge, Massachusetts: Ballinger .

Phillips, P. C. B. (1986). "Understanding spurious regressions in econometrics, *Journal of Econometrics*, 33, 311–40.

Phillips, P. C. B. and S. Ouliaris (1988). "Testing for cointegration using principal components methods," *Journal of Economic Dynamics and Control*, 12, 205–30.

Pierce, D. A., and L. D. Haugh (1977). "Causality in temporal systems," *Journal of Econometrics*, 5, 265–93.

Prescott, E. C. (1986). "Theory ahead of business-cycle measurement," in K. Brunner and

A. H. Meltzer (eds) *Real Business Cycles, Real Exchange Rates and Actual Policies*, Carnegie-Rochester Conference Series on Public Policy, volume 25.

Sargent, T. J. (1979). *Macroeconomic Theory*. New York: Academic Press.

Sargent, T. J., and C. A. Sims (1977). "Business cycle modelling without pretending to have too much a priori economic theory," in C. A. Sims (ed) *New Methods in Business Cycle Research: Proceedings from a Conference*, Federal Research Bank of Minneapolis, Minnesota.

Schmidt, P., and P. C. B. Phillips (1989). "Testing for a unit root in the presence of deterministic trends," Cowles Foundation Discussion Paper 933.

Sims, C. A. (1972). "Money, Income and Causality," *American Economic Review*, 62, 540–52.

Sims, C. A. (1974). "Seasonality in regression," *Journal of the American Statistical Association*, 69, 618–26.

Wallis, K. F. (1974). "Seasonal adjustment and relations between variables," *Journal of the American Statistical Association*, 69, 18–31.

Whittle, P. (1963). *Prediction and Regulation by Linear Least-Square Methods*. New Jersey: Van Nostrand Reinhold.

Zadeh, L. A., and C. A. Desoer (1963). *Linear System Theory: The State-Space Approach*. New York: McGraw-Hill.

15

Estimating Linear Quadratic Models with Integrated Processes

Allan W. Gregory, Adrian R. Pagan, and Gregor W. Smith

> But unlike the economic theoretician, who usually works with general classes of functions, [the builder of econometric models] must work with particular functional forms (e.g., linear quadratic, exponential.) (Bergstrom 1967, p. 3)

Introduction

When Rex Bergstrom wrote his 1967 monograph, *ad hoc* specification dominated in econometric research. Nowhere was this truer than in dynamics. The intervening 20 years have seen some progress in rectifying this situation: intertemporal optimizing theory has been utilized to suggest suitable dynamic specifications and a literature has emerged describing classes of models that seem appropriate for many economic data series. The former development tends to be described as the "Euler equation approach," while the latter deals with the class of error correction models (ECM). At a very general level it is hard to reconcile the two traditions, but if one follows Bergstrom's pragmatism in adopting specific functional forms for agents' utility and production functions, it is possible to achieve a synthesis. Nickell (1985) did just this, showing that Euler equations derived from quadratic objective functions could be recast as error correction models, so that the approaches are isomorphic. Each has its advantages. The Euler equation approach enables interpretation of the estimated parameters as those associated with objective functions, whilst the ECM methodology allows the "data to speak for itself," and is therefore compatible with a number of possible objective functions.

What was most striking about the trends cited above was the implication that the nature of the forcing variables faced by agents determined the appropriate *specification* for estimating equations. Concurrently with the emergence of this principle, work by Engle and Granger (1987), Phillips (1987), Sims et al (1990) *inter alia*, showed that *estimation theory and procedures* must be adapted for the type of data econometricians use. Consequently, it is an obvious step to integrate the themes. It is this quest which motivates the current paper. Surprisingly, there is little research on the interface, the most prominent exception being Dolado et al. (1991), although one can find reference to some of the issues scattered through applied papers such as Ilmakunnas (1989), and the book by Pesaran (1987).

The paper[1] is organized as follows. We set out the models studied and describe different representations of them that are found in the literature. Then we look at some general issues of estimability and identifiability of parameters in these models. It is shown that the ability to identify parameters is dependent upon the nature of the forcing variables, and that it is quite likely that one of the parameters, the discount factor, cannot be estimated with much accuracy. Hence, the common practice of presetting this parameter has theoretical support. Broadly, the third section is concerned with the ability to find consistent estimators of the unknown parameters, and ignores questions of inference. The fourth section rectifies this by applying ideas in the literature concerned with the estimation of cointegrating vectors, for example Phillips and Hansen (1990), Johansen (1988) and Park (1988), that describe estimators which enable hypothesis tests to be conducted in a standard way on the cointegrating vector. One interesting difference between our situation and that in the literature on estimation with integrated variables is the way in which we arrive at an ECM representation. In Engle and Granger and in Phillips and Hansen, the ECM is derived as a *consequence* of cointegration between variables, and it is the cointegrating vector which is of prime importance. All other parameters are regarded as nuisance parameters and are effectively ignored by the use of robust estimation techniques. But, when an ECM is a consequence of a theoretical specification, as in the models studied in this paper, the "nuisance" parameters become of interest, and some modifications to standard methods of estimation need to be made to allow for this fact. Finally, we evaluate the proposed estimators by a small simulation study.

The Model and Its Representations

As mentioned earlier, intertemporal optimizing models vary according to the choice of function to be optimized, but a popular variant has been the linear–quadratic adjustment cost model in which a decision maker solves the following problem in an attempt to track a target value y_s^* over time

$$\min_{\{\mathbf{y}_s\}} E_t \sum_{s=t}^{\infty} \beta^{s-t}[\delta(\mathbf{y}_s - \mathbf{y}_s^*)^2 + (\mathbf{y}_s - \mathbf{y}_{s-1})^2], \tag{1}$$

where the expectation is taken with respect to information available to an agent at time t ($\mathscr{F}_t$).[1] The target variable is $y_t^* = \mathbf{x}_t'\theta + e_t$, where e_t is a white-noise error known to the decision maker, while $\mathbf{x}_t$ is a $q \times 1$ vector of forcing variables.[3] It is presumed that the error e_t appears in $\mathscr{F}_t = \{e_t, y_{t-j}, \mathbf{x}_{t-j+1}\}_{j=1}^{\infty}$, but is not known to an investigating econometrician, whose information set is therefore a subset of $\mathscr{F}_t, \mathscr{G}_t$. The popularity of this model is evident in the literature concerning choice of factor of production levels, for example Kennan (1979), Nickell (1987), Layard and Nickell (1986), and Wren-Lewis (1986), for which y_t would be the level of employment (or hours worked) and $\mathbf{x}_t$ variables such as output and the real wage.

The first-order condition for the optimization problem is the Euler equation

$$\Delta y_t = \beta E_t \Delta y_{t+1} + c(y_t - y_t^*), \tag{2}$$

where $c = -\delta$ and E_t is the expectation taken with respect to $\mathscr{F}_t$. As is well known, both roots of the characteristic equation of this second-order difference equation are positive and they lie on either side of unity. Denote the stable root of the quadratic $\beta z^2 - (1 + \beta + \delta)z + 1 = 0$ by λ, leading to the forward solution to (2) of

$$y_t = \lambda y_{t-1} + (1 - \lambda)(1 - \beta\lambda)E_t \sum_{s=t}^{\infty} (\beta\lambda)^{s-t} y_s^*. \tag{3}$$

Equations (2) and (3) form the basis of estimation techniques advanced for the linear/quadratic model. As with all rational expectations models (Wickens 1982), there are two general approaches to estimation. In the first, $E_t\,\Delta y_{t+1}$ is replaced by $\Delta y_{t+1} + \eta_{t+1}$, where $E_t(\eta_{t+1}) = 0$, and equation (2) could be written as

$$\Delta y_t = \beta\,\Delta y_{t+1} + c(y_t - \mathbf{x}_t'\theta) + v_t, \tag{4}$$

where $v_t = \beta\eta_{t+1} - ce_t$ has the property that $E(v_t\,|\,\mathcal{G}_t) = 0$. As suggested by McCallum (1976), instrumental variable (IV) estimators of the coefficients of equation (4) might be performed with instruments drawn from $\mathcal{G}_t$.

Alternatively, if an assumption is made about how $\mathbf{x}_t$ is generated, the unknown expectation in (3) may be found and an estimating equation derived. There are two cases of particular interest to us about how $\mathbf{x}_t$ evolves, and the corresponding solved versions of (3) would be[4]

Case 1 $\quad (1 - \rho_1 L)x_t = \varepsilon_t,\ E_{t-1}(\varepsilon_t) = 0$

$$\Delta y_t = (\lambda - 1)(y_{t-1} - x_{t-1}\theta) + (1 - \lambda)\theta[(1 - \rho_1\beta\lambda)^{-1}(1 - \beta\lambda)x_t - x_{t-1}] + (1 - \beta\lambda)(1 - \lambda)e_t. \tag{5}$$

Case 2 $\quad (1 - \rho_2 L)(1 - L)x_t = \varepsilon_t,\ E_{t-1}(\varepsilon_t) = 0$

$$\Delta y_t = (\lambda - 1)(y_{t-1} - x_{t-1}\theta) + (1 - \beta\lambda\rho_2)^{-1}(1 - \lambda)\,\Delta x_t'\theta + (1 - \beta\lambda)(1 - \lambda)e_t. \tag{6}$$

If x_t is integrated of order one (I(1)) we would get (5) with $\rho_1 = 1$, while if it is of order two (I(2)), we would get (6) with $\rho_2 = 1$. Because it is central to later work it is useful to rewrite the special case of (5) when $\rho_1 = 1$ as (5′).

$$\Delta y_t = (\lambda - 1)(y_{t-1} - x_{t-1}\theta) + (1 - \lambda)\,\Delta x_t\theta + (1 - \beta\lambda)(1 - \lambda)e_t, \tag{5′}$$

or in the equivalent form of the partial adjustment model

$$y_t = \lambda y_{t-1} + (1 - \lambda)x_t\theta + (1 - \beta\lambda)(1 - \lambda)e_t. \tag{7}$$

In turn (7) is usefully reparameterized in the format of Bewley (1979)

$$y_t = -[\lambda/(1 - \lambda)]\,\Delta y_t + x_t\theta + (1 - \beta\lambda)e_t. \tag{8}$$

Equation (8) is important since it demonstrates that θ is the cointegrating vector between y_t and x_t as all other variables in (8) are I(0). Depending on the context, any one of (5′), (7) or (8) will be adopted when working with case 1.

Some General Issues of Estimation and Identification

Estimation procedures for these models vary according to whether they are "single equation" or "systems of equations" oriented. In the former instance, attention is focused upon either the Euler equation (4) or the "solved" forms in (5) and (6). In the latter, if $|\rho_1| < 1$ it is apparent that ρ_1 enters both the equation for y_t and that for x_t, and this points to the likelihood that joint estimation of the two equations would be profitable. Of the "single equation" proponents, two proposals stand out: those by Kennan (1979) and Dolado et al. (1991).

Kennan (1979) was essentially concerned with case 1 ($|\rho_1| < 1$), but where x_t followed a pth order autoregression and was strictly exogenous. With a higher order autoregression of order p, (5) would contain terms $x_t, \ldots, x_{t-p+1}$. He proposed regressing y_t against $y_{t-1}, x_t, \ldots, x_{t-p+1}$ to obtain an estimator of λ, solving for $\hat{\delta}$ from the polynomial connecting (λ, β, δ) after prespecifying β, and then regressing $\delta^{-1}(\Delta y_t - \beta\, \Delta y_{t+1}) + y_t$ against x_t (see (4)) to find $\hat{\theta}$. Of course if one knows that $p = 1$, both θ and λ could have been estimated directly from (5), replacing ρ_1 by $\hat{\rho}_1$, the OLS estimator of ρ_1 from $x_t = \rho_1 x_{t-1} + \varepsilon_t$.

Kennan observes that some corrections need to be made to standard errors owing to the use of "generated regressors," see Newey (1984) and Pagan (1984), in finding $\hat{\theta}$. A further difficulty arises when $\rho_1 = 1$, caused by the fact that the regressors y_{t-1} and x_t are cointegrated. This feature means that the regressor cross-product matrix in his first-stage regression to find λ, namely that associated with (7), is asymptotically singular, and that fact precludes the estimators of both parameters from attaining the T-convergence rate normally associated with integrated regressors. Park and Phillips (1988) deal with this complication by a "co-ordinate rotation." In general, if z_{1t} and z_{2t} are cointegrated with cointegrating vector α, so that $z_{1t}\alpha + \zeta_t$, the relation $z_{1t}\gamma_1 + z_{2t}\gamma_2$ can be re-expressed as $(\gamma_1\alpha + \gamma_2)z_{2t} + \zeta_t\gamma_1$, where the two "new" regressors, z_{2t} and ζ_t, are respectively I(1) and I(0). Then γ_1 would be estimated $T^{1/2}$ consistently whereas $(\gamma_1\alpha + \gamma_2)$ is estimated T-consistently. Equating $z_{1t} = y_{t-1}$ and $z_{2t} = x_t$, inspection of (7) and (8) shows that $\gamma_1 = \lambda$, $\alpha = \theta$ and $\gamma_2 = (1 - \lambda)\theta$. "Co-ordinate rotation" therefore gives the correct asymptotics directly and means the estimation of (8) rather than (7). Consequently, if one wanted to proceed with Kennan's approach, it would seem best to work with the latter equation to determine θ and λ.

Retaining the restriction that $\rho_1 = 1$, Dolado et al. (1991) note that the ordering in Kennan's procedure might be reversed. Under these circumstances y_t is I(1), the long-run response of y_t to x_t in (5) is θ, and the regression of y_t against x_t consistently estimates this long-run response. Having found θ, they then suggest that one might consistently estimate δ and β by applying instrumental variables (IV) to (4) with instruments selected from $\mathcal{G}_t$.

The sequential estimation strategy espoused by Dolado et al., which is rooted in the two-step approach in Engle and Granger (1987), and which seeks to exploit different convergence rates for estimators of parameters of variables exhibiting different degrees of integration, is an interesting one. However, it is clearly important to know what its limits would be. One concern that is immediate with all of these models is whether the parameters can be identified. Identification issues in the linear quadratic model are rarely treated explicitly, although a parameter that seems to have been difficult to estimate has been the discount factor β. Some authors set it to a prespecified number, for example Kennan (1979). Others do this but suggest it is estimable, for example, Blanchard and Melino (1986, p. 389) who comment, "We could in principle estimate β. Recent papers indicate that obtaining accurate estimates of β in models such as ours is difficult. Our choice of $\beta = 0.99$ is arbitrary. Varying β between 0.95 and 1.00 has however very little effect on the estimated parameters." Only a few actually estimate it, recent examples being Ilmakunnas (1989) and Dolado et al (1991). Such a diverse set of responses does raise the possibility that there may be a problem of identifiability with this parameter, and we therefore proceed to examine this question, firstly in the context of (5), and subsequently treating estimation in the more general environment of (6).

That there is a serious identification problem for some of the parameters of (5) should be immediately apparent from (5), when $\rho_1 = 1$ and θ is a scalar, as there are three unknown parameters β, δ, and θ, but only two regressors (see (7)). This seems to explain why those authors who preset β do so, as they invariably work with the solved equation (5). Those who seem to believe that β is estimable, e.g. Dolado et al. proceed instead from (4), with the additional assumption that θ can be consistently estimated from some other source. Indeed, θ *can* be consistently estimated from the regression of y_t against x_t, provided x_t is I(1) (Stock (1987)). However, since equation (4) uses less information than (5), it is hard to see how it is therefore possible to estimate more parameters. Some reconciliation of these views is needed, and we turn to that task now.

Dolado et al. (1991) have as a maintained assumption that x_t is strictly exogenous in both cases 1 and 2, i.e. the correlation between ε_t and e_t is zero. *Assuming that θ is known* they would recommend estimation of δ and β in case 1 by performing IV on (4) with instruments $z_{t-1} = y_{t-1} - x_{t-1}\theta$ and Δy_{t-1} for z_t and Δy_{t+1} respectively.[5] For this scenario we now show that only one of the two parameters β and δ in (4) is in fact identifiable.

As all the variables in (4) are I(0), a requirement for asymptotic identification of the parameters of (4) is that the "relevance" condition be satisfied, namely that the covariance matrix between instruments and regressors is nonsingular.[6] When $\rho_1 = 1$, $z_t = y_t - x_t\theta = (1 - \lambda L)^{-1}[(1 - \lambda)(1 - \beta\lambda)e_t - \theta\lambda\varepsilon_t]$, and, under standard assumptions, the covariance matrix converges to

$$\begin{bmatrix} E(\Delta y_{t-1}\,\Delta y_{t+1}) & E(\Delta y_{t-1} z_t) \\ E(z_{t-1}\,\Delta y_{t+1}) & E(z_{t-1} z_t) \end{bmatrix} = \begin{bmatrix} (\lambda-1)^2\gamma_2 - \theta(1-\lambda)^2 a + (\lambda-1)d & (\lambda-1)\gamma_2 + \theta(1-\lambda)a + d \\ (\lambda-1)\gamma_1 & \gamma_1 \end{bmatrix}, \quad (9)$$

where $a = E(\Delta x_{t-1} z_t)$, $\gamma_k = E(z_t z_{t-k})$ and $d = (1 - \beta L)^2(1 - \lambda)^2\lambda\sigma_e^2$. Clearly this matrix is singular. Of course one can still estimate unidentified models, although estimators cannot be consistent and, as Phillips (1989) shows, the distribution of *both* of the IV estimators of β and δ will be rendered nonstandard.[7].

It is interesting to speculate about the identifiability of β when $|\rho_1| < 1$. *If* $\boldsymbol{\theta}$ *is known* there are two regressors and two parameters in (5), suggesting that β might be identified. Pesaran (1987, pp. 134–47) deals with identification issues in Euler equations such as (2), although some modification is needed to fit the variant that he conducts an identification investigation on. Specifically, he excludes e_t from the conditional expectation in (2). Consequently, replacing $y_t - y_t^*$ by $y_t - x_t'\theta - e_t = z_t - e_t$, his version of (2) would be $\Delta y_t = \beta E_t(\Delta y_{t+1}) + cz_t - ce_t$. After allowing z_t to be a stationary AR(r) process, he gives a necessary condition for identification as $r \geqslant 2$, suggesting that when z_t is only a first-order autoregressive process, there will be identification difficulties. In fact, when $\rho_1 = 1$, $z_t = (1 - \lambda L)^{-1}[(1 - \lambda)(1 - \beta\lambda)e_t - \theta\lambda\varepsilon_t]$, and therefore it is an AR(1); the lack of identifiability predicted by an application of Pesaran's condition therefore agrees with our finding. Such an outcome should be contrasted with what happens when $\rho_1 \neq 1$. Then, $(1 - \lambda L)(1 - \rho_1 L)z_t = \{(1 - \lambda)(1 - \beta\lambda)(1 - \rho_1 L)e_t\} + \{[(1 - \beta\lambda)(1 - \lambda)/(1 - \rho_1\lambda\beta) - 1] + \lambda L\}\varepsilon_t\theta$, making z_t an ARMA(2,1) process. Applying Pesaran's rule, the necessary condition for β and δ to be identified is therefore satisfied. The reduction from an ARMA(2,1), when $\rho_1 \neq 1$, to an AR(1), when $\rho_1 = 1$, occurs because the MA(1) in the latter case becomes $-\lambda\,\Delta\varepsilon_t\theta + (1 - \lambda)(1 - \beta\lambda)\,\Delta e_t$, and the common unit root to both the AR(2) and the MA(1) cancels. In summary, once $\rho_1 = 1$ it is no longer possible to separately identify β and δ.[8]

Modification to these conclusions is needed if x_t is allowed to evolve as in case 2. Suppose that θ and ρ_2 are known (ρ_2 can be consistently estimated by regressing Δx_t against Δx_{t-1}), and focus on the simple IV estimator discussed previously. The forcing variable becomes

$$z_t = (1 - \lambda L)^{-1}[(1 - \lambda)(1 - \beta\lambda)e_t - \theta\lambda(1 - \rho_2\beta\lambda)^{-1}(1 - \rho_2\beta)\,\Delta x_t],$$

and the fact that Δx_t is an AR(1) means that z_t will be an ARMA(2, 1), satisfying the necessary condition for identification. It seems likely that this will be sufficient as well, although it is hard to verify the conjecture. Perhaps a more relevant concern is not whether there is a complete failure of identifiability, but whether the estimation problem is sufficiently well determined to enable precise estimation of β and δ even in very large samples. One way to address this issue is to conceive of the demonstrated failure of identifiability when $\rho_2 = 0$ (case 2 coincides with case 1) as arising from perfect collinearity between the instruments, thereby leading to a singular correlation matrix. Then it may be asked how far away from singularity the correlation matrix between instruments and regressors becomes as ρ_2 increases. There seems little to be said analytically about this feature, as the covariance matrix is a complex function of β, δ, ρ_2, σ_e^2 and σ_ε^2. For this reason we have simply computed the eigenvalues of the correlation matrix for many configurations of case 2, finding that the smallest eigenvalue was always less than 0.1. For example, in the Monte Carlo "basic experiment" described later in equation (20), and with $(1 - \rho_2 L)\,\Delta x_t = \varepsilon_t$, the smallest eigenvalues are 0.01 ($\rho_2 = 0.5$), 0.05 ($\rho_2 = 0.8$) and 0.07 ($\rho_2 = 0.9$).[9] This finding points to the extreme difficulty of *jointly* estimating both β and δ. To see that the source of the collinearity is due to β, assume that β is known, form $\beta\,\Delta y_{t+1}$, and move it to the left-hand side of (4), after which δ may be estimated by IV with z_{t-1} as an instrument for z_t. Then the corresponding eigenvalues (now the correlation coefficients between the two variables) would be 0.5, 0.49, and 0.48 respectively.

A different view of the estimability of β is to be had from the ECM (6). Again fixing θ and ρ_2, estimation would proceed by linearizing (6) around some initial estimators of λ and β, performing a regression to get updated estimates of these parameters, and continuing to iterate this sequence until convergence. At the termination of iterations $\hat{\delta}$ is recoverable by solving the polynomial $\hat{\beta}\hat{\lambda}^2 - (1 + \hat{\beta} + \hat{\delta})\hat{\lambda} + 1 = 0$. The precision of estimation depends upon the covariance matrix of the derivatives of (6) with respect to λ and β, and these derivatives are

$$[-(1 - \rho_2\beta\lambda)^{-1}(\rho_2\beta - 1)\,\Delta x_t'\theta + z_{t-1}]$$

and $-(1 - \rho_2\beta\lambda)^{-2}\rho_2\lambda(1 - \lambda)\,\Delta x_t'\theta$ respectively, where

$$z_t = (1 - \lambda L)^{-1}[(1 - \lambda)(1 - \beta\lambda)e_t - \theta\lambda(1 - \rho_2\beta\lambda)^{-1}(1 - \rho_2\beta)\,\Delta x_t].$$

Correlation between these terms is high for values of ρ_2 near zero, but weakens quickly as ρ_2 increases. For the example mentioned above, which led to a near-singular matrix in the IV case, the correlation between the derivatives is -0.8 when $\rho_2 = 0.1$ but -0.28 when $\rho_2 = 0.5$.

This feature shows that the ECM has performed a successful reparameterization so as to ensure a low correlation between regressors, whereas the Euler equation variation (4) does not do this. Despite that fact, the ability to estimate β accurately depends not just upon the correlation between derivatives but also their variances; in particular we are interested in the magnitude of the variance of the derivative of (6) with respect to β. Setting $\rho_2 = 0$ (case 1) makes the variance identically zero, and so β is not identified, but it is equally apparent that the variance will tend to be small unless ρ_2 is quite large. Moreover, this variance will tend to be much smaller than that of the derivative with respect to λ unless ρ_2 is large, illustrating the point that it is β which is generally hard to estimate. In the basic experiment being referred to the ratio of the variance of the β-derivative to that for the λ-derivative is 40 when $\rho_2 = 0.5$ and 13 when $\rho_2 = 0.8$.

As ρ_2 approaches unity, both derivatives become I(1) processes, creating the potential for sharp estimation. Some care has to be taken with the argument, however. If $\beta = 1$, it can be seen from the formula for z_t that this variable would be I(0), and so both derivatives are dominated by terms in $\Delta x_t\theta$, i.e. they would be cointegrated, meaning that only one of the parameters could be estimated T-consistently. Interestingly enough, if one reverts to estimating from the Euler equation, it will be β that can be estimated T-consistently, as it attaches to an I(1) variable Δy_{t+1}, whereas δ is associated with the I(0) variable z_t.[10] It is hard to know what to make of this case. Theoretically β could not be unity, since then the transversality condition in the optimization fails to be satisfied, although the fact that it is generally in the range 0.96–0.99 indicates that the limiting case might be of interest as an approximation. Moreover, it also seems unlikely that most x_t variables would be I(2), at least after a log transformation. Nevertheless one should keep this extreme configuration in mind as a counter example about the ablity to estimate β, even if one's presumption is that the difficulties in estimating β documented above point in the direction of presetting it. It is hard to escape the feeling that this is exactly what happens in applied studies, with the discount rate being fixed after poor estimates are obtained in initial (or previous) investigation. Our analysis might therefore be seen as providing a pragmatic justification for fixing β in applied work with the linear–quadratic model.

Systems estimation has been outlined in Hansen and Sargent (1980) (when $|\rho_1| < 1$), and has been extensively used in the literature, see for example Sargent

(1978). If $\rho_1 = 1$, θ would be the cointegrating vector, and in principle any estimators of such a vector could be utilized, for example Johansen (1988), Phillips (1991a), and Park (1988), although there are other parameters to be estimated here, namely δ, and that may demand a modified response. For the objectives of this section however, it is sufficient to note that, as all the discussion given previously concerning identification of δ and β proceeded under the assumption that ρ_2 was known, it must apply equally to systems estimators.

Estimation of the Linear/Quadratic Model

In this section we consider the estimation of the unknown parameters in (4) and (5′), i.e. it is assumed that a unit root appears in the equation describing the evolution of $\mathbf{x}_t$ and that this fact is known to an investigator. It is also assumed that the $\mathbf{x}_t$ are not cointegrated; if they are, a prior transformation needs to be made to extract the I(1) and I(0) components. As the analysis closely follows that for case 1, mention of case 2 will be made only when necessary. Because the discussion in the previous section pointed to several difficulties in estimating β, it will be treated as known throughout this section.

Single Equation Estimation from the Euler Equation

With β assumed known, (4) could be redefined as

$$\psi_t = c(y_t - \mathbf{x}_t'\theta) + v_t, \tag{10}$$

where $\psi_t = \Delta y_t - \beta\, \Delta y_{t+1}$ and $c = -\delta$. A simple estimator of the two unknown parameters θ and c is available from the logic of Engle and Granger's (1987) two-step method. First, θ is estimated by regressing y_t against $\mathbf{x}_t$ to produce $\tilde{\theta}$, and then c is estimated by doing instrumental variables of ψ_t against $y_t - \mathbf{x}_t'\tilde{\theta}$ to produce $\tilde{c}$. The regression to get $\tilde{\theta}$ is essentially from (8), where the error term is $-(1-\lambda)^{-1}\lambda\, \Delta y_t + (1-\beta\lambda)e_t$. As $\Delta y_t = (\lambda - 1)z_{t-1} + (1-\lambda)\,\Delta\mathbf{x}_t'\theta + (1-\beta\lambda)(1-\lambda)e_t$ from (5′), and z_t was shown in the previous section to be a stationary AR(1), it follows that $T(\tilde{\theta} - \theta_0)$ has a limiting distribution, provided that $\boldsymbol{\varepsilon}_t$ and e_t are restricted as in Phillips and Hansen (1990). It is then an easy matter to demonstrate that $T^{1/2}(\tilde{c} - c_0)$ will be asymptotically normally distributed, provided that this is so for the IV estimator using instruments based on the true θ.

Now, it is well known that $\tilde{\theta}$ will not be asymptotically normally distributed when $\mathbf{x}_t$ is I(1) unless $\mathbf{x}_t$ is strongly exogenous, necessitating some adjustments to it in order that inferences about θ can be made from the t-statistics associated with the regression. There are a number of suggested adjustments, for example Park's (1988) "canonical cointegrating regressions" method or the "fully modified estimator" of Phillips and Hansen (1990). As it is the latter which is adopted in this paper, a brief description of its *modus operandi* seems in order.

Consider equation (8) and the equation describing $\Delta\mathbf{x}_t$, collected below as (11a) and (11b),

$$y_t = \mathbf{x}_t'\theta + \xi_t, \tag{11a}$$

$$\Delta\mathbf{x}_t = \boldsymbol{\varepsilon}_t, \tag{11b}$$

where $\xi_t = -(1-\lambda)^{-1}\lambda\,\Delta y_t + (1-\beta\lambda)e_t$. Two corrections to $\tilde{\theta}$ are made by Phillips and Hansen. First, they correct a "bias" in $T(\tilde{\theta}-\theta)$ due to endogeneity of $\Delta\mathbf{x}_t$. This involves replacing y_t by $y_t^+ = y_t - \hat{\Omega}_{12}\hat{\Omega}_{22}^{-1}\,\Delta\mathbf{x}_t$, where $\hat{\Omega}$ is an estimator of Ω, the "long run covariance matrix of $\zeta_t' = [\xi_t, \Delta\mathbf{x}_t]$,"[11] and regressing y_t^+ against $\mathbf{x}_t$ to produce $\theta^* = (\sum \mathbf{x}_t\mathbf{x}_t')^{-1}\sum \mathbf{x}_t y_t^+$. A further correction is then made for "autocorrelation bias" by modifying θ^* to $\hat{\theta}_{\mathrm{PH}} = \theta^* - (\sum \mathbf{x}_t\mathbf{x}_t')^{-1}Tg$, where

$$g = \hat{\Delta}\begin{bmatrix} 1 \\ -\hat{\Omega}_{22}^{-1}\quad \hat{\Omega}_{21} \end{bmatrix} \tag{11c}$$

and $\hat{\Delta}$ is a consistent estimator of $\Delta = \sum_{k=0}^{\infty} E(\Delta\mathbf{x}_0, \zeta_k')$.[13] After these modifications, t-statistics formed with $\hat{\theta}_{\mathrm{PH}}$ are asymptotically normally distributed.

Some comments on this estimator are in order, particularly since it forms the backbone of many of the other estimators that we study. First, it applies immediately to case 2, since (8) would just be augmented by an extra I(0) term $[(1-\lambda\beta\rho_2)^{-1} \times (1-\lambda) - 1]\,\Delta\mathbf{x}_t'\theta$, and by its very nature the estimator adapts to serial correlation in $\Delta\mathbf{x}_t$. Second, the procedure works *only* if it is known that there is a unit root in the $\mathbf{x}_t$ equation and that root is *prescribed* rather than estimated – see Phillips and Hansen (1990, p. 103).

Now, if $\mathbf{x}_t$ had been an I(0) process, it would have been desirable to exploit the nonlinearity in parameters that characterizes (10). To do so involves the linearization of (10) around some initial consistent estimators, say $\tilde{\theta}$ and $\tilde{c}$, to give

$$w_t = \tilde{z}_t c + (\tilde{\delta}\mathbf{x}_t')\theta + v_t, \tag{12}$$

where $\tilde{z}_t = y_t - \mathbf{x}_t'\tilde{\theta}$; $w_t = \psi_t - \tilde{c}\mathbf{x}_t'\tilde{\theta}$ and $v_t = v_t - \mathbf{x}_t'(\theta - \tilde{\theta})(c - \tilde{c})$. This expansion is exact as the second derivatives of the function with respect to θ and c are zero, and it is only the cross-derivative which is nonzero. Equation (12) suggests the possibility of producing another estimator of θ by regressing w_t against $\tilde{\delta}\mathbf{x}_t$. A complication, however, is the presence of the I(0) term $z_t c$ on the right-hand side of (12), although an obvious solution, employed by Hansen (1989), is to purge (12) of that term by subtracting $\tilde{z}_t\tilde{c}$ from both sides, making the new dependent variable $\mathbf{w}_t - \tilde{z}_t\tilde{c}$, and then to run a regression of $(w_t - \tilde{z}_t\tilde{c})$ against $(\tilde{\delta}\mathbf{x}_t)$ to find an estimator of θ. Conceivably, one might iterate this process.

Although this estimation strategy described above is a straightforward application of classical nonlinear regression methods, its properties are not immediately obvious. For this reason, an alternative derivation of (12), which aids understanding and is very useful, is to return to (4) and invert it, obtaining

$$y_t = \mathbf{x}_t'\theta + \delta^{-1}(\beta\,\Delta y_{t+1} - \Delta y_t + v_t). \tag{13}$$

If δ was known, $\boldsymbol{\theta}$ might be estimated from the regression

$$y_t + \delta^{-1}\psi_t = \mathbf{x}_t'\theta + \delta^{-1}v_t, \tag{14}$$

or

$$\delta y_t + \psi_t = \delta\mathbf{x}_t'\theta + v_t. \tag{15}$$

Replacing δ by $\tilde{\delta}$ in (15) makes the dependent variable $\tilde{\delta}y_t + \psi_t = \psi_t + \tilde{\delta}\mathbf{x}_t'\tilde{\theta} + \tilde{\delta}(y_t - \mathbf{x}_t'\tilde{\theta}) = w_t - \tilde{z}_t\tilde{c}$, and (15) is therefore equivalent to (12), where the error term in the latter absorbs the terms created by the shift from δ to $\tilde{\delta}$. Hence, the new estimator of $\boldsymbol{\theta}$ arising from linearization can be computed from the regression of $y_t + \tilde{\delta}^{-1}(\Delta y_t - \beta\,\Delta y_{t+1})$ against $\mathbf{x}_t$.[14] Of course, just like $\tilde{\theta}$, some adjustments need to be made to enable standard inferential procedures to pertain, but that can be accommodated by applying the Phillips–Hansen technology to

$$y_t + \tilde{\delta}^{-1}(\Delta y_t - \beta\,\Delta y_{t+1}) = \mathbf{x}_t'\theta + \zeta_t \tag{16a}$$

$$\Delta\mathbf{x}_t = \boldsymbol{\varepsilon}_t, \tag{16b}$$

rather than to (11a) and (11b). The resulting estimator will be designated $\hat{\theta}_{\mathrm{E}}$, with E to represent the fact that it derives from the Euler equation. Notice that in case 1, $y_t - \mathbf{x}_t'\theta$ in (8) and (13) must be identical, so the difference between $\hat{\theta}_{\mathrm{PH}}$ and $\hat{\theta}_{\mathrm{E}}$ resides solely in the fact that $\delta\boldsymbol{\psi}_t$ is purged from the right-hand side of (8) when constructing $\hat{\theta}_{\mathrm{E}}$. *Prima facie*, it might be expected that the resulting estimator of θ, $\hat{\theta}_{\mathrm{E}}$, would have better small-sample behavior than $\hat{\theta}_{\mathrm{PH}}$, as it uses prior knowledge about the structure of the error term in (13), rather than requiring that the long-run covariance adjustment described earlier do all the work.

In the analysis above, attention has centered upon how to estimate θ in such a way as to be able to utilize standard test statistics. Corresponding to each way of estimating θ would be alternative estimators of $z_t = y_t - \mathbf{x}_t'\theta$, and these would generate different IV estimators of δ. In all cases however, the choice of instruments could be made according to the principles of GMM estimation set out in Hansen (1982), although because of the one-dependent nature of the error v_t, the optimal instruments involve all past lags of Δy_t and z_t – see Hansen and Singleton (1990). Thus, there is more than one way of setting up the IV estimator. In all instances however, the fact that θ can be estimated T-consistently means that $T^{1/2}(\hat{\delta} - \delta_0)$ will have a limiting normal distribution whose exact covariance matrix will depend on the type of IV estimator selected. Notice that the one-dependent nature of v_t makes it necessary to do a robust computation of the standard errors of $\hat{\delta}$ in order to make proper inferences.

Single Equation Estimation from the ECM

If the expectation is solved for, estimation can be done with the ECM's (5) or (6). Here the information that $\mathbf{x}_t$ is known to possess a unit root has been exploited in settling on a specification, and so prior knowledge of a unit root is extremely important to this approach. Just as for the Euler equation discussion, β will be taken to be known so that the task is to estimate θ and λ in case 1 ($\rho_1 = 1$); once λ has been quantified δ can be recovered by factorizing the polynomial $(1 - \lambda z)(1 - \lambda z^{-1}) = \beta z^2 - (1 + \beta + \delta)z + 1$. An initial consistent estimator of λ, $\tilde{\lambda}$, could be found by Kennan's method, i.e. regress y_t against y_{t-1} and $\mathbf{x}_t$ and use the estimated coefficient on y_{t-1}, but there would be other alternatives such as 2SLS on (8), with instruments y_{t-1} and $\mathbf{x}_t$ for Δy_t and $\mathbf{x}_t$ – see Bewley (1979) – or OLS on (5) with $\boldsymbol{\theta}$ replaced by $\tilde{\boldsymbol{\theta}}$. It is the last of these options that we select.

Linearizing (5) around $\tilde{\theta}$ and $\tilde{\lambda}$ gives

$$y_t - \mathbf{x}_t'\tilde{\theta}\tilde{\lambda} = [\tilde{z}_{t-1} - \Delta\mathbf{x}_t'\tilde{\theta}]\lambda + (1 - \tilde{\lambda})\mathbf{x}_t'\theta + u_t, \tag{17}$$

where $u_t = \mathbf{x}_t'(\theta - \tilde{\theta})(\lambda - \tilde{\lambda}) + (1 - \beta\lambda)(1 - \lambda)e_t$. If $\mathbf{x}_t$ was I(0), one would perform the regression in (17) to get updated estimates of θ and λ and, if the u_t were normally distributed, this two-step estimator would be asymptotically efficient relative to the MLE. Because $z_{t-1} - \Delta\mathbf{x}_t'\theta$ is I(0) in case 1 ($\rho_1 = 1$), rather than perform the full regression in (17), one might proceed with the following sequential estimator.[15] First, $[\tilde{z}_{t-1} - \Delta\mathbf{x}_t'\tilde{\theta}]\lambda$ is moved to the left-hand side of (17) and θ is estimated. Second, with that estimate of θ, θ^*, replacing θ, move $(1 - \tilde{\lambda})\mathbf{x}_t'\theta^*$ to the left-hand side of (17) and determine λ by a regression of $y_t - (1 - \tilde{\lambda})\mathbf{x}_t'\theta^*$ against $(z_{t-1}^* - \Delta\mathbf{x}_t'\theta^*)$.

To relate this way of estimating θ to those presented previously, observe that the regression equation it is based upon is

$$(1 - \tilde{\lambda})^{-1}[y_t - \mathbf{x}_t'\tilde{\theta}\tilde{\lambda} - (\tilde{z}_{t-1} - \Delta\mathbf{x}_t'\tilde{\theta})\tilde{\lambda}] = \mathbf{x}_t'\theta + \eta_t. \tag{18}$$

In (18), the left-hand side is $(1 - \tilde{\lambda})^{-1}[y_t - \tilde{\lambda}y_{t-1}] = y_t + (1 - \tilde{\lambda})^{-1}\tilde{\lambda}\,\Delta y_t$, and this would be identical to the left-hand side of (8) except that λ has been replaced by $\tilde{\lambda}$. Comparing (18) with (11a) reveals that the estimator of θ differs from $\tilde{\theta}$ in the fact that the disturbance term in (11a) has been purged of a known component. The factor extracted differs from that for $\tilde{\theta}_{\mathrm{E}}$ (see (16b)), because of the different informational assumptions. If the process generating $\mathbf{x}_t$ is exactly known, the error term in any $(y_t, \mathbf{x}_t)$ regression can be reduced to a function of the "econometrician error" alone. Without this knowledge, there is a remaining component that depends on the "expectation error" as well.

Now this connection means that θ can be estimated by applying the Phillips–Hansen estimator to (8) and (11b), after adding $(1 - \tilde{\lambda})^{-1}\tilde{\lambda}\,\Delta y_t$ to both sides of (8). The resulting system is

$$y_t + (1 - \tilde{\lambda})^{-1}\tilde{\lambda}\,\Delta y_t = \mathbf{x}_t'\theta + \boldsymbol{\eta}_t. \tag{19a}$$

$$\Delta\mathbf{x}_t = \boldsymbol{\varepsilon}_t, \tag{19b}$$

and the estimator of θ will be designated $\hat{\theta}_{\mathrm{ECM}}$.[16] To get $\tilde{\lambda}_{\mathrm{ECM}}$, the second part of the sequential procedure is implemented with z_t being regressed against $[\tilde{z}_{t-1} - \Delta\mathbf{x}_t'\tilde{\theta}]$ to produce $\hat{\lambda}_{\mathrm{ECM}}$. Because of the T-consistency of $\hat{\theta}_{\mathrm{ECM}}$, the asymptotic distribution of $\hat{\lambda}_{\mathrm{ECM}}$ is the same as if θ was known. If case 2 is entertained, (8) would have an extra term $[(1 - \lambda\beta\rho_2)^{-1} - 1]\,\Delta\mathbf{x}_t'\theta$ in it, which would change the linearized equation. Nevertheless, by rearranging the terms into those which are I(1) and those which are I(0), it is simple to apply the same sequential approach to the estimation of θ and λ (although different formulae would emerge). There is an additional complication though, caused by the use of an initial consistent estimator of ρ_2. This induces a "generated regressor" effect into the regression determining $\hat{\lambda}_{\mathrm{ECM}}$, and a correction to the covariance matrix needs to be done following the formulae in Newey (1984). Actually, because ρ_2 appears in both (8) and in the equation generating $\Delta\mathbf{x}_t$ it might be sensible to adopt a systems estimator to exploit the efficiency gains coming from such cross-equation restrictions.

Systems Estimation

The estimators described in the previous two subsections are single equation estimators in the sense that they estimate the parameters of (4) or (8), ignoring the equation for $\Delta \mathbf{x}_t$, except insofar as information on $\Delta \mathbf{x}_t$ is used to perform "bias adjustments." As the parameters to be determined are essentially the cointegrating vector θ and the "adjustment parameter" δ, there may be some gains to jointly estimating the system. For this to be so, $\Delta \mathbf{x}_t$ would have to possess an autoregressive structure, such as in case 2. Johansen (1988) describes a LIML-type joint estimator of θ and λ when $(y_t, \mathbf{x}_t)$ follow a finite-order VAR, Phillips (1991a) discusses FIML estimation of the parameters θ, λ, and ρ_2, and Phillips (1991b) outlines a spectral estimator of θ and λ. Conceptually, it is hard to apply the first two of these procedures to the estimation of parameters of the Euler equation, as the vector $(y_t, \mathbf{x}_t)$ does not follow a finite-order VAR owing to the MA(1) in the composite error term of (4). Hence, the spectral estimator looks most appealing, as it does not need to explicitly estimate the parameters of the autocorrelation process of $\Delta \mathbf{x}_t$.

A similar problem arises with the ECM version. Take case 2 and replace Δx_t in (6) by $(1 - \rho_2 L)^{-1}\varepsilon_t$. Multiplying (6) by $(1 - \rho_2 L)$ gives a VAR in (y_t, x_t) but with a disturbance term of the form $(1 - \beta\lambda\rho_2)^{-1}(1 - \lambda)\varepsilon_t'\theta + (1 - \rho_2 L)(1 - \beta\lambda)(1 - \lambda)e_t$ for the y_t equation, i.e. an MA(1) again. Consequently, the assumption of Johansen's method, namely that these errors are white noise, will be invalid. Moreover, it is not possible to replace this composite error with a single error term and then to proceed to maximum likelihood estimation, see Phillips (1988). These facts raise interesting problems about joint estimation of λ and θ by systems methods that deserve fuller exploration. Most work with systems approaches has begun with the presumption that there is a finite-order VAR for $(y_t, \mathbf{x}_t)$ and then derived an ECM representation that is compatible with such a VAR. Utilizing theoretical analysis to derive the ECM reverses this sequence and highlights the fact that there may be no finite-order VAR which encapsulates the theoretical model. Hence, estimation methods that emphasize a VAR structure are not necessarily appropriate to estimation of the linear quadratic model.

A Monte Carlo Study of the Estimators

A brief investigation was made of the sampling properties of the proposed estimators, with special emphasis being placed upon the correspondence of the size of test statistics with the theoretical predictions of the asymptotic theory. Specifically, the prediction is that the recentered estimators of θ should have t-values that behave like a standard normal deviate in large samples. To assess this prediction, one thousand replications of each experiment were performed, and the proportion of times the t-values exceeded the critical values associated with the 10, 5, and 1 percent levels of significance of a standard normal are reported. These are taken to indicate the true sizes of the test. All computation was done with programs written in the GAUSS language.

The basic experiment consists of the two equations

$$\Delta y_t + (\lambda - 1)(y_{t-1} - x_{t-1}\theta) + (1 - \lambda)\theta\,\Delta x_t + (1 - \beta\lambda)(1 - \lambda)e_t \qquad (20a)$$

$$\Delta x_t = \varepsilon_t, \qquad (20b)$$

where $[e_t, \varepsilon_t]$ are drawn from a bivariate normal distribution with covariance matrix

$$\Sigma = \begin{pmatrix} \sigma_{ee} & \sigma_{e\varepsilon} \\ \sigma_{\varepsilon e} & \sigma_{\varepsilon\varepsilon} \end{pmatrix} \tag{20c}$$

and the parameters θ, δ, and Σ vary across experiments.[17] West (1986) has a similar experimental design. Our basic experiment puts $\theta = 1$, $\delta = 0.5$, and

$$\Sigma = \begin{pmatrix} 1 & 0.5 \\ 0.5 & 1 \end{pmatrix}, \tag{20d}$$

meaning that the forcing variable x_t is actually an endogenous variable with zero drift. For ease of reference, estimators are given a designation that refers to the procedure that generated them. Hence $\tilde{\theta}_{\text{OLS}}$ is the OLS estimator $\tilde{\theta}$ described from the regression in (11a); $\hat{\theta}_{\text{PH}}$ is based on this OLS estimator but now centered properly as suggested in Phillips and Hansen (1990); $\hat{\theta}_{\text{E}}$ is the Phillips–Hansen estimator of θ from (16) while $\hat{\delta}_{\text{E}}$ is the IV estimator from (4) with θ replaced by $\hat{\theta}_{\text{E}}$; and $\hat{\theta}_{\text{ECM}}$ and $\hat{\delta}_{\text{ECM}}$ are the error correction model variants arising out of (19). For the IV estimator of δ, the instruments employed were Δy_{t-1}, Δy_{t-2}, and $\tilde{z}_{t-1}$. The estimator $\tilde{\theta}_{\text{OLS}}$ is included in order to illustrate the effects of ignoring the integration in x_t upon the sizes of test statistics.

Table 15.1 records the outcomes for the initial experiment and is intended to show how the sizes of the test statistics are related to variation in the cost of adjustment. Based on this initial experiment, the ECM estimators work well with samples of 200 observations, and are acceptable even with $T = 100$. As expected, the OLS estimator, being uncentered, has a large size distortion that can be reduced considerably by the Phillips–Hansen modifications. However, $\hat{\theta}_{\text{PH}}$ still has bias in its size relative to the ECM-based estimator. What is striking, and surprising, is the poor performance of $\hat{\theta}_{\text{E}}$, particularly as compared to $\hat{\theta}_{\text{PH}}$. One possibility is that the long-run covariance matrix of the disturbances in (16) is very different from that for (11), as the E and PH estimators derive from these equation systems respectively. Any such differences may make one harder to estimate. Now the error term in (16a) would be (ignoring terms of $o_p(1)$)

$$\zeta_t = (e_t - \lambda\beta e_{t+1}) - \delta^{-1}\beta\theta(1-\lambda)\varepsilon_{t+1}, \tag{21}$$

and it therefore possesses an MA(1) structure, as contrasted with the error of (11a), $(-\theta\lambda\varepsilon_t + \delta\lambda e_t)(1 - \lambda L)^{-1}$, which is an AR(1). However, despite this difference in format, both the long-run covariance matrices of (16) and (11) have identical determinants, $\delta^2\lambda^2(\sigma_{ee}\sigma_{\varepsilon\varepsilon} - \sigma_{e\varepsilon}^2)/(1-\lambda)^2$, which become singular as $\delta \to 0$; the determinant values are 0.64, 0.29, 0.20, 0.10, and 0.06 for $\delta = 10, 1, 0.5, 0.2, 0.1$. Ultimately, then, although we would expect a breakdown of *both* estimators as δ becomes small, the equivalence of the determinants means that this feature cannot explain the differential performance of the two estimators.

It is also the case that the numerical values of their respective Phillips–Hansen adjustments are very similar. For example, in the basic experiment, the first adjustment, i.e. $\Omega_{12}\Omega_{22}^{-1}$, is -0.705 (E) and -0.765 (PH), changing to -1.5159 (E) and

Table 15.1 Size of test statistics as the cost of adjustment term varies

	$T = 100$			$T = 200$		
	0.1	0.05	0.01	0.1	0.05	0.01
1. $\theta = 1, \delta = 0.5, \Sigma = \begin{pmatrix} 1 & 0.5 \\ 0.5 & 1 \end{pmatrix}$						
$\tilde{\theta}_{\text{OLS}}$	0.24	0.16	0.06	0.27	0.18	0.07
$\hat{\theta}_{\text{PH}}$	0.16	0.10	0.03	0.14	0.08	0.02
$\hat{\theta}_{\text{E}}$	0.04	0.02	0.01	0.03	0.01	0.00
$\hat{\theta}_{\text{ECM}}$	0.14	0.08	0.02	0.11	0.05	0.02
$\hat{\delta}_{\text{E}}$	0.09	0.04	0.01	0.08	0.05	0.02
$\hat{\delta}_{\text{ECM}}$	0.10	0.04	0.01	0.10	0.04	0.01
2. $\theta = 1, \delta = 0.2, \Sigma = \begin{pmatrix} 1 & 0.5 \\ 0.5 & 1 \end{pmatrix}$						
$\tilde{\theta}_{\text{OLS}}$	0.31	0.22	0.10	0.34	0.25	0.11
$\hat{\theta}_{\text{PH}}$	0.16	0.09	0.03	0.14	0.08	0.02
$\hat{\theta}_{\text{E}}$	0.03	0.01	0.00	0.01	0.00	0.00
$\hat{\theta}_{\text{ECM}}$	0.15	0.09	0.02	0.12	0.06	0.02
$\hat{\delta}_{\text{E}}$	0.11	0.07	0.03	0.10	0.06	0.02
$\hat{\delta}_{\text{ECM}}$	0.07	0.03	0.01	0.07	0.04	0.01
3. $\theta = 1, \delta = 10, \Sigma = \begin{pmatrix} 1 & 0.5 \\ 0.5 & 1 \end{pmatrix}$						
$\tilde{\theta}_{\text{OLS}}$	0.14	0.08	0.00	0.13	0.07	0.02
$\hat{\theta}_{\text{PH}}$	0.15	0.08	0.03	0.10	0.06	0.02
$\hat{\theta}_{\text{E}}$	0.09	0.05	0.01	0.07	0.04	0.01
$\hat{\theta}_{\text{ECM}}$	0.10	0.06	0.01	0.08	0.05	0.02
$\hat{\delta}_{\text{E}}$	0.82	0.78	0.70	0.69	0.65	0.56
$\hat{\delta}_{\text{ECM}}$	0.23	0.20	0.15	0.17	0.14	0.08

-1.6659 (PH) as δ changes from 0.5 to 0.2.[18] Consequently, the adjustments performed are approximately equal for each estimator, so that it cannot be the adjustment which explains differing sampling performance, focusing attention upon the OLS estimators of θ that form the base of each of the E and PH estimators. Designating these by $\hat{\theta}^{\text{E}}_{\text{OLS}}$ and $\hat{\theta}^{\text{PH}}_{\text{OLS}}$ respectively, where $\hat{\theta}^{\text{E}}_{\text{OLS}}$ is found from OLS applied to (16a) and $\hat{\theta}^{\text{PH}}_{\text{OLS}}$ comes from (11a), the experiments having $\delta = 0.5$ or 0.2 produce a bias in $\hat{\theta}^{\text{PH}}_{\text{OLS}}$ which is negative, whereas that for $\hat{\theta}^{\text{E}}_{\text{OLS}}$ is positive. Because the first Phillips–Hansen adjustment terms are negative and are subtracted from $\hat{\theta}^{\text{E}}_{\text{OLS}}$ and $\hat{\theta}^{\text{PH}}_{\text{OLS}}$, this means that the adjustment actually works in the wrong direction for the E estimator, causing an increase rather than a reduction in size distortion. This situation changes when $\delta = 10$; for that configuration $\hat{\theta}^{\text{E}}_{\text{OLS}}$ does indeed have the requisite negative bias. Increasing the sample size also eventually changes the sign of the bias, with correct size being attained for statistics based on $\hat{\theta}_{\text{E}}$ when there are upward of 5,000 observations (1,000 for $\hat{\theta}_{\text{PH}}$).

Exactly why one obtains a positive bias in $\hat{\theta}^{\text{E}}_{\text{OLS}}$ is unclear. Because the two estimators differ only in the dependent variable, one possibility is that the troubles of the E-estimator stem from the use of $\tilde{\delta}$ in constructing the dependent variable of (16a). However, replacing the estimate of δ with its true value does not change the result. Another explanation is suggested by the observation that the error term in (21) is an MA(1) with a negative parameter, as this has caused similar bias problems when testing for a unit root (Schwert 1987). Such an explanation works for a comparison of the first and third experiments in table 15.1 in that the MA(1) parameter is -0.126, -0.457, and -0.376 when $\delta = 10, 0.5$, and 0.2, but it fails when comparing the first and second experiments. Another factor, however, comes into play – the R^2 of the regression in (16a), for finite n, is lower with $\delta = 0.2$ than with $\delta = 0.5$, since the variance of the error term is higher – and it is known that the small sample bias of the OLS estimator of θ is positively related to the R^2, see Banerjee et al. (1986). So a joint consideration of both effects seems crucial in producing a satisfactory account of the outcomes of table 15.1. Turning away from estimating θ to δ, the outcomes are reversed with both $\hat{\delta}_E$ and $\hat{\delta}_{ECM}$ having more accurate test sizes with small values of δ. As δ rises (the cost of adjustment falls), the rejection frequency rises dramatically, especially for $\hat{\delta}_E$, the reason being that the instruments become very poor as both Δy_t and z_t resemble white-noise processes.

Table 15.2 reveals what happens as the degree of endogeneity of x_t increases. To achieve such an effect the covariance matrix Σ is altered to

$$\Sigma = \begin{pmatrix} 1 & 0.7 \\ 0.7 & 1 \end{pmatrix}. \tag{22}$$

All results appear to be insensitive to this change. Our final experiment in table 15.3

Table 15.2 Size of test statistics as endogeneity increases

	$T = 100$			$T = 200$		
	0.10	0.05	0.01	0.10	0.05	0.01
1. $\theta = 1, \delta = 0.5, \Sigma = \begin{pmatrix} 1 & 0.5 \\ 0.5 & 1 \end{pmatrix}$						
$\tilde{\theta}_{OLS}$	0.24	0.16	0.06	0.27	0.18	0.07
$\hat{\theta}_{PH}$	0.16	0.10	0.03	0.14	0.08	0.02
$\hat{\theta}_E$	0.04	0.02	0.01	0.03	0.01	0.00
$\hat{\theta}_{ECM}$	0.14	0.08	0.02	0.11	0.05	0.02
$\hat{\delta}_E$	0.09	0.04	0.01	0.08	0.05	0.02
$\hat{\delta}_{ECM}$	0.10	0.04	0.01	0.10	0.04	0.01
2. $\theta = 1, \delta = 0.5, \Sigma = \begin{pmatrix} 1 & 0.7 \\ 0.7 & 1 \end{pmatrix}$						
$\tilde{\theta}_{OLS}$	0.24	0.16	0.06	0.27	0.19	0.07
$\hat{\theta}_{PH}$	0.15	0.10	0.03	0.14	0.08	0.02
$\hat{\theta}_{IV}$	0.03	0.01	0.01	0.02	0.00	0.00
$\hat{\theta}_{ECM}$	0.14	0.08	0.02	0.10	0.05	0.02
$\hat{\delta}_{IV}$	0.10	0.04	0.01	0.09	0.04	0.01
$\hat{\delta}_{ECM}$	0.08	0.05	0.02	0.10	0.04	0.01

Table 15.3 Size of test statistics as the long-run response changes

	$T = 100$			$T = 200$		
	0.10	0.05	0.01	0.10	0.05	0.01
1. $\theta = 1, \delta = 0.5, \Sigma = \begin{pmatrix} 1 & 0.5 \\ 0.5 & 1 \end{pmatrix}$						
$\tilde{\theta}_{\mathrm{OLS}}$	0.24	0.16	0.06	0.27	0.18	0.07
$\hat{\theta}_{\mathrm{PH}}$	0.16	0.10	0.03	0.14	0.08	0.02
$\hat{\theta}_{\mathrm{E}}$	0.04	0.02	0.01	0.03	0.01	0.00
$\hat{\theta}_{\mathrm{ECM}}$	0.14	0.08	0.02	0.11	0.05	0.02
$\hat{\delta}_{\mathrm{E}}$	0.09	0.04	0.01	0.08	0.05	0.02
$\hat{\delta}_{\mathrm{ECM}}$	0.10	0.04	0.01	0.10	0.04	0.01
2. $\theta = 10, \delta = 0.5, \Sigma = \begin{pmatrix} 1 & 0.5 \\ 0.5 & 1 \end{pmatrix}$						
$\tilde{\theta}_{\mathrm{OLS}}$	0.26	0.18	0.07	0.29	0.20	0.06
$\hat{\theta}_{\mathrm{PH}}$	0.09	0.04	0.01	0.03	0.02	0.01
$\hat{\theta}_{\mathrm{E}}$	0.02	0.00	0.00	0.01	0.00	0.00
$\hat{\theta}_{\mathrm{ECM}}$	0.12	0.08	0.02	0.10	0.05	0.02
$\hat{\delta}_{\mathrm{E}}$	0.11	0.07	0.03	0.10	0.05	0.02
$\hat{\delta}_{\mathrm{ECM}}$	0.02	0.01	0.00	0.02	0.00	0.00

examines the influence of the value of the long-run response, θ. It highlights the inadequacies in our earlier explanations of the positive bias in $\hat{\theta}_{\mathrm{E}}$, as that now increases slightly (as a proportion of θ), despite the fact that both the MA(1) parameter in the error term has declined (in abolute terms) and R^2 has increased. The ECM estimator of θ continues to perform well, emphasizing the gains from knowing how Δx_t is generated. What is odd in this table is the failure of the ECM estimator of δ. Given that θ is very accurately estimated by $\hat{\theta}_{\mathrm{ECM}}$, $\hat{\lambda}$ is effectively the OLS estimate from (17) after fixing θ, and we would therefore expect good performance for $\hat{\delta}_{\mathrm{ECM}}$. Exactly why this outcome is observed is a subject for future study.

Conclusion

The paper has examined the estimation of equations coming from linear quadratic optimization models when the forcing variables are integrated. After demonstrating that there is frequently a lack of identification for some of the parameters in such models, we fixed one of them – the discount rate – and proceeded to look at how estimators of the remaining parameters could be derived. By the nature of Euler equation solutions, there are two sets of parameters to be estimated; one associated with I(1) variables and the other with I(0) variables. Previous literature has largely concentrated upon the estimation of the parameters attached to I(1) variables, the cointegrating vector. Unfortunately, standard procedures for this have undesirable side effects upon the estimation of the I(0) variable parameters. Nevertheless, simple adjustments are implemented to overcome this problem.

We devise two general classes of estimators for the unknown parameters, corresponding to the two procedures normally used for estimating models with rational expectations. The first of these works with the Euler equation (E) and is found by replacing the unknown expectation with the observed value of the variables expectations are being formed about. The second solves for the expectation; in our context this leads to an error correction model, and the derived estimator is termed an ECM-estimator. In all instances some corrections must be made to the estimators of the long-run response in order to allow for standard inferences. Within the category of E-estimators, we investigated two different approaches aimed at effecting such adjustment, but differing by the amounts of information exploited about the structure of the error term.

A final section puts all these estimators to the test in a simple simulation study. It is found that the ECM-estimator of the long-run response generally works very well, while E-estimators are much less reliable. Within the E-estimator class it was found that attempting to exploit knowledge about the structure of the error term in the estimation equation was generally harmful, although we were unable to determine exactly why this was so. When estimating adjustment cost terms, the situation is not so simple. In fact, it sometimes seems as if there is an inverse relation between the ability to estimate long-run responses and adjustment parameters.

Some interesting questions emerged from the study. Normally an Euler equation estimator is preferred in many rational expectation estimation contexts, since it does not require the specification of an expectation generating process, and hence it exhibits a degree of robustness. Its poor performance in many of the experiments here might therefore be viewed as rather disturbing for applied research. But it has to be realized that the robustness property cited above is much less advantageous for determining the long-run response when there are integrated regressors. Then, to consistently estimate the long-run response it is only necessary to determine which *integrated* variables appear in the expectations generating process; all others may be subsumed within an error term. This fact is not to deny that E-estimators are appealing; the adjustment cost parameters attach to I(0) variables and an incorrect specification of expectations means the ECM method will be working with a misspecified model, and so inconsistent estimators of those parameters will be found. In these circumstances an E estimator is very attractive. Since the best estimator of the adjustment cost parameters frequently seems to come from the Euler equation, while the best estimator for the long-run response is that from the ECM, the possibility is raised of using each estimator for the task at which it has a comparative advantage. Whether this conclusion holds up to further analysis will be dealt with in future work. Another extension is to models with expectations that do not derive from Euler equations. The estimation methods advanced here would continue to apply if conditions can be found that would enable the solution of models with expectations and integrated variables; an important advantage of the linear quadratic model is that a substantial literature can be drawn upon for that purpose. Wickens (1992) takes up the latter problem elsewhere in this volume.

Notes

1. We are grateful to Neil Ericsson, Bruce Hansen, Hashem Pesaran, and anonymous referees for discussion on this material.

2. Pesaran (1991) derives results when the cost function is augmented by higher order adjustment terms such as $(\Delta^2 y_s)^2$.
3. It would be possible to allow e_t to be serially correlated provided it remains an integrated process of order zero. This last restriction cannot be relaxed as it would mean that the error term in "regressions" would be the same order of integration as the regressors.
4. x_t is taken to be a scalar here for expositional purposes.
5. Actually, in their simulation study they have four instruments: Δy_{t-1}, z_{t-1}, Δy_{t-2}, and z_{t-2}. It is not hard to show that the result we give is invariant to the number of instruments. Therefore Dolado et al.'s first experiment is attempting to estimate an unidentified model, and one would expect the poor results they obtain. When β is fixed though, and only δ is being estimated, one should get good results; indeed such an outcome is apparent from their table 1 (actually they fix β at unity rather than the true value of 0.97). Notice that the assumption of a known θ is for convenience only. If the model cannot be identified even when θ is known, the situation will be worse when θ needs to be estimated.
6. This point is emphasized in the context of models such as these by Pesaran (1987, p. 193).
7. He mentions that, by conditioning upon $\hat{\beta}$, i.e. forming $\Delta y_t - \hat{\beta}\,\Delta y_{t+1}$ as a dependent variable, it would be possible to get asymptotic normality for an IV estimator of δ.
8. Even though β and δ may be identified when θ is known, the conclusion does not extend to the situation when θ is unknown, as there are then three parameters in (5) but only two regressors, y_{t-1}, and x_t, as x_{t-1} cancels. Consequently, one of the three parameters cannot be identified even when $\rho_1 < 1$. In many contexts θ will in fact be known. For example, if y_t and x_t are logs of variables, and the ratio of the levels is a constant, θ would be unity. Notice that the "counting rule" just used is only a necessary condition, as evidenced by the case $\rho_1 = 1$ discussed in the text, where there were two parameters and two regressors, but only a single parameter was identified.
9. The eigenvalues were found by estimating the correlation matrix from 2,500 observations generated according to the theoretical model. This introduces a slight error. For example, when $\rho_2 = 0$, the smallest eigenvalue is truly zero, but computed from the simulation it was 2.5×10^{-5}. However, this discrepancy is clearly not important for the point we wish to make. Programs to perform the simulations and eigenvalue computations were done in GAUSS.
10. Dolado et al. (1991) were the first to notice the curious result that, when $\beta = 1$, z_t is I(0), whereas for $\beta \neq 1$ it is I(1).
11. If ζ_t is a covariance stationary process, the long-run covariance matrix is proportional to the spectral density at the origin.
12. Actually, the first adjustment also removes serial correlation but only in ζ_t; the second adjustment is intended to compensate for serial correlation in ε_t.
13. It is interesting to observe that this is exactly the regression employed by Kennan (1979) for estimating θ.
14. It is easy to see that $T^{-1}\Sigma \mathbf{x}_t \boldsymbol{\eta}_t - T^{-1}\Sigma \mathbf{x}_t(1 - \beta\lambda)e_t$ is $o_p(1)$ (case 1, $\rho_1 = 1$), owing to the $T^{1/2}$ consistency of $\tilde{\lambda}$ and the fact that $T^{-1}\Sigma \mathbf{x}_t\,\Delta y_t$ converges in law to a random variable. Consequently, the disturbance term in (19a) can be regarded as $(1 - \beta\lambda)e_t$.
15. The fact that $z_{t-1} - \Delta \mathbf{x}_t'\theta$ is I(0) and $\mathbf{x}_t$ is I(1) means that the regressors are asymptotically uncorrelated, thereby enabling a sequential approach.
16. It is easy to show that the two estimators of θ formed by regressing $y_t - \delta^{-1}\psi_t$ and $y_t - \tilde{\delta}^{-1}\psi_t$ against $\mathbf{x}_t$ are asymptotically identical owing to the fact that $T^{-3/2}\Sigma \mathbf{x}_t'\psi_t$ converges to zero.
17. λ is a function of δ once β is prescribed, and the latter is set to 0.97 in these experiments. All long-run covariance matrices are estimated as in Newey and West (1987) using $T^{1/3}$ lags.
18. Because there is no serial correlation in the equation for Δx_t, the second of the Phillips–Hansen adjustments should be zero. It was found that both adjustments were well estimated even with quite small sample sizes, although some care had to be taken in the Euler equation case, as the error term in (16a) is an MA(1) and therefore one would wish

to give weights of unity to the lag-0 and lag-1 autocovariances but zero to all others. The Newey–West formula does not do this, but repeating the computations with the exact estimate of the long-run variance did not change any conclusions.

References

Banerjee, A., J. J. Dolado, D. F. Hendry, and G. W. Smith (1986). "Exploring equilibrium relationships through static models: some Monte Carlo evidence," *Oxford Bulletin of Economics and Statistics*, 48, 253–77.

Bergstrom, A. R. (1967). *The Construction and Use of Economic Models*. London: English Universities Press.

Bewley, R. A.(1979). "The direct estimation of the equilibrium response in a linear dynamic model," *Economics Letters*, 3, 357–62.

Blanchard, O. J., and A. Melino (1986). "The cyclical behaviour of prices and quantities: the case of the automobile market," *Journal of Monetary Economics*, 17, 379–407.

Dolado, J. J., J. W. Galbraith, and A. Banerjee (1991). "Estimating intertemporal quadratic adjustment models with integrated series," *International Economic Review*, 32, 919–36.

Engle, R. F., and C. W. Granger (1987). "Co-integration and error correction: representation, estimation and testing," *Econometrica*, 49, 1057–72.

Hansen, L. P. (1982). "Large sample properties of generalized method of moments estimators," *Econometrica*, 50, 1029–54.

Hansen, B. (1989). "Testing for structural change of unknown form in models with non-stationary regressors," mimeo, University of Rochester.

Hansen, L. P., and T. J. Sargent (1980). 'Formulating and estimating dynamic linear rational expectations models," *Journal of Economic Dynamics and Control*, 2, 7–46.

Hansen, L. P., and K. J. Singleton (1990). 'Efficient estimation of asset pricing models with moving average errors," National Bureau of Economic Research Technical Paper 86.

Ilmakunnas, P. (1989). "Survey expectations vs. rational expectations in the estimation of a dynamic model: demand for labour in Finnish manufacturing," *Oxford Bulletin of Economics and Statistics*, 51, 297–314.

Johansen, S. (1988). "Statistical analysis of cointegration vectors," *Journal of Economic Dynamics and Control*, 2, 231–54.

Kennan, J. (1979). "The estimation of partial adjustment models with rational expectations," *Econometrica*, 47, 1441–55.

Layard, R., and S. Nickell (1986). "Unemployment in Britain," *Economica*, 53, S121–70.

McCallum, B. (1976). "Rational expectations and the natural rate hypothesis: some consistent estimates," *Econometrica*, 44, 43–52.

Newey, W. K. (1984). "A method of moments interpretation of sequential estimators," *Economics Letters*, 14, 201–6.

Newey, W. K., and K. D. West (1987). "A simple positive semi-definite heteroskedasticity and autocorrelation consistent covariance matrix," *Econometrica*, 49, 703–8.

Nickell, S. (1985). "Error correction, partial adjustment and all that: an expository note," *Oxford Bulletin of Economics and Statistics*, 47, 119–29.

Nickell, S. (1987). "Dynamic models of labour demand," in O. Ashenfelter and R. Layard (eds) *Handbook of Labour Economics*. Amsterdam: North-Holland.

Pagan, A. R. (1984). "Econometric issues in the analysis of regressions with generated regressors," *International Economic Review*, 25, 221–47.

Park, J. Y. (1988). "Canonical co-integrating regressions," Center for Analytic Economics, Working Paper 88–29, Cornell University.

Park, J. Y., and P. C. B. Phillips (1988). "Statistical inference in regressions with integrated processes: part 1," *Econometric Theory*, 4, 468–97.

Pesaran, H. (1991). "Costly adjustment under rational expectations: a generalization," *Review of Economics and Statistics*, LXXIII, 353–8.
Pesaran, H. (1987). *The Limits to Rational Expectations*. New York: Blackwell.
Phillips, P. C. B. (1987). "Time series regression with a unit root," *Econometrica*, 55, 277–301.
Phillips, P. C. B. (1988). "Multiple regression with integrated time series," *Contemporary Mathematics*, 80, 79–104.
Phillips, P. C. B. (1989). "Partially identified econometric models," *Econometric Theory*, 5, 181–240.
Phillips, P. C. B. (1991a). "Optimal inference in cointegrated systems," *Econometrica*, 59, 283–306.
Phillips, P. C. B. (1991b). "Spectral regression for co-integrated time series," in W. Barnett, J. Powell, and G. Tauchen (eds) *Nonparametric and Semiparametric Methods in Economics and Statistics*, pp. 413–35. Cambridge: Cambridge University Press.
Phillips, P. C. B., and B. E. Hansen, (1990). "Statistical inference in instrumental variables regression with I(1) processes," *Review of Economic Studies*, 57, 99–125.
Sargent, T. J. (1978). "Estimation of dynamic labour demand schedules under rational expectations," *Journal of Political Economy*, 86, 1009–44.
Schwert, G. W. (1987). "Effects of model misspecification on tests for unit roots in macro-economic data," *Journal of Monetary Economics*, 20, 73–103.
Sims, C. A., J. Stock, and M. W. Watson (1990). "Inference in linear time series models with some unit roots," *Econometrica*, 58, 113–44.
West, K. D. (1986). "Full versus limited information estimation of a rational expectations model: some numerical comparisons," *Journal of Econometrics*, 33, 367–85.
Wren-Lewis, S. (1986). "An econometric model of U.K. manufacturing employment using survey data on expected output," *Journal of Applied Econometrics*, 1, 297–316.
Wickens, M. R. (1982). "The efficient estimation of econometric models with rational expectations," *Review of Economic Studies*, 49, 817–38.
Wickens, M. R. (1992). "Rational expectations and integrated variables," this volume, pp. 317–336.

16

Reducing Parameter Numbers in Econometric Modeling

E. J. Hannan

Introduction

Since there will never be any attainable true system generating the data, the best that can be hoped for is for such understanding of the structure of the system to be available that a *very restricted* model class can be successfully used. The measure of success here could be predictive ability. Here, by a model class, we mean a family of probabilistic structures listed by means of a fixed number of parameters. It is probably true that the most successful econometric modeling is of this kind. However, there is not much that we can say about that and here we shall be concerned with discussing often-used model classes and variants of these that may reduce parameter numbers.

One main reason for reducing parameter numbers is to obtain a description of the structure of the data that has a reasonably direct interpretation. Of course, a good fit can always be obtained, but that guarantees little, since we may merely be closely modeling impermanent features of the data. To be sure, also, we may use objective methods to choose the degree of fit, but the objection remains. It is the implementation of the fitted model, its usefulness for us, that, it seems, demands a reasonable number of fitted parameters, i.e. a reasonably simple and comprehensible model. It must also be said that models with large numbers of parameters may present great computational difficulties, for example numerical instabilities.

In the next section a brief discussion of the structure of linear systems will be given which will form a basis for later discussion, for example of the methods of Tiao and Tsay (1989). Further detail on linear systems can be found in Hannan and Deistler (1988) and we refer to that also for technical terminology used here and not explained. In the third section, we discuss choice of a model class and a model from that class. A proper understanding of the costs both of fitting parameters and of multiplying model classes is essential.

One means of reducing parameter numbers is to fit a large model, say an autoregression–regression (ARX) model that is easy to fit, and then to approximate to that, controlling the approximation error. We discuss this in the fifth section. In the sixth section, we deal with a method of variate transformation that might reduce the order of an ARX model. Finally, adaptive methods will be described where the model fitted is time-dependent. These seem important both because they reduce the complexity of the fitted structure and because they are more realistic.

The account given below will necessarily be brief. It is intended as an introductory survey. Where possible references will, however, be given.

The Structure of Linear Systems

As a basis for the discussion let us begin from a class of s component series, $\mathbf{y}(t)$, and component series $\mathbf{z}(t)$ satisfying

$$\mathbf{y}(t) = \sum_{0}^{\infty} K(j)\boldsymbol{\varepsilon}(t-j) + \sum_{1}^{\infty} L(j)\mathbf{z}(t-j),\ K(0) = I_s. \tag{1}$$

It may be that $z(t)$ is independent on the history of the y process to time t. Note that $(t-1)$ is the latest time point for which the $\mathbf{z}$ vector occurs in (1). The s-component $\varepsilon(t)$ sequence is to satisfy $E\{\boldsymbol{\varepsilon}(t)\} = 0$, $E\{\boldsymbol{\varepsilon}(s)\boldsymbol{\varepsilon}(t)'\} = \delta_{s,t}\Sigma$, $\Sigma > 0$.

For convenience, we assume that

$$\sum_{1}^{p} \|(K(j)\|^2 < \infty, \quad \sum_{1}^{\infty} \|(L(j)\|^2 < \infty, \tag{2}$$

which means that the first component on the right-hand side in (1) is well defined as a limit in mean square and we assume that the same is true for the second. These conditions (2) mean that we are essentially considering here the stationary case. In fact, a great deal of what is said extends to the case where, in particular, (1) would hold only after some initial sequence had been differenced in some way so as to produce $\mathbf{y}(t)$. We shall occasionally refer to that situation in what follows but for the main part shall retain the conditions (2).

Consider the block Hankel matrix $\mathscr{H} = [K(i+j-1), L(i+j-1)]$ where the (i,j)th, $sx(s+m)$, block is shown, $i,j = 1,2,3,\ldots$. Each row of $\mathscr{H}$ lies in l_2, the linear space of all square summable sequences. Let H_0 be a submatrix of rows of $\mathscr{H}$ that span the linear space spanned by all rows of $\mathscr{H}$. We assume H_0 is minimal, i.e. no row can be omitted without losing that property. (We emphasize that we are talking of rows, not blocks of rows.) Let H_1 be the first block of s rows of $\mathscr{H}$ and partition H_0 as $[B, D, H_2]$, where B is made up of the first s columns and D of the next m. Now $H_1 = CH_0$ and $H_2 = AH_0$. The first of these is obvious and the second follows from the fact that eliminating the first $s+m$ columns of $\mathscr{H}$ leaves us with a matrix of rows of $\mathscr{H}$. Put $\mathbf{x}(t) = H_0\xi_{t-1}$, $\xi_t' = (\boldsymbol{\varepsilon}(t)', \mathbf{z}(t)', \boldsymbol{\varepsilon}(t-1)', \mathbf{z}(t-1)', \ldots)$. Then $\mathbf{x}(t+1) = B\boldsymbol{\varepsilon}(t) + D\mathbf{z}(t) + H_2\xi_{t-1} = A\mathbf{x}(t) + D\mathbf{z}(t) + B\boldsymbol{\varepsilon}(t)$. Also from (1), $\mathbf{y}(t) = H_1\xi_{t-1} + \boldsymbol{\varepsilon}(t) = C\mathbf{x}(t) + \boldsymbol{\varepsilon}(t)$ and we obtain the state space form

$$\mathbf{x}(t+1) = A\mathbf{x}(t) + D\mathbf{z}(t) + B\boldsymbol{\varepsilon}(t), \quad \mathbf{y}(t) = C\mathbf{x}(t) + \boldsymbol{\varepsilon}(t). \tag{3}$$

The only arbitrary element in (3) is the choice of H_0, and we fix that, in a natural way, by choosing the first linearly independent set discovered as we examine the rows of $\mathscr{H}$ from top to bottom. If we are to finitely parameterize (3), we must assume H_0 has finitely many rows, i.e. the rank of $\mathscr{H}$ is finite. Call it n, which is spoken of as the order or McMillan degree. If $r(u, j)$ is the jth row, $j = 1, \ldots, s$, in the uth blocks of rows, $u = 1, 2, \ldots$, then H_0, with the choice just described, always consists of rows

$$r(u, j), \qquad u = 1, \ldots, n_j; \quad j = 1, \ldots, s; \quad \Sigma n_j = n. \tag{4}$$

This means that all jth rows in a block are included up to the n_jth block and none thereafter. (This follows from the fact that the jth row in the $(k + 1)$th block is the part of the jth row in the kth block got by eliminating the first $s + m$ columns). It also means that H_0, with this method of choice, is specified by the n_j, which are known as the Kronecker indices. The dimension $d(n_1, n_2, \ldots, n_s)$ of the space of all systems, (3), i.e. of all $\mathscr{H}$, for given n_j is given in Hannan and Deistler (1988, p. 63) and there is no purpose in repeating it here. This dimension is the number of freely varying elements in A, B, C, D with this choice of H_0, i.e. the number of elements not identically 0 or 1. If $\mathbf{y}(t)$ is replaced by $M\mathbf{y}(t)$, for some nonsingular matrix M, then the n_j may be permuted but the set of them remains unchanged. If $n_1 \leqslant n_2 \leqslant \cdots \leqslant n_s$ then, for the given set of the n_j, the dimension d will be minimal, but this is of no real interest because M is unknown and will, in general, involve as many parameters as are saved by this reordering of the n_j. Call $V(n_1, n_2, \ldots, n_s)$ the set of all systems (3) for given n_j. This is mapped in a one-to-one manner onto a set in $d(n_1, n_2, \ldots, n_s)$-dimensional space by the freely varying elements, i.e. it is appropriately co-ordinatized by them. (Of course there is also Σ, whose co-ordinatization is obvious). Of course, the V spaces are nonintersecting for different sets of n_j. Thus we have an essentially unique complete description of all finite-order systems (1). It is an elementary piece of manipulation to show that if $k(z) = \sum_0^\infty K(j)z^{-j}$, $l(z) = \sum_1^\infty L(j)z^{-j}$, then

$$[k(z), l(z)] = C[zI_n - A]^{-1}[B, D] + [I_s, 0], \tag{5}$$

which is clearly rational. Conversely if $k(z)$, $l(z)$ are matrices of rational functions then $n < \infty$. (It should be mentioned that in Hannan and Deistler (1988), $k(z)$, $l(z)$ are defined with z replacing z^{-1}. It is more convenient to use the above definition here.) In this case, where $k(z)$, $l(z)$ are rational, the condition $\det k(z) \neq 0$, $|z| > 1$, is necessary and sufficient in order that the $\varepsilon(t)$ in (1) and (3) should be the linear prediction errors. For conciseness below, we shall assume that $\det k(z) \neq 0$, $|z| \geqslant 1$. This additional restriction seems of no importance, The requirement inherent in (2) that $k(z)$ be analytic for $|z| \geqslant 1$ is of importance and relates to the stationarity requirement discussed above. Of course, (3) is an appropriate formulation even without that stationarity requirement. Indeed a case occurring commonly in econometrics would be that where $k(z)$, $l(z)$ have poles on $|z| = 1$, but are still rational. One may then still achieve (3) and (5), though now A will have eigenvalues on $|z| = 1$. In the stationary ARMA case, for example, when $\mathbf{z}(t)$ does not occur, the spectral density matrix of $\mathbf{y}(t)$ is $(2\pi)^{-1}k(e^{iw})\Sigma k(e^{(w)})^*$ which is thus parameterized by the n_j and the "free" parameters in k, l, Σ. Of course, now also Σ is the prediction error covariance matrix and (3) is the "prediction error state space form." We emphasize again that the structure theory, involving the n_j, has nothing essential to do with stationarity, in this rational transfer function, finite-order case, in particular.

If $s = 1$ then $V(n)$ consists of structures of the form

$$\sum_0^n \alpha(j)\mathbf{y}(t-j) = \sum_1^n \delta(j)\mathbf{z}(t-j) + \sum_0^n \beta(j)\boldsymbol{\varepsilon}(t-j), \quad \alpha(0) = \beta(0) = 1. \tag{6}$$

Then also $k(z) = \Sigma\beta(j)z^{n-j}/\Sigma\alpha(j)z^{n-j}$, $l(z) = \Sigma\delta(j)z^{n-j}/\Sigma\alpha(j)z^{n-j}$ and have the polynomials $a(z) = \Sigma\alpha(j)z^i$, $b(z) = \Sigma\beta(j)z^i$, $d(z) = \Sigma\delta_j z^i$ are relatively prime, i.e. have no common zero. This is because n is the McMillan degree and hence minimal for such a representation. The form (6) is called the ARMAX representation.

One way we can possibly economize on parameters is by further subdividing the $V(n_1, \ldots, n_s)$. For example, for $s = 1$ we could replace the upper limits of summation, n, in (6) by p, q, r (reading from left to right) where now $n = \max(p, q, r)$. Of course, in introducing more model classes we are, in other ways, making the situation more complex. For $s > 1$ the range of possibilities is much greater as we explain further in the fourth section.

An Inferential Principle

It is clearly impossible to construct one set of principles for all statistical problems. For one thing *ad hoc* methods will always be important in relation to very complicated situations. Here we present some ideas of a general nature due to Rissanen (1986, 1989). They seem important both in practice and as a basis for understanding the problems of this paper.

Rissanen's idea is that we are presented with data and models, or model classes. Given a fully specified, probablistic model, the data can be encoded in a manner that, on average, gives a shortest code length. That model is to be preferred that gives the shortest average code length. This is a formal definition of the notion of "reduction of data" which Fisher (1944, p. 1) states as one of the ways of saying what statistics is about. One additional thing must be said about Rissanen's idea, and that is that, subject to general prior understanding, the code must be decodable, for otherwise silly codes, giving one bit as the code for the data, are possible. The prior understanding may involve technical aspects of the encoding, the order in which components are to be sent and so on.

It is impossible here to enter into the details of the costing of the encoding, which are not trivial to explain. Taking the $V(n_1, \ldots, n_s)$ as the model classes we agree to encode the n_j first, then $\boldsymbol{\theta}$ and then the data. Terms in the cost that are independent of the n_j or $\boldsymbol{\theta}$ can be ignored. Thus this is true of the $\mathbf{z}(t)$ which we treat as fixed numbers. To the first order of accuracy we obtain an expression

$$s \log n + \tfrac{1}{2}d(n_1, \ldots, n_s) \log T + (T/2) \log \det \hat{\Sigma}(n_1, \ldots, n_s), \tag{7}$$

where the first term is the cost of encoding the n_j, the next of encoding the vector $\hat{\theta}$, and the last the cost of encoding the data using the model $\hat{\theta}$, which is the maximum likelihood estimator given the n_j. In fact, log might be $\log_2$, but that is an irrelevant change. The expression (7) has been obtained on the basis of a fictitious likelihood obtained by treating the $\boldsymbol{\varepsilon}(t)$ as Gaussian. $\hat{\Sigma}$ is the maximum likelihood, ML, estimator of Σ. Of course $\mathbf{y}(t)$ must be quantized and truncated at some maximum value so $P(\mathbf{y} \mid \boldsymbol{\theta}, \mathbf{z})$ is a discrete density so that (7) involves an approximation using a Gaussian likelihood and a suitable fine quantization and suitably large truncation point. Also $\boldsymbol{\theta}$ has been quantized. Generally the first term is insignificant compared to the other two. If it is omitted and we multiply by $2T^{-1}$, then what is usually called BIC is obtained, namely

$$\log\det\hat{\Sigma}(n_1,\ldots,n_s)+\frac{d(n_1,\ldots,n_s)\log T}{T}. \tag{8}$$

Nevertheless, (7) gives us a way of thinking about the problem discussed in the last section, where a finer and finer subdivision of the $V(n_1,\ldots,n_s)$ might be considered, for as this is done the first term will rise and the second fall. For example, changing from (6) to the case where the upper limits are p, q, r with $n=\max(p,q,r)$ increases the first term in (7) from $\log n$ to about $3\log n$, but the second term declines to $\frac{1}{2}(p+q+r)\log T$, from $(3n/2)\log T$. In relation to this, it should be said that a sensible algorithm would determine n first and then, given n, examine $p, q, r\leqslant n$, $\max(p,q,r)=n$. Also Pötscher (1990) has shown the following, for $s=1$ when $\mathbf{z}(t)$ does not occur, i.e. the ARMA case. Then in examining BIC when the data are generated by an ARMA process, the algorithm can be stopped at the first *relative* minimum, $\hat{n}$, and asymptotically that will be consistent. If p, q, $\max(p,q)=\hat{n}$ are then to be examined, the criterion $2\log\hat{n}+\log[\min(p_0q_0)]+[(p+q)/2]\log T+(T/2)\log\hat{\sigma}^2_{p,q}$ should be used. It may be that then the last term is only slightly increased, for some $p\neq q$, while a fall in the first two terms, relative to $\log\hat{n}+\hat{n}\log T$, will outweigh the rise in the prediction variance term and $p\neq q$ will be preferred. Of course, in most considerations the first term in (7) has been ignored in the past.

The MDL (minimum description length) criterion, (7), could be replaced by one in which a prior is introduced for $\boldsymbol{\theta}$ and the last term becomes $-\log[\pi(\boldsymbol{\theta})P(\mathbf{y}\mid\boldsymbol{\theta},\mathbf{z})]$ where $\pi(\boldsymbol{\theta})$ is the prior and $P(\mathbf{y}\mid\boldsymbol{\theta},\mathbf{z})$ is the density for $\mathbf{y}(t)$. Since $\pi(\hat{\boldsymbol{\theta}})P(\mathbf{y}\mid\hat{\boldsymbol{\theta}},\mathbf{z})\leqslant\Sigma\pi(\boldsymbol{\theta})P(\mathbf{y}\mid\boldsymbol{\theta},\mathbf{z})$, Rissanen proposes to replace (7) by the "stochastic complexity,"

$$-\log\sum_{n_1\ldots n_s}\sum\int P(\mathbf{y}\mid\boldsymbol{\theta},\mathbf{z})\pi(n_1,\ldots,n_s;\boldsymbol{\theta})\,d\boldsymbol{\theta}. \tag{9}$$

The problem of choosing a suitable prior then arises. We cannot discuss all of this further here.

An alternative to Rissanen's ideas is proposed by Akaike (1969, 1977). See also Findley (1985). Akaike's method is directed at the minimization of $-E_0\{\log[P(\mathbf{y})/\boldsymbol{\theta}_j]\}$ over model classes specified by the $\boldsymbol{\theta}_j$. Here E_0 denotes an expectation using the true distribution. If $\hat{\boldsymbol{\theta}}_j$ is the ML estimator for the jth model class we might use $-\log P(\mathbf{y}/\hat{\boldsymbol{\theta}}_j)$ to estimate the minimum of $-E_0\{\log[P(\mathbf{y})/\boldsymbol{\theta}_j]\}$ over the jth class. Akaike's formula, AIC, is based on a first-order correction to the bias in this estimate, ignoring bias terms independent of j. The general formula is of the form, in our Gaussian context, so as to compare with (7), and ignoring second-order terms,

$$T/2\log\det\hat{\Sigma}(n_1,\ldots,n_s)+d(n_1,\ldots,n_s). \tag{10}$$

Akaike's procedure never chooses fewer parameters than Rissanen's.

One problem with both of these procedures is that of putting into the prescription of the model classes all of the, in some cases half thought out, understanding the investigator may have, including understanding about final objectives. (It is also difficult to prescribe a probability law for a stochastic process, which means that the Gaussian case is commonly forced upon us.) The failure to spell all of this out may lead to a tendency to too few parameters being chosen, as minor features may be ignored unless there is special emphasis. However, this does not relate to the present context, where too many parameters tends to be the problem.

In the next section a procedure due to Tiao and Tsay (1989), closely related to the use of $V(n_1, \ldots, n_s)$, will be discussed.

Subdivision of the $V(n_1, \ldots, n_s)$ Spaces

We may put (see (5)), for given n_j,

$$[kz, lz] = a(z)^{-1}[b(z), d(z)],$$
$$a(z) = \Sigma A(j)z^j, \quad b(z) = \Sigma B(j)z^j, \quad d(z) = \Sigma D(j)^{zj}. \tag{11}$$

As has been said earlier it is $k(z^{-1})$, $l(z^{-1})$ which, when represented in a new form (1), with the factors still matrices of polynomials, give rise to an ARMAX representation. However, $k(z)$, $l(z)$, as now defined, are easier to discuss. In fact $a(z)$, $b(z) - a(z)$, and $d(z)$ are most easily described. The diagonal elements of $a(z)$ are of degree n_j and have the coefficient of the highest power of z as unity. Also, for all i, j,

$$\text{degree}[b_{ij}(z) - a_{ij}(z)] = \text{degree } d_{ij}(z) = n_i - 1$$
$$\text{degree } a_{ij}(z) \leqslant n_i, j \leqslant i, \text{degree } a_{ij}(z) < n_i, j > i \tag{12}$$
$$\text{degree } a_{ij}(z) < n_j, i \neq j.$$

The number $d(n_1, \ldots, n_s)$ can be calculated from these formulas. The n_i thus determine the row degrees and the number of "free" parameters, i.e. those not identically 0 or 1. They are not analogous to p, q, r for $s = 1$ but to n, of course, which is the only n_j for $s = 1$. Thus, as with $s = 1$, it would be possible to consider further restrictions than those posed by (12), in other words to subdivide the $V(n_1, \ldots, n_s)$ spaces. A suitable such subdivision would involve zero restrictions on the *low*-degree terms in $a(z)$, $b(z)$, $d(z)$ (since these become the high degree terms when $k(z^{-1})$, $l(z^{-1})$ are considered. (See below (6).) Of course, the restrictions could even be by individual elements and not necessarily row-wise. The final choice would be made by the analogue of (7). The procedure would be computationally troublesome.

An alternative procedure related to this is proposed by Tiao and Tsay (1989). This also seems computationally troublesome and, instead of using a procedure, like (7), depends on hypothesis-testing methods related to canonical correlation procedures. (See below (16) for a little more detail concerning these.) Tiao and Tsay (1989) begin from an ARMA model in the form

$$\sum_0^p A(j)\mathbf{y}(t-j) = \sum_0^q B(j)\boldsymbol{\varepsilon}(t-j), \quad A(0) = B(0) = I_s. \tag{13}$$

There are problems with this set-up for $s > 1$ since, without further requirements, there will be many models, even for the same p, q, giving the same transfer function from $\boldsymbol{\varepsilon}(t)$ to $\mathbf{y}(t)$. The points where this lack of uniqueness holds will constitute lower dimensional submanifolds in the full parameter space, and it will be very unlikely that the maximum of the likelihood will lie in one of these submanifolds. However, it is quite likely that it will be very near one of them and when that is so, problems of numerical stability may arise for iterative estimation algorithms. In any case, neglecting this problem, the idea is to reduce the parameter numbers below $(p + q)s^2$ by replacing $\mathbf{y}(t)$ by $\boldsymbol{\eta}(t) = M\mathbf{y}(t)$, where M is chosen so as to reduce (13) to a form where $\boldsymbol{\eta}_i(t)$ is expressed only in terms of $\mathbf{y}(t-j), j \leqslant p_i$, $\boldsymbol{\varepsilon}(t-j), j \leqslant q_i$, $i = 1, \ldots, s$, where p_i, q_i are as small as possible. The technique used to discover such relations is to regress the vector $\mathbf{y}_m(t) = (\mathbf{y}(t-1)', \ldots, \mathbf{y}(t-m)')'$ on $\mathbf{y}_k(t-l)$ for various m, k, l and to seek for "null"vectors by the standard canonical correlation procedure, i.e. vectors for which the canonical correlations are near zero. Unless $k \geqslant m$, there will be zero canonical correlations. Tiao and Tsay (1989) in their examples use $k = m$. If a "null" vector is found for a given m, l, then we may use this to define an $\boldsymbol{\eta}_i(t)$ for $m = p_i$, $l = q_1 + 1$. We do not go into further details concerning the final choice of $\boldsymbol{\eta}(t)$, which involves searching over a table of m, l values in particular.

Subjective elements enter into the procedure. It does not lead to an efficient estimation method, though it would be a first step in such a method. It is elaborate. It seems, in a not fully effective way, to be trying to obtain something like the Kronecker indices, but perhaps also a little more.

It is a fact that multivariate ARMAX models have been little used, because of their complexity, the multiplication of parameter numbers they lead to, and the large computational problem. In the next section we discuss an alternative method.

Model Order Reduction

There is a large literature surrounding the ideas to be briefly discussed here. Some references are Aoki (1987), Glover (1984), and Wahlberg (1987). To make things more concrete let us begin from an ARX model

$$\sum_{0}^{p} A(j)\mathbf{y}(t-j) = \sum_{0}^{p} D(j)\mathbf{z}(t-j) + \boldsymbol{\varepsilon}(t), \qquad A(0) = I_s. \tag{14}$$

This is easy to fit because the procedure is basically a regression, and indeed is susceptible to recursive procedures (the Levinson, Whittle type algorithms) on p, which itself can be chosen via a formula of the type of (7). However, the number of parameters is $2ps^2$ (apart from those in Σ), which can be very large unless s is 2 or 3 at most. An optimal fit will nevertheless have been found, in terms of (7). Of course, the fitting procedure is essentially a prediction error method, and any approximation to the fitted model must increase the estimated prediction error as measured by $\hat{\Sigma}_p$. Even then, one must be careful because the relevant prediction is outside of the observation range and some features of the variation of the data over the observation range may be impermanent so that the sacrifice of the description of them will cost nothing for real prediction. For purposes of understanding, one might seek to replace the fitted model by some approximant. Many techniques might be used. For example, viewing (14) as a model wherein $\mathbf{y}(t)$ is regressed on $\mathbf{y}(t-j)$, $\mathbf{z}(t-j)$, $j = 1, \ldots, p$, one might effect a canonical correlation analysis, seeking to retain only the components in a singular value decomposition for the matrix of regression coefficients that are of not too small a magnitude.

A second procedure is to approximate to (14) by an ARMAX structure of much lower order than the order, ps, of (14). There are various ways you might do this but we discuss only one of these here. It also involves the singular value decomposition, but of the Hankel matrix. The method need not commence from an ARX model. There seems to have been no comparison, in that context, with the first approximation procedure mentioned above.

The structure (14) can be put in state space form (3), for example with

$$A = \begin{bmatrix} 0 & I_s & \cdots & 0 & 0 \\ \vdots & \vdots & \cdots & \vdots & \vdots \\ 0 & 0 & \cdots & 0 & I_s \\ -A(p) & -A(p-1) & \cdots & -A(2) & -A(1) \end{bmatrix}, \quad D = \begin{bmatrix} L(1) \\ \vdots \\ L(p) \end{bmatrix}, \quad B = \begin{bmatrix} K(1) \\ \vdots \\ K(p) \end{bmatrix}$$

$$\mathbf{C} = [I_s, 0 \ldots 0]. \tag{15}$$

Here also $k(z) = (\Sigma A(j)z^{-j})^{-1}$, $l(z) = k(z)\sum_1^p D(j)z^{-j}$. The $k(z)$, $l(z)$ also define the Hankel matrix. One procedure is to construct a new state space representation, of lower order, by constructing an approximating Hankel matrix to the Hankel matrix $\mathscr{H}$ for (15). This may be done via a singular value decomposition for $\mathscr{H}$. (See Hannan (1987), for some discussion and references.) A more direct procedure is as follows, which we present only for the AR case, where $Z(t)$ is not present. (We do this since a reasonable procedure for the ARX case will be very complicated because of the possibly complicated nature of the autocovariance structure of the $Z(t)$.) The matrices $P = \sum_0^\infty A^j B\Sigma B'(A')^j$, and $Q = \sum_0^\infty (A')^j \mathbf{C}'\mathbf{C}A^j$ are called the reachability and observability Gramians. $P = E\{x(t)x(t)'\}$. They satisfy $APA' + B\Sigma B' = P$, and $A'QA + C'C = Q$, which may be used to calculate them, since these are linear equations for P, Q. (See Wahlberg (1987), for other computational references.) Now construct M as follows. Cholesky factorize Q as $R'R$ and put $RPR' = U'\Lambda^2 U$ where U is orthogonal and Λ is diagonal with $\lambda_1 \geqslant \lambda_2 \geqslant \cdots \geqslant \lambda_n$, $n = ps$, down the main diagonal. The λ_i are the singular values of $\mathscr{H}$. Transform the state space representations corresponding to (15), using $M = \Lambda^{-1}U'R$, so that $\tilde{\mathbf{x}}(t) = M\mathbf{x}(t)$, $\tilde{A} = MAM^{-1}$, $\tilde{B} = MB$, $\tilde{C} = \mathbf{C}M^{-1}$. Of course k is then unchanged.

Then $\tilde{\mathbf{x}}(t+1) = \tilde{A}\tilde{\mathbf{x}}(t) + \tilde{B}\boldsymbol{\varepsilon}(t)$, $\mathbf{y}(t) = \tilde{C}\tilde{\mathbf{x}}(t) + \boldsymbol{\varepsilon}(t)$. The approximation procedure consists of omitting those rows of $\tilde{\mathbf{x}}(t)$, $\tilde{A}$, $\tilde{B}$, and columns of $\tilde{A}$, $\tilde{C}$ for which the corresponding λ_i are small. Of course, the λ_i are the variances of the components of $\tilde{\mathbf{x}}(t)$ so that we are omitting state variables with smaller variance from the model, which seems reasonable. If $\tilde{k}$ is the resulting transfer function then $\|k - \tilde{k}\|_\infty \leqslant 2\sum_{k+1}^n \lambda_i$, where λ_k is the last λ_i retained. Here $\|f(z)\|_\infty$ is, for any $f(z)$, the supremum over ω of the maximum singular value of $f(e^{i\omega})$. Thus one may achieve an order reduction by a method for which the magnitude of the approximation to k is controlled.

One problem is that the singular value decomposition of $\mathscr{H}$ may not be fully relevant because the appropriate metric in the space to which $\mathscr{H}$ operates may not have been used. This is discussed in Wahlberg (1987) under the heading of "frequency weighted balanced reduction." The term "balanced truncation" is also used, the word "balance" coming from the reduction of P, Q to the same form. In the ARMA case, where $\mathbf{z}(t)$ does not occur, we have, from (1),

$$\mathbf{y}^{(t+1)} = \mathscr{H}\xi_t + \mathscr{K}\boldsymbol{\varepsilon}^{(t+1)}, \tag{16}$$

where ξ_t was defined above (3) and $\mathbf{y}^{(t)} = (\mathbf{y}(t)', y(t+1)', \ldots)'$, and similarly $\boldsymbol{\varepsilon}^{(t)}$, while $\mathscr{K} = [K(i-j)]$, the (i, j)th block being shown with $K(l) = 0, l < 0$. The relation (16) shows the metric that is appropriate in this case, since an appropriate singular value decomposition will be that corresponding to the canonical correlation analysis for the regression relation (16). Indeed, (16) shows one reason why the Hankel matrix is important, for it transfers the influence of the present and past to the future. One can see what the metric might be by considering the classical multivariate regression problem $Y = XB + E$, where Y is $T \times p$, X is $T \times q$ and B is $q \times p$. To reduce $\hat{B}$ to a diagonal form we consider $\det[\mu Y'Y - Y'X(XX')^{-1}X'Y]$ and choose the μ and the corresponding vectors for which this determinant is zero. These μ values are the canonical correlations. Equivalently, we are considering

$$\{\mu I_p - [(Y'Y)^{-1/2}\hat{B}'(X'X)^{1/2}][(Y'Y)^{-1/2}\hat{B}'(X'X)^{1/2}]^{-1}\}, \quad \hat{B} = (X'X)^{-1}(X'Y),$$

and the relevant metrics are those defined by $Y'Y$ and $X'X$. For some further information concerning this, the reader may consult Hannan (1987) and references therein.

This model reduction procedure will lead to an ARMA model replacing an AR, for example, and one may ask why an ARMA model is not fitted in the first place, since the method just described will not be optimal in the case where there is a true ARMA model. The answer is that there is no true ARMA model, that fitting an ARMA model using (7) may lead to confusingly many parameters and that the method described is designed to sacrifice some "fit" in a controlled way, so as to retain only main features of the data as measured by the λ_j. However, it must be said that the discussion in the preceding paragraph, below (16), is relevant. Unfortunately, a more detailed discussion cannot be given here.

Variate Transformations to Reduce Order in an ARX

As we have already said, (14) avoids the complexities and potential instabilities of a vector ARMAX estimation procedure. Here we discuss a further procedure by which we may seek to reduce the parameter numbers in (14). The discussion will be presented in terms of the AR model

$$\sum_0^p A(j)\mathbf{y}(t-j) = \boldsymbol{\varepsilon}(t), \tag{17}$$

but the ARX case may be included by replacing $\mathbf{y}(t)$ in (17) by $(\mathbf{y}(t), \mathbf{z}(t)')'$, with $\mathbf{z}(0) = 0$. The idea, due to Wahlberg (Wahlberg and Hannan 1992) is to replace $\mathbf{y}(t-j)$ in (17) by a filtered form, $\mathbf{u}_j(t)$, of $\mathbf{y}(t)$, the filters being chosen to reduce p, it is hoped.

In the following, we present formulas as if all calculations are done in Toeplitz fashion, i.e. as if $\mathbf{y}(t)$ is part of an infinite sequence that happens to be zero for $t \leqslant 0$ or $t > T$. This fiction means that Toeplitz calculations have bad effects, but these can be reduced by using a taper as in Dahlhaus (1983).

Consider the case where $\mathbf{y}(t)$ is ARMA so that $k(z) = a(z)^{-1}b(z)$. Of course, we could then fit an ARMA model. We use these here only to motivate the method to be used. The order, p, necessary for a good approximation will be determined by the nearness of zeros of det $k(z)$ to the unit circle. If they can be moved well away, then a moderate value of p may suffice. The transformation $w = (z - a)/(1 - az)$, $|a| < 1$ maps the unit disk onto itself and the unit circle onto itself. The constant, a, is available to adjust the transformation for a particular case. On this basis it is suggested, remembering that z^{-1} is also the backwards shift, that

$$\mathbf{u}_j(t) = \frac{K}{z - a}\left(\frac{1 - az}{z - a}\right)^{j-1} \mathbf{y}(t); \quad K = (1 - a^2)^{1/2}, \qquad |a| < 1, j \geqslant 1 \tag{18}$$

be formed and the regression

$$\sum_0^p G_j \mathbf{u}_j(t) = \mathbf{e}(t), \quad E\{\mathbf{e}(s)\mathbf{e}(t)'\} = \delta_{st}\Omega, \qquad \Omega > 0, \tag{19}$$

be substituted for (17). Here $\mathbf{u}_0(t) = \mathbf{y}(t)$. The factor $K(z - a)^{-1}$ occurs in (18) because its squared modulus is the Jacobian of the transformation from $e^{i\omega}$ to $e^{i\upsilon} = (e^{i\omega} - a)/(1 - a\,e^{i\omega})$. The Levinson–Whittle algorithm, which allows (19) to be calculated recursively on p, still obtains (see Wahlberg and Hannan (1992), for the algorithm for this case). Thus

$$\frac{1}{T}\sum_t \mathbf{u}_j(t)\mathbf{u}_k(t)' = c_{k-j}, \qquad k, j \geqslant 1 \tag{20}$$

where the summation is over all t, in the left-hand term.

The determination of a is effected so as to minimize the calculated error mean square, $\hat{\sigma}_p^2$ let us say, and $\hat{p}$ is determined so as to minimize $\log \hat{\sigma}_p^2 + (p + 1) \log T/T$, $p \leqslant P$. A Gauss–Newton iteration to calculate $\hat{a}$ is described in Wahlberg and Hannan.

Adaptive Estimation

It is very likely that a substantial reduction in parameter numbers could be achieved by using a nonlinear model. For some references see Franke et al. (1984). This topic is too large to be discussed here. The episodic nature of some nonlinear phenomena also abound. The topic briefly treated in this last section attempts to deal with this. It is not quite a procedure for reducing parameter numbers, but rather one whereby a small number of parameters will be used locally in time to replace the use of a very elaborate model for the whole observed time period. Of course, the methods have initially been developed as an on-line procedure and, in the electrical engineering literature from which many of the ideas come, real-time calculations are important.

Many very fine algorithms, e.g. lattice calculations, have been developed for this last purpose. They would rarely be significant in an econometric context. Extensive discussions of the methods are given in Ljung and Söderström (1983), and Young (1984). It is surprising that little use seems to have been made of the method in economics. We shall present the techniques for the scalar case without input, $\mathbf{z}(t)$, but these restrictions are not essential. Also adaptive AR procedures, only, will be discussed, though ARMA models have been treated, but perhaps rarely used. One way to approach the problem is to consider the model

$$\sum_{0}^{p_t} \alpha_{p,t}(j)\mathbf{y}(t-j) = \boldsymbol{\varepsilon}(t), \quad E\{\boldsymbol{\varepsilon}(s)\boldsymbol{\varepsilon}(t)\} = \delta_{st}\sigma_t^2, \tag{21}$$

where now the model is evolving with time. As a result not all of the data back to time $t = 1$ should be used. One procedure is to choose the $\hat{\alpha}_{p,t}(j)$ to minimize

$$\sum_{s=1}^{t} \lambda_t(s)\left[\sum_{0}^{p} \alpha_{p,t}(j)\mathbf{y}(s-j)\right] \tag{22}$$

subject to initial values being given for $s - j < 0$. The $\lambda_t(s)$, called forgetting factors, are chosen to be of the form

$$\lambda_t(s) = a_s \prod_{s+1}^{t} \lambda(u), \quad \lambda_t(t) = a_t, \tag{23}$$

The a_t enable $\lambda_t(s)$ to be tailored to give a more desirable shape. If $\lambda(u) \equiv \lambda$, $0 < \lambda < 1$, then the forgetting is exponential. The calculations may be effected in an iterative fashion. Thus if $\boldsymbol{\theta}_t$ is the vector of $\hat{\alpha}_{p,t}(j)$, then

$$\boldsymbol{\theta}_t = \boldsymbol{\theta}_{t-1} + a_t P_t \mathbf{x}(t)e(t), \quad \mathbf{e}_p(t) = \mathbf{y}(t) - \boldsymbol{\theta}_{t-1}'\mathbf{x}(t) \tag{24}$$

where $\mathbf{x}(t)' = (\mathbf{y}(t-1), \mathbf{y}(t-2), \ldots, \mathbf{y}(t-p))$ and

$$P_t = \lambda(t)^{-1}\{P_{t-1} - [\lambda(t)a_t^{-1} + \mathbf{x}(t)'P_{t-1}\mathbf{x}(t)]^{-1}P_{t-1}\mathbf{x}(t)\mathbf{x}(t)'P_{t-1}\}. \tag{25}$$

The remaining matter needing discussion is the choice of p_t as a function of t. Let $\hat{\sigma}_t^2(p)$ be the estimate of the residual mean square at time t. Let $\mathbf{e}_p(t)$ be the "honest" prediction error defined in (24). (It is "honest" because the predictor depends only on data to time $t - 1$). Then a modification of the procedure in the third section, due to Rissanen (1986), leads to the use of a criterion

$$\frac{1}{t}\sum_{s=1}^{t-1} [\log \hat{\sigma}_p^2(s) + \mathbf{e}_p(s+1)^2/\hat{\sigma}_p^2(s)] \tag{26}$$

for the case of no forgetting and a fixed true model structure. However, with forgetting, this does not perform well (Hannan et al. 1989). An alternative is to use

$$\log \hat{\sigma}_p^2(t) + p[\log f(t)]/f(t);$$

$$\hat{\sigma}_p^2(t) = f(t)^{-1}\Sigma\lambda_t(s)\hat{\boldsymbol{\varepsilon}}_{p,t}(s)^2, \quad \hat{\boldsymbol{\varepsilon}}_{p,t}(s) = \sum_0^p \hat{\alpha}_{p,t}(j)\mathbf{y}(s-j).$$

$$f(t) = \sum_1^t \lambda_t(s) = \lambda(t)f(t-1) + a_t, \quad f(0) = 0. \tag{27}$$

The quantity $f(t)$ is a measure of the amount of data used to time t. Of course, p_t is chosen to minimize (27). Reasonably efficient calculations for these algorithms are discussed in Hannan et al. (1989).

In principle, these procedures could be elaborated to deal with the complex structure of the second section. However, it is most likely that these would be used in an adaptive context. One would expect the p_t values to be small so that few parameters are involved. They are changing but may change slowly. The methods are essentially prediction error methods and are suitable for short-term prediction procedures. They are far from being structural.

Conclusion

This has been a very brief survey of a very large topic, designed to provide broad information, and some references, for the reader. Not all of the procedures will ultimately prove to be useful. However, some of them surely will. It seems to this author that such surveys, perhaps better written than this one, are needed, so great is the scope now, even of our little part of science. A sympathetic understanding is needed from the reader, as well as an open and enquiring mind, for detail has to be limited and the discussion brief. This discussion is also theoretical and there is a distaste abroad for theory, the circle having turned through 180° over 20 years or so. (Perhaps a 90° turn was needed.) A more extensive and effective survey would also present a great deal of data analysis.

References

Akaike, H. (1969). "Fitting autoregressive models for prediction," *Annals of the Institute of Statistical Mathematics*, 21, 243–47.

Akaike, H. (1977). "On entropy maximisation principle," in P. Krishnaiah (ed.) *Applications of Statistics*, pp. 27–41. Amsterdam, North-Holland.

Aoki, M. (1987). *State Space Modelling of Time Series*. New York: Springer-Verlag.

Dahlhaus, R. (1983). "Spectral analysis with tapered data," *Journal of Time Series Analysis*, 4, 163–76.

Findley, D. F. (1985). "On the unbiasedness property of AIC for exact or approximating linear stochastic time series models," *Journal of Time Series Analysis*, 6, 229–52.

Fisher, R. A. (1944). *Statistical Methods for Research Workers* (10th edn). Edinburgh, Oliver and Boyd.

Franke, J., W. Härdle, and D. Martin (1984) *Robust and Non-Linear Time Series Analysis*. New York: Springer-Verlag.

Glover, K. (1984). "All optimal Hankel-norm approximations of linear multivariable systems and their L^∞-error bounds," *International Journal of Control*, 39, 1115–93.

Hannan, E. J. (1987). "Rational transfer function approximation," *Statistical Science*, 2, 135–61.

Hannan, E. J., and M. Deistler (1988). *Statistical Theory of Linear Systems*. New York: Wiley.

Hannan, E. J., A. McDougall, and D. S. Poskitt (1989). "Recursive estimation of autoregression," *Journal of the Royal Statistical Society*, B, 51, 217–34.

Ljung, L., and T. Söderström (1983). *Theory and Practice of Recursive Identification*. Cambridge, Massachusetts: MIT Press.

Pötscher, B. (1990). "Estimation of autoregressive moving average order given an infinite number of models and approximation of spectral densities," *Journal of Time Series Analysis*, 11, 165–79.

Rissanen, J. (1986). "Stochastic complexity and modelling," *Annals of Statistics*, 14, 1080–100.

Rissanen, J. (1989). *Stochastic Complexity in Statistical Inquiry*. New Jersey: World Scientific.

Tiao, G. C., and R. S. Tsay (1989). "Model specification in multivariable time series," *Journal of the Royal Statistical Society*, 51, 157–214.

Wahlberg, B. (1987). *On the Identification and Approximation of Linear Systems*. Linköping: Department of Electrical Engineering, Linköping University.

Wahlberg, B., and E. J. Hannan (1992). "Parametric signal modelling using Laguerre filters," *Annals of Applied Probability*, forthcoming.

Young, P. C. (1984). *Recursive Estimation and Time Series Analysis*. New York: Springer-Verlag.

17

Semiparametric Efficiency Bounds for Linear Time-Series Models

Lars P. Hansen

Introduction

In this paper, we deduce a semiparametric efficiency bound for a class of linear time-series models that imply multiperiod conditional moment restrictions. Models in this class are commonly encountered in macroeconomics and finance. The conditional moment restrictions are parametrized by a finite-dimensional vector, and this vector is the focal point of the estimation problem. Knowledge of this parameter vector does not, however, determine uniquely the entire stochastic law of motion for the time series. To remain flexible on the remaining peripheral aspects of the law of motion, we admit a rich array of parameterizations, each of which reflects a different form of prior information. Following Stein (1956), a semiparametric efficiency bound is the *supremum* of the asymptotic covariance matrices of the parameters of interest taken over the rich array of alternative parameterizations of the entire model. The class of admissible parameterizations turns out to be infinite-dimensional, which explains the term *semiparametric*. In this paper, we assume that the underlying stochastic process is stationary and normally distributed, but we impose only very weak restrictions on the temporal dependence beyond the conditional moment restrictions.

This paper has several important antecedents. The basic approach is due to Stein (1956). Levit (1975) deduced the efficiency bound implied by a finite number of unconditional moment restrictions, and Chamberlain (1987) deduced the efficiency bound implied by a finite number of conditional moment restrictions. Both Levit and Chamberlain conducted their analysis assuming the data are generated from an independent and identically distributed process. In both cases method-of-moments type estimators either attain or approximate the efficiency bound. On a related vein, Stoica et al. (1985) showed that the efficiency bound for instrumental variables estimators of autoregressive parameters in finite-parameter ARMA models is equal to the asymptotic covariance matrix of the maximum likelihood estimator of these same parameters. Finally, Hansen (1985) suggested a general martingale approximation method for deducing efficiency bounds for classes of generalized method-of-moments estimators for dependent data generating processes that are stationary.

The main result in this paper is that the semiparametric efficiency bound for finite-parameter maximum likelihood estimators coincides with the generalized method-of-moments efficiency bound reported in Hansen (1985). This establishes a certain type of duality that extends aspects of the analysis in Levit (1975) and Chamberlain (1987) to dependent processes. It also gives an alternative interpretation of the efficiency bound calculations suggested in Hansen (1985).

This paper is organized as follows. The second through fifth sections specify the estimation problem under investigation. Convenient mathematical constructs are introduced, the underlying probability model is presented and alternative finite-dimensional parameterizations are described. In the sixth section we define the semiparametric efficiency bound for our estimation problem and show how to compute it using regression methods. More precisely, the vectors of likelihood scores for the parameters of interest are regressed onto the rich array of *possible* likelihood scores for the peripheral features of the model. The space of potential regression errors is characterized and interpreted in the seventh section. We then use this characterization in the eighth section to establish that the semiparametric efficiency bound is identical to the generalized method-of-moments efficiency bound.

Mathematical Preliminaries

Throughout this paper, we use lag operators that map the space of covariance stationary stochastic processes into itself. As is often the case, transform methods are valuable for characterizing and restricting admissible classes of lag operators. Transforms of lag operators are functions with power series expansions that converge inside the unit circle of the complex plane. In this section, we construct alternative normed linear spaces of transforms and describe properties of these spaces.

First we introduce some notation. Define $\mathscr{U} \equiv \{\zeta \in \mathbb{C}: |\zeta| < 1\}$ and $\mathscr{U}^c \equiv \{\zeta \in \mathbb{C}: |\zeta| \leqslant 1\}$. Let $\mathscr{A}^2$ be the space of analytic functions with power series expansions on $\mathscr{U}$ that have square summable real coefficients, and $\mathscr{M}^2$ be the space of $(n \times n)$ matrices of functions in $\mathscr{A}^2$. It follows from the maximum modulus principle that the maximum modulus of an analytic function occurs at the boundary of a domain, for example see Saks and Zygmund (1971, p. 163). If the domain is $\{\zeta \in \mathbb{C}: |\zeta| \leqslant \delta\}$ for δ in (0, 1), then the maximum modulus occurs on the circle $\{\zeta \in \mathbb{C}: |\zeta| = \delta\}$. With this in mind, for $m = [m_{jk}]$ we define

$$\|m_{jk}\|_\infty \equiv \lim_{\delta \to 1} \max_{|\zeta| = \delta} |m_{jk}(\zeta)|. \tag{1}$$

and, abusing notation slightly,

$$\|m\|_\infty \equiv \max \{ \|m_{jk}\|_\infty : j, k = 1, 2, \ldots, n\}. \tag{2}$$

The limit on the right-hand side of (1) is always well defined because the maximum is monotone in δ, although this limit may be infinite. We let $\mathscr{M}^\infty$ be the subspace of $\mathscr{M}^2$ containing functions for which $\|m\|_\infty$ is finite. Note that $\| \ \|_\infty$ defines a norm on $\mathscr{M}^\infty$.

We consider, in turn, three successively smaller subspaces of $\mathscr{M}^\infty$, each of which will be used to restrict families of admissible lag operators. Let $\mathscr{M}^c$ denote the subspace of $\mathcal{M}^\infty$ consisting of all matrix functions that are continuous on $\mathcal{U}^c$. For m in $\mathcal{M}^c$,

$$\|m_{jk}\|_\infty = \max_{|\zeta|=1} |m_{jk}(\zeta)|. \tag{3}$$

Recall that functions in $\mathcal{A}^2$ have derivatives with convergent power series expansions on $\mathcal{U}$. For a matrix m in $\mathcal{M}^2$, let m' denote the corresponding matrix of derivatives. Define $\mathcal{S}^2 \equiv \{m \in \mathcal{M}^c : m' \in \mathcal{M}^2\}$ and $\mathcal{S}^\infty \equiv \{m \in \mathcal{S}^2 : m' \in \mathcal{M}^\infty\}$.

Any member m of $\mathcal{M}^c$ can be used to construct a lag operator on the space of n-dimensional covariance stationary stochastic processes. Let the power series expansion for m be denoted

$$m(\zeta) = \sum_{j=0}^{\infty} \mu_j(\zeta)^j, \tag{4}$$

and let $\{\mathbf{y}_t\}$ be an n-dimensional covariance stationary process. Then

$$m(L)\mathbf{y}_t \equiv \sum_{j=0}^{\infty} \mu_j \mathbf{y}_{t-j} \tag{5}$$

is a well-defined mean-square limit of Cesaro sums, and the resulting stochastic process $\{m(L)\mathbf{y}_t\}$ is covariance stationary.

In some of our analysis, we will restrict the admissible lag operators to be invertible. Let $\mathcal{N}^c$ be the subset of matrix functions in $\mathcal{M}^c$ that are nonsingular on the entire domain $\mathcal{U}^c$. For any element m of $\mathcal{N}^c$, $(m)^{-1}$ is also in $\mathcal{N}^c$. In such circumstances, the corresponding lag operator $m(L)$ has a one-sided inverse on the space of n-dimensional covariance stationary stochastic processes.

One-dimensional Parameterizations of the Probability Model

In this section, we describe a probability model for a vector time series $\{\mathbf{y}_t\}$. The model is specified with sufficient generality to accommodate the estimation problem considered in the remaining sections of this paper. We then introduce one-dimensional parameterizations of this probability model and investigate properties of the maximum likelihood estimator of the scalar parameter. Most importantly, we give a characterization of the scalar stationary process of scores that approximate the scores of the likelihood function. Although in this section we focus exclusively on one-dimensional parameterizations, later we show how to construct higher-dimensional parameterizations from a vector of one-dimensional parameterizations.

The underlying probability model for $\{\mathbf{y}_t\}$ is given by:

$$a_0(L)\mathbf{y}_t = b_0(L)\mathbf{w}_t + \mathbf{c}_0 \tag{6}$$

subject to the following two restrictions.

1. Assumption 1: $a_0 \in \mathcal{N}^c$, $b_0 \in \mathcal{N}^c$ and $\mathbf{c}_0 \in \mathbb{R}^n$.

2. Assumption 2: $\{\mathbf{w}_t\}$ is an n-dimensional Gaussian white noise with covariance matrix I.

Among other things, assumption 1 guarantees that the operators $a_0(L)$ and $b_0(L)$ have one-sided inverses. Hence $\{\mathbf{y}_t\}$ can be expressed in terms of $\{\mathbf{w}_t\}$ and conversely:

$$\mathbf{w}_t = b_0(L)^{-1}a_0(L)\mathbf{y}_t - b_0(1)^{-1}\mathbf{c}_0 \tag{7}$$

$$\mathbf{y}_t = a_0(L)^{-1}b_0(L)\mathbf{w}_t + a_0(1)^{-1}\mathbf{c}_0. \tag{8}$$

In light of moving-average representation (8) and assumption 2, $\{\mathbf{y}_t\}$ is a stationary Gaussian process. In the concluding section, we discuss extensions to the case in which $\{\mathbf{w}_t\}$ is a conditionally homoskedastic sequence of martingale differences.

We find it convenient to characterize the stochastic process $\{\mathbf{y}_t\}$ in terms of the triple $(a_0, b_0, \mathbf{c}_0)$. Let $\mathscr{T}$ be the product space $\mathscr{M}^c \times \mathscr{M}^c \times \mathbb{R}^n$. An implication of assumption 1, is that $(a_0, b_0, \mathbf{c}_0)$ is in $\mathscr{T}$. We construct a norm on $\mathscr{T}$ as follows:

$$\|(a, b, \mathbf{c})\| = \max\{\|a\|_\infty, \|b\|_\infty, |\mathbf{c}|\} \tag{9}$$

where $|\mathbf{c}|$ is the Euclidean norm of the vector $\mathbf{c}$. Hence $\mathscr{T}$ is a normed linear space.

Consider a one-dimensional parameterization of $(a_0, b_0, \mathbf{c}_0)$. We view this parameterization as a one-dimensional curve that passes through the point $(a_0, b_0, \mathbf{c}_0)$. More formally, this curve is a function $\mathscr{Q}$ mapping an open set $\mathscr{O}$ of $\mathbb{R}$ into $\mathscr{T}$ where $\mathscr{O}$ contains zero. Since $\mathbb{R}$ and $\mathscr{T}$ are normed linear spaces, we can define a notion of differentiation.

Restriction 1: $\mathscr{Q}$ is differentiable on $\mathscr{O}$, and $\mathscr{Q}(0) = (a_0, b_0, \mathbf{c}_0)$.

Our choice of $\alpha = 0$ as the index for the correct probability model is made for notational covenience. In light of assumption 1, the open set $\mathscr{O}$ can be constructed so that both a_α and b_α are in $\mathscr{N}^c$ for α in $\mathscr{O}$. Since $\mathscr{Q}$ is differentiable at $\alpha = 0$, we can define a member $(Da_0, Db_0, D\mathbf{c}_0)$ of $\mathscr{T}$ to be its derivative at that point. It is understood that this derivative depends on the choice of parameterization $\mathscr{Q}$.

Imagine using this one-dimensional parameterization to construct a maximum likelihood estimator of the true value of α ($\alpha = 0$) and hence of $(a_0, b_0, \mathbf{c}_0)$. The large-sample properties of finite-dimensional Gaussian likelihood estimators for linear time-series models have been studied extensively, see for example Walker (1964), Dunsmuir and Hannan (1976), and Dunsmuir (1979). We give a brief (and informal) derivation of the score process for the log-likelihood functions because this process will play an essential part in our analysis.

The time t contribution to the Gaussian likelihood evaluated at the true parameter value is constructed in terms of two objects, the forecast error $\mathbf{v}_t$ of $\mathbf{y}_t$ given $\mathbf{y}_{t-1}, \mathbf{y}_{t-2}, \ldots, \mathbf{y}_1$ and the covariance matrix of $\mathbf{v}_t$. The process $\{\mathbf{v}_t : t \geqslant 1\}$ is, in general, not stationary because the dimension of the conditioning information set increases over time. For this reason, we follow the usual practice of approximating $\mathbf{v}_t$ by the forecast error of $\mathbf{y}_t$ given the semi-infinite record $\mathbf{y}_{t-1}, \mathbf{y}_{t-2}, \ldots$, see for example Caines (1988, chapter 7). These two forecast errors often differ because they are constructed using distinct conditioning information sets. The advantage to using the semi-infinite record as a conditioning information set is that the resulting forecast error, process $\{a_0(0)^{-1}b_0(0)\mathbf{w}_t\}$, is stationary by assumption. For our purposes, this difference is asymptotically negligible, so that in deriving the score process it is more convenient to use the stationary or steady-state approximation. We make some additional comments on the validity of this approximation at the end of the section.

So far we have described the steady-state approximation only for a true probability model. Given a parameterization $\mathcal{Q}$ of $(a_0, b_0, \mathbf{c}_0)$, we build a parameterization $\boldsymbol{\psi}_t$ of $\mathbf{w}_t$ via

$$\boldsymbol{\psi}_t(\alpha) = b_\alpha(L)^{-1}a_\alpha(L)\mathbf{y}_t - b_\alpha(1)^{-1}\mathbf{c}_\alpha \tag{10}$$

where $\mathcal{Q}(\alpha) = (a_\alpha, b_\alpha, \mathbf{c}_\alpha)$. Note that for each α, $\{\boldsymbol{\psi}_t(\alpha)\}$ is a stationary stochastic process. It follows from (7) that

$$\mathbf{w}_t = \boldsymbol{\psi}_t(0). \tag{11}$$

More generally, $a_\alpha(0)^{-1}b_\alpha(0)\boldsymbol{\psi}_t(\alpha)$ is the steady-state approximation to the forecast error of $\mathbf{y}$ given $\mathbf{y}_{t-1}, \mathbf{y}_{t-2}, \ldots, \mathbf{y}_1$ for parameter value α. The corresponding covariance matrix for this approximate forecast error is $a_\alpha(0)^{-1}b_\alpha(0)b_\alpha(0)'a_\alpha(0)^{-1\prime}$. The time t contribution to the steady-state approximation to the log-likelihood function is

$$-\tfrac{1}{2}\boldsymbol{\psi}_t(\alpha)\cdot\boldsymbol{\psi}_t(\alpha) - \tfrac{1}{2}\log\{\det[a_\alpha(0)^{-1}b_\alpha(0)b_\alpha(0)'a_\alpha(0)^{-1\prime}]\}, \tag{12}$$

Since $\mathcal{Q}$ is differentiable on $\mathcal{O}$, $\boldsymbol{\psi}_t$ is mean-square differentiable on $\mathcal{O}$ and the corresponding score variable is obtained by differentiating (12) with respect to α and evaluating the derivative at $\alpha = 0$. In so doing we obtain

$$\mathbf{s}_t = -\mathbf{w}_t\cdot D\boldsymbol{\psi}_t(0) + E[\mathbf{w}_t\cdot D\boldsymbol{\psi}_t(0)], \tag{13}$$

where $D\boldsymbol{\psi}_t(0)$ satisfies the recursion

$$Da_0(L)\mathbf{y}_t = b_0(L)D\boldsymbol{\psi}_t(0) + Db_0(L)\mathbf{w}_t + D\mathbf{c}_0. \tag{14}$$

Solving (14) for $D\boldsymbol{\psi}_t$ gives

$$\begin{aligned} D\boldsymbol{\psi}_t(0) &= b_0(L)^{-1}[Da_0(L)\mathbf{y}_t - D\mathbf{c}_0 - Db_0(L)\mathbf{w}_t] \\ &= b_0(L)^{-1}[Da_0(L)a_0(L)^{-1}b_0(L) - Db_0(L)]\mathbf{w}_t \\ &\quad + b_0(1)^{-1}Da_0(1)a_0(1)^{-1}\mathbf{c}_0 - b_0(1)^{-1}D\mathbf{c}_0 \\ &= m^d(L)\mathbf{w}_t + \mathbf{c}_d. \end{aligned} \tag{15}$$

where

$$m^d(\zeta) \equiv b_0(\zeta)^{-1}[Da_0(\zeta)a_0(\zeta)^{-1}b_0(\zeta) - Db_0(\zeta)], \tag{16}$$

$$\mathbf{c}_d \equiv b_0(1)^{-1}Da_0(1)a_0(1)^{-1}\mathbf{c}_0 - b_0(1)^{-1}D\mathbf{c}_0. \tag{17}$$

Notice that the function m^d is in $\mathcal{M}^c$. Substituting (15) into (13) gives an alternative expression for $\mathbf{s}_t$:

$$s_t = -\mathbf{w}_t \cdot [m^d(L)\mathbf{w}_t + \mathbf{c}_d] + \mathrm{Tr}[m^d(0)]. \tag{18}$$

Relations (16) through (18) give a general characterization for an asymptotic score process $\{s_t\}$ which will be used extensively throughout this paper. This process is of interest because, among other things, the asymptotic variance of the maximum likelihood estimator is the reciprocal of $E(s_t^2)$.

By exploiting properties of normally distributed random vectors, we decompose s_t into three orthogonal components:

$$\mathbf{s}_t = \mathbf{s}_t^1 + \mathbf{s}_t^2 + \mathbf{s}_t^3, \tag{19}$$

where

$$s_t^1 = -\mathbf{w}_t \cdot [m^d(0)\mathbf{w}_t] + \mathrm{Tr}\,[m^d(0)], \tag{20}$$

$$s_t^2 = -\mathbf{w}_t \cdot \{[m^d(L) - m^d(0)]\mathbf{w}_t\}, \tag{21}$$

$$s_t^3 = -\mathbf{w}_t \cdot \mathbf{c}_d. \tag{22}$$

With this decomposition in mind, we construct three orthogonal Hilbert spaces. Let

$$H_1 = \{h : h = \mathbf{w}_t' W \mathbf{w}_t - \mathrm{Tr}(W) \quad \text{for some } n \times n \text{ matrix } W\} \tag{23}$$

$$H_2 = \{h : h = \mathbf{w}_t \cdot [m(L)\mathbf{w}_{t-1}] \quad \text{for some } m \in \mathscr{M}^2\} \tag{24}$$

$$H_3 = \{h : h = \mathbf{w}_t \cdot \mathbf{c} \quad \text{for some } \mathbf{c} \in \mathbb{R}^n\}. \tag{25}$$

Then s_t^1 is in H_1, s_t^2 is in H_2 and s_t^3 is in H_3. Consequently, $\mathbf{s}_t$ is in the Hilbert space $H \equiv H_1 \oplus H_2 \oplus H_3$.

Our derivation of the score process for the likelihood function is admittedly informal. For instance, we have not demonstrated the validity of using a stationary approximation. Such demonstrations do exist in the time series literature, see for example Dunsmuir and Hannan (1976) and Dunsmuir (1979). To apply their analyses, we must impose somewhat stronger restrictions on the parameterization $\mathscr{Q}$ and on the time series model $(a_0, \ell_0, \mathbf{c}_0)$. Dunsmuir and Hannan (1976) derived a central limit theorem for quasi-maximum likelihood estimators obtained by maximizing a frequency domain approximation to the likelihood function (see their theorem 5). Their result applies to our estimation environment if we assume that $\mathscr{Q}$ maps $\mathscr{O}$ into $\mathscr{S}^2 \times \mathscr{S}^2 \times \mathbb{R}^n$, which is a subspace of $\mathscr{T}$, and that $\mathscr{Q}$ is twice differentiable. The derivatives are only required to be in $\mathscr{T}$ and not necessarily in its subspace $\mathscr{S}^2 \times \mathscr{S}^2 \times \mathbb{R}^n$.[1]

Dunsmuir and Hannan (1976) focused on the asymptotic distribution of parameter estimators with time t scores in $H_2 \oplus H_3$.[2] Dunsmuir (1978) extended their central limit theorem to cover more general situations in which the time t scores of interest also have components in H_1 (see his theorem 2.1). His result applies to our set-up if

$\mathcal{Q}$ maps $\mathcal{O}$ into $\mathcal{S}^{\infty} \times \mathcal{S}^{\infty} \times \mathbb{R}^n$ and is twice differentiable. The derivatives, however, are only required to be in $\mathcal{T}$.

By reducing the space of admissible lag operators (say from $\mathcal{M}^c$ to $\mathcal{S}^{\infty}$), in effect we limit further the temporal dependence of the time series $\{\mathbf{y}_t\}$. Such reductions may not be problematic because even the more restrictive assumptions accommodate a rich collection of linear time-series models. We introduced these reductions only to ensure that a convenient set of *sufficient* conditions are satisfied for the central limit theorems reported in Dunsmuir and Hannan (1976) and Dunsmuir (1979) to apply. In our derivation of the scores, we choose to use $\mathcal{T}$ instead of the more restrictive spaces to incorporate some additional flexibility, but what is important for our subsequent analysis is characterization (16) through (18) of the score process.

Conditional Moment Restrictions

In this section we introduce the multiperiod conditional moment restrictions used to identify and estimate the parameter vector of interest. Such restrictions are commonly encountered in applications in macroeconomics and finance, see for example Hansen and Sargent (1991) and Hansen and Singleton (1991). We model these conditional moment restrictions as comprising the first l equations of the n-equation system (6).

Let a_{01} and b_{01} be the upper $l \times n$ block of a_0 and b_0 respectively, and let $\mathbf{c}_{01}$ be the upper l-dimensional subvector of $\mathbf{c}_0$. It follows from (6) that

$$a_{01}(L)\mathbf{y}_t = b_{01}(L)\mathbf{w}_t + \mathbf{c}_{01}. \tag{26}$$

As a device for restricting the time series and identifying the parameters of interest, we assume:

Assumption 3: b_{01} is a matrix polynomial of order $\tau - 1$.

To see that assumption 3 can be interpreted as a τ-period conditional moment restriction, let J_t be the information set (sigma algebra) generated by $\mathbf{y}_t, \mathbf{y}_{t-1}, \ldots$ or equivalently by $\mathbf{w}_t, \mathbf{w}_{t-1}, \ldots$. An implication of assumption 3 is that

$$E[a_{01}(L)\mathbf{y}_t - \mathbf{c}_{01} | J_{t-\tau}] = 0. \tag{27}$$

Conditional moment restriction (27) has no empirical content unless additional restrictions are imposed on a_{01} and $\mathbf{c}_{01}$. We assume that $(a_{01}, \mathbf{c}_{01})$ is parameterized by a k-dimensional vector $\boldsymbol{\beta}_0$. Let $\mathcal{Q}^*$ be a mapping from an open subset $\mathcal{O}^*$ of $\mathbb{R}^k$ containing $\boldsymbol{\beta}_0$ into $\mathcal{T}$ such that

$$b_\beta = b_0, \tag{28}$$

$$[0, I_{n-l}]a_\beta = [0, I_{n-l}]a_0, \tag{29}$$

and

$$[0, I_{n-l}]\mathbf{c}_\beta = [0, I_{n-l}]\mathbf{c}_0 \tag{30}$$

for all $\boldsymbol{\beta}$ in $\mathcal{O}^*$.

Assumption 4: $\mathscr{Q}^*$ is continuously differentiable, satisfies (28)–(30) on $\mathscr{O}^*$ and $\mathscr{Q}^*(\boldsymbol{\beta}_0) = (a_0, b_0, \mathbf{c}_0)$.

Following logic that is entirely analogous to that presented in the third section, there is a k-dimensional score vector process $\{\mathbf{r}_t^*\}$ associated with this parameterization that is stationary. As in the third section, it can be demonstrated that the entries in $\mathbf{r}_t^*$ are in H. Since the only components of parameterization $\mathscr{Q}^*$ that are not degenerate are the ones that pertain to a_{01} and $\mathbf{c}_{01}$, it follows from (16)–(18) that entry j of $\mathbf{r}_t^*$ can be represented as

$$-\mathbf{w}_t \cdot \{b^-(L)[\imath_j^*(L)\mathbf{w}_t + \boldsymbol{\rho}_j^*]\} + \operatorname{Tr}[b^-(0)\imath_j^*(0)] \tag{31}$$

where b^- is the $n \times l$ left block of $(b_0)^{-1}$ and

$$\imath_j^*(L)\mathbf{w}_t + \boldsymbol{\rho}_j^* = Da_{01}(L)\mathbf{y}_t - D\mathbf{c}_{01}. \tag{32}$$

The derivatives on the right-hand side of (29) are taken with respect to the jth entry of $\boldsymbol{\beta}_0$, $\imath_j^*$ is an $l \times n$ matrix of functions continuous on $\mathscr{U}^c$ and $\boldsymbol{\rho}_j^*$ is in $\mathbb{R}^l$.

Assumption 4 gives information that can be used to identify and estimate the parameter vector β_0. Parameterization $\mathscr{Q}^*$ provides an extensive amount of additional *a priori* information as evidenced by (28)–(30). In particular, b_{01} and the second block of $n - l$ equations in (6) must be known *a priori*. Estimation using $\mathscr{Q}^*$ is a parametric maximum likelihood problem, and the asymptotic covariance matrix for the resulting estimator of β_0 is given by inverse of $E(\mathbf{r}_t^*\mathbf{r}_t^{*\prime})$. The estimation problem of interest to us, however, is one in which the prior information given in (28)–(30) is eliminated. This problem is semiparametric in nature, because eliminating prior information about the $n - l$ remaining equations, in effect, introduces an infinite-dimensional nuisance parameter into the estimation. In the next section, we construct a large family of one-dimensional parameterizations that, when combined appropriately, removes the prior information embedded in (28)–(30).

Basis Parameterizations

In the previous section we presented a k-dimensional parameterization of the conditional moment restrictions. In this section we describe a set of one-dimensional parameterizations that provide a *basis* for multiple-dimensional parameterizations of the remaining aspects of the model. These basis parameterizations are divided into three subsets. Parameterizations in subset j have time t score random variables in H_j. For each parameterization, we compute the scores using formulas (16)–(18).

The members of the first collection of parameterizations have scores in H_1. Let

$$b_\alpha(\zeta) = b_0(\zeta)(I + \alpha W), \tag{33}$$

where W is any $n \times n$ matrix. The corresponding parameterization of the entire model is $\mathscr{Q}(\alpha) = (a_0, b_\alpha, \mathbf{c}_0)$. For this parameterization $Db_0(\zeta)$ is $b_0(\zeta)W$, and the time t score is

$$\mathbf{s}_t = -\mathbf{w}_t' W \mathbf{w}_t + \operatorname{Tr}(W) \tag{34}$$

which is in H_1. By changing W we generate a finite-dimensional linear space G_1 of time t score random variables. Note that $G_1 = H_1$.

Members of the second collection of parameterizations have scores in H_2. These parameterizations focus on ℓ_0 while maintaining the order restriction given in assumption 3. Let $0 < j < \tau$, and

$$\ell_\alpha(\zeta) = \ell_0(\zeta) + \alpha W \zeta^j. \tag{35}$$

The corresponding parameterization for the entire model is $\mathscr{Q}(\alpha) = (a_0, \ell_\alpha, \mathbf{c}_0)$. For this parameterization $D\ell_0(\zeta) = W\zeta^i$, and the time t score is

$$\mathbf{s}_t = -\mathbf{w}_t \cdot [\ell_0(L)^{-1} W \mathbf{w}_{t-j}], \tag{36}$$

which is in H_2. We obtain a finite-dimensional collection of such parameterizations by changing the matrix W and letting j vary between zero and τ exclusive of the end points.

Next we consider a related family of parameterizations of ℓ_0 that also maintain the order restriction given in assumption 3. Let V be any $n \times n$ matrix such that the upper $l \times n$ matrix contains all zeros. Hence V satisfies

$$[I_l, 0]V = 0. \tag{37}$$

Let $j \geqslant \tau$, and

$$\ell_\alpha(\zeta) = \ell_0 + \alpha V \zeta^j. \tag{38}$$

The corresponding parameterization is $\mathscr{Q}(\alpha) = (a_0, \ell_\alpha, \mathbf{c}_0)$. For this parameterization $D\ell_0(\zeta) = V\zeta^j$, and the time t score is

$$\mathbf{s}_t = -\mathbf{w}_t \cdot [\ell_0(L)^{-1} V \mathbf{w}_{t-j}], \tag{39}$$

which is in H_2. We obtain an infinite-dimensional collection of such parameterizations by varying V subject to (37) and varying $j \geqslant \tau$.

Let G_2 denote the linear space of all finite linear combinations of time t scores of the form (36) and (39). This space is not closed but is a subspace of H_2. To justify looking at this space, we expand the collection of parameterizations by taking finite linear combinations. Let $s_t^1, s_t^2, \ldots, s_t^m$ be any m basis scores of the form given in (36) and (39), $\mathscr{Q}_1, \mathscr{Q}_2, \ldots, \mathscr{Q}_m$ be the corresponding parameterizations, and $\theta_1, \theta_2, \ldots, \theta_m$ be any real m real numbers. A parameterization $\mathscr{Q}$ with time t score:

$$\mathbf{s}_t = \sum_{j=1}^{m} \theta_j \mathbf{s}_t^j \tag{40}$$

is given by

$$\mathscr{Q}(\alpha) = \left[\sum_{j=1}^{m} \theta_j \mathscr{Q}_j(\alpha)\right] + \left(1 - \sum_{j=1}^{m} \theta_j\right)(a_0, \ell_0, \mathbf{c}_0). \tag{41}$$

Parameterization $\mathscr{Q}$ is differentiable on the intersection of the $\mathcal{O}_j$ and $\mathscr{Q}(0) = (a_0, b_0, \mathbf{c}_0)$ and hence satisfies restriction 1.

Members of the third collection of parameterizations have scores in H_3. These parameterizations focus on the lower $l - n$ subvector of $\mathbf{c}_0$. Let

$$\mathbf{c}_\alpha = \mathbf{c}_0 + \alpha \mathbf{u}, \tag{42}$$

where $\mathbf{u}$ is $\mathbb{R}^n$ has zeros in the first l positions. Hence $\mathbf{u}$ is any vector in $\mathbb{R}^n$ that satisfies:

$$[I_l, 0]\mathbf{u} = 0. \tag{43}$$

The corresponding parameterization is $\mathscr{Q}(\alpha) = (a_0, b_0, \mathbf{c}_\alpha)$. For this parameterization $D\mathbf{c}_0 = \mathbf{u}$, and the time t score is

$$\mathbf{s}_t = -\mathbf{w}_t \cdot [b_0(1)^{-1}\mathbf{u}], \tag{44}$$

which is in H_3. Let G_3 denote the finite-dimensional linear space of score variables of the form (44) for any $\mathbf{u}$ in $\mathbb{R}^n$ satisfying (43).

By mimicking construction (41) we build a family Θ of one-dimensional parameterizations with scores that are linear combinations of scores in G_1, G_2, and G_3. The resulting linear space of time t score random variables is given by $G = G_1 \oplus G_2 \oplus G_3$. This space is not closed because G_2 need not be closed.

The collection Θ of one-dimensional parameterizations is devised to loosen restrictions (28) and (30) imposed by parameterization $\mathscr{Q}^*$. It turns out not to be necessary to loosen restrictions (29) on the lower $(n - l) \times n$ submatrix of a_0 because one-dimensional parameterizations of this lower block result in time t scores in the mean-square closure of G. As we will see in the next section, adding such parameterizations will not alter the semiparametric efficiency bound for estimators of β_0.

Efficiency Bound

In this section we combine the parameterizations described in sections four and five to construct a family Π of finite-dimensional parameterizations of $(a_0, b_0, \mathbf{c}_0)$. We then define a semiparametric efficiency bound for this class of parameterizations.

Let $\mathbf{e}_j$ be a $(2k)$-dimensional vector of zeros except in position j where there is a one, and let $\mathscr{Q}_1, \mathscr{Q}_2, \ldots, \mathscr{Q}_k$ be any k parameterizations in Θ. Using these objects together with $\mathscr{Q}^*$ introduced in the fourth section, we construct a $2k$-dimensional parameterization $\mathscr{P}$:

$$\mathscr{P}(\gamma) = \mathscr{Q}_1(\gamma \cdot \mathbf{e}_1) + \mathscr{Q}_2(\gamma \cdot \mathbf{e}_2) + \cdots + \mathscr{Q}_k(\gamma \cdot \mathbf{e}_k) + \mathscr{Q}^*([0, I_k]\gamma) - (k)(a_0, b_0, \mathbf{c}_0). \tag{45}$$

Then $\mathscr{P}$ is a continuously differentiable function mapping $\mathbb{R}^{2k}$ into $\mathscr{T}$ in the neighborhood of $\gamma_0 \equiv (0, \beta_0)$, and $\mathscr{P}(\gamma_0) = (a_0, b_0, \mathbf{c}_0)$. The score vector for this parameterization can be written as $[\mathbf{r}_t', \mathbf{r}_t^{*\prime}]'$ where $\mathbf{r}_t$ is a k-dimensional random vector with entries in G. Entry j of $\mathbf{r}_t$ is the score random variable for $\mathscr{Q}_j$.

Suppose that $[\mathbf{r}_t', \mathbf{r}_t^{*\prime}]'$ has a nonsingular covariance matrix. Then the asymptotic covariance matrix for the maximum likelihood estimator of γ_0 is the inverse of this covariance matrix. Our interest is in the lower right $k \times k$ submatrix of this inverse. Using the partitioned inverse formula, this submatrix can be computed as the inverse of the covariance matrix $\text{cov}(\mathscr{P})$ of the vector of errors obtained by performing the population regression of $\mathbf{r}_t^*$ onto $\mathbf{r}_t$, where formally

$$\text{cov}(\mathscr{P}) \equiv E\mathbf{r}_t^*\mathbf{r}_t^{*\prime} - E\mathbf{r}_t^*\mathbf{r}_t'(E\mathbf{r}_t\mathbf{r}_t')^{-1}E\mathbf{r}_t\mathbf{r}_t^{*\prime}. \tag{46}$$

To construct a semiparametric efficiency bound for estimators of β_0, we follow Stein (1956) and compute a least upper bound on the asymptotic covariance matrices of maximum likelihood estimators of β_0 for alternative parameterizations $\mathscr{P}$. Let Π be the family of all parameterizations $\mathscr{P}$ of the form given by (45), and let

$$\text{INF} = \inf\{\text{cov}(\mathscr{P}) : \mathscr{P} \in \Pi\} \tag{47}$$

whenever such a greatest lower bound exists. Then the semiparametric efficiency bound is

$$\text{SUP} = (\text{INF})^{-1} \tag{48}$$

as long as INF is nonsingular. Calculating this bound entails finding (or at least approximating) the least informative $(2k)$-dimensional parameterization of the model to use in constructing a maximum likelihood estimator of β_0.

The optimization problem on the right-hand side of (47) requires ranking positive semidefinite matices. We use the familiar partial ordering in which a first matrix is greater than or equal to the second matrix if the difference between the first and second matrix is positive semidefinite. Although this ordering is not complete, the collection Π is sufficiently rich that a greatest lower bound always exists.

As emphasized by Stein (1956), the solution to optimization problem (47) can be deduced by projecting each entry of $\mathbf{r}_t^*$ onto the closure G^* of G and forming the covariance matrix of the projection errors. This covariance matrix is INF. To understand why this regression yields a valid solution, construct a k-dimensional sequence $\{\mathbf{r}_t^j : j = 1, 2, \ldots\}$ with entries in G that converge in mean-square (coordinate by coordinate) to the projection of $\mathbf{r}_t^*$ onto $\mathbf{G}^*$. Since each entry of $\mathbf{r}_t^j$ is in G^*, $(\mathbf{r}_t^j, \mathbf{r}_t^{*\prime})'$ is the time t score vector of parameterization $\mathscr{P}_j$ in Π. Furthermore, the sequence of covariance matrices $\{\text{cov}(\mathscr{P}_j) : j = 1, 2, \ldots\}$ converges to the covariance matrix of the vector of errors in projecting $\mathbf{r}_t^*$ onto G^*. Consequently, this candidate for INF can always be approximated. Furthermore, it is a lower bound because the covariance matrix for the vector of errors in projecting $\mathbf{r}_t^*$ onto any vector $\mathbf{r}_t$ with entries in G must be less than or equal to the covariance matrix of the vector of errors for the projection of $\mathbf{r}_t^*$ onto G^*.

All of the parameterizations used in defining INF in (47) are $(2k)$-dimensional where k is the dimension of β_0. As is typically the case, this dimensionality restriction is made only as a matter of convenience. Note that the projection of $\mathbf{r}_t^*$ onto G^* necessarily coincides with the projection of $\mathbf{r}_t^*$ onto the span of a k-dimensional vectors of random variables in G^*. For instance, the k-dimensional random vector can be the projection of $\mathbf{r}_t^*$ onto G^*. Since $(2k)$-dimensional parameterizations give sufficient flexibility to approximate the projection of $\mathbf{r}_t^*$ onto G^*, expanding the dimension of the admissible parameterizations will not alter the efficiency bound.

Projection Errors

It follows from the analysis in the previous section that the efficiency bound SUP can be calculated by deducing the error in projecting $\mathbf{r}_t^*$ onto G^*. Since the entries of $\mathbf{r}_t^*$ are in H, the vectors of projection errors are in the orthogonal complement F of G^* relative to H. In this section we characterize F.

Let $\mathbf{e}_t$ be the disturbance vector for the l-dimensional subsystem of equations that depend on the parameter vector β_0:

$$\mathbf{e}_t \equiv \mathscr{b}_{01}(L)\mathbf{w}_t = \mathscr{a}_{01}(L)\mathbf{y}_t - \mathbf{c}_{01}. \tag{49}$$

In light of conditional moment restriction (27), this disturbance vector satisfies

$$E(\mathbf{e}_t \mid J_{t-\tau}) = 0. \tag{50}$$

Let X be the space of l-dimensional random vectors that are finite linear combinations of $\mathbf{y}_{t-\tau}, \mathbf{y}_{t-\tau-1}, \ldots$ translated by an element of $\mathbb{R}^l$, and let X^* be the mean-square closure of X. In light of (50), any random vector $\mathbf{x}_{t-\tau}$ in X^* satisfies the unconditional moment restriction

$$E(\mathbf{e}_t \cdot \mathbf{x}_{t-\tau}) = 0. \tag{51}$$

We can think of the set X as containing an extensive collection of instrumental variables that can be used to estimate $\boldsymbol{\beta}_0$. It turns out that random vectors in the mean-square closure X^* can be used to represent the linear space F.

Proposition 1 $F = \{h : h = w_t \cdot [\mathscr{b}_{01}(L^{-1})' x_{t-\tau}]$ *for some* $x_{t-\tau}$ *in* $X^*\}$.

Proof Given the orthogonal decompositions of G and H, it suffices to compute the orthogonal complement F_j of G_j relative to H_j for $j = 1, 2, 3$. The space F is then given by $F_1 \oplus F_2 \oplus F_3$. We consider in turn F_j for $j = 1, 2, 3$.

We have already remarked that G_1 and H_1 are the same space. Consequently, F_1 contains only the zero random variable.

Next consider F_2, and let h be any member of F_2. Since h is in H_2, $h = w_t \cdot [m(L)w_{t-1}]$ for some m in $\mathscr{M}^2$. This random variable is orthogonal to G_2 if, and only if, it is orthogonal to the time t scores used to generate G_2. Hence

$$E\{[m(L)w_{t-1}] \cdot [\mathscr{b}_0(L)^{-1} W w_{t-j}]\} = 0 \quad \text{for } 0 < j < \tau \text{ and any } n \times n \text{ matrix } W; \tag{52}$$

and

$$E\{[m(L)w_{t-1}] \cdot [\mathscr{b}_0(L)^{-1} V w_{t-j}]\} = 0$$
$$\text{for } j \geq \tau \text{ and any } n \times n \text{ matrix } V \text{ such that } [I_l, 0]V = 0. \tag{53}$$

Orthogonality conditions (52) and (53) are most conveniently represented using Fourier transforms. Recall that Fourier transforms of the coefficients of the power series expansion of m and $\mathscr{b}_0$ are obtained from the values of these functions on the unit circle of the complex plane.[3] Recall that the unit circle can be parameterized as

$\{\exp(i\omega):\omega \in (-\pi, \pi]\}$. The Fourier representation of (52) is

$$(1/2\pi)\int_{-\pi}^{\pi} \operatorname{Tr}\{W'\mathscr{b}_0[\exp(i\omega)]^{-1\prime}m[\exp(-i\omega)]\}\exp[(i\omega)(j-1)]\,d\omega = 0, \qquad 0 < j < \tau \quad (54)$$

and any $n \times n$ matrix W. Given the flexibility in choosing W, (54) is equivalent to

$$(1/2\pi)\int_{-\pi}^{\pi} \mathscr{b}_0[\exp(i\omega)]^{-1\prime}m[\exp(-i\omega)]\exp[(i\omega)(j-1)]\,d\omega = 0, \qquad 0 < j < \tau. \quad (55)$$

Similarly, the Fourier representation for (53) is

$$(1/2\pi)\int_{-\pi}^{\pi} \operatorname{Tr}\{V'\mathscr{b}_0[\exp(i\omega)]^{-1\prime}m[\exp(-i\omega)]\}\exp[(i\omega)(j-1)]\,d\omega = 0, \qquad j \geqslant \tau \quad (56)$$

and any $n \times n$ matrix V such that $[I_l, 0]V = 0$. Given the flexibility in choosing V, (56) is equivalent to

$$[0, I_{n-l}](1/2\pi)\int_{-\pi}^{\pi} \mathscr{b}_0[\exp(i\omega)]^{-1\prime}m[\exp(-i\omega)]\exp[(i\omega)(j-1)]\,d\omega = 0, \qquad j \geqslant \tau. \quad (57)$$

Orthogonality conditions (55) amd (57) imply restrictions on the Fourier coefficients of the matrix function χ defined by

$$\chi(\omega) \equiv \mathscr{b}_0[\exp(i\omega)]^{-1\prime}m[\exp(-i\omega)]. \quad (58)$$

In particular, the Fourier coefficients for $\{\exp[(-i\omega)j]:j \geqslant 0\}$ are zero in the lower $(n-l) \times n$ block of χ and the Fourier coefficients for $\{\exp[(-i\omega)j]:0 \leqslant j < \tau - 1\}$ are zero in the $l \times n$ block of χ. As a result χ can be represented as

$$\chi(\omega) = \exp(i\omega)m^*[\exp(i\omega)] + \begin{bmatrix} \exp[-i\omega(\tau-1)]\mathscr{f}[\exp(-i\omega)] \\ 0 \end{bmatrix} \quad (59)$$

where m^* is in $\mathscr{M}^2$ and $\mathscr{f}$ is an $l \times n$ matrix of functions in $\mathscr{A}^2$. We solve for m by substituting (58) into (59) and premultiplying both sides of (59) by $\mathscr{b}_0[\exp(i\omega)]'$:

$$\begin{aligned} m[\exp(-i\omega)] &= \exp(i\omega)\mathscr{b}_0[\exp(i\omega)]'m^*[\exp(i\omega)] \\ &\quad + \mathscr{b}_0[\exp(i\omega)]'\begin{bmatrix} \exp[-i\omega(\tau-1)]\mathscr{f}[\exp(-i\omega)] \\ 0 \end{bmatrix} \\ &= \exp(i\omega)\mathscr{b}_0[\exp(i\omega)]'m^*[\exp(i\omega)] \\ &\quad + \exp[-i\omega(\tau-1)]\mathscr{b}_{01}[\exp(i\omega)]'\mathscr{f}[\exp(-i\omega)]. \end{aligned} \quad (60)$$

Recall that ℓ_{01} is a polynomial of degree $\tau - 1$. Consequently ℓ^* is also a polynomial of degree $\tau - 1$ where

$$\ell^*(\zeta) = \zeta^{\tau-1}\ell_{01}(\zeta^{-1})',$$

and $\ell^*[\exp(-i\omega)]f[\exp(-i\omega)]$ has a one-sided Fourier expansion in terms of $\{\exp[-(i\omega)j]: j \geqslant 0\}$. Furthermore, $\exp(i\omega)\ell_0[\exp(i\omega)]'m^*[\exp(i\omega)]$ has a one-sided Fourier expansion in terms of $\{\exp[(i\omega)j]: j > 0\}$. Finally, since m has a power series expansion, $m[\exp(-i\omega)]$ has a one-sided Fourier expansion in terms of $\{\exp[-(i\omega)j]: j \geqslant 0\}$. Therefore,

$$\exp(i\omega)\ell_0[\exp(i\omega)]'m^*[\exp(i\omega)] = 0, \tag{61}$$

$$m(\zeta) = \ell^*(\zeta)f(\zeta), \tag{62}$$

$$h = \mathbf{w}_t \cdot [\ell_{01}(L^{-1})'f(L)\mathbf{w}_{t-\tau}]. \tag{63}$$

It is straightforward to reverse the argument and demonstrate that any h of the form given in (63) is in F_2.

Finally, consider F_3 and let h be any member of F_3. Then h is in H_3 and hence can be represented as $\mathbf{w}_t \cdot \mathbf{c}$ for some $\mathbf{c}$ in $\mathbb{R}^n$. Since the random variable h must also be orthogonal to G_3,

$$E\{(\mathbf{c} \cdot \mathbf{w}_t)[\ell_0(1)^{-1}\mathbf{u}] \cdot \mathbf{w}_t\} = \mathbf{c}'\ell_0(1)^{-1}\mathbf{u} = 0, \tag{64}$$

for any $\mathbf{u}$ such that $[I_l, 0]\mathbf{u} = 0$, or equivalently,

$$[0, I_{n-l}]\ell_0(1)^{-1\prime}\mathbf{c} = 0. \tag{65}$$

Equality (63) holds if, and only if,

$$\mathbf{c} = \ell_{01}(1)'\boldsymbol{\phi} \quad \text{for some } \boldsymbol{\phi} \text{ in } \mathbb{R}^n. \tag{66}$$

Therefore,

$$h = \mathbf{w}_t \cdot [\ell_{01}(1)'\boldsymbol{\phi}]. \tag{67}$$

It is straightforward to reverse the logic to show that any h of the form given in (65) is in F_3.

Adding together the h terms of the form given in (63) and (67) gives the desired representation of F because $f(L)\mathbf{w}_{t-\tau} + \boldsymbol{\phi}$ is in X^* and all members of X^* can be represented in this fashion.

Proposition 1 provides an important link between a class X of admissible instrumental variables to be used in estimating the parameter vector $\boldsymbol{\beta}_0$ and the space of random variables in the orthogonal complement F. To understand this link better, note that the disturbance vector process $\{\mathbf{e}_t\}$ is, in general, serially correlated, as is the product process $\{\mathbf{e}_t \cdot \mathbf{x}_{t-\tau}\}$. Following Gordin (1969) and Hansen (1985), a central limit approximation for the product process can be obtained by first finding a sequence $\{\mathbf{f}_t\}$ of stationary martingale differences such that

$$(1/T)^{1/2} \sum_{t=1}^{T} \{\mathbf{e}_t \cdot \mathbf{x}_{t-\tau} - \mathbf{f}_t\} \tag{68}$$

converges in mean-square to zero as $T \to \infty$, and then applying Billingsley's (1961) central limit theorem for martingales. A process $\{\mathbf{f}_t\}$ that satisfies (68) is

$$\mathbf{f}_t = \mathbf{w}_t \cdot [\ell_{01}(L^{-1})'\mathbf{x}_{t-\tau}], \tag{69}$$

see for example Hansen (1985). Notice that $\mathbf{f}_t$ is in F. Therefore, members of F can be used to generate martingale difference approximations (in the sense of (69)) to dot products of the structural disturbance vector $\mathbf{e}_t$ and random vectors in X^*. We use this characterization of F in the following section.

Dual Efficiency Problem

In this section we show that the efficiency bound described in the sixth section is the same as the efficiency bound for generalized method-of-moments (GMM) estimators given in Hansen (1985). To establish this result we use the characterization of the score vector $\mathbf{r}_t^*$ given in (31) and (32) together with the characterization of F given in proposition 1.

We formulate the GMM efficiency problem as follows. Using the parameterization introduced in the fourth section, let

$$\boldsymbol{\varepsilon}_t(\beta) = [I_l, 0][a_\beta(L)\mathbf{y}_t - \mathbf{c}_\beta]. \tag{70}$$

Note that $\boldsymbol{\varepsilon}_t(\beta_0) = \mathbf{e}_t$ so that $\boldsymbol{\varepsilon}_t$ can be viewed as a parameterization of the l-dimensional system of conditional moment restrictions. Let d_t be the $l \times k$ matrix of (mean-square) derivatives of $\boldsymbol{\varepsilon}_t$ evaluated at $\boldsymbol{\beta}_0$. It follows from (32) that column j of d_t is then given by $\imath_j^*(L)\mathbf{w}_t + \boldsymbol{\rho}_j^*$.

Random vectors in X can be used to construct unconditional moment conditions as in (51). To estimate the parameter vector $\boldsymbol{\beta}_0$ using GMM, we select k of these vectors. With this in mind, let $Z = X^k$ where X^k is the k-fold Cartesian product of X. We find it convenient to represent elements of Z as $(l \times k)$ matrices. Each random matrix $z_{t-\tau}$ in Z can be used to construct k unconditional moment conditions:

$$E(z_{t-\tau}'\mathbf{e}_t) = 0. \tag{71}$$

Hansen (1982) investigated the large-sample properties of GMM estimators that solve (at least asymptotically) sample counterparts to moment equations such as (71).

Let $\text{cov}^*(z_{t-\tau})$ denote the asymptotic covariance matrix for the GMM estimator indexed by $z_{t-\tau}$. The GMM efficiency problem is to find the greatest lower bound INF* for the asymptotic covariance matrices of these alternative GMM estimators:

$$\text{INF}^* = \inf\{\text{cov}^*(z_{t-\tau}) : z_{t-\tau} \text{ in } Z\} \tag{72}$$

We refer to minimization problem (72) as the *dual* to problem (47). It turns out that the *dual* efficiency bound for GMM estimators coincides with the *primal* efficiency bound for parametric maximum likelihood estimators. Among other things, this means that the solutions to the *dual* solution discussed in Hansen (1985) and Hansen and Singleton (1991) are also solutions to the primal problem.

Proposition 2 *If there exists a $z_{t-\tau}$ in Z such that $E(z'_{t-\tau}d_t)$ is nonsingular, then* SUP = INF*.

Proof To establish that SUP and INF* are the same, we first show how to compute INF* using martingale difference approximations as described by Hansen (1985). A martingale difference approximation for $\{z'_{t-\tau}\mathbf{e}_t\}$ is a k-dimensional process $\{\boldsymbol{\lambda}_t\}$ of stationary and ergodic martingale differences for which

$$(1/T^{1/2}) \sum_{t=1}^{T} (z'_{t-\tau}\mathbf{e}_t - \boldsymbol{\lambda}_t) \tag{73}$$

converges in mean-square to zero as $T \to \infty$. Since each column of the k columns of $z_{t-\tau}$ can be represented as $\mathbf{x}_{t-\tau}$ for some $\mathbf{x}_{t-\tau}$ in X, each of the k entries of $\boldsymbol{\lambda}_t$ are given by formula (69). Hence we use (69) to construct a function $\Lambda: Z \to F^k$ where F^k in the k-fold Cartesian product of F and $\Lambda(z_{t-\tau}) = \boldsymbol{\lambda}_t$. Let F^z be the image of Z under Λ. Although F^z is a proper subset of F^k, the mean-square closure of F^z is F^k.

To characterize the bound INF*, we find a random vector $\mathbf{f}_t^d$ in F^k such that

$$E[\Lambda(z_t)\mathbf{f}_t^{d\prime}] = E(z'_{t-\tau}d_t) \quad \text{for} \quad \mathbf{f}_t^d = \Lambda(z_{t-\tau}) \text{ and } z_{t-\tau} \text{ in } Z. \tag{74}$$

The GMM efficiency bound is given by

$$\text{INF}^* = [E(\mathbf{f}_t^d\mathbf{f}_t^{d\prime})]^{-1} \tag{75}$$

as long as there exists at least one index $z_{t-\tau}$ such that $E(z'_{t-\tau}d_t)$ is nonsingular (see lemma 4.4 in Hansen (1985)). To establish that SUP and INF* are equal, it suffices to show that the random vector $\mathbf{f}_t^*$ of errors in projecting the entries of $\mathbf{r}_t^*$ onto G^* satisfies (74).

Since the entries of $\mathbf{r}_t^* - \mathbf{f}_t^*$ are in G^*, they are orthogonal to F^*. Hence

$$E[\Lambda(z_{t-\tau})\mathbf{r}_t^{*\prime}] = E[\Lambda(z_{t-\tau})\mathbf{f}_t^{*\prime}] \text{ for all } z_{t-\tau} \text{ in } Z. \tag{76}$$

As was noted in (31), entry j of $\mathbf{r}_t^*$ can be represented as

$$-\mathbf{w}_t \cdot \{\ell^-(L)[\imath_j^*(L)\mathbf{w}_t + \boldsymbol{\rho}_j^*]\} + \text{Tr}\,[\ell^-(0)\imath_j^*(0)], \tag{77}$$

and as was stated in proposition 1, entry m of $\Lambda(z_t)$ can be represented as

$$\mathbf{w}_t \cdot [\ell_{01}(L^{-1})'\mathbf{x}_{t-\tau}] \tag{78}$$

for some $\mathbf{x}_{t-\tau}$ in X^*. Since ℓ^- is the left-hand $n \times l$ submatrix of ℓ^{-1},

$$\ell^-(\zeta)'\ell_{01}(\zeta)' = I_l. \tag{79}$$

The expected cross-product between entry j of $\mathbf{r}_j^*$ and entry m of $\boldsymbol{\lambda}(z_t)$ satisfies

$$E[\{\ell^-(L)[\imath_m^*(L)\mathbf{w}_t + \boldsymbol{\rho}_m^*]\}\cdot\{\ell_{01}(L^{-1})'\mathbf{x}_{t-\tau}\}] = E\{[\imath_m^*(L)\mathbf{w}_t + \boldsymbol{\rho}_m^*]\cdot\mathbf{x}_{t-\tau}\}. \tag{80}$$

Equality (80) can be established using the same Fourier transform approach that was used in the previous section. Thus

$$E[\boldsymbol{\lambda}(z_t)\mathbf{r}_t^{*\prime}] = E(z_{t-\tau}'d_t). \tag{81}$$

It follows from (76) and (81) that $\mathbf{f}_t^*$ satisfies (74). Therefore the two efficiency bounds are identical.

Concluding Remarks

1 The duality result (proposition 2) extends the familiar asymptotic equivalence of two-stage least squares and limited-information maximum likelihood estimators to dynamic simultaneous equations models in which a subset of equations has disturbance terms that are multiperiod forecast errors.

2 Proposition 2 also generalizes a result in Stoica et al. (1985). They showed that the efficiency bound for instrumental variables estimators of the autoregressive parameters for a univariate ARMA model is the same as the maximum likelihood asymptotic covariance matrix for those parameters. In contrast to the set-up in this paper, their estimation problem is fully parametric.

3 Since INF* = SUP, it is possible to exploit characterizations of INF* given in Hansen (1985) and the algorithms for computing that bound suggested in Hansen and Singleton (1991) when using maximum likelihood estimation methods. For instance, the semiparametric efficiency bound can be used in conjunction with maximum likelihood methods to obtain more conservative statistical inferences that take account of uncertainty in the peripheral features of the model. Alternatively, this bound can be compared to the asymptotic covariance matrix of the parameters of interest to assess the efficiency gains attributable to the finite parameterization of the peripheral features of the model.

4 By examining the GMM efficiency problem it is possible to characterize when the semiparametric counterpart to the Fisher information matrix is nonsingular. As long as there exists a matrix $z_{t-\tau}$ in Z such that $E(z_{t-\tau}'d_t)$ is nonsingular, the Fisher information matrix will be nonsingular as well. The existence of such a matrix is the familiar requirement that there be an appropriately rich set of valid instrumental variables to identify the parameter vector of interest.

5 The assumption that the white-noise process is Gaussian can be replaced by an assumption that this process is a conditionally homoskedastic martingale difference sequence. It is already known that the GMM efficiency bound is still the same (Hansen 1985). If the normal likelihood function is used without assuming that the noise process is Gaussian, much of the analysis of finite-parameter (quasi) maximum likelihood estimation still applies as long as the one-step-ahead covariance

can be parameterized independently of the remaining features of the probability model, see for example Bergstrom (1972) and Dunsmuir and Hannan (1976). As was shown by MaCurdy (1982), however, the conditional homoskedasticity assumption potentially can be exploited to obtain additional efficiency gains.

6 In this paper we assumed that the moving-average function $\mathscr{b}_0$ is nonsingular on $\mathscr{U}^*$ and hence cannot be singular on the unit circle of the complex plane. Hansen et al. (1988) showed how to compute GMM efficiency bounds when unit roots are present in the moving-average polynomial. This suggests that it may be possible to extend proposition 2 in this paper to accommodate more general $\mathscr{b}_0$ functions.

7 One important class of applications is excluded from our estimation environment. Suppose that the conditional moment restrictions can be interpreted as the Euler equations for a quadratic optimization problem. In addition, suppose that $l = n$ so that these equations, when solved appropriately, determine the stochastic process $\{\mathbf{y}_t\}$. Hence $\mathscr{a}_0(\zeta)$ and $\mathscr{a}_{01}(\zeta)$ coincide. The functions $\mathscr{a}_0(\zeta)$ derived from the Euler equations will typically be singular at points in U. The duality result given in proposition 2 no longer applies, and there will be an efficiency wedge between maximum likelihood and GMM estimators. The reason is that to implement maximum likelihood estimation one must solve the *unstable roots* (the zeros of $\mathscr{a}_0(\zeta)$) forward, in effect solving the Euler equation system. The resulting solution imposes additional restrictions across $\mathscr{a}_0(\zeta)$ and $\mathscr{b}_0(\zeta)$. Of course, GMM estimation also could be applied after solving the unstable roots forward as suggested in Hansen and Sargent (1982). Such GMM procedures would probably eliminate the efficiency wedge.

8 In this paper we have made *ad hoc* comparisons of estimators by examining their asymptotic covariance matrices. Such a criterion (ranking estimators by their asymptotic covariance matrices) implies that parametric maximum likelihood estimators can be dominated by *superefficient* estimators designed to perform extremely well for particular probability models, see for example Ibragimov and Has'minskii (1981, chapter 1). In other estimation environments, it is well known that parametric maximum likelihood estimators are asymptotically optimal under a local minimax criterion. It should be possible to extend the analysis in this paper along the lines of Levit (1975) and Chamberlain (1987) to establish the minimiax counterpart to proposition 2.

Notes

An earlier version of this paper was presented at the Econometric Society North American Meetings in the summer of 1988. Part of the paper was completed while the author was Visiting Research Professor in the Graduate School of Business at Stanford University. This research was supported in part by a grant from the National Science Foundation. Conversations with John Heaton and Ken Singleton were helpful in writing this paper. Comments on an earlier draft by Peter C. B. Phillips, Doug Steigerwald, and an anonymous referee are gratefully acknowledged.

1. Assumption C1 in Dunsmuir and Hannan (1976) is implied by the fact that $\mathscr{Q}$ is twice differentiable, and assumption C2 is implied by the fact that $\mathscr{a}_\alpha$ and $\mathscr{b}_\alpha$ are in $\mathscr{S}^2$. Dunsmuir and Hannan also established a central limit result that avoids the frequency domain approximation to the likelihood function (see corollary 3). This results requires additional smoothness restrictions.

2. As will be evident subsequently, the components of the time t scores in H_1 will drop out of our calculations, so our analysis also focuses on $H_2 \oplus H_3$.
3. Strictly speaking, this statement is only valid for functions in $\mathscr{A}^2$ that are continuous on $\mathscr{U}^c$. For other functions in $\mathscr{A}^2$, the values on the unit circle can be defined as radial limits as the radius increases to one. These limits converge almost everywhere on the unit circle.

References

Bergstrom, A. R. (1972). "The covariance matrix of the limited information maximum likelihood estimator," *Econometrica* 40, 899–901.

Billingsley, P. (1961). "The Lindeberg–Levy theorem for martingales," *Proceedings of the American Mathematical Society*, 12, 788–92.

Chamberlain, G. (1987). "Asymptotic efficiency in estimation with conditional moment restrictions," *Journal of Econometrics*, 34, 305–34.

Caines, P. E. (1988). *Linear Stochastic Systems*. New York: John Wiley & Sons.

Dunsmuir, W. (1978). "A central limit theorem for parameter estimation in stationary vector time series and its application to models for signal observed with noise," *Annals of Statistics*, 7, 490–506.

Dunsmuir, W., and E. J. Hannan (1976). "Vector linear time series models," *Advances in Applied Probability*, 8, 339–64.

Gordin, M. I. (1969). "The central limit theorem for stationary processes," *Soviet Mathematics Doklady*, 1174–6.

Hansen, L. P. (1982). "Large sample properties of generalized method of moments estimators," *Econometrica*, 50, 1029–54.

Hansen, L. P. (1985). "A method for calculating bounds on the asymptotic covariance matrices of generalized method of moments estimators," *Journal of Econometrics*, 30, 203–38.

Hansen, L. P., J. C. Heaton, and M. Ogaki (1988). "Efficiency bounds implied by multi-period conditional moment restrictions," *Journal of the American Statistical Association*, 83, 863–71.

Hansen, L. P., and T. J. Sargent (1982). "Instrumental variables procedures for estimating linear rational expectations models," *Journal of Monetary Economics*, 9, 263–96.

Hansen, L. P., and T. J. Sargent (1991). "Exact linear rational expectations models: specification and estimation," in *Rational Expectations Econometrics, Underground Classics in Economics*, chapter 3, pp. 45–75. Boulder, Colorado: West View Press.

Hansen, L. P., and K. J. Singleton (1990). "Efficient estimation of linear asset pricing models with moving-average errors," NBER Technical Working Paper 86.

Hansen, L. P., and K. J. Singleton (1991). "Computing semi-parametric efficiency bounds for linear time series models," in W. Barnett, J. Powell, and G. Tauchen (eds) *Nonparametric and Semiparametric Methods in Economics and Statistics*, chapter 15, pp. 387–412. New York: Cambridge University Press.

Ibragimov, I. A., and R. Z. Has'minskii (1981). *Statistical Estimation: Asymptotic Theory*. Berlin: Springer-Verlag.

Levit, B. Y. (1975). "On the efficiency of a class of non-parametric estimates," *Theory of Probability and Its applications*, 2, 723–40.

MaCurdy, T. E. (1982). "Using information on the moments of disturbances to increase the efficiency of estimation," manuscript.

Saks, S., and A. Zygmund (1971). *Analytic Functions*. New York: Elsevier Publishing Co.

Stein, C. (1956). "Efficient nonparametric testing and estimation," *Proceedings of the Third Berkeley Symposium on Mathematics and Statistics of Probability*, 1, 187–95.

Stoica, P., Soderstrum, T., and Friedlander, B. (1985). "Optical instrumental variable estimates of the AR parameters of an ARMA process," *IEEE Transactions on Automatic Control*, 1066–74.

Walker, A. M. (1964). "Asymptotic properties of least squares estimates of parameters of a stationary non-deterministic time series," *Journal of the Australian Mathematical Society*, 4, 363–84.

18

Evaluating Dynamic Econometric Models by Encompassing the VAR

David F. Hendry and Grayham E. Mizon

Introduction

It is a pleasure to participate in a volume in honor of Rex Bergstrom given his many contributions to econometrics in general, and to the modeling of small econometric systems in particular (see *inter alia* Bergstrom (1984) and Bergstrom and Wymer (1976)). Most of the models considered by Rex are formulated in continuous time with inference done via discrete time ARMA specifications. Since the particular structural models that Rex analyzed empirically are parsimoniously parameterized, the question arises as to whether they are capable of encompassing general ARMA specifications. This paper provides a framework within which questions of this type can be addressed.

A number of modeling strategies have been advocated for analyzing relationships between economic time series – see for example Hendry (1987), Leamer (1987), Sims (1980), the reviews by Pagan (1987, 1989), and the discussions in Phillips (1991) and Phillips and Loretan (1991). Though these authors have differences of emphasis, and on some issues substantive differences of opinion, they all agree that econometric models need to be evaluated rigorously. For example, in so far as the approach of Sims is to find data coherent models which eschew the imposition of "incredible" *a priori* restrictions, it can be interpreted as an essential first stage in a multistage modeling strategy which seeks to develop models that are congruent with all the available information. Similarly, Hendry and Mizon (1990) argue for seeking models that are congruent with the available information. Necessary conditions for any model to be congruent include data coherency, constant parameters, valid weak exogeneity of any unmodeled variables for parameters of interest, consistency with *a priori* theory, and data admissibility. In addition, any model claiming to be structural must have invariant parameters and be able to parsimoniously encompass the associated unrestricted system; all of these aspects can be evaluated.

This paper derives linear dynamic structural econometric models (SEMs) by a series of reductions from an associated general congruent linear vector autoregressive representation (VAR) to establish a valid basis for inference (see Mizon (1989) and Spanos (1986, 1989b), who terms this basis the Haavelmo distribution, after Haavelmo (1944)). The analysis applies whether the variables being modeled are stationary or nonstationary, though in the latter case an adequate representation of nonstationarity must be found prior to testing structural hypotheses, unless nonstandard distribution theory is to be used (Park and Phillips (1988, 1989), Sims et al. (1990)). When more than one model is available, their performance can be compared by testing which, if any, parsimoniously encompasses the associated VAR or open system: checking whether a SEM is a valid reduction of a congruent VAR is a powerful way to evaluate it. Monfort and Rabemananjara (1990) make a similar proposal for modeling VARs in stationary variables using the theory of asymptotic least squares, and formally derive the appropriate testing theory. Here, the focus is on hypotheses of nonstationarity, constancy, and encompassing.

An additional motivation for the analysis is to provide a feasible method for evaluating the performance of large-scale macroeconomic models. Although the need for rigorous model evaluation is no less for empirical macroeconometric systems than it is for single equations and small-scale models, the lack of degrees of freedom renders whole model evaluation difficult, if not impossible in some cases. The approach described below allows tests of whether particular sectors of large-scale models are capable of encompassing a congruent VAR representation involving all the variables relevant to each sector.

In the present context, the world "model" is ambiguous, since it could denote the activity (to model), a theoretical entity, an empirical representation (in which sense the VAR is an empirical model of the DGP), or a synonym for a set of simultaneous equations. To discriminate between these possible meanings, we refer to the VAR as a system (following Hendry et al. (1988)) and use the acronym SEM for any structural representation, including sets of simultaneous equations.

The next section presents the framework for analyzing VARs and SEMs involving stationary and nonstationary variables. The third section discusses the formulation and estimation of SEMs, and exogeneity conditions, in the context of the entailed reductions. The encompassing hypotheses implied by such SEMs relative to each other and to an embedding VAR are considered in the fourth section. An empirical application analyzes the relationship between UK money, prices, incomes, and interest rates in the fifth section, and the sixth section concludes the paper. Clements and Mizon (1991) present a further application.

VAR Models for Stationary and Nonstationary Data

Formulation

The general system considered for an $N \times 1$ vector of time-series variables $\mathbf{x}_t$ is

$$\mathbf{A}(L)\mathbf{x}_t = \boldsymbol{\psi}\mathbf{D}_t + \mathbf{v}_t \qquad \text{where } \mathbf{v}_t \sim IN(\mathbf{0}, \Sigma), \tag{1}$$

corresponding to:

$$\mathbf{x}_t | \sigma(\mathbf{X}_{t-1}^1) \sim N(-\mathbf{A}^*(L)\mathbf{x}_{t-1} + \boldsymbol{\psi}\mathbf{D}_t, \Sigma) \qquad \text{for } t = 1, 2, \ldots, T, \tag{2}$$

when $\sigma(\mathbf{X}_{t-1}^1)$ is the sigma field generated by $\mathbf{X}_{t-1}^1 = \{\mathbf{x}_1, \mathbf{x}_2, \ldots, \mathbf{x}_{t-1}\}$, and $\mathbf{D}_t$ contains deterministic components (constant, trend, and centered seasonal dummy variables). In (1):

$$\mathbf{A}(L) = \sum_{j=0}^{p} \mathbf{A}_j L^j = \mathbf{I}_N + \mathbf{A}^*(L)L,$$

which is a pth-order matrix polynomial in the lag operator L with $\mathbf{A}_0 = \mathbf{I}_N$. Also, $\{\mathbf{A}_j\}$ and Σ are unrestricted, except that the latter is a symmetric $N \times N$ covariance matrix; the initial values $\mathbf{x}_{1-p}, \mathbf{x}_{2-p}, \ldots, \mathbf{x}_0$ are fixed, and p is finite, so that moving average components are excluded. These assumptions, together with those about independence, normality, and homoscedasticity, are made to simplify the analysis, and none of them is a fundamental restriction. Their relaxation would complicate the algebra without yielding valuable additional insights. However, the assumption that $\{\mathbf{A}_1, \ldots, \mathbf{A}_p, \boldsymbol{\psi}, \Sigma)$ are constant is fundamental, and will be scrutinized below.

Equation (1) can be reparameterized as

$$\Delta \mathbf{x}_t = \sum_{i=1}^{p-1} \mathbf{\Pi}_i \Delta \mathbf{x}_{t-i} + \mathbf{\Pi} \mathbf{x}_{t-p} + \boldsymbol{\psi} \mathbf{D}_t + \mathbf{v}_t, \tag{3}$$

where $\mathbf{\Pi}_i = -(\mathbf{I}_N + \sum_{j=1}^{i} \mathbf{A}_j)$ and $\mathbf{\Pi} = -(\mathbf{I}_N + \sum_{j=1}^{p} \mathbf{A}_j) = -\mathbf{A}(1)$, and $\mathbf{\Pi}$ is the matrix of long-run responses: see for example Johansen and Juselius (1990). Although $\mathbf{v}_t \sim IN(\mathbf{0}, \Sigma)$, and so is stationary, the N variables in $\mathbf{x}_t$ need not all be stationary. For example, if $p = 1$ and $\mathbf{\Pi} = \mathbf{0}$, then (3) consists of N random walks, possibly with drifts and quadratic trends. Temporarily ignoring any deterministic nonstationarities, the rank of $\mathbf{\Pi}$ determines how many level variables x_{it} are stationary, and how many are integrated of first order (denoted I(1): see Granger (1986) and Engle and Granger (1987)) so that Δx_{it} is stationary. It is assumed throughout that none of the roots of $\det(\mathbf{A}(L)) = 0$ are inside the unit circle, so that explosive variables are excluded.

Letting v denote the rank of $\mathbf{\Pi}$, there are three cases:

1. $v = N$ so that all N variables in $\mathbf{x}_t$ are I(0) and hence stationary if there are no deterministic regime shifts or trends in $\mathbf{D}_t$;
2. $v = 0$ so that the N variables in $\mathbf{x}_t$ are I(1), and $\Delta \mathbf{x}_t$ is stationary (apart from the possibility of a deterministic trend); and
3. $0 < v < N$, in which case there are $(N - v)$ linear combinations of $\mathbf{x}_t$, which act as common (stochastic) trends, and v cointegrated linear combinations of $\mathbf{x}_t$.

In this last case, $\mathbf{\Pi}$ can be factored into $-\boldsymbol{\alpha}\boldsymbol{\beta}'$ where both $\boldsymbol{\alpha}$ and $\boldsymbol{\beta}$ are $N \times v$ matrices of rank v, $\boldsymbol{\beta}$ containing the v cointegrating vectors, and $\boldsymbol{\alpha}$ being the loadings matrix (also known as the adjustment parameters), such that the linear combinations $\boldsymbol{\beta}'\mathbf{x}_t$ are I(0) (Johansen 1988, 1991, Hylleberg and Mizon 1989). To ensure that, e.g. I(2) variables are excluded, let $\boldsymbol{\alpha}_\perp$ and $\boldsymbol{\beta}_\perp$ be matrices which are orthogonal to $\boldsymbol{\alpha}$ and $\boldsymbol{\beta}$ respectively, and:

$$\mathbf{\Psi} = (\partial \mathbf{A}(z)/\partial z)|_{z=1}$$

which is the mean lag matrix. Then $\boldsymbol{\alpha}_\perp' \mathbf{\Psi} \boldsymbol{\beta}_\perp$ should have rank $N - v$ (Johansen 1988).

Phillips (1991) shows the importance for modeling integrated variables of determining the order of integration of each variable and the dimension of the cointegrating space v, and using this knowledge in the estimation and testing of the cointegrated system. Not to do so can result in nonoptimal inference. It is also critical that the nature of the deterministic variables in $\mathbf{D}_t$ be established if valid inferences are to be drawn, particularly when $\mathbf{x}_t$ is I(1). For example, Johansen and Juselius (1990) show that the distribution of the likelihood ratio test statistic for determining the dimension of the cointegrating space varies depending on the presence, or absence, of constant terms in the system, and also varies depending on whether the constant terms are restricted to lie in the space orthogonal to the loadings matrix $\boldsymbol{\alpha}$, i.e. whether the vector of constants $\boldsymbol{\psi}_1 = \boldsymbol{\alpha\beta}_0$ say.

These considerations suggest that modeling might begin by determining the time-series properties of each variable separately, using univariate tests for the order of integration (and possible presence of deterministic trends and/or seasonals) such as Dickey–Fuller, augmented Dickey–Fuller, and Phillips' z statistics (Dickey and Fuller 1979, 1981, Phillips and Perron 1988). However, analysis of the relationships between the variables in $\mathbf{x}_t$ also must be undertaken in the context of a congruent VAR like (3), to assess the validity of single equation methods (Spanos 1989a, Phillips 1991, Phillips and Loretan 1991). This is particularly important when $\mathbf{x}_t$ is I(1), since the determination of ν requires analysis of the N-variable system.

Even when $\mathbf{x}_t$ is I(0), it remains important to have a general congruent system underlying the analysis, and advantageous to adopt a general-to-specific modeling strategy. The alternative strategy of starting from a specific (perhaps *a priori* theory determined) system, and then subjecting that to misspecification testing, is seen to be flawed when it is realized that the first "significant" misspecification test statistic invalidates all preceding inferences, subject to probabilities of type 1 error. Further, as noted in Ericsson and Hendry (1989), and demonstrated in Mizon (1989), empirical evidence can corroborate more than one model, even though the models may be based on conflicting theories. A general-to-specific modeling strategy, on the other hand, first seeks to find a congruent statistical system, to provide a valid basis for conditional inference, and then tests and compares alternative *a priori* theories within this well-grounded statistical framework. These properties of congruent SEMs in the class defined in (3) and of a general-to-specific modeling strategy are exploited below, which also seeks to extend the analysis in Hendry et al. (1988), to I(1) variables.

Estimation and Hypothesis Testing in VARs

Despite the practical importance of allowing for deterministic variables, and of establishing the precise form in which they enter models of the class in (3), deterministic components will be ignored in this and the next two sections in order to simplify the analysis and concentrate attention on the relationships between the variables in $\mathbf{x}_t$. A further notational simplification is obtained by writing (1) in companion form as

$$\mathbf{x}_t^+ = \mathbf{A}^+\mathbf{x}_{t-1}^+ + \boldsymbol{\varepsilon}_t, \qquad \text{where } \mathbf{x}_t^+ = \begin{pmatrix} \mathbf{x}_t \\ \mathbf{x}_{t-1} \\ \vdots \\ \mathbf{x}_{t-p} \end{pmatrix},$$

$$\mathbf{A}^+ = \begin{pmatrix} -\mathbf{A}_1 & -\mathbf{A}_2 & \dots & -\mathbf{A}_{p-1} & -\mathbf{A}_p & \mathbf{0} \\ \mathbf{I} & \mathbf{0} & \dots & \mathbf{0} & \mathbf{0} & \mathbf{0} \\ \dots & \dots & \dots & \dots & \dots & \dots \\ \mathbf{0} & \mathbf{0} & \dots & \mathbf{0} & \mathbf{I} & \mathbf{0} \end{pmatrix}, \qquad \boldsymbol{\varepsilon}_t = \begin{pmatrix} \mathbf{v}_t \\ \mathbf{0} \\ \vdots \\ \mathbf{0} \end{pmatrix}, \tag{4}$$

Using $\boldsymbol{\Pi} = -\boldsymbol{\alpha}\boldsymbol{\beta}'$, the corresponding representation for (3) is

$$\mathbf{f}_t = \boldsymbol{\Pi}^*\mathbf{f}_{t-1} + \boldsymbol{\varepsilon}_t, \qquad \text{where } \mathbf{f}_t = \begin{pmatrix} \Delta\mathbf{x}_t \\ \vdots \\ \Delta\mathbf{x}_{t-p+1} \\ \boldsymbol{\beta}'\mathbf{x}_{t-p} \end{pmatrix},$$

$$\boldsymbol{\Pi}^* = \begin{pmatrix} \boldsymbol{\Pi}_1 & \boldsymbol{\Pi}_2 & \cdots & \boldsymbol{\Pi}_{p-1} & -\boldsymbol{\alpha}\boldsymbol{\beta}' & -\boldsymbol{\alpha} \\ \mathbf{I} & \mathbf{0} & \ldots & \mathbf{0} & \mathbf{0} & \mathbf{0} \\ \ldots & \ldots & \ldots & \ldots & \ldots & \ldots \\ \mathbf{0} & \mathbf{0} & \ldots & & \boldsymbol{\beta}' & \mathbf{I} \end{pmatrix}. \tag{5}$$

In (4) and (5), $\boldsymbol{\varepsilon}_t \sim IN(\mathbf{0}, \boldsymbol{\Omega})$, where $\boldsymbol{\Omega}$ is non-negative definite, but singular. In general, $\mathbf{x}_t^+$ is I(1) but an important property of (5) is that $\mathbf{f}_t$ is I(0). The system could be reformulated by rearranging and partitioning $\mathbf{x}_t$ into $(\mathbf{x}'_{at}:\mathbf{x}'_{bt})'$ where $\Delta\mathbf{x}'_{at}$ and $\mathbf{x}'_t\boldsymbol{\beta}$ are I(0), the former corresponding to the equations with unit roots (Phillips 1991). Then, letting $\mathbf{z}'_t = (\Delta\mathbf{x}'_{at}:\mathbf{x}'_t\boldsymbol{\beta})$, and $\mathbf{w}'_t = (\mathbf{z}'_t:\mathbf{z}'_{t-1}:\ldots:\mathbf{z}'_{t-p})$, the system $\mathbf{w}_t = \mathbf{P}\mathbf{w}_{t-1} + \boldsymbol{\zeta}_t$ yields an isomorphic representation of (5). Thus, the long-run solution for the system can be defined in terms of $E[\mathbf{z}_t]$ where $E[\cdot]$ denotes expectation with respect to the system. This formulation is easily generalized to incorporate identities as below.

In the case that $\mathbf{x}_t$ is I(1) and there are no cointegrating vectors (i.e. $v = 0$ so that $\boldsymbol{\Pi} = \mathbf{0}$), (4) is of the form of (10) in Phillips and Durlauf (1986), with $\mathbf{A}^+$ replacing their $\mathbf{A}$. Hence, the limiting distribution of the least squares estimator of $\mathbf{A}^+$ can be obtained from their theorem 3.2, and that of $\boldsymbol{\Omega}$ from their theorem 3.3. These theorems apply for errors $\boldsymbol{\varepsilon}_t$ generated by more general processes than those considered in this paper, e.g. vector ARMA processes with some heteroscedasticity. Further, although the conventional statistics for testing hypotheses about $\mathbf{A}^+$ do not have the usual limiting distributions, Phillips and Durlauf (1986) provide test statistics which do have limiting χ^2 distributions.

Alternatively, if it is known that $\boldsymbol{\Pi} = \mathbf{0}$, and this information is used, then (5) becomes a VAR in the I(0) variables $\Delta\mathbf{x}_t$ for which the usual methods of estimation and hypothesis testing apply. This latter point re-emphasizes the importance of determining the orders of integration of the variables in $\mathbf{x}_t$ and of the dimension of the cointegrating space v at the start of modeling. The same point applies, perhaps with more importance, in cases where $\mathbf{x}_t$ is I(1), but $0 < v < N$. In such cases, if it is known that v cointegrating vectors exist, it is possible to estimate the parameters of (5) with $\boldsymbol{\alpha}$ and $\boldsymbol{\beta}$ of rank v, using the maximum likelihood procedure of Johansen (1988), and it is also possible to test hypotheses (including certain hypotheses about $\boldsymbol{\alpha}$ and $\boldsymbol{\beta}$) using test statistics which have limiting χ^2 distributions.

When the locations of the unit roots or values of $\boldsymbol{\beta}$ are unknown, a two-step approach is required, with the Johansen (1988) procedure as the first step, after which the I(0) formulation is based on estimated cointegrating vectors. Since the variances of estimated $\boldsymbol{\beta}_i$ are a smaller order in T than the variances of estimated coefficients of I(0) variables, it is legitimate to condition inferences on them as in Engle and Granger (1987) and Stock (1987).

Finally, in the stationary case, when $\mathbf{\Pi}$ has full rank N, and so in parameterization (4), all of the eigenvalues of $\mathbf{A}^+$ have modulus less than unity, estimation and hypothesis testing are standard. In particular, since $E[\mathbf{f}_{t-1}\boldsymbol{\varepsilon}_s'] = \mathbf{0}\ \forall s > t$, the second moments of $\mathbf{f}_t$, namely $\mathbf{M} = E[\mathbf{f}_t\mathbf{f}_t']$ and $\mathbf{M}_1 = E[\mathbf{f}_t\mathbf{f}_{t-1}']$, are given by the following:

$$\mathbf{M} = \mathbf{\Pi}^*\mathbf{M}\mathbf{\Pi}^{*\prime} + \mathbf{\Omega}, \qquad \mathbf{M}_1 = \mathbf{\Pi}^*\mathbf{M}, \tag{6}$$

so that

$$\text{vech}\,(\mathbf{M}) = (\mathbf{I} - \mathbf{\Pi}^* \otimes \mathbf{\Pi}^{*\prime})^{-1}\,\text{vech}\,(\mathbf{\Omega}), \tag{7}$$

when vech $(\cdot)$ is a column vector operator. If there were unit roots, the inverse in (7) would not exist. The sample estimators of these moments are $\hat{\mathbf{M}} = T^{-1}\mathbf{F}'\mathbf{F}$, $\hat{\mathbf{M}}_1 = T^{-1}\mathbf{F}'\mathbf{F}_1$ when $\mathbf{F}' = (\mathbf{f}_1\mathbf{f}_2, \ldots, \mathbf{f}_T)$, so that from Hannan (1970, chapter 4), under our assumptions:

$$\sqrt{T}\,\text{vech}\,(\hat{\mathbf{M}} - \mathbf{M}) \to_d N(\mathbf{0}, \mathbf{C}). \tag{8}$$

Govaerts (1986) obtains $\mathbf{C}$ when $\mathbf{\Pi}^* = \mathbf{Q}\mathbf{\Lambda}\mathbf{Q}^{-1}$ and $\mathbf{\Lambda}$ is block diagonal with complex and possibly repeated roots.

With this review of the relevant results on estimation and testing in stationary and nonstationary VARs as background, it is now possible to consider the relationship between SEMs and both VARs (which have no exogenous variables) and open systems (which condition on nonmodeled variables).

SEMs: Formulation and Estimation

Closed Systems

A key property of (5) is that it defines the conditional means and variances of all the I(0) variables, which we express succinctly as $E[\mathbf{f}_t|\mathbf{f}_{t-1}] = \mathbf{\Pi}^*\mathbf{f}_{t-1}$ and $\text{Var}\,(\mathbf{f}_t|\mathbf{f}_{t-1}) = \mathbf{\Omega}$. Thus, in I(0) space, the VAR can be interpreted as a model of these conditional means and variances. Given that background, the class of SEM considered has the form

$$\mathbf{\Phi}\mathbf{f}_t = \mathbf{u}_t, \tag{9}$$

where $\mathbf{\Phi}$ is an $n \times N^*$ matrix of structural parameters with $N^* = Np + v$ and $n \leq N$, subject to normalization and sufficient *a priori* identifying restrictions. The identification of the structural parameters must be determined relative to the congruent statistical systems for $\{\mathbf{f}_t\}$, namely (5), and not simply in the context of the SEM (9) (Spanos 1990). Since (4) and (5) are alternative parameterizations of the original congruent statistical system, there is no loss of generality in considering structural models in terms of $\mathbf{f}_t$ rather than $\mathbf{x}_t^+$.

Equations (5) and (9) imply that

$$\mathbf{\Phi}\mathbf{f}_t = \mathbf{\Phi}\mathbf{\Pi}^*\mathbf{f}_{t-1} + \mathbf{\Phi}\boldsymbol{\varepsilon}_t = \mathbf{u}_t, \tag{10}$$

from which two important subclasses of models emerge, depending on whether or not (9) is dynamically misspecified. The errors $\mathbf{u}_t$ are usually assumed by investigators to be serially uncorrelated, and yet this will only be the case if $\mathbf{\Phi\Pi}^* = \mathbf{0}$ so that $\mathbf{u}_t = \mathbf{\Phi}\boldsymbol{\varepsilon}_t$. A more common form of stating this condition for the correct dynamic specification of (9) is $E[\mathbf{f}_{t-1}\mathbf{u}_t'] = \mathbf{0}$, which is an instrument validity condition. If $\mathbf{\Phi\Pi}^* = \mathbf{0}$, then (9) is dynamically well specified, but this condition cannot be known to hold *a priori* and so has to be tested relative to (5), which has been designed to be congruent.

The second subclass arises when $\mathbf{\Phi\Pi}^* \neq \mathbf{0}$, so that (9) is dynamically misspecified in that $\mathbf{u}_t$ will be serially correlated, and hence potentially all other inferences about the elements of $\mathbf{\Phi}$ are invalidated. A particular problem that might arise in the present context is that some dynamic misspecification may involve omitted I(1) variables which, if undetected, could induce spurious regressions. Whilst analysis of other features of the SEM (9), using test statistics which are robust to temporal dependence and heterogeneity might be contemplated (as in Domowitz and White (1982) and White (1989)), the fact that $\mathbf{\Phi}$ is inconsistently estimated by regression invalidates this class of inferences, which in any case are inefficient relative to those which are undertaken in the context of a dynamically correctly specified model. This is an especially serious drawback when testing constancy and invariance claims about putative structural parameters.

Let $\mathbf{\Phi} = (\mathbf{\Gamma}_0, \mathbf{\Gamma}_1, \ldots, \mathbf{\Gamma}_{p-1}, \mathbf{\Gamma})$, then from (5), (9) is:

$$\mathbf{\Gamma}_0 \,\Delta\mathbf{x}_t = -\sum_{i=1}^{p-1} \mathbf{\Gamma}_i \,\Delta\mathbf{x}_{t-i} - \mathbf{\Gamma}\boldsymbol{\beta}'\mathbf{x}_{t-p} + \mathbf{u}_t. \tag{9'}$$

Since (5) is congruent by hypothesis, then so is (9′) if the identifying restrictions on $\mathbf{\Phi}$ are valid (Hatanaka 1975, Monfort and Rabemananjara 1990). Indeed, (9′) simply provides a parsimonious interpretation of the conditional mean and variance of $\mathbf{x}_t$ noted above, in terms of nonlinear restrictions on $\mathbf{\Pi}^*$, rather than the linear restrictions associated with exclusion and noncausality claims. Note that $\boldsymbol{\beta}$ is an invariant under the class of linear transformations considered here.

An important distinction that must be made in (9′) is whether or not all the variables involved are I(0). If the SEM is correctly specified, then in case 1, $\mathbf{\Gamma}$ can take any value; in case 2, $\mathbf{\Gamma} = \mathbf{0}$, so only differenced variables enter; and in case 3, $\mathbf{\Gamma} = \boldsymbol{\gamma}$, which is $n \times v$. If the SEM is not correctly specified, there are two possible situations: (a) the I(1) components are misspecified (for example, the formulation of $\mathbf{\Gamma}$ might preclude cointegrating combinations being included in (9′); and (b) only the I(0) terms are incorrectly formulated (short-term dynamics are incorrect). In practice, investigators must be aware of such possible misspecifications and should investigate each of the issues.

Although the correct dynamic specification cannot be known, there are clear advantages to be gained from attempting to ensure that the system being used is dynamically well specified and that the models thereof are congruent with the system. However, nothing prevents investigators either from asserting that the $\mathbf{u}_t$ of their SEM is well specified, or from actually applying the standard test statistics to such models (see for example Pesaran and Deaton (1978) for an empirical illustration). Moreover, an important encompassing prediction of one model might well be the presence of autocorrelation in the errors of a rival specification (see Ericsson and Hendry (1985) for an example).

Open Systems

The class specified so far in (9) consists of *a priori* restricted closed systems or VARs which do not condition on potentially exogenous variables. For this class, restrictions are largely concerned with dynamic structure, and in particular with hypotheses of Granger noncausality and simplified dynamics. In fact, the only hypotheses not concerned with dynamics and constancy (or invariance: see Frisch (1938) and Aldrich (1989)) are restrictions on the contemporaneous covariance matrix $\boldsymbol{\Sigma}$. Although it is important to have a congruent VAR like (5) as a valid basis for conditional inference, it is unusual for economic theories to be concerned with closed models, and theories typically regard some variables as being determined exogenously. For example, in demand for money studies it is often assumed that the income variable, and possibly the interest rate, are exogenous, in that the econometric analyses are undertaken in the context of the distribution of money demand conditional on income and the interest rate. We provide later an empirical example in which income and the interest rate do appear to be weakly exogenous for the parameters of the money demand equation.

The treatment of some variables as weakly exogenous (Engle et al. 1983) can be valid by construction, particularly when the underlying distributions are normal and the parameters of interest are those of the relevant conditional distributions. This is not the case for all variables though, and so there are occasions when it is important to test exogeneity hypotheses. For example, invalid conditioning can result in parameter nonconstancy when there are changes in the process generating the conditioning variables. Hence apparent structural change in conditional submodels can provide an indirect test of weak exogeneity hypotheses – see Anderson and Mizon (1989) for further discussion of this point, and for alternative ways of dealing with parameter nonconstancy and structural change. The empirical illustration includes changes in government policies and in a major commodity price, which induce parameter nonconstancy in the closed VAR, and so lead us to introduce dummy variables to deal with these specific events.

Of equal importance when $\mathbf{x}_t$ is I(1) are cross-equation links induced by the presence in several equations of a common cointegrating combination $\boldsymbol{\beta}_i'\mathbf{x}_t$ where $\boldsymbol{\beta}_i'$ is the i row of $\boldsymbol{\beta}'$. If the same $\boldsymbol{\beta}_i'\mathbf{x}_t$ enters the j and k equations, then the contemporaneous values of the $\mathbf{x}_t$ with nonzero coefficients in $\boldsymbol{\beta}_i'\mathbf{x}_t$ cannot be weakly exogenous for the parameters of the i equation, since the resulting parameters cannot be variation free. Failure to account for such linkages can seriously affect the validity of inference as documented by Phillips (1991) and Phillips and Loretan (1991). This form of failure of weak exogeneity also occurs in the empirical example, and throws light on both earlier successful money demand studies and the difficulty experienced by other investigators in establishing excess demand influences on inflation in UK macroeconomic models.

For an open system incorporating I(1) nonmodeled variables to be well defined in terms of I(0) modeled variables, all nonstationarity inherited from the nonmodeled variables must be mapped into cointegrating vectors. If the locations of the unit roots and cointegrating vectors are known, the system as a whole can be mapped into I(0) space, using the transformed partition of $\mathbf{x}_t$ into $\mathbf{z}_t = (\Delta\mathbf{x}_{at}':\mathbf{x}_t'\boldsymbol{\beta})'$ noted above.

Thereafter, conventional asymptotics apply. If the locations of the unit roots are unknown, but the conditional distribution of the modeled variables given the nonmodeled is stationary, the analysis proceeds as in Johansen (1992). Partition $\Delta \mathbf{x}_t$ into $(\Delta \mathbf{x}'_{1t} : \Delta \mathbf{x}'_{2t})'$, where the $\Delta \mathbf{x}_{2t}$ are to be treated as weakly exogenous for the parameters of interest $\boldsymbol{\mu}$, deemed throughout to include $\boldsymbol{\alpha}$ and $\boldsymbol{\beta}$. Factorize the joint sequential density $D_X(\Delta \mathbf{x}_t | \mathbf{f}_{t-1}, \boldsymbol{\theta})$ of $\Delta \mathbf{x}_t$ accordingly as

$$D_X(\Delta \mathbf{x}_t | \mathbf{f}_{t-1}, \boldsymbol{\theta}) = D_{X_1|X_2}(\Delta \mathbf{x}_{1t} | \Delta \mathbf{x}_{2t}, \mathbf{f}_{t-1}, \boldsymbol{\theta}_1) D_{X_2}(\Delta \mathbf{x}_{2t} | \mathbf{f}_{t-1}, \boldsymbol{\theta}_2), \tag{11}$$

noting that information on the cointegrating vectors is retained by $\mathbf{f}_{t-1}$. Then, $\Delta \mathbf{x}_{2t}$ is weakly exogenous for $\boldsymbol{\mu}$ if $\boldsymbol{\mu}$ depends on $\boldsymbol{\theta}_1$ alone, and $\boldsymbol{\theta}_1$ and $\boldsymbol{\theta}_2$ are variation free. Such a requirement is violated if both $\boldsymbol{\theta}_1$ and $\boldsymbol{\theta}_2$ depend on the same $\{\boldsymbol{\beta}_i\}$. Since

$$\boldsymbol{\alpha\beta}'\mathbf{x}_t = \begin{bmatrix} \boldsymbol{\alpha}_{11} & \boldsymbol{\alpha}_{12} \\ \boldsymbol{\alpha}_{21} & \boldsymbol{\alpha}_{22} \end{bmatrix} \begin{bmatrix} \boldsymbol{\beta}'_{11} & \boldsymbol{\beta}'_{12} \\ \boldsymbol{\beta}'_{21} & \boldsymbol{\beta}'_{22} \end{bmatrix} \begin{bmatrix} \mathbf{x}_{1t} \\ \mathbf{x}_{2t} \end{bmatrix} = \begin{bmatrix} \boldsymbol{\alpha}_{11} & \boldsymbol{\alpha}_{12} \\ \boldsymbol{\alpha}_{21} & \boldsymbol{\alpha}_{22} \end{bmatrix} \begin{bmatrix} \boldsymbol{\beta}'_{11}\mathbf{x}_{1t} + \boldsymbol{\beta}'_{12}\mathbf{x}_{2t} \\ \boldsymbol{\beta}'_{21}\mathbf{x}_{1t} + \boldsymbol{\beta}'_{22}\mathbf{x}_{2t} \end{bmatrix}, \tag{12}$$

and since conditioning $\Delta \mathbf{x}_{1t}$ on $\Delta \mathbf{x}_{2t}$ creates the error correction mechanism (ECM) $\{\boldsymbol{\alpha}_{12} - \boldsymbol{\Sigma}_{12}\boldsymbol{\Sigma}_{22}^{-1}\boldsymbol{\alpha}_{22}\}\{\boldsymbol{\beta}'_{21}\mathbf{x}_{1t} + \boldsymbol{\beta}'_{22}\mathbf{x}_{2t}\}$, then necessary conditions for the weak exogeneity of $\Delta \mathbf{x}_{2t}$ for $(\boldsymbol{\alpha}_{11} : \boldsymbol{\beta}_{11} : \boldsymbol{\beta}_{12})$ are that $\boldsymbol{\alpha}_{21} = \mathbf{0}$ and that $\{\boldsymbol{\alpha}_{12} - \boldsymbol{\Sigma}_{12}\boldsymbol{\Sigma}_{22}^{-1}\boldsymbol{\alpha}_{22}\} = \mathbf{0}$. These are testable from the procedure in Johansen (1988, 1992) and Johansen and Juselius (1990). However, linking short-run parameters with some of the $\{\boldsymbol{\beta}_i\}$ need not matter for inferences about long-run parameters of interest. One of the advantages of testing SEMs against closed VARs is that exogeneity hypotheses can be tested, rather than merely being asserted, as in the conventional specification of SEMs.

For SEMs defined on conditional distributions, where certain variables are validly regarded as weakly exogenous as in (11), the relevant underlying congruent statistical system is a VAR, which has the role usually played by the unrestricted reduced form equations. However, the order of specification has been reversed in that the SEM arises as a valid reduction of the system, rather than the reduced form being derived from the SEM and then treated as unrestricted. *A priori* restrictions from economic theory, even though they may be expressed as restrictions on the structural equations, are constraints which can be tested as hypotheses on the parameters of the open system. The likelihood ratio testing principle provides an obvious method to test these structural overidentifying restrictions. However, since they are being tested relative to a congruent system (which could be a VAR if no conditioning assumptions were imposed), the modeling is not being done with a structure which is (over)identified on the basis of incredible restrictions. Rather, the credibility of the *a priori* structural information is being directly assessed relative to a statistically well specified or congruent system: see Hendry et al. (1988) for further details in a stationary context.

In addition to being able to test the ability of any particular SEM to encompass a congruent system, it is important to be able to assess the relative merits of alternative structural models. The next section develops a theory for testing rival structural models.

Encompassing

Closed Systems
Consider rival SEMs of the form

$$H_a: \mathbf{\Phi}_a \mathbf{f}_t = \mathbf{u}_{at}, \qquad H_b: \mathbf{\Phi}_b \mathbf{f}_t = \mathbf{u}_{bt}, \tag{13}$$

which are (over)identified relative to the congruent statistical system (5), where $\mathbf{\Phi}_a$ and $\mathbf{\Phi}_b$ are $n_a \times N^*$ and $n_b \times N^*$ respectively. Two cases must be distinguished: whether the SEMs are complete or not (i.e. whether n_a and n_b equal n); and whether the SEMs are in I(0) space or not. The importance of the latter is to ensure that the correct critical values of tests are used in practice (e.g. not conventional ones if the VAR is I(1) and the SEM is I(0)); we assume a mapping to I(0) prior to testing encompassing hypotheses. The former raises more subtle issues when the SEMs are incomplete; in particular, they must be explaining the same set of variables (Hendry 1986). Here, we restrict attention to complete systems.

The error covariance matrices of each specification in (13) are given by $\mathbf{\Sigma}_{aa} = \mathbf{\Phi}_a \mathbf{M} \mathbf{\Phi}_a'$ and $\mathbf{\Sigma}_{bb} = \mathbf{\Phi}_b \mathbf{M} \mathbf{\Phi}_b'$ respectively, so that H_a dominates in H_b in generalized variance (or likelihood) if $\det(\mathbf{\Sigma}_{aa}) \leq \det(\mathbf{\Sigma}_{bb})$. Although generalized variance dominance provides a natural criterion for model comparisons, it is only a necessary condition for H_a to encompass H_b (denoted $H_a \mathscr{E} H_b$). When the DGP for $\mathbf{x}_t$ is not known, the congruent statistical system, in this case the VAR (5), provides a framework within which the properties of H_a and H_b can be evaluated. In particular, the VAR defines a common probability space within which the rival models can be compared.

Let γ_b denote the vector of parameters in $\mathbf{\Phi}_b$ which characterizes H_b, noting that the value of γ_b is implied by (5), and is a function of $\mathbf{\Pi}^*$ and $\mathbf{\Sigma}$. Let γ_p denote what H_a predicts γ_b to be when H_a is assumed to be the DGP. Then H_a encompasses $H_b(H_a \mathscr{E} H_b)$ if and only if $(\gamma_b - \gamma_p) = \mathbf{0}$.

Both H_a and H_b are nested within the VAR (5), which we denote by $H_i \subset$ VAR. It is clear that the VAR automatically encompasses H_i by virtue of each H_i being a reduction of the VAR. The issue of interest here is whether either of H_a or H_b encompasses the VAR. If so, since a simple model is accounting for the results of a more general model within which it is nested, we call this parsimonious encompassing of the VAR, denoted $H_a \mathscr{E}_p$ VAR, or $H_b \mathscr{E}_p$ VAR. For further details on encompassing, see Hendry and Richard (1982, 1989), Mizon (1984), and Mizon and Richard (1986).

The main difficulty in establishing encompassing theorems about SEMs is that their exogeneity assumptions may differ, so that the models are not in a common probability space. This problem does not arise with closed systems if either H_a or H_b asserts that $E_i[\mathbf{u}_{it}\mathbf{f}_{t-1}'] = \mathbf{0}$ for $i =$ a, b where E_i denotes expectations with respect to model i. Consider the case when $i =$ a. Since $E_a[\mathbf{u}_{at}\mathbf{f}_{t-1}'] = \mathbf{0}$ implies that the derived error $\{\mathbf{u}_{at}\}$ is an innovation against the past of the process, from (13) and (5):

$$E[\mathbf{\Phi}_a \mathbf{f}_t \mathbf{f}_{t-1}'] = \mathbf{\Phi}_a \mathbf{\Pi}^* E[\mathbf{f}_{t-1}\mathbf{f}_{t-1}'] \tag{14}$$

must be zero for all t, and hence:

$$\mathbf{\Phi}_a \mathbf{\Pi}^* = \mathbf{0}. \tag{15}$$

This is precisely the earlier condition for the absence of dynamic misspecification.

If (15) holds, then H_a is a valid reduction of the VAR and hence H_a parsimoniously encompasses the VAR. Conversely, if (15) does not hold, H_a cannot encompass the VAR since H_a can be rejected against the VAR in that elements of $\mathbf{f}_{t-1}$ must be relevant to H_a in addition to the variables included through its definition in (13). If neither modeler accepts the validity of the instruments used by the other, or there are insufficient instruments to identify the joint or nesting hypothesis, considerable problems can ensue and cross-model encompassing may not be testable (Ericsson 1983). Thus, conditional on the proprietor of H_a accepting lagged variables as legitimate potential explanatory variables:

Theorem 1 $H_a \mathscr{E}$ VAR *if and only if* $\mathbf{\Phi}_a\mathbf{\Pi}^* = \mathbf{0}$.

A consequence of theorem 1, is the following.

Theorem 2 *If* $H_a \mathscr{E}_p$ VAR *and* $H_i \subset$ VAR, *then* $H_a \mathscr{E} H_i$.

Thus, we use the VAR as a catalyst for allowing encompassing comparisons between SEMs. The converse of theorem 2 is false in that $H_a \mathscr{E} H_i$ could hold without $H_a \mathscr{E}_p$ VAR (e.g. because $H_i \subset H_a$), but by requiring congruence, H_a would be rejected against the VAR in our framework. Hence, to encompass rival models, it is sufficient for H_a to be congruent and $H_a \mathscr{E}_p$ VAR.

Since $\mathbf{\Pi}^*$ is generally singular, the set $\{\mathbf{\Phi}_i|\mathbf{\Phi}_i\mathbf{\Pi}^* = \mathbf{0}; \mathrm{i} = \mathrm{a, b}, \ldots\}$ will usually have more than one element, and hence many models could satisfy the encompassing property in theorem 1, and be mutually encompassing. The appendix provides a four-equation example. Thus, the theorem defines an equivalence class of mutually encompassing models, which may nevertheless correspond to apparently antagonistic theoretical specifications, all of which can be identifiable conditional on their *a priori* restrictions. In this sense, therefore, the claim in Sims (1980) that structural identifying information is "incredible" is sustainable: since the equivalence class members are observationally equivalent, how could "prior" information about particular members ever be acquired?

The resolution to this conundrum in our framework rests on the applicability of the Lucas critique (Frisch 1938, Haavelmo 1944, Lucas 1976, Aldrich 1989). Moreover, such a resolution supplies a constructive application of what is often used as a destructive empirical criticism. Specifically, coefficients $\mathbf{\Phi}_i$ in the set $\{\mathbf{\Phi}_i|\mathbf{\Phi}_i\mathbf{\Pi}^* = \mathbf{0}\}$ which are not merely reparameterizations of each other cannot all be invariant to changes in the parameters of the DGP, since they are different functions of those parameters. Thus, policy regime changes will induce changes in some of the parameter sets, destroying the observational equivalence, and hence mutual encompassing, which held in a constant parameter world. Succinctly, if nature experiments enough for us, only that representation which corresponds to the actual structure of behaviour will remain constant, and hence its parameters be super exogenous. For further results on testing the Lucas critique, see Engle and Hendry (1989) and Favero and Hendry (1989).

Open Systems

The basic difficulty for open system encompassing, from (11) above, is that SEMs may differ in their specification of exogeneity. The resolution proposed here is a two-step test:

1. Test each closed model against the VAR using theorem 2.
2. Test the validity of the weak exogeneity reduction of each closed model.

1 If both SEMs encompass the VAR, then they are observationally equivalent; if neither does, both are rejected relative to the VAR; and if one does then it is an acceptable parameterization. The condition for a closed SEM to encompass a closed VAR in I(0) form coincides with the well-known condition for the validity of over-identifying restrictions, namely $\mathbf{\Phi\Pi^*} = \mathbf{0}$. This requirement is tested below using a likelihood ratio statistic. The same form of test applies in a congruent open system with valid conditioning variables, subject to noting the prior reduction to I(0).

2 The aspect of weak exogeneity that is most easily tested in I(1) systems is the presence of cointegrating vectors in several relationships, and this is investigated empirically below from the estimates of $\boldsymbol{\alpha}$.

An Empirical Illustration

The empirical example is for a VAR which interrelates money, prices, incomes, and interest rates in the UK. The measure of money, denoted by M, is quarterly M1 over the period 1963 through 1984, where the precise dates depend on the lag lengths of the models to be analyzed. The income measure (Y) is constant price total final expenditure (TFE), the price measure (P) is the implicit deflator of TFE and the interest rate (R) is the three-month local authority bill rate. All variables (other than R) are seasonally adjusted and lower case letters denote logarithms of capitals.

The first important choice concerns the functional form specification of the VAR, and here three issues require note. First, preliminary analysis revealed a high degree of non-constancy in any system involving the level of R_t (rather than r_t), primarily due to a large increase in the residual variance of the equation for R_t over the sample period. Thus, although Trundle (1982) showed the advantages of R_t over r_t as a regressor in money-demand equations in the UK, because of the system context and the restriction to a linear analysis, we decided to use r_t as the interest rate variable in the system.

Secondly, the VAR must be interpreted as having been marginalized with respect to all other relevant variables, which here include exchange rates, commodity prices, capital and labor inputs, and fiscal policy measures. Consequently, there remain no explanatory factors for one of the levels of p_t and m_t, necessitating that the remaining measure enter only in differences. Given the requirement that the money variable had to be real money to maintain long-run homogeneity with respect to prices, the system could be interpreted at this stage as determining either of m_t or p_t.

Finally, to account for the level of y_t, a linear trend was used as a proxy for the combined effects of input growth and technical progress, although this is not a very satisfactory resolution of a difficult problem. Thus, the selected VAR involved the four variables $(m_t - p_t, \Delta p_t, y_t, r_t)$. Their time series graphs are shown in figure 18.1(a–d) and suggest that $(m_t - p_t, \Delta p_t, r_t)$ are near I(1), whereas y_t is closer to being stationary around a trend over the sample considered here.[1]

The next set of issues concerns the substantial number of regime changes which occurred over the sample period. On the domestic scene, these include the Competition and Credit Control Regulations of 1971, the attempt by the Heath government to

Figure 18.1(a) **Real M1 in the UK** ($m - p$)

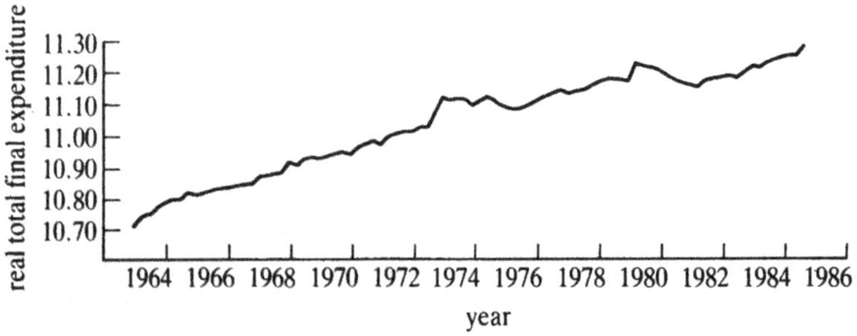

Figure 18.1(b) **Real total final expenditure in the UK** (y)

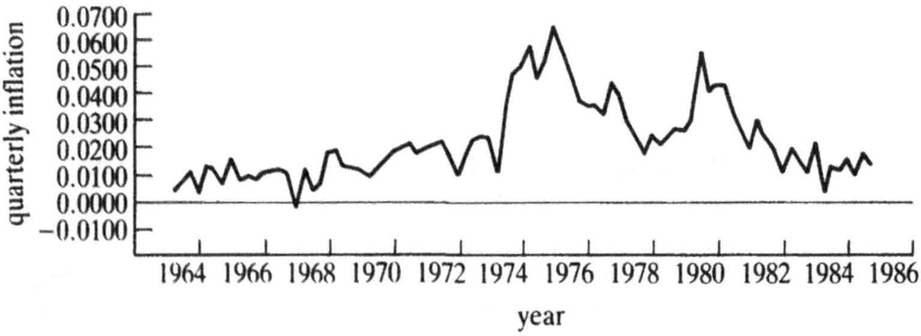

Figure 18.1(c) **Quarterly rate of inflation in the UK** (Δp)

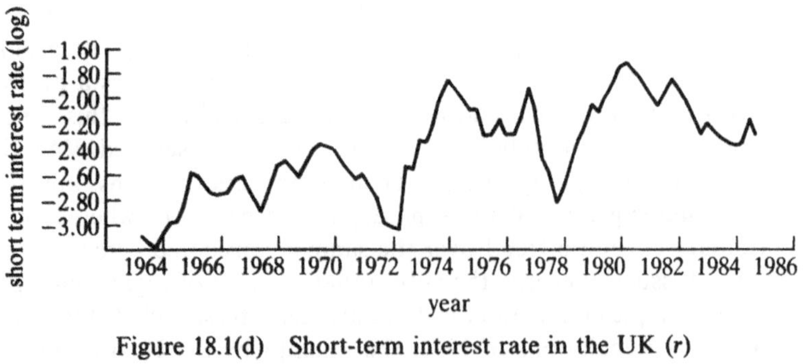

Figure 18.1(d) **Short-term interest rate in the UK** (r)

"go for growth" in 1973, the change in the rate of value added tax (VAT) from 8 percent to 15 percent in 1979, the abandonment of exchange controls in that year, and the tight monetary policy introduced by the Thatcher government after 1979. Internationally, we note the UK's decision to follow the shift from fixed to floating exchange rates in 1971, and the oil crises in late 1973 and again in 1979, with the important difference that the UK became essentially self-sufficient in oil between those two dates. It is possible that the VAR might need dummy variables for any or all of these changes; since the dummies would enter unrestrictedly in the VAR, but restrictedly in the model thereof, encompassing the VAR by a structural model should be challenging.

The first stage of the analysis checked for the degree of integratedness of the individual series. Such univariate evidence can at best provide a rough guide since the associated tests are conditional on untested, and usually unlikely, auxiliary hypotheses concerning constancy of the parameters in the scalar representations. Nevertheless, an augmented Dickey–Fuller (ADF) test, including a trend, was conducted for each series, with the lag length selected to remove any manifest residual serial correlation (Dickey and Fuller 1979, 1981). Table 18.1 records the full-sample outcomes.[2]

Table 18.1 Augmented Dickey–Fuller statistics

Variable	$m - p$	Δp	y	r
Longest lag	5	2	6	1
Coefficient	−0.140	−0.126	−0.139	−0.191
"t"-statistic	−3.68	−1.89	−3.70	−3.41

In contrast to the interpretation of the graphs, the statistics in table 18.1 suggest that at the 5 percent level, $(m_t - p_t, y_t, r_t)$ are nearly stationary around a trend, whereas Δp_t appears to be I(1). However, none of the tests is significant at the 2.5 percent level, and the recursively computed ADF "t"-statistics in figure 18.2(a–d)

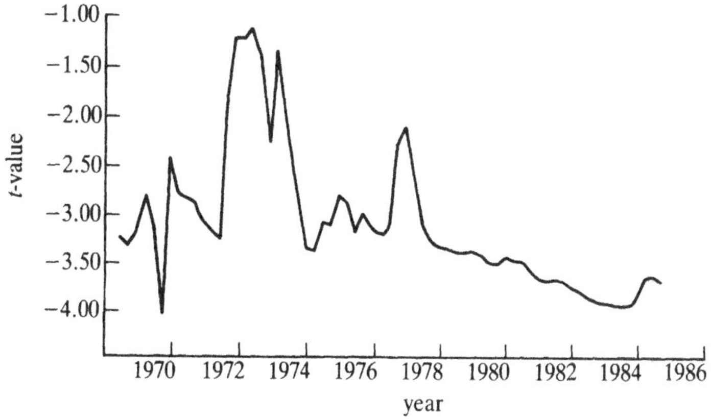

Figure 18.2(a) Time series of t-values in ADF unit root test for $m - p$

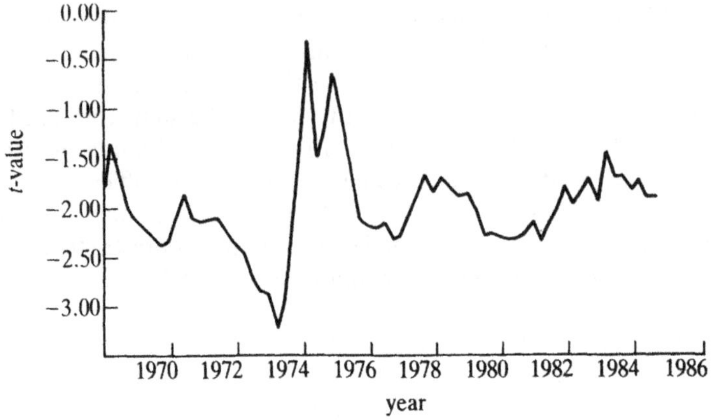

Figure 18.2(b) Time series of t-values for ADF unit root test on Δp

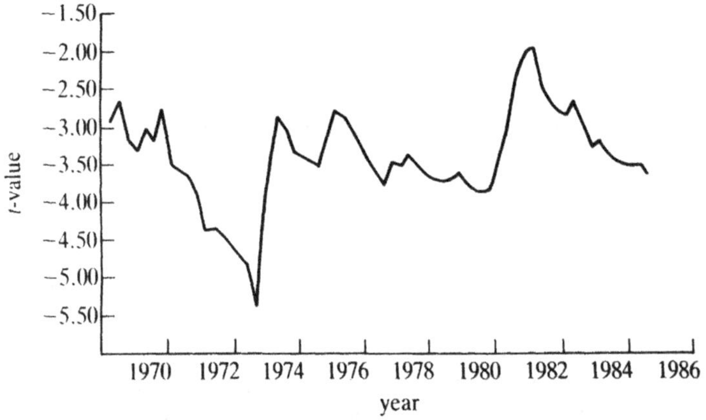

Figure 18.2(c) Time series of ADF test for y adjusted for the Oil Crisis

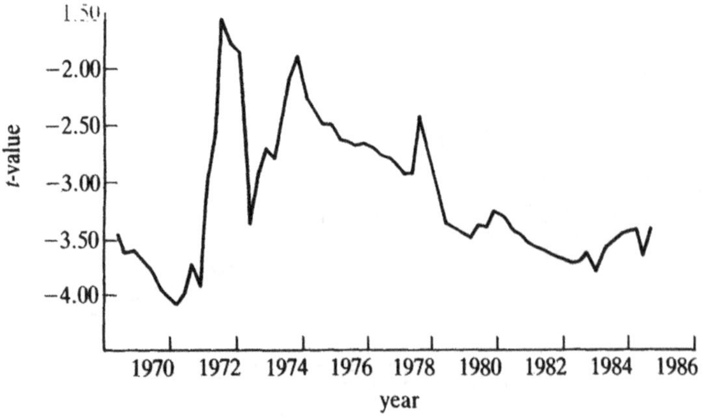

Figure 18.2(d) Time series of t-values for ADF unit root test for r

reveal these to be highly variable, such that both reject and not-reject decisions occurred for most variables. While considerable variance is certainly to be expected under the null of a unit root, inferences from these scalar representations in small samples do not seem to be reliable.

A better basis for the analysis is to directly investigate cointegration in the VAR, using the procedure suggested by Johansen (1988). If it is granted that none of the series is I(2) or higher, then the number of noncointegrated components of the four series reveals the number of nonstationary combinations of variables and hence the number of unit roots. Four lags were allowed for each variable, and a constant and linear trend were included in each equation, making 18 variables per equation and 72 in total. Most lagged variables had elements which were significant at the conventional 5 percent level in at least one equation.

To conduct the cointegration analysis, the VAR is reparameterized in differences except for the levels of the variables at the longest lag, which have the matrix of coefficients $\boldsymbol{\Pi} = -\boldsymbol{\alpha}\boldsymbol{\beta}'$, where $\boldsymbol{\alpha}$ and $\boldsymbol{\beta}$ are $N \times v$ for $0 \leq v \leq N$ cointegrating vectors as in the second section. The maximum likelihood estimator of $\boldsymbol{\Pi}$, subject to the rank restriction imposed via $\boldsymbol{\alpha}\boldsymbol{\beta}'$, is obtained by solving an eigenvalue problem where $\boldsymbol{\beta}$ is the matrix of eigenvectors and the associated ordered eigenvalues are denoted by $1 \geq \lambda_1 \geq \cdots \geq \lambda_v \geq \cdots \geq \lambda_N \geq 0$. When $\boldsymbol{\Pi}$ is unrestricted, all N eigenvalues are retained and the log-likelihood function depends on $-\frac{1}{2}T\sum_{i=1}^{N} \ln(1-\lambda_i)$, whereas when $\boldsymbol{\Pi}$ has rank v, the log-likelihood is a function of the v largest $\{\lambda_i\}$: $-\frac{1}{2}T\sum_{i=1}^{v} \ln(1-\lambda_i)$, $v = 0, 1, \ldots, N$.

This analysis is conditional on knowing v. Since the v largest eigenvalues deliver the cointegration vectors, $\lambda_{v+1} \cdots \lambda_N$ should be zero for the noncointegrating combinations or unit roots. Twice the log of the likelihood ratio for the hypothesis of $N - v$ unit roots, or at most v cointegrating relations (denoted H_v) against the unrestricted alternative is given by twice the difference between these expressions, leading to the test statistic $\eta(v) = -T\sum_{i=v+1}^{N} \ln(1-\lambda_i)$, $v = 0, 1, \ldots, N-1$.

Thus, H_0 is not rejected if $\eta(0)$ is insignificant, but is rejected in favour of H_1 – at least one cointegrating vector – if $\eta(0)$ is significant, and so on. This yields a testing sequence terminating at the last significant $\eta(v)$, corresponding to $N - v$ unit roots and v cointegrating vectors.

Alternatively, tests of the null of $N - v$ unit roots against the alternative of $N - v - 1$ unit roots could be based on the largest $\{\lambda_v\}$ using $\zeta(v-1) = -T\ln(1-\lambda_v)$, called the max statistic. As with scalar unit-root tests, a small value of λ_v implies that the unit root hypothesis cannot be rejected at the v stage. The null of $N - v$ unit roots is rejected if $\zeta(v)$ is significant at the desired level. Thus, $\zeta(v-1)$ tests H_{v-1} against H_v. Under the null hypothesis that rank $(\boldsymbol{\Pi}) = v$, so that the eigenvalues in question are zero, both $\eta(v)$ and $\zeta(v-1)$ have nonstandard distributions which are functionals of Brownian motion, but critical values for these tests have been tabulated by Johansen (1988), Johansen and Juselius (1990) and Osterwald-Lenum (1992) *inter alia*, see table 18.2.

Critical values for these tests when the VAR contains both a constant and a trend unrestrictedly are tabulated in Osterwald-Lenum (1992). The largest eigenvalue is significant at the 5 percent level on the trace test, and the two largest on the max test. Thus, we proceed on the provisional basis that there are two cointegrating relationships, and two unit roots, corresponding to the hypothesis that rank $(\boldsymbol{\Pi}) = 2$. An alternative interpretation of these tests is that there is little cost to deleting the

Table 18.2 Cointegration test statistics

v	λ_v	$\zeta(v-1)$	$\eta(v-1)$
4	0.0038	0.32	0.32
3	0.0716	6.17	6.48
2	0.2663	25.70	32.19
1	0.4186	45.01	77.20

two linear combinations of the levels given by $v = 4$ and $v = 3$, judged in the metric of I(1) distributions: here that would also be true in an I(0) metric, where such likelihood ratio tests would be $\chi^2(4)$.

Table 18.3 records (in rows) the eigenvectors $\boldsymbol{\beta}'$ for the two largest eigenvalues, normalized by the relevant diagonal term, augmented by the remaining two eigenvectors, $\mathbf{v}_3$ and $\mathbf{v}_4$:

Table 18.3 Cointegration coefficients

Vector	$m-p$	Δp	r	y
$\boldsymbol{\beta}_1$	1.00	5.94	0.966	−0.648
$\boldsymbol{\beta}_2$	0.011	1.00	0.003	−0.283
$\mathbf{v}_3$	−3.43	−25.3	1.00	1.14
$\mathbf{v}_4$	−0.48	−0.90	−0.005	1.00

Figure 18.3(a–d) records the time series of the four cointegration relationships $\boldsymbol{\beta}_i'\mathbf{x}_t$ and $\mathbf{v}_i'\mathbf{x}_t$, of which only the first two corresponding to the two largest eigenvalues are stationary. Interpreting the evidence, the first cointegrating vector (i.e. $m - p = -5.9\,\Delta p - 0.97r + 0.65y$) is close to the long-run solution of the money demand equation found in Hendry (1979, 1988), but with a smaller income coefficient. The sum of $\boldsymbol{\beta}_1$ and $\boldsymbol{\beta}_2$ is $m - p = -6.9\,\Delta p - 0.97r + 0.93y$, which is closer and seems to eliminate the trend. The second cointegrating vector suggests that inflation is stationary but influenced by deviations of output from trend. This is contrary to the scalar evidence, but more in keeping with intuition about inflation being I(0) rather than I(1) in the UK over the postwar period.[3]

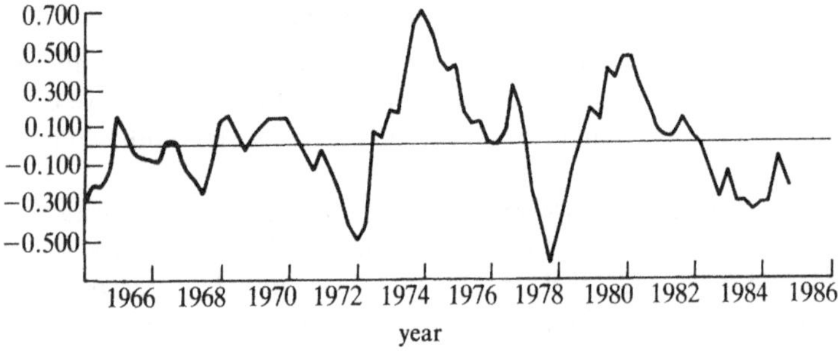

Figure 18.3(a) First cointegration relationship

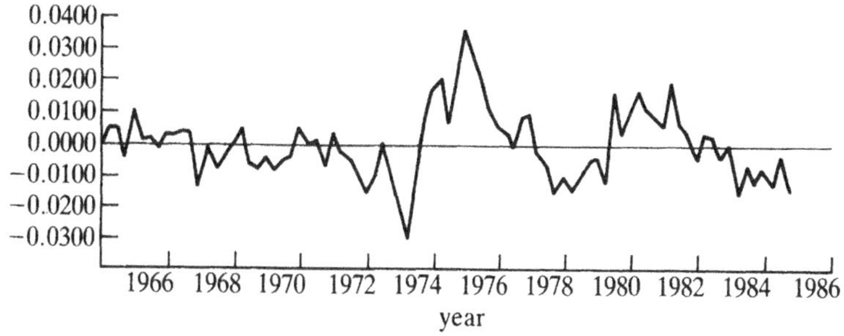

Figure 18.3(b) Second cointegration relationship

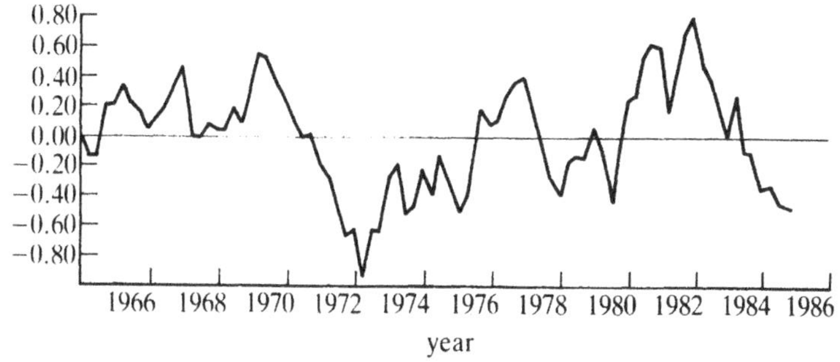

Figure 18.3(c) Third cointegration relationship

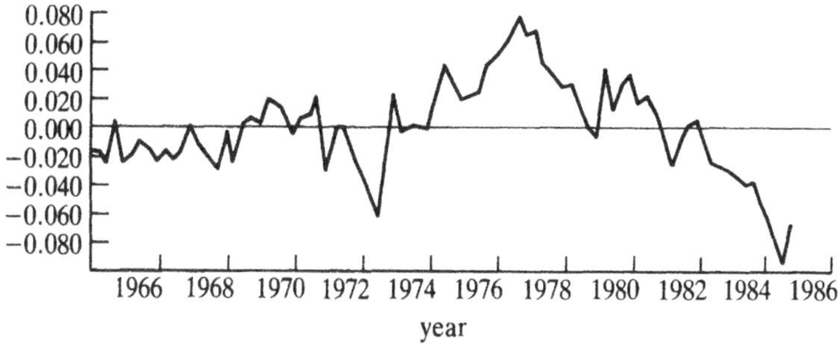

Figure 18.3(d) Fourth cointegration relationship

Next, the adjustment coefficients $\boldsymbol{\alpha}$ corresponding to the standardized $\boldsymbol{\beta}$ are shown in table 18.4, again augmented by those corresponding to the $\mathbf{v}_i$ above.

Table 18.4 Adjustment coefficients for vectors (1) through (4)

Equation	(1)	(2)	(3)	(4)
$m - p$	−0.102	0.017	0.008	−0.013
Δp	0.025	−0.54	−0.001	−0.002
r	−0.016	−3.01	−0.098	0.089
y	0.017	0.39	−0.002	−0.029

The main effect of the first cointegrating vector (i.e. the long-run demand for money) is on $(m-p)_t$ with relatively small effects on the other three variables. Interestingly, although Δp_t and r_t do not appear to cointegrate despite their relatively similar time profiles, the α-coefficient in the second cointegrating vector is large for r_t, so that there is a strong feedback effect from the excess-demand/inflation disequilibrium onto interest rates. This evidence reveals an economy in which real money is determined by inflation, interest rates and income; inflation is influenced by deviations of income from trend; interest rates are affected by inflation and excess demand; and income is trend-dominated but affected by inflation.

Following the cointegration analysis and transformation to I(0) (except that the level of r_{t-2} was retained), the VAR equations were tested for the relevance of the lagged variables, the randomness and normality of the residuals, and the constancy of the coefficients. Some of the longer lagged regressors in the initial unrestricted specification were not significant at the 5 percent level, and in the final run, we retained only those regressors which were significant either in the VAR or in the econometric model. It is unclear whether this should increase or lower the power of the encompassing tests against the VAR. However, the constancy tests revealed that the regime shifts discussed above perceptibly changed some of the VAR parameters, so two dummy variables were introduced. The first, called DOUT, sought to capture the impact of the major positive domestic policy shocks to output in 1972/3 and 1979, whereas the second, called DOIL, was for the initial impact of the two oil crises.[4] To allow for linear functions of the variables which could occur in the SEM, the cointegrating vectors (denoted ECM_{1_t}, ECM_{2_t}), as well as differences of variables were included in the data set, augmenting it to nine endogenous variables in the system: $(\Delta(m-p)_t, \Delta r_t, \Delta^2 p_t, \Delta y_t, \mathrm{ECM}_{1_t}, \mathrm{ECM}_{2_t}, r_t, \Delta(m-p-y)_t, \Delta p_t)$, determined by four stochastic equations and five identities. The cointegrating vectors were defined empirically as[5] $\mathrm{ECM}_{1_t} = \Delta(m-p-y)_t + 7.0\,\Delta^2 p_t + 0.7\,\Delta r_t + \mathrm{ECM}_{1_{t-1}}$, and $\mathrm{ECM}_{2_t} = 1.0\,\Delta^2 p_t - 0.28\,\Delta(y_t - 0.005t) + \mathrm{ECM}_{2_{t-1}}$.

The resulting VAR seemed congruent with the data evidence, and was simplified to eliminate redundant variables. Table 18.5 reports F-tests for the significance of each regressor in the simplified VAR (i.e. F-tests for the associated column of coefficients being zero).

Table 18.5 F-tests on retained regressors

DOUT	DOIL	$\mathrm{ECM}_{1_{t-1}}$	Δr_{t-1}	Δp_{t-1}	Δy_{t-1}	$\Delta(m-p-y)_{t-1}$
9.48**	3.68**	6.33**	0.98	3.53*	0.20	1.30
Δp_{t-2}	r_{t-2}	$\mathrm{ECM}_{2_{t-1}}$	Δp_{t-3}	Δp_{t-4}	$\Delta(m-p)_{t-2}$	
2.07	1.01	2.55*	0.85	1.78	2.16	

Notes: * denotes significance at the 5 percent level; ** at the 1 percent level, treating the statistics as having central $F(4, 69)$ distributions under the null of zero coefficient vectors.

Owing to the five identities involved, the apparent significance of any given variable depends on which other linear combinations involving it are retained (e.g. it could be incorrect to ignore the overall effects from Δy_{t-1} given its presence in $\Delta(m-p-y)_{t-1}$ merely because neither lag is individually significant). The importance of the error correction terms is clear, however. Overall, there are 56 coefficients in this I(0)-parsimonious VAR.

Next, table 18.6 records χ^2 tests for the VAR residuals being white noise and normally distributed, asymptotically distributed as $\chi^2(12)$ and $\chi^2(2)$ respectively under the relevant null.

Table 18.6 Statistics for white noise and normal residuals

	$\Delta(m-p)_t$	Δp_t	Δy_t	Δr_t
$\chi^2(12)$	14.00	10.22	15.70	14.89
$\chi^2(2)$	5.10	2.63	2.39	2.39

Finally, figure 18.4(a–d) records the complete sequence of "breakpoint" Chow (1960) statistics scaled by their 5 percent critical values, testing the constancy of the coefficients in each equation. For each break point, these statistics correspond to what an investigator selecting that point would have calculated, and the scaling by the associated 5 percent critical value is merely for ease of interpretation, and does not correspond to an overall significance level for the complete sequence of tests (see Hendry (1989) for how the sequence is calculated).

On the basis of this evidence, the simplified VAR has acceptably constant

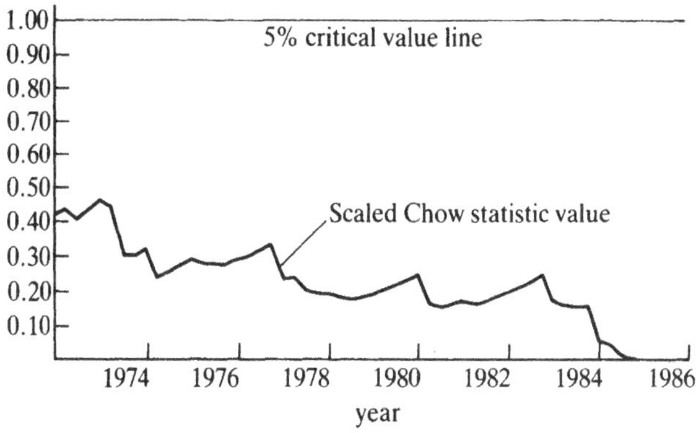

Figure 18.4(a) Scaled "break-point" Chow test for $\Delta(m-p)$

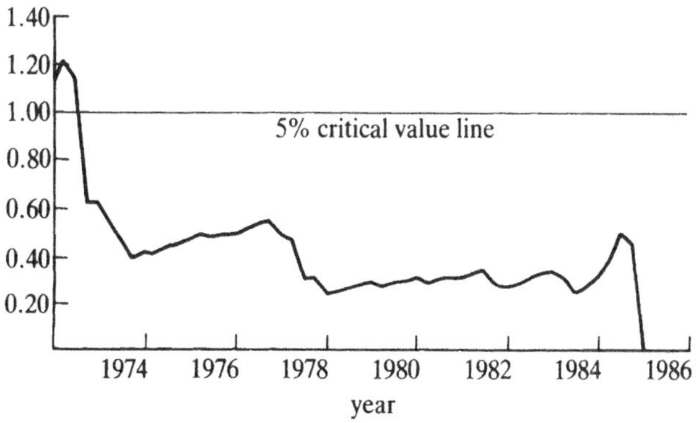

Figure 18.4(b) Scaled "break-point" Chow test for Δr

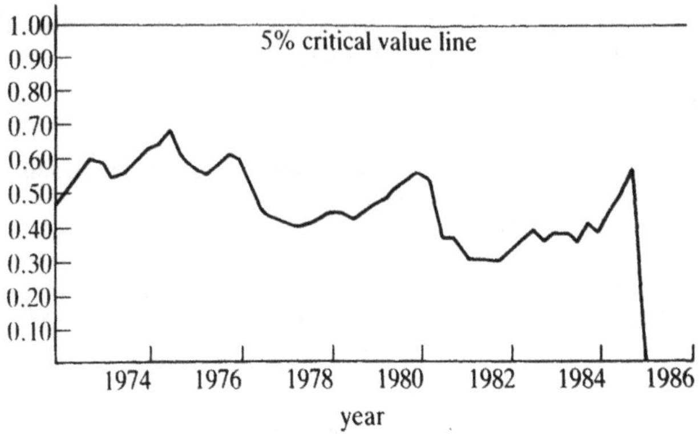

Figure 18.4(c) Scaled "break-point" Chow test for Δy

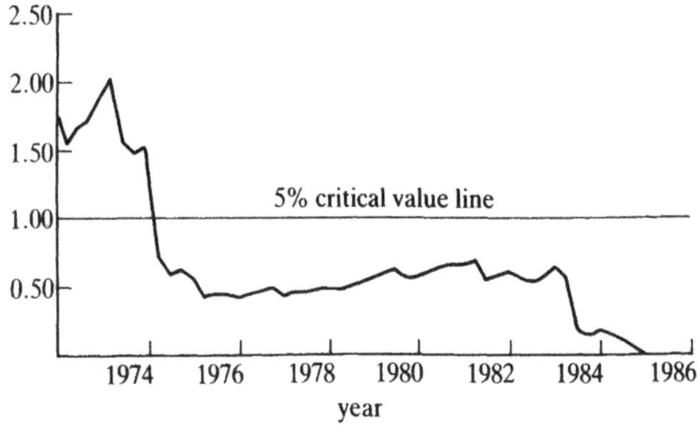

Figure 18.4(d) Scaled "break-point" Chow test for $\Delta^2 p$

coefficients and approximately white-noise, normally distributed errors. Thus, it is a data coherent system against which it is worth testing the econometric model (see Hendry et al. (1988) for further details on this aspect of system modeling). Since the earlier cointegration analysis is not invalidated by these additional tests, it is reasonable to use the cointegrating linear combinations as explanatory factors, a feature which would be precluded by a VAR specified in differences only.

The fourth stage was the formulation of the SEM to be tested for encompassing the VAR. This model (table 18.7) was based on a previously established equation for money demand (Hendry 1979, Trundle 1982, Hendry 1985), augmented by an equation for determining the interest rate dependent on inflation, and two marginal equations for income and inflation, both incorporating the second cointegrating vector. The resulting four-equation SEM was augmented by the five identities to determine the values of the two cointegrating vectors, Δp_t, r_t, and $\Delta(m - p - y)_t$. Full-information maximum likelihood (FIML) estimation yielded the following equations; the exact sample period was 1964(2) through 1984(4), with an F-test of parameter constancy test based on a separate run retaining the last 12 observations:

Table 18.7 Econometric model

$$
\begin{array}{lllll}
\Delta(m-p)_t & = -0.196 & -\ 0.520\,\Delta^2 p_t & -\ 0.082\,\Delta r_t & -\ 0.195\,\Delta(m-p-y)_{t-1} \\
 & \ \ (0.018) & \ \ (0.339) & \ \ (0.027) & \ \ (0.072) \\
 & -\ 0.095\mathrm{ECM}_{1_{t-1}} & & & \\
 & -\ (0.009) & & & \\
\Delta r_t & = -0.395 & +\ 7.63\,\Delta^2 p_t & +\ 0.162\,\Delta r_{t-1} & +\ 1.55\,\Delta y_{t-1} \\
 & \ \ (0.128) & \ \ (2.68) & \ \ (0.096) & \ \ (0.87) \\
 & -\ 0.141 r_{t-2} & & +\ 2.40\,\Delta p_{t-1} & \\
 & \ \ (0.046) & & \ \ (1.16) & \\
\Delta y_t & = \ \ 1.03 & +\ 0.043\mathrm{DOUT} & +\ 0.338\mathrm{ECM}_{2_{t-1}} & -\ 0.184\,\Delta y_{t-1} \\
 & \ \ (0.47) & \ \ (0.006) & \ \ (0.16) & \ \ (0.087) \\
 & -0.448\,\Delta^2 p_{t-1} & & -\ 0.300\,\Delta p_{t-4} & +\ 0.262\,\Delta(m-p)_{t-2} \\
 & \ \ (0.163) & & \ \ (0.093) & \ \ (0.058) \\
\Delta^2 p_t & = -0.707 & +\ 0.018\mathrm{DOIL} & -\ 0.235\mathrm{ECM}_{2_{t-1}} & -\ 0.236\,\Delta^2 p_{t-1} \\
 & \ \ (0.196) & \ \ (0.004) & \ \ (0.065) & \ \ (0.086)
\end{array}
$$

The structural and derived reduced form residual standard errors are given in table 18.8.

Table 18.8 Residual standard errors

Model	$\Delta(m-p)$	Δr	Δy	Δp
SEM	0.0127	0.109	0.0104	0.0058
VAR	0.0159	0.110	0.0101	0.0057

The money demand equation is close to (a linear transform of) that estimated by ordinary least squares in Hendry (1988), despite Δp_t and r_t being treated as endogenous here due to estimation by FIML. Such an outcome is consistent with the validity of the conditional estimates reported in that paper, which were shown to be super-exogenous to changes in the conditioning processes (Engle and Hendry 1989). Further, the weak exogeneity of Δp_t and r_t for the parameters of the money demand function is supported by the absence of the first cointegrating vector from the remaining equations. Only I(1) data-based restrictions, such as those due to earlier research and the cointegration analysis, were imposed, since I(0) restrictions almost costlessly reduce degrees of freedom and hence reduce the critical value of the encompassing test statistic.

The equation for r_t involves a strong dependence on current and past inflation (virtually one-for-one to $\Delta^2 p_t$ when inflation is adjusted to annual rates), a small dependence on past income growth and a significant feedback from r_{t-2}, suggesting that r_t is in fact stationary. Adding $\mathrm{ECM}_{2_{t-1}}$ to the interest rate equation yielded only a small coefficient despite the results from the cointegration analysis.

Income appears to be stationary around a trend, with deviations influenced by past inflation and changes in inflation and real money growth. The dummy for economic policy changes plays a large role.

Finally, the equation for inflation is a first-order autoregression in $\Delta^2 p_t$ with the deviation of income from trend having a positive influence. DOUT and DOIL were each restricted to enter only the relevant equation. The model as a whole is interpretable, embodies the cointegration information and is highly parsimonious compared to the VAR. Figure 18.5(a–d) shows the time series of fitted values and outcomes from the solved model in table 18.7 (i.e. the one-step ahead predictions against outcomes) in units of $\Delta(m-p)_t$, Δp_t, Δy_t, and Δr_t for clarity.

The key statistic, given the motivation for the present study, is the value of the encompassing test against the simplified VAR. Since the SEM has 22 parameters, this test, which is equivalent to a test of the over-identifying restrictions, is given by $\chi^2(34) = 22.87$. Such an outcome is well below the 5 percent critical value, notwithstanding the relatively small sample size, the fact that the VAR was simplified to eliminate redundant variables, and the large number of restrictions imposed. Thus, the econometric model encompasses the VAR, and offers a much smaller dimensional yet congruent data representation. As a final test, albeit both within-sample and essentially entailed by the equivalent test on the VAR, the $F(48, 66)$ test of parameter constancy over the final three years yielded 0.72, and so is also well below its 5 percent critical value.

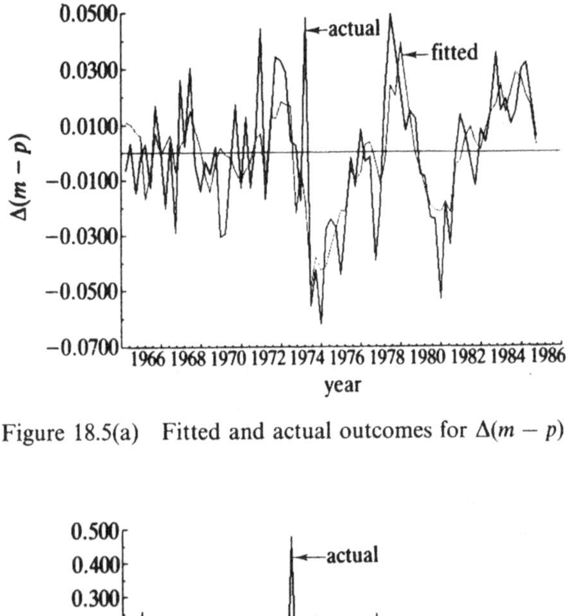

Figure 18.5(a) Fitted and actual outcomes for $\Delta(m-p)$

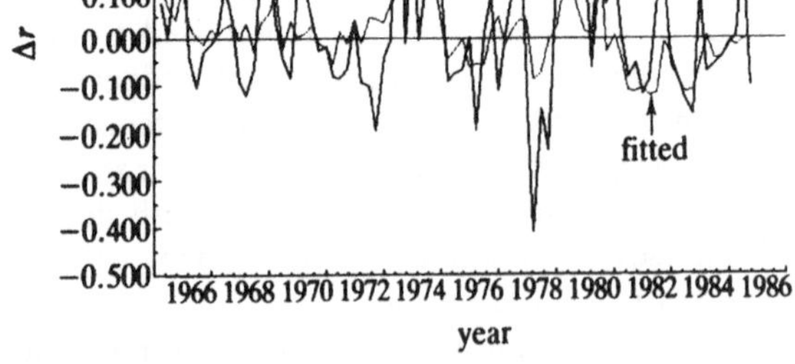

Figure 18.5(b) Fitted and actual outcomes for Δr

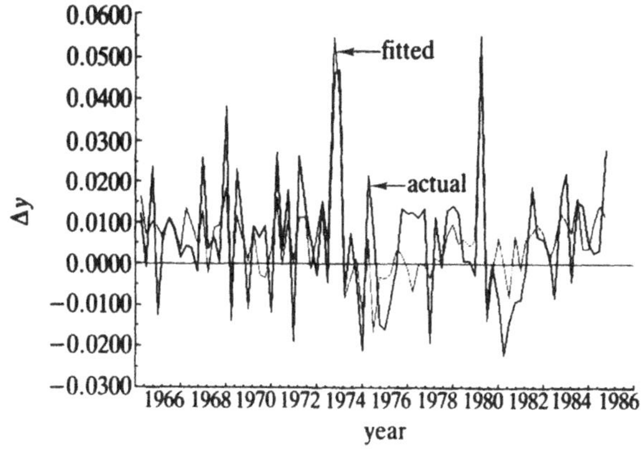

Figure 18.5(c) Fitted and actual outcomes for Δy

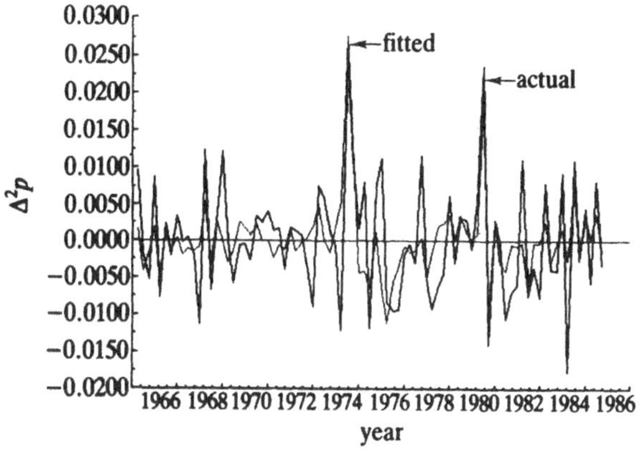

Figure 18.5(d) Fitted and actual outcomes for $\Delta^2 p$

Conclusions

A framework was proposed for developing valid structural models which encompass the underlying VAR, when the levels data are I(1) but include cointegrated combinations. The method commences from a VAR formulated in terms of suitably transformed data variables, such that linearity, approximate normality, and parameter constancy are at least logically possible. Then it investigates the rank of the cointegration space using the techniques proposed by Johansen (1988, 1991). On the basis of that evidence, the system is transformed to an I(0) representation and tested for congruency. Tests for open and closed models to encompass their unrestricted systems are considered, and encompassing conditions are established. The reduction of a closed system to an open one necessitates valid weak exogeneity of the conditioning variables for the parameters of interest, entailing the absence of cointegrating information in the relevant marginal system. In the case that the complete system is modeled, the encompassing condition coincides with the usual test for the validity of over-identifying information, but conducted against a baseline which has previously been demonstrated to be data-coherent. Recursive procedures are used to investigate the constancy of inferences across the whole sample period.

An empirical example of modeling money demand in the UK illustrates the feasibility of the approach. Two cointegrating vectors are established, the first of which corresponds to a long-run money demand equation similar to that found by earlier single equation research. The resulting VAR in I(0) space is deemed adequately constant and data-coherent, after creating two special effects dummy variables, to make system modeling worthwhile. A structural representation is postulated, building on earlier research, and shown to parsimoniously encompass the VAR. Given the dearth of valid and applicable system evaluation statistics (Chong and Hendry 1986), the proposed test seems a useful addition to the macro-modeler's toolkit, in so far as it is applicable to encompassing within sectors or nearly decomposable blocks of large systems: the equations in such blocks can be tested for encompassing the entailed VAR which does not involve any dubious exogeneity assertions for its validity.

Finally, the absence of cross-equation influences from the first cointegration vector further supports the weak exogeneity of the contemporaneous variables in the money demand model for the contingent plan parameters which Hendry (1988) found to be invariant to regime shifts over the sample period. Conversely, the presence in both the inflation and the output equations of a common cointegrating vector, thereby violating weak exogeneity, may help explain the difficulty previously experienced by UK researchers in establishing a significant impact of excess demand on inflation (Hendry 1981).

Appendix A: An Illustrative Example of Mutually Encompassing SEMs

Consider a four-variable process involving $(y_{1t}, y_{2t}, z_{1t}, z_{2t})$; since the issues do not depend on stationarity or its absence, we neglect that difficulty here and only consider a stationary case. The companion form representation is $\mathbf{f}_t = \Pi^* \mathbf{f}_{t-1} + \boldsymbol{\varepsilon}_t$, and we take the exemplar

$$\begin{bmatrix} y_{1t} \\ y_{2t} \\ z_{1t} \\ z_{2t} \\ y_{1t-1} \\ y_{2t-1} \\ z_{1t-1} \end{bmatrix} = \begin{bmatrix} \pi_{11} & \pi_{12} & \pi_{13} & 0 & 0 & 0 & 0 \\ 0 & \pi_{22} & \pi_{23} & \pi_{24} & 0 & 0 & 0 \\ 0 & 0 & \pi_{33} & 0 & 0 & 0 & 0 \\ 0 & 0 & 0 & 0 & 0 & 0 & 0 \\ 1 & 0 & 0 & 0 & 0 & 0 & 0 \\ 0 & 1 & 0 & 0 & 0 & 0 & 0 \\ 0 & 0 & 1 & 0 & 0 & 0 & 0 \end{bmatrix} \begin{bmatrix} y_{1t-1} \\ y_{2t-1} \\ z_{1t-1} \\ z_{2t-1} \\ y_{1t-2} \\ y_{2t-2} \\ z_{1t-2} \end{bmatrix} + \begin{bmatrix} \varepsilon_{1t} \\ \varepsilon_{2t} \\ \varepsilon_{3t} \\ \varepsilon_{4t} \\ 0 \\ 0 \\ 0 \end{bmatrix} \tag{A1}$$

Thus, y_{1t} and y_{2t} are autocorrelated and intercorrelated, z_{1t} is autocorrelated, and z_{2t} is white noise. The last three equations are identities, so only the first four have errors. The z terms are not Granger-caused by the y terms, although the intercorrelation structure of the $\boldsymbol{\varepsilon}_t$ process has not been specified. The underlying behavioral equation for y_{1t} is, in fact,

$$y_{1t} = \theta_1 y_{1t-1} + \theta_2 y_{2t-1} + \theta_3(z_{1t} - z_{2t}) + u_{1t}, \tag{A2}$$

where the z_{it} are strongly exogenous for the θ_i. We only discuss that equation.

Consider the arbitrary $\boldsymbol{\phi}$ vector $(1:\phi_2:\phi_3:\phi_4:\phi_5:\phi_6:\phi_7)'$, premultiply (A1) by $\boldsymbol{\phi}'$ and set $\boldsymbol{\phi}'\Pi^* = \mathbf{0}'$, then there are four non-null equations:

$$\begin{aligned} \pi_{11} + \phi_5 = 0; \qquad \pi_{12} + \phi_2\pi_{22} + \phi_6 = 0; \\ \pi_{13} + \phi_2\pi_{23} + \phi_3\pi_{33} + \phi_7 = 0; \qquad \phi_2\pi_{24} = 0. \end{aligned} \tag{A3}$$

Consider the equation corresponding to (A1). If $\boldsymbol{\phi}'\Pi^*$ is to vanish, $\phi_2 = 0$ is essential: no valid model of y_{1t} can include y_{2t}. Equally, $\phi_5 = -\pi_{11}$ and $\phi_6 = -\pi_{12}$ are required. However, ϕ_4 is free and the only remaining equation in (A3) is $\pi_{13} + \phi_3\pi_{33} + \phi_7 = 0$. Thus, when $\pi_{33} \neq 0$, possible models for y_{1t} include:

1. $\boldsymbol{\phi}' = (1:0:0:0:-\pi_{11}:-\pi_{12}:-\pi_{13})$, with error ε_{1t}.
2. $\boldsymbol{\phi}' = (1:0:0:-\lambda:-\pi_{11}:-\pi_{12}:-\pi_{13})$, with error $\varepsilon_{1t} - \lambda\varepsilon_{4t}$.
3. $\boldsymbol{\phi}' = (1:0:-\pi_{13}/\pi_{33}:0:-\pi_{11}:-\pi_{12}:0)$, with error $\varepsilon_{1t} - (\pi_{13}/\pi_{33})\varepsilon_{3t}$.
4. $\boldsymbol{\phi}' = (1:0:-\pi_{13}/\pi_{33}:\lambda:-\pi_{11}:-\pi_{12}:0)$, with error $\varepsilon_{1t} - (\pi_{13}/\pi_{33})\varepsilon_{3t} + \lambda\varepsilon_{4t}$.

When $\lambda = \pi_{13}/\pi_{33} = \theta_3$, (4) reproduces (A2) and hence $u_{1t} = \varepsilon_{1t} - \theta_3\varepsilon_{3t} + \theta_3\varepsilon_{4t}$. Conversely, 1 is equation (1) of the VAR (A1). Similar principles apply to the y_{2t} equation.

Even in this simple example, many models can, but also many cannot, achieve historical encompassing of the VAR, and as such are observationally equivalent: selecting between those listed (1)–(4) above cannot be achieved by this form of encompassing.

Notes

The research for this paper was undertaken in 1989, and the first version completed in December 1989. The financial support for this research from the UK Economic and Social Research Council Macroeconomic Research Consortium (ESRC grant B01250024) is gratefully acknowledged. We are indebted to Mike Clements, Rob Engle, Bernadette Govaerts, Tony Hall, Bruce Hansen, Teun Kloek, Søren Johansen, Guy Laroque, Françoise Maurel, Adrian Pagan, Peter Phillips, Jean-François Richard, Aris Spanos and Ken Wallis for helpful comments on earlier drafts.

1. Since all four modeled variables are of interest, figures occur in *blocks* of four numbered successively.
2. All of the empirical calculations reported here were undertaken using PC-GIVE 6.01: see Hendry (1989).
3. The degree of integratedness of a time series is not necessarily an intrinsic property and could change over historical periods; hyperinflation is one example, but the switch from fixed to floating exchange rates also could have altered the integratedness of exchange rates, etc.
4. DOUT equalled unity in 1972(4), 1973(1), and 1979(2) and was zero elsewhere; DOIL equalled unity in 1973(3), 1973(4) and 1979(3).
5. An interest elasticity of 0.9 did not prove data coherent, whereas 0.7 did, so despite the initial cointegration evidence, the latter was used.

References

Aldrich, J. (1989). "Autonomy," *Oxford Economic Papers*, 41, 15–34.

Anderson, G. J., and G. E. Mizon (1989). "What can statistics contribute to the analysis of economic structural change?," chapter 1 in P. Hackl (ed.) *Statistical Analysis and Forecasting of Economic Structural Change*. Berlin: Springer-Verlag.

Bergstrom, A. R. (1984). "Monetary, fiscal and exchange rate policy in a continuous time econometric model of the United Kingdom," in P. Malgrange and P. Muet (eds) *Contemporary Macroeconomic Modelling*. Oxford: Basil Blackwell.

Bergstrom, A. R., and C. R. Wymer (1976). "A model of disequilibrium neoclassical growth and its application to the United Kingdom," in A. R. Bergstrom (ed.) *Statistical Inference in Continuous Time Econometric Models*, pp. 267–327. Amsterdam: North-Holland.

Chong, Y. Y., and D. F. Hendry (1986). "Econometric evaluation of linear macro-economic models," *Review of Economic Studies*, 53, 671–90 (reprinted in Granger (1990) *op. cit.*).

Chow, G. C. (1960). "*Tests of equality between sets of coefficients in two linear regressions*," *Econometrica*, **28**, 591–605.

Clements, M. P., and G. E. Mizon (1991). "Empirical analysis of macroeconomic time series: VAR and structural models," *European Economic Review*, 35, 887–932.

Dickey, D. A., and W. A. Fuller (1979). "Distribution of the estimators for autoregressive time series with a unit root," *Journal of the American Statistical Association*, 74, 427–31.

Dickey, D. A., and W. A. Fuller (1981). "Likelihood ratio statistics for autoregressive time series with a unit root," *Econometrica*, 49, 1057–72.

Domowitz, I., and H. White (1982). "Misspecified models with dependent observations," *Journal of Econometrics*, 20, 35–58.

Engle, R. F., and C. W. J. Granger (1987). "Cointegration and error-correction: representation, estimation and testing," *Econometrica*, 55, 251–76.

Engle, R. F., and D. F. Hendry (1989). "Testing super exogeneity and invariance in regression models," forthcoming, *Journal of Econometrics*.

Engle, R. F., D. F. Hendry, and J.-F. Richard (1983). "Exogeneity," *Econometrica*, 51, 277–304.

Ericsson, N. R. (1983). "Asymptotic properties of instrumental variables statistics for testing non-nested hypotheses," *Review of Economic Studies*, 50, 287–303.

Ericsson, N. R., and D. F. Hendry (1985). "Conditional econometric modelling: an application to new house prices in the United Kingdom," chapter 11 in A. C. Atkinson and S. Fienberg (eds) *A Celebration of Statistics*. New York: Springer-Verlag.

Ericsson, N. R., and D. F. Hendry (1989). "Encompassing and rational expectations: how sequential corroboration can imply refutation," International Finance Discussion Paper 354, Board of Governors of the Federal Reserve System, June 1989.

Favero, C., and D. F. Hendry (1989). "Testing the Lucas critique," A. W. Phillips Lecture at the 1989 Australasian Meeting of the Econometric Society, forthcoming, *Econometric Reviews*.

Frisch, R. (1938). "*Statistical versus* theoretical relations in econometric macrodynamics," in *Autonomy of Economic Relations*, memorandum published in 1948, University of Oslo.

Govaerts, B. (1986). *Applications of the Encompassing Principle to Linear Dynamic Models*, Ph.D. Thesis, Université Catholique de Louvain.

Granger, C. W. J. (1969). "Investigating causal relations by econometric models and cross-spectral methods," *Econometrica*, 37, 224–38.

Granger, C. W. J. (1986). "Developments in the study of cointegrated economic variables," *Oxford Bulletin of Economics and Statistics*, 48, 213–28.

Granger, C. W. J. (ed) (1990) *Modelling Economic Series: Readings in Econometric Methodology*. Oxford: Oxford University Press.

Haavelmo, T. (1944). "The probability approach in econometrics," *Econometrica*, 12, Supplement, 1–118.

Hannan, E. J. (1970). *Multiple Time Series*. New York: John Wiley and Sons.

Hatanaka, M. (1975). "On the global identification of the dynamic simultaneous equations model with stationary disturbances," *International Economic Review*, 16, 545–54.

Hendry, D. F. (1979). "Predictive failure and econometric modelling in macroeconomics: the transactions demand for money," chapter 9 in P. Ormerod (ed.) *Modelling the Economy*. London: Heinemann Educational Books.
Hendry, D. F. (1981). "Econometric evidence in the appraisal of UK monetary policy," pp. 1–21 in volume 3 of *The Third Report of the Select Committee of the House of Commons on The Treasury and Civil Service*. London: HMSO.
Hendry, D. F. (1985). "Monetary economic myth and econometric reality," *Oxford Review of Economic Policy*, 1, 72–84.
Hendry, D. F. (1986). "Encompassing in linear dynamic stationary processes," mimeo, Nuffield College, Oxford.
Hendry, D. F. (1987). "Econometric methodology: a personal perspective," chapter 10 in T. F. Bewley (ed.) *Advances in Econometrics*, pp. 29–48. Cambridge: Cambridge University Press.
Hendry, D. F. (1988). "The encompassing implications of feedback *versus* feedforward mechanisms in econometrics," *Oxford Economic Papers*, 40, 132–49.
Hendry, D. F. (1989). *PC-GIVE: An Interactive Econometric Modelling System*. Oxford: Oxford Institute of Economics and Statistics.
Hendry, D. F., and G. E. Mizon (1990). "Procrustean econometrics: or stretching and squeezing data," pp. 121–36 in C.W.J. Granger (1990) *op cit*.
Hendry, D. F., A. J. Neale, and F. Srba (1988). "Econometric analysis of small linear systems using PC-FIML," *Journal of Econometrics*, 38, 203–26.
Hendry, D. F., and J.-F. Richard (1982). "On the formulation of empirical models in dynamic econometrics," *Journal of Econometrics*, 20, 3–33.
Hendry, D. F., and J.-F. Richard (1989). "Recent developments in the theory of encompassing," in B. Cornet and H. Tulkens (eds) *Contributions to Operations Research and Econometrics. The Twentieth Anniversary of CORE*, pp. 393–440. Cambridge, Massachusetts: MIT Press.
Hylleberg, S., and G. E. Mizon (1989). "Cointegration and error correction mechanisms," *Econometric Journal* (Conference Supplement), 99, 113–25.
Johansen, S. (1988). "Statistical analysis of cointegration vectors," *Journal of Economic Dynamics and Control*, 12, 231–54.
Johansen, S. (1991). "Estimation and hypothesis testing of cointegration vectors in Gaussian vector autoregressive models," *Econometrica*, 59, 1551–80.
Johansen, S. (1992). "Cointegration in partial systems and the efficiency of single equation analysis," *Journal of Econometrics*, 52, 389–402.
Johansen, S., and K. Juselius (1990). "Maximum likelihood estimation and inference on cointegration – with applications to the demand for money," *Oxford Bulletin of Economics and Statistics*, 52, 169–210.
Leamer, E. E. (1987). "Econometric metaphors," in T. F. Bewley (ed.) *Advances in Econometrics*, pp. 1–28. Cambridge: Cambridge University Press.
Lucas, R. E. (1976). "Econometric policy evaluation: a critique," in K. Brunner and A. H. Meltzer (eds) *The Phillips Curve and Labor Markets*, pp. 19–46. Amsterdam: North-Holland.
Mizon, G. E. (1984). "The encompassing approach in econometrics," in D. F. Hendry and K. F. Wallis (eds) *Econometrics and Quantitative Economics*, pp. 135–72. Oxford: Basil Blackwell.
Mizon, G. E. (1989). "The role of econometric modelling in economic analysis," *Revista Española de Económia*, 6, 167–91.
Mizon, G. E., and J.-F. Richard (1986). "The encompassing principle and its application to non-nested hypothesis tests," *Econometrica*, 54, 657–78.
Monfort, A., and R. Rabemananjara, (1990). "From a VAR model to a structural model, with an application to the wage–price spiral," *Journal of Applied Econometrics*, 5, 203–27.
Osterwald-Lenum, M. (1992). "A note with quantiles of the asymptotic distribution of the maximum likelihood cointegration rank test statistics: four cases," *Oxford Bulletin of Economics and Statistics*, 54, 461–72.
Pagan, A. R. (1987). "Three econometric methodologies: a critical appraisal," *Journal of Economic Surveys*, 1, 3–24 (reprinted in C.W.J. Granger (1990), *op. cit.*).
Pagan, A. R. (1989). "Twenty years after: econometrics, 1966–1986," in B. Cornet and

H. Tulkens (eds) *Contributions to Operations Research and Econometrics. The Twentieth Anniversary of CORE*, pp. 319–83. Cambridge, Massachusetts: MIT Press.
Park, J. Y., and P. C. B. Phillips (1988). "Statistical inference in regressions with integrated processes: part I," *Econometric Theory*, 4, 468–98.
Park, J. Y., and P. C. B. Phillips (1989). "Statistical inference in regressions with integrated processes: part II," *Econometric Theory*, 5, 95–132.
Pesaran, M. H., and A. S. Deaton (1978). "Testing non-nested nonlinear regression models," *Econometrica*, 46, 677–694.
Phillips, P. C. B. (1991). "Optimal inference in cointegrated systems," *Econometrica*, 59, 283–306.
Phillips, P. C. B., and S. N. Durlauf (1986). "Multiple time series regression with integrated processes," *Review of Economic Studies*, 53, 473–95.
Phillips, P. C. B., and M. Loretan (1991). "Estimating long run economic equilibria," *Review of Economic Studies*, 58, 407–36.
Phillips, P. C. B., and P. Perron (1988). "Testing for a unit root in time series," *Biometrika*, 75, 335–46.
Sims, C. A. (1980). "Macroeconomics and reality," *Econometrica*, 48, 1–48 (reprinted in Granger (1990) *op. cit.*).
Sims, C. A., J. H. Stock and M. W. Watson (1990). "Inference in linear time series models with some unit roots," *Econometrica*, 58, 113–44.
Spanos, A. (1986). *Statistical Foundations of Econometric Modelling.* Cambridge: Cambridge University Press.
Spanos, A. (1989a). "Unit roots and their dependence on the implicit information set," *Advances in Econometrics*, 8, 271–92.
Spanos, A. (1989b). "On re-reading Haavelmo: a retrospective view of econometric modeling," *Econometric Theory*, 5, 405–29.
Spanos, A. (1990). "The simultaneous equations model revisited: statistical adequacy and identification," *Journal of Econometrics*, 44, 87–105.
Stock, J. H. (1987). "Asymptotic properties of least-squares estimators of co-integrating vectors," *Econometrica*, 55, 1035–56.
Trundle, J. (1982). "The demand for M1 in the UK," Bank of England Discussion Paper.
White, H. (1989). *Estimation, Inference, and Specification Analysis.* Cambridge: Cambridge University Press .

19

Empirical Implications of Arbitrage-free Asset Markets

S. Maheswaran and Christopher A. Sims

Introduction

Price changes for a durable good with small storage costs must, in a frictionless competitive market, be in some sense unpredictable – or so it seems intuitively. After all, if the good were reliably predicted to rise rapidly in price, one would think the current price should be bid up by speculators eager to cash in on the predicted capital gains, while if it were reliably predicted to fall rapidly in price, owners of the good would sell their holdings to avoid the predicted capital losses. These market reactions to predicted price rises or falls should prevent the occurrence of reliably predicted rises or falls. This intuitive idea has sometimes been formalized as the hypothesis that the price P_t of such a good should be a martingale relative to information observable by market participants, i.e. that, if X_t is data which becomes available at t,

$$E[P_{t+s}|X_u, u \leq t] = P_t, \tag{1}$$

for any $s > 0$.

But as emphasized by Lucas (1978) and by Leroy (1973), among others, (1) emerges from such models only under extremely restrictive assumptions.

In a classic paper, Harrison and Kreps (1979) showed that elimination of arbitrage opportunities would, in a market for assets traded continuously in time, force relative prices of assets to follow stochastic processes *equivalent* (in a technical measure-theoretic sense) to a martingale process. However, this result is not in conflict with the findings of Lucas and Leroy that asset prices in equilibrium models do not in general follow martingale processes. The martingale-equivalence result is empty in a discrete-time model, because in such a model practically any stochastic process is equivalent to a martingale. Even in continuous-time models the martingale equivalence result by itself places only weak restrictions on the observable behavior of asset prices.

If it is only the martingale equivalence property, not (1) (the martingale property itself), that is implied by theoretical analysis of arbitrage-free markets, then is it happenstance that econometric tests of (1) often show it to be close to correct? And is the intuitive notion that speculators should eliminate predictable price changes simply fallacious? We show that, with a continuous data record on prices, there are classes of behavior for prices that are inconsistent with martingale equivalence. Roughly speaking, we show that martingale equivalence restricts the nature of price behavior over fine time intervals, ruling out paths that show increasingly erratic behavior of rates of change over smaller and smaller time units if this erratic behavior can be to some extent predicted.

We attempt to make the paper readable at two levels. A reader should be able to understand the nature of our claims about the testable implications of arbitrage-freeness without having a firm enough grounding in the theory of continuous-time stochastic processes to understand our proofs. Thus, in some sections of the paper, we explain at an elementary level concepts necessary to understanding the claimed results, while in other parts of the paper we make arguments that assume a more mathematically sophisticated reader. While we refer to Jacod and Shiryayev (1987) for standard results, the treatment there is terse; readers approaching the subject for the first time might consult Protter (1990) or Dothan (1990).

Martingale Equivalence

In an appendix we state the technical definition of equivalence of probability measures and provide a concise derivation of the martingale equivalence result[1]. Here we characterize the result more intuitively. If we are given some events to which probabilities can be attached, we may consider two different probability distributions on them, μ and ν, each of which attaches a probability $\mu(S)$ or $\nu(S)$ to each event S. We say μ is *absolutely continuous* with respect to ν, or ν *dominates* μ, if every event with probability zero under ν has probability zero under μ, i.e. $\upsilon(S) = 0 \Rightarrow \mu(S) = 0$. If the implication goes the other way as well, so μ dominates ν also, then the two probabilities are *equivalent*. The events S are conditions which we may be able to observe. To say that μ and ν are equivalent is just to say that there is no event we could observe which would tell us with certainty that one or the other of the two probability models is correct. Such an event would be one which was impossible under one model (say $\mu(S) = 0$), but still possible under the other model ($\nu(S) \neq 0$), which is exactly what equivalence of probability measures rules out.

If a price $P(t)$ can be observed over an interval, say $[0, 1]$, we say it follows the stochastic process μ if μ is a probability measure over events defined as sets of possible observed time paths for P. Roughly speaking, P follows a process equivalent to a martingale process if there is a martingale process such that no possible observable behavior of P can allow us to tell with certainty whether we are observing the martingale process or the actual probability distribution of P, and vice versa – if we observed a Q generated by the martingale process, there would be no possible observation that could rule out Q having been generated by the P process.

If we can observe P only at discrete intervals, say $t = j/n$, $j = 1, \ldots, n$, equivalence to a martingale places no restrictions at all on the observable behavior of the P. The Wiener process martingale $W(t)$, defined by its properties that $W(t) - W(s) \sim N(0, t - s)$ and that changes in W over nonoverlapping time intervals are independent, gives $W(j/n)$, $j = 1, \ldots, n$ a joint normal distribution with nonsingular covariance matrix. This means, of course, that the vector of W values at the n points j/n has a PDF that is continuous and nonzero over the whole of n-dimensional Euclidean space $\mathbb{R}^n$. But any distribution on $\mathbb{R}^n$ which has an everywhere nonzero PDF is equivalent to the Lebesgue measure, and hence all such distributions are mutually equivalent. Thus any stochastic process which gives $P(j/n)$, $j = 1, \ldots, n$ a nonzero PDF over all of $\mathbb{R}^n$ is equivalent over those n discrete t-values to the Gaussian process generated by sampling a Wiener process at those values of t. This covers most of the stochastic processes used in practical time-series modeling – all ARIMA processes with Gaussian disturbances, for example.

When P can be observed at every point of the $[0, 1]$ interval, equivalence to a martingale is not an empty condition. For example, a Wiener process puts zero probability on the event that $P(\cdot)$ is differentiable over $[0, 1]$. Some commonly used continuous-time stochastic models (e.g. stochastic differential equations of higher than first order) imply that $P(\cdot)$ is differentiable with probability one. Thus it is easy to write down a convenient continuous-time model that is not equivalent to a Wiener process.

However, the class of all continuous-time martingales is large, and it turns out that most commonly used, convenient models for continuous-time stochastic processes are at least absolutely continuous with respect to *some* continuous-time martingale, even though many are not absolutely continuous with respect to a Wiener process. That is, defining observable behavior for prices that has zero probability under *every* martingale process is not easy. Consider a process whose time paths have continuous derivatives with probability one, for example. We know such a process is not absolutely continuous with respect to a Wiener process, but it is absolutely continuous with respect to a different martingale.

In particular, suppose μ is the probability measure for the differentiable process and suppose that we generate a sequence of random times t_j, $j = 1, \ldots, \infty$, from a Poisson process that makes the probability of an event generating a new t_j 0.01 per unit time. (That is, at any date t, the PDF of the time s until the next t_j is $0.01e^{-0.01s}$.) We define a new process as follows. To generate a random time path for the new process, first draw a time path for P from the μ distribution, then a sequence of t_j from the Poisson process. Modify the initially drawn P path by adding a discontinuous jump of height $-100\dot{P}(t_j)$ at each of the random times t_j. ($\dot{P}$ is the derivative of the original P with respect to t.) The resulting process will have differentiable time paths, except for occasional random jumps, and will be a martingale. Given the way we have chosen the jump process, the odds are about 100 to 1 against observing any jump over the interval $[0, 1]$. Thus, the kind of behavior we always observe under μ – differentiable time paths of P over $[0, 1]$ – is usually observed over that interval under the martingale process we have constructed. The differentiable process is absolutely continuous with respect to the martingale we constructed from it, because if the differentiable process is the truth, we will never observe a path of P over $[0, 1]$ which allows us to be certain that the process is not the martingale we constructed. Of course, there is some probability under the martingale process that we will observe a discontinuous jump in P on $[0, 1]$, and in that case we could be sure we were not observing the differentiable process, so the martingale is not absolutely continuous with respect to the differentiable process.

An Observable Criterion for Failure of Martingale Equivalence

If the highly predictable behavior over short time intervals of a differentiable process is not ruled out by martingale equivalence, what kind of price behavior could we observe that would allow us to conclude that martingale equivalence fails? One kind of price behavior that would allow such a conclusion can be characterized as follows. For any process X that is a local martingale[2] there is an associated positive, increasing process $[X, X]_t$ called the (optional) *quadratic variation*[3] in X. We refer the reader to Jacod and Shiryayev (1987, section 4e) for a formal definition, as it requires some technical apparatus. However, it can be understood through the following definition of an estimator of it and through a statement of some of its properties. We define[4]

$$\widehat{[X,X]}_t^h = \sum_{j=1}^{[t/h]} [X(jh) - X((j-1)h)]^2, \qquad \widehat{[X,X]}_t = \lim_{h\to 0} \{\widehat{[X,X]}_t^h\}, \tag{2}$$

where the notation "$[t/h]$" means "the largest integer less than or equal to t/h."

Jacod and Shiryayev (1987, theorem 4.47) show that the term in brackets on the right-hand side of (2) converges in probability as $h \to 0$ to $[X, X]_t$ when X is a local martingale. This does not imply that it converges for any single sample path, but it does imply that the probability of paths such that the limit on the right-hand side of (2) exists and is something other than $[X, X]_t$ is zero. A martingale has zero quadratic variation with probability one if and only if it is a trivial constant martingale. (See Jacod and Shiryayev (1987, proposition 4.50).)

Let $\mathscr{S}_t$ be the set of all finite sequences $\{s_i\}_{i=1}^n$, $0 < s_i < s_{i+1} < t$, all $i = 1, \ldots, n-1$. The total variation in X over $[0, t]$ is then defined as

$$V_X(t) = \sup_{\{s_j\} \text{ in } \mathscr{S}_t} \left\{ \sum_{j=1}^n |X(s_j) - X(s_{j-1})| \right\}. \tag{3}$$

Theorem *If X is a local martingale, with probability one there is no interval* $[0, t]$ *with* $t > 0$ *such that* $[X, X]_t = 0$ *and* $V_X(t) = \infty$.

Proof See appendix.

Thus we have the desired criterion for an observed time path that could not have come from a martingale process: a path for which our estimate shows zero quadratic variation over some interval but that has unbounded variation (in the usual sense) over the interval.

A local martingale also cannot have infinite quadratic variation over finite intervals. This provides a second criterion for an observed time path that cannot have come from a martingale process.

Implementing a check for these conditions with real data raises some problems. Both (2) and (3) include limit operations. In practice, we never have truly continuous records of asset prices, so we cannot actually compute these limits. We must be content with computing (2) for a finite sequence of n which grow larger and (3) for a finite sequence of increasingly fine partitions. We would look for the finite sequence of right-hand sides of (2) to be shrinking while a finite sequence of right-hand sides of (3) is increasing. Of course, this can never give us the certainty about failure of the no-arbitrage condition that would be possible with a truly continuous data record.

However, the fact that actual data cannot truly leave us certain that observed prices are not drawn from a martingale-equivalent process does not fatally weaken our results. The results carry the same kind of weight as a standard consistency proof. Just as, with an infinite sample, we can be certain that data are generated by an autoregression with a unit root, with a continuous record we can be certain that an observed price process is not martingale-equivalent. Just as our samples are in fact finite, they are in fact not truly continuous. Knowing what methods would give us certainty in an infinite sample (consistent estimation procedures) is a useful guide to good procedure in finite samples; similarly knowing what methods would give us certainty with a truly continuous record is a useful guide to good procedure with actual fine-time-unit, but discrete, data.

Convenient Parametric Models Not Absolutely Continuous with Respect to Martingales

Since our conclusions cannot be certain, we will want to place probabilistic error bounds on them. To do so, we will need to formulate a parametric model for the stochastic process followed by an observed asset price that includes both stochastic processes equivalent to martingales and stochastic processes that are not.

We first note that there is a well-known class of processes some of which, over finite intervals with probability one, generate infinite quadratic variation and others of which, with probability one, generate zero quadratic variation and infinite total variation. What Mandelbrot and Van Ness (1968) call "fractional Brownian motions" have the property that when their parameter H satisfies $0 < H < 0.5$, quadratic variation is infinite with probability one, and when $0.5 < H < 1$, with probability one, quadratic variation is 0 and total variation is infinite. Much of the literature on fractional Brownian motion emphasizes the "long dependence" properties of such processes – the slow rate at which their autocovariance functions decay toward zero at infinity or the unboundedness of the spectral density or its derivative at 0. We focus instead on the processes' fine-time-unit properties – the unboundedness of the derivative of the autocovariance function at 0 or the slow decay toward zero at infinity of the spectral density function.

Because the fractional Brownian motions tie the long-dependence properties of the process to the same parameter that determines its fine-time-unit behavior, they do not form a practically useful parametric family for modeling asset prices. Building on work in Maheswaran (1990a, 1990b), we show in the appendix that if X is a Gaussian process with moving average representation

$$X(t) = \int a(t-s)\,\mathrm{d}W(s), \tag{4}$$

if $a(s)/s^p$ converges to some $\varepsilon > 0$ as $s \to 0$ from above, and if $a(s)$ is otherwise smooth, then for $-0.5 < p < 0$, not only $[X, X]$ but our estimate $\widehat{[X, X]}$ is infinite, with probability one. Also, if $0 < p < 0.5$, then with probability one, $[X, X]$ and $\widehat{[X, X]}$ are zero, while V_X is infinite. (Note that our p corresponds to $H - 0.5$ in the notation of Mandelbrot and Van Ness.)

This result opens up a range of practical modeling alternatives. For example, one could construct any convenient parametric family of functions $b(\cdot\,;\beta)\colon \mathbb{R}^+ \to \mathbb{R}$

satisfying $b(0; \beta) = 1$, b differentiable in its first argument t for all $t > 0$ and right-differentiable at $t = 0$, and $\int t^2 b(t; \beta)^2 \, dt < \infty$. Then, letting a in (4) satisfy

$$a(s) = \gamma s^p b(s; \beta), \tag{5}$$

one has a convenient parametric family of stationary, Gaussian processes allowing infinite quadratic variation ($-0.5 < p < 0$), martingale-equivalent behavior ($p = 0$), zero quadratic variation combined with infinite total (first-order) variation ($0 < p \leq 0.5$), and zero quadratic variation combined with bounded total variation ($1 \geq p > 0.5$).

For technical reasons it may be worth noting that processes of the class parameterized in (5) are, for $-0.5 < p < 0.5$, $p \neq 0$ not only not absolutely continuous with respect to any martingale measure, they are not semimartingales. That this is true follows directly from the definition of a semimartingale as the sum of a local martingale and a process whose paths have bounded total variation. Since much of the convenient apparatus of stochastic calculus fails to apply outside the realm of semimartingales, we should observe that we have here an example where assuming that an asset price follows a semimartingale is a substantive restriction, not a mere regularity condition.

Comparing Smoothness and Variation-discrepancy as Criteria for Failure of the No-arbitrage Condition

A price process P whose time paths are almost surely absolutely continuously differentiable in t is not equivalent to a martingale and offers a simply defined arbitrage opportunity.[5] Suppose we have a proposed rule for choosing over the interval $0 \leq t \leq 1$ a time path $A(t)$ for holdings of the asset whose price is $P(t)$ and also a path $N(t)$ for holdings of the numeraire asset. Whatever the rule may be, we can improve on its performance with zero risk by changing the original $N(t)$ path to $N(t) - \delta \dot{P}(t)$ for any $\delta > 0$. To satisfy the original wealth constraint, the new path $A^*(t)$ for holdings of the non-numeraire asset will have to satisfy

$$\mathrm{d}A^*(t) = \mathrm{d}A(t) + \delta \frac{\mathrm{d}[\dot{P}(t)]}{P(t)}. \tag{6}$$

But it is easy to check, integrating by parts, that (6) implies[6]

$$P(t)A^*(t) + N(t) - \delta \dot{P}(t) = P(t)A(t) + N(t) + \delta P(t) \int_0^t \left(\frac{\dot{P}(s)}{P(s)} \right)^2 \mathrm{d}s. \tag{7}$$

The left-hand side of (7) is just the value of the portfolio under the new rule, and the right-hand side shows that it strictly exceeds the value under the old rule. Harrison et al. (1984) show that arbitrage opportunities exist for differentiable paths even when they are not absolutely continuously differentiable.

However, as we have already observed, this kind of deviation from the no-arbitrage condition cannot be detected with certainty from a finite span of data. As the period over which we observe differentiability lengthens, it would be reasonable for us to be more and more confident that the discontinuous jumps in P that would reconcile observed differentiability with martingale behavior will never occur. But no finite span of observation can make us certain of this, even with a continuous data record.

In contrast, the type of deviation from martingale equivalence we focus on in this paper, which we may as well call "variation discrepancy", can be identified with certainty from a finite span of data. It is true that checking for variation discrepancy requires observation at arbitrarily fine time units, but of course verifying differentiability also requires observation at arbitrarily fine time units.

The nature of arbitrage strategies that would exploit the failure of martingale equivalence via variation discrepancy is an interesting question. As we show in the appendix, for price processes whose logs are of the form (4), with a given by (5) with $-0.5 < p < 0.5$, $p \neq 0$, it is possible to construct trading rules based on the observed history of prices that obtain arbitrarily low ratios of standard deviation of return to mean return. The idea is that one trades at uniform time intervals h, always investing in the asset when the expected price change over the next interval of length h is positive, in the numeraire otherwise. The mean return from such a strategy over a fixed interval goes to infinity as the trading interval h goes to zero. The standard deviation of the return remains bounded.

As is also shown in the appendix, this possibility implies the existence of an arbitrage opportunity in the time-zero contingent claims market. The idea is that though none of these investment strategies is risk-free, as the risk becomes arbitrarily small their time-zero value as a random payout must eventually exceed the time-zero price of the capital necessary to implement them.

In the appendix we also construct purely risk-free arbitrage strategies entirely in the spot market. The idea is to choose h and the fraction of the portfolio invested in the asset to make the probability of loss over $(0, 0.5)$ 0.25, say. Then, if there is a gain by time $t = 0.5$, hold the numeraire until $t = 1$. Otherwise, recalibrate h and the fraction of the portfolio invested so that the probability of failing to be above the initial $t = 0$ level of wealth by $t = 0.75$ is less than 0.125. Repeat this indefinitely, at each date $t = 1 - 2^{-j}$, stopping if a profit has been achieved, otherwise intensifying the transaction rate so that the probability of not achieving a profit over the next interval of length 2^{-j-1} is less than 2^{-j-2}. This achieves a profit over the interval $(0, 1)$ with probability one, using only a fixed initial investment.

Conclusion

We have shown that there are stable probability models for price behavior that are outside the semimartingale class and that may have a role in financial market modeling when absence of arbitrage opportunities is not a foregone conclusion. We hope to have encouraged the interest of other researchers who may help to discover the ultimate usefulness of these ideas.

Appendix

A Measure-Theoretic Derivation of Martingale Equivalence We consider two assets, one the numeraire and the other, which we call c, whose spot price in terms of the numeraire is given by P_t for t in $[0, 1]$. We assume that there are some traders in the market who hold both assets and who care about the total value of their portfolio at $t = 1$, but not about their asset holdings at intermediate points in time.[7] There is a probability space Ω and a sigma-field $\mathscr{F}$ of subsets of Ω. The information structure, common across all agents, is defined by the increasing family of sigma-fields $\{\mathscr{F}_t\colon t$ in $[0,1]\}$ with $\mathscr{F}_1 = \mathscr{F}$. We suppose that trading is allowed in arbitrary contingent claims on the numeraire asset and c, subject to the requirement that an asset traded at t can be contingent only on events in $\mathscr{F}_t$.

Let $\delta^c, \delta^n\colon \mathscr{F} \to \mathbb{R}^n$ denote set functions such that $\delta^n(A)$ and $\delta^c(A)$ are the prices at time zero of one unit of the numeraire asset or c, respectively, delivered at $t = 1$ contingent on the true state of the world ω lying in A. Since one unit of either asset can be delivered regardless of the state of the world at $t = 1$ by simply holding it from $t = 0$ to $t = 1$, we must have $\delta^n(\Omega) = 1$, $\delta^c(\Omega) = P_0$. We also assume $\delta^c, \delta^n \geq 0$ for all arguments, as usual for a price. We take the absence of arbitrage opportunities to imply that each δ be a measure. That is, it must be true that $\delta(\varnothing) = 0$ and that, for any countable class $\{A_j\}$ of disjoint sets in $\mathscr{F}$,

$$\delta\left(\bigcup A_j\right) = \sum \delta(A_j). \tag{A1}$$

If (A1) did not hold, there would be some class of claims, contingent on a set of mutually exclusive events, that could be bought separately at a total price different from the price of an equivalent claim contingent on the union of the separate contingencies. In other words, two equivalent bundles of goods would have different prices, which is exactly an arbitrage opportunity.[8]

Now suppose that there is no set A in $\mathscr{F}$ such that $\delta^n(A) = 0$ and $\delta^c(A) > 0$. For this condition to fail would imply that there is some contingency under which the numeraire is valueless but the other asset is still valuable. This condition means that δ^c is absolutely continuous with respect to δ^n. It is a standard result in measure theory that under these conditions there is an integrable function (the Radon–Nikodym derivative) $Q\colon \Omega \to \mathbb{R}$ satisfying

$$\forall A \text{ in } \mathscr{F},\ \delta^c(A) = \int_A Q(\omega)\delta^n(\mathrm{d}\omega). \tag{A2}$$

Now it is well known that for any sub-σ-field $\mathscr{F}_t$ of $\mathscr{F}$, there is an integrable, $\mathscr{F}_t$-measurable function $E_t[Q\,|\,\cdot\,]$ on Ω with the property that

$$\forall A \text{ in } \mathscr{F}_t,\ \delta^c(A) = \int_A E_t[Q\,|\,\omega]\delta^n(\mathrm{d}\omega). \tag{A3}$$

We will proceed to show that with probability one, $P_t = E_t[Q]$.

To do so we have to extend our δ terms to pricing rules for a wider class of payouts than the simple unit contingent payouts for which they are already defined. It is natural to suppose that countable linear combinations of contingent payouts can be priced, with a payout of $\lambda_i > 0$ units of the numeraire for ω in A_i, priced at

$$\pi\left(\sum \lambda_i \mathscr{I}(\omega; A_i)\right) = \sum \lambda_i \delta^n(A_i). \tag{A4}$$

Here we have represented the payout as a linear combination of indicator functions on Ω, with π a "pricing function" delivering current prices of payouts specified as functions on Ω. That this type of payout be priced this way is also a consequence of a no-arbitrage assumption, assuming that contingent claims are infinitely divisible. From (A4), π already has the form of an integral, and we can extend π uniquely to all positive δ^n-measurable functions on Ω by using one further property of arbitrage: if a payout f on Ω dominates another payout g in the sense that $f(\omega) > g(w)$ for all ω except for a set of δ^n-measure 0, then $\pi(f) \geq \pi(g)$. Given this, it must be true[9] that

$$\pi(f) = \int f(\omega)\delta^n(d\omega) \tag{A5}$$

for any $\mathscr{F}$-measurable f.

Consider an arbitrary set A in $\mathscr{F}_t$. We consider how to value a claim to a unit of c contingent on A. We have two feasible ways of delivering one unit of c at $t = 1$ contingent on A: buy at $t = 0$ a claim to one unit of c contingent on A, or buy at $t = 0$ an asset that pays P_t units of the numeraire good at t, contingent on A being realized at t. The proceeds from this asset can be used at t to purchase a unit of c if A has been realized. We know how to price these two assets. The outright contingent claim to c is worth, at $t = 0$, by (A2)

$$\delta^c(A) = \int_A E_t[Q\,|\,\omega]\delta^n(d\omega) \tag{A6}$$

while the claim to the P_t payout contingent on A is worth, by (A5),

$$\pi(P_t\mathscr{I}(\omega; A)) = \int_A P_t(\omega)\delta^n(d\omega). \tag{A7}$$

Since absence of arbitrage opportunities implies (A6) = (A7) for all A in $\mathscr{F}_t$, $P_t = E_t[Q]$ on a set of δ^n-measure one.

Observe that so far we have not made any use of the notion of a true or "physical" probability distribution on Ω. To do so, we need to add an assumption about the relation between δ^n-measure and true probability. It is natural to suppose they are equivalent, so that no value is given to delivery of a unit of the numeraire contingent on an event of zero probability, and some positive value is given to delivery contingent on any event that has nonzero probability. Then the P_t stochastic process, which we have shown to be a martingale under the δ^n measure, is equivalent to a martingale under the true probability measure.

Properties of Processes with MA Kernel Behaving like s^p Near the Origin Consider a process X of the form (4) with a of the form (5), satisfying

1. $b(0) \neq 0$;
2. $b(s)$ right-continuous in s at $s = 0$;
3. $b'(s)$ exists and is bounded and continuous;
4. $-0.5 < p < 0.5$.

(Here we have suppressed the argument β in (5).) It is convenient to define $\Delta_h X(t) = X(t) - X(t - h)$.

Lemma 1 *For an X satisfying* (1)–(4) *in the above list, for every integer j*

$$R_h(j) = h^{-(2p+1)}\,\mathrm{Cov}\,(\Delta X_h(t), \Delta X_h(t-jh)) \xrightarrow[h\to 0]{} R(j); \tag{A8}$$

and there exists a $C > 0$, *not dependent on h, such that for all* $j > 0$,

$$Cj^{p-1} > |R_h(j)| \quad \textit{for } -0.5 < p < 0, \tag{A9}$$

$$Cj^{2p-1} > |R_h(j)| \quad \text{for } 0 < p < 0.5. \tag{A10}$$

Proof $\Delta_h X(t)$ has moving average kernel $\alpha_h(s)$, with $\alpha_h(s) = a(s)$, $0 \le s < h$, $\alpha_h(s) = a(s) - a(s-h)$ for $s \ge h$. Thus we can write, for $j \ge 1$,

$$\begin{aligned} h^{2p+1}R_h(j) = {} & \int_0^h b(s)s^p[(s+jh)^p b(s+jh) - (s+jh-h)^p b(s+jh-1)]\,\mathrm{d}s \\ & + \int_h^\infty [b(s)s^p - b(s-h)(s-h)^p] \\ & \times [(s+jh)^p b(s+jh) - (s+jh-h)^p b(s+jh-h)]\,\mathrm{d}s. \end{aligned} \tag{A11}$$

For $j = 0$, the first term in (A11) is replaced by $\int_0^h b(s)^2 s^p\,\mathrm{d}s$.

Suppose that, in (A11) or the corresponding expression for $j = 0$, we make the change in variables $s = vh$. Then it is straightforward to check that, by the boundedness of b and its derivative, the two integrals in (A11) behave like h^{2p+1} as $h \to 0$ for any fixed j.[10] (Checking this does require noting that $v^p - (v-1)^p$ behaves like v^{p-1} as $v \to \infty$, and is thus integrable for $p < 0.5$.) Further, there is a constant $C > 0$ such that the first integral on the right-hand side of (A11) is bounded above in absolute value by

$$Ch^{2p+1}\int_0^1 v^p|(v+j)^p - (v+j-1)^p|\,\mathrm{d}v < Ch^{2p+1}j^{p-1} \tag{A12}$$

for $j \ge 2$, where the generic "C" may be different on the two sides of (A12). This follows by noting that, using a Taylor expansion of the second factor in the middle expression of (A13) below,

$$|(v+j)^p - (v+j-1)^p| = j^p\left|\left(\frac{v}{j}+1\right)^p - \left(\frac{v-1}{j}+1\right)^p\right| \cong pj^{p-1}. \tag{A13}$$

With the same change of variable, we can bound the second integral on the right-hand side of (A11) by

$$\begin{aligned} Ch^{2p+1}\int_1^\infty v^{p-1}(v+j)^{p-1}\,\mathrm{d}v &= Ch^{2p+1}\int_1^\infty (v^2+vj)^{p-1}\,\mathrm{d}v \\ &\le Ch^{2p+1}j^{2p-1}. \end{aligned} \tag{A14}$$

Here as before we use a generic constant "C" that may take on different values in different expressions. Note that when $p < 0$, (A12) becomes the effective bound on (A10), while when $p > 0$, (A14) is the effective bound.

Lemma 2 *For* $p > 0, \widehat{[X,X]}_1^h \xrightarrow{\text{a.s.}} 0$ *as* $h \to 0$.

Proof From (A8), it is easy to conclude that

$$E[\widehat{[X,X]}_1^h] = E\left[\sum_{j=1}^{h-1} \Delta_h X(jh)^2\right] \quad \text{behaves like } h^{2p} \text{ as } h \to 0. \tag{A15}$$

Since $\widehat{[X,X]}_1 > 0$ with probability one, the fact that h^{2p} in (A15) goes to zero with h for $p > 0$ implies that for this case $\widehat{[X,X]}_1^h$ converges in probability to zero as $h \to 0$. By choosing a sequence h_j that converges fast enough to zero ($h_j = \delta^j$ for any $0 < \delta < 1$, for example) we can make the convergence almost sure.[11]

Lemma 3 *For* $p < 0, \widehat{[X,X]}_1^h \xrightarrow{\text{a.s.}} \infty$ *as* $h \to 0$.

Proof First we need the following lemma.

Lemma 4 *For X and Z jointly Gaussian,*

$$\text{Cor}\,(X^2, Z^2) = (\text{Cor}\,(X, Z))^2. \tag{A16}$$

where "Cor" means "correlation".

For $p < 0$, (A9) and (A10) imply that R_h is absolutely summable. Then (A8)–(A11) can be used, together with (A16), to show

$$h^{-4p-1}\,\text{Var}\,(\widehat{[X,X]}_1^h) \xrightarrow[h \to 0]{} \varepsilon, \tag{A17}$$

where ε is some constant ≥ 0. Thus the ratio of the mean of $[X, X]_1^h$ to its standard deviation behaves like $h^{-0.5}$ and goes to infinity as $h \to 0$. This guarantees that $[X, X]_1^h$ converges in probability to infinity as $h \to 0$ for $p < 0$. Again, by choosing a sequence of h values converging rapidly enough to zero, we can attain convergence with probability one.

It remains then to show the following lemma.

Lemma 5 *The paths of X will be of unbounded variation when* $0 < p < 0.5$.

Proof Observe that

$$V_X^h(1) = \sum_{j=1}^{h-1} |\Delta_h X(j/h)|. \tag{A18}$$

The individual random variables in the sums on the right-hand side of (A9) and (A10) have expected value bounded below by a term of the form $Ch^{p+0.5}$, $C > 0$, so the entire term has expectation bounded below by a $Ch^{p-0.5}$ term that goes to infinity as $h \to 0$.

For jointly Gaussian random variables Y and Z with correlation ρ, Cor $(|Y|, |Z|)$ behaves like ρ^2 as $\rho \to 0$. This, together with (A9), allows us to conclude that the standard deviation of $V_x^h(1)$ behaves like h^{1-2p} for small h and thus again to conclude that we have convergence in probability to infinity, with convergence almost surely if the h sequence is taken to converge quickly enough to zero.

Arbitrage Strategies Since non-martingale-equivalent price processes must present arbitrage opportunities, it is interesting to explore what these might be. For spot prices Q_t whose logarithms q_t follow processes of the type considered here, we can construct arbitrage strategies as follows. First we observe the properties of the following type of investment. At date 0, invest \$1 (one unit of the numeraire) in the asset if $E_0[\Delta_h q_h] > 0$, hold on to the \$1 (invest it in the numeraire) otherwise. Continue to follow this rule, investing the entire current accumulation of wealth in the asset when $E_t[\Delta_h q_{t+h}] > 0$, keeping it in the numeraire otherwise, with the portfolio being adjusted according to this rule at each date t that is an exact integral multiple of h. Over the fixed interval $[0, \gamma]$, if W_t is the value of the portfolio at date t, we have[12]

$$E_0[\log W_\gamma] = \frac{\gamma}{2h} E_0[E_t[q_{t+h} - q_t] | E_t[q_{t+h} - q_t] > 0]. \tag{A19}$$

Now $E_t[q_{t+h} - q_t]$ is the "explained part" of $\Delta_h q_{t+h}$, based on all information in the continuous record of q up to time t. It therefore has larger variance than the best predictor of $\Delta_h q_{t+h}$ based on $\Delta_h q_t$ alone. By (A8), we know that the latter variance behaves like h^{2p+1}, and is thus bounded below, for $p \neq 0$ and small h, by Bh^{2p+1} for some $B > 0$. Assuming q is Gaussian, (A19) is just the expectation of a truncated Gaussian variable and is therefore proportional to the standard deviation of the variable. From the form of (A19), we can see that it is bounded below by $B_1 h^{p-0.5}$ for some $B_1 > 0$, so long as $p \neq 0$. With $-0.5 < p < 0.5$, we can thus conclude that the expected return over the interval $[0, \gamma]$ is arbitrarily large for h small enough.

To determine the variance of the return, we denote the return over one h-length interval as

$$y_{t+h} = \Delta q_{t+h} \cdot \mathscr{I}(E_t[\Delta q_{t+h}] > 0), \tag{A20}$$

where $\mathscr{I}(\cdot)$ is a random variable taking on the value one when its argument is true and zero otherwise. Then the autocovariance function of y satisfies, for $|i - j| \geq 1$,

$$|\mathrm{Cov}(y_{ih}, y_{jh})| \leq \begin{cases} K|i-j|^{p-1}h^{2p+1}, & -0.5 < p < 0, \\ K|i-j|^{2p-1}h^{2p+1}, & 0 < p < 0.5. \end{cases} \tag{A21}$$

This set of inequalities follows from (A9) and (A10) and the fact that, for any two jointly Gaussian random variables X and Y with correlation coefficient ρ and any functions f and g such that $|f(X)|$ and $|g(Y)|$ have finite first and second moments, the correlation of $f(X)$ and $g(Y)$ is $O(\rho)$ as $\rho \to 0$. The variance of W_γ is the variance of the sum of the y_{ih} terms over the $(0, \gamma)$ interval and is thus bounded by

$$\frac{\gamma}{h} \sum_{j=-\gamma/h}^{\gamma/h} Kj^{\pi-1}h^{2p+1}, \tag{A22}$$

where $\pi = p$ for $p < 0$, $\pi = 2p$ for $p > 0$. This is in turn bounded above by

$$\frac{\gamma}{h} K\left(\frac{\gamma}{h}\right)^{\pi} h^{2p+1} = \begin{cases} O(h^p), & p < 0, \\ O(1) & p > 0, \end{cases} \tag{A23}$$

where the value of the constant K may shift between its occurrences in (A22) and (A23). Since we found above that the expected return is bounded below by $B_1 h^{p-0.5}$, we can apply (A23) to find that the ratio of expected return to its standard deviation goes to infinity as $h \to 0$, behaving as $h^{p-0.5}$ for $0 < p < 0.5$ and as $h^{0.5(p-1)}$ for $-0.5 < p < 0$.

The strategies we have outlined here do not directly produce a risk-free gain, of course, since there is always some nonzero variance to the return they provide. They can be used to develop strictly risk-free arbitrage opportunities in two ways. First, in the presence of contingent claims markets, it must be true that as risk goes to zero while expected return remains bounded below, the value of contingent claims to the payout must converge to a number greater than the initial capital required. Thus there will be an arbitrage opportunity in the contingent claims market.

To produce an arbitrage opportunity in the spot market, we apply a strategy that looks like the classic doubling strategies for martingale processes. Apply the strategy outlined above over the time interval $(0, 0.5)$, with h and the fraction of the initial portfolio committed to the investment strategy in this initial period chosen so that the probability of losing any money over the interval is less than 0.25. If at $t = 0.5$ we have made a profit, we stop and hold our winnings until $t = 1$. Otherwise, we readjust h and the fraction of our portfolio invested so that the probability of our wealth being below the initial $t = 0$ level at $t = 0.75$ is less than 0.125. That is, we choose h so that the expected gain over $(0.5, 0.75)$ is high enough, and the variance low enough, that we will be above the initial wealth level at $t = 0.75$ with probability 0.875. Now we repeat this indefinitely, at each time $1 - 2^{-j}$ either stopping, because we have achieved a profit, or intensifying the rate of trading so as to increase the expected rate of return and make the probability of failing to achieve a profit by the end of the next interval of length 2^{-j-1} less than 2^{-j-2}. It is easily seen that the probability of never achieving a profit during the time interval $(0, 1)$ is zero. Further, the total number of transactions required to implement the strategy will be finite, though there is no deterministic upper bound on the number of transactions that will be required.

Proof of the theorem First we need another result.

Lemma 6 *A purely discontinuous local martingale X that has a.s. no more than a single point of discontinuity has locally integrable variation.*

This lemma may appear more obvious than it is. A martingale with a randomly timed jump consists in general of two components, the jump part and a "compensator" with continuous sample paths. The work in the proof is to show that the compensator, besides being continuous, necessarily has finite variation.

Proof Let T be the stopping time defined as the date at which X jumps. Then the "sums of jumps" process for X is

$$\sum_{s \leq t} \Delta X = \begin{cases} 0, & t < T, \\ X(T) - X(T_-), & t \geq T. \end{cases} \tag{A24}$$

This processes is obviously a.s. of finite variation. It is also locally of absolutely integrable total variation. To see this, observe that we can define the sequence of stopping times

$$T_n = \inf\{t\colon |X(t)| > n\} \tag{A25}$$

so that $T_n \to \infty$ a.s. and the stopped martingales X^{T_n} are all absolutely integrable.[13] To simplify notation we denote X^{T_n} by X_n. We have

$$X_n(T) = (X_n(T) - X_n(T_-)) + X_n(T_-). \tag{A26}$$

$X_n(T)$ and $X_n(T_-)$ are by construction absolutely integrable, which implies that the term in brackets must be also. Thus the process

$$\sum_{s \leq t} \Delta X_n = \left(\sum_{s \leq t} \Delta X \right)^{T_n} \tag{A27}$$

is absolutely integrable and the process $\sum \Delta X$ itself is locally absolutely integrable (i.e. in $\mathscr{A}_{\text{loc}}$). But then, by Jacod and Shiryaev (1987, theorem 3.18), there is a predictable process

$$\left(\sum_{s \leq t} \Delta X \right)^p \text{ in } \mathscr{A}_{\text{loc}}, \tag{A28}$$

unique up to an evanescent set, such that

$$\left(\sum_{s \leq t} \Delta X \right) - \left(\sum_{s \leq t} \Delta X \right)^p \tag{A29}$$

is a local martingale. By the uniqueness of (A28), the process displayed in (A29) must be X itself (up to an evanescent set). Otherwise, the difference between X and (A29) would be a nonzero local martingale with no discontinuities, and the assumption of pure discontinuity for X implies it contains no such component. Since both terms in (A29) have been verified to lie in $\mathscr{A}_{\text{loc}}$, their difference, X, is in $\mathscr{A}_{\text{loc}}$ also.

Now consider the result we are aiming for, restated here.

Theorem *If X is a local martingale, with probability one there is no interval $[0, t]$ with $t > 0$ such that $[X, X]_t = 0$ and $V_X(t) = \infty$.*

Proof Consider the stopping time $T = \inf\{t: [X, X]_t > 0\}$. The stopped process X^T is a local martingale with at most one discontinuity – a possible jump at T. Therefore, by the lemma, it has bounded variation with probability one. Since $[0, T]$ is the longest interval on which $[X, X]$ remains zero, we have proved the result.

Notes

Research for this paper was supported in part by NSF grant SES 8722451. The advice of Kerry Back, anonymous referees, and the editor has improved the paper, for which the authors are grateful.

1. Our approach uses a slightly different set of primitives than the original Harrison–Kreps approach. By defining an arbitrage opportunity more broadly, we are able to use measure-theoretic structure more heavily and avoid explicitly introducing a topology on payoff functions.
2. The word "local" here is used in the special sense of continuous-time stochastic process theory. We do not attempt to define it here, but readers unfamiliar with it can note that a martingale is also locally a martingale and can refer to Jacod and Shiryayev (1987) for more detail.
3. We will henceforth simply call this the quadratic variation.
4. Note that this estimate is a random variable chosen to approximate another random variable – $[X, X]_t$ – and not a conventional statistical estimator of a nonrandom parameter.
5. This assertion might seem to contradict the earlier claim that we can never be sure that a smooth price process is not drawn from a martingale-equivalent process. The arbitrage opportunity demonstrated here depends on it being *certain* that the price process is differentiable.
6. From (6) we have

$$A^*(t) - A^*(0) = A(t) - A(0) + \delta \int_0^t \frac{\ddot{P}(s)}{P(s)} ds$$

$$= A(t) + \delta \left.\frac{\dot{P}(s)}{P(s)}\right|_0^t + \int_0^t \left(\frac{\dot{P}(s)}{P(s)}\right)^2 ds$$

   This yields (7) when multiplied by $P(t)$.

7. This rules out assets that have dividend or interest payments or that provide a utility yield as they are held. The martingale equivalence result proved below can be extended to assets that do have such yields. Yields must occcur in a continuous flow rather than as discrete payouts at isolated dates, but otherwise the extension puts little restriction on the nature of yields. Such an extension is displayed in Sims (1984).
8. We should observe, though, that it is probably more conventional to require only that *finite* collections of contingent claims sell at the same price as a claim contingent on the union of the contingencies they represent. Countable additivity is then derived from a separate assumption of continuity in some topology on the space of return functions.
9. Note that $\pi(f)$ may be infinite if f is unbounded.
10. By "$f(h)$ behaves like $g(h)$ as $h \to 0$", we mean there is a constant $0 < C < \infty$ such that $f(h) | g(h) \to C$ as $h \to 0$.

11. $E[|X_j|] = O(\delta(j))$, where $\delta(j)$ decreases monotonically to 0 as $j \to \infty$, implies $P[|X_j| > \varepsilon] = O(\delta(j))$. By choosing $k(j)$ to increase rapidly enough in j, e.g. so that $k(j) = \delta^{-1}(2^{-j})$, we can make $P[|X_{k(j)}| > \varepsilon] = O(2^{-j})$, and thus guarantee that

$$\sum_{j=i}^{\infty} P[|X_{k(j)}| > \varepsilon] \xrightarrow[i \to \infty]{} 0, \quad \text{i.e. } X_{k(j)} \xrightarrow{\text{a.s.}} 0.$$

12. Since $\log(W_0) = 0$, $\log(W_y)$ is the sum of the changes in logs of W over the length-h decision intervals. The unconditional probability that $E_t[q_{t+h} - q_t] > 0$ is 0.5, and the expected change in the log portfolio value during periods when it is kept entirely invested in the numeraire is 0. Thus the right-hand side of (A17) is just the unconditional expectation of the change in log portfolio value over a typical interval, multiplied by the number of intervals. This argument does depend on E_0 being the same as unconditional expectation, which requires that the process "start up" at time 0 with zero innovation process before that.
13. As per the standard notation in the probability literature, if X is a process and T is a stopping time, we take X^T to mean the "stopped" process defined as $X^T(t) = X(t \wedge T)$, with $t \wedge T = \min(t, T)$. Furthermore, the prévisible (sometimes called the predictable) projection of a process X is denoted by $(X)^p$. See Jacod and Shiryayev (1987) for details.

References

Dothan, M. U. (1990). *Prices in Financial Markets.* Oxford: Oxford University Press.

Harrison, J. M., R. Pitbladdo, and S. M. Schaefer (1984). "Continuous price processes in frictionless markets have infinite variation," *Journal of Business*, 57, 353–65.

Harrison, J. M., and D. Kreps (1979). "Martingales and arbitrage in multiperiod securities markets," *Journal of Economic Theory*, 20, 381–408.

Leroy, S. F. (1973). "Risk aversion and the martingale behavior of stock prices," *International Economic Review*, 14, 436–46.

Jacod, J., and A. N. Shiryayev (1987). *Limit Theorems for Stochastic Processes.* Berlin: Springer-Verlag.

Lucas, R. E., Jr (1978). "Asset prices in an exchange economy," *Econometrica*, 46, 1429–46.

Maheswaran, S. (1990a). "Semimartingales and small time dynamics of prices," discussion paper, Olin School of Business, Washington University, St Louis.

Maheswaran, S. (1990b). "Predictable short-term variation in asset prices: theory and evidence," discussion paper, Olin School of Business, Washington University, St Louis.

Mandelbrot, B. B., and J. W. Van Ness (1968). "Fractional Brownian motions, fractional noises, and applications," *SIAM Review*, 10, October.

Protter, P. (1990). *Stochastic Integration and Differential Equations: A New Approach.* Berlin: Springer-Verlag.

Sims, C. (1984). "Martingale-like behavior of asset prices," discussion paper, University of Minnesota Center for Economic Research.

20

Rational Expectations and Integrated Variables

Michael R. Wickens

Introduction

In the mid-1970s, when Rex Bergstrom and I were colleagues at Essex, rational expectations (RE) was starting to displace other expectational assumptions and we frequently discussed its merits. These days, modeling expectations as rational has become part of the standard *impedimenta* of the applied econometrician and has largely displaced other expectational assumptions. Much has been written on the econometrics of RE, but virtually all of this work predates the recent interest in nonstationary time series and integrated series.[1] The purpose of this paper is to consider the problem of solving and estimating rational expectations equations with integrated series.

The paper is organized as follows. In the second section, the solution of the model is derived on the assumption that the forcing variables are I(1) and are predetermined. Although a particular dynamic model with future expectations is chosen, the results are capable of both specialization and generalization. It is shown that the model admits more than one solution, but only two are of interest, the globally stable and the saddlepath solutions. A brief review of the problems of estimating dynamic models with I(1) variables is presented in the third section. The merits of the Wickens and Breusch (1988) estimator, which is a development of the Bewley transformation, are advanced and are supported by some new analytic results on its asymptotic distribution which is shown to permit standard inference. In the fourth section, the single equation estimation of RE models is considered. Both the substitution and the errors in variable methods are discussed. Small-sample evidence on alternative single equation estimators of ordinary dynamic model and RE models is presented in the fifth section. Some conclusions about the best way to estimate RE models are drawn in the sixth section.

The Model and its Solution

For the most part attention will be focused on the problems of solving and estimating the following rational expectations model[2]:

$$y_t = \alpha E_t y_{t+1} + \delta y_{t-1} + \beta x_t + e_t, \qquad (1)$$

where x_t is a predetermined, nonstationary, or I(1), process

$$\Delta x_t = \eta + \sum_{s=0}^{\infty} \phi_s e_{t-s} + \sum_{s=0}^{\infty} \theta_s \varepsilon_{t-s}, \tag{2}$$

with $\phi_0 = 0$, $\theta_0 = 1$, $\sum_{s=0}^{\infty} \phi_s^2 < \infty$, $\sum_{s=0}^{\infty} \theta_s^2 < \infty$ and $\sum_{s=0}^{\infty} \phi_s z^s$, $\sum_{s=0}^{\infty} \theta_s z^s$ analytic functions on the open disk. The error terms e_t and ε_t are assumed to be mutually and serially uncorrelated variables with zero means and variances σ^2 and ω^2 respectively. In forming expectations at time t, agents know e_t and ε_t, but the econometrician does not. It is also assumed that the econometrician does not know how equation (1) has arisen; in particular, the values of α and δ are unknown.[3] It is straightforward to impose the extra restriction that e_t and ε_t are also unknown to the agent, see Wickens (1986).

In solving RE models it is usually assumed that x_t is strongly, or strictly, exogenous, implying that $\phi_i = 0$ for all i. In this section, a weaker assumption is considered, that x_t is predetermined, which allows $\phi_i \neq 0$ $(i > 0)$. The results of this section all apply without modification when x_t is strictly exogenous. This is not true for estimation where the assumption of strictly exogenous x_t brings considerable simplification. When x_t is strictly exogenous, the assumption that Δx_t is generated by a moving average process rather than by an autoregressive or ARMA process does not impose any restrictions if equation (2) is invertible. Nevertheless, as we shall see later, there is particular interest in the case where Δx_t is strongly exogenous and is generated by an AR(1). It is also straightforward to extend the results to the case of a number of exogenous variables; only in one situation, multiple integrated x with drift (i.e. co-trending x), are modifications to the estimation method required.

A detailed analysis of the solution and estimation of equation (1) is available in Wickens (1986) for the case where x_t is strongly exogenous and stationary. More general models are also considered, such as where there is more than one future expectation (i.e. $E_t y_{t+1}$, $E_t y_{t+2}$, etc.), higher order lags in y_t and where expectations are dated $t - 1$ or before (e.g. $E_{t-1} y_t$). Since different problems arise in each case, the analysis becomes quite lengthy. This is the reason for focusing on a single case here.

The solution to equations (1) and (2) can be obtained in several different ways, see Pesaran (1987) for a survey. Here the variant of Muth's method of undetermined coefficients developed by Whiteman (1983) will be used, as it makes the nature of the nonunique solutions more transparent. The general solution of y_t can be written[4]

$$\Delta y_t = c + \sum_{s=0}^{\infty} a_s e_{t-s} + \sum_{s=0}^{\infty} b_s \varepsilon_{t-s}, \tag{3}$$

where $A(z) = \sum_{s=0}^{\infty} a_s z^s$ and $B(z) = \sum_{s=0}^{\infty} b_s z^s$ contain no roots inside the unit circle. If L is the lag operator $L^s x_t = x_{t-s}$ for any x_t, $s \geq 0$, then (2) and (3) can be written

$$\Delta x_t = \eta + u_t + v_t, \tag{4}$$

$$\Delta y_t = c + A(L) e_t + B(L) \varepsilon_t, \tag{5}$$

where $u_t = \phi(L) e_t$, $v_t = \theta(L) \varepsilon_t$, $\phi(L) = \sum_{s=0}^{\infty} \phi_s L^s$ and $\theta(L) = \sum_{s=0}^{\infty} \theta_s L^s$. After first differencing, equation (1) can be written

$$\Delta y_t = \frac{1}{1-\alpha}[\alpha E_t \, \Delta y_{t+1} - \alpha E_{t-1} \, \Delta y_t + \delta \, \Delta y_{t-1} + \beta \, \Delta x_t + \Delta e_t]. \tag{6}$$

Next we replace y_t and x_t in (6). Using the Weiner–Kolmogorov prediction formulas for u_t gives

$$\begin{aligned} E_t u_{t+s} &= \sum_{s=0}^{\infty} \phi_{s+i} e_{t-i} = [L^{-s}\phi(L)]^{+} e_t \\ &= L^{-s}\left[\phi(L) - \sum_{i=0}^{s-1} \phi_i L^i\right] e_t. \end{aligned} \tag{7}$$

It follows, therefore, that

$$E_t \, \Delta y_{t+1} = c + L^{-1}[A(L) - a_0]e_t + L^{-1}[B(L) - b_0]\varepsilon_t, \tag{8}$$

$$E_{t-1} \, \Delta y_t = c + [A(L) - a_0]e_t + [B(L) - b_0]\varepsilon_t. \tag{9}$$

From (4), (5), (8), and (9), equation (6) can be expressed in terms of the fundamental innovations e_t and ε_t as

$$\begin{aligned} (1-\alpha)[c + A(L)e_t + B(L)\varepsilon_t] = {} & \alpha\{c + L^{-1}[A(L) - a_0]e_t + [B(L) - b_0]\varepsilon_t\} \\ & - \alpha\{c + [A(L) - a_0]e_t + [B(L) - b_0]\varepsilon_t\} \\ & + \delta\{c + LA(L)e_t + LB(L)\varepsilon_t\} \\ & + \beta[\eta + \phi(L)e_t + \theta(L)\varepsilon_t] + (1 - L)e_t. \end{aligned} \tag{10}$$

The method of undetermined coefficients evaluates c, $A(L)$, and $B(L)$ by equating the terms on each side of equation (10) with respect to the constants and the terms in e_t and ε_t. As a result, we obtain

$$c = \frac{\beta\eta}{1 - \alpha - \delta}, \tag{11}$$

$$A(z) = \frac{(1-z)(\alpha a_0 - z) - \beta z \phi(z)}{\alpha - z + \delta z^2}, \tag{12}$$

$$B(z) = \frac{\alpha b_0(1-z) - \beta z \theta(z)}{\alpha - z + \delta z^2}. \tag{13}$$

It follows that, if x_t has no deterministic trend (i.e. $\eta = 0$) then neither does y_t (i.e. $c = 0$); in this case both possess only stochastic trends. a_0 and b_0 are free parameters yet to be determined.

Equations (12) and (13) are analytic for $|z| < 1$ if and only if the roots of $\alpha - z + \delta z^2 = 0$ lie on or outside the unit circle. For each root inside the unit circle, $A(z)$ and $B(z)$ have a removable singularity at that root, see Whiteman (1983, p. 7). Denoting the roots λ_1 and λ_2, there are three possibilities:

1. The globally stable model: $|\lambda_1|, |\lambda_2| \geq 1$, which implies $\alpha - 1 + \delta \geq 0$ and $1 \geq 2\delta$.
2. The saddlepath solution: $|\lambda_1| \geq 1$ and $|\lambda_2| < 1$, which implies that $\alpha - 1 + \delta \leq 0$.
3. The globally unstable solution: $|\lambda_1|, |\lambda_2| < 1$, which implies that $\alpha - 1 + \delta \geq 0$ and $1 \leq 2\delta$.

In general it will not be known *a priori* which solution occurs, and since this is important for the choice of estimation method, preliminary estimation will be required.[5]

The globally stable solution, case 1, is nonunique in the sense that any path (i.e. values of a_0 and b_0) will allow equilibrium to be restored following a disturbance. From (11)–(13), the solution for y_t can be written

$$\Delta y_t = \frac{\beta\eta}{1-\alpha-\delta} + \frac{(\alpha a_0 - L)(1-L) - \beta L\phi(L)}{\alpha - L + \delta L^2} e_t + \frac{\alpha b_0(1-L) - \beta L\theta(L)}{\alpha - L + \delta L^2} \varepsilon_t, \quad (14)$$

implying

$$y_t = \frac{1}{\alpha} y_{t-1} - \frac{\delta}{\alpha} y_{t-2} - \frac{\beta}{\alpha} x_{t-1} + a_0 e_t - \frac{1}{\alpha} e_{t-1} + b_0 \varepsilon_t. \quad (15)$$

Thus the solution is a stable backward-looking difference equation in y_t. Having derived the solution, it is apparent that (15) can be obtained directly from (1) by substituting $E_t y_{t+1} = y_{t+1} - \xi_{t+1}$ (where $\xi_{t+1} = a_0 e_{t+1} + b_0 \varepsilon_{t+1}$ is the innovation in y_{t+1}), redating the equation at time $t-1$ and solving for y_t. It may be noted that the solution has the same form as (13) for x_t stationary, see Wickens (1986).

The saddlepath solution, case 2, is the one of most interest to us. This solution has a removable singularity at the unstable root λ_2 that provides restrictions on a_0 and b_0, and make the solution unique. Imposing the condition that $A(z)$ and $B(z)$ be analytic at $z = \lambda_2$, and recalling that $\alpha - z + \delta z^2 = \delta(\lambda_1 - z)(\lambda_2 - z)$, implies

$$\lim_{z \to \lambda_2} (\lambda_2 - z)A(z) = \frac{(\alpha a_0 - \lambda_2)(1-\lambda_2) - \beta\lambda_2\phi(\lambda_2)}{\delta(\lambda_1 - \lambda_2)} = 0 \quad (16)$$

$$\lim_{z \to \lambda_2} (\lambda_2 - z)B(z) = \frac{\alpha b_0(1-\lambda_2) - \beta\lambda_2\theta(\lambda_2)}{\delta(\lambda_1 - \lambda_2)} = 0 \quad (17)$$

from which it follows that

$$a_0 = [\lambda_2 + \beta\lambda_2\phi(\lambda_2)/(1-\lambda_2)]/\alpha, \quad (18)$$

$$b_0 = \beta\lambda_2\theta(\lambda_2)/\alpha(1-\lambda_2) \quad (19)$$

Substituting (11)–(13) and the expressions for a_0 and b_0 into (5) gives

$$\Delta y_t = \frac{\beta\eta}{1-\alpha-\delta} + \frac{1}{\delta(\lambda_1 - L)}\Delta e_t + \frac{\beta\lambda_2\phi(\lambda_2)(1-L)/(1-\lambda_2) - \beta L\phi(L)}{\delta(\lambda_1 - L)(\lambda_2 - L)} e_t$$
$$+ \frac{\beta\lambda_2\theta(\lambda_2)(1-L)/(1-\lambda_2) - \beta L\theta(L)}{\delta(\lambda_1 - L)(\lambda_2 - L)} \varepsilon_t. \tag{20}$$

Thus

$$\delta(\lambda_1 - L)\,\Delta y_t = \frac{\beta\eta}{1-\lambda_2} + \Delta e_t + \frac{\beta}{1-\lambda_2}\left[L + (1-L)\frac{1-\lambda_2\phi(\lambda_2)L^{-1}\phi(L)^{-1}}{1-\lambda_2 L^{-1}}\right]u_t$$
$$\times \frac{\beta}{1-\lambda_2}\left[L + (1-L)\frac{1-\lambda_2\theta(\lambda_2)L^{-1}\theta(L)^{-1}}{1-\lambda_2 L^{-1}}\right]v_t. \tag{21}$$

Defining $L^{-s}u_t = E_t u_{t+s}$, it can be shown that[6]

$$\frac{1-\lambda_2\phi(\lambda_2)L^{-1}\phi(L)^{-1}}{1-\lambda_2 L^{-1}} u_t = \sum_{s=0}^{\infty} \lambda_2^s E_t u_{t+s}, \tag{22}$$

and hence that

$$\delta\lambda_1\,\Delta y_t - \delta\,\Delta y_{t-1} = \frac{\beta\eta}{1-\lambda_2} + \Delta e_t + \frac{\beta}{1-\lambda_2}\left[\Delta x_{t-1} - \eta + \sum_{s=0}^{\infty}\lambda_2^s E_t\,\Delta^2 x_{t+s}\right], \tag{23}$$

which can be rewritten as

$$y_t = \frac{1}{\lambda_1} y_{t-1} + \frac{\beta}{\delta\lambda_1}\sum_{s=0}^{\infty}\lambda_2^s E_t x_{t+s} + \frac{1}{\delta\lambda_1} e_t. \tag{24}$$

Thus the stable root λ_1 has been solved backwards and the unstable root λ_2, forwards. Again, when x_t is stationary, the form of the solution is the same as (24), see Wickens (1986). The dynamics of y_t can also be expressed as the partial adjustment model $\Delta y_t = (1 - \lambda_1^{-1})[\bar{y}_t - y_{t-1}]$ where $\bar{y}_t$ is a forward-looking target

$$\bar{y}_t = \frac{\beta}{\delta(\lambda_1 - 1)}\sum_{s=0}^{\infty}\lambda_2^s E_t x_{t+s} + \frac{1}{\delta(\lambda_1 - 1)} e_t. \tag{25}$$

The adjustment dynamics following a permanent change in $E_t x_{t+s}$ can now be given the following interpretation: the change alters $\bar{y}_t$ and causes a jump onto the saddlepath, after which y_t reaches the new long-run equilibrium along the saddlepath by partial adjustment to $\bar{y}_t$.

In case 3, both roots are unstable. This implies that $A(z)$ and $B(z)$ will each contain two singularities – at λ_1 and λ_2. For $A(z)$ and $B(z)$ to be analytic, we require $\lim_{z\to\lambda_i}(\lambda_i - z)A(z) = 0$ and $\lim_{z\to\lambda_i}(\lambda_i - z)B(z) = 0$ for $i = 1, 2$. Thus four conditions must be satisfied. But as there are only two free parameters, a_0 and b_0, it is not possible to make both $A(z)$ and $B(z)$ analytic. Hence no solution for y_t exists.

All of these results are invariant on whether the particular x_t process is predetermined, not predetermined or strictly exogenous. There is, however, one case of particular interest to which attention may be drawn, namely, where x_t is strictly exogenous and is generated by an autoregressive process. If, for example, x_t is an AR(1), then $\phi_i = 0$ and $\theta_i = \theta^i$ for all i. In this case

$$\frac{1 - \lambda_2\theta(\lambda_2)L^{-1}\theta(L)^{-1}}{1 - \lambda_2 L^{-1}} = \frac{1}{1 - \theta\lambda_2}, \tag{26}$$

and so (24) can be written

$$y_t = \frac{1}{\lambda_1} y_{t-1} + \frac{\beta}{\delta\lambda_1(1 - \lambda_2)(1 - \theta\lambda_2)}(x_t - \theta\lambda_2 x_{t-1}) + e_t. \tag{27}$$

Although (27) is a well-defined solution, it presents a potential identification problem. Assuming that θ is identified from (4) and noting that λ_1 is also identified, there are still three parameters (β, δ, λ_2) to be identified but only two coefficients (those of x_t and x_{t-1}) to use.[7] Lack of identifiability is not, however, a general feature.[8]

Estimating Dynamic Equations with Integrated Variables

The problem of estimating equation (1) when x_t is I(1) can be divided into two parts: the problem of estimating a dynamic equation which has I(1) variables, and the modifications that are required to apply these methods to an RE model. In this section we discuss the first issue. We comment briefly on the various estimators that have been proposed, and then suggest an alternative one-step estimator for which inference can be based on standard asymptotic distributions.

To illustrate the discussion we consider the estimation of the dynamic equation

$$y_t = \alpha y_{t-1} + \beta x_t + \gamma x_{t-1} + e_t, \tag{28}$$

where y_t and x_t are I(1), with or without drift, and e_t is NID(0, σ^2) and is independent[9] of x_t. The difficulty here is that OLS estimates of the coefficients of (28), although consistent, have nonstandard distributions. This makes inference problematical since standard asymptotic distributions will no longer provide satisfactory approximations to the small-sample distribution which is unknown and will usually need to be calculated on a case-by-case basis, typically using simulation methods. As a result, a literature has developed on how one might be able to use standard asymptotic approximations.

The basic idea is to seek a transformation of the data that leaves us with stationary variables. Inference concerning the coefficients of the transformed variables can then be made using standard distribution theory. The various different methods that have been proposed can be grouped into four types, two involve systems estimation and two single equation estimation.

1 The full-information structural systems estimator of Phillips (1990, 1991), Phillips and Loretan (1991). Apart from the first equation, which is the cointegrating regression, the system is created by adding equations for the right-hand side variables in which all the variables are transformed to stationarity by imposing their unit roots. The resulting estimates all have either a normal or a mixed normal asymptotic distribution, which permits standard inference.

2 The restricted system VAR estimator of Johansen (1988, 1989) and Johansen and Juselius (1988). First, the unrestricted VAR is estimated by OLS and the number of cointegrating regressions and common stochastic trends is established. Then the system is re-estimated, imposing the cointegrating vector restrictions. The restrictions on the cointegrating vector or on the loadings of the cointegrating vectors can be tested by either likelihood ratio or Wald tests. In this approach, emphasis is not usually placed on tests of individual coefficients, but on the implications that restrictions on individual coefficients have for the system as a whole. Nevertheless, once the cointegrating vectors are imposed, conditional on these, the remaining coefficients will be distributed asymptotically of normal.

3 Corrected single equation estimation, Phillips (1990), Phillips and Hansen (1990) and Phillips and Loretan (1991). Corrections are made to the variables in the regression which, in effect, are implicit in the FIML estimator of Phillips.

4 Multistep estimation, for example the two-step estimator of Engle and Granger (1987) and the three-step estimator of Engle and Yoo (1990). The first step is to estimate the cointegrating regression. The second is to estimate an error correction model (ECM) in which all of the variables are transformed to stationarity. The third step involves additional regressors as a result of taking a Newton approximation to the full likelihood from the second step.

Estimators 1–3 were originally designed mainly to estimate and permit inference on the cointegrating vector(s). With suitable, fairly trivial modifications, all three can be used to estimate all of the coefficients of a dynamic model, and Johansen and Juselius (1988) have done this. In contrast, apart from their simplicity, one attraction of the multistep estimators is that they are designed explicitly to estimate the full dynamics. And by combining the second stage with estimators 1–3, estimates of the full dynamics can be obtained for these estimators too.

It will be shown, however, that by employing the method proposed by Wickens and Breusch (1988) it is possible to estimate a full dynamic model in one step in such a way as to permit standard inference. For comparison, we begin by describing the Engle–Granger two-step estimator in more detail. Next we state the Wickens–Breusch (WB) estimator and then derive its asymptotic distribution.

As explained above, in step one of the two-step estimator, the cointegrating regression, or long-run model

$$y_t = \theta x_t + u_t \tag{29}$$

is estimated by OLS, where $\theta = (\beta + \gamma)/(1 - \alpha)$, and

$$u_t = -[\alpha/(1-\alpha)]\,\Delta y_t - [\gamma/(1-\alpha)]\,\Delta x_t + [1/(1-\alpha)]e_t. \tag{30}$$

In step two, the error correction model (ECM)

$$\Delta y_t = \beta \, \Delta x_t - (1 - \alpha)\hat{u}_{t-1} + \tilde{e}_t \tag{31}$$

is estimated by OLS, where $\hat{u}_t$ is the residual from (30) and

$$\tilde{e}_t = e_t + (1 - \alpha)(\hat{u}_{t-1} - u_{t-1}).$$

In step one, because the regressors in (29) are I(1) and $\hat{u}_t$ is I(0), the estimator of θ is $O_p(T^{-1})$ and hence is super-consistent, but unless x is I(1) with drift, its asymptotic distribution is not normal but is a nonstandard functional of Brownian motion, see Phillips (1987), Park and Phillips (1988, 1989), West (1988) and Sims et al. (1990). In step two, the estimators of α and β are $O_p(T^{-1/2})$ and are asymptotically normal. It may be noted that the estimator of γ obtained from $(1 - \alpha)\theta - \beta$ will also be $O_p(T^{-1/2})$ and asymptotically normal as its distribution is dominated by the slower converging estimators, see Sims et al. (1990).

A weakness of the Engle and Granger estimator is that it may have poor small-sample properties as a result of the estimator of θ in step one having substantial bias due to omitting the short-run dynamics. Banerjee et al. (1986) provide Monte Carlo evidence in support of this. The bias is likely to be greater the more highly correlated are x_t and u_t; for example, when adjustment is slow (i.e. α is close to unity). The third step in the Engle and Yoo (EY) estimator provides a correction for this bias. In the present example, the corrected EY estimator of θ is $\tilde{\theta} = \hat{\theta} + \hat{\lambda}/(1 - \hat{\alpha})$ where $\hat{\lambda}$ is the coefficient from the regression of $\tilde{e}_t$ on x_{t-1}. In other words, it is as though x_{t-1} were omitted from the cointegrating regression (29).

The WB estimator employs the same basic idea as the Bewley (1979) estimator. This is to rewrite the original dynamic equation in a form where the only level variables are those in the cointegrating regression and the other variables are in difference form. Thus (28) becomes

$$y_t = \theta x_t - [\alpha/(1 - \alpha)] \, \Delta y_t - [\gamma/(1 - \alpha)] \, \Delta x_t + [1/(1 - \alpha)] e_t. \tag{32}$$

This is then estimated by instrumental variables using the regressors of (28) as instrumental variables. The resulting estimates of θ, etc. are identical to the ones that would be obtained if (28) were estimated by OLS and then these estimates were used to solve for θ. This estimator can be used to obtain consistent long-run parameter estimates, whether y_t and x_t are I(1) or I(0). But if y_t and x_t are I(1) then, like the OLS estimator of θ from (29), this estimator of θ is also superconsistent as it is $O_p(T^{-1})$. Of more interest is the fact that this estimator of θ has a mixed normal distribution in large samples and that the estimators of α, β, and γ are asymptotically normal. The proofs of these results are given in the appendix.[10]

Although proposed here as an entirely different estimator to the two-step method, by basing the estimate of u_t used in the second step ECM estimation on the WB estimator of θ instead of the cointegrating regression, it would be possible to use the WB estimator to give a modified two-step estimator. In general, this modified two-step estimator would be different from the WB estimator, but for equation (28) the estimates would be identical. The similarity arises because (32) is just a transformed version of (28) with no restrictions imposed. But if (28) excludes x_{t-1}, then this imposes a restriction on the ECM which is, of course, ignored when estimated by OLS. To see this, rewrite (31) as

$$\Delta y_t = \beta \, \Delta x_t - (1 - \alpha)(y_{t-1} - \theta x_{t-1}) + \tilde{e}_t. \tag{33}$$

When x_{t-1} is excluded from (28), it would be possible to estimate α, β, and θ from (33) in one step by taking account of the restriction $\theta = \alpha/(1 - \beta)$. But if x_{t-1} is included in (28), then $\theta = (\alpha + \gamma)/(1 - \beta)$ and (33) could now be estimated unrestrictedly by OLS with Δx_t, y_{t-1} and x_{t-1} as regressors. The new restriction is used to estimate γ.

To summarize these results, although until recently the literature has been more concerned with the long-run than the short-run parameters of dynamic models, it is always possible to obtain a full-information estimator of both. It appears that if unit root and cointegration restrictions are imposed, the full-information estimator will have an asymptotic distribution that is either a mixture of normals or a normal. This permits standard distributions to be used in inference. An alternative to full information is single equation estimators and a number of these exist. Some have nonstandard asymptotic distributions, but by using various combinations of stationarity transformations, correction terms and multistep methods, it is possible to obtain single equation estimators that allow standard inference procedures to be employed. While the Engle–Granger two-step estimator is the one that is most widely used due to its simplicity, it has been argued that the one-step Wickens–Breusch estimator, which is also simple to use, may be preferable. These results form the basis for the choice of alternative estimators for RE models that are examined in the next section.

Estimating Rational Expectations Models

Full-information estimators of RE models will generally exist but they will usually involve complex calculations. It is therefore of interest to ask whether alternative estimators can be found for equation (1) which are simple to compute – such as a single equation estimator – permit standard asymptotic inference, and have good small-sample properties.

In the terminology of Wickens (1982), rational expectations models can be estimated by two methods: the substitution (S) method and the errors in variables (EIV) method. In the S method, the expectations variables are replaced by their solution expressed in terms of observable variables. The complete system can then be estimated by full-information methods, taking into account the cross-equation restrictions produced by the substitutions. The resulting estimator will be asymptotically efficient. Less efficient estimators that ignore restrictions can also be found for the S method, but the main purpose of this method is to derive a fully efficient estimator. In contrast, the objective of the EIV method is to obtain a simpler, but less efficient, estimator. Though again, the EIV method can yield a fully efficient estimator too. In the EIV method the expectations variables are replaced by their realized values, thereby creating an error which is incorporated into the disturbance term, hence the analogy with the errors in variables problem. Single equation instrumental variable or GMM estimation can now be employed to give a consistent but less efficient estimator. The main concern here is in deriving simple single equation estimators and this leads naturally, but not exclusively, to focusing on the EIV method, but we shall also comment on how to obtain fully efficient estimators.

Apart from the usual problems of nonlinear estimation, there is another drawback to efficient estimation: it is necessary to know the type of solution that occurs, whether it is globally stable and hence nonunique, or a saddlepath solution and therefore unique. Often this will be known *a priori*, especially if the equation is derived as an Euler equation from a formal intertemporal optimizing problem. But if it is not, then the first step is to try to determine the type of solution by preliminary consistent estimation. Having decided on this, fully efficient estimation becomes possible. Another advantage of using simpler, and in general less-efficient single equation methods, is that the type of solution need not be determined prior to estimation.[11] Nevertheless, we shall proceed by considering first the estimation of the globally stable model and then that of the saddlepath solution.

Case 1: the globally stable model

The full solution is given by equation (15) and can be written

$$y_t = \frac{1}{\alpha} y_{t-1} - \frac{\delta}{\alpha} y_{t-2} - \frac{\beta}{\alpha} x_{t-1} + \eta_t, \tag{34}$$

where $\eta_t = a_0 e_t - (1/\alpha)e_{t-1} + b_0 \varepsilon_t$ is an unrestricted MA(1) process. First we consider the S method of estimation. Clearly, as no expectation terms appear in (34), no substitutions are required and so the equation can be estimated immediately using one of the methods described in the previous section. Given our previous discussion, fully efficient estimation is straightforward – at least in principle – and there is no need to go further into the details of this. Instead we focus on the two-step and WB estimators.

For the two-step estimator, we need the cointegrating regression and the ECM associated with (34). These are

$$y_t = \theta x_t + u_t, \tag{35}$$

where $\theta = \beta/(1 - \alpha - \delta)$ and

$$\Delta y_t = \frac{\delta}{\alpha} \Delta y_{t-1} + \frac{(1 - \alpha - \delta)}{\alpha} [y_{t-1} - \theta x_{t-1}] + \eta_t. \tag{36}$$

OLS can be used in the first stage to estimate θ, and will be super-consistent, but it cannot be used in the second step due to the fact that η_t is an MA(1) process and will be correlated with both regressors due to the presence of y_{t-1}. In principle, the obvious single equation estimator to use in the second step is a GMM estimator such as the ordinary IV estimator, with the Hansen and Hodrick (1980) estimator of the covariance matrix of the coefficients in order to take account of the MA error term. As the MA error is backward-looking, Theil's generalized IV estimator would be more efficient as it takes account of the serial correlation. In practice, the problem with GMM estimation is finding suitable instrumental variables. Here a natural choice is y_{t-2} and x_{t-1} and their lagged values.

The EIV method can be applied to the original model, equation (1). Replacing $E_t y_{t+1}$ by y_{t+1} and incorporating the resulting measurement (or innovation) error $\xi_{t+1} = y_{t+1} - E_t y_{t+1}$ into the disturbance term gives

$$y_t = \alpha y_{t+1} + \delta y_{t-1} + \beta x_t + \omega_t, \tag{37}$$

where $\omega_t = e_t - \alpha \xi_{t+1}$. For the globally stable solution, $\xi_{t+1} = a_0 e_{t+1} + b_0 \varepsilon_{t+1}$, hence $\omega_t = e_t - \alpha(a_0 e_{t+1} + b_0 \varepsilon_{t+1}) = -\alpha \eta_{t+1}$ which was defined above. In other words, (37) is just another way of writing the globally stable solution (15). Although this expression could have been obtained without going through the process of solving the model, the extra information acquired through doing so is the fact that ω_t is an *unrestricted* MA(1) if the globally stable solution occurs. It is immediately obvious that (37) would also be obtained if the saddlepath solution arose. But, to anticipate later results, it can be shown that then ξ_{t+1} would be defined differently and ω_t would no longer be an unrestricted MA(1). Thus whether ω_t is an unrestricted or a restricted MA(1) is another way to express the difference between the two types of solution[12]. In either case estimation can proceed without taking account of such restrictions, and this would be correct in the globally stable case.

As well as being a different way of expressing the solution of the RE model, (37) can be used to provide an alternative second step estimating equation to (36) which has the attraction of being more suitable when α is small, namely,

$$\Delta y_t = \frac{\alpha}{1-\alpha} \Delta y_{t+1} - \frac{(1-\alpha-\delta)}{1-\alpha} [y_{t-1} - \theta x_t] - \frac{\alpha}{1-\alpha} \eta_{t+1} \tag{38}$$

As Δy_{t+1} and Δy_t are correlated with η_{t+1}, GMM estimation will be required again. Valid instruments are x_t and y_{t-1} and their lags. The ordinary IV estimator with the Hansen and Hodrick (1980) covariance matrix is again a possible GMM estimator. Given the forward nature of the MA error term in (38), two more efficient GMM estimators are the asymptotically equivalent Hayashi and Sims (1983) forward filter estimator and the two-stage least squares (2S2SLS) estimator of Cumby et al. (1983). Since (36) and (38) involve only stationary variables, all of the GMM estimators discussed above will be asymptotically normal.

So far the discussion has focused on two-step estimation. We now consider the use of the one-step WB estimator. This involves rewriting (37) as

$$y_t = \frac{\alpha}{1-\alpha-\delta} \Delta y_{t+1} - \frac{\delta}{1-\alpha-\delta} \Delta y_t + \theta x_t - \frac{\alpha}{1-\alpha-\delta} \eta_{t+1}. \tag{39}$$

Clearly (38) and (39) are just alternative transformations of (37) – and after redating, with (36) they are also alternative transformations of (34). Moreover, (39) can be estimated by the same types of GMM estimators as (38). Now, however, there is no need for the first step estimation. Given the results in the appendix about the asymptotic distribution of the WB estimator, it seems reasonable to conjecture that asymptotically these GMM estimators of θ will have a mixed normal distribution, and that the remaining estimates will be normal. Thus the advantages of the WB estimator discussed in the previous section seem to carry over to the estimation of RE models.

Case 2: the saddlepath solution

The discussion of this case can be briefer than before because many of the issues that arise have already appeared. The solution is given by (24) and involves a distributed lead function in $E_t x_{t+s}$. We consider both the S and EIV methods.

The S method involves using the Weiner–Kolmogorov formulas, equation (8), to replace $E_t x_{t+s}$ in (24). To obtain a fully efficient estimator joint estimation of the resulting equation with (4) taking account of the cross-equation restrictions introduced by the substitution and the cointegrating restrictions and the unit roots must be performed. In general, this is quite a complex nonlinear computational problem even with modern computing technology. It is simplified somewhat if x_t, or Δx_t, are generated by an AR(n) process, but, as explained above, the case where the greatest simplification occurs lacks identifiability, i.e. when $n = 1$. Rather than pursue these issues we turn to the EIV method and single equation estimation.

Unlike the globally stable case, here the EIV method greatly simplifies matters. With one important difference it is exactly the same as before. Thus we start with (1) and replace expectations with realizations to obtain (37) once more. The difference is that now a_0 and b_0 are no longer free parameters but are determined by (18) and (19). It is these restrictions that make the saddlepath solution unique. Substituting these expressions for a_0 and b_0 implies that the disturbance in (37) becomes the *restricted* MA(1):

$$\omega_t = e_t - [\lambda_2 + \beta\lambda_2\phi(\lambda_2)/(1-\lambda_2)]e_{t+1} - [\beta\lambda_2\theta(\lambda_2)/(1-\lambda_2)]\varepsilon_{t+1}. \tag{40}$$

If one is willing to ignore these restrictions on ω_t and treat it as an unrestricted MA, then estimation is exactly as before: we can use either a two-step estimator with (38) as the second-stage model, or the WB single equation estimator based on (39). We would then be ignoring the type of solution entirely.[13] An alternative fully efficient estimator is also obtainable by estimating (39) jointly with (4) and taking account of the cross-equation restrictions implied by (40). Again, this involves a more complex computational problem, though, perhaps, less difficult than before.

Simulation Evidence

In this section, small sample evidence is presented on the distributions of various single equation estimators of the dynamic model, equation (28), and on alternative two-step and WB estimators of the RE model, equation (1). Monte Carlo evidence is provided on the estimators of the dynamic model, but the evidence for the RE estimators is based on a single artificial sample.

Single equation estimators of dynamic models The data generating process for the simulations is the following dynamic model $y_t = \alpha y_{t-1} + \beta x_t + e_t$, $\Delta x_t = \rho\,\Delta x_{t-1} + \varepsilon_t$, where e_t is distributed NID(0, σ^2) and ε_t is NID(0, ψ^2). The parameter settings are $\theta = \beta/(1-\alpha) = 1$, $\rho = 0.3$, $\sigma = 0.05$, $\psi = 0.005$, $T = 80$, and α is varied to permit different degrees of persistence. Three different estimators are considered: the Engle–Granger two-step estimator, the WB estimator, and the Engle–Yoo three-step estimator.

In table 20.1 selected significance points for the three estimates of $\hat{\theta}$ are reported

Table 20.1 Significance points for $\hat{\theta}$

	0.010	0.025	0.050	0.100	0.500	0.900	0.950	0.975	0.990
					$\alpha = 0.9$				
2S(EG)	0.327	0.406	0.470	0.531	0.774	0.873	0.891	0.899	0.909
	0.011	0.010	0.009	0.009	0.008	0.006	0.004	0.003	0.002
WB	0.904	0.937	0.957	0.967	0.998	1.03	1.04	1.06	1.09
	0.002	0.002	0.003	0.004	0.006	0.004	0.003	0.002	0.001
3S(EY)	0.877	0.912	0.929	0.953	0.992	1.02	1.03	1.04	1.06
	0.002	0.002	0.003	0.004	0.006	0.004	0.003	0.002	0.001
					$\alpha = 0.6$				
2S(EG)	0.834	0.863	0.875	0.904	0.962	0.982	0.986	0.988	0.991
	0.002	0.002	0.003	0.004	0.006	0.004	0.003	0.002	0.001
WB	0.985	0.989	0.991	0.994	1.00	1.01	1.01	1.01	1.02
	0.001	0.002	0.003	0.004	0.006	0.004	0.003	0.002	0.001
3S(EY)	0.978	0.986	0.989	0.993	0.999	1.00	1.01	1.01	1.01
	0.002	0.002	0.003	0.004	0.006	0.004	0.003	0.002	0.001
					$\alpha = 0.3$				
2S(EG)	0.950	0.960	0.968	0.975	0.990	0.996	0.997	0.998	0.999
	0.001	0.002	0.003	0.004	0.006	0.004	0.003	0.002	0.001
WB	0.992	0.994	0.995	0.997	1.00	1.00	1.00	1.01	1.01
	0.001	0.002	0.003	0.004	0.006	0.004	0.003	0.002	0.001
3S(EY)	0.990	0.994	0.995	0.996	1.00	1.00	1.00	1.01	1.01
	0.001	0.002	0.003	0.004	0.006	0.004	0.003	0.002	0.001

for 1000 replications for alternative values[14] of α. For each set of significance points, their Monte Carlo standard errors are reported in the second row. Despite the relatively small number of replications, the standard errors indicate that the significance points are quite well determined. The results show that in terms of median unbiasedness, dispersion and skewness the WB estimator of θ performs best. This superiority is greater the larger the value of α, which reflects the argument made earlier than omitting the short-run dynamics creates a bigger misspecification in the cointegrating regression (29) the slower the dynamic adjustment. The results also show that the asymptotic distribution theory offers a good approximation, and this is better for the WB estimator than for the Engle–Yoo three-step estimator.

Estimators of the RE model The artificial sample is generated from the Euler equation of the following intertemporal optimization problem and so relates to the saddlepath solution. Consider minimizing the quadratic cost function $E_t \sum_{s=0}^{\infty} (1+\rho)^{-s}[\gamma(y_{t+s} - y^*_{t+s})^2 + (\Delta y_{t+s})^2]$ with respect to y_t, where $\rho < 1$ and the target is $y^*_t = \theta x_t + u_t$. This gives the Euler equation

$$y_t = \nu E_t y_{t+1} + \nu(1+\rho)y_{t-1} + \nu(1+\rho)\gamma\theta x_t + \nu(1+\rho)\gamma u_t, \qquad (41)$$

where $\nu = 1/[1 + (1+\gamma)(1+\rho)]$. Comparing equations (1) and (41), $\alpha = \nu$, $\delta = \alpha(1+\rho)$, $\beta = \delta\gamma\theta$, $\theta = \beta/(1 - \alpha - \delta)$ and $e_t = \delta\gamma u_t$; furthermore, the roots $\lambda_1, \lambda_2 = [1 \pm \sqrt{(1 - 4\alpha\delta)}]/2\delta$. In this example it is assumed that x_t is strictly exogenous and is generated by the ARIMA(1, 1, 1) process

$$\Delta x_t = \xi \, \Delta x_{t-1} + \varepsilon_t + \phi \varepsilon_{t-1}, \tag{42}$$

which is a special case of (2). Using (18) and (19), the restrictions imposed by the saddlepath solution on a_0 and b_0 are found to be $a_0 = \lambda_2/\alpha$ and $b_0 = \beta\lambda_2(1 + \phi\lambda_2)/[\alpha(1 - \lambda_2)(1 - \xi\lambda_2)]$. Series for y_t and x_t are created by drawing independent random samples for e_t and ε_t which are NID(0, σ^2) and NID(0, ψ^2). The parameter values chosen were $T = 80$, $\theta = 1$, $\rho = 0.1$, $\gamma = 1.0$, $\xi = 0.3$, $\phi = 0.4$, $\sigma = 0.01$, and $\psi = 0.05$.

Two different sets of two-step estimates were calculated. Both were based on estimating θ from the cointegrating regression (35), but in the second step one estimated (36) using OLS which is not consistent, and the other used the ordinary IV estimator with instruments y_{t-2}, Δy_{t-2}, x_{t-1}, Δx_{t-1}, Δx_{t-2}, Δx_{t-3} which is consistent. Three different versions of the WB estimator were calculated. All involved estimating equation (39) by GMM and used the same instruments as above. The three GMM estimators were the ordinary IV, the Hayashi–Sims and the 2S2SLS estimators. In an attempt to isolate the effect of the innovation error introduced by the EIV method, an additional set of estimates was obtained in which the true values of $E_t y_{t+1}$ were treated as observable. The resulting equation was then estimated by the WB method using the ordinary IV estimator.

The results are reported in table 20.2.[15] Ignoring the last row for the moment, all give good estimates of the long-run coefficient θ, but none give anything approaching reasonable estimates of the short-run parameters. The two approaches give different results from each other, but within each class the estimates are very similar. The two-step estimators are by far the worst in terms of absolute bias. The last line of table 20.2 gives a clue to the cause of these poor estimates. Here the true value of $E_t y_{t+1}$ generated by the simulation has been used instead of y_{t+1}; this is not, of course, an option available in practice. A considerable improvement occurs in the estimates of the short-run parameters, which suggests that the main cause of the poor estimates is a failure to instrument y_{t+1} adequately. Once this problem is removed, the WB estimator performs quite well. Other samples based on these parameter values gave qualitatively similar results. So clear-cut are these results

Table 20.2 Alternative estimates of equation (41)

	θ	α	β	δ
True value	1.000	0.3125	0.3438	0.3438
Two-step estimators				
OLS	0.974	2.658	−2.332	0.737
IV	0.974	2.903	−2.617	0.784
EIV–WB estimators				
IV	0.981	−0.085	0.814	0.25
HS	0.976	−0.083	0.818	0.248
2S2SLS	0.982	−0.070	0.815	0.241
IV(Ey)	0.978	0.384	0.256	0.355

that there seems little value in carrying out a full Monte Carlo simulation to determine their sampling variation. Experiments with other parameter values did not perform very differently. A possible implication is that it may be necessary for the estimator to take more explicit account of the information in the innovation error. This suggests that full-information methods may be required after all.

Conclusions

The solution of RE models with I(1) forcing variables has been obtained and is found to be similar to that with I(0) variables. Although the two standard approaches to estimating RE models (namely the substitution and errors in variables methods) can be used, the presence of I(1) variables requires a number of changes. These are similar to those required to estimate dynamic equations with I(1) variables which are not RE models. The main alternative ways of estimating such dynamic models are reviewed. Since the objective is to find suitable single equation estimators for RE models, attention was focused on single equation estimators and especially on two multistep estimators, the Engle–Granger two-step estimator and the Engle–Yoo three-stage estimator. An alternative single equation estimator, the Wickens–Breusch estimator, was also considered. One advantage of this estimator is that it is calculated in one step. More importantly, and unlike the Engle–Granger estimator, it is shown that the WB estimator has an asymptotic distribution of the long-run parameters that is a mixture of normals and hence allows standard inference. Monte Carlo evidence shows that the WB estimator is marginally better than the three-step estimator and that its asymptotic distribution is a good approximation to its finite-sample distribution. In contrast, the two-step estimator is badly biased and skewed.

It is shown that a modification to the Engle–Granger two-step estimator is required when applied to the RE model; an IV or GMM estimator is required in the second stage in order to achieve consistency. The WB estimator is particularly suited to the errors in variables approach. It usually requires IV estimation, but given the additional presence of moving average errors, a GMM estimator such as the Hayashi–Sims or 2S2SLS estimator seems preferable. Small-sample evidence on the performance of these various single equation estimators based on a single artificial sample shows that all give good estimates of the long-run parameters, but none performs well in estimating the short-run parameters. Since using the rational expectations themselves produces such improved estimates, this suggests that the problem is the difficulty of finding adequate instrumental variables for the realized values of the rationally expected variables. A possible solution is to use a full-information estimator instead, as this will take account of the innovation error. This conjecture merits further investigation. In another paper in this volume Gregory et al., considering the case of endogenous x_t, advocate fixing the discount rate *a priori.*

Appendix

We wish to determine the asymptotic distribution of the Wickens–Breusch estimator. Consider the dynamic model

$$y_t = \alpha y_{t-1} + \beta x_t + e_t, \tag{A1}$$

where x_t is I(1), being strictly exogenous and generated by

$$\Delta x_t = \varepsilon_t, \tag{A2}$$

with $e_t \sim \text{iid}(0, \sigma^2)$, $\varepsilon_t \sim \text{iid}(0, \omega^2)$, and e_t and ε_t independent. These assumptions are restrictive, and the effects of generalizing them will be considered later. Equation (A1) can be rewritten as

$$y_t = \theta x_t - [\alpha/(1-\alpha)]\,\Delta y_t + [1/(1-\alpha)]e_t \tag{A3}$$

$$= \delta' z_t + u_t, \tag{A4}$$

where $z_t = (x_t, \Delta y_t)$, $\delta' = (\delta_1, \delta_2) = [\theta, -\alpha/(1-\alpha)]$, $\theta = \beta/(1-\alpha)$ and $u_t = [1/(1-\alpha)]e_t$. We wish to determine the asymptotic distribution of the IV estimator of δ using $w_t = (x_t, y_{t-1})$ as the instruments.

We shall make use of the results on convergence in probability of Phillips (1987) and Park and Phillips (1988, 1989) – see also Sims et al. (1990) and Stock (1987). The particular results we use are stated here without proof. The following notation is taken from Phillips (1987): $\Rightarrow$ denotes weak convergence of the associated probability measure to a possibly stochastic limit. $V(t)$ and $W(t)$ denote Weiner processes. Integrals such as $\int_0^1 W(s)\,\mathrm{d}W(s)$ are written in stylized form as $\int W\,\mathrm{d}W$.

$$T^{-2}\sum_1^T [C(L)x_t]^2 \Rightarrow C(1)^2\omega^2 \int W^2,$$

$$T^{-1}\sum_1^T x_t[C(L)\varepsilon_t] \Rightarrow \omega^2\left[C(1)\int W\,\mathrm{d}W + c_0\right],$$

$$T^{-1}\sum_1^T x_{t-1}[C(L)\varepsilon_t] \Rightarrow C(1)\omega^2 \int W\,dW,$$

$$T^{-1}\sum_1^T x_t[C(L)e_t] \Rightarrow C(1)\sigma\omega \int W\,\mathrm{d}V,$$

where $T^{-1/2}\sum_1^{[Tr]} e_t \Rightarrow \sigma V(r)$, $T^{-1/2}\sum_1^{[Tr]} \varepsilon_t \Rightarrow \omega W(r)$. $\sum_0^\infty |s|^{1/2}|c_s| < \infty$, $C(L) = \sum_0^\infty c_s L^s$ and [Tr] is the integer part of Tr.

With these results, and noting that (A1) can be written as

$$y_t = (1-\alpha L)^{-1}[\beta x_t + e_t], \tag{A5}$$

it can be shown that

1. $T^{-2}\sum_1^T x_t^2 \Rightarrow \omega^2 \int W^2,$

2. $T^{-2}\sum_1^T x_t y_{t-1} = T^{-2}\sum_1^T x_t\{(1-\alpha L)^{-1}[\beta x_{t-1} + e_{t-1}]\} \Rightarrow \theta\omega^2 \int W^2,$

3. $T^{-1}\sum_{1}^{T} x_t e_t \Rightarrow \sigma\omega \int W \,\mathrm{d}V,$

4. $T^{-1}\sum_{1}^{T} y_{t-1} e_t = T^{-1}\sum_{1}^{T} \{(1-\alpha L)^{-1}[\beta x_{t-1} + e_{t-1}]\} e_t \Rightarrow \theta\sigma\omega \int W \,\mathrm{d}V,$

5. $T^{-1}\sum_{1}^{T} x_t \,\Delta y_t = T^{-1}\sum_{1}^{T} x_t \{(1-\alpha L)^{-1}[\beta \,\Delta x_t + \Delta e_t]\} \Rightarrow \theta\omega^2 \left[\int W \,\mathrm{d}W + 1\right],$

6. $T^{-1}\sum_{1}^{T} y_{t-1} \,\Delta y_t = T^{-1}\sum_{1}^{T} \{(1-\alpha L)^{-1}[\beta x_{t-1} + e_{t-1}]\}$

$$\times \{(1-\alpha L)^{-1}[\beta \,\Delta x_t + \Delta e_t]\} \Rightarrow \theta^2\omega^2 \int W \,\mathrm{d}W - \sigma^2/(1+\alpha).$$

The IV estimator of δ, $\hat{\delta}$, can be written

$$(\hat{\delta} - \delta) = (\Sigma w_t' z_t)^{-1} \Sigma w_t' e_t/(1-\alpha). \tag{A6}$$

Hence

$$\begin{bmatrix} \hat{\theta} - \theta \\ \hat{\delta}_2 - \delta_2 \end{bmatrix} = K \begin{bmatrix} (\Sigma y_{t-1}\,\Delta y_t)(\Sigma x_t e_t) - (\Sigma x_t \,\Delta y_t)(\Sigma y_{t-1} e_t) \\ (\Sigma x_t y_{t-1})(\Sigma x_t e_t) - (\Sigma x_t^2)(\Sigma y_{t-1} e_t) \end{bmatrix}, \tag{A7}$$

where $K^{-1} = (1-\alpha)[(\Sigma x_t^2)(\Sigma y_{t-1}\,\Delta y_t) - (\Sigma x_t y_{t-1})(\Sigma x_t \,\Delta y_t)]$. Using 1–6, it can be shown that

$$T(\hat{\theta} - \theta) \Rightarrow \left[\sigma \int W \,\mathrm{d}V\right] \Big/ \left[(1-\alpha)\omega \int W^2\right] \equiv MN. \tag{A8}$$

Thus $T(\hat{\theta} - \theta)$ is asymptotically a mixture of normal distributions (MN). In contrast, substituting 1–6 in (A7) would give $\hat{\delta}_2 - \delta_2 = 0$. In 1–6, however, terms $O_p(T^{-1/2})$ have been omitted. Had they been retained, then it would have been clear that $\hat{\delta}_2 - \delta_2$ is not zero but $O_p(T^{-1/2})$, implying that $T^{1/2}(\hat{\delta}_2 - \delta_2)$ is asymptotically normal. Thus inference about θ and δ_2 (and hence α and β) can be conducted using standard distributions.

As indicated above, these results are qualitatively unchanged for a less restrictive set-up. For example, adding further lags of x_t to (A1) will not affect the result that $T(\hat{\theta} - \theta)$ has a limiting normal distribution and the estimates of the coefficients of Δy_t and Δx_t and their lags are $O_p(T^{-1/2})$, and hence are asymptotically normal. Similarly, when e_t and ε_t are not serially independent, then again it can be shown that $T(\hat{\theta} - \theta)$ has a limiting normal distribution and $\hat{\delta}_2 - \delta_2$ is $O_p(T^{-1/2})$. At first sight, a more far-reaching restriction is the assumption that x_t is strictly exogenous – e_t and ε_t are uncorrelated. However, if we define $\zeta_t = e_t - \lambda\varepsilon_t$, where ζ_t is independent of ε_t, then (A1) can be rewritten as

$$y_t = \alpha y_{t-1} + \beta x_t + \lambda \,\Delta x_t + \zeta_t. \tag{A9}$$

The problem is therefore reduced to that of adding lagged values of x_{t-1} to (A1). It will be noted, however, that had (A1) included x_{t-1}, then (A9) would be indistinguishable from (A1); in other words, if e_t and ε_t are correlated then, given (A2), the process assumed to generate x_t here, (A1) with x_{t-1} included, is not identified. But if $\Delta x_t = D(L)\varepsilon_t$ then, depending on $D(L)$, and on the lag structure of x_t in (A1), identification need not be a problem. An alternative approach is to use the systems version of the WB estimator on (A1) and (A2) jointly, see Wickens and Breusch (1988).

Notes

This research was supported by a grant from the ESRC. The author would like to thank Peter Phillips for his many helpful suggestions. Further thanks are also due to Soren Johansen, Adrian Pagan, Andrew Scott and the referees for their valuable comments on an earlier draft.

1. Pesaran (1987) has provided a comprehensive survey of this literature for the case of stationary time series. See also Broze et al. (1986).
2. It is assumed throughout that y_t and x_t have been de-meaned.
3. Equations like (1) commonly arise as Euler equations in an intertemporal optimization problem. For example, Dolado et al. (1989) and Gregory et al. (1990) consider explicitly the case where (1) is obtained as a result of minimizing a quadratic cost function. Further details of this can be found in the fifth section.
4. When x_t is I(0), y_t replaces Δy_t in (3), see Wickens (1986).
5. In many situations, the type of solution will be in fact be known. An example is the Euler equation interpretation of (1) given in note 1, where uniqueness requires the saddlepath solution 2. It will be noted that in this case $\alpha - 1 + \delta = -\gamma\delta/(1 + \alpha + \gamma) \leq 0$ and so solution 2 is guaranteed.
6. See Hansen and Sargent (1980) or Whiteman (1983, p. 57).
7. Dolado et al. (1990) and Gregory et al. (1990) resolve this problem by assuming that α is known.
8. More generally, when x_t is an AR(n) process, identification would require the number of lags of x_t in equation (1) to be at least n, see Pesaran (1987).
9. Some of the estimators we shall discuss apply under more general assumptions about the error process. Most of the results are extended to the case of x_t a vector in an obvious way.
10. The asymptotic distribution of IV estimators for other models with I(1) variables has also been considered by Dolado et al. (1989), Phillips and Hansen (1990), and Rau (1990).
11. See Wickens (1986) for further details.
12. It may be observed that, although the saddlepath solution can be given a backward representation, the resulting equation will have an unstable root. It is not uncommon that when estimating a dynamic model an unstable root is found. This is sometimes interpreted as a flaw in the model, the estimator or the program. It may, however, be an indication of an omitted forward-looking expectation.
13. In fact, it is possible to test for the type of solution. Since estimates of all of the coefficients of the original model, equation (1), are obtained, it is possible to estimate the roots of the system from these and hence to test for the number of unstable roots.
14. The simulations were computed using a modified version of a Gauss program by J. Galbraith.
15. The Hayashi–Sims and 2S2SLS estimates were computed using the Gauss program SEREM written by Robertson and Scott (1990).

References

Banerjee, A., J. J. Dolado, D. F. Hendry, and G. W. Smith (1986). "Exploring equilibrium relationships in econometrics through static models: some Monte Carlo evidence," *Oxford Bulletin of Economics and Statistics*, 253–77.

Bewley, R. A. (1979). "The direct estimation of the equilibrium response in a linear dynamic model," *Economic Letters*, 3, 357–62.

Broze, L., C. Gourieroux, and A. Szafarz (1986). "Solutions of dynamic linear rational expectations models," *Econometrica.*

Cumby, R. E., J. Huizinga, and M. Obstfeld (1983). "Two-step two-stage least squares estimation in models with rational expectations," *Journal of Econometrics*, 21, 333–55.

Dolado, J. J., N. R. Ericsson, and J. J. Kremers (1989). "Inference in conditional dynamic models with integrated variables," Paper presented to the European Meeting of the Econometric Society, Munich.

Dolado, J. J., J. W. Galbraith, and A. Banerjee (1990). "Estimating Euler equations with integrated series," revision to Oxford Applied Economics Discussion Paper 81.

Engle, R. F., and C. W. J. Granger (1987). "Cointegration and error correction: representation, estimation and testing," *Econometrica*, 55, 251–76.

Engle, R. F., and B. S. Yoo (1990). "Cointegrated economic time series: a survey with new results," revision of a paper presented to the European Meeting of the Econometric Society, Copenhagen 1987.

Gregory, A. W., A. R. Pagan, and G. W. Smith (1990). "Estimating Euler equations from linear quadratic models."

Hansen, L. P., and R. Hodrick (1980). "Forward exchange rates as optimal predictors of future spot rates: an econometric analysis," *Journal of Political Economy*, 88, 829–53.

Hansen, L. P., and T. J. Sargent (1980). "Formulating and estimating dynamic linear rational expectations models," *Journal of Economics Dynamics and Control*, 2, 7–46.

Hayashi, F., and C. W. Sims (1983). "Nearly efficient estimation of time series models with predetermined, but not exogenous instruments," *Econometrica*, 51, 783–98.

Johansen, S. (1988). "Statistical analysis of cointegration vectors," *Journal of Economics Dynamics and Control*, 12, 231–54.

Johansen, S. (1989). *Likelihood based inference on cointegration. Theory and applications*, Lecture notes, University of Copenhagen.

Johansen, S., and K. Juselius (1988). "Hypothesis testing for cointegration vectors – with application to the demand for money in Denmark and Finland," Discussion Paper 88-05, University of Copenhagen.

Pagan, A. R., and M. R. Wickens (1989). "A survey of some recent econometric methods," *Economic Journal*, 99.

Park, J. Y., and P. C. B. Phillips (1988). "Statistical inference in regressions with integrated processes: part 1," *Econometric Theory*, 4, 468–97.

Park, J. Y., and P. C. B. Phillips (1989). "Statistical inference in regressions with integrated processes: part 2," *Econometric Theory*, 5, 95–131.

Pesaran, M. H. (1987). *Limits to rational expectations.* London: Basil Blackwell.

Phillips, P. C. B. (1987). "Time series regression with a unit root," *Econometrica*, 55, 277–301.

Phillips, P. C. B. (1988). "Reflections on econometric methodology," *Economic Record*, 64, 344–59.

Phillips, P. C. B. (1990). "Joint estimation of equilibrium coefficients and short-run dynamics," forthcoming as a Problem in *Econometric Theory.*

Phillips, P. C. B. (1991). "Optimal inference in cointegrated systems," *Economics*, forthcoming.

Phillips, P. C. B., and B. E. Hansen (1990). "Statistical inference in instrumental variables regression with I(1) processes," *Review of Economic Studies.*

Phillips, P. C. B., and M. Loretan (1991). "Estimating long run equilibria," *Review of Economic Studies.*

Rau, Hsiu-hua (1990). "The joint estimation of long run coefficients and short run dynamics," mimeo, Yale University.

Robertson, D., and A. Scott (1990). "SEREM. A software package for the estimation of rational expectations models," Centre for Economic Forecasting Discussion Paper 03-90, London Business School.

Sims, C. A., J. H. Stock, and M. W. Watson (1990). "Inference in linear time series models with some unit roots," *Econometrica*, 58, 113–44.

Stock, J. H. (1987). "Asymptotic properties of least squares estimates of cointegration vectors," *Econometrica*, 55, 1035–56.

West, K. D. (1988). "Asymptotic normality when regressors have a unit root," *Econometrica*, 56, 1397–418.

Whiteman, C. H. (1983). *Linear Rational Expectations Models: A User's Guide*. Minnesota: University of Minnesota Press.

Wickens, M. R. (1982). "The efficient estimation of econometric models with rational expectations," *Review of Economic Studies*, 49, 55–67.

Wickens, M. R. (1986). "The estimation of linear models with future rational expectations by efficient and instrumental variables methods," CEPR Discussion Paper 111.

Wickens, M. R., and T. S. Breusch (1988). "Dynamic specification, the long run and the estimation of transformed regression models," *Economic Journal*, 98, 189–205.

Part V

Empirical Applications

21

The Stochastic Behavior of Mineral-Commodity Prices

Terence D. Agbeyegbe

Introduction

It is generally accepted that there are many theories of mineral-commodity price formation. On the one hand, we have Hotelling (1931) style models that predict systematic increases in real metal prices. These models are based on fundamentals such as supply, demand, and asset-holding decisions and they suggest that price movements are predictable. When we add to the models the possibility that new discoveries and technical change can lower prices, the expected pattern of price movement is no longer so simple, but it is still systematic.

On the other hand, we have random walk and martingale models of price formation that suggest that price changes are unpredictable. Briefly, if the current price is the expected value of the future price, the price sequence follows a martingale process. For such a process, a trading strategy that is based upon a knowledge of past prices cannot be expected to yield a return in excess of a buy and hold position. This argument is usually adopted to explain the stochastic behavior of commodities prices when mineral commodities are traded in auction markets such as the London Metal Exchange and The Commodity Metal Exchange (COMEX) in New York. When an exchange is formed, the possibility of speculation is introduced. For example, the annual volume of trading in silver on COMEX alone is 50 times the annual volume of new-mine production. Markets where speculation plays an important role should result in speculation being a "fair game," in particular, the expected profits to the speculator should be zero. This suggests that the appropriate model of price movement is a martingale. In the special case where a detailed specification of the economic conditions is made, such that the distributions of one-period returns repeat themselves through time, we obtain a random walk model. On this point see Fama (1970).

Predictions from the two sorts of models are therefore very different. But should we care? Perhaps so. Producers and consumers need to form forecasts for planning purposes and the nature of their forecast will depend on which class of model is more appropriate. Moreover, only empirical tests are capable of distinguishing among competing models: a model that predicts systematic increases and a model that predicts that prices are unpredictable. This paper can be viewed as an attempt to do just that.

Notice that the idea that mineral commodities prices have quadratic time trends is now new. A well-known result is that mineral-commodity prices follow U-shaped price paths (see for example Schultze (1974), Gilbert (1978), Heal (1981), Pindyck (1978), and Slade (1982a)). The theoretical models of Schultze, Slade (who extends the work of Schultze), and Heal rely on technical progress to produce the result, whereas Pindyck relies on exploration, and Gilbert relies on market structure. These theoretical models compatible with U-shaped price paths pave important implications. For example, Slade's (1982a), investigation of the long-run behavior of natural-resource commodity prices was an attempt at reconciling the theoretical predictions of increasing real Hotelling (1931) style models with the empirical findings of falling prices for these commodities. By deriving a theoretical model for relative price movements for the case of exogenous technical change, and endogenous change in the grade of ores mined, she was able to obtain a result that suggested that the time path for relative prices will be U-shaped. This implied price movement was in fact tested for aluminum, copper, iron, lead, nickel, silver, tin, zinc, coal, natural gas, and petroleum for a period covering 1870 through 1978.

The results indicate that the model parameters for quadratic trends were statistically significant for 11 out of the 12 commodities, the exception being lead. Results complementary to this were obtained by Smith (1979), and others, in other analyses of natural-resource commodity price aggregates.

My analysis differs from the previous literature in at least four ways. First, I employ two different approaches to investigating the order of the polynomial in time. The first approach involves regressing the first difference of each series against a constant, time, and six of its own lags, to correct for serial correlation in the error terms. The advantage of this approach is that I am able to obtain "correct" standard errors. Such an approach has been used by Stock and Watson (1989) in their study of the evidence on money–income causality. This approach is different from that of Slade (1982a), who examines the "t"-statistics on the time and time-squared coefficients, obtained from regressing the level of each series on a constant, time, and time squared. This approach assumes that the error terms for the price equations are uncorrelated. A modification involving additional variables, namely dummy variables, has also been considered by Mueller and Gorin (1985) and Slade (1985). As noted by Slade (1985) such an approach is "somewhat curious" and "it is not clear why the effects of cartels, wars and depressions should be U (or inverted U) shaped". For this reason. I have not included dummy variables.

The second approach is due to Park and Choi (1988). It is generally accepted that the behavior of standard statistics, such as the F statistics, depends on whether the errors of the generating process are stationary or integrated. This suggests that the standard statistics are invalid to test for time trends prior to unit roots tests. Since this problem is not resolved even when the tests are based on differenced regressions, there is a need for a different test for time trends. Notice that the first approach to testing for time trends is justified only when the stochastic component of a given time series is integrated and has a unit root. If this component is stationary, the first differences generate a moving average type process possessing a unit root which is not invertible and cannot be approximated with an autoregressive process. The approach of Park and Choi, which I adopt, does not rely on the unit root hypothesis.

Second, compared to the earlier literature, the models of price paths I investigate are more general with respect to the assumption made about the error terms. For example, Slade (1988) considers a very simple first-order stochastic difference equation with normal errors. This assumption on the distribution of the error term is quite restrictive.

Third, I employ both univariate and multivariate tests of unit roots. Unlike previous researchers working on metal price movements, I investigate the possibility that the mineral resource prices might have up to two unit roots and time trends up to the second order. The test for a second unit root is simply a test for a unit root in the first difference of the series. The multivariate tests made it possible to investigate the issue of cointegration among the many price series.

Fourth, in contrast to Slade (1988) who analyzed an equation that nests a simple Hotelling model and a random walk model, I analyze an equation that nests a model which generates a U-shaped path and a random walk model. In other words the equation allows for the joint presence of time trends and unit roots. This model is presented in the next section.

Interest in unit roots is not merely one of statistical curiosity, but one that has some potential implications in the modeling of commodity price movements. For example, recent papers by MacDonald and Taylor (1988), Agbeyegbe (1989b, 1992) among others, have explored results linking unit roots and cointegration theories to testing the market efficiency hypothesis in the London Metal Exchange.

It is also the case that the use of spectral analysis techniques in modeling commodity prices requires stationarity assumptions. It is therefore important to investigate the correct detrending transformation for the price series. These are made possible with unit root tests. For an empirical example, see Slade (1982b). Phillips (1988) has recently shown how spectral methods may be usefully employed in regressions for certain nonstationarity time series.

There are other studies of mineral commodity price movements that do not involve the U-shaped price path. See, for example, Barnett and Morse (1963), Heal and Barrow (1979, 1981), Smith (1981), and Agbeyegbe (1989a) among others.

The plan of the paper is as follows: the next section provides two simple economic models. The models demonstrate that the price path of mineral-commodity prices follows a U-shape path and a random walk with drift. The third section provides univariate and multivariate unit roots tests and tests of common trends. The fourth section is concerned with the empirical results, and finally there is the concluding section.

Stochastic Behavior of Prices in Efficient Markets

In this section two possible models of metal price movements are introduced. The first is a version of the simple Hotelling (1931) model and the second is a random walk with drift model. My presentation of the first model follows that of Heal (1981). Since Hotelling's (1931) work, it is now generally accepted that under certain conditions, a necessary (though not sufficient) condition for efficient use of a resource is that the difference between its price and marginal extraction cost should rise over time at the rate of interest. This is identical to saying that

$$(p_t - M_t) = (p_0 - M_0)\exp(rt), \tag{1}$$

where p_t is the price of the resource at time t, M_t is the marginal extraction cost at time t, and r is the rate of interest. Dropping the dependence on t, this may be rewritten as

$$\frac{\dot{p}}{p} = r\frac{(p - M)}{p} + \frac{\dot{M}M}{Mp}, \tag{2}$$

where the dot represents the time derivative. Equation (2) states that the price of the resource should rise at a rate which is the weighted average of the interest rate and the rate of change of marginal extraction costs. The weights of the interest rate and the cost changes are respectively the contribution of royalty and cost to price.

In viewing equation (2), notice that the first term on the right-hand side is positive, whereas the second will be negative if costs are falling and positive if costs are rising. In fact, one might expect that costs would fall over an initial period during which the development of the resource is being opened up and during which there is technical progress. In the long-run, however, decline in the grade of ore mined would force costs up. Additionally, notice that one would initially expect the royalty element in prices to be low, and hence the first term on the right of equation (2) to be small.

The above discussion leads to the following conclusion about the movement of prices. Initially $\dot{p}/p$ is likely to be negative, owing to the second term in equation (2) being negative and the first term small, but in the long-run $\dot{p}/p$ would be positive. In sum, in an efficient market, prices thus fall initially, but rise in the longer term generating a U-shaped path.

An alternate model for the movement of prices is the random walk model. Samuelson (1965) provided a proof that properly anticipated prices fluctuate randomly. The random walk and the submartingale models are special cases of the expected return or "fair game" efficient markets model. Following Fama (1970), a market is called "efficient", if prices at any point in time "fully reflect" available information. Expected return models are developed under the assumptions that the conditions of market equilibrium can be stated in terms of expected returns and that equilibrium expected returns are formed on the basis of an information set, which is "fully reflected" in prices at the current times. These "fair game" models rule out the possibility of trading systems based on information in the information set (up to the current period) that have expected profits or returns in excess of the equilibrium expected profits or returns.

Let $\{p_t\}$ represent a univariate data generating process for the spot price of the various mineral prices. In nonrigorous terms, I define a martingale process, as a $\{p_t\}$ which satisfies $E(p_{t+1}|I) = p_t$, where E is the ordinary expectations operator, p_t, is the price at time t and I_t is the information set reflected in market prices. This representation can be obtained by assuming that individuals arbitrage between commodities and assets whose return is zero. An alternate representation of price movements which does not assume that the expected value of the returns on an asset is the submartingale model. Under the assumption that risk-neutral individuals arbitrage between commodities and a riskless asset yielding a constant positive return, commodities prices obey the submartingale

$$E(p_{t+1}|I_t) \geq p_t. \tag{3}$$

The earlier literature dealing with tests of the submartingale process consisted invariably of tests in a form consistent with a random walk with positive drift. Define $\{u_t\}$ to be residuals in the following model:

$$p_t = \mu + p_{t-1} + u_t. \tag{4}$$

μ is a drift parameter. For now assume $\{u_t\}$ is a white-noise process. Equation (4) informs us that $\{p_t\}$ is a pure random walk with drift.

I depart from previous literature by considering a formulation that nests a model which generates a U-shaped path and a random walk model with drift. The formulation allows for the joint presence of time trends and unit roots and is based on the idea that the commodities prices obey a submartingale, equation (3), with the commodities prices being generated by deterministic trend terms with independent and identically distributed noise. The formulation is initially based on the parameterization

$$p_t = \mu + \beta t + \alpha p_{t-1} + u_t, \tag{5}$$

Equation (5) allows for a random walk with drift, when $\beta = 0$ and $\alpha = 1$. Nonzero β and $\alpha = 1$ generates a quadratic trend model with unit root. In the next section, I consider an alternate parameterization, equation (10), which encompasses both models and permits unit roots tests even when the time series exhibit trend reversion characteristics. Before considering this formulation, I consider various formulations and tests for the movement of commodities prices. These are outlined in the next section.

Univariate and Multivariate Tests on Unit Roots with Time Trends

The tests employed are those of Dickey and Fuller (1979, 1981), Phillips and Perron (1988), and Perron (1988), Stock and Watson (1988a, 1989) and Schmidt and Phillips (1989). I call the model represented by equation (4) the null model.

Dickey–Fuller Tests

This test is based on the augmented OLS regression

$$\Delta p_t = \mu + \beta t + \gamma p_{t-1} + \sum_{i=1}^{r} \delta_i \Delta p_{t-i} + u_t, \tag{6}$$

where r is chosen to eliminate autocorrelation and Δ denotes first difference.

Under the null, the hypothesis of interest is $\gamma = \alpha - 1 = 0$, where α is defined by the alternative model

$$p_t = \mu + \beta(t - T/2) + \alpha p_{t-1} + u_t, \tag{7}$$

where T is the sample size.

The Dickey–Fuller (1976) test is performed by comparing the usual regression "t"-statistic with the tables of critical values given in Fuller (1976, p. 373) for τ_τ. I call this test T1.

In Dicky and Fuller (1981), they extended this work. I report likelihood ratio tests of the unit root hypothesis based on that extension. The test statistic is based on restricted residual sum of squares, RRSS, from the regression model

$$\Delta p_t = \mu + \sum_{i=1}^{r} \delta_i \Delta p_{t-i} + u_t \tag{8}$$

and the unrestricted residual sum of squares, URSS, from equation (6).

The likelihood ratio statistic is defined as

$$\Phi_3 = [(\text{RRSS} - \text{URSS})/2]/[\text{URSS}/(T - 3 - r)]. \tag{9}$$

The critical values of this statistic are available in Dickey and Fuller (1981, table VI). I call this test T2.

Phillips and Perron Tests

Schwert (1987) has noted that the Dickey–Fuller (1979) testing procedure can lead to misleading inferences when moving average terms are present in the first-difference representation of the process. Alternate testing procedures are due to Phillips (1987), Phillips and Perron (1988), and Perron (1988). These tests involve making a nonparametric rather than an autoregressive correction of the Fuller type, for short-run dependence. The tests are based on equation (7). The $\{u_t\}$ are now not necessarily white noise. Under the null, $\alpha = 1$ and $\beta = 0$. The test statistics I adopt are $Z(\tilde{\alpha})$, $Z(t_{\tilde{\alpha}})$ and $Z(\Phi_3)$ (see Perron and Phillips (1987)).

Stock and Watson Tests

I now briefly discuss the Stock and Watson (1988a, 1988b) tests for common trends that I use in this paper.[1] The reader is referred to Stock and Watson (1988a, 1988b) for details. Their test of cointegration determines the number of common stochastic trends in a system of integrated variables. Let P_t denote an $n \times 1$ time series variable. They developed testing procedures for testing the null hypothesis that P_t has $k \leq n$ common stochastic trends, against the alternative that it has $m < k$ common trends. It is based on the idea that if there exist some common stochastic trends that are shared by more than two integrated processes, then the system is cointegrated in the sense of Engle and Granger (1987). The statistic they propose is based on the modified least squares regression coefficient matrix of the first-order vector autoregression, which is shown to be free of nuisance parameters. I employ the $q_f^{\tau}(k, m)$ statistic. Critical values of this statistic are given in Stock and Watson (1988a). When $n = 1$, I call this test T3.

I also consider a modified statistic, $q_f^{\tau^2}(k, m)$. This statistic is computed exactly as is the $q_f^{\tau}(k, m)$ statistic, except that the data are first detrended using a quadratic as well as a linear time trend. The advantage of this statistic is that it enables us to test for k versus m unit roots when there might be a quadratic term under the null or the alternative. Critical values from a Monte Carlo experiment are reported in Stock and Watson (1989). When $n = 1$, I call this test QT1. I have also briefly examined the Stock–Watson $q_f^{\tau}[\Delta p]$, test of a second unit root, allowing for the alternative that the series is stationary in first differences around a linear time trend. This is test T4.

The Schmidt and Phillips Test

Schmidt and Phillips (1989), noted that the Dickey–Fuller and the semiparametric correction methods of the Z tests are not well designed for testing trend reversion under the alternative. They argued that in the nonaugmented version of the Dickey–Fuller test based on the regression $p_t = \mu + \beta t + \alpha p_{t-1} + u_t$, linear trend is allowed under the null with $\beta = 0$ (nonzero β generates a quadratic trend), whereas under the alternative the linear trend requires nonzero β. Thus the test allows for linear trend under the alternative by including in the regression a variable that is irrelevant under the null. Their conjecture that this may result in some loss of power in finite sample is supported by Monte Carlo evidence in a later part of their paper. Additionally, they mention that the distributions of the test statistics in the above regression are independent of α but depend on β under both the null and the alternative hypotheses.

Their unit root tests for models with a higher order polynomial trend are based on the alternative parameterization

$$p_t = \sum_{j=0}^{k} a_j t^j + x_t, \qquad x_t = \alpha x_{t-1} + u_t. \tag{10}$$

where x_t is the stochastic part of p_t, x_0 is taken as fixed and the u_t are assumed to be iid $N(0, \sigma^2)$. k is the order of the polynomial. This parameterization with $k = 1$ has previously been considered by Bhargava (1986). Under the null hypothesis, $\alpha = 1$.

The regression that defines the test statistics is

$$\Delta p_t = \sum_{j=0}^{k-1} c_j t^j + \phi \tilde{S}_{t-1} + \text{error}, \tag{11}$$

where $\tilde{S}_t$ are the residuals from the model (10) in levels, but where the parameters have been estimated from the model in differences. The test statistics are $\tilde{\rho} = T\tilde{\phi}$ and $\tilde{\tau}$, the usual t-statistics for $\phi = 0$ in (11). The critical values of these statistics are available in Schmidt and Phillips (1989). I call $\tilde{\rho}$ QT2 and $\tilde{\tau}$ QT3. See Schmidt and Phillips (1989) for a detailed discussion of these tests.

Empirical Results

In this section, I present my empirical results. The series I have chosen are four major mineral commodities produced in North America: pig iron, copper, lead, and zinc. The historical data on actual prices are taken from Manthy's (1978) book. These are the prices for which the longest annual series are available.[2] They cover the years from 1871 through 1973, and were obtained from his table MP-6.

I begin by investigating the order of the polynomial in time. I present results, given in column 1 of table 21.1, on the coefficients of the constant in a regression of the first difference of each series against a constant, and six of its own lags. Column 2 presents results on the coefficients of time in the same regressions with a time trend. The results from columns 1 and 2 of table 21.1 suggest that all the metal prices except that of lead are adequately characterized by a quadratic time trend. These results are comparable to those of Slade (1982a), based on deflated prices, but different from

Table 21.1 Point estimates and standard errors coefficients for fitted quadratic trends for all four commodities[a]

	Standard test (difference)		*Standard test (Slade's approach)*		*New regression[b] (Park–Choi)*	
Series	constant	time	time	time^2	constant	time
Pig iron	1.25$^+$	0.061*	−1.86**	0.03**	−1.62	0.046*
	(0.79)	(0.03)	(0.18)	(0.09)	(1.67)	(0.03)
Copper	0.44	0.36**	−0.72**	0.01**	−0.76	0.022*
	(0.36)	(0.01)	(0.08)	(0.001)	(0.72)	(0.01)
Lead	0.12	0.006	−0.12**	0.002**	−0.13	0.004
	(0.14)	(0.01)	(0.03)	(0.00)	(0.28)	(0.01)
Zinc	0.22	0.013*	−0.14**	0.002**	−0.22	0.006
	(0.20)	(0.01)	(0.027)	(0.000)	(0.43)	(0.01)

[a] + Denotes significance at the 90 percent confidence level.
* Denotes significance at the 95 percent level.
** Denotes significance at the 99 percent level.
[b] The estimates are based on the regression

$$\Delta p_t = \sum_{j=0}^{q-1} d_j t^j + \text{error}, \quad \text{where } q = 2.$$

Table 21.2 $G_\Delta(k, q)$ test statistics

Commodity	$m = 0$	$m = 2$	$m = 4$
Pig iron	3.1886	3.3256	2.9544
Copper	3.7099	3.5659	3.7088
Lead	0.9388	0.8730	0.8870
Zinc	1.2112	1.2672	1.0217

The regression that defines the test statistic is given in the footnotes to table 21.1. Under the null hypothesis H_0: $d_k = \cdots = d_{q-1} = 0$. In the paper, $k = 1$ and $q = 2$. Critical values: 10 percent: 2.706; 5 percent: 3.841; 2 percent: 5.412; 1 percent: 6.635 (Source: chi-squared (1) tables]. m is the number of sample autocorrelations used in the tests.

those obtained by using the specification adopted by Slade (1982a), see table 21.1, columns 3 and 4. Coefficient and standard error estimates from the regression $\Delta p_t = \mu + \beta t + \text{error}$, are given in columns 5 and 6. The results for the $G_\Delta(1, 2)$ statistics are given in table 21.2. The G_Δ-test rejects the null of some time coefficient being insignificant if the statistic is large. The statistic has a limiting chi-squared distribution if the stochastic component of $\{p_t\}$ is integrated and it is asymptotically zero when this component is stationary around a deterministic trend. See Park and Choi (1988) for detailed discussion of the derivation of this statistic. In contrast to previous results, the results in table 21.2 suggest that at the 10 percent significance level, both the lead and zinc prices are not characterized by a quadratic time trend. Copper and pig iron are adequately characterized by a quadratic time trend.

Table 21.3 presents results for the point estimates and standard errors of unit root coefficients for all four commodities. These estimates are based on equation (7). For example, zinc has a point estimate of 0.707 and a standard error of 0.075. Tables 21.4 and 21.5 present results on tests of a single unit root. Columns 1, 2, and 3 of table 21.4 are the Dickey–Fuller, the likelihood ratio and the Stock–Watson q_f^τ tests for a single root when there might be a trend term. At the 1 percent significance level, the results of the univariate tests do not lead to rejection of the unit root hypothesis for pig iron, copper, and lead prices. There is some conflict with the results as they relate to zinc prices. In columns 1 and 2 of table 21.4, we see that, at the 5 percent significance level, the unit root hypothesis is not rejected for zinc prices. These results are to be contrasted with those reported in column 3, which do not support the unit root hypotheses at this significance level. They are, however, consistent with the Phillips and Perron tests, table 21.5, and they seem to confirm the objections of Schwert (1987).

In examining table 21.5, we see that, at the conventional significance levels reported, the evidence based on the Phillips and Perron tests will not lead to a rejection of

Table 21.3 Point estimates and standard errors of unit root coefficients for all four commodities, 1871–1973

Series	*Estimate*	*Standard error*
Pig iron	0.942	0.033
Copper	0.966	0.040
Lead	0.873	0.048
Zinc	0.707	0.075

Table 21.4 Tests for the presence of unit roots, 1871–1973

Commodity	T1 D–F "*t*"	T2 D–F Φ_3	T3 $q_f^\tau[p]$
Pig iron	−1.787	3.367	−6.792
Copper	−0.303	3.697	−3.954
Lead	−2.564	3.796	−14.674
Zinc	−1.653	3.516	−31.392

Critical values for T1: 10 percent: −3.15; 5 percent: −3.45; 2.5 percent: −3.73; 1 percent: −4.04.
Critical values for T2: 10 percent: 5.47; 5 percent: 6.49; 2.5 percent: 7.44; 1 percent: 8.73.
Critical values for T3: 10 percent: −18.2; 5 percent: −21.7; 2.5 percent: −24.8; 1 percent: −29.2.
Source for T1 is Fuller (1976).
Source for T2 is Dickey and Fuller (1981).
Source for T3 is Stock and Watson (1988a).
The $q_f^\tau[p]$ denotes the $q_f^\tau(1, 0)$ statistics from Stock and Watson (1988a).
$r = 4$.

Table 21.5 Tests for the presence of unit roots, 1871–1973

$Z(\tilde{\alpha})$ test statistics

	α	$m = 0$	$m = 2$	$m = 4$
Pig iron	0.942	−5.951	−5.436	−5.089
Copper	0.966	−3.486	−3.773	−2.640
Lead	0.873	−13.10	−14.63	−13.13
Zinc	0.707	−30.21	−21.86	−21.70

Critical values: 10 percent: −18.3; 5 percent: −21.8; 2.5 percent: −25.1; 1 percent: −29.5. Source: Fuller (1976).
m is the number of sample autocorrelations used in the nonparametric tests.[3]

$Z(t_{\tilde{\alpha}})$ test statistics

	α	$m = 0$	$m = 2$	$m = 4$
Pig iron	0.942	−1.776	−1.703	−1.651
Copper	0.966	−0.843	−0.897	−0.673
Lead	0.872	−2.658	−2.798	−2.662
Zinc	0.707	−3.934	−3.362	−3.350

Critical values: 10 percent: −3.12; 5 percent: −3.41; 2.5 percent: −3.66; 1 percent: −3.96. Source: Fuller (1976).

$Z(\Phi_3)$ test statistics

	α	$m = 0$	$m = 2$	$m = 4$
Pig iron	0.942	3.053	2.902	2.778
Copper	0.966	2.040	2.064	1.950
Lead	0.873	3.982	4.486	3.996
Zinc	0.707	8.241	3.769	3.642

Critical values: 10 percent: 5.34; 5 percent: 6.26; 2.5 percent: 7.16; 1 percent: 8.27. Source: Dickey and Fuller (1981).

the unit root model for all the metal prices except zinc. The results on zinc are inconclusive. It should be pointed out that, though these statistics have the same asymptotic distribution as the statistics due to Fuller (1976) and Dickey–Fuller (1979, 1981), Monte Carlo experiments by Schwert (1989) show that they have different finite-sample distributions. I am therefore not surprised to notice that the results from the various tests are mixed.

I next consider table 21.6. Column 1 is the modified Stock–Watson $q_f^{\tau}[p]$ test for a single unit root when there might be a quadratic time trend. Columns 2 and 3 contain results on the Schmidt and Phillips $\tilde{\rho}$ and $\tilde{\tau}$ tests for a unit root, which allows for a quadratic trend under both the null and alternative, without introducing parameters that are irrelevant under either. Column 4 is the Stock–Watson $q_f^{\tau}[p]$ test of a second unit root, allowing for the alternative that the series is stationary in first differences around a linear time trend. At the conventional significance levels, the tests do not lead to a rejection of the hypothesis of a unit root with quadratic

Table 21.6 Tests for the presence of unit roots when there might be a quadratic time trend and test for a second unit root, 1871–1973

	QT1 $q_f^{\tau^2}[p]$	QT2 $\tilde{\rho}$	QT3 $\tilde{\tau}$	T4 $q_f^{\tau}[\Delta p]$
Pig iron	−21.321	−12.048	−2.550	−115.121
Copper	−17.570	−12.129	−2.067	−99.194
Lead	−22.642	−18.762	−3.162	−91.472
Zinc	−58.734	−55.633	−5.850	−152.187

Critical values for QT1: 10 percent: −24.1; 5 percent: −27.9; 1 percent: 35.5.
Ctitical values for QT2: 10 percent: −20.4; 5 percent: −23.7; 2.5 percent: −26.6; 1 percent: −30.4.
Critical values for QT3: 10 percent: −3.31; 5 percent: −3.60; 2.5 percent: −3.84; 1 percent: −4.16.
Critical values for T4: 10 percent: −24.1; 5 percent: −27.9; 1 percent: −35.5.
Source for QT1 is Stock and Watson (1989).
Source for QT2 is Schmidt and Phillips (1989).
Source for QT3 is Schmidt and Phillips (1989).
Source for T4 is Stock and Watson (1988a).
The $q_f^{\tau^2}[p]$ denotes the $q_f^{\tau^2}(1, 0)$ statistics from Stock and Watson (1989).
The $q_f^{\tau}[\Delta p]$ denotes the $q_f^{\tau}(1, 0)$ statistics from Stock and Watson (1988a).

time trend for pig iron, copper, and lead. The hypothesis is rejected for zinc. The results in column 4 suggest no series contains two unit roots.

Slade (1988) has investigated the unit root properties of several major North American commodities for the years 1906–1973. These include copper, pig iron, lead, bauxite, silver, petroleum, and coal. The tests based on the ordinary t statistics and the g statistics of Berenbluth and Webb (1973) support the presence of unit roots in all commodities except petroleum. Notice, firstly, that zinc is not among the commodities Slade (1988) investigated and secondly, that the tests employed by Slade do not compare favorably with the tests I have used in this paper. More specifically, if a unit root is present in the commodity price time series process then the regression considered by Slade becomes essentially spurious in the sense of Granger and Newbold (1974) and Phillips (1986). The use of these tests is therefore invalid.

I now turn to the multivariate tests. In testing for common trends, I need a multivariate representation. In considering this representation, I initially adopted the U-shaped time path representation for relative prices suggested by Gilbert (1978), Pindyk (1978) and Slade (1982a). Specifically, I assumed that the data are characterized by a quadratic time trend and at most as many unit roots as variables. This representation is for the whole system, the four metal prices.

The multivariate tests are given in table 21.7. The earlier univariate results for zinc prices do not conclusively support the view that the data are characterized by a unit root process. In view of these results, I investigated subsystems not involving zinc prices. In examining these results, notice that tests for cointegration among the series, pig iron, copper, and lead (reported in table 21.7) generally fail to reject the null that the pig iron, copper, and lead are not cointegrated. These results are true for any combination of these commodity prices. These led me to accept that the multivariate representations have as many unit roots as variables. A result that suggests that these series do not have stochastic trends in common.

Table 21.7 Multivariate tests, 1871–1973

System	Unit roots under null and alternative	$q_f^{\tau}(k, k-1)$	$q_f^{\tau^2}(k, k-1)$
TA Pb, Cu	2 vs 1	−16.321	−22.132
TB Cu, Fe	2 vs 1	−29.685	−24.368
TC Pb, Cu, Fe	3 vs 2	−25.765	−26.690

Fe = Pig iron; Cu = copper; Pb = lead; and Zn = zinc.
Based on q_f^{τ}:
Critical values for TA and TB: 10 percent: −26.7; 5 percent: −30.8; 1 percent: −39.2.
Critical values for TC: 10 percent: −34.6; 5 percent: −39.0; 1 percent: −48.7.
Source for TA, TB and TC is Stock and Watson (1988a, 1989).[4]
Based on $q_f^{\tau^2}$:
Critical values for TA and TB: 10 percent: −32.5; 5 percent: −36.9; 1 percent: −46.0.
Critical values for TC: 10 percent: −41.0; 5 percent: −45.3; 1 percent: −55.7.
Source for TA, TB and TC is Stock and Watson (1988a, 1989).

Conclusion

I characterized the time trend and unit root properties of mineral-resource prices for some selected commodities. I also conducted tests for the presence of a single unit root when there might be a quadratic time trend in the data. In my analysis, I employed both univariate and multivariate tests of unit roots. I also investigated the possibility that the mineral resource prices might have up to two roots and time trends up to the second order.

The univariate tests led me to obtain the following characterization for the univariate metal price series. Pig iron, lead, and copper prices are adequately represented as processes with single unit roots and quadratic time trend. Zinc prices do not contain unit roots. This empirical finding of a unit root and quadratic time trend for some of the commodities is very interesting. It suggests that in the short run the unanticipated component of price movements dominates the process but in the long run, some systematic movement is detectable and is of the sort we might expect from theory. The systematic trends, however, are probably too irregular to be arbitraged away (given that there are holding costs). The present results are therefore consistent with both the random walk theory and the Hotelling-style models.

The multivariate tests led me to conclude that pig iron, copper, and lead do not have common stochastic trends. Thus, in modeling the long-run behavior of natural-resource commodity prices, it might be more appropriate to assume separate sets of fundamentals for each commodity.

There are several issues that have not been addressed in this paper. First, it should be noted that my analysis was conducted in discrete time. An alternate approach would be to investigate the stochastic behavior of prices in continuous time. Arguments in favor of formulating and estimating models in continuous time are given in the important writings of Professor Bergstrom (1966, 1976, 1984), and elsewhere. Professor Bergstrom has noted that there is a need for formulating econometric models in which variables are treated as continuous functions of time. This is so since the variables that occur in most econometric models are, by and large, the result of large numbers of microeconomic decisions taken by different individuals at different point of time. These may be regarded as continuous functions of time. Professor Bergstrom's treatment of nonstationary continuous-time models is contained in Bergstrom (1985, 1986).

Second, this paper assumes a stable underlying data generating process for the commodities. The important issue of testing for unit roots in models with structural change has not been addressed. It is possible, in some of the commodities examined, that the data generating process for prices has changed at least once over the sample period. This type of change can affect the conclusion reached in the paper. Perron (1989), for example, rejects the unit root hypothesis for most USA macroeconomic time series when a structural break is allowed in the data for the Great Depression or the oil price shock of 1973. A useful approach for further analysis is to adopt the testing procedure suggested by Park (1988) who extends Phillips (1987) unit roots tests to accommodate models with multiple structural changes as well as deterministic polynomial time trend of an arbitrary order.

Third, this paper considered only four commodities. Future work might usefully extend the analysis to cover more major commodities. Slade (1982a), for example, examined the price behavior of several commodities, these included aluminum, copper, iron, lead, nickel, silver, tin, zinc, coal, natural gas, and petroleum.

Notes

I would like to thank Professor P. C. B. Phillips, the referees, Professors R. G. Cummings, D. Golbe, M. Schranz, and E. Seeley for helpful comments that have improved the presentation of the present version of the paper. I am responsible for any remaining errors.

1. There are other multivariate tests for common trends in the literature. For example Baillie and Bollerslev (1989) have applied a multivariate test for unit roots due to Johansen (1988) to test for the presence of stochastic trend among a set of seven daily spot and forward exchange rates. Baillie (1989) has applied this test to commodity prices.
2. Notes on the sources and construction of Manthy's historical series are contained in Manthy (1978, pp. 212–213). The index for pig iron prices is constructed by weighting the prices of five types of pig iron (basic, Bessemer, foundary-northern, foundary-southern, and malleable), by their 1951–3 average production. The actual prices for copper, lead, and zinc are in terms of average cents per pound. For this paper, I have settled for the longest series given in his book, 104 observations. Shiller and Perron (1985) have shown that the power of unit root tests depends on the span of available data.
3. There is some ambiguity in the appropriate choice of lag truncation number. The test statistics are reported for various lags so that sensitivities in the results of the tests are apparent. Also note that in the computation of our test statistics. I have followed Perron and Phillips (1987) and have adopted a consistent estimator proposed by Newey and West (1987). The results make use of the finite sample correction of Perron (1988).
4. My thanks to Mark Watson for providing me with the Gauss program for computing the Stock and Watson tests for common trends.

References

Agbeyegbe, T. D. (1989a). "Interest rates and metal price movements: further evidence," *Journal of Environmental Economic Management*, 16, 184–92.

Agbeyegbe, T. D. (1989a). "Seasonal unit roots, metal prices and the efficiency of the London Metal Exchange," mimeo, Hunter College.

Agbeyegbe, T. D. (1992). "Common stochastic trends: Some evidence from the London Metal Exchange," *Bulletin of Economic Research*, 44, 141–51.

Baillie, R. T., and T. Bollerslev (1989). "Common stochastic trends in a system of exchange rates," *Journal of Finance*, 44, 167–81.

Baillie, R. T. (1989). "Commodity prices and aggregate inflation," *Carnegie-Rochester Conference Series on Public Policy*, 31, 185–240.

Barnett, H. D., and C. Morse (1963). *Scarcity and Growth*. Baltimore. Johns Hopkins University Press.

Berenbluth, I. I., and G. I. Webb (1973). "A new test for autocorrelated errors in the linear regression model," *Journal of the Royal Statistical Society* **B** 35, 33–50.

Bergstrom, A. R. (1966). "Non-recursive models as discrete approximations to systems of stochastic differential equations," *Econometrica*, 34, 173–82.

Bergstrom, A. R. (ed.) (1976). *Statistical Inference in Continuous-Time Economic Models*. Amsterdam: North-Holland.

Bergstrom, A. R. (1984). "Continuous-time stochastic models and issues of aggregation over time," in Z. Griliches and M. D. Intrilligator (eds) *Handbook of Econometrics*, volume 2. Amsterdam: North-Holland.

Bergstrom, A. R. (1985). "The estimation of parameters in non-stationary higher-order continuous-time dynamic models," *Econometric Theory*, 1, 369–85.

Bergstrom, A. R. (1986). "The estimation of open higher order continuous-time dynamic models with mixed stock and flow data," *Econometric Theory*, 2, 350–73.

Bhargava, A. (1986). "On the theory of testing for unit roots in observed time series with a unit root," *Review of Economic Studies*, 369–84.

Dickey, D. A., and W. A. Fuller (1979). "Distribution of the estimators for autoregressive time series with a unit root," *Journal of the American Statistical Association*, 74, 427–31.

Dickey, D. A., and W. A. Fuller (1981). "Likelihood ratio statistics for autoregressive time series with a unit root," *Econometrica*, 49, 1057–72.

Engle, R. F., and C. W. J. Granger (1987). "Cointegration and error correction: representation, estimation and testing," *Econometrica*, 55, 251–76.

Fama, E. F. (1970). "Efficient capital markets: a review of theory and empirical work," *Journal of Finance*, 25, 383–417.

Fuller, W. A. (1976). *Introduction to Statistical Time Series*. New York: John Wiley.

Gilbert, R. J. (1978). "Dominant-firm pricing policy in a market for an exhaustible resource," *Bell Journal of Economics* 9, 385–95.

Granger, C. W. J., and P. Newbold (1974). "Spurious regressions in econometrics," *Journal of Econometrics*, 74, 111–20.

Heal, G. M. (1981). "Scarcity, efficiency and disequilibrium in resource markets," *The Scandinavian Journal of Economics*, 83, 334–51.

Heal, G. M., and M. M. Barrow (1979). "The relationship between interest rates and metal price movements," *Revues in Economic Studies* 48, 161–81.

Heal, G. M., and M. M. Barrow (1981). "Empirical investigation of the long-term movement of resource prices: a preliminary report," *Economic Letters*, 7, 95–103.

Hotelling, H. (1931). "The economics of exhaustible resources," *Journal of Political Economics*, 39, 137–75.

Johansen, S. (1988). "Statistical analysis of cointegration vectors," *Journal of Economic Dynamics and Control*, 12, 231–54.

MacDonald, R., and Taylor, M. P. (1988). "Metal prices, efficiency and cointegration: some evidence from the London Metal Exchange," *Bulletin of Economic Research*, 40, 235–39.

Manthy, R. (1978). *Natural Resource Commodities – A Century of Statistics*. Baltimore: Johns Hopkins University Press.

Mueller, M. J., and D. R. Gorin (1985). "Informative trends in natural-resource commodity prices: a comment on Slade," *Journal of Environmental Economic Management* 12, 83–9.

Newey, W. K., and K. D. West (1987). "A simple positive semi-definite, heteroscedasticity and autocorrelation consistent covariance matrix," *Econometrica*, 55, 703–8.

Park, J. Y. (1988). "Testing for unit roots in models with structural change," Center for Analytical Economics, Working Paper, 88-10.

Park, J. Y., and B. Choi (1988). "A new approach to testing for a unit root," Center for Analytical Economics, Working Paper, 88-23.

Perron, P. (1988). "Trends and random walks in macroeconomic time series: further evidence from a new approach," *Journal of Economic Dynamics and Control*, 12, 297–332.

Perron, P. (1989). "The great crash, the oil price shock, and the unit root hypothesis," *Econometrica*, 57, 1361–401.

Perron, P., and P. C. B. Phillips (1987). "Does GNP have a unit root? A re-evaluation," *Economic Letters*, 23, 139–45.

Phillips, P. C. B. (1986). "Understanding spurious regressions in econometrics," *Journal of Econometrics*, 33, 311–40.

Phillips, P. C. B. (1987). "Time series regression with a unit root," *Econometrica*, 55, 277–302.

Phillips, P. C. B. (1988). "Spectral regression for cointegrated time series," forthcoming in W. Barnett (ed.) *Nonparametric and Semiparametric Methods in Economics and Statistics*. Cambridge: Cambridge University Press.

Phillips, P. C. B., and P. Perron (1988). "Testing for a unit root in time series regression," *Biometrika*, 75, 335–46.

Pindyck, R. S. (1978). "The optimal exploration and production of non-renewable resources," *Journal of Political Economy*, 86, 841–62.

Samuelson, P. A. (1965). "Proof that properly anticipated prices fluctuate randomly," *Industrial Management Review*, 6, 41–9.

Schultze, W. D. (1974). "The optimal use of non-renewable resources: the theory of extraction," *Journal of Environmental Economic Management*, 1, 53–73.

Schmidt, P., and P. C. B. Phillips (1989). "Testing for a unit root in the presence of deterministic trends," Cowles Foundation Discussion Paper, 933.

Schwert, G. (1987). "Effects of model specification on tests for unit roots in macroeconomic data," *Journal of Monetary Economics*, 20, 73–103.

Schwert, G. (1989). "Tests for unit roots: a Monte-Carlo investigation," *Journal of Business and Economic Statistics*, 7, 147–60.

Shiller, R. J., and P. Perron (1985). "Testing the random walk hypothesis: power versus frequency of observation," *Economic Letters*, 18, 381–6.

Slade, M. E. (1982a). "Trends in natural-resource commodity prices: an analysis of the time domain," *Journal of Environmental Economic Management*, 9, 122–37.

Slade, M. E. (1982b). "Cycles in natural-resource commodity prices: an analysis of the frequency domain," *Journal of Environmental Economic Management*, 9, 138–48.

Slade, M. E. (1985). "Noninformative trends in natural resource commodity prices: U-shaped price path exonerated," *Journal of Environmental Economic Management*, 12, 181–92.

Slade, M. E. (1988). "Grade selection under uncertainty: least cost last and other anomalies," *Journal of Environmental Economic Management*, 15, 189–205.

Smith, V. K. (1979). "Natural resource scarcity: a statistical analysis," *Review of Economic Statistics*, 61, 423–7.

Smith, V. K. (1981). "The empirical relevance of Hotelling's model for natural resources," *Resources and Energy*, 3, 105–17.

Stock, J. H., and M. W. Watson (1988a). "Testing for common trends," *Journal of American Statistics Association*, 83, 1097–107.

Stock, J. H., and M. W. Watson (1988b). "Testing for common trends," Discussion Paper, Harvard University, Kennedy School of Government.

Stock, J. H., and M. W. Watson (1989). "Interpreting the evidence on money–income causality," *Journal of Econometrics*, 40, 161–81.

22

Continuous-Time Econometric Modeling and the Issue of Capital Liberalization

Giancarlo Gandolfo and Pier Carlo Padoan

Introduction

This paper[1] examines the consequences of the liberalization of capital movements in the Italian economy. The analysis is carried out using the fifth version of the Italian continuous-time model (Gandolfo and Padoan 1990), a model whose first version (Gandolfo and Padoan 1980, Gandolfo 1981) was inspired by the work of Rex Bergstrom and Clifford Wymer (1976). Our model is a medium-term disequilibrium model specified and estimated as a set of stochastic differential equations which stresses real and financial accumulation in an open and highly integrated economy. This version includes a detailed specification of the financial sector as well as the endogenous determination of the exchange rate.

The use of a continuous-time econometric model turns out to be very helpful for the analysis of the problem at hand. In fact, international capital movements are modeled according to the portfolio adjustment view. Hence they are considered as the flow deriving from the adjustment of the actual to the desired stock of net foreign assets. Thus, one needs in the first place a rigorous estimation of the associated speed of adjustment independently of the sampling interval. This estimation can be obtained only through the continuous-time approach to econometric modeling. In this context, capital liberalization takes the form of an increase in the adjustment speed of net foreign assets to their (partial) equilibrium value. The analysis of the consequences of this increase is carried out at two levels. First, stability and sensitivity analysis about the steady state of the model identify a source of instability in the increase in question. Possible stabilizing factors are also considered. In the second place, the systemic consequences of capital liberalization are considered by carrying out several simulations with different degrees of capital liberalization. These include the case of perfect capital mobility. The behavior of the variables of the model is then compared with that obtained in the control solution. The usual caveats apply to this type of exercise (Lucas' critique, etc. See, however, Gandolfo and Padoan (1984, section II.4 of appendix II), where these problems are examined in detail.

The plan of the paper is as follows. In the second section we examine the problem of modeling the liberalization of capital movements. In the third section we give an overview of the capital movements equation in the context of our model. Stability and sensitivity analysis are treated in the fourth section, and simulation results in the fifth section. A sixth section concludes the paper.

Modeling Capital Liberalization

At the moment, it seems that neither economic theory nor empirical research have much to tell us on this problem. As regards economic theory, on the one hand we have the Mundellian time-honoured analysis of perfect capital mobility, on the other the literature on foreign exchange crises.

The Mundellian analysis (Mundell 1963) assumes perfect capital mobility and examines the effectiveness of monetary and fiscal policy under fixed and flexible exchange rates. Under fixed exchange rates, perfect capital mobility implies the ineffectiveness of monetary policy and the full effectiveness of fiscal policy. The opposite is true under flexible exchange rates. These propositions are almost 30 years old, but later studies have not added much to them. The refinements include the distinction between perfect capital mobility and perfect asset substitutability, the reintroduction of some effectiveness of fiscal policy through changes in the real money supply due to exchange-rate changes, etc. (Gandolfo 1987, section 16.6). The literature on foreign exchange crises points out that the removal of capital controls may give rise to speculative attacks in a regime of adjustable peg. These attacks may cause the exhaustion of international reserves thus forcing parity realignments. Besides, in the presence of perfect capital mobility, accommodating realignments (namely realignments that completely offset the cumulated loss of competitiveness) may cause undesirable oscillations in the exchange rate and vicious circle phenomena (Wyplosz 1986, Driffill 1988, Obstfeld 1988). This would increase the frequency of realignments, hence undermining the credibility of the exchange-rate arrangements. The conclusion is that one cannot rely solely on realignments of real exchange rates to eliminate external disequilibria.

As regards *empirical research*, only limited empirical work is available on the effects of capital liberalization on the macroeconomic system. Most of this research has been carried out in relation to the problems of the developing countries. In these countries, in fact, the issue of opening up domestic economies through the liberalization of trade and capital movements has been of perennial concern to policy makers. An interesting result of these studies (Khan and Zahler 1983, 1985) is that the liberalization of capital movements not accompanied by the liberalization of trade flows may destabilize the economic system.

The main problem in both theoretical and empirical analysis is how to model capital controls (and liberalization). In our opinion, the effect of capital controls is embodied in the value of the adjustment speed of the actual to the desired stock of net foreign assets. This follows from our way of modeling capital flows and from a precise hypothesis. The hypothesis is that the desired stock of net foreign assets depends on fundamentals while the adjustment speed reflects institutional features like capital controls. Tight capital controls determine a low adjustment speed. Freedom of capital movements is reflected in a very high value of the adjustment speed. In addition, we believe that the effects of capital liberalization should be studied in a macroeconomic general equilibrium framework where the dynamic aspects are fully considered. In fact, capital movements are influenced by (and influence) the behavior of the whole macroeconomy.

The Mark V version of the Italian continuous-time model is well suited to our purpose. It is, in fact, an economy-wide dynamic macroeconometric model that considers the interrelationships among stocks and flows, real and financial variables, prices, and quantities. The model also considers the links and feedbacks between market-determined and policy-determined variables. Our analysis is closely related to that of Jonson et al. (1982), who use the Reserve Bank of Australia continuous-time model to examine the case of fast capital flows, among others. To this purpose they increase the adjustment speed of the actual to the desired stock of net foreign assets and perform sensitivity and simulation analyses. Their results, however, are not directly comparable to ours (besides the different institutional setting). The reason is that they consider a modest increase in the adjustment speed. The corresponding mean time lag is one quarter, which is not really perfect capital mobility. The theoretical models, in fact, identify perfect capital mobility with an (almost) instantaneous adjustment, which means a very low mean time lag. In our exercises we have assumed a mean time lag of one day. Nevertheless, the methodology that we follow is essentially similar to that of the Jonson–McKibbin–Trevor paper.

The Model and the Capital Movement Equation

The model is a nonlinear system of stochastic differential equations (see the appendix). This system has been linearized about sample means for estimation purposes. Tables 22.1 and 22.2 give the parameter estimates, and table 22.3 gives the main results of sensitivity analysis under flexible exchange rates. For a full description of the model see Gandolfo and Padoan (1990).

Let us now examine the capital flow equation briefly. This is equation (A12) of the model:

$$D \log \mathrm{NFA} = \alpha_{24} \log (\mathrm{N\hat{F}A}/\mathrm{NFA}) + \alpha_{25} \log (\mathrm{PMGS_f} \cdot E \cdot \mathrm{MGS}/\mathrm{PXGS} \cdot \mathrm{XGS}), \qquad \alpha_{25} < 0, \quad (1)$$

where

$$\mathrm{N\hat{F}A} = \gamma_{11} e^{\beta_{19}[i_f + \log(FR/E) - i_{\mathrm{TIT}}]} (PY)^{\beta_{20}} (\mathrm{PF_f} \cdot E \cdot \mathrm{YF})^{-\beta_{21}}. \quad (2)$$

The equation has a twofold nature. The first component is the adjustment of the stock of net foreign assets (NFA) to its desired value $\mathrm{N\hat{F}A}$. The latter reflects the portfolio balance view, in which the scale variables are proxied by the domestic (PY) and foreign ($\mathrm{PF_f} \cdot E \cdot \mathrm{YF}$) money incomes. Besides the scale variables, the level of $\mathrm{N\hat{F}A}$ is determined by the interest differential corrected for exchange rate expectations. These are proxied by the ratio of the forward to the spot exchange rate (FR/E). We know that under imperfect asset substitutability the expected exchange rate differs from the forward premium by the relative risk premium. This is implicitly present in our equation as discussed in Gandolfo and Padoan (1990).

The interest differential term is also included in the interest rate equation. This is consistent with the idea that the domestic interest rate moves to close the discrepancy between its current value and the covered interest parity value. In fact, under perfect mobility and infinite elasticity of arbitrage funds the relation $i_{\mathrm{TIT}} = i_f + (FR - E)/E$ should hold. Considerations of imperfect capital mobility can, however, explain the

Table 22.1 Estimated adjustment parameters

Parameter	Entering equation number	Point estimate (a)	Asymptotic standard error (b)	(c) = (a)/(b)	Mean time lag (quarters)	Standard error of mean time lag
α_1	(1)	1.147	0.214	5.37	0.872	0.162
α_2	(1)	0.114	0.041	2.77		
α_3	(2)	1.003	0.178	5.64	0.997	0.177
α_4	(2)	0.112	0.014	8.14		
α_5	(4)	0.927	0.157	5.90	1.079	0.183
α_6	(4)	0.329	0.125	2.62		
α_7	(4)	0.021	0.010	2.05		
α_8	(5)	0.869	0.142	6.09	1.149	0.188
α_9	(5)	0.618	0.219	2.81		
α_{10}	(6)	1.879	0.273	6.88	0.532	0.077
α_{11}	(6)	0.573	0.058	9.88		
α_{12}	(7)	0.493	0.111	4.44	2.028	0.459
α_{13}	(7)	0.313	0.114	2.75		
α_{14}	(7)	0.122	0.058	2.07		
α_{15}	(8)	0.340	0.113	3.02	2.941	0.974
α_{16}	(9)	0.383	0.103	3.71	2.611	0.704
α_{17}	(10)	0.030	0.007	4.17		
α_{18}	(10)	0.073	0.003	25.68	13.698	0.593
α_{19}	(10)	0.181	0.007	27.13		
α_{20}	(10)	0.049	0.004	13.78		
α_{21}	(10)	0.085	0.004	21.73		
α_{22}	(11)	0.140	0.026	5.35	7.143	1.335
α_{23}	(11)	−2.904	0.516	5.63		
α_{24}	(12)	0.091	0.032	2.84	10.989	3.869
α_{25}	(12)	−0.182	0.029	6.15		
α_{26}	(13)	4.095	0.938	4.36	0.244	0.056
α_{27}	(14)	0.155	0.055	2.81	6.452	2.296
α_{28}	(15)	0.401	0.110	3.61	2.494	0.691
α_{29}	(15)	−3.410	0.654	5.21		
α'	(2)	0.059	0.004	15.71	16.949	1.079
η	(3)	0.083	0.025	3.27		

presence of a gap between the two members. This, in turn, gives rise to a (policy managed) movement of i_{TIT} aimed at the reduction of the gap.

The second element in the equation refers to capital movements which are not strictly related to portfolio considerations, but rather to trade flows. The ratio of the value of imports to the value of exports is meant to capture the effect of commercial credits on the capital account. A trade deficit – i.e. $(\text{PMGS}_f \cdot E \cdot \text{MGS}/\text{PXGS} \cdot \text{XGS}) > 1$, hence $\log(\quad) > 0$ – is partly financed through commercial credits from abroad. This gives rise to an increase in foreign liabilities ($D \log \text{NFA} < 0$).

Stability and Sensitivity

The (local) stability of the model has been examined by using the linear approximation about the steady state. The model has two exchange rate regimes (fixed and floating

Table 22.2 Other estimated parameters

Parameter	*Entering equation number*	*Point estimate (a)*	*Asymptotic standard error (b)*	(*c*) = (*a*)/(*b*)
β_1	(1)	−1.296	0.299	4.33
β_2	(1)	0.0*		
β_3	(1), (7), (10)	2.237	0.968	2.31
β_4	(1), (7), (10)	1.135	0.109	10.43
β_5	(1), (7), (10)	1.480	0.164	9.01
β_6	(4)	0.672	0.140	4.81
β_7	(4)	0.547	0.101	5.41
β_8	(4)	1.166	0.158	7.38
β_9	(5)	0.378	0.082	4.58
β_{10}	(5)	0.659	0.128	5.14
β_{11}	(5)	0.945	0.112	8.49
β_{12}	(7)	0.330	0.047	6.94
β_{13}	(7)	0.501	0.046	10.87
β_{14}	(7)	0.0*		
β_{15}	(8)	0.480	0.081	5.92
β_{16}	(8)	0.404	0.070	5.79
β_{17}	(9)	0.629	0.041	15.45
β_{18}	(11)	−2.340	0.294	7.96
β_{19}	(12)	9.026	3.281	2.75
β_{20}	(12)	1.0*		
β_{21}	(12)	1.0*		
β_{22}	(14)	1.101	0.048	22.92
λ_4	(9)	0.019	0.001	16.94
δ_1	(13)	0.103	0.049	2.08
δ_2	(13)	−0.092	0.080	1.14
δ_3	(13)	0.367	0.081	4.51
δ_4	(13)	0.065	0.031	2.02
δ_5	(16)	−0.390	0.376	1.04
δ_6	(16)	−0.126	0.200	0.63
δ_7	(16)	0.927	0.188	4.92
δ_8	(16)	0.282	0.038	7.39
γ_1	(1)	0.764	0.005	152.72
γ_2	(1), (7), (10)	0.0006	0.0007	0.83
γ_3	(2)	6.011	0.288	20.84
γ_4	(4)	0.089	0.107	0.82
γ_5	(4), (6)	1.009	0.061	16.60
γ_6	(5)	0.199	0.197	1.01
γ_7	(7)	1.264	0.226	5.58
γ_8	(8)	1.061	0.022	48.88
γ_9	(9)	0.742	0.017	42.51
γ_{10}	(11)	0.0095	0.0004	20.67
γ_{11}	(12)	0.00036	0.00007	4.95
γ_{12}	(14)	0.134	0.048	2.80
γ_{13}	(15)	0.252	0.007	33.94
γ_{14}	(16)	1.0*		
γ_{15}	(16)	1.147	0.213	5.37

* = value imposed.

Table 22.3 Sensitivity analysis with respect to selected parameters under flexible exchange rates

Root (μ)	$\partial\mu/\partial\alpha_5$	$\partial\mu/\partial\alpha_8$	$\partial\mu/\partial\alpha_{14}$	$\partial\mu/\partial\alpha_{15}$	$\partial\mu/\partial\alpha_{16}$	$\partial\mu/\partial\alpha_{24}$	$\partial\mu/\partial\beta_6$	$\partial\mu/\partial\beta_7$	$\partial\mu/\partial\delta_8$
0.3109	−0.3153	−1.1513				2.9454			
−0.0009							0.0987	−0.0054	
−0.0751							0.239	−0.076	
−0.1675 ±0.0219i		0.0476	0.3585						
−0.2595 ±0.4111i		−0.5064							
−0.3737 ±0.0591i				0.4899	−0.2342				−0.3068

exchange rates), as the sample period covers 1960(4)–1984(4). This requires the computation of two steady states (one for each regime) and, consequently, of two linear approximations. The model is practically stable under both regimes, which show no appreciable difference as regards stability. In fact, all the complex roots have negative real parts and all but one real characteristic root are negative. However, the positive root is not significantly different from zero at the 5 percent level. We therefore conclude that the hypothesis of stability cannot be rejected.

There is, however, a possible interpretation of this positive root suggested by sensitivity analysis. Table 22.3 gives the main results of sensitivity analysis under flexible exchange rates; in this table we present only the results concerning the parameters that crucially affect stability. This table shows a large and positive partial derivative of the possibly positive root with respect to α_{24} (the adjustment speed of net foreign assets). Such a result implies that an increase in α_{24} would cause an increase in this root, hence instability for sufficiently high values of α_{24}. This result holds also under fixed exchange rates. Under flexible exchange rates it is possible to suggest an explanation for this phenomenon. Let us first note that our use of the forward exchange rate as a proxy for the expected spot rate may also be seen as representing rational expectations. Then, if we couple a very high adjustment speed ($\alpha_{24} \to \infty$) with rational expectations we are in a well-known context. Efficient asset markets with rational expectations imply that the equilibrium state has the saddle-point property, hence at least one positive root. The presence of only one positive root is related to our choice of using also other types of expectations in addition to rational expectations. This is a deliberate choice due to our eclectic approach (discussed in detail in Gandolfo and Padoan (1990) and confirmed by the estimates).

There is, however, more to it than that. With $\alpha_{24} \to \infty$ we have perfect capital mobility which, as shown above, implies instability unless we can rely on rational expectations causing the model to jump on a stable path. Since we do not have generalized rational expectations (see above), full capital liberalization may have a destabilizing impact on the model *ceteris paribus*. We wish to stress the *ceteris paribus* clause, because by (directly or indirectly) acting on other parameters one might counteract this destabilizing effect. Sensitivity analysis indicates some possible stabilizing effects. Both an increase in α_5 (the adjustment speed of imports) and an increase in α_8 (the adjustment speed of exports) have a stabilizing effect on the positive root. The implication is that the destabilizing impact on an increase in capital mobility may be offset by an increase in goods mobility. When one frees capital movements, one must also have free trade in goods and services.

Simulation Results

Some further indications on the effects of higher capital mobility may be obtained through simulation analysis. The behavior of the control solution has been compared with that of versions in which some parameters have been altered to represent capital liberalization. These exercises have been performed by using the original nonlinear model. In fact, the parameters being estimated are those of the original nonlinear differential model. Hence we can use this nonlinear model for simulation rather than the linear approximation. The starting point was the first quarter of 1980 to have, in principle, five years of in-sample behavior for comparison. The spirit of the exercise is to "rerun history," asking what would have happened had capital movements been liberalized at that point. This, hopefully, can give us further information on the adjustment of the Italian economy, as described by our model, to a new institutional regime.

Higher capital mobility has been simulated by imposing an increase in α_{24}, the adjustment speed of net foreign assets, and eliminating capital controls from the equation of real imports.[2] Let us note that an increase in α_{24} would probably be accompanied by an increase in α_{18} and perhaps in α_{17}. These parameters, however, do not affect stability in an appreciable way (they do not, in fact, appear in table 22.3). Thus we decided not to consider these changes for the sake of brevity.

The value of α_{24} has been set to different values, starting from $\alpha_{24} = 0.2$, which is the bifurcation value of the parameter derived from sensitivity analysis discussed above. The highest value considered is $\alpha_{24} = 90$, i.e. a mean time lag of one day, an assumption of (almost) perfect capital mobility. The behavior of the model does not change significantly from a qualitative point of view. By this we mean that the basic features of the reaction mechanism triggered by the increase of α_{24} do not change with the value of the adjustment speed. The only difference lies in the intensity of the movements of the variables. We decided, therefore, to present for each of the first two cases considered (see below) the results obtained with $\alpha_{24} = 90$, i.e. the case of full capital liberalization. The analysis of the effects of capital liberalization has been carried out considering different hypotheses about exchange rate expectations and the policy reactions to exchange rate movements.

Case 1

The model is altered only as regards the elimination of capital controls from the import equation and the increase in α_{24}.

The main result of the simulations is that, after a period of apparently stable behavior, the dynamic path of some variables, notably the exchange rate, becomes explosive. We may distinguish between an impact effect and an adjustment mechanism (see figure 22.1). The increase in α_{24} leads to an immediate increase in NFA which causes an appreciation of the exchange rate E (impact effect). This is a well-known effect in portfolio models (Gandolfo 1987, section 18.8.3.3). The change in E, in turn, leads to a decrease in the interest rate (i_{TIT}) and to an increase in the level of international reserves (R). This is the consequence of the "leaning against the wind"

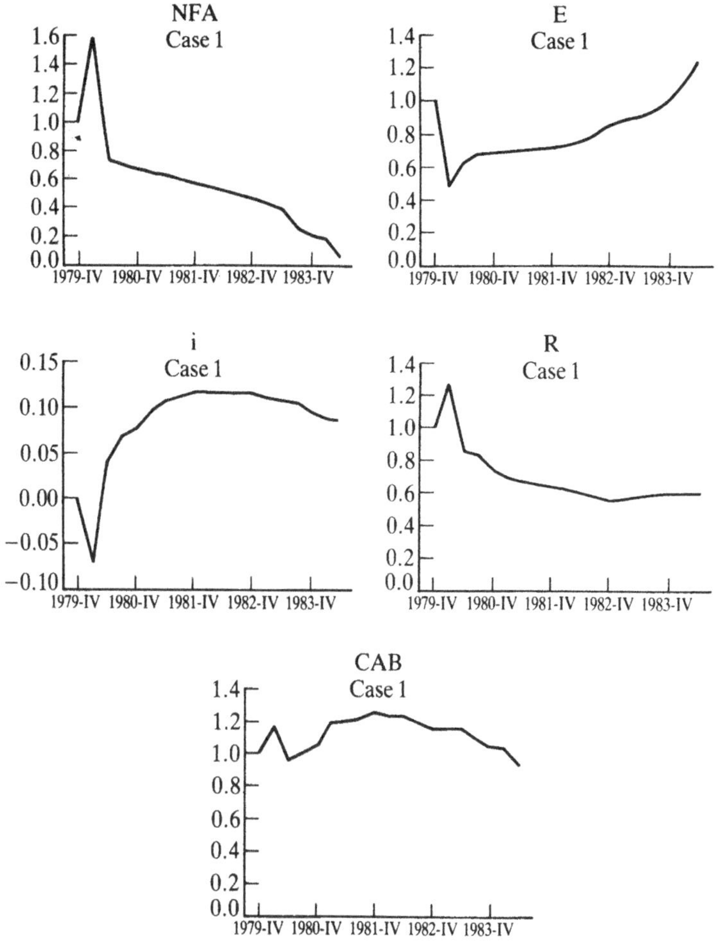

Figure 22.1 Simulations of Case 1

components present in both equations. These components cause the interest rate to increase (decrease) and international reserves to decrease (increase) when the change in the exchange rate ($D \log E$) is positive (negative). Finally, improvement of the terms of trade associated with the decrease in E produces an improvement in the current account. From this point onwards, a reaction mechanism involving mainly the interest rate and the level of international reserves is set into motion.

The level of R is now higher than the target value which depends on the value of imports (now lower because of the appreciation of the exchange rate). As a consequence, the level of reserves tends to decrease. The level of the interest rate, on the contrary, is pushed upwards by two elements. One is the appreciation of the spot exchange rate relative to the forward rate which increases the target value of i_{TIT}. The other is the monetary squeeze caused by the decrease in international reserves through the money supply equation. The increase in i_{TIT} leads to a decrease in the accumulation of net foreign assets.

The decrease in NFA pushes towards the depreciation of the exchange rate. This effect is partially offset by the behavior of the current account (which is improving). At this stage the economy is apparently following a stable path characterized by a lower exchange rate and a higher interest rate. One important real effect is a relatively lower level of fixed investment produced by the tighter monetary and credit conditions. After about three years, however, the pressure for a higher exchange rate overcomes the opposing forces. The exchange rate starts a depreciating movement which soon becomes explosive. The results confirm the widespread view that a decrease in capital controls leads initially to a higher stock of net foreign assets. They also confirm the similarly widespread opinion that the economy can be kept on a relatively stable path with appropriate interest rate and exchange rate policies. This latter opinion, unfortunately, is true only for a few years, and does not hold in the longer run. What this exercise shows, in fact, is that the new regime leads to the build up of market pressures concentrating on the exchange rate which eventually become unsustainable.

Case 2

The role of policy interventions associated with the "leaning against the wind" component was crucial in the previous case. A second group of simulations has been carried out by eliminating this component from the two policy equations (interest rate and international reserves). A second major modification is related to exchange rate expectations which are represented by the ratio of the forward to the spot exchange rate. The forward rate was kept exogenous in the previous simulation and this fact might have somewhat distorted the result of the exercise.

Different ways out were available, including the possibility of introducing an equation for the endogenous determination of the forward exchange rate. We decided to adopt another solution, which has the advantage of minimizing changes in the structures of the model and avoiding the introduction of new parameters. Expected exchange rate changes were proxied by the rate of change of E, $D \log E$, which replaced $\log(FR/E)$ in both the interest rate and the capital movements equation. This amounts to assuming perfect foresight (the divergence between i_{TIT} and $i_{\mathrm{f}} + D \log E$ does, however, remain due to imperfect asset substitutability). In this case too the experiment of capital liberalization leads to an explosive movement of the exchange rate (see figure 22.2). This movement, however, occurs much earlier (and with a much greater reaction in the variables considered) than in the previous case (see figure 22.2). The increase in α_{24} produces, as before, an increase in NFA and an appreciation of the exchange rate. The absence of leaning-against-the-wind components leaves the interest rate unchanged while international reserves slowly increase. Easier monetary conditions cause the current account to deteriorate. This is due to both higher imports and lower exports (which are inversely related to credit and hence money supply growth). The rather marked deterioration in the current account puts a pressure on the exchange rate, which starts a very rapid devaluation course. As a consequence, the economy starts a cumulative process which eventually explodes. The devaluation is generated by the deterioration in the overall balance of payments. This is the result of stock–flow interactions as well as of different adjustment speeds in the balance of payments components. Let us consider, in fact, the relatively low adjustment speeds of real imports and exports. We can then understand that the favorable quantity effect of the devaluation on trade flows will be felt much more slowly than the adverse terms-of-trade effect. This leads to a further

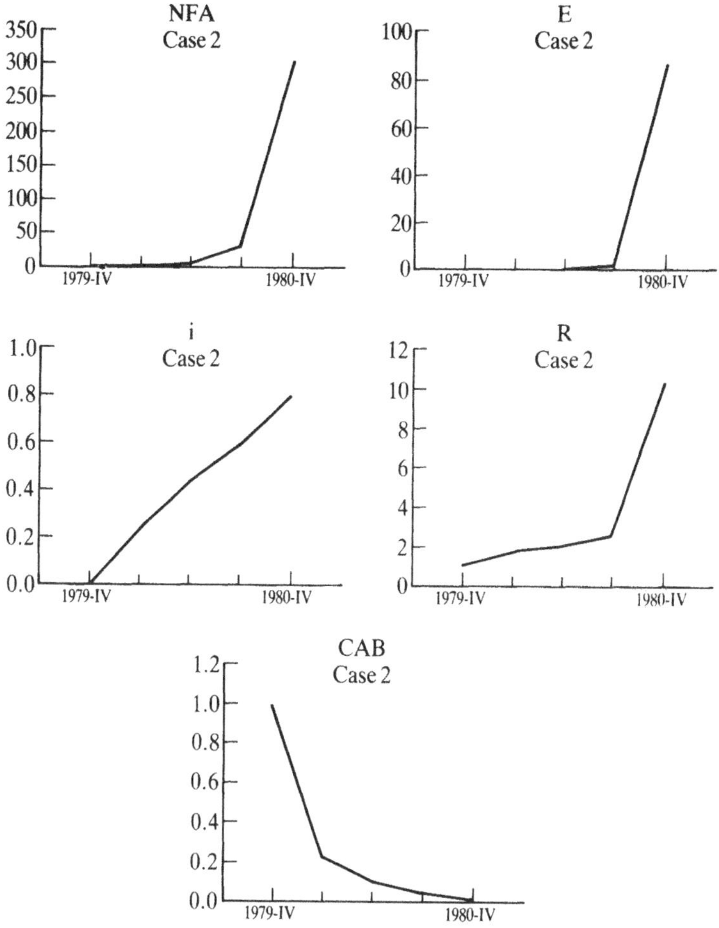

Figure 22.2 Simulations of Case 2

devaluation which is accepted by the monetary authorities, since the leaning-against-the-wind components have been suppressed. On the contrary, the central bank accumulates reserves to reach the target value for *R*. This value, in fact, keeps on increasing due to the increasing value of imports determined by the depreciation of the exchange rate. Higher reserves lead to easier monetary conditions and further current account deterioration.

Case 3

Our final exercise includes the joint liberalization of capital movements and trade flows. The basic model is modified as in case 1 with the addition of an increase in the adjustment speed of both imports and exports of goods and services. Accordingly, both α_5 and α_8 are set equal to 15, i.e. a mean time lag of roughly one week. Lower values of α_5 and α_8, i.e. longer mean time lags, did not alter the results significantly. As sensitivity analysis indicates, an increase in α_5 and α_8 exerts a stabilizing effect on the model. The main result of the simulation (see figure 22.3) is that the behavior of the model is more stable. After four years, nevertheless, the unstable movement of

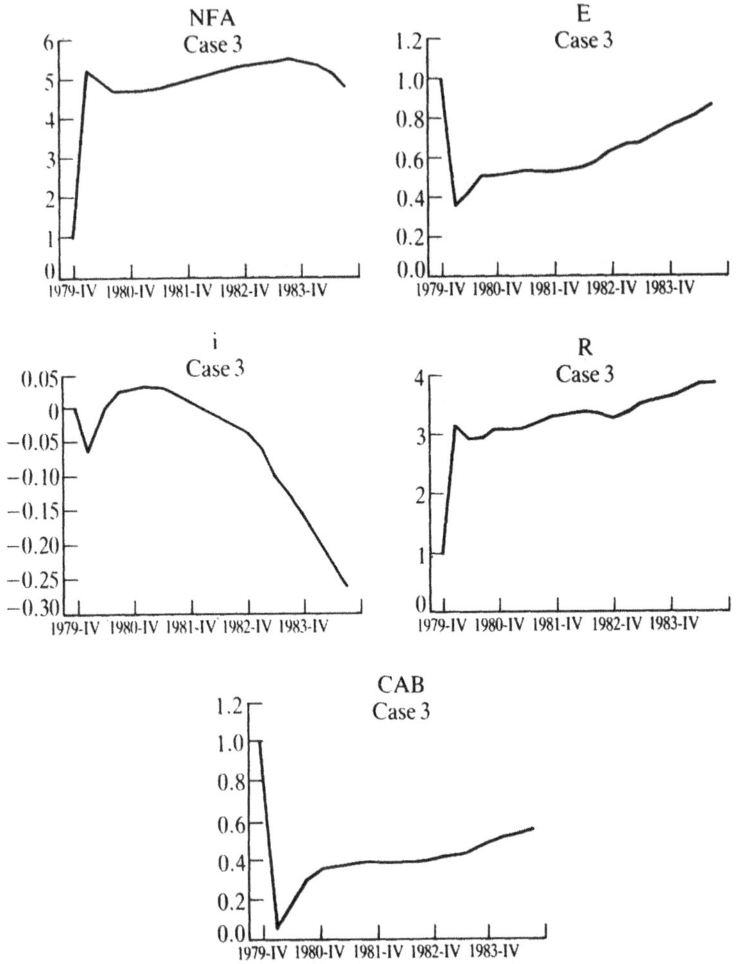

Figure 22.3 Simulations of Case 3

the exchange rate emerges as in the previous cases. The behavior of the system, however, is different. As in case 1, the increase in α_{24} leads to an immediate increase in NFA, which causes an appreciation of the exchange rate. This, in turn, leads to a decrease in the interest rate and to an increase in the level of reserves. The current account, on the contrary, heavily deteriorates as the increase in the quantity of imports is larger than the increase in the quantity of exports. Following this "impact effect" the model sets itself onto a path characterized by the following properties. The level of reserves stays at the new, higher, level as required by the higher level of imports. This determines a higher money stock which leads to a lower interest rate and hence to lower desired net foreign assets ($\widehat{NFA}$). This effect is offset, however, by the lower level (revaluation) of the exchange rate which pushes up NFA. The consequence is a stable behavior of NFA. Simultaneously, the current account is improving thanks to the catching up of XGS in spite of the negative effect of the lower level of *E* on exports. If the improvement in the current account had been faster, it could have offset the pressure on the exchange rate. This pressure is due to a level of E which is inconsistent with trade competitiveness. In the end the pressure on the exchange rate leads to instability.

This final experiment confirms that an increase in the adjustment speed of trade flows mitigates the destabilizing effects of financial liberalization. The system, however, still displays instability at the new, more deregulated, regime. This suggests that in future research we should consider further changes to the model, in particular to the policy rules.

Conclusion

In this paper we have discussed the advantages of using small econometric models specified and estimated in continuous time for the analysis of the effects of capital liberalization. We have argued that this class of models offers the possibility of giving rigorous empirical content to several theoretical and empirical issues emerging from research on capital liberalization. After briefly discussing the literature on capital liberalization, we have analyzed this problem within our model of the Italian economy. Hence we do not claim that our results have general theoretical validity.

Sensitivity analysis has shown that an increase in the adjustment speed of the stock of net foreign assets would lead to an unstable dynamic behavior. This result has been confirmed through simulation exercises which assume the presence or absence of leaning-against-the-wind intervention and different specifications of exchange rate expectations. Exchange market interventions are crucial to keep the model on an *apparently* stable path. This path is characterized by large capital inflows, a higher level of the interest rate and an appreciated currency. (Note that these features are exactly those displayed by the Italian economy in the present stage of capital liberalization.) After a three-year period, however, a violent currency crisis develops which eventually leads to the collapse of the system. Rational expectations and absence of interventions lead to the crisis in a shorter time span. On the contrary, the contemporaneous liberalization of financial and goods markets increases the stability of the system as sensitivity analysis had already suggested. While simulation results should not be taken at face value, given the somewhat mechanical nature of this kind of exercise, they do reveal potential sources of instability. They also point out the opportunity of implementing accompanying measures to avoid the breaking out of financial crises in the liberalization process.

Appendix

The equations of the model are as follows.

Private consumption

$$D \log C = \alpha_1 \log(\hat{C}/C) + \alpha_2 \log(M/M_d), \qquad \text{(A1)}$$

$$\hat{C} = \gamma_1 \, e^{\beta_1 D \log Y}(P/\mathrm{PMGS_f} \cdot E)^{\beta_2}(Y - T/P), \beta_1 \gtrless 0, \beta_2 \gtreqless 0;$$

$$M_d = \gamma_2 \, e^{-\beta_3 i_{\mathrm{TIT}}} P^{\beta_4} Y^{\beta_5}, \beta_3 \gtrless 0.$$

Rate of growth in fixed capital stock

$$Dk = \alpha_3[\alpha' \log(\hat{K}/K) - k] + \alpha_4 Da, \qquad \hat{K} = \gamma_3 \tilde{Y}, \qquad \gamma_3 = \kappa/u. \tag{A2}$$

Expected output

$$D \log \tilde{Y} = \eta \log(Y/\tilde{Y}). \tag{A3}$$

Imports

$$D \log \mathrm{MGS} = \alpha_5 \log(\mathrm{M\hat{G}S}/\mathrm{MGS}) + \alpha_6 \log(\hat{V}/V) + \alpha_7 \mathrm{PCC}, \tag{A4}$$

$$\mathrm{M\hat{G}S} = \gamma_4 P^{\beta_6}(\mathrm{PMGS_f} \cdot E)^{-\beta_7} Y^{\beta_8}, \qquad \hat{V} = \gamma_5 \tilde{Y}.$$

Exports

$$D \log \mathrm{XGS} = \alpha_8 \log(\mathrm{X\hat{G}S}/\mathrm{XGS}) - \alpha_9 Da, \tag{A5}$$

$$\mathrm{X\hat{G}S} = \gamma_6(\mathrm{PXGS}/\mathrm{PF_f} \cdot E)^{-\beta_9} \mathrm{YF}^{\beta_{10}}(\gamma_3 \mathrm{Y}/\mathrm{K})^{-\beta_{11}}.$$

Output

$$D \log Y = \alpha_{10} \log(\tilde{Y}/Y) + \alpha_{11} \log(\hat{V}/V). \tag{A6}$$

Price of output

$$D \log P = \alpha_{12} \log(\hat{P}/P) + \alpha_{13} Dm + \alpha_{14} \log(M/M_\mathrm{d}), \tag{A7}$$

$$\hat{P} = \gamma_7(\mathrm{PMGS_f} \cdot E)^{\beta_{12}} W^{\beta_{13}} \mathrm{PROD}^{-\beta_{14}}.$$

Price of exports

$$D \log \mathrm{PXGS} = \alpha_{15} \log(\mathrm{P\hat{X}GS}/\mathrm{PXGS}), \qquad \mathrm{P\hat{X}GS} = \gamma_8 P^{\beta_{15}}(\mathrm{PF_f} \cdot E)^{\beta_{16}}. \tag{A8}$$

Money wage rate

$$D \log W = \alpha_{16} \log(\hat{W}/W), \qquad \hat{W} = \gamma_9 P^{\beta_{17}} \mathrm{e}^{\lambda_4 t}. \tag{A9}$$

Interest rate

$$Di_{\mathrm{TIT}} = \alpha_{17} \log(M_\mathrm{d}/M) + \alpha_{18}[i_\mathrm{f} + \log(FR/E) - i_{\mathrm{TIT}}] + \alpha_{19} D \log E + \alpha_{20} Dr + \alpha_{21} Dh, \tag{A10}$$

Bank advances

$$D \log A = \alpha_{22} \log(\hat{A}/A) + \alpha_{23} Dk, \qquad \alpha_{23} \gtrless 0, \tag{A11}$$

$$\hat{A} = \gamma_{10} \mathrm{e}^{\beta_{18} i_{\mathrm{TIT}}} M, \qquad \beta_{18} \gtrless 0.$$

Net foreign assets

$$D \log \text{NFA} = \alpha_{24} \log (\hat{\text{NFA}})/\text{NFA}) + \alpha_{25} \log (\text{PMGS}_f \cdot E \cdot \text{MGS}/\text{PXGS} \cdot \text{XGS}),$$

$$\alpha_{25} < 0, \tag{A12}$$

$$\hat{\text{NFA}} = \gamma_{11} e^{\beta_{19}[i_f + \log(FR/E) - i_{\text{TIT}}]}(PY)^{\beta_{20}}(\text{PF}_f \cdot E \cdot \text{YF})^{-\beta_{21}}.$$

Monetary authorities' reaction function on money supply

$$Dm = \alpha_{26}(\hat{m} - m) + \delta_3 Dh + \delta_4 Dr, \tag{A13}$$

$$\hat{m} = m^* + \{\delta_1[D \log (PY) - (\rho_P + \rho_Y)] + \delta_2 Di_{\text{TIT}}\}, \qquad \delta_1 \gtrless 0, \delta_2 \gtrless 0.$$

Taxes

$$D \log T = \alpha_{27} \log (\hat{T}/T), \qquad \hat{T} = \gamma_{14}(PY)^{\beta_{22}}. \tag{A14}$$

Public expenditure

$$D \log G = \alpha_{28} \log (\gamma_{13} Y/G) + \alpha_{29} D \log Y, \qquad \alpha_{29} \gtrless 0. \tag{A15}$$

Monetary authorities' reaction function on international reserves

$$D \log R = b\delta_5 \log (E_e/\mathbf{E}) + (1 - b)\delta_6 \log (\hat{E}/E) - \delta_7 D \log E + \delta_8 \log (\hat{R}/R), \tag{A16}$$

$$\hat{E} = \text{PXGS}/\gamma_{14}\text{PF}_f, \ \hat{R} = \gamma_{15}\text{PMGS}_f \cdot E \cdot \text{MGS}, \ b = \begin{cases} 1 \text{ under fixed exchange rates,} \\ 0 \text{ under floating exchange rates.} \end{cases}$$

Inventories

$$\text{DV} = Y + \text{MGS} - C - \text{DK} - \text{XGS} - G. \tag{A17}$$

Fixed capital stock

$$D \log K = k. \tag{A18}$$

Rate of growth in money supply

$$m = D \log M. \tag{A19}$$

Public sector borrowing requirement

$$DH = PG - T. \tag{A20}$$

Rate of growth in international reserves

$$r = D \log R. \tag{A21}$$

Rate of growth in bank advances

$$a = D \log A. \tag{A22}$$

Rate of growth in H

$$h = D \log H. \qquad \text{(A23)}$$

Balance of payments

$$\text{PXGS} \cdot \text{XGS} - \text{PMGS}_f \cdot E \cdot \text{MGS} + (\text{UT}_a - \text{UT}_p) - \text{DNFA} - \text{DR} = 0. \qquad \text{(A24)}$$

Variables of the model

The endogenous variables are listed below.

A	= nominal stock of bank advances
a	= proportional rate of growth of A
C	= private consumption expenditure in real terms
E	= lira–dollar spot exchange rate
G	= public expenditure in real terms
H	= public sector borrowing requirement
h	= proportional rate of change of H
i_{TIT}	= domestic nominal interest rate
K	= stock of fixed capital in real terms
k	= proportional rate of change of K
M	= nominal stock of money (M2)
m	= proportional rate of change of M
MGS	= imports of goods and services in real terms
NFA	= nominal stock of net foreign assets
P	= domestic price level
PXGS	= export price level
R	= nominal stock of international reserves
r	= proportional rate of change of R
T	= nominal taxes
V	= stock of inventories in real terms
W	= money wage rate
XGS	= exports of goods and services in real terms
Y	= real net domestic product and income
Y	= expected real net domestic product and income.

The exogenous variables are as follows.

E_C	= official lira–dollar parity under fixed exchange rates
FR	= forward exchange rate
i_f	= foreign nominal interest rate
PF_f	= foreign competitors' export price level (in foreign currency)
PMGS_f	= import price level (in foreign currency)
PROD	= labour productivity
t	= time
$(\text{UT}_a - \text{UT}_p)$	= net unilateral transfers, in nominal terms
YF	= real world income.

Notes

1. We wish to thank (with the usual disclaimer) two anonymous referees for their useful comments. Research support from the University of Rome "La Sapienza" and the Ministry of the University and of Scientific and Technological Research is gratefully acknowledged.
2. The introduction of capital control variables in the equation for real imports reflected an attempt to account for clandestine capital movements. An earlier study (Gandolfo 1977) found significant empirical evidence for this phenomenon in the Italian economy on the import side. Clandestine outflows are positively related to controls on international capital movements.

References

Bergstrom, A. R. (ed.) (1976). *Statistical Inference in Continuous Time Economic Models.* Amsterdam: North-Holland.

Bergstrom, A. R. (1984). "Continuous time stochastic models and issues of aggregation over time," in: Z. Griliches, and M. D. Intriligator (eds) *Handbook of Econometrics*, volume 2, chapter 20. Amsterdam: North-Holland.

Bergstrom, A. R., and C. R. Wymer (1976). "A model of disequilibrium neoclassical growth and its application to the United Kingdom," in A. R. Bergstrom (ed.) (1976) 267–327.

Driffill, J. (1988). "The stability and sustainability of the European Monetary System with perfect capital markets," in F. Giavazzi, S. Micossi, and M. Miller (eds) *The European Monetary System.* Cambridge: Cambridge University Press.

Gandolfo, G. (1977). "Esportazioni clandestine di capitali e sovrafatturazione delle importazioni," *Rassegna Economica*, 41, 1515–26.

Gandolfo, G. (1981). *Qualitative Analysis and Econometric Estimation of Continuous Time Dynamic Models.* Amsterdam: North-Holland.

Gandolfo, G. (1987). *International Economics II.* Berlin: Springer-Verlag.

Gandolfo, G., and P. C. Padoan (1980). "A macrodynamic model of the Italian economy: theory and empirical results," in J. Gutenbaum, and M. Niezgódka (eds) *Applications of Systems Theory to Economics, Management and Technology*, pp. 217–40. Warsaw: Polish Scientific Publishers.

Gandolfo, G., and P. C. Padoan (1984). *A Disequilibrium Model of Real and Financial Accumulation in an Open Economy.* Berlin: Springer-Verlag.

Gandolfo, G., and P. C. Padoan (1990). "The Italian continuous time model: theory and empirical results," *Economic Modelling* 7, April.

Jonson, P. D., W. J. McKibbin, and R. G. Trevor (1982). "Exchange rates and capital flows: a sensitivity analysis," *Canadian Journal of Economics*, 1, 669–92.

Khan, M., and R. Zahler (1983). "The macroeconomic effects of changes in barriers to trade and capital flows: a simulation analysis," *IMF Staff Papers* 30, 223–82.

Khan, M., and R. Zahler (1985). "Trade and financial liberalization given external shocks and inconsistent domestic policies," *IMF Staff Papers* 32, 22–55.

Mundell, R. A. (1963). "Capital mobility and stabilization policy under fixed and flexible exchange rates," *Canadian Journal of Economics and Political Science* 29, 475–85.

Obstfeld, M. (1988). "Competitiveness, realignments and speculation: the role of financial markets," in F. Giavazzi, S. Micossi, and M. Miller (eds) *The European Monetary System.* Cambridge: Cambridge University Press.

Wymer, C. R., various dates, TRANSF, RESIMUL, CONTINEST, PREDIC, APREDIC computer programs and relative manuals; supplement 3 on solution of nonlinear differential equation systems.

Wyplosz, C. (1986). "Capital controls and balance of payments crisis," *Journal of International Money and Finance* 5, 167–79.

23

Economies of Scale in the New Zealand Electricity Distribution Industry

David E. A. Giles and Nicolas S. Wyatt

Introduction

The New Zealand electricity industry is currently undergoing a process of deregulation, and there is considerable interest in its future structure. This industry is divided into three horizontal layers, dealing with the generation, high-voltage transmission, and final distribution of electricity. Although a few distributors generate a significant proportion of their requirements, there has been no trend towards vertical integration. Generation and transmission are currently under the control of the Electricity Corporation of New Zealand (ECNZ), from whom the various regional Electricity Supply Authorities (ESAs) purchase bulk electricity, and transmit it from ECNZ's substations to the end users.[1] This study focuses on these ESAs and examines whether there are economies of scale in the distribution of electricity in New Zealand.

At the time of our sample there were 60 ESAs in New Zealand,[2] a mountainous country comprising two principal islands, with a population of approximately 3.3 million people. Some 70 percent of the population live in the North Island (44,281 square miles), the Auckland metropolitan area accounting for 840,000 people, while in the South Island (58,093 square miles) the largest urban centre is Christchurch (population 300,000). Constitutionally, the ESAs are of two types – Electric Power Boards (EPBs), which are independent statutory bodies run by boards elected from the area over which the ESA has a franchise; and the Municipal Electricity Departments (MEDs), which are the trading arms of territorial local government and are managed by committees of the relevant local council. Each ESA has an area franchise and an associated obligation to supply electricity without discrimination. Only licensed firms may distribute electricity. Strictly, these franchises do not exclude the operation of competitors, but in practice only one franchise has been issued for each area.

Debate over the scale of electricity distributors in New Zealand has raged for years. The geographical features of the country are unusually relevant, but given the number of consumers and the relatively small annual output (19,444 GWh in 1986/87), it is not surprising that the appropriateness of 60 or so ESAs has been questioned. A Royal Commission headed by Stanton (1959) concluded that the (then 83) ESAs were technically efficient, but would be improved by amalgamations. So 26 supply areas were recommended, but without explicit reference to (economic) scale economies.

The latter were explored to some extent by Jones (1987) and with respect to the Christchurch region by McCutcheon et al. (1987). None of these studies employs any formal econometric analysis.

Several technical and organizational factors influence economies of scale in electricity distribution. Organizational economies may arise at the firm level as a result of staff specialization and staff control costs. Below some size a firm may not be able to employ the optimal resources, while beyond some other size the firm faces increasing costs in controlling these resources. Organizational economies can arise from increasing the specialization of managerial staff – the benefits of a larger firm depend on the gains from having this expertise "in house" in terms of cost and firm-specific knowledge gained. Conversely, organizational diseconomies may develop beyond a certain firm size, perhaps because of increasing communication problems, the difficulty of maintaining consistent objectives, and the potential for managerial "slack."

The principal technical economies are in distribution equipment, which lead to economies of density, economies in capacity expansion, and economies in the provision of capacity to meet peak requirements. An increase in equipment capacity leads to a less than proportionate rise in equipment cost. Larger capacity equipment also yields lower system costs as higher voltage operation lowers system energy losses. These factors contribute to economies of density. As the number of customers, and energy demand, rises for a given area, average cost falls. Supply security can also be improved when density rises. Several low-voltage networks can be interconnected with open switches to provide different flow paths, so that a fault that might otherwise cut off supply can be bypassed. Such benefits are exhausted at a certain scale of operation by the requirement to keep separate the networks supplied by each ECNZ substation. All of this points to the potential for scale economies in this industry – the extent to which such economies are in fact present or are exhausted is, of course, an empirical issue.

Econometric studies of scale economies in electricity industry in other countries focus primarily on generation rather than distribution, and reflect the vertically integrated nature of this industry elsewhere, see for example Christensen and Greene (1976), Betancourt and Edwards (1987), and Sing (1987). Other relevant studies include those of Neuberg (1977), Heuttner and Landon (1978), Aivazian et al. (1987), and some of the material discussed by Weiss (1975). A typical finding is that the average cost curves exhibit extensive "flat" regions – i.e. there is a wide range of outputs consistent with essentially constant returns to scale.

In this paper we use a Translog cost model and cross-section data for the 1986/87 financial year to estimate economies of scale in the distribution of electricity in New Zealand. The ESAs have a statutory obligation to supply electricity and are price takers in the purchase of bulk electricity from ECNZ (this being their major operating cost). An econometric model of cost, rather than production, is appropriate given that the firms are cost minimizers rather than profit maximizers.[3] The model and data used are described in the next two sections. The fourth section discusses the results; and our conclusions are given in the final section.

The Model

Costs for the firms in this industry are of the form

$$C = f(Y, P, I), \tag{1}$$

where C denotes total cost, Y is output, $\mathbf{P}$ is a vector of n input prices, and $\mathbf{I}$ is a vector of m additional industry-specific variables. In formulating such a relationship, it is assumed that output and input prices are exogenous, and that (for a given technology) firms adjust input levels so as to minimize costs of production. Given the comments at the end of the last section, and our use of cross-section data, such assumptions seem reasonable in this case. In common with other related studies, we use the Translog function (e.g. Christensen et al. (1971, 1973)) to formalize (1):

$$\begin{aligned} \ln C = {} & \alpha_0 + \alpha_y \ln Y + \tfrac{1}{2}\gamma_{yy}(\ln Y)^2 + \sum_{i=1}^{n} \gamma_{yi} \ln Y \ln P_i \\ & + \frac{1}{2}\sum_{i=1}^{n}\sum_{j=1}^{n} \gamma_{ij} \ln P_i \ln P_j + \sum_{i=1}^{n} \alpha_i \ln P_i + \sum_{k=1}^{m} \beta_k \ln I_k \\ & + \frac{1}{2}\sum_{k=1}^{m}\sum_{g=1}^{m} \beta_{kg} \ln I_k \ln I_g + \sum_{k=1}^{m} \beta_{ky} \ln I_k \ln Y \\ & + \sum_{k=1}^{m}\sum_{i=1}^{n} \theta_{ki} \ln I_k \ln P_i, \end{aligned} \tag{2}$$

where $\gamma_{ij} = \gamma_{ji}$ and $\beta_{kg} = \beta_{gk}$. The attractions of this functional form are that it is flexible enough to represent quite general production structures; it imposes no restrictions on factor substitutability; and it allows economies of scale to vary with output. To ensure that (2) is consistent with a well-behaved production function, it must be homogeneous of degree one in input prices, which implies

$$\begin{gathered} \sum_{j=1}^{n} \gamma_{ij} = \sum_{i=1}^{n}\sum_{j=1}^{n} \gamma_{ij} = \sum_{i=1}^{n} \gamma_{ij} = 0, \\ \sum_{i=1}^{n} \gamma_{yi} = 0, \qquad \sum_{i=1}^{n} \alpha_i = 1, \qquad \sum_{i=1}^{n} \theta_{ki} = 0; \qquad k = 1, \ldots, m. \end{gathered} \tag{3}$$

The symmetry of the γ_{ij} terms follows from Young's theorem, given that the cost function is continuously twice differentiable. If X_i is the quantity of input i, applying Shephard's lemma, the associated input cost share equations are

$$S_i = (P_i X_i / C) = \alpha_i + \gamma_{yi} \ln Y + \sum_{j=1}^{n} \gamma_{ij} \ln P_j + \sum_{k=1}^{m} \theta_{ki} \ln I_k, \qquad i = 1, \ldots, n. \tag{4}$$

Adding normally distributed error terms, our full model comprises equation (2) and the equations (4). The model is estimated by joint maximum likelihood (ML), with all of the mentioned parameter restrictions imposed. The well-known singularity of the contemporaneous error covariance matrix associated with such allocation models is allowed for in the usual way – one of the share equations is dropped from the system, the coefficient estimates being invariant to the choice of this equation. Our primary interest is the measurement of scale economies. As is conventional, such economies are defined in terms of the relationship between cost and output along the expansion path. That is, with fixed input prices (and industry-specific variables) and costs minimized at each output level. Specifically, we define them as the ratio of average to marginal costs:

$$\text{SCALE} \equiv (\partial \ln C/\partial \ln Y)^{-1} = \left[\alpha_y + \gamma_{yy} \ln Y + \sum_{i=1}^{n} \gamma_{yi} \ln P_i + \sum_{k=1}^{m} \beta_{ky} \ln I_k\right]^{-1}, \quad (5)$$

so there are scale economies (diseconomies) if SCALE is greater (less) than unity. The requirement that SCALE declines monotonically, as Y increases, holds if and only if $\gamma_{yy} > 0$. Given estimates of the parameters, and fixing the values of input prices and the industry-specific variables, setting (5) to unity and solving for Y allows the calculation of the output level at which such a firm's average cost is minimized. Dividing this output level into the total value of industry output suggests the number of such firms that are consistent with average cost minimization.

Data

Our sample comprises 60 cross-section data points for the 1986/87 financial year; the latest available. Output is defined as total retail sales of electricity (kWh). The sample is characterized by a conglomeration of ESAs with small output – 52 of the 60 firms had an annual output of 500 GWh or less. Of the remainder, one (Auckland) had an output nearly seven times as great as this, more than ten times the average output, and only slightly less than the combined outputs of the next three largest ESAs.[4]

Total cost is the simple sum of four input costs; those associated with labor, capital, electricity purchased, and other. The last of these is measured as total reported expenditure in the year in question, less expenditures on labor, capital, and on purchasing and (if applicable) generating electricity, less expenditures relating to the retailing of appliances. Accordingly, these "other" costs essentially relate to maintenance and operation, administration, loan interest, and depreciation. In the case of labor, total salaries and wages were adjusted to exclude amounts associated with any electricity generation or appliance sales, or capitalized in particular capital projects. Figures for the historic value of each ESA's assets were inflated and depreciated to allow for a life of 30 years for most distribution equipment. Different capital items were treated separately with respect to depreciation rates and method of depreciation (diminishing value or straight line). This breakdown distinguished between distribution equipment; distribution and transmission buildings; public lighting; land; offices, stores, and workshops; loose tools, plant, and furniture; motor vehicles; and other capital items. Aggregate capital figures were then constructed. The cost of purchasing electricity includes that associated with purchases from ECNZ, plus any from firms involved in cogeneration or from other ESAs. Generation costs (in the few cases, where relevant) were excluded from the analysis to ensure comparability across ESAs. A commensurate value was calculated and included in total electricity costs in such cases. Such values were calculated taking account of the structure of the bulk supply tariff, which distinguishes between winter zone and anytime demands; between day and night energy rates; and between location in the North and South Islands.

Input prices were defined as follows. The prices of labor and "other" inputs are the associated expenditures divided by the number of employees. Three possible definitions of the price of capital inputs were considered: total capital value divided by circuit kilometers of distribution line; the value of capital divided by the combined amount of circuit kilometers of distribution line plus kVA transformer capacity, expressed as circuit kilometer "equivalents"; a constant capital price across ESAs.[5] Two alternative measures of the price of electricity purchased were considered: total electricity cost divided by total electricity purchased and generated (cents/kWh); and constant values of 2.8084 cents/kWh for South Island ESAs, and 3.4318 cents/kWh for North Island ESAs, reflecting the average energy components in the wholesale electricity tariff.

Finally, we consider up to five industry-specific variables. Two of these are dummy variables for the "type" of ESA ($\ln(I_1) = 1$, EPB; $= 0$, MED); and for ESA location ($\ln(I_2) = 1$, North Island; $= 0$, South Island). We also considered the load factor (I_3) and density. Two possible measures of the latter were considered – I_4 = number of consumers per square kilometer of licensed area; or I_4 = number of consumers per circuit kilometer of distribution line. Also considered was a regional dummy variable ($\ln(I_5) = 1$, urban; $= 0$, rural). Further details of the data and their construction are given by Wyatt et al. (1989).

Results

Joint ML estimation and the other computations were undertaken with the TSP package (Hall et al. 1988). Equation (2) was constrained to avoid the multicollinearity that would otherwise arise because $\ln(I_i) = (\ln(I_i))^2$ $(i = 1, 2, 5)$. Not all of β_1, β_2, β_5, β_{11}, β_{22}, and β_{55} are identifiable in our model and so the relevant terms were coded as $1.5\beta_i \ln(I_i)$ $(i = 1, 2, 5)$. When all of the industry-specific variables (however defined) were included in the model, the results were economically implausible: the estimates of γ_{yy} were negative. A sequence of nested model tests revealed the load factor to be the main source of this problem,[6] although when it is removed from the model we were still unable to obtain plausible results with a significant rural–urban effect. Accordingly, we discarded these two regressors. A formal model-selection procedure was then used to determine the final specification of the model. Akaike's information criterion (AIC) was used to discriminate between the non-nested specifications that arise with the alternative definitions of density and the prices of capital and electricity purchased. With the variable definitions fixed, a sequence of nested likelihood ratio tests (LRTs) was used to determine whether the model should be simplified further by deleting other industry-specific variables. These asymptotic tests were applied in the manner described by Mizon (1977) so as to control their true size.

This procedure favored the first of the measures of density and electricity price, and the second measure of capital price. With these definitions, the results of our LRTs appear in table 23.1. Two non-nested specifications cannot be rejected, so the final selection is again based on AIC, resulting in the retention of density and the "type" of ESA as the industry-specific variables. The lack of significance of the North–South dummy apparently reflects the fact that the electricity purchase price variable is already capturing the relevant effects. The ML estimates of the model's parameters appear in table 23.2.

Table 23.1 Tests of nested hypotheses

Model specification tests

Industry-specific variables included

Maintained hypothesis	*Restricted hypothesis*	LRT[a]	v	AIC
(I_1, I_2, I_4)	(I_1, I_2)	N.A.[b]	—	—
(I_1, I_2, I_4)	(I_2, I_4)	11.97	7	−16.97
(I_2, I_4)	I_2	N.A.[b]	—	—
(I_2, I_4)	I_4	20.26[c]	6	—
(I_1, I_2, I_4)	(I_1, I_4)	8.76	7	−17.03
(I_1, I_4)	I_4	23.46[c]	6	—
(I_1, I_4)	I_1	N.A.[b]		

Homotheticity test[d]

Maintained hypothesis	*Restrictions*	LRT	v
See table 23.2	$\gamma_{y1} = \gamma_{y2} = \gamma_{y3} = 0$	20.40[c]	3

[a] LRT is asymptotically χ^2 with v degrees of freedom.
[b] Not acceptable. Estimated coefficients conflict with prior economic theory.
[c] Significant at the 1 percent level or higher.
[d] Homogeneity restrictions are nested within homotheticity restrictions, so the former are rejected. Testing separately for homogeneity also leads to rejection: LRT = 21.86 ($v = 6$).

Each variable enters the model in several forms. The overall significance of the industry-specific variables has been established via the LRTs. Individually, many of the parameters are also significant. Signing the parameters is not trivial. The relevant issue is the sign of the partial derivative of C with respect to the variable of interest. Equivalently, we can sign the associated elasticity, which is more easily derived, given the form of (2). For example, we expect $\partial \ln C/\partial \ln Y$ (= 1/SCALE) and $\partial \ln C/\partial \ln P_i$ $(= S_i)$ $(i = 1, \ldots, 4)$ to be positive; and in the case of "density", $\partial \ln C/\partial \ln I_4 < 0$. The anticipated sign for the ESA "type" dummy variable is ambiguous. Using the estimated parameters from table 23.2, we have evaluated each of these derivatives at each point in the sample. There are no exceptions to the anticipated signs, and the estimated shares are all positive fractions. Given the imposition of the restriction $\sum_i \gamma_{yi} = 0$, homotheticity of the underlying production function would imply $\gamma_{y1} = \gamma_{y2} = \gamma_{y3} = 0$. Adding the additional restrictions $\gamma_{yy} = \beta_{1y} = \beta_{4y} = 0$ implies homogeneity of the production function. Homotheticity and homogeneity are both rejected by LRTs (see table 23.1), and so are not imposed in the following analysis. Ordering the data by increasing value of output, there is no evidence of heteroskedasticity in the residuals. However, to be conservative, all reported standard errors and tests are based on White's (1980) heteroskedasticity-consistent covariance matrix estimator.

Estimated scale economy measures appear in table 23.3. These are obtained from (5) in two ways – first, as is conventional, $\overline{\text{SCALE}}$ is calculated with all variables except output fixed (here, to their sample means); and secondly, SCALE is calculated at each individual sample point.[7] The latter figures are interesting, but the former are of primary importance and only on these can cross-firm comparisons be based. The point estimates of $\overline{\text{SCALE}}$ suggest there are economies of scale in this industry

Table 23.2 Maximum likelihood estimates

Parameter	*Estimate (asymptotic "t"-value)*	*Parameter*	*Estimate (asymptotic "t"-value)*
α_0	7.775 (0.93)	α_1	−0.060 (−0.16)
α_y	0.661 (0.75)	α_2	−1.170 (−2.91)
γ_{yy}	0.031 (0.58)	α_3	2.155 (4.68)
γ_{y1}	−0.004 (−0.51)	β_1	−0.148 (−0.08)
γ_{y2}	−0.018 (−1.59)	β_4	0.267 (0.46)
γ_{y3}	0.023 (2.05)	β_{44}	0.001 (0.02)
γ_{22}	0.197 (8.01)	β_{14}	−0.068 (−0.88)
γ_{32}	−0.168 (−7.17)	β_{1y}	−0.037 (−0.24)
γ_{42}	−0.013 (−0.42)	β_{4y}	−0.002 (−0.06)
γ_{33}	0.183 (4.64)	θ_{11}	−0.010 (−0.39)
γ_{43}	−0.000 (−0.02)	θ_{12}	0.150 (3.20)
γ_{41}	−0.018 (−0.83)	θ_{13}	−0.126 (−3.33)
		θ_{41}	0.002 (0.41)
		θ_{42}	−0.028 (−3.09)
		θ_{43}	0.024 (2.90)

Equation:	ln C	S_1	S_2	S_3
R^2	0.964	0.661	0.485	0.433

Note: Estimates of remaining parameters are derivable from the homogeneity and symmetry restrictions. Asymptotic "*t*"-values (in parentheses) are standard normally distributed. The asymptotic standard errors on which these are based are calculated using White's heteroskedasticity-consistent covariance matrix estimator.

– numerically, all of these values exceed unity, except for that of Auckland, the ESA with by far the largest output. The Wald test is used to test the hypothesis of unitary economies of scale. In fact, we test if the reciprocal of SCALE (from (5)) is unity. The hypothesis of interest is formulated in this equivalent way to minimize the distortion of the true size of the Wald test (from the nominal size chosen) in finite samples. This choice is based on the results of Gregory and Veall (1985) and Phillips and Park (1988). The results obtained appear in table 23.3, where we see that for 26 cases the $\overline{\text{SCALE}}$ estimates are significantly greater than unity. No such estimate is significantly less than unity – even at the level of output experienced by the

Table 23.3 Scale economy measures

	Supply authority	*Output* (10^9 kWh)	$\overline{SCALE}$	*SCALE*
1	Ashburton	0.158	1.090 (3.85)**	1.093 (1.35)
2	Auckland	3.426	0.988 (0.01)	1.016 (0.02)
3	Bay of Islands	0.194	1.082 (3.11)*	1.080 (1.12)
4	Bay of Plenty	0.402	1.057 (0.70)	1.067 (0.43)
5	Bluff	0.017	1.177 (1.41)	1.146 (1.36)
6	Buller	0.082	1.114 (3.43)*	1.117 (1.46)
7	Cambridge	0.087	1.112 (3.56)*	1.119 (1.42)
8	Central Canterbury	0.427	1.055 (0.61)	1.066 (0.50)
9	Central Hawkes Bay	0.082	1.114 (3.44)*	1.101 (1.59)
10	Central Waikato	0.486	1.050 (0.44)	1.061 (1.05)
11	Christchurch	1.475	1.014 (0.01)	1.012 (0.01)
12	Dannevirke	0.070	1.120 (3.08)*	1.124 (2.11)
13	Dunedin	0.731	1.037 (0.15)	1.018 (0.02)
14	Egmont	0.191	1.082 (3.17)*	1.086 (2.03)
15	Franklin	0.248	1.073 (2.06)	1.075 (1.83)
16	Hamilton	0.136	1.095 (4.10)**	1.082 (2.77)*
17	Hawkes Bay	0.565	1.045 (0.30)	1.058 (0.65)
18	Horowhenua	0.257	1.072 (1.91)	1.094 (2.28)
19	Hutt Valley	0.967	1.027 (0.07)	1.058 (0.71)
20	Invercargill	0.216	1.078 (2.65)	1.073 (5.03)**
21	Kaiapoi	0.022	1.166 (1.57)	1.162 (1.45)
22	King Country	0.086	1.112 (3.54)*	1.092 (1.20)
23	Manwatu-Oroua	0.306	1.066 (1.32)	1.076 (1.43)
24	Marlborough	0.178	1.085 (3.46)*	1.091 (1.04)
25	Napier	0.076	1.117 (3.26)*	1.122 (2.64)
26	Nelson	0.109	1.103 (4.00)**	1.105 (6.30)**
27	New Plymouth	0.272	1.070 (1.71)	1.050 (0.22)
28	North Auckland	0.417	1.055 (0.64)	1.062 (0.64)
29	North Canterbury	0.198	1.081 (3.03)*	1.082 (0.78)
30	Otago	0.157	1.090 (3.86)**	1.079 (0.78)
31	Otago Central	0.204	1.080 (2.90)*	1.083 (0.61)
32	Palmerston North	0.180	1.085 (3.42)*	1.072 (2.91)*
33	Port Hills	0.079	1.115 (3.36)*	1.106 (3.48)*
34	Poverty Bay	0.207	1.080 (2.84)*	1.083 (1.15)
35	Riccarton	0.049	1.134 (2.42)	1.147 (1.57)
36	Rotorua	0.285	1.068 (1.55)	1.080 (1.65)
37	South Canterbury	0.260	1.072 (1.87)	1.079 (0.68)
38	Southland	0.424	1.055 (0.62)	1.046 (0.14)
39	Taranaki	0.250	1.073 (2.03)	1.078 (0.98)
40	Tararua	0.046	1.136 (2.33)	1.134 (1.69)
41	Tasman	0.297	1.067 (1.42)	1.080 (0.76)
42	Taumarunui	0.021	1.169 (1.53)	1.140 (1.94)
43	Taupo	0.162	1.089 (3.78)*	1.058 (0.10)
44	Tauranga MED	0.056	1.128 (2.65)	1.120 (1.55)
45	Taurange EPB	0.349	1.061 (0.98)	1.075 (1.69)
46	Te Awamutu	0.102	1.106 (3.89)**	1.111 (2.02)
47	Thames Valley	1.062	1.024 (0.05)	1.029 (0.08)
48	Thames-Coromandel	0.030	1.154 (1.82)	1.115 (1.51)
49	Timaru	0.120	1.100 (4.09)*	1.108 (3.43)*
50	Wairarapa	0.195	1.082 (3.08)*	1.089 (1.43)
51	Wairoa MED	0.019	1.171 (1.49)	1.159 (1.42)

continued

Table 23.3 *(continued)*

Supply authority	*Output* (10^9 kWh)	$\overline{SCALE}$	*SCALE*
52 Wairoa EPB	0.038	1.144 (2.07)	1.130 (1.55)
53 Waitaki	0.146	1.092 (4.01)**	1.100 (1.35)
54 Waitemata	1.280	1.019 (0.02)	1.030 (0.16)
55 Waitomo	0.113	1.102 (4.04)**	1.097 (1.39)
56 Wanganui-Rangatikei	0.351	1.061 (0.97)	1.060 (0.55)
57 Wellington	0.837	1.032 (0.10)	1.020 (0.04)
58 West Coast	0.118	1.100 (4.09)**	1.113 (1.08)
59 Whakatane	0.038	1.143 (2.08)	1.130 (1.63)
60 Whangarei	0.092	1.109 (3.69)*	1.104 (2.80)*
Average	0.324	1.088	1.087

Note: $\chi^2_{(1)}$ Wald-test values appear in parentheses. These are calculated using White's heteroskedasticity-consistent covariance matrix estimator.

* Significantly different from unity at 10 percent level.

** Significantly different from unity at 5 percent level.

Auckland ESA, there is no significant evidence that scale economies have been exhausted. This reinforces the earlier comment that there is evidence of scale economies in New Zealand electricity distribution.

The average cost (AC) curve implied by our estimated Translog model appears in figure 23.1, evaluated with all variables other than output set to their sample means. It exhibits the typical "flat" region mentioned in the first section: AC is minimized ($\overline{\text{SCALE}} = 1$) at an annual output of 2,315 GWh, but casual observation suggests that any output in the range 500–3,500 GWh is essentially consistent with minimum AC. In 1986/87, total output for the industry was 19,444 GWh, so we see that eight or nine "typical" ESAs with equal output would have ensured AC minimization. Taking account of the flat section of the AC curve suggests that up to 39 such ESAs would not have been inconsistent with this objective. This number can be formalized by noting that the asymptotic standard error associated with the AC-minimizing number of "typical" firms (8.4) is 19.855, so a 90 percent confidence interval puts an upper bound of 41 on this number of ESAs.

As a sensitivity test of our results we respecified the model to include only three input costs: the cost of electricity was discarded, as being largely beyond the control of ESAs, total cost was redefined accordingly, and the complete analysis was replicated. The preferred model specification used the second definitions of density and capital price, and the North–South dummy variable was retained. Our broad conclusions were unaltered: average cost was minimized at 1,748 GWh per year, implying 11 firms in the industry; a 90 percent confidence interval on this number of firms allows for up to 40 ESAs without departing significantly from AC-minimization; more than half of the $\overline{\text{SCALE}}$ and SCALE estimates were significantly greater than unity, and only one was numerically (but not significantly) less. Full details are given by Wyatt et al. (1989).[8]

Finally, we consider the (Allen) partial elasticities of substitution between the four factor inputs, which for the Translog model are defined as $\sigma_{ii} = (\gamma_{ii} + S_i^2 - S_i)/S_i^2$; $i = 1, \ldots, 4$, and $\sigma_{ij} = (\gamma_{ij} + S_iS_j)/S_iS_j$; $i, j = 1, \ldots, 4$; $i \neq j$.

We also consider the cost (price) elasticities of factor demand: $\eta_{ij} = S_j\sigma_{ij}$;

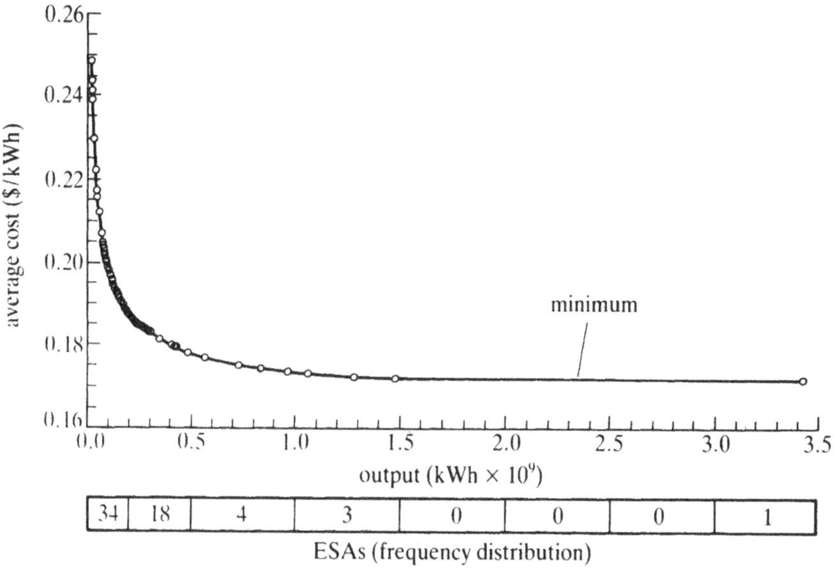

Figure 23.1 Estimated TRANSLOG AC curve

$i, j = 1, \ldots, 4$. (These formulas are given by Berndt and Wood (1975).)

Estimates of these elasticities, together with asymptotic standard errors, appear in table 23.4. These estimates are reported for the firms with the largest and smallest output levels in our sample, to summarize the extent to which the results depend on the sample values. With one exception (labor when output is at its maximum), all inputs are own-price responsive. However, these responses are generally not significant – the only significant own-cost elasticities are for capital and for labor when output is small.

As is frequently the case in studies of the energy sector, capital and labor are found to be substitutes, and significantly so for small output levels. The signs of the other elasticities suggest that while the labor and "other" inputs are complements, all other pairs of factors are substitutable to some degree. However, none of these effects is statistically significant.

Conclusions

This paper uses a Translog cost model to estimate economies of scale in electricity distribution in New Zealand. We find evidence that the number of firms currently in the industry is greater than that consistent with average cost minimization. Our results indicate that, at the output levels associated with more than a third of the firms in our sample, there are significant scale economies, and that these economies are not (significantly) exhausted even at the highest sample value. Not surprisingly, the number of Electricity Supply Authorities in New Zealand has attracted attention over the years. Our results show this attention to be justified – with figure 23.1 in mind, and calculating the total industry cost with eight identical firms operating at AC-minimizing output, we find that would be a 15.5 percent reduction in this total

Table 23.4 Estimated elasticities

Partial elasticities of factor substitution (σ_{ij})

(i, j)	*Labor*		*Capital*		*Electricity*		*Other*	
	max	min	max	min	max	min	max	min
Labor	15.76	−4.10*						
	(14.05)	(1.31)						
Capital	0.19	0.64*	−0.10	−0.26*				
	(0.75)	(0.33)	(0.07)	(0.14)				
Electricity	−0.43	0.69	0.10	0.06	−0.31	−0.34		
	(3.20)	(0.70)	(0.13)	(0.13)	(0.43)	(0.22)		
Other	−10.12	−2.54	0.58	0.36	0.97	0.98	−6.46	−6.14
	(13.48)	(4.29)	(1.00)	(1.52)	(1.50)	(1.12)	(17.74)	(19.28)

Cost elasticities of factor demand (η_{ij})

(i, j)	*Labor*		*Capital*		*Electricity*		*Other*	
	max	min	max	min	max	min	max	min
Labor	0.52	−0.44*	0.12	0.27*	−0.13	0.29	−0.50	−0.12
	(0.46)	(0.14)	(0.46)	(0.14)	(0.97)	(0.30)	(0.66)	(0.20)
Capital	0.01	0.07*	−0.06	−0.11*	0.03	0.03	0.03	0.02
	(0.02)	(0.04)	(0.04)	(0.06)	(0.04)	(0.05)	(0.05)	(0.07)
Electricity	−0.02	0.07	0.06	0.03	−0.09	−0.15	0.05	0.05
	(0.11)	(0.08)	(0.08)	(0.05)	(0.13)	(0.09)	(0.07)	(0.05)
Other	−0.33	−0.28	0.36	0.15	0.29	0.41	−0.32	−0.29
	(0.44)	(0.46)	(0.62)	(0.64)	(0.45)	(0.47)	(0.87)	(0.91)

Note: "max" and "min" relate to firms with the largest and smallest outputs in the sample. Figures in parentheses are asymptotic standard errors based on White's heteroskedasticity – consistent covariance matrix estimator.

* Significant at the 10 percent level.

cost relative to that which prevailed in our 1986/87 sample. Even reducing the number of firms from 60 to 40 implies an 8 percent reduction in total industry cost on this basis.[9]

Such figures must be treated cautiously. Our model has been specified carefully but it cannot capture the full detail of this industry. The firms in it are not homogeneous. Each has its individual features, which of course preclude the attainment of the hypothetical situations just described. We offer no prescription for the amalgamation of Supply Authorities. Clearly, there are important geographic, technical, and social constraints that would have to be taken into account. Since this study was undertaken, several major changes to the New Zealand electricity distribution industry have been announced and the final impact of these changes is unclear. Subject to the constraints noted, our results suggest the likely future shape of the industry if Supply Authorities were to rationalize their activities in a more competitive environment.

Notes

The second author is now with Transpower New Zealand Ltd. This paper is based on work undertaken in the preparation of the more general report by Wyatt et al. (1989). We would like to thank Patrick Caragata for suggesting this study and for his ongoing support during its execution. We are also grateful to Max Brown and Andrew Duncan for their substantial input, to Judith Giles for numerous helpful discussions, and to the New Zealand Ministries of Energy and Commerce for supporting this study. We would like to thank members of the Electricity Supply Association of New Zealand for their many helpful comments and suggestions during the course of our research, and the referee for several constructive comments on an earlier draft. This paper is the responsibility of the authors, and any views expressed should not be attributed to their employers.

1. Six major industrial users purchase bulk electricity direct from the national grid. They are excluded from this study.
2. Recently, this number has been reduced to 52, and negotiations for further amalgamations are in progress.
3. Recent changes to the industry include the potential for ESAs to bargain directly with ECNZ over the price of bulk electricity and changes to taxation arrangements for ESAs. In addition, the New Zealand Government has recently announced that ESAs will be corporatized, so in future they should be more profit-oriented.
4. All of our analysis was repeated with the Auckland observation excluded from the sample. The numerical estimates changed only slightly from those reported below, and none of the conclusions was altered.
5. In this case the implications of the estimation results are, of course, independent of the figure chosen.
6. There is evidence of multicollinearity, in terms of both the simple and multiple correlations between this variable and the other regressors.
7. As the estimate of γ_{yy} in table 23.2 is positive, the $\overline{\text{SCALE}}$ estimates decrease monotonically with increasing output. This is not the case for SCALE, of course.
8. That paper also reports some tentative, and only partially successful, attempts to model the ESAs as dual-output firms, supplying both "energy" (in kWh) and "power" (in kW). This was motivated by the peak-load problem and the ESAs' limited ability to smooth their loads. The aggregate scale economy estimates obtained were totally consistent with those reported here.
9. In the case of our three-input model these industry cost savings are estimated to be 21 percent and 17.5 percent respectively.

References

Aivazian, V. A., J. L. Callen, M. W. L. Chan, and D. C. Mountain (1987). "Economies of scale versus technological change in the natural gas transmission industry," *Review of Economics and Statistics*, 69, 556–61.

Berndt, E. R., and D. O. Wood (1975). "Technology, prices and the derived demand for energy," *Review of Economics and Statistics*, 57, 259–68.

Betancourt, R. R., and J. H. Y. Edwards (1987). "Economies of scale and the load factor in electricity generation," *Review of Economics and Statistics*, 69, 551–6.

Christensen, L. R., and W. H. Greene (1976). "Economies of scale in U.S. electric power generation," *Journal of Political Economy*, 84, 655–76.

Christensen, L. R., D. W. Jorgensen, and L. J. Lau (1971). "Conjugate duality and the transcendental logarithmic production function," (abstract), *Econometrica*, 39, 255–6.

Christensen, L. R., D. W. Jorgensen, and L. J. Lau (1973). "Transcendental logarithmic production frontiers," *Review of Economics and Statistics*, 55, 28–45.

Gregory, A. W., and M. R. Veall (1985). "Formulating Wald tests of nonlinear restrictions," *Econometrica*, 53, 1465–8.

Hall, B. H., R. Schnake, and C. Cummins (1988). *Time Series Processor Version 4.1 User's Manual*. Palo Alto: TSP International.

Heuttner, D. A., and Landon, J. A. (1978). "Electric utilities: scale economies and diseconomies," *Southern Economic Journal*, 44, 892–912.

Jones, M. A. (1987). *Forced Amalgamation of New Zealand Local Bodies and Power Supply Authorities.* Christchurch: Finlay, Kitching & Associates.

McCutcheon, I. A., R. J. Adams, D. J. Binns, and D. S. Scott (1987). *Report of the Study Team Appointed to Examine the Organisation of the Electricity Supply Authorities in the Greater Canterbury Region.* Christchurch: Canterbury Study Team.

Mizon, G. E. (1977). "Inferential procedures in non-linear models: an application in a U.K. industrial cross section study of factor substitution and returns to scale," *Econometrica*, 45, 1221–42.

Neuberg, L. G. (1977). "Two issues in the municipal ownership of electric power distribution systems," *Bell Journal of Economics*, 8, 303–23.

Phillips, P. C. B., and J. Y. Park (1988). "On the formulation Wald tests of nonlinear restrictions," *Econometrica*, 56, 1065–83.

Sing, M. (1987). "Are combinations gas and electric utilities multiproduct natural monopolies?," *Review of Economics and Statistics*, 69, 392–8.

Stanton Royal Commission (1959). *Report of the Commission of Enquiry into the Distribution of Electricity.* Wellington: Government Printer.

Weiss, L. W. (1975). "Antitrust in the electric power industry," in A. Phillips (ed.) *Promoting Competition in Regulated Markets.* Washington: Brookings Institution.

White (1980). "A heteroskedasticity-consistent covariance matrix and a direct test for heteroskedasticity," *Econometrica*, 48, 721–46.

Wyatt, N. S., M. R. Brown, P. J. Caragata, A. J. Duncan, and D. E. A. Giles (1989). *Performance Measures and Economies of Scale in the New Zealand Electricity Distribution System.* Wellington: Ministry of Energy.

24

Long-run Equilibrium Estimation and Inference: A Nonparametric Application

V. B. Hall and R. G. Trevor

Introduction

Phillips (1991a) has demonstrated that the long-run parameters of a continuous-time error correction model (ECM) involving nonstationary variables can be estimated from a corresponding discrete-time ECM. He derives theoretical results for a first-order stochastic differential equation system, driven by quite general stationary errors. The vector of variables is integrated of order one (an I(1) process), with the multiple long-run relationships being given by the cointegrating vectors. This theoretical work is an extension of the Phillips (1991c) results for a discrete-time ECM with a single cointegrating relationship.

He suggests frequency domain procedures of the type due to Hannan (1963) for estimation and inference, anticipating they would provide significant computational advantages over methods traditionally used for continuous-time models.[1] In particular, he considers the very significant problems associated with temporal aggregation (see for example Bergstrom (1984)), the problems of selecting short-run dynamics, and the complexities of nonlinear estimation would not arise. This is due to the generality afforded by the nonparametric treatment of regression errors in frequency domain procedures.

A further key element of Phillips' paper is that spectral estimates of the cointegrating parameters are asymptotically equivalent to the corresponding maximum likelihood estimates. Moreover, the nuisance parameters introduced into the limiting distributions by the presence of nonstationary processes have only scale effects. It is therefore possible to carry out conventional asymptotic chi-squared hypothesis testing.

In light of the above, the principal aim of this paper is to present some initial estimates and inferences based on Phillips' theoretical results and suggested empirical procedures. The innovative aspects are: (1) it provides an early application of this methodology to macroeconomic time-series data,[2] thereby giving initial evidence on both the potential gains and difficulties relative to traditional methods; (2) it extends the Engle and Granger (1987) type scalar cointegration methods to vector cases, in a way which is not conditional on the precise modeling of short-run dynamics as is required, for example, in the maximum likelihood procedure developed by Johansen (1988, 1991); and (3) it illustrates the outcome of some simple hypothesis tests on the long-run parameter values. This is possible because Wald test statistics involving coefficients on the I(1) regressors are not misleading. It therefore overcomes a major limitation of the Engle–Granger procedure.

More specifically, our application is to a vector of Australian data on household disposable income, and aggregate and disaggregated consumer expenditure. The long-run consumer expenditure equations estimated could help to underpin a full continuous-time or discrete-time macroeconomic model, once satisfactory long-term relationships have been developed in other key areas.

We have chosen a restricted vector of Australian data as suitable for this study, as it is not the purpose of this paper either to estimate a "best" long-run (or short-run) consumption function, or to test alternative forms of underlying consumption theory. Previous Australian studies, such as those undertaken by Freebairn (1976), Williams (1979), Anstie et al. (1983), Johnson (1983), and McKibbin and Richards (1988), have not focussed on long-run cointegrating relationships.

Hence, the three stages in our empirical work involve: firstly, testing each variable for its order of integration and for the presence of any deterministic trend; secondly, testing for the number of cointegrating relationships amongst the variables; and thirdly, from the discrete data set, estimating and conducting tests on the coefficients of the appropriate cointegrated system. The two methods used are the Hannan efficient and band spectral estimators suggested by Phillips.

A fourth stage, that of estimating the corresponding short-run dynamic equations conditional on these nonparametric estimates of the long-run relationships, is left for future work.

From a methodological point of view, we have employed consistent hypothesis testing procedures whenever possible. At the first (unit root) stage, this involves checking to ensure results are consistent for the real, nominal, and implicit deflator forms of each consumption and income variable. At the second (cointegration) stage, this means using nonunivariate cointegration tests for both aggregate and disaggregated data sets, and relying on unit root test findings with respect to trend and drift.

Relevant aspects of the econometric theory and estimation procedures are the subject of the next section, empirical results are presented in the third section, and our concluding comments appear in the final section.

Econometric Theory and Estimation Procedures

Following the treatment in Phillips (1991a), let $\mathbf{y}(t)$ be an n-vector I(1) process in continuous time and let $\boldsymbol{\mu}(t)$ be an n-vector stationary time series. The vectors $\mathbf{y}(t)$ and $\boldsymbol{\mu}(t)$ are partitioned into the n_1 and n_2 subvectors as follows

$$\mathbf{y}(t) = \begin{bmatrix} \mathbf{y}_1(t) \\ \mathbf{y}_2(t) \end{bmatrix}, \qquad \boldsymbol{\mu}(t) = \begin{bmatrix} \boldsymbol{\mu}_1(t) \\ \boldsymbol{\mu}_2(t) \end{bmatrix} \tag{1}$$

On the assumption that there are n_1 cointegrating relationships between these n variables (that is, there are n_1 linearly independent linear combinations of the n elements of the $\mathbf{y}(t)$ vector which are stationary), the data generating mechanism for

$\mathbf{y}(t)$ is therefore the cointegrated system

$$\mathbf{y}_1(t) = B\mathbf{y}_2(t) + \boldsymbol{\mu}_1(t), \tag{2}$$

$$D\mathbf{y}_2(t) = \boldsymbol{\mu}_2(t). \tag{3}$$

Equation (2) gives the long-run relationship between the variables. This relationship is perturbed by stationary deviations, which may represent short-run (or stationary) dynamics, measurement error and temporal aggregation errors as well as the innovations. Differentiation of equation (2) (in the sense of Phillips (1991a, pp. 969–70)) leads to $D\mathbf{y}_1(t) = B\boldsymbol{\mu}_2(t) + D\boldsymbol{\mu}_1(t)$ which may be combined with equations (2) and (3) to yield

$$D\mathbf{y}(t) = -EA\mathbf{y}(t) + \boldsymbol{\omega}(t), \tag{4}$$

$$E = \begin{bmatrix} I \\ 0 \end{bmatrix}, \qquad A = [I, -B], \qquad \boldsymbol{\omega}(t) = \begin{bmatrix} \boldsymbol{\mu}_1(t) + B\boldsymbol{\mu}_2(t) + D\boldsymbol{\mu}_1(t) \\ \boldsymbol{\mu}_2(t) \end{bmatrix}$$

and E is an $(n_1 + n_2) \times n_1$ array and A is $n_1 \times (n_1 + n_2)$.

Equation (4) is a continuous-time analog of a triangular format ECM. In this formulation, the matrix E is known; it is only the B submatrix of the coefficient matrix A which is to be estimated.

Phillips proves that every continuous-time ECM of the form of equation (4) generates an exact discrete model that may be written in the discrete-time triangular ECM format

$$\Delta\mathbf{y}_t = -EA\mathbf{y}_{t-1} + \boldsymbol{\varepsilon}_t, \tag{5}$$

where the discrete data are recordings of the instantaneous data at equispaced points in time, and Δ is the difference operator.[3]

The long-run equilibrium coefficients B, incorporated in the matrix A, are the same in both the continuous-time and discrete-time ECMs. There are no identification or aliasing problems. The only requirements on the error processes are stationarity and the existence of a continuous spectral density matrix. In particular, any short-run dynamics are absorbed into these error processes.

Equation (5) could be estimated by maximum likelihood or instrumental variables. Both of these techniques would require a precise formulation of the residual processes. However, given the quite general conditions placed on these processes, a non-parametric treatment of the residuals is appropriate. Hence, spectral regression methods provide a suitable estimation strategy.

Two such estimators are suggested in Phillips (1991a). These are the Hannan efficient and band spectral estimators. Equation (5) may be reduced to

$$\mathbf{z}_t = EB\mathbf{x}_t + \boldsymbol{\varepsilon}_t, \qquad \mathbf{z}_t = \begin{bmatrix} \mathbf{y}_{1t} \\ \Delta\mathbf{y}_{2t} \end{bmatrix}, \qquad \mathbf{x}_t = \mathbf{y}_{2t-1}. \tag{6}$$

Now if $\boldsymbol{\beta}$ is defined as the column vector containing the stacked rows of B, then the Hannan efficient estimators are

$$\tilde{\boldsymbol{\beta}} = \left[\frac{1}{2M}\sum_{k=-M+1}^{M} E'F_{\varepsilon\varepsilon}^{-1}\left(\frac{\pi k}{M}\right)E \otimes F_{xx}\left(\frac{-\pi k}{M}\right)\right]^{-1}$$
$$\times\left[\frac{1}{2M}\sum_{k=-M+1}^{M}\left\{E'F_{\varepsilon\varepsilon}^{-1}\left(\frac{\pi k}{M}\right)\otimes I_{n_2}\right\}f_{zx}\left(\frac{-\pi k}{M}\right)\right], \tag{7}$$

$$\operatorname{var}(\tilde{\boldsymbol{\beta}}) = \frac{1}{T}\left[\frac{1}{2M}\sum_{k=-M+1}^{M} E'F_{\varepsilon\varepsilon}^{-1}\left(\frac{\pi k}{M}\right)E \otimes F_{xx}\left(\frac{-\pi k}{M}\right)\right]^{-1}. \tag{8}$$

In these equations, the $F(\cdot)$ functions denote smoothed periodogram estimates of the respective spectral density matrices, using a rectangular window and a band of width π/M for M integer. Correspondingly, $f(\cdot)$ is the vectorization of $F(\cdot)$ obtained by stacking the rows of $F(\cdot)$ into a column vector.

This estimator is essentially generalized least squares (GLS) applied in the frequency domain; the "covariance matrices" of the variables are adjusted for the "covariance matrix" of the residuals. This is done by averaging over the whole spectrum. The role of the E matrix is simply to pick out the relevant rows and columns of equation (6) which correspond to the long-run coefficients in the B matrix.

Asymptotically, the important parts of the GLS weighting scheme are those that incorporate the long-run behavior of the data. Accordingly, band spectral estimators based on spectral estimates at the origin may be used, and can be written as

$$\tilde{\boldsymbol{\beta}}_0 = [E'F_{\varepsilon\varepsilon}^{-1}(0)E \otimes F_{xx}(0)]^{-1}[\{E'F_{\varepsilon\varepsilon}^{-1}(0)\otimes I_{n_2}\}f_{zx}(0)], \tag{9}$$

$$\operatorname{var}(\tilde{\boldsymbol{\beta}}_0) = \frac{2M}{T}[E'F_{\varepsilon\varepsilon}^{-1}(0)E \otimes F_{xx}(0)]^{-1}. \tag{10}$$

Phillips (1991a) shows that these estimators are asymptotically equivalent to the maximum likelihood estimator of B in equation (5). They therefore share all the advantages of maximum likelihood, with one major additional advantage. Maximum likelihood requires explicit modeling of the error process in equation (5). In particular the estimates would be conditional on a specific parameterization of the short-run dynamics – a subject on which economic theory is often silent.

The limit distributions of these two spectral regression estimators involve nuisance parameters due to the presence of integrated processes. However, the nuisance parameters involve only scale effects, so conventional asymptotic Wald tests may be constructed.

The null hypothesis $R\boldsymbol{\beta} = \mathbf{r}$ may be tested by the statistics

$$S = (R\tilde{\boldsymbol{\beta}} - \mathbf{r})'[R\operatorname{var}(\tilde{\boldsymbol{\beta}})R']^{-1}(R\tilde{\boldsymbol{\beta}} - \mathbf{r})$$

or

$$S_0 = (R\tilde{\boldsymbol{\beta}}_0 - \mathbf{r})'[R\operatorname{var}(\tilde{\boldsymbol{\beta}}_0)R']^{-1}(R\tilde{\boldsymbol{\beta}}_0 - \mathbf{r}) \tag{11}$$

corresponding to the two estimators. Each statistic has a χ^2 distribution with rank (R) degrees of freedom.

Three additional issues are of particular importance for the implementation of this approach. These involve establishing effective procedures for computation of the spectral regressions; determining the order of cointegration; and choosing initial estimates of the residuals for the GLS procedure.

Hannan (1970) provides formulas for spectral regression which are computationally more tractable than equations (7) through (10). For instance, the Hannan efficient estimator in equation (7) may be more conveniently computed by

$$\tilde{\boldsymbol{\beta}} = \left[\frac{1}{M}\sum_{k=0}^{M} \delta_k\{E'u_{\varepsilon\varepsilon}(\cdot)E \otimes c_{xx}(\cdot) - E'v_{\varepsilon\varepsilon}(\cdot)E \otimes q_{xx}(\cdot)\}\right]^{-1}$$

$$\times \operatorname{vec}\left[\frac{1}{M}\sum_{k=0}^{M} \delta_k\{E'u_{\varepsilon\varepsilon}(\cdot)c_{zx}(\cdot) - E'v_{\varepsilon\varepsilon}(\cdot)q_{zx}(\cdot)\}\right], \qquad (12)$$

$$F(\cdot) = \tfrac{1}{2}(c(\cdot) - iq(\cdot)), \qquad u = (c + qc^{-1}q)^{-1},$$

$$v = -c^{-1}q(c + qc^{-1}q)^{-1}, \qquad \delta_k = \begin{cases} 1, & k \neq 0, M, \\ 0.5, & k = 0, M. \end{cases}$$

On the issue of the number of cointegrating vectors, Johansen (1988, 1991) provide a likelihood ratio test capable of determining the order of cointegration. His method can also provide estimates of, and hypothesis tests on, both long-run and short-run parameters. A potentially important limitation of his procedure is that the maximum likelihood estimates produced are conditional on the specific parameterization of the model. For instance, Johansen's theory allows only for VAR-type dynamics. However, in the absence of a well-developed nonparametric test for *multiple* cointegrating relationships, in this study we have relied on Johansen's cointegration tests.

Finally, both spectral estimators require an initial estimate of B in order to construct the residual spectral density estimate $F_{\varepsilon\varepsilon}(\cdot)$. This also raises the question of iterating on the estimate of B. Such choices, together with the choice of method to calculate the spectral density matrices, may affect the finite-sample performance of the estimators. They will not, however, affect the asymptotic properties of the estimators. For the purposes of this application, it was decided to use both OLS and Johansen estimates as initial values for B, and to examine the implications of multiple iterations.[4]

Empirical Results

Data

It seemed appropriate to commence with estimating some long-run relationships between consumption expenditure and income. This was not only because it could reasonably be expected from recent work by Engle and Granger (1987) (and by a number of others) for the USA that such series would be I(1), but also because it is widely believed that long-run relationships exist between consumption and income variables. The general long-run equations (13) and (14) specified below are consistent with a variety of economic theoretic specifications, including forms of Keynesian and permanent income hypotheses.[5]

Some theoretical models postulate a long-run relationship between real permanent income, and real consumption of nondurables and service flows from durables.[6]

As no official measures of these variables exist for Australia, household disposable income and consumption expenditure series were used. This choice will not affect our parameter estimates, given the nonparametric nature of our estimator and provided the measurement errors are stationary.

The 14 variables we consider are defined in table 24.1. Each series consists of 118 quarterly (seasonally adjusted) observations in logarithmic form, from 1959(3) through 1988(4). The constant price series are at average 1984/85 prices.[7]

Table 24.1 Variable descriptions

Variable	*Description*
C	Aggregate real private final consumption expenditure
CHD	Real private consumption expenditure on household durables
CMV	Real private consumption expenditure on motor vehicles
CND	Real private consumption expenditure on nondurables
YHD	Real household disposable income (=YHD$/PC)
C$	Aggregate nominal private final consumption expenditure
CHD$	Nominal private consumption expenditure on household durables
CMV$	Nominal private consumption expenditure on motor vehicles
CND$	Nominal private consumption expenditure on nondurables
YHD$	Nominal household disposable income
PC	Implicit deflator for aggregate private final consumption expenditure
PCHD	Implicit deflator for private consumption expenditure on household durables
PCMV	Implicit deflator for private consumption expenditure on motor vehicles
PCND	Implicit deflator for private consumption expenditure on nondurables

Possible long-run relations amongst our variables at the aggregate level would include

$$C = \beta_1 \text{YHD} \tag{13}$$

and its nominal equivalent.

The corresponding vector form for real disaggregated consumption would be

$$\begin{bmatrix} \text{CHD} \\ \text{CMV} \\ \text{CND} \end{bmatrix} = \begin{bmatrix} \beta_2 \\ \beta_3 \\ \beta_4 \end{bmatrix} [\text{YHD}]. \tag{14}$$

Two particular advantages of equation (14) for our purposes are that it provides a useful illustration for the Phillips estimation procedures in multivariate form, and allows for the testing of a range of restrictions on the parameter values (e.g. $\beta_1 = 1$, $\beta_2 = \beta_3 = \beta_4$, and $\beta_2 = \beta_3 = \beta_4 = 1$).

Unit Root Tests for Stationarity

Testing for the order of integration of individual data series is seldom a straightforward exercise (see for example Pagan and Wickens (1989, section I.2.1)). Broadly speaking, it is known that the tests are sensitive to the presence of deterministic drift or time trends, and to departures from residuals which are independently and identically distributed (IID).

Based on a general equation of the form

$$w_t = \delta + \gamma t + \alpha w_{t-1} + v_t \tag{15}$$

our procedure was to test each series (and their first and second differences) for a unit root, with and without drift and linear time trends, under a sequence of nested hypotheses. Particular care was taken to ensure our unit root test results were consistent for the real, nominal, and implicit deflator forms of each consumption and income variable, as this kind of consistency check seldom seems to have been reported in previous empirical work.

Many of the tests available in the literature are modifications to the original Dickey–Fuller (Dickey and Fuller (1979, 1981)) tests, for situations where the residuals are not IID.[8]

However, consistent with the nonparametric approach adopted in this paper, we employed initially the tests as modified by Phillips and Perron (1988) and Perron (1988). To test a given order of integration, say one unit root versus none, we start by estimating equation (15). First the hypothesis that $\alpha = 1$ is tested by the $Z(\alpha)$ and $Z(t_\alpha)$ statistics; it would be rejected if the statistic were more negative than the critical value. If this hypothesis is not rejected, the joint hypothesis that $\alpha = 1$ and $\gamma = 0$ is tested by the $Z(\Phi_3)$ statistic; it is rejected if it exceeds the critical value. In the event that this hypothesis is not rejected, the joint hypothesis that $\alpha = 1$, $\gamma = 0$, and $\delta = 0$ is tested by the $Z(\Phi_2)$ statistic; it is rejected if it exceeds the critical value. If this hypothesis also is not rejected, equation (15) is re-estimated under the constraint that $\gamma = 0$. Based on the constrained estimates, the hypothesis that $\alpha = 1$ is again tested by $Z(\alpha)$ and $Z(t_\alpha)$ statistics (with different critical values). If this hypothesis is not rejected, the joint hypothesis that $\alpha = 1$ and $\delta = 0$ would be tested using the $Z(\Phi_1)$ statistic.

In all cases the hypotheses of two or more unit roots were unambiguously rejected by the Phillips–Perron (PP) tests. Under the conditions of equation (15), empirical results for the single unit root case are therefore presented in table 24.2. The lags reflect the number of terms in the Newey and West (1987) variance calculation used in the PP adjustments. At lag zero, the statistics are essentially the unadjusted Dickey–Fuller statistics.

Results in table 24.2 show that all the series are I(1) with drift (and no time trend), except for the CMV series which is I(1) with no drift. The latter result is confirmed by the statistics derived from the restricted version of equation (15), the point estimate of the root from the constrained model being 0.9556. As a consistency check, tests were conducted on the (log-levels) of the implicit price deflator series. In all cases these were found to be I(1).[9]

Further consistency checks, involving the augmented Dickey–Fuller (ADF), Dickey–Pantula (ADP), and Stock–Watson (SW) tests were then undertaken.[10] These tests are parametric extensions to the original Dickey–Fuller tests. Each of these tests requires an autoregressive (AR) parametric adjustment in order to adjust for serial dependency in the residuals of equation (15). Following Schwert (1987) we used AR adjustments of length 4 and 12.[11]

Table 24.2 Phillips–Perron unit root test statistics

Test	*Lag*	C	CHD	CMV	CND	YHD	C$	CHD$	CMV$	CND$	YHD$
α		0.9955	0.9659	0.9423	0.9956	0.9701	0.9652	0.9543	0.8425	0.9674	0.9622
$Z(\alpha)$	0	−0.47	−3.82	−6.46	−0.45	−3.35	−3.99	−5.21	−17.68	−3.74	−4.30
	5	−0.67	−7.09	−6.51	−0.35	−2.52	−5.12	−7.45	−19.15	−4.78	−4.90
	10	−0.43	−7.79	−5.73	−0.25	−2.62	−5.90	−8.81	−18.44	−5.50	−5.83
	15	−0.28	−7.74	−4.54	−0.24	−2.64	−6.33	−9.15	−16.21	−5.94	−6.40
$Z(t_\alpha)$	0	−0.25	−1.32	−1.82	−0.24	−1.31	−4.12	−2.98	−3.12	−4.31	−2.38
	5	−0.33	−1.84	−1.83	−0.19	−1.14	−2.86	−2.71	−3.23	−2.84	−2.32
	10	−0.23	−1.93	−1.72	−0.14	−1.17	−2.70	−2.75	−3.18	−2.66	−2.32
	15	−0.15	−1.93	−1.54	−0.13	−1.17	−2.67	−2.77	−3.00	−2.62	−2.34
$Z(\Phi_3)$	0	2.68	0.87	2.68	2.79	2.13	17.36	6.90	4.80	20.03	4.76
	5	2.45	1.69	2.68	2.95	2.35	6.69	4.68	5.17	6.89	4.10
	10	2.74	1.86	2.63	3.12	2.31	5.41	4.52	4.99	5.44	3.68
	15	2.98	1.85	2.64	3.14	2.31	5.04	4.52	4.43	5.00	3.59
$Z(\Phi_2)$	0	47.59	11.62	2.26	58.09	14.11	307.20	49.82	7.86	383.91	103.92
	5	42.92	7.30	2.26	61.71	18.60	90.99	21.46	7.72	103.19	76.41
	10	48.64	6.89	2.29	65.38	17.93	61.89	16.49	7.78	68.98	54.51
	15	53.19	6.91	2.45	65.85	17.80	52.69	15.67	8.09	57.60	46.54

Critical values are given in Fuller (1976) and Dickey and Fuller (1981). At the 1 percent level they are −29.50, −3.96, 8.27 and 6.09 for $Z(\alpha)$, $Z(t_\alpha)$, $Z(\Phi_3)$, and $Z(\Phi_2)$ respectively.

The ADF and ADP results show our variables to be I(2) in almost all cases for an AR correction of 12, and in about half of the cases for an AR correction of 4. However, there was a marked lack of consistency in the inferences drawn from these tests applied to each set of real, nominal, and implicit deflator measures. For example, the ADF tests with an AR correction of 4 suggest that the logs of nominal and real consumption of household durables are I(1), but that the log of the implicit price deflator is I(2). Since these variables are related by a simple identity, at least one of these inferences must be erroneous.[12]

Given this outcome, results from a univariate version of the SW q_f test were then examined. For AR corrections of both 4 and 12, variables were consistently I(1), thereby confirming the outcomes from the PP tests.

It can therefore be said with reasonable confidence that all the real, nominal, and implicit deflator variables of interest to us are I(1).[13] For the second stage of our empirical work, this meant that the following groupings of variables were then examined: (1) real aggregate consumption (C and YHD); (2) real disaggregated consumption (CHD, CMV, CND and YHD); (3) nominal aggregate consumption (C$ and YHD$); and (4) nominal disaggregated consumption (CHD$, CMV$, CND$ and YHD$).

Testing for the Number of Cointegrating Vectors

For a long-run relationship to exist between a set of variables which are I(1), there must be one or more cointegrating vectors. In the context of our application, failure to find one cointegrating vector for C and YHD (or C$ and YHD$) would mean a simple aggregate long-run consumer expenditure equation is not estimable. On the other hand, the finding of one cointegrating vector allows estimation to proceed legitimately. Similarly, establishing the existence of three cointegrating vectors for either the real or nominal disaggregated groups of variables would support the estimation of three equations.

Johansen's (1988, 1991) trace and maximum eigenvalue likelihood ratio tests were used to establish the number of cointegrating vectors, and the corresponding estimates of the cointegrating vectors were also used as one set of starting values for the spectral estimation procedure results reported in the next subsection.

As was done in Johansen's empirical work (Johansen and Juselius 1988, 1990), we first determined the order of the VAR model for each group of variables, using a likelihood ratio test.[14] For the four cases above, the outcomes were VAR(1), VAR(3), VAR(2), and VAR(3) respectively. In line with our research strategy of conducting the same hypothesis tests consistently across our aggregate and disaggregate data sets, nonunivariate cointegration tests were used in the two aggregate cases where there could at most be a single cointegrating vector.

Johansen's tests for the number of cointegrating vectors were applied to each of these VAR models. Initially one uses the trace statistic to test the null hypothesis that there are at most zero cointegrating relationships. Should that be rejected, tests for successively higher orders of cointegration are applied until an acceptance occurs.[15] Maximum eigenvalue tests are used in conjunction with this sequence of trace tests. Each maximum eigenvalue statistic is used to test the null hypothesis that there are P cointegrating vectors against the alternative that there are $P + 1$ cointegrating vectors.

Results are presented in table 24.3. Each order of cointegration statistic presented

Table 24.3 Johansen's order of cointegration statistic

						Critical values			
Aggregate			Disaggregated			Trace		Max. eigenvalue	
P	Real	Nominal	P	Real	Nominal	2.5%	5%	2.5%	5%
—			0	60.08	79.60	50.4	47.2	29.3	27.2
—			1	35.45	32.90	32.3	29.5	23.0	20.8
0	10.21	31.57	2	17.22	13.45	17.3	15.2	15.8	14.0
1	4.68	0.02	3	3.65	0.05	5.3	4.0	5.3	4.0

Critical values are given in Johansen (1991) and Johansen and Juselius (1990). The statistic tests the hypothesis that there *at most* P cointegrating vectors.

in the table is the value of the trace statistic for the null hypothesis of at most P cointegrating vectors. The difference between the values at P and $P + 1$ gives the value of the maximum eigenvalue statistic for the null hypothesis of P cointegrating vectors.

Conditional on the particular VAR corrections for serial dependence, the outcomes of these tests at the 5 percent level of significance are[16]: (1) there is no evidence against there being no cointegration between aggregate real consumption and household disposable income; (2) for the real disaggregated group of variables, there are three cointegrating vectors; (3) aggregate nominal consumption is cointegrated with household disposable income; and (4) for the nominal disaggregated group of variables, the evidence is less clear cut. There are either two or three cointegrating vectors. For the maximum eigenvalue statistic of 13.4, the null hypothesis of two cointegrating vectors is narrowly unable to be rejected, the critical value being 14.0. However, both test statistics clearly fail to provide evidence against three cointegrating vectors.

Consequently, for *real* consumer expenditure an aggregate equation should not be estimated, but a vector equation including three disaggregated components should be estimated.

In contrast, results for the *nominal* variables suggest that it would be appropriate to estimate the aggregate model. A disaggregated model including either two or three cointegrating vectors could be estimated. We proceeded with three cointegrating vectors.[17]

However, before turning to the spectral estimates and tests of long-run coefficients work in the next subsection, it is necessary to comment further on what is perhaps our major surprising result – the finding of no cointegration between aggregate real consumption and household disposable income.[18] There are *two* main puzzles: whether this result is consistent with that for the aggregate nominal variables; and whether it is consistent with economic theoretic notions of a long-run relationship between consumption and income.

There would seem at least the following possible explanations: (1) the real variables, as measured, are in fact not cointegrated over the sample period; (2) despite substantial progress having occurred in recent years, existing tests are still inadequate to cover all situations; (3) the long-run relationship between consumption and income depends on other nonstationary variables; and (4) there are sizeable (nonstationary) measurement errors in the real data set. These could be in the deflators for consumer durables during periods of rapid technological change, and/or in the household disposable income variable during periods of significant inflation.

The deflator for durable goods view is based on there having been substantial technological innovation in consumer durables. For example, technical innovations in household durables over our estimation period include clothes washers and dryers, dish washing machines, microwave ovens, home entertainment centers, video machines and computers, and central heating and air conditioning. There are likely to have been significant changes in the degree of durability of some items. Perhaps more importantly, there are likely to be severe problems in measuring the real expenditures on these goods – the same constant dollar amount buys a much higher quality item today than it did previously. The latter case has been argued in principle and demonstrated empirically by Baily and Gordon in the context of measurement of investment in computers. For example, as expressed in Baily and Gordon (1988, p. 386):

> Goods where technological progress has been rapid have falling relative prices and increasing sales volumes. The use of base-period prices overweights the growth of these dynamic commodities in years following the base year and underweights them in years preceding the base year. [...]Constant-dollar base-weighted investment series imply that the computer industry disappears as you go back a few years, and it explodes and takes over the total as you go forward in time.

The income based view of mismeasurement has been argued and illustrated empirically for Australia by Anstie et al. (1983). Real "economic" income is defined by them as that income which may be consumed while leaving real wealth intact. In essence, they argue that the Australian Statistician's definition of household disposable income is inadequate in the face of inflation and that it should be modified by an inflation adjusted wealth measure. That is, measured income needs to be adjusted downwards by the value of the inflation tax on nominal assets. However, our unit root results suggest that the log of the implicit price deflator is I(1), so inflation will be a stationary variable and an unlikely explanation for the lack of cointegration between the real aggregate variables.

Unfortunately, neither of these two sources of mismeasurement are unique to the Australian data. Moreover, any complete explanation of our no cointegration result also needs to resolve the puzzle of the inconsistent aggregate real and nominal outcomes. These outcomes of no cointegration in the real case, and cointegration in the nominal case, would only be consistent if the nominal long-run income elasticity is not unity.[19] However, all the estimates of this elasticity presented in the next subsection are unambiguously unity, and cointegration of the real variables is also rejected when a unitary elasticity is imposed.

Our finding in the previous subsection of inconsistent inferences, arising from parametric ADF unit root tests on the components of identities between (the logs of) aggregate nominal, real, and implicit price deflator data, suggests that a similar problem may be occurring with the parametric Johansen tests for the number of cointegrating vectors in the aggregate real and nominal data sets. Figure 24.1 shows the log levels of real aggregate consumption and real disposable income, as well as the estimated (nonstationary) residual from the Johansen "cointegrating" relationship. Figure 24.2 shows the analogous variables from the nominal aggregate data

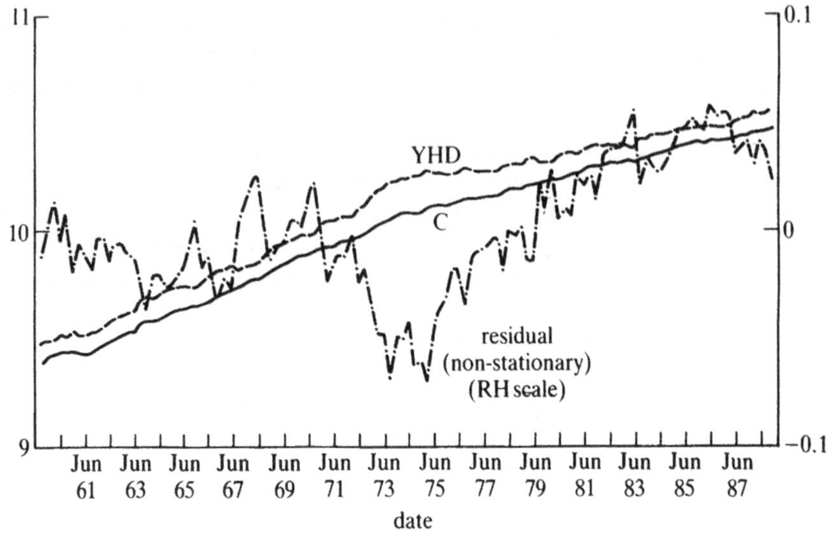

Figure 24.1 Cointegrating equation: real aggregate data

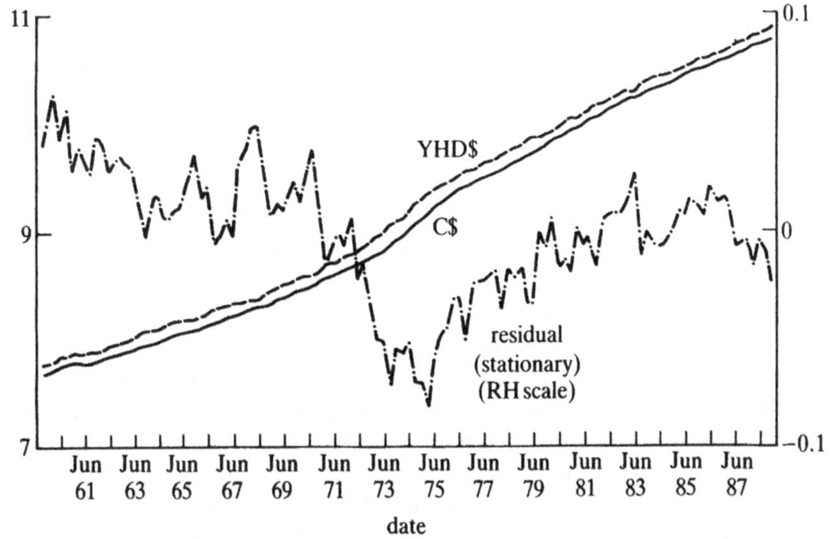

Figure 24.2 Cointegrating equation: nominal aggregate data

set, where the cointegrating residual is stationary. The two residuals are compared in figure 24.3.

Visually, there appears to be little difference in the stationarity of the two residuals, yet the Johansen test results infer otherwise. This suggests that some parametric adjustment (such as introducing a polynomial in time) to the VAR model of the real aggregate data underlying the Johansen procedure may produce different inferences. Yet such adjustments would not satisfy the criteria of internal consistency

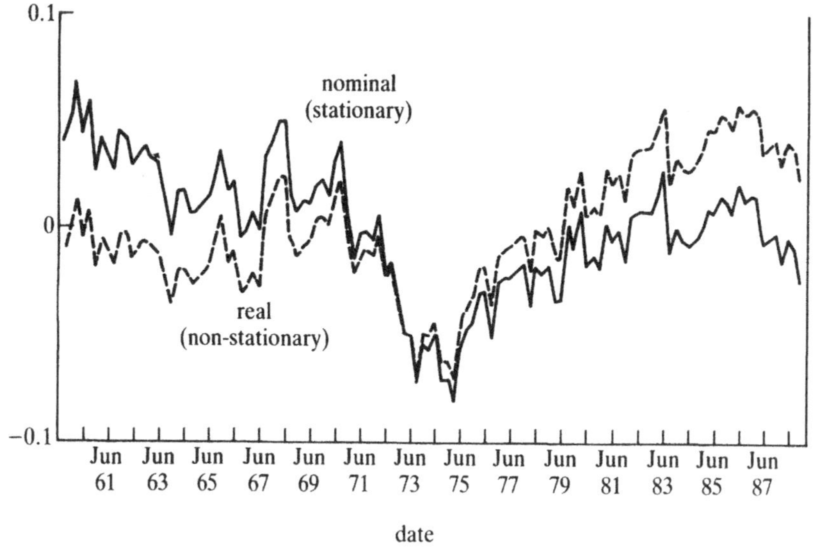

Figure 24.3 Cointegration residuals: aggregate data

– there is no evidence of time trends in our unit root tests, and the existence of a deterministic trend in the real cointegrating relationship would imply that a similar trend existed in the nominal cointegrating relationship.

Consequently, for the purposes of this paper, these puzzles have to remain unresolved. For the sake of completeness, however, we will present the estimation and hypothesis testing results from the "noncointegrated" real aggregate data set along with the results from the cointegrated real disaggregated and nominal aggregate and disaggregated data sets.

Spectral Estimates and Tests of Long-run Coefficients

Given the number of cointegrating vectors established in the previous subsection, it is now necessary to make a normalization of these in order to write models in the form of equations (2) and (3). Since the spectral estimates are not maximum likelihood, they will not be invariant to normalization – this, of course, is a feature shared with other potential estimators. It seemed sensible in our application to make the standard normalization that consumption is a function of income, as illustrated in equations (13) and (14). The disaggregated cointegration vectors can be written with each disaggregated consumption component as a function of the other two components and income. These can be solved for the "reduced form" in which each consumption component is a function of income only.

For each model, two obvious restrictions that we test are that the income elasticities of consumption expenditure are jointly unity and that they are jointly equal.

As indicated in the second section, both spectral techniques require an initial estimate of the coefficients. Two sets of initial values are used: one being the OLS estimates of equation (6)[20]; the other being the Johansen estimates of the cointegrating vector (appropriately normalized). In each case, the effects of multiple iterations were evaluated by taking the number of iterations to nine. Empirical results from the final

Table 24.4 Long-run parameter estimates

Equation	OLS estimate	OLS initial values: Band spectral	OLS initial values: Hannan efficient	Johansen estimate	Johansen initial values: Band spectral	Johansen initial values: Hannan efficient
C	0.9841	0.9890 (0.0790)	0.9649 (0.0134)	0.9527	0.9890 (0.0790)	0.9649 (0.0134)
CHD	1.4008	1.4008 (0.1752)	1.2999 (0.0295)	1.4160	1.4008 (0.1752)	1.3000 (0.0295)
CMV	0.8970	0.9127 (0.3889)	0.9251 (0.0706)	0.7785	0.9127 (0.3889)	0.9252 (0.0706)
CND	0.9580	0.9630 (0.0901)	0.9582 (0.0130)	1.1075	0.9630 (0.0901)	0.9583 (0.0130)
C$	1.0057	1.0054 (0.0225)	1.0011 (0.0048)	1.0151	1.0054 (0.0225)	1.0011 (0.0048)
CHD$	0.9756	0.9758 (0.0539)	0.9472 (0.0080)	0.9596	0.9758 (0.0539)	0.9472 (0.0080)
CMV$	0.8047	0.8045 (0.0536)	0.8177 (0.0172)	0.7981	0.8045) (0.0536)	0.8177 (0.0172)
CND$	1.0180	1.0176 (0.0290)	1.0209 (0.0045)	1.0314	1.0176 (0.0290)	1.0209 (0.0045)

Each entry is the point estimate of the coefficient on household disposable income in the relevant equation. Where Wald test statistics are asymptotically χ^2, estimated standard errors are given in parentheses. For the spectral methods, the estimates are from the ninth iteration.

Table 24.5 Wald tests of restrictions

	All coefficients unity				*All coefficients equal*			
	OLS		*Johansen*		*OLS*		*Johansen*	
	Band spectral	*Hannan efficient*	*Band spectral*	*Hannan efficient*	*Band spectral*	*Hannan efficient*	*Band spectral*	*Hannan efficient*
Real aggregate	0.8892	0.0089	0.8892	0.0089	—	—	—	—
Real disaggregated	0.0339	0.0000	0.0339	0.0000	0.0267	0.0000	0.0267	0.0000
Nominal aggregate	0.8101	0.8181	0.8101	0.8181	—	—	—	—
Nominal disaggregated	0.0006	0.0000	0.0006	0.0000	0.0066	0.0000	0.0066	0.0000

Each entry is the marginal significance level of the test statistic. At the 5% level of significance, a hypothesis with a marginal level of significance less than 0.0500 would be rejected.

iteration are presented in tables 24.4 and 24.5. Table 24.4 provides the band spectral and Hannan efficient parameter estimates and relevant standard errors, for each of the two sets of initial values. Wald test statistics for the two types of restrictions are presented in table 24.5.

On methodological issues, it can be concluded that: (1) our estimates are not substantially affected by iterations beyond the first (for example, for the Hannan efficient estimates based on OLS initial values, there was only one parameter which changed by more than 1 percent between the first and ninth iterations – the change was actually less than 2 percent); (2) even though two of the three initial values given by the Johansen and OLS estimators differ substantially in the real disaggregated case, this has negligible effect on the frequency domain estimates; (3) the band spectral estimates appear less precise, in the sense that they have larger standard errors. This is because an adjustment has been made to take into account that there are effectively "fewer" observations used in their estimation[21]; and (4) the VAR parameterization inherent in the Johansen estimator can have significant impacts on the estimates of long-run parameters. There are, for example, a number of nontrivial differences between the (parametric) Johansen and the (nonparametric) spectral estimates in table 24.4.

With respect to the economic implications of our results: (1) it is generally the case that the estimated long-run income elasticities of consumption are sensible in magnitude, ranging from around 0.8 to about 1.0; (2) in the case of real disaggregated consumption, the various estimates of the income elasticity for expenditure on household durables are all substantially larger than unity. This is consistent with the view in the previous subsection that the lack of cointegration between the real aggregate variables could be due to measurement errors in the deflators for consumer durables during periods of rapid technological change. Perhaps not surprisingly, both the hypotheses of equality and of unity of the coefficients are rejected by the joint tests. When these two tests are redone on the nondurables and motor vehicles coefficients alone, the hypothesis of equality cannot be rejected for either set of estimates, but that of unity can be rejected for the Hannan efficient estimates[22]; (3) the long-run nominal income elasticity of consumption is unambiguously unity; and (4) the nominal income elasticity estimates for disaggregated consumption are distinctly different from those for their real counterparts. The two of most interest are for household durables and motor vehicles. The lower nominal estimates are consistent with our comments about possible measurement problems in the real durables data. In each case the hypotheses of equality and of unity of the coefficients are unambiguously rejected.

Concluding Comments

We have taken an important first step towards evaluating empirically whether the theoretical framework and methods suggested by Phillips (1991a) should be used to estimate long-run relations (in continuous time).

In terms of statistical procedures adopted, it has been demonstrated that the spectral regression estimates were relatively straightforward to compute, that a few iterations of the spectral estimators may be all that is required, and that the spectral estimates have not been sensitive to alternative initial estimates.

Our application has also highlighted the potential importance of nonparametric estimators. In the univariate case, for parametric (autoregressive) based corrections, the unit root test results were somewhat confusing and internally inconsistent. This is in complete contrast to the results from the (Phillips–Perron) tests with nonparametric corrections, which were internally consistent. In the multivariate area also, a number of the nonparametric (spectral regression) estimates of the long-run coefficients were markedly different from the parametric (vector autoregressive) Johansen estimates. Monte Carlo work, building on the contributions of Schwert (1987), Phillips and Ouliaris (1990), and Corbae (1990), would allow an evaluation of conditions under which the nonparametric methods might be more generally superior.

Empirically, the long-run consumption function estimates obtained are sufficiently realistic for it to be worthwhile exploring conditional short-run dynamic relations. A number of cautionary comments about data measurement had to be made along the way, and careful judgement had to be exercised during the course of several of the test procedures. The test procedures we used were consistent across our aggregate and disaggregated data sets, and between the unit root and cointegration stages of our investigation. This methodological stance could have contributed to our major surprising result, namely that the null of no cointegration between aggregate real consumer expenditure and household disposable income cannot be rejected. Some unresolved empirical issues relating to aggregate *real* consumer expenditure have been referred to. However, overall the outcomes have certainly been sufficiently encouraging for the examination of other macroeconomic and financial data sets to be justified, and for the testing of long-run relationships more rigorously grounded in economic theory. Setting such relations more explicitly into a fuller macroeconomic model with either discrete or continuous dynamics could also be considered.

Notes

We are grateful to Peter Phillips and three referees for their perceptive comments on earlier versions. The paper also benefited in its initial stages from comments made by Lew Evans, Arthur Grimes, and John McDermott during a presentation to the February 1990 Conference of the New Zealand Association of Economists.

1. Major contributions to the continuous-time literature have recently been reviewed in Phillips (1991a, section 1) and Bergstrom (1988). The complexities of formulating and estimating empirical macroeconomic models have been illustrated for the UK, Australia, and New Zealand in Bergstrom and Wymer (1976), Jonson et al. (1977) and Bailey et al. (1987).
2. During the revision stages of this paper, it was brought to our attention that Corbae (1990) has recently reported empirical results based on the techniques suggested in Phillips (1991c) for a single cointegrating vector ECM. Corbae examines a permanent income hypothesis consumption function, similar to that estimated by Campbell (1987) in the time domain. A principal result from Corbae's Monte Carlo work was the powerful support for "... the bias and and efficiency gains from conducting [Phillips (1991c)] systems spectral estimation over [Engle (1974)] single equation estimation" (Corbae (1990, p. 176)).
3. The proposition also has a converse. For every discrete-time cointegrated system such as equation (5), there is an underlying continuous system such as equations (2) and (3) which gives rise to it. Phillips (1991b) shows that all that is required

for optimal estimation of the long-run coefficients is consistent estimation of the long-run covariance matrix of the system residuals. Hence, given the estimation technique used here, it matters little for the estimation of the long-run parameters whether the underlying dynamics are continuous or discrete. However, everything depends on the estimation procedure used.

4. We do not explicitly examine differing methods of constructing the spectral density matrices. Nevertheless, we do control for some of the choices available by using both the Hannan efficient and band spectral estimators.
5. For example, equation (13) is consistent with the long-run equilibrium of the continuous time consumption function specified in Bergstrom and Wymer (1976, pp. 269–72).
6. See for example Hall (1978), Flavin (1981), and Campbell (1987). Note that the error correction modeling structure we use is consistent both with present value models and with models that postulate adjustment to long-run equilibrium. See for example Campbell and Shiller (1987, 1988).
7. The data are taken from the dX NIF data set supplied by EconData. The nondurables series are the sums of the series for food, rent, and other nondurables. The real, nominal, and implicit price deflator series were double checked for consistency with each other, as were the aggregate and disaggregated consumption expenditure series. All the econometric calculations were carried out on a microcomputer using the programming facilities of the RATS package.
8. These include extensions to adjust for seasonality. See, for example Dickey et al. (1984), Engle et al. (1989) and Hylleberg et al. (1990). Because our quarterly data are seasonally adjusted, conventional unit root tests are employed.
9. For the series PCMV, the outcome was I(1) with a time trend.
10. See Said and Dickey (1984), Dickey et al. (1986), Dickey and Pantula (1987), and Stock and Watson (1988).
11. Based on a Monte Carlo analysis, Schwert suggests correcting for an AR of order k, where $k = \text{int}\{4(T/100)^{1/4}\}$ or $k = \text{int}\{12(T/100)^{1/4}\}$, and T is the number of observations.
12. The inconsistency of the inferences from ADF tests on the components of identities between (the logs of) aggregate nominal, real and implicit price deflator data for Australia may be found in other studies also. (See for example the results reported in Hargreaves (1990, table 2).) This is a puzzling result, and the stochastic properties of the Australian data are worthy of further investigation. Peter Phillips has suggested a possible explanation, based on Phillips and Ouliaris (1990). The ADF test is asymptotically equivalent to the PP $Z(t_\alpha)$ statistic. Both have less power than the $Z(\alpha)$ test, as the rate of divergence under the alternative is greater for $Z(\alpha)$ than the ADF.
13. All further calculations were performed on data in de-meaned form.
14. We considered a maximum of six lags and applied the small-sample correction of Sims (1980).
15. The maximum number of cointegrating relationships within a group of I(1) variables is one less than the number of variables. Should no acceptance be found in the sequence of tests, the inference would be that the variables are I(0). This would call into question the results of earlier unit root tests.
16. We followed the convention that tests can only reject or fail to reject null hypotheses. Evidence against a null hypothesis need only be provided by either of the two tests.
17. Johansen and Juselius (1990), when analyzing their Finnish data, were faced with a similar situation. They also chose the higher order of cointegration.
18. The result continues to hold when our aggregate data are expressed in per capita terms. This finding is not inconsistent with the conclusions cautiously expressed in McKibbin and Richards (1988, pp. 11, 25–26).
19. The nominal cointegrating equation may be written as

$$(C + \text{PC}) = \beta(\text{YHD} + \text{PC}) + \xi$$

and may be rearranged as a real cointegrating equation of the form

$$C = \beta \text{YHD} + (\beta - 1)\text{PC} + \xi$$

with the additional I(1) term $(\beta - 1)$PC.

20. These estimates will differ slightly from those of Engle and Granger (1987), since our regressors are lagged.
21. Fewer is in the sense that only a small part of each observation is used, namely that part which corresponds to the long-run trend. In our case, this adjustment increases the standard errors approximately tenfold.
22. For the band spectral and Hannan efficient estimators, the marginal significance levels for the hypothesis of unity of the two coefficients are 0.8002 and 0.0010 respectively, while those for the hypothesis of equality are 0.9097 and 0.6579.

References

Anstie, R. K., M. R. Gray, and A. R. Pagan (1983). "Inflation and the consumption ratio," in A. R. Pagan and P. K. Trivedi (eds) *The Effects of Inflation: Theoretical Investigations and Australian Evidence.* Canberra: Centre for Economic Policy Research, Australian National University.

Bailey, R. W., V. B. Hall, and P. C. B. Phillips (1987). "A model of output, employment, capital formation and inflation," in G. Gandolfo and F. Marzano (eds) *Keynesian Theory, Planning Models and Quantitative Economics*, volume II, pp. 703–67. Milano: Giuffrè-Editore.

Baily, M. N., and R. J. Gordon (1988). "The productivity slowdown, measurement issues, and the explosion of computer power," *Brookings Papers on Economic Activity*, 2, 347–431.

Bergstrom, A. R. (1984). "Continuous time stochastic models and issues of aggregation over time," in Z. Griliches and M. D. Intriligator (eds). *Handbook of Econometrics*, volume II, pp. 1145–212. Amsterdam: North-Holland.

Bergstrom, A. R. (1988). "The history of continuous time econometric models," *Econometric Theory*, 4, 365–83.

Bergstrom, A. R., and C. R. Wymer (1976). "A model of disequilibrium neoclassical growth and its application to the United Kingdom," in A. R. Bergstrom (ed.) *Statistical Inference in Continuous Time Economic Models.* Amsterdam: North-Holland.

Campbell, J. Y. (1987). "Does saving anticipate declining labor income? An alternative test of the permanent income hypothesis," *Econometrica*, 55, 1249–73.

Campbell, J. Y., and R. J. Shiller (1987). "Cointegration and tests of present value models," *Journal of Political Economy*, 95, 1062–88.

Campbell, J. Y., and R. J. Shiller (1988). "Interpreting cointegrated models," *Journal of Economic Dynamics and Control*, 12, 505–22.

Corbae, D. (1990). "A reexamination of the consumption function using frequency domain regressions," in *Essays in Dynamic Macroeconomics*, chapter IV. Yale University PhD Dissertation.

Dickey, D. A., W. R. Bell, and R. B. Miller (1986). "Unit roots in time series models," *American Statistician*, 40, 12–26.

Dickey, D. A., and W. A. Fuller (1979). "Distribution of the estimators for autoregressive time series with a unit root," *Journal of the American Statistical Association*, 74, 427–31.

Dickey, D. A., and W. A. Fuller (1981). "Likelihood ratio statistics for autoregressive time series with a unit root," *Econometrica*, 49, 1057–72.

Dickey, D. A., D. P. Hasza, and W. A. Fuller (1984). "Testing for unit roots in seasonal time series," *Journal of the American Statistical Association*, 79, 355–67.

Dickey, D. A., and S. G. Pantula (1987) "Determining the order of differencing in autoregressive processes," *Journal of Business and Economic Statistics*, 5, 455–61.

Engle, R. F. (1974). "Band spectrum regression," *International Economic Review*, 15, 1–11.

Engle, R. F., and C. W. J. Granger (1987). "Co-integration and error correction: representation, estimation and testing," *Econometrica*, 55, 251–76.

Engle, R. F., C. W. J. Granger, and J. J. Hallman (1989). "Merging short- and long-run forecasts: an application of seasonal cointegration to monthly electricity sales forecasting," *Journal of Econometrics*, 40, 45–82.

Flavin, M. A. (1981). "The adjustment of consumption to changing expectations about future income," *Journal of Political Economy*, 89, 974–1009.

Freebairn, J. W. (1976). "Determinants of consumption," in W. E. Norton and D. W. Stammer (eds) *Conference in Applied Economic Research: Papers and Proceedings*. Sydney: Reserve Bank of Australia.

Fuller, W. A. (1976). *Introduction to Statistical Time Series*. New York: Wiley.

Hall, R. E. (1978). "Stochastic implications of the life cycle–permanent income hypothesis: theory and evidence," *Journal of Political Economy*, 86, 971–87.

Hannan, E. J. (1963). "Regression for time series," in M. Rosenblatt (ed.) *Time Series Analysis*, pp. 17–37. New York: John Wiley and Sons.

Hannan, E. J. (1970). *Multiple Time Series*. New York: John Wiley and Sons.

Hargreaves, C. (1990). "Money demand modelling in Australian economy-wide models: some preliminary analyses," Department of Economics, University of New England. Presented to Economic Modelling Bureau of Australia June 1990 Conference.

Hylleberg, S., R. F. Engle, C. W. J. Granger, and B. S. Yoo (1990). "Seasonal integration and cointegration," *Journal of Econometrics*, 44, 215–38.

Johansen, S. (1988). "Statistical analysis of cointegration vectors," *Journal of Economic Dynamics and Control*, 12, 231–54.

Johansen, S. (1991). "Estimation and hypothesis testing of cointegration vectors in Gaussian vector autoregressive models," *Econometrica*, 59, 1551–80.

Johansen, S., and K. Juselius (1988). "Hypothesis testing for cointegration vectors – with an application to the demand for money in Denmark and Finland," Institute of Economics, University of Copenhagen.

Johansen, S., and K. Juselius (1990). "Maximum likelihood estimation and inference on cointegration – with applications to the demand for money," *Oxford Bulletin of Economics and Statistics*, 52, 169–210.

Johnson, P. (1983). "Life-cycle consumption under rational expectations: some Australian evidence," *Economic Record*, 59, 345–50.

Jonson, P. D., E. R. Moses, and C. R. Wymer (1977). "The RBA76 model of the Australian economy," in W. E. Norton (ed.) *Conference in Applied Economic Research*. Sydney: Reserve Bank of Australia.

McKibbin, W. J., and A. J. Richards (1988). "Consumption and permanent income: the Australian case," Research Discussion Paper 8808, Reserve Bank of Australia.

Newey, W. K., and K. D. West (1987). "A simple positive semi-definite heteroskedasticity and autocorrelation consistent covariance matrix," *Econometrica*, 55, 703–8.

Pagan, A. R., and M. R. Wickens (1989). "A survey of some recent econometric methods," *Economic Journal*, 99, 962–1025.

Perron, P. (1988). "Trends and random walks in macroeconomic time series," *Journal of Economic Dynamics and Control*, 12, 297–332.

Phillips, P. C. B. (1991a). "Error correction and long run equilibrium in continuous time," *Econometrica*, 59, 967–80.

Phillips, P. C. B. (1991b). "Optimal inference in cointegrated systems," *Econometrica*, 59, 283–306.

Phillips, P. C. B. (1991c). "Spectral regression for cointegrated time series," in W. Barnett, J. Powell and G. Tauchen (eds) *Nonparametric and Semiparametric Methods in Economics and Statistics*. New York: Cambridge University Press.

Phillips, P. C. B., and S. Ouliaris (1990). "Asymptotic properties of residual based tests for cointegration," *Econometrica*, 58, 165–93.

Phillips, P. C. B., and P. Perron (1988). "Testing for a unit root in time-series regression," *Biometrika*, 75, 335–46.

Said, S. E., and D. A. Dickey (1984). "Testing for unit roots in autoregressive moving average models of unknown order," *Biometrika*, 71, 599–608.

Schwert, G. W. (1987). "Effects of model misspecification on tests for unit roots in macroeconomic data," *Journal of Monetary Economics*, 20, 73–103.

Sims, C. A. (1980). "Macroeconomics and reality," *Econometrica*, 48, 1–48.

Stock, J. H., and M. W. Watson (1988). "Testing for common trends," *Journal of the American Statistical Association*, 83, 1097–107.

Williams, R. A. (1979). "Household saving and consumption," in W. E. Norton and I. W. Little (eds) *Conference in Applied Economic Research.* Sydney: Reserve Bank of Australia.

Index

Printed and bound by CPI Group (UK) Ltd, Croydon, CR0 4YY

16/04/2025

14658825-0005